Texts in Computing

Volume 15

Design and Analysis of Purely Functional Programs
Third Edition

Texts in Computing Series Editor
Ian Mackie   mackie@lix.polytechnique.fr

Design and Analysis of Purely Functional Programs
Third Edition

Christian Rinderknecht

ISBN 978-1-84890-059-2

College Publications
Scientific Director: Dov Gabbay
Managing Director: Jane Spurr
Department of Computer Science
King's College London, Strand, London WC2R 2LS, UK

http://www.collegepublications.co.uk

Cover produced by Laraine Welch

Contents

Foreword

This book addresses *a priori* different audiences whose common interest is functional programming.

For undergraduate students, we offer a very progressive introduction to functional programming, with long developments about algorithms on stacks and some kinds of binary trees. We also study memory allocation through aliasing (dynamic data-sharing), the role of the control stack and the heap, automatic garbage collection (GC), the optimisation of tail calls and the total allocated memory. Program transformation into tail form, higher-order functions and continuation-passing style are advanced subjects presented in the context of the programming language Erlang. We give a technique for translating short functional programs to Java.

For postgraduate students, each functional program is associated with the mathematical analysis of its minimum and maximum cost (efficiency), but also its average and amortised cost. The peculiarity of our approach is that we use elementary concepts (elementary calculus, induction, discrete mathematics) and we systematically seek explicit bounds in order to draw asymptotic equivalences. Indeed, too often textbooks only introduce Bachmann notation $\mathcal{O}(\cdot)$ for the dominant term of the cost, which provides little information and may confuse beginners. Furthermore, we cover in detail proofs of properties like correctness, termination and equivalence.

For the professionals who do not know functional languages and who must learn how to program with the language XSLT, we propose an introduction which dovetails the part dedicated to undergraduate students. The reason of this unusual didactic choice lies on the observation that XSLT is rarely taught in college, therefore programmers who have not been exposed to functional programming face the two challenges of learning a new paradigm and use XML for programming: whereas the former puts forth recursion, the latter obscures it because of the inherent verbosity of XML. By learning first an abstract functional language, and then XML, we hope for a transfer of skills towards the design and implementation in XSLT without mediation.

This book has also been written with the hope of enticing the reader into theoretical computing, like programming language semantics, formal logic, lattice path counting and analytic combinatorics.

I thank Nachum Dershowitz, François Pottier, Sri Gopal Mohanty, Walter Böhm, Philippe Flajolet, Francisco Javier Barón López, Ham Jun-Wu and Kim Sung Ho for their technical help.

Most of this book was written while I was working at Konkuk University (Seoul, Republic of Korea) with the Department of Internet and Multimedia, from 2005 to 2012. Some parts were added from 2013 to 2014, while I was visiting the Department of Programming Languages and Compilers at the Eötvös Loránd University (Budapest, Hungary) — also known as ELTE.

Please inform me of any error at `rinderknecht@free.fr`.

Budapest, Hungary.
24th June 2025.

Christian Rinderknecht

Chapter 1

Introduction

This is an overview of the topics developed in the rest of the book.

1.1 Rewrite systems

String-rewriting Let us play with a string of white and black beads, like $\circ \bullet \bullet \bullet \circ \circ \bullet$, and the game (Dershowitz and Jouannaud, 1990, Dershowitz, 1993) consists in removing two adjacent beads and replace them with only one according to some rules, for example

$$\bullet \circ \xrightarrow{\alpha} \bullet \qquad \circ \bullet \xrightarrow{\beta} \bullet \qquad \bullet \bullet \xrightarrow{\gamma} \circ$$

The rules α, β and γ make up a simple *string-rewriting system*. Rules α and β can be conceived as 'A black bead absorbs a white bead next to it'. The goal of this game is to end up with as few beads as possible, so our example may lead to the *rewrites*

$$\circ\bullet\bullet\boxed{\bullet\circ}\circ\bullet \xrightarrow{\alpha} \circ\bullet\bullet\boxed{\bullet\circ}\bullet \xrightarrow{\alpha} \boxed{\circ\bullet}\bullet\bullet \xrightarrow{\beta} \bullet\bullet\boxed{\bullet\bullet} \xrightarrow{\gamma} \bullet\boxed{\bullet\circ} \xrightarrow{\alpha} \boxed{\bullet\bullet} \xrightarrow{\gamma} \circ$$

where the part of the string to be rewritten next is framed.

Other compositions of the rules lead to the same result $\circ$ as well. Some others bring all-white strings, the simplest being $\circ\circ$. Some others lead to $\bullet$. Strings that can not be further rewritten, or *reduced*, are called *normal forms*. These observations should prompt us to wonder whether all strings have a normal form; if so, if it is unique and, furthermore, if it is either all-white or black-only.

First, let us note that the system is *terminating*, that is, there is no infinite chain of rewrites, because the number of beads strictly decreases in all the rules, although this is not a necessary condition in general, for instance, $\circ \bullet \xrightarrow{\beta'} \bullet\circ\circ$ would preserve termination because the composition

1

$\beta\alpha\alpha$ would be equivalent to the original rule β. In particular, this means that any string has a normal form. Furthermore, notice how the parity of the number of black beads is invariant through each rule and how there is no rewrite rule for two adjacent white beads. Therefore, if there are $2p$ initial black beads, then composing rules α and β lead to an all-black string, like ● ● ● ●, which can be reduced by applying rule γ to contiguous pairs of beads into an all-white string made of p beads. Otherwise, the same all-black string can be reduced by applying alternatively γ and β on the left end or γ and α on the right end, yielding ○. Similarly, if there is an initial odd number of black beads, we always end up with one black bead. It suffices to consider the rewrites ○○ $\xleftarrow{\gamma}$ ● ● ○ $\xrightarrow{\alpha}$ ● ● $\xrightarrow{\gamma}$ ○ to see that normal forms are not unique. Systems where normal forms are unique are called *confluent*.

If we add the rule ○ ○ $\xrightarrow{\delta}$ ○, the result of the game is always one bead, whose colour depends on the original parity of the black beads as before, and any strategy is successful. To see why, let us consider first that two non-overlapping parts of a string can be rewritten in parallel, that is to say, the order in which they are applied is irrelevant. The interesting cases occur when two applications of rules (maybe of the same rule) lead to different strings because they overlap. For instance, ○ ○ $\xleftarrow{\gamma}$ ● ● ○ $\xrightarrow{\alpha}$ ● ●. The important point is that ○ ○ and ● ● can be rewritten into ○ at the next step by δ and γ, respectively.

In general, what matters is that all pairs of strings resulting from the application of overlapping rules, called *critical pairs*, can be rewritten to the same string, to wit, they are *joinable*. In our example, all interactions occur on substrings consisting of three beads (because the left-hand sides of the rules are made of exactly two beads), so we must examine in FIGURE 1.1 eight cases, which we can order as if counting in binary from 0 to 7, (○) being interpreted as 0 and (●) as 1. In all the cases, the divergences are joinable in one step at most.

$$
\begin{array}{c}
\circ\circ \xleftarrow{\delta} \circ\circ\circ \xrightarrow{\delta} \circ\circ \\[4pt]
\circ\bullet \xleftarrow{\delta} \circ\circ\bullet \xrightarrow{\beta} \circ\bullet \\[4pt]
\bullet \xleftarrow{\alpha} \bullet\circ \xleftarrow{\beta} \circ\bullet\circ \xrightarrow{\alpha} \circ\bullet \xrightarrow{\beta} \bullet \\[4pt]
\circ \xleftarrow{\gamma} \bullet\bullet \xleftarrow{\beta} \circ\bullet\bullet \xrightarrow{\gamma} \circ\circ \xrightarrow{\delta} \circ \\[4pt]
\bullet\circ \xleftarrow{\alpha} \bullet\circ\circ \xrightarrow{\delta} \bullet\circ \\[4pt]
\bullet\bullet \xleftarrow{\alpha} \bullet\circ\bullet \xrightarrow{\beta} \bullet\bullet \\[4pt]
\circ \xleftarrow{\delta} \circ\circ \xleftarrow{\gamma} \bullet\bullet\circ \xrightarrow{\alpha} \bullet\bullet \xrightarrow{\gamma} \circ \\[4pt]
\bullet \xleftarrow{\beta} \circ\bullet \xleftarrow{\gamma} \bullet\bullet\bullet \xrightarrow{\gamma} \bullet\circ \xrightarrow{\alpha} \bullet
\end{array}
$$

Figure 1.1: The critical pairs are all joinable

In general, it is not necessary for critical pairs to be joinable in one rewrite just after the divergence, but to be joinable after any number of rewrites. This property is called *local confluence*. Together with termination, it implies that *every* string has exactly one normal form, which is a strong property entailing confluence.

The system we defined is *ground*, that is, it involves no variables. Variables allow a finite system to denote an infinite number of ground rules if the elements making up the strings are infinite, but also to reduce the size of a finite ground system. For instance, the previous example is equivalent to

$$\bullet \circ \xrightarrow{\alpha} \bullet \qquad\qquad \circ\, x \xrightarrow{\beta+\delta} x \qquad\qquad \bullet\, \bullet \xrightarrow{\gamma} \circ$$

where $x \in \{\circ, \bullet\}$. If we accept multiple occurrences of a variable on the left-hand side of a rule, a so-called *non left-linear rule*, we can further decrease the size of the system as follows:

$$x\, x \xrightarrow{\gamma+\delta} \circ \qquad\qquad x\, y \xrightarrow{\alpha+\beta} \bullet$$

There is now an *implicit order over the rules*, which is the order of writing (from left to right, top to bottom): the rule $\gamma + \delta$ must be examined first for a match with a part of the current string, because it is included in the second (set $x = y$ in $\alpha + \beta$ and we obtain the same left-hand side as $\gamma + \delta$).

Term-rewriting Up to now, only string-rewriting systems have been played with. More general are the *term-rewriting systems* (Baader and Nipkow, 1998), where a *term* is a mathematical object possibly featuring tuples, integers and variables. Let us consider the following totally ordered system

$$(0, m) \to m; \qquad (n, m) \to (n - 1, n \cdot m); \qquad n \to (n, 1). \qquad (1.1)$$

where rules are separated by a semi-colon and the last one is ended by a period. Arithmetic operators $(-)$ and $(\cdot)$ are defined outside the system, and m and n are variables denoting natural numbers. Would the rules not be ordered as they are laid out, the second rule would match any pair. Instead, it can be assumed that $n \neq 0$ in the second rule. We can easily see that all compositions of rewrites starting with a natural number n end with the *factorial* of n, that is, $1 \cdot 2 \cdot 3 \cdots n$, or simply $n!$:

$$n \to (n, 1) \to \cdots \to (0, n!) \to n!, \quad \text{for } n \in \mathbb{N}.$$

Let us note $(\xrightarrow{n})$ the composition of $(\to)$ repeated n times:

$$(\xrightarrow{1}) := (\to); \qquad (\xrightarrow{n+1}) := (\to) \circ (\xrightarrow{n}), \quad \text{with } n > 0.$$

The symbol ':=' is the definitional equality, meaning: 'is, by definition'. The *transitive closure* of $(\rightarrow)$ is defined as $(\twoheadrightarrow) := \bigcup_{i>0}(\overset{i}{\rightarrow})$. In the present case, the factorial coincides with the transitive closure of $(\rightarrow)$, namely, $n \twoheadrightarrow n!$. Let $(\overset{*}{\rightarrow})$ be the reflexive-transitive closure of $(\rightarrow)$, that is, $(\overset{*}{\rightarrow}) := (=) \cup (\twoheadrightarrow)$.

A confluent system defines a *partial function*, and it is then convenient to name it; for example, $c(1, d(n))$ is a term constructed with *function names* c and d, as well as variable n. A tuple tagged with a function name, like $f(x, y)$, is called a *function call*. The components of the tuples are then called *arguments*, for example $d(n)$ is the second argument of the call $c(1, d(n))$. It is possible for a function call to hold no arguments, like $d()$. For a given system, we restrict the left-hand sides of rules to be calls to the same function being defined.

1.2   Trees for depicting terms

The topological understanding of a function call or a tuple is the finite *tree*. A tree is a hierarchical layout of information and FIG-URE 1.2 shows the shape of one. The disks are called *nodes* and the segments which connect two nodes are called *edges*. The top-most node (with a diameter) is called the *root* and the bottommost ones ($\bullet$) are called the *leaves*. All nodes except the leaves are

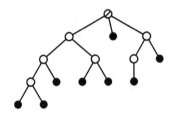

Figure 1.2: Shape of a tree

seen to downwardly connect to some other nodes, called *children*. Up-wardly, each node but the root is connected to another node, called its *parent*. Depending on the context, a node can also denote the whole tree of which it is the root. Any node except the root is the root of a *proper subtree*. A tree is its own subtree. The children of a node x are the roots of *immediate subtrees* with respect to the tree rooted at x. Any two different immediate subtrees are disjoint, that is, no node from one connects to a node in the other. A group of trees is a *forest*.

Trees can be used to depict terms as follows. A function call is a tree whose root is the function name and the chil-dren are the trees denoting the arguments. A tuple can be considered as having an invisible function name represented by a node with a period (.) in the tree, in which case the components of the tuple are its children. For example, the tree in FIGURE 1.3 has root f and leaves 0, x, 1 and y. Note how variables x and y are set in italics to differentiate them

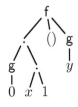

Figure 1.3

from function names x and y, set in sans-serif. For example $d((), e([1]))$ can be interpreted as a tree of root d and whose first immediate subtree is the representation of the empty tuple (), and the second immediate subtree corresponds to $e([1])$. FIGURE 1.3 represents the tree corresponding to $f((g(0), (x, 1)), (), g(y))$. The number of arguments of a function is called *arity*. Functions with the same name but different arities are permitted; for instance, we could have both $c(a())$ and $c(a(x), 0)$. This is called *overloading*. To distinguish the different uses, the arity of the function should be indicated after a slash, for example $c/1$ and $c/2$.

1.3 Purely functional languages

We only want to consider confluent systems because they define partial functions. This property can be trivially enforced by setting an order on the rules, as we did in previous examples. Another restriction we impose is for normal forms to be *values*, to wit, they do not contain any function call which can be further reduced. These two constraints define a *purely functional language* (Hughes, 1989, Hinsen, 2009). Notice that we do not require by construction that a system terminates. Not doing so enables more expressivity, at the expense of some more work to prove termination case by case.

We would like to further constrain the computation of function calls by imposing that arguments are rewritten before the call is. This strategy is named *call-by-value*. Unfortunately, it enables otherwise terminating programs to not terminate. For instance, let us consider

$$f(x) \xrightarrow{\alpha} 0. \qquad g() \xrightarrow{\beta} g().$$

We have $f(g()) \xrightarrow{\alpha} 0$ but $f(g()) \xrightarrow{\beta} f(g()) \xrightarrow{\beta} \ldots$ Despite this inconvenience, we shall retain call-by-value because it facilitates some analyses. (As an illustration of a reduction strategy more powerful than call-by-value, see the purely functional language Haskell (Doets and van Eijck, 2004).) Also it allows us to restrict the shape of the left-hand sides, called *patterns*, to one, outermost function call, since we expect the arguments to be fully evaluated, that is, to be values. For instance, we disallow a rule like

$$\text{plus}(x, \text{plus}(y, z)) \rightarrow \text{plus}(\text{plus}(x, y), z).$$

If the system is also terminating, we say that $(\xrightarrow{*})$ defines an *evaluation*, or *interpretation*, of the terms. For example, the factorial fact/1 can be defined by the ordered system

$$\text{fact}(0) \rightarrow 1; \qquad \text{fact}(n) \rightarrow n \cdot \text{fact}(n - 1). \tag{1.2}$$

Thus $\mathsf{fact}(n) \twoheadrightarrow n!$ and the system details how to reduce step by step $\mathsf{fact}(n)$ to its value.

Most functional languages allow *higher-order function* definitions, whereas standard term-rewriting systems do not. Such an example would be the following higher-order functional program, where $n \in \mathbb{N}$:

$$\mathsf{f}(g, 0) \to 1; \qquad \mathsf{f}(g, n) \to n \cdot g(g, n - 1). \qquad \mathsf{fact}_1(n) \to \mathsf{f}(\mathsf{f}, n).$$

Note that these two definitions are not recursive, yet $\mathsf{fact}_1/1$ computes the factorial. An adequate theoretical framework to understand higher-order functions is the λ-*calculus* (Hindley and Seldin, 2008, Barendregt, 1990). In fact, the λ-calculus features prominently in the semantics of programming languages, whether they are functional or not (Winskel, 1993, Reynolds, 1998, Pierce, 2002, Friedman and Wand, 2008, Turbak and Gifford, 2008). Here, we prefer to work with rewrite systems because they offer native pattern matching, whilst in the λ-calculus we would have to encode it as a cascade of conditionals, which have themselves to be encoded by means of more elementary constructs.

In the following, we show how to express linear data structures in a purely functional language and how to run our programs on a computer.

Stacks   Let us consider the abstract program

$$\mathsf{cat}(\mathsf{nil}(), t) \overset{\alpha}{\to} t; \qquad \mathsf{cat}(\mathsf{cons}(x, s), t) \overset{\beta}{\to} \mathsf{cons}(x, \mathsf{cat}(s, t)).$$

It defines the function $\mathsf{cat}/2$ that concatenates two *stacks*. Functions $\mathsf{nil}/0$ and $\mathsf{cons}/2$ are *data constructors*, that is, functions that are *not* defined by any system: their irreducible calls model data, so they are values and are allowed in patterns as arguments. The function call $\mathsf{nil}()$ denotes the empty stack, and $\mathsf{cons}(x, s)$ is the stack obtained by putting the item x on top of the stack s, an action commonly referred as *pushing x on s*. A non-empty stack can be thought of as a finite series of items that can only be accessed sequentially from the top, as suggested by the analogy with a stack of material objects, like cubes or plates.

Let T be the set of all possible terms and $S \subseteq T$ be the set of all stacks. Formally, S can by defined by *induction* as the smallest set $\mathcal{S}$ such that

- $\mathsf{nil}() \in \mathcal{S}$;

- if $x \in T$ and $s \in \mathcal{S}$, then $\mathsf{cons}(x, s) \in \mathcal{S}$.

Note that, in rule β, if s is not a stack, the recursion implies that the function $\mathsf{cat}/2$ is partial, not because the rewrites never end, but because the normal form is not a value. In operational terms, the interpreter fails to rewrite the call for some arguments.

Let us set the following abbreviations:

- $[] := \mathsf{nil}()$,

- $[x\,|\,s] := \mathsf{cons}(x, s)$,

after the convention of the programming language **Prolog** (Sterling and Shapiro, 1994, Bratko, 2000). For instance, we may write $[1\,|\,[2\,|\,[3\,|\,[]]]]$ instead of $\mathsf{cons}(1, \mathsf{cons}(2, \mathsf{cons}(3, \mathsf{nil}())))$. We can further abbreviate the notations as follows:

- $[x_1, x_2, \ldots, x_n\,|\,s] := [x_1\,|\,[x_2\,|\,\ldots\,[x_n\,|\,s]]]$,

- $[x] := [x\,|\,[]]$.

For example, $[1\,|\,[2\,|\,[3\,|\,[]]]]$ is more compactly written as $[1, 2, 3]$. Our rewrite system for **cat/2** now becomes a bit more legible:

$$\mathsf{cat}([], t) \xrightarrow{\alpha} t; \qquad \mathsf{cat}([x\,|\,s], t) \xrightarrow{\beta} [x\,|\,\mathsf{cat}(s, t)]. \qquad (1.3)$$

Finally, let us illustrate it with the following evaluation:

$$\mathsf{cat}([1, 2], [3, 4]) \xrightarrow{\beta} [1\,|\,\mathsf{cat}([2], [3, 4])] \xrightarrow{\beta} [1\,|\,[2\,|\,\mathsf{cat}([], [3, 4])]] \xrightarrow{\alpha} [1, 2, 3, 4].$$

Abstract syntax trees Depending on the context, we may use the arborescent depiction of terms to bring to the fore certain aspects of a computation. For example, it may be interesting to show how parts of the output (the right-hand side) are actually *shared* with the input (the left-hand side), or how much of the data remains invariant through a given rule. The former notion supposes that terms reside in some sort of space and that they can be referred to from other terms. That abstract space serves as a model of a computer *memory*. Consider for instance in FIGURE 1.4 the same definition of **cat/2** as given in (1.3). The arrows on certain edges denote some data sharing. When trees are used to visualise terms, they are called *abstract syntax trees* (AST). When some trees share subtrees, the whole forest is called a *directed acyclic graph* (DAG).

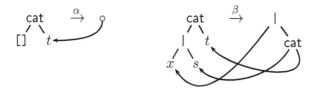

Figure 1.4: Definition of **cat/2** with directed acyclic graphs

1.4   Analysis of algorithms

The branch of theoretical informatics (or *computer science*) devoted to the mathematical study of the efficiency of programs has been pioneered by Donald Knuth, who named it *analysis of algorithms* (Sedgewick and Flajolet, 1996, Knuth, 1997). Given a function definition, this approach consists basically in three steps:

1. defining a measure on the arguments, which represents their size;

2. defining a measure on time, which abstracts the wall-clock time;

3. expressing the abstract time needed to compute calls to that function in terms of the size of its arguments.

This function models the efficiency and is called the *cost* (the lower the cost, the higher the efficiency). For example, when sorting objects, also called *keys* in this context, by comparing them, the input size is the number of keys and the abstract unit of time is often one comparison, so the cost is the mathematical function which associates the number of keys and the number of comparisons to sort them.

Exact cost   Rewrite systems enable a rather natural notion of cost for functional programs: it is the number of rewrites to reach the value of a function call, assuming that the arguments are values. In other words, it is the number of calls needed to compute the value. To gain some generality, we need to relate the cost to a measure of the size of the input. In the case of stacks, this is the number of items it contains. For instance, let us recall the concatenation of two stacks in definition (1.3):

$$\mathsf{cat}([\,],t) \xrightarrow{\alpha} t; \qquad \mathsf{cat}([x\,|\,s],t) \xrightarrow{\beta} [x\,|\,\mathsf{cat}(s,t)].$$

We observe that t is invariant, so the cost depends only on the size of the first argument. Let C_n^{cat} be the cost of the call $\mathsf{cat}(s,t)$, where n is the size of s. Rules α and β respectively lead to the equations

$$C_0^{\mathsf{cat}} \stackrel{\alpha}{=} 1 \qquad C_{n+1}^{\mathsf{cat}} \stackrel{\beta}{=} 1 + C_n^{\mathsf{cat}},$$

which, together, yield $C_n^{\mathsf{cat}} = n + 1$.

Extremal costs   When considering sorting programs based on comparisons, the cost varies depending on the algorithm and it also often depends on the original partial ordering of the keys, thus size does not capture all aspects needed to assess efficiency. This quite naturally leads to consider bounds on the cost: for a given input size, we seek the configurations of the input that minimise and maximise the cost, respectively called *best case* and *worst case*. For example, some sorting algorithms have their worst case when the keys are already sorted, others when they are sorted in reverse order, etc.

Average cost Once we obtain bounds on a cost, the question about the *average* or *mean cost* (Vitter and Flajolet, 1990) (Knuth, 1997, §1.2.10) arises as well. It is computed by taking the arithmetic mean of the costs for all possible inputs of a given size. Some care is necessary, as there must be a finite number of such inputs. For instance, to assess the mean cost of sorting algorithms based on comparisons, it is usual to assume that the input is a series of n *distinct keys* and that the sum of the costs is taken over all its *permutations*, thus divided by $n!$, the number of permutations of size n. The uniqueness constraint actually allows the analysis to equivalently, and more simply, consider the permutations of $(1, 2, \ldots, n)$. Some sorting algorithms, like *merge sort* (Knuth, 1998a, §5.2.4) (Cormen et al., 2009, §2.3) or *insertion sort* (Knuth, 1998a, §5.2.1) (Cormen et al., 2009, §2.1), have their average cost *asymptotically equivalent* to their maximum cost, that is, for increasingly large numbers of keys, the ratio of the two costs become arbitrarily close to 1. Some others, like *Quicksort* (Knuth, 1998a, §5.2.2) (Cormen et al., 2009, §7), have the growth rate of their average cost being of a lower magnitude than the maximum cost, on an asymptotic scale (Graham et al., 1994, §9).

Online versus off-line Sorting algorithms can be distinguished depending on whether they operate on the whole series of keys, or key by key. The former are said *off-line*, as keys are not sorted while they are coming in, and the latter are called *online*, as the sorting process can be temporally interleaved with the input process. For example, insertion sort is an online algorithm, whereas Quicksort is not because it is an instance of the divide-and-conquer strategy that splits the whole data set. This distinction is pertinent in other contexts, as with algorithms that are intrinsically *sequential*, instead of enabling some degree of *parallelism*, e.g., a database is updated by a series of atomic requests, but requests on non-overlapping parts of the data might be performed in parallel.

Amortised cost Sometimes an update is costly because it is delayed by an imbalance in the data structure that calls for an immediate remediation, but this remediation itself may lead to a state such that subsequent operations are faster than if the costly update had not happen. Therefore, when considering a series of updates, it may be overly pessimistic to cumulate the maximum costs of all the operations considered in isolation. Instead, *amortised analysis* (Okasaki, 1998a) (Cormen et al., 2009, §17) takes into account the interactions between updates, so a lower maximum bound on the cost is derived. Note that this kind of analysis is inherently different from the average case analysis, as its object is the composition of different functions instead of independent calls to the same function on different inputs. Amortised analysis is a worst case analysis of a sequence of updates, not of a single one.

Aggregate analysis   As an example, let us consider a counter enumerating the integers from 0 to n in binary by updating an array containing bits (Cormen et al., 2009, §17.1). In the worst case, an increment leads to inverting all the bits. The number m of bits of n can be found as follows. Let $n := \sum_{i=0}^{m-1} b_i 2^i$, where the b_i are the bits and $b_{m-1} = 1$. By definition of b_{m-1}, the lower bound for n is 2^{m-1}. The upper bound is attained when all the bits are 1, that is, $2^{m-1} + 2^{m-2} + \ldots + 2^0$. Let us call S_{m-1} that sum. By simplifying the expression $S_{m-1} = 2S_{m-1} - S_{m-1}$, we obtain $S_{m-1} = 2^m - 1$. Gathering the bounds, we thus have:

$$2^{m-1} \leqslant n < 2^m \Rightarrow m - 1 \leqslant \lg n < m \Rightarrow m = \lfloor \lg n \rfloor + 1, \qquad (1.4)$$

where $\lfloor x \rfloor$ (*floor of x*) is the greatest integer less than or equal to x and $\lg n$ is the binary logarithm of n. The cost of the n increments is thus bounded from above by $n \lg n + n \sim n \lg n$, as $n \to \infty$.

A little observation reveals that this upper bound is overly pessimistic, as carry propagation clears a series of rightmost bits to 0, so the next addition will flip only one bit, the following two etc. as shown in FIGURE 1.5a on the facing page, where bits about to be flipped at the next increment are set in boldface type. Counting the flips *vertically* reveals that the bit corresponding to 2^0, that is, the rightmost bit, flips every time. The bit of 2^1 flips once every two increments, so, from 0 to n, it flips $\lfloor n/2^1 \rfloor$ times. In general, the bit of 2^k flips $\lfloor n/2^k \rfloor$ times. Therefore, the total number of flips $F(n)$ in a sequence of n increments is

$$F(n) := \sum_{k \geqslant 0} \left\lfloor \frac{n}{2^k} \right\rfloor. \qquad (1.5)$$

The sum is actually always finite, as illustrated in FIGURE 1.5b on the next page. There, we can see *diagonally* that 1-bits at position j appear in positions $j-1$ down to 0, so account for $2^j + 2^{j-1} + \cdots + 2^0 = 2^{j+1} - 1$. In all generality, let $n := 2^{e_r} + \cdots + 2^{e_1} + 2^{e_0} > 0$, with $e_r > \cdots > e_1 > e_0 \geqslant 0$ and $r \geqslant 0$. The naturals e_i are the positions of the 1-bits in the binary

n	Bits of n	Flips
0	0 0 0 0 **0**	0
1	0 0 0 **0 1**	1
2	0 0 0 **1 0**	3
3	0 0 **0 1 1**	4
4	0 0 **1 0 0**	7
5	0 0 1 **0 1**	8
6	0 0 1 **1 0**	10
7	0 **0 1 1 1**	11
8	0 **1 0 0 0**	15
9	0 1 0 **0 1**	16
10	0 1 0 **1 0**	18
11	0 1 **0 1 1**	19
12	0 1 **1 0 0**	22
13	0 1 1 **0 1**	23
14	0 1 1 **1 0**	25
15	**0 1 1 1 1**	26
16	1 0 0 0 **0**	31

(a) Bit flips

k	$\lfloor n/2^k \rfloor$	Bits	$\sum_{i=0}^{k} \lfloor n/2^i \rfloor$
0	22	1 0 1 1 0	22
1	11	0 1 0 1 1	33
2	5	0 0 1 0 1	38
3	2	0 0 0 1 0	40
4	1	0 0 0 0 1	41

(b) $F(n) = \sum_{i \geqslant 0} \lfloor n/2^i \rfloor$, with $n = 22$

Figure 1.5: Counting bits vertically and diagonally

notation of n. The power 2^{e_r} corresponds to the leftmost bit in the binary expansion of n, so $e_r + 1$ is equal to the number of bits of n, which is known from equation (1.4):

$$e_r = \lfloor \lg n \rfloor. \tag{1.6}$$

We can now give a closed form for $F(n)$ as follows:

$$F(n) = \sum_{i=0}^{r} (2^{e_i+1} - 1) = 2n - \nu_n, \tag{1.7}$$

where $\nu_n := r+1$ is the sum of the bits of n, or, equivalently, the number of 1-bits. It is called many names, like *population count*, *sideways sum*, *bit sum* or *Hamming weight*; for example, in FIGURE 1.5b, we can read $F(22) = 41 = 2 \cdot 22 - 3$. Furthermore, we have the following intuitive tight bounds for any $n > 0$:

$$1 \leqslant \nu_n \leqslant \lfloor \lg n \rfloor + 1,$$

because equality (1.6) establishes that $\lfloor \lg n \rfloor + 1$ is the number of bits of the number n. Therefore, $2n - \lfloor \lg n \rfloor - 1 \leqslant F(n) \leqslant 2n$. L'Hospital rule entails that $\lim_{n \to +\infty} (\lg n / n) = \lim_{n \to +\infty} (1/n \ln 2) = 0$, where $\ln n$ is the *natural logarithm*. Therefore,

$$F(n) \sim 2n, \text{ as } n \to \infty.$$

Two enumerations (counting vertically and diagonally) have shown that the exact total number of flips is of a lower (logarithmic) magnitude than expected.

This example resorts to a particular kind of amortised analysis called *aggregate analysis*, because it relies on enumerative combinatorics (Stanley, 1999a,b, Martin, 2001) to reach its result (it aggregates positive partial amounts, often in different manners, to obtain the total cost). A visually appealing variation on the previous example consists in determining the average number of 1-bits in the binary notation of the integers from 0 to n (Bush, 1940).

1.5   Inductive proofs

Let us remark that $\mathsf{cat}([1], [2, 3, 4]) \twoheadrightarrow [1, 2, 3, 4] \twoheadleftarrow \mathsf{cat}([1, 2], [3, 4])$. It is enlightening to create *equivalence classes* of terms that are joinable. These classes then define an equivalence relationship ($\equiv$) as follows:

$a \equiv b$ if there exists a unique value v such that $a \overset{*}{\to} v$ and $b \overset{*}{\to} v$.

For instance, $\mathsf{cat}([1, 2], [3, 4]) \equiv \mathsf{cat}([1], [2, 3, 4])$. The relation ($\equiv$) is indeed an equivalence because it is

- *reflexive*: $a \equiv a$;
- *symmetric*: if $a \equiv b$, then $b \equiv a$;
- *transitive*: if $a \equiv b$ and $b \equiv c$, then $a \equiv c$.

If we want to prove equivalences with variables ranging over infinite sets, like $\mathsf{cat}(s, \mathsf{cat}(t, u)) \equiv \mathsf{cat}(\mathsf{cat}(s, t), u)$, we need some *induction principle*.

Well-founded induction   We define a *well-founded order* (Winskel, 1993) on a set A as being a binary relation ($\succ$) which does not have any *infinite descending chains*, to wit, no $a_0 \succ a_1 \succ \ldots$ The *well-founded induction principle* then states that, for any predicate $\aleph$,

$$\forall a \in A. \aleph(a) \text{ is implied by } \forall a.(\forall b.a \succ b \Rightarrow \aleph(b)) \Rightarrow \aleph(a).$$

Because there are no infinite descending chains, any subset $B \subseteq A$ contains minimal elements $M \subseteq B$, that is, there is no $b \in B$ such that

$a \succ b$, if $a \in M$. In this case, proving by well-founded induction degenerates into proving $\aleph(a)$ for all $a \in M$. When $A = \mathbb{N}$, this principle is called *mathematical (complete) induction* (Buck, 1963). *Structural induction* is another particular case where $t \succ s$ holds if, and only if, s is a proper *subterm* of t, namely, the abstract syntax tree of s is included in the tree of t and $s \neq t$.

Sometimes, a restricted form is enough. For instance, we can define $[x \mid s] \succ s$, for any term x and any stack $s \in S$. Both x and s are *immediate subterms* of $[x \mid s]$. There is no infinite descending chain since $[]$ is the unique minimal element of S: no s satisfies $[] \succ s$; so the basis is $t = []$ and $\forall t.(\forall s.t \succ s \Rightarrow \aleph(s)) \Rightarrow \aleph(t)$ degenerates into $\aleph([])$.

Termination   When defining our purely functional language, we allowed programs to not terminate. We could actually have imposed some syntactic restrictions on recursive definitions in order to guarantee the termination of all functions. A well-known class of such terminating functions makes exclusively use of a bridled form of recursion called *primitive recursion* (Robinson, 1947, 1948).

Unfortunately, many useful functions do not fit, easily or at all, in this framework and, as a consequence, most functional languages leave to the programmers the responsibility to check the termination of their programs. For theoretical reasons, it is not possible to provide a general criterion for termination, but some rules exist that cover many usages.

Consider the following example where $m, n \in \mathbb{N}$:

$$
\begin{aligned}
\mathsf{ack}(0, n) &\xrightarrow{\theta} n + 1; \\
\mathsf{ack}(m + 1, 0) &\xrightarrow{\iota} \mathsf{ack}(m, 1); \\
\mathsf{ack}(m + 1, n + 1) &\xrightarrow{\kappa} \mathsf{ack}(m, \mathsf{ack}(m + 1, n)).
\end{aligned}
$$

This is a simplified form of Ackermann's function, an early example of a total computable function which is not primitive recursive. It makes use of double recursion and two parameters to grow values as towers of exponents, for example,

$$
\mathsf{ack}(4, 3) \twoheadrightarrow 2^{2^{2^{65536}}} - 3.
$$

It is not obviously terminating, because if the first argument does decrease, the second largely increases.

Let us define a well-founded ordering on pairs, called *lexicographic order*. Let $(\succ_A)$ and $(\succ_B)$ be well-founded orders on the sets A and B. Then $(\succ_{A \times B})$ defined as follows on $A \times B$ is well-founded:

$$
(a_0, b_0) \succ_{A \times B} (a_1, b_1) :\Leftrightarrow a_0 \succ_A a_1 \text{ or } (a_0 = a_1 \text{ and } b_0 \succ_B b_1). \quad (1.8)
$$

If $A = B = \mathbb{N}$ then $(\succ_A) = (\succ_B) = (>)$. To prove that $\mathsf{ack}(m, n)$ terminates for all $m, n \in \mathbb{N}$, first, we must find a well-founded order on the calls $\mathsf{ack}(m, n)$, that is, the calls must be totally ordered without any infinite descending chain. Here, a lexicographic order on $(m, n) \in \mathbb{N}^2$ extended to $\mathsf{ack}(m, n)$ works:

$$\mathsf{ack}(a_0, b_0) \succ \mathsf{ack}(a_1, b_1) :\Leftrightarrow a_0 > a_1 \text{ or } (a_0 = a_1 \text{ and } b_0 > b_1).$$

Clearly, $\mathsf{ack}(0, 0)$ is the minimum element. Second, we must prove that $\mathsf{ack}/2$ rewrites to smaller calls. We are only concerned with rules ι and κ. With the former, we have the inequality

$$\mathsf{ack}(m + 1, 0) \succ \mathsf{ack}(m, 1).$$

With rule κ, we have the following inequalities:

$$\mathsf{ack}(m + 1, n + 1) \succ \mathsf{ack}(m + 1, n),$$
$$\mathsf{ack}(m + 1, n + 1) \succ \mathsf{ack}(m, p),$$

for all values p, in particular when $\mathsf{ack}(m + 1, n) \twoheadrightarrow p$. □

A series of examples of termination proofs for term-rewriting systems has been published by Dershowitz (1995), Arts and Giesl (2001). An accessible survey is provided by Dershowitz (1987). Knuth (2000) analysed some famously involved recursive functions.

Associativity   Let us recall the definition (1.3) of the concatenation of two stacks:

$$\mathsf{cat}([\,], t) \xrightarrow{\alpha} t; \qquad \mathsf{cat}([x \,|\, s], t) \xrightarrow{\beta} [x \,|\, \mathsf{cat}(s, t)].$$

and let us prove the associativity of $\mathsf{cat}/2$, which we express formally as

$$\mathsf{CatAssoc}(s, t, u) : \mathsf{cat}(s, \mathsf{cat}(t, u)) \equiv \mathsf{cat}(\mathsf{cat}(s, t), u)$$

where s, t and u are stack values.

The goal here is to use the rewrite system as an abstract machine to prove a property, with the timely help of the induction principle. Precisely, we want to rewrite each side of the equivalence we wish to prove until we either find the same term (equality), or we use the induction hypothesis (equivalence). We want to be free to choose a rewrite amongst those possible for a given term, and this freedom is entailed by the joint termination and confluence of the rewrite system defining the functions: we always assume they hold when proving properties of such functions.

We apply the well-founded induction principle to the structure of s, so we must establish

- the basis $\forall t, u \in S.\mathsf{CatAssoc}([\,], t, u)$;

- step $\forall s, t, u \in S.\mathsf{CatAssoc}(s, t, u) \Rightarrow \forall x \in T.\mathsf{CatAssoc}([x\,|\,s], t, u)$.

Underlining the call being rewritten, the base case is:

$$\underline{\mathsf{cat}}([\,], \mathsf{cat}(t, u)) \overset{\alpha}{\to} \mathsf{cat}(t, u) \overset{\alpha}{\leftarrow} \mathsf{cat}(\underline{\mathsf{cat}}([\,], t), u).$$

Let us assume now $\mathsf{CatAssoc}(s, t, u)$, called the *induction hypothesis*, and let us prove $\mathsf{CatAssoc}([x\,|\,s], t, u)$, for any term x. We have:

$$\begin{aligned}
\underline{\mathsf{cat}}([x\,|\,s], \mathsf{cat}(t, u)) &\overset{\beta}{\to} [x\,|\,\mathsf{cat}(s, \mathsf{cat}(t, u))] \\
&\equiv [x\,|\,\mathsf{cat}(\mathsf{cat}(s, t), u)] \qquad \mathsf{CatAssoc}(s, t, u) \\
&\overset{\beta}{\leftarrow} \underline{\mathsf{cat}}([x\,|\,\mathsf{cat}(s, t)], u) \\
&\overset{\beta}{\leftarrow} \mathsf{cat}(\underline{\mathsf{cat}}([x\,|\,s], t), u).
\end{aligned}$$

Thus $\mathsf{CatAssoc}([x\,|\,s], t, u)$ holds and $\forall s, t, u \in S.\mathsf{CatAssoc}(s, t, u)$. $\qquad \square$

Note that we matched here an expression, namely $\mathsf{cat}([x\,|\,s], \mathsf{cat}(t, u))$, instead of a value, as is normally done with the call-by-value evaluation strategy, because we work with equivalences and we assumed that the system is terminating and confluent, so *any reduction strategy will do*.

1.6 Implementation

Translation to Erlang It is always enjoyable to have computers actually evaluate our function calls. We briefly introduce here Erlang, a functional language that contains a pure core (Armstrong, 2007). A *module* is a collection of function definitions. The syntax of Erlang is very close to our formalism and our previous rewrite systems become

```
-module(mix).
-export([cat/2,fact/1]).

cat(   [],T) -> T;
cat([X|S],T) -> [X|cat(S,T)].

fact(N) -> f(fun f/2,N).

f(_,0) -> 1;
f(G,N) -> N * G(G,N-1).
```

The differences are the headers and the lexical conventions of setting variables in big capitals and to mute unused variables in patterns with an underscore (_). Moreover, the expression fun f/2 denotes f/2 when used in stead of a value. From the Erlang shell, we can compile and run some examples:

```
1> c(mix).
{ok,mix}
2> mix:cat([1,2,3],[4,5]).
[1,2,3,4,5]
3> mix:fact(30).
265252859812191058636308480000000
```

Note that Erlang features exact integer arithmetic and that the order of
the definitions is irrelevant.

Translation to Java   Functional programs on stacks can be systematically translated into Java, following designs similar to those initially published by Felleisen and Friedman (1997), Bloch (2003) and Sher (2004).
This operation should transfer some interesting properties proved on the
source to the target language: the whole point hinges on how the mathematical approach presented earlier, both with structural induction and
functional programming, leads to trusted Java programs and, therefore,
constitutes a solid bridge between mathematics and computer science.

   Of course, the programs discussed in this book are extremely short
and the topic at hand thus resorts to 'programming in the small', but,
from the vantage point of software engineering, these functional programs
can then be considered as *formal specifications* of the Java programs, and
inductive proofs may be thought as instances of *formal methods*, like the
ones used to certify telecommunication protocols and critical embedded
systems. Therefore, this book may be used as a prerequisite to a software
engineering course, but also to an advanced programming course.

Design Pattern   The design pattern in Java which models a stack
relies on polymorphic methods and abstract and generic classes. The
following class Stack captures the essence of a stack:

```
// Stack.java
public abstract class Stack<Item> {
  public final NStack<Item> push(final Item item) {
    return new NStack<Item>(item,this); }
}
```

A stack is empty or not and the class Stack is abstract because it asserts
that both are stacks and that they share common functionalities, like the
method push, which is a wrapper around the constructor of non-empty
stacks, NStack, so both empty and non-empty stacks are augmented by
the same method. The argument item of push is declared **final** because

we want it to be constant in the body of the method, following the functional paradigm. The empty stack [] is mapped to an extension `EStack` of `Stack`, capturing the relationship 'An empty stack is a stack'. The class `EStack` contains no data.

```
// EStack.java
public final class EStack<Item> extends Stack<Item> {}
```

The non-empty stack is logically encoded by `NStack`, another subclass of `Stack`:

```
// NStack.java
public final class NStack<Item> extends Stack<Item> {
  private final Item head;
  private final Stack<Item> tail;

  public NStack(final Item item, final Stack<Item> stack) {
    head = item; tail = stack; }
}
```

The field `head` models the first item of a stack and `tail` corresponds to the rest of the stack (so `NStack` is a recursive class). The constructor just initialises these. Importantly, both are declared `final` to express that we do not expect reassignments after the first instantiation. Just as in our functional language, every time a new stack is needed, instead of modifying another with a side-effect, a new one is created, perhaps reusing others as constant components.

Concatenation of stacks As an example, let us recall definition (1.3) on page 7 for concatenating two stacks:

$$\mathsf{cat}([], t) \overset{\alpha}{\to} t; \qquad \mathsf{cat}([x \,|\, s], t) \overset{\beta}{\to} [x \,|\, \mathsf{cat}(s, t)].$$

The translation into our Java class hierarchy is as follows. The first argument of `cat/2` is a stack, corresponding to `this` inside our classes `EStack` and `NStack`. Therefore, the translation of `cat/2` is an abstract Java method in class `Stack`, with one parameter (the second of `cat/2`):

```
public abstract Stack<Item> cat(final Stack<Item> t);
```

Rule α applies only if the current object represents [], so the corresponding translation is a method of `EStack`. Dually, rule β leads to a method of `NStack`. The former returns its argument, so the translation is

```
public Stack<Item> cat(final Stack<Item> t) { return t; }
```

The latter returns an object of NStack corresponding to $[x \mid cat(s,t)]$. It is built by translating this stack from the bottom up: translate $cat(s,t)$ and then push x. Let us recall that s is the tail of $[x \mid s]$ on the left-hand side of rule β, hence $[x \mid s]$ is this and s corresponds to this.tail, or, simply, tail. Similarly, x is head. Finally,

```
public NStack<Item> cat(final Stack<Item> t) {
  return tail.cat(t).push(head);
}
```

Part I

Linear Structures

Chapter 2

Fundamentals

2.1 Concatenating

In the introduction, we did not explain the design of cat/2, the function which concatenates its two stack arguments. Let us start from scratch and proceed slowly.

Consider writing a function join/2 doing the same thing as cat/2. First, the requirement should be expressed in English as a function which takes two stacks and computes a stack containing all the items of the first stack followed by all the items of the second one, while retaining the relative order of the items. A requirement would be incomplete without some examples. For instance,

$$\text{join}([3,5],[2]) \twoheadrightarrow [3,5,2].$$

We should try some extreme cases, that is, special configurations of the arguments, in order to understand more precisely what is expected from this function. Both arguments being stacks, a hint comes naturally to mind because it is well known that stacks must either be empty or non-empty. This simple observation leads to consider four distinct cases: both stacks are empty; the first is empty and the second is not; the first is not empty and the second is; both are not empty:

$$\text{join}([\,],[\,])$$
$$\text{join}([\,],[y\,|\,t])$$
$$\text{join}([x\,|\,s],[\,])$$
$$\text{join}([x\,|\,s],[y\,|\,t])$$

It is important not to rush to write the right-hand sides and wonder: Are some cases left out? No, because there are exactly two arguments which

21

can each be either empty or not, leading to exactly $2 \cdot 2 = 4$ cases. Then, we write the corresponding canvas:

$$\mathsf{join}([\,], [\,]) \rightarrow \boxed{};$$
$$\mathsf{join}([\,], [y \,|\, t]) \rightarrow \boxed{};$$
$$\mathsf{join}([x \,|\, s], [\,]) \rightarrow \boxed{};$$
$$\mathsf{join}([x \,|\, s], [y \,|\, t]) \rightarrow \boxed{}.$$

Let us ponder which rule looks easier, because there is no reason to complete them in order if we do not want to. When reading the patterns, a clear mental representation of the situation should arise. Here, it seems that the first rule is the easiest because it contains no variable at all: what is the stack made of all the items of the (first) empty stack followed by all the items of the (second) empty stack? Since the empty stack, by definition, contains no item, the answer is the empty stack:

$$\mathsf{join}([\,], [\,]) \rightarrow [\,];$$
$$\mathsf{join}([\,], [y \,|\, t]) \rightarrow \boxed{};$$
$$\mathsf{join}([x \,|\, s], [\,]) \rightarrow \boxed{};$$
$$\mathsf{join}([x \,|\, s], [y \,|\, t]) \rightarrow \boxed{}.$$

Perhaps we might wonder whether this case should be dropped. In other words, is it a meaningful case? Yes, because the English description of the behaviour of $\mathsf{join}/2$ mandates the result be always a stack made of items of other stacks (the arguments), so, in the absence of any items to 'put' in the result, the final stack 'remains' empty.

It should be evident enough that the second and third rules are symmetric, because appending a non-empty stack to the right of an empty stack is the same as appending it to the left: the result is always the non-empty stack in question.

$$\mathsf{join}([\,], [\,]) \rightarrow [\,];$$
$$\mathsf{join}([\,], [y \,|\, t]) \rightarrow [y \,|\, t];$$
$$\mathsf{join}([x \,|\, s], [\,]) \rightarrow [x \,|\, s];$$
$$\mathsf{join}([x \,|\, s], [y \,|\, t]) \rightarrow \boxed{}.$$

The last rule is the trickiest. What does the pattern in the left-hand side of the rule reveal about the situation? That both stacks are not empty, more precisely, the top of the first stack is denoted by the variable x, the corresponding rest (which can either be empty or not) is s, and similarly for the second stack and y and t. Are these bricks enough for building the right-hand side, that is, the next step towards the result? We understand that appending two stacks p and q preserves in the result the total order of the items present in both, but also the relative order of the items of p

with respect to the items of q. In other words, the items of $p = [x \,|\, s]$ must be present in the result before the items of $q = [y \,|\, t]$ and the items from p must be in the same order as in p (same for q). With this ordering in mind, it is perhaps natural sketching the following:

$$\mathsf{join}([x \,|\, s], [y \,|\, t]) \rightarrow \square\, x \,\square\, s \,\square\, y \,\square\, t \,\square.$$

In one rewrite step, can the item x be placed in its final place, that is, in a position from where it does not need to be moved again? The answer is yes: it must be the top of the result.

$$\mathsf{join}([x \,|\, s], [y \,|\, t]) \rightarrow [x \,|\, \square\, s \,\square\, y \,\square\, t \,\square].$$

What about the other top, variable y? It should remain on top of t:

$$\mathsf{join}([x \,|\, s], [y \,|\, t]) \rightarrow [x \,|\, \square\, s \,\square\, [y \,|\, t]].$$

What is the relationship between s and $[y \,|\, t]$? We may be tempted by

$$\mathsf{join}([x \,|\, s], [y \,|\, t]) \rightarrow [x \,|\, [s \,|\, [y \,|\, t]]].$$

which is flawed. The reason is that, while we may allow stacks to be used as items for other stacks (in other words, stacks can be arbitrarily embedded in other stacks), s should not be used as an item here, as it is when it is used as a top in $[s \,|\, [y \,|\, t]]$. Let us consider the running example $\mathsf{join}([3, 5], [2])$: here, the left-hand side of the rule in question bounds x to 3, s to $[5]$, y to 2 and t to $[]$, therefore the corresponding putative right-hand side $[x \,|\, [s \,|\, [y \,|\, t]]]$ is actually `[3|[[5]|[2|[]]]]`, differing from the result `[3|[5|[2|[]]]]` in that `[5]` is not 5.

How can s and $[y \,|\, t]$ be concatenated? Of course, this is exactly the purpose of the function $\mathsf{join}/2$ currently being defined. Therefore, what we need here is a *recursive call* (underlined below):

$$\mathsf{join}([], []) \rightarrow [];$$
$$\mathsf{join}([], [y \,|\, t]) \rightarrow [y \,|\, t];$$
$$\mathsf{join}([x \,|\, s], []) \rightarrow [x \,|\, s];$$
$$\mathsf{join}([x \,|\, s], [y \,|\, t]) \rightarrow [x \,|\, \underline{\mathsf{join}(s, [y \,|\, t])}].$$

Correctness and completeness It is extremely common that, in the course of designing a function, we focus on some aspect, some rule, and then on some other part of the code, and we may miss the forest for the trees. When we settle for a function definition, the next step is to check whether it is correct and complete with respect to the conception we had of its expected behaviour.

We say that a definition is *correct* if all function calls that can be
rewritten in one step can be further rewritten in the expected result, *and*
if every failing call was expected to fail. By failure, we mean that a *stuck
expression* is reached, that is, an expression containing a function call
which can not be further rewritten.

We say that a definition is *complete* if all function calls that we
expect *a priori* to be computable are indeed computable. In other words,
we must also check that the definition enables rewriting into a value any
input we deem acceptable.

How do we check that the last definition of join/2 is correct and
complete? If the concept of 'expected result' is not formally defined,
typically by means of mathematics, we resort to *code review* and *testing*.
One important aspect of the reviewing process consists in verifying again
the left-hand sides of the definition and see if all possible inputs are
accepted or not. In case some inputs are not matched by the patterns,
we must justify that fact and record the reason in a comment. The left-
hand sides of join/2 match all the combinations of two stacks, whether
they are empty or not, and this is exactly what was expected: no more,
no less. The next step is to inspect the right-hand sides and wonder
twofold:

1. Are the right-hand sides rewritten into the expected type of value,
   for all function calls?

2. Are the function calls being provided the expected type of arguments?

These checks stem from the fact that some functional languages, like
Erlang, do not include *type inference* at compile-time. Other functional
languages, like OCaml and Haskell, would have their compilers automatically establish these properties. The examination of the right-hand sides
in the definition of join/2 confirms that

- the right-hand sides of the first three rules are stacks containing
  the same kind of items as the arguments;

- the arguments of the unique recursive call in the last rule are stacks
  made of items from the parameters;

- assuming that the recursive call has the expected type, we deduce
  that the right-hand side of the last rule is a stack made of items
  from the arguments.

As a conclusion, the two questions above have been positively answered.
Notice how we had to assume that the recursive call already had the type

we were trying to establish for the current definition. There is nothing wrong with this reasoning, called *inductive*, and it is rife in mathematics. We shall revisit it in different contexts.

The following stage consists in testing the definition. This means to define a set of inputs which lead to a set of outputs and failures that are all expected. For example, it is expected that join([], []) → [], so we could assess the validity of this statement by running the code, and the function call indeed passes the test. How should we choose the inputs meaningfully? There are no general rules, but some guidelines are useful. One is to consider the empty case or the smaller case, whatever that means in the context of the function. For example, if some argument is a stack, then let us try the empty stack. If some argument is a nonnegative integer, then let us try zero. Another advice is to have at least *test cases*, that is, some function calls whose values are known, which exert each rule. In the case of join/2, there are four rules to be covered by the test cases.

Improvement   Once we are convinced that the function we just defined is correct and complete, it is often worth considering again the code for improvement. There are several directions in which improvements, often called *optimisations* although the result may not be optimal, can be achieved:

- Can we rewrite the definition so that in all or some cases it is faster?

- Is there an equivalent definition which uses less memory in all or some cases?

- Can we shorten the definition by using fewer rules (perhaps some are useless or redundant) or shorter right-hand sides?

- Can we use less parameters in the definition? (This is related to memory usage.)

Let us reconsider join/2:

$$join([], []) \rightarrow [];$$
$$join([], [y\,|\,t]) \rightarrow [y\,|\,t];$$
$$join([x\,|\,s], []) \rightarrow [x\,|\,s];$$
$$join([x\,|\,s], [y\,|\,t]) \rightarrow [x\,|\,join(s, [y\,|\,t])].$$

and focus our attention on the two first rules, whose common point is to have the first stack being empty. It is clear now that the right-hand sides are, in both rules, the second stack, whether it is empty (first rule) or not (second rule). Therefore, there is no need to discriminate on the structure of the second stack when the first one is empty and we can equivalently write

$$\mathsf{join}([\,],t) \to t, \text{ where } t \text{ is a stack};$$
$$\mathsf{join}([x\,|\,s],[\,]) \to [x\,|\,s];$$
$$\mathsf{join}([x\,|\,s],[y\,|\,t]) \to [x\,|\,\mathsf{join}(s,[y\,|\,t])].$$

Note how the new definition does not formally ascertain that t is a stack – hence the comment – so it is not strictly equivalent to the original definition: now $\mathsf{join}([\,],5) \to 5$. Let us compromise by favouring the conciseness of the latter definition or assume type inference.

Let us consider next the two last rules and look for common patterns. It turns out that, in the penultimate rule, the first stack is matched as $[x\,|\,s]$ but nothing is done with x and s except *rebuilding* $[x\,|\,s]$ in the right-hand side. This suggests that we could simplify the rule as follows:

$$\mathsf{join}([\,],t) \to t;$$
$$\mathsf{join}(s,[\,]) \to s, \text{ where } s \text{ is a non-empty stack};$$
$$\mathsf{join}([x\,|\,s],[y\,|\,t]) \to [x\,|\,\mathsf{join}(s,[y\,|\,t])].$$

It is important to check that changing $[x\,|\,s]$ into s does not affect the pattern matching, that is to say, exactly the same inputs which used to match the pattern are still matching it. Indeed, it is possible in theory that the new s matches an empty stack. Can we prove that s is never empty? The left-hand side of the penultimate rule matches only if the previous rule did not match, in other words, rules are tried in the order of the writing, that is, top-down. Therefore, we know that s can not be bound to the empty stack, because $[\,]$ is used in the previous rule *and* the second parameter can be any stack. Nevertheless, as happened before, s is not necessarily a stack anymore, for instance, $\mathsf{join}(5,[\,]) \to 5$. Again, we will ignore this side-effect and choose the conciseness of the latter definition.

In the last rule, we observe that the second argument, matched by $[y\,|\,t]$, is simply passed over to the recursive call, thus it is useless to distinguish y and t and we can try

$$\mathsf{join}([\,],t) \to t;$$
$$\mathsf{join}(s,[\,]) \to s;$$
$$\mathsf{join}([x\,|\,s],t) \to [x\,|\,\mathsf{join}(s,t)].$$

(Can t be empty?) Again, we must make sure that t can not match an empty stack: it can not be empty because, otherwise, the previous pattern would have matched the call. As it is, the penultimate pattern is included in the last, that is, all input matched by the penultimate could be matched by the last, which leads us to consider whether the definition would still be correct if t could be empty after all. Let us label the rules as follows:

$$\mathsf{join}([\,], t) \xrightarrow{\alpha} t;$$
$$\mathsf{join}(s, [\,]) \xrightarrow{\beta} s;$$
$$\mathsf{join}([x\,|\,s], t) \xrightarrow{\gamma} [x\,|\,\mathsf{join}(s, t)].$$

Let s be some stack containing n items, which we write informally as $s = [x_0, x_1, \ldots, x_{n-1}]$. (Informally because of the ellipsis.) The subscript i in x_i is the *position* of the item in the stack, the top being at position 0. Then we would rewrite in one step

$$\mathsf{join}(s, [\,]) \xrightarrow{\beta} s.$$

Had rule β been erased, we would have had instead the series

$$
\begin{aligned}
\mathsf{join}(s, [\,]) \;&\xrightarrow{\gamma}\; [x_0\,|\,\mathsf{join}([x_1, \ldots, x_{n-1}], [\,])] \\
&\xrightarrow{\gamma}\; [x_0\,|\,[x_1\,|\,\mathsf{join}([x_2, \ldots, x_{n-1}], [\,])]] \\
&=\; [x_0, x_1\,|\,\mathsf{join}([x_2, \ldots, x_{n-1}], [\,])] \\
&\xrightarrow{\gamma}\; [x_0, x_1\,|\,[x_2\,|\,\mathsf{join}([x_3, \ldots, x_{n-1}], [\,])]] \\
&=\; [x_0, x_1, x_2\,|\,\mathsf{join}([x_3, \ldots, x_{n-1}], [\,])] \\
&\;\;\vdots \\
&\xrightarrow{\gamma}\; [x_0, x_1, \ldots, x_{n-1}\,|\,\mathsf{join}([\,], [\,])] \\
&\xrightarrow{\alpha}\; [x_0, x_1, \ldots, x_{n-1}\,|\,[\,]] \\
&=\; [x_0, x_1, \ldots, x_{n-1}] \\
&=\; s.
\end{aligned}
$$

In short, we found $\mathsf{join}(s, [\,]) \twoheadrightarrow s$. This means that rule β is useless, since its removal allows us to reach the same result s, although more slowly: n steps by rule γ plus 1 by rule α, instead of one step by rule β. We are hence in a situation where we discover that the original definition was already specialised for speed when the second stack is empty. If we remove rule β, the program is shorter but becomes slower in that special case.

This kind of dilemma is quite common in programming and there is sometimes no clear-cut answer as to what is the best design. Perhaps another argument can here tip the scale slightly in favour of the removal. Indeed, whilst the removal slows down some calls, it makes the number of rewrites easy to remember: it is the number of items of the first stack plus 1; in particular, the length of the second argument is irrelevant. So let us settle for a new definition with a new name:

$$\mathsf{cat}([\,], t) \xrightarrow{\alpha} t;$$
$$\mathsf{cat}([x\,|\,s], t) \xrightarrow{\beta} [x\,|\,\mathsf{cat}(s, t)].$$

Let us note that cat(5, []) fails again, as it does in the original version.

When programming medium or large applications, it is recommended to use evocative variables, like StackOfProc, instead of enigmatic ones, like s. But in this presentation we are mostly concerned with short programs, not software engineering, so short variables will do. Nevertheless, we need to opt for a naming convention so we can easily recognise the type of the variables across function definitions.

Tail form   As the rewrite of cat(s, []) shows, the right-hand side of rule β of cat/2 features a call with the *context* $[x \,|\, \_]$, the mark $\_$ standing for the location of the call cat(s, t). When all the right-hand sides of a definition are either values, or arithmetic expressions, or expressions made only of data constructors, or one function call whose arguments are values or arithmetic expressions or data constructors, it is said to be in *tail form*.

We may wonder whether a tail form variant is necessary or not and we will discuss this issue later. At the moment, let us take this as a stylistic exercise and, instead of presenting a systematic transformation, let us envisage a pragmatic approach. In the case of cat/2, as stated above, the only context is $[x \,|\, \_]$ and the operator ($|$) is not associative, that is, $[x \,|\, [y \,|\, z]] \not\equiv [[x \,|\, y] \,|\, z]$. The idea is to add another parameter in which we will store the values from the context, and when the input is exhausted, we will rebuild the context from that parameter, called an *accumulator*. Here, we want a new function cat/3 whose definition has the shape

$$\mathsf{cat}([\,], t, \underline{u}) \rightarrow \boxed{};$$
$$\mathsf{cat}([x \,|\, s], t, \underline{u}) \rightarrow \boxed{}.$$

The new parameter u is the accumulator in question. Since we want to store many x in it, it must be a stack. Furthermore, its initial value should be the empty stack, otherwise extraneous items would be found in the result. Therefore, the definition in tail form, equivalent to cat/2 and named cat$_0$/2, calls cat/3 with the extra argument $[\,]$:

$$\mathsf{cat}_0(s, t) \rightarrow \mathsf{cat}(s, t, [\,]).$$

Let us go back to cat/3 and push x on u:

$$\mathsf{cat}([\,], t, u) \xrightarrow{\alpha} \boxed{};$$
$$\mathsf{cat}([x \,|\, s], t, u) \xrightarrow{\beta} \mathsf{cat}(s, t, [x \,|\, u]).$$

What is the accumulator with respect to the expected result? We already know that it can not be a partial result, because ($|$) is not associative.

So some more work has to be done with u *and* t, but, first, we should understand what u contains at this point and unfolding a call, with a piece of paper and a pencil, is quite enlightening.

Let s be a stack of n items $[x_0, x_1, \ldots, x_{n-1}]$. We have the following:

$$\mathsf{cat}(s, t, []) \xrightarrow{\beta} \mathsf{cat}([x_1, \ldots, x_{n-1}], t, [x_0])$$
$$\xrightarrow{\beta} \mathsf{cat}([x_2, \ldots, x_{n-1}], t, [x_1, x_0])$$
$$\vdots$$
$$\xrightarrow{\beta} \mathsf{cat}([], t, [x_{n-1}, x_{n-2}, \ldots, x_0])$$
$$\xrightarrow{\alpha} \boxed{}.$$

Therefore, u in the left-hand side of rule α is bound to a stack which contains the same items as the original first argument s, but in *reverse order*. In other words, given the call $\mathsf{cat}(s, t, [])$, the parameter u in the first pattern of $\mathsf{cat}/3$ holds s reversed. What can we do with u and t in order to reach the result?

The key is to realise that the answer depends on the contents of u, which, therefore, needs to be matched more accurately: is u empty or not? This leads to split rule α into α_0 and α_1:

$$\mathsf{cat}([], t, []) \xrightarrow{\alpha_0} \boxed{};$$
$$\mathsf{cat}([], t, [x \mid u]) \xrightarrow{\alpha_1} \boxed{};$$
$$\mathsf{cat}([x \mid s], t, u) \xrightarrow{\beta} \mathsf{cat}(s, t, [x \mid u]).$$

Notice that rules α_0 and α_1 could be swapped, as they filter completely distinct cases. The right-hand side of rule α_0 is easy to guess: it must be t, since it corresponds to the case when we want to append the empty stack to t:

$$\mathsf{cat}([], t, []) \xrightarrow{\alpha_0} t;$$
$$\mathsf{cat}([], t, [x \mid u]) \xrightarrow{\alpha_1} \boxed{};$$
$$\mathsf{cat}([x \mid s], t, u) \xrightarrow{\beta} \mathsf{cat}(s, t, [x \mid u]).$$

How do we relate t, x and u in rule α_1 with the result we are looking for? Given the rewrite $\mathsf{cat}(s, t, []) \twoheadrightarrow \mathsf{cat}([], t, [x \mid u])$, we know that $[x \mid u]$ is s reversed, so item x is last in s and it should be on top of t in the result. What should we do with u?

The key is to realise that we need to start the same process again, that is, we need another recursive call:

$$\mathsf{cat}([], t, []) \xrightarrow{\alpha_0} t;$$
$$\mathsf{cat}([], t, [x \mid u]) \xrightarrow{\alpha_1} \mathsf{cat}([], [x \mid t], u);$$
$$\mathsf{cat}([x \mid s], t, u) \xrightarrow{\beta} \mathsf{cat}(s, t, [x \mid u]).$$

To test the correctness of this definition, we can try a small example:

$$\mathsf{cat}([1,2,3],[4,5],[\,]) \xrightarrow{\beta} \mathsf{cat}([2,3],[4,5],[1])$$
$$\xrightarrow{\beta} \mathsf{cat}([3],[4,5],[2,1])$$
$$\xrightarrow{\beta} \mathsf{cat}([\,],[4,5],[3,2,1])$$
$$\xrightarrow{\alpha_1} \mathsf{cat}([\,],[3,4,5],[2,1])$$
$$\xrightarrow{\alpha_1} \mathsf{cat}([\,],[2,3,4,5],[1])$$
$$\xrightarrow{\alpha_1} \mathsf{cat}([\,],[1,2,3,4,5],[\,])$$
$$\xrightarrow{\alpha_0} [1,2,3,4,5].$$

As a conclusion, the tail form version of $\mathsf{cat}/2$, called $\mathsf{cat}_0/2$, requires an auxiliary function $\mathsf{cat}/3$ with an accumulator whose purpose is to reverse the first argument:

$$\mathsf{cat}_0(s,t) \xrightarrow{\alpha} \mathsf{cat}(s,t,[\,]).$$
$$\mathsf{cat}([\,],t,[\,]) \xrightarrow{\beta} t;$$
$$\mathsf{cat}([\,],t,[x\,|\,u]) \xrightarrow{\gamma} \mathsf{cat}([\,],[x\,|\,t],u);$$
$$\mathsf{cat}([x\,|\,s],t,u) \xrightarrow{\delta} \mathsf{cat}(s,t,[x\,|\,u]).$$

We also know what to do when the context is not made of a call to some associative operator: push the values of the variables it contains and when the input stack is empty, pop these and use them to fill the context, which is then evaluated. We will revisit this method.

Efficiency The number of steps to rewrite $\mathsf{cat}_0(s,t)$ into a value is greater than with $\mathsf{cat}(s,t)$, as we guessed while writing the previous example. Indeed, assuming that s contains n items, we have

- one step to obtain $\mathsf{cat}(s,t,[\,])$, by rule α;
- n steps to reverse s in the accumulator, by rule δ;
- n steps to reverse the accumulator on top of t, by rule γ;
- one step when the accumulator is finally empty, by rule β.

Thus, the total number of steps is $2n + 2$, which is twice the cost of the previous version. Why the difference between $\mathsf{cat}/2$ and $\mathsf{cat}_0/2$? The operation applied to the accumulator consists in pushing an item onto a stack and has to be undone later: the accumulator is not a partial result but a *temporary stack* used to hold the items of the first stack in reverse order. We shall find many occurrences of this situation. Meanwhile, it is important to remember that a tail form variant of a function operating on stacks may lead to a slower program. Moreover, the definition we derived in tail form may be longer, as illustrated by $\mathsf{cat}_0/2$: four rules instead of two.

The rewrites $\mathsf{cat}_0([1, 2, 3], [4, 5]) \twoheadrightarrow [1, 2, 3, 4, 5]$ seen above can be abstractly conceived as a product (composition) of rules: $\alpha \cdot \delta^n \cdot \gamma^n \cdot \beta$, or, simply, $\alpha \delta^n \gamma^n \beta$. This expression is called the *execution trace* and its length is the number of rules $\mathcal{C}_n^{\mathsf{cat}_0}$ of $\mathsf{cat}_0(s, t)$, given that the length of a rule is 1, hence $|\alpha| = |\beta| = |\gamma| = |\delta| = 1$ and the length of the composition of two rules is the sum of their lengths: $|\alpha \cdot \delta| = |\alpha| + |\delta|$. Therefore, we have the following:

$$\mathcal{C}_n^{\mathsf{cat}_0} = |\alpha \delta^n \gamma^n \beta| = |\alpha| + |\delta^n| + |\gamma^n| + |\beta| = 1 + |\delta| \cdot n + |\gamma| \cdot n + 1$$
$$= 2n + 2.$$

Digression Let us reconsider the definition (1.2) of $\mathsf{fact}/1$ on page 5:

$$\mathsf{fact}(0) \xrightarrow{\alpha} 1;$$
$$\mathsf{fact}(n) \xrightarrow{\beta} n \cdot \mathsf{fact}(n - 1).$$

For instance, we have

$$\mathsf{fact}(3) \xrightarrow{\beta} 3 \cdot \mathsf{fact}(3 - 1) \qquad = 3 \cdot \mathsf{fact}(2)$$
$$\xrightarrow{\beta} 3 \cdot (2 \cdot \mathsf{fact}(2 - 1)) = 3 \cdot (2 \cdot \mathsf{fact}(1))$$
$$\xrightarrow{\alpha} 3 \cdot (2 \cdot (1)) \qquad = 6 = 3!$$

It is often clearer to implicitly compose intermediary arithmetic operations ($=$) with the current rewrite and write in short

$$\mathsf{fact}(3) \xrightarrow{\beta} 3 \cdot \mathsf{fact}(2) \xrightarrow{\beta} 3 \cdot (2 \cdot \mathsf{fact}(1)) \xrightarrow{\alpha} 3 \cdot (2 \cdot (1)) = 6.$$

Note how the last rewrite ($\xrightarrow{\alpha}$) must be followed by a series of multiplications $3 \cdot (2 \cdot 1)$ because each individual multiplication had to be delayed until $\mathsf{fact}(1)$ be computed. This could have been anticipated because the call to $\mathsf{fact}/1$ in the right-hand side of the rewrite rule ($\xrightarrow{\beta}$), that is, the underlined text in

$$\mathsf{fact}(n) \xrightarrow{\beta} n \cdot \underline{\mathsf{fact}(n - 1)}$$

has the non-empty context '$n * \_$'. To understand why this is important, let us consider a slightly longer series of rewrites:

$$\mathsf{fact}(5) \xrightarrow{\beta} 5 \cdot \mathsf{fact}(4)$$
$$\xrightarrow{\beta} 5 \cdot (4 \cdot \mathsf{fact}(3))$$
$$\xrightarrow{\beta} 5 \cdot (4 \cdot (3 \cdot \mathsf{fact}(2)))$$
$$\xrightarrow{\beta} 5 \cdot (4 \cdot (3 \cdot (2 \cdot \mathsf{fact}(1))))$$
$$\xrightarrow{\alpha} 5 \cdot (4 \cdot (3 \cdot (2 \cdot (1)))).$$

It is clear that each rewrite by ($\xrightarrow{\beta}$) yields a longer expression. Let us focus now only on the shapes of these expressions:

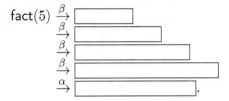

This phenomenon suggests that a great deal of space, that is, computer *memory*, is needed to keep the expressions before the final, long arithmetic computations. The example leads to induce that the larger term occurring in the computing of fact(n) is the one just before ($\xrightarrow{\alpha}$) and its size is likely to be proportional to n, since all the integers from n to 1 had to be kept until the end.

A tail form version $\mathsf{fact_0}/1$ would be

$$\mathsf{fact_0}(n) \to \mathsf{fact_0}(n, 1), \text{ if } n \geqslant 1.$$
$$\mathsf{fact_0}(1, a) \to a;$$
$$\mathsf{fact_0}(n, a) \to \mathsf{fact_0}(n - 1, a \cdot n).$$

Here, in contrast with $\mathsf{cat}/3$, the operation applied to the accumulator is associative (a multiplication) and the accumulator is, at all times, a partial result. Instead of delaying the multiplications, exactly one multiplication is going to be computed at each rewrite, thus, in the end, nothing remains to be done: there is no instance of the context to resume. This kind of definition is thus in tail form.

Notice that the cost of $\mathsf{fact_0}/1$ is $n + 1$, whilst the cost of $\mathsf{fact}/1$ is n, so, contrary to $\mathsf{cat_0}/2$ and $\mathsf{cat}/2$, the tail form here does not significantly increases the cost. This is due to the nature of the operations on the accumulator, which do not require to be reversed or undone.

The previously considered function call $\mathsf{fact_0}(5)$ is evaluated thusly:

$$
\begin{aligned}
\mathsf{fact_0}(5) &\xrightarrow{\alpha} \mathsf{fact_0}(5, 1), &&\text{since } 5 > 1, \\
&\xrightarrow{\gamma} \mathsf{fact_0}(5 - 1, 1 \cdot 5) &&= \mathsf{fact_0}(4, 5) \\
&\xrightarrow{\gamma} \mathsf{fact_0}(4 - 1, 5 \cdot 4) &&= \mathsf{fact_0}(3, 20) \\
&\xrightarrow{\gamma} \mathsf{fact_0}(3 - 1, 20 \cdot 3) &&= \mathsf{fact_0}(2, 60) \\
&\xrightarrow{\gamma} \mathsf{fact_0}(2 - 1, 60 \cdot 2) &&= \mathsf{fact_0}(1, 120) \\
&\xrightarrow{\beta} 120.
\end{aligned}
$$

The reason why $\mathsf{fact_0}(5) \equiv \mathsf{fact}(5)$ is that

$$(((1 \cdot 5) \cdot 4) \cdot 3) \cdot 2 = 5 \cdot (4 \cdot (3 \cdot (2 \cdot 1))). \tag{2.1}$$

This equality holds because, in general, for all numbers x, y and z,

1. the multiplication is associative: $x \cdot (y \cdot z) = (x \cdot y) \cdot z$;

2. the number 1 is neutral with respect to $(\cdot)$: $x \cdot 1 = 1 \cdot x = x$.

To show exactly why, let us write $(\overset{1}{=})$ and $(\overset{2}{=})$ to denote, respectively, the use of associativity and neutrality, then lay out the following equalities leading from the left-hand side to the right-hand side of the purported equality (2.1):

$$(((1 \cdot 5) \cdot 4) \cdot 3) \cdot 2 \overset{2}{=} ((((1 \cdot 5) \cdot 4) \cdot 3) \cdot 2) \cdot 1$$
$$\overset{1}{=} (((1 \cdot 5) \cdot 4) \cdot 3) \cdot (2 \cdot 1)$$
$$\overset{1}{=} ((1 \cdot 5) \cdot 4) \cdot (3 \cdot (2 \cdot 1))$$
$$\overset{1}{=} (1 \cdot 5) \cdot (4 \cdot (3 \cdot (2 \cdot 1)))$$
$$\overset{1}{=} 1 \cdot (5 \cdot (4 \cdot (3 \cdot (2 \cdot 1))))$$
$$\overset{2}{=} 5 \cdot (4 \cdot (3 \cdot (2 \cdot 1))). \quad \square$$

Furthermore, if we do not want to rely upon the neutrality of 1, we could define another equivalent function $\mathsf{fact}_1/1$ which sets the initial call to $\mathsf{fact}_1(n-1, n)$, instead of $\mathsf{fact}_0(n, 1)$, and stops when the number is 0, instead of 1:

$$\mathsf{fact}_1(n) \overset{\alpha}{\rightarrow} \mathsf{fact}_1(n-1, n), \text{ if } n > 0.$$
$$\mathsf{fact}_1(0, a) \overset{\beta}{\rightarrow} a;$$
$$\mathsf{fact}_1(n, a) \overset{\gamma}{\rightarrow} \mathsf{fact}_1(n-1, a \cdot n).$$

The same example now runs as

$$\mathsf{fact}_1(5) \overset{\alpha}{\rightarrow} \mathsf{fact}_1(5-1, 5) \quad = \mathsf{fact}_1(4, 5)$$
$$\overset{\gamma}{\rightarrow} \mathsf{fact}_1(4-1, 5 \cdot 4) \quad = \mathsf{fact}_1(3, 20)$$
$$\overset{\gamma}{\rightarrow} \mathsf{fact}_1(3-1, 20 \cdot 3) \quad = \mathsf{fact}_1(2, 60)$$
$$\overset{\gamma}{\rightarrow} \mathsf{fact}_1(2-1, 60 \cdot 2) \quad = \mathsf{fact}_1(1, 120)$$
$$\overset{\gamma}{\rightarrow} \mathsf{fact}_1(1-1, 120 \cdot 1) = \mathsf{fact}_1(0, 120)$$
$$\overset{\beta}{\rightarrow} 120.$$

This new version relies on the following equality which can be proved only by means of associativity: $(((5 \cdot 4) \cdot 3) \cdot 2) \cdot 1 = 5 \cdot (4 \cdot (3 \cdot (2 \cdot 1)))$.

The number of rewrites of $\mathsf{fact}_0/1$ is almost the same as with $\mathsf{fact}/1$, precisely one more step due to the rule α. But the former presents an advantage in terms of memory usage, as long as it is assumed that all integers within a certain range occupy the same space. This means that, for instance, that the memory needed to store the number 120 is the same as for the number 5. Then the shape of the previous rewrites:

$$\mathsf{fact_0}(5) \xrightarrow{\alpha} \boxed{}$$
$$\xrightarrow{\gamma} \boxed{}$$
$$\xrightarrow{\gamma} \boxed{}$$
$$\xrightarrow{\gamma} \boxed{}$$
$$\xrightarrow{\gamma} \boxed{}$$
$$\xrightarrow{\beta} \boxed{}.$$

It seems probable that this version uses a constant chunk of memory, while fact/1 uses an increasing amount of memory, more precisely a space proportional to n when computing $n!$. (In the following sections, we shall see that a more precise model of memory allocation is provided by abstract syntax trees.) This phenomenon has been anticipated by the keen reader who noticed that there is no context for the calls in the rules defining $\mathsf{fact_0}/2$, so there are no delayed computations that accumulate until the last step. As a conclusion, $\mathsf{fact_0}/1$ is always preferable to fact/1.

The previous discussions on obtaining equivalent definitions which are in tail form suppose to consider programs as some kind of data. At this point, it is a methodological standpoint only and we do not mean that functions can be processed as stacks (we shall come back on this later when discussing higher-order functions and continuation-passing style), but, more informally, we mean that definitions can be transformed into other definitions and that this is often an excellent method, as opposed to trying to figure out from scratch the final definition. It would have been probably more difficult to write the tail form variant of cat/2 without having first designed the version not in tail form.

It is in general not a good idea to start head-on by defining a function in tail form because it may either be unnecessary or lead to a mistake since these kinds of definitions are usually more involved. In the following sections and chapters, we will explain when tail form definitions are useful and how to obtain them using a systematic method.

Let us consider a simple case by defining a function last/1 such that $\mathsf{last}(s)$ computes the last item of the non-empty stack s. The correct approach is to forget about tail forms and aim straight at the heart of the problem. We know that s can not be empty, so let us start with the following left-hand side:

$$\mathsf{last}([x\,|\,s]) \rightarrow \boxed{}.$$

Can we reach the result in one step? No, because we do not know whether x is the sought item: we need to know more about s. This additional information about the structure of s is given by more precise patterns:

s can be empty or not, that is: $s = []$ or $s = [y\,|\,t]$. We then have:

$$\mathsf{last}([x\,|\,[]]) \rightarrow \boxed{};$$
$$\mathsf{last}([x\,|\,[y\,|\,t]]) \rightarrow \boxed{}.$$

The first pattern can be simplified as follows:

$$\mathsf{last}([x]) \rightarrow \boxed{};$$
$$\mathsf{last}([x\,|\,[y\,|\,t]]) \rightarrow \boxed{}.$$

The first right-hand side is easy to guess:

$$\mathsf{last}([x]) \rightarrow x;$$
$$\mathsf{last}([x\,|\,[y\,|\,t]]) \rightarrow \boxed{}.$$

In the last rule, how do x, y and t relate to the result? Can we reach it in one step? No, despite we know that x is *not* the result, we still don't know whether y is, so we have to start over again, which means a recursive call is required:

$$\mathsf{last}([x]) \rightarrow x;$$
$$\mathsf{last}([x\,|\,[y\,|\,t]]) \rightarrow \mathsf{last}(\boxed{}).$$

Note how knowing that some specific part of the input is not useful to build the output is useful knowledge. We can not call recursively $\mathsf{last}(t)$ because t may be empty and the call would then fail, meaning that the answer was actually y. Therefore, we must call with $[y\,|\,t]$ to give y the chance to be the last:

$$\mathsf{last}([x]) \rightarrow x;$$
$$\mathsf{last}([x\,|\,[y\,|\,t]]) \rightarrow \mathsf{last}([y\,|\,t]).$$

As we advocated previously, the next phase consists in testing this definition for correctness and completeness, using meaningful examples (covering extreme cases and all the rules at least once). For the sake of the argument, let us assume that $\mathsf{last}/1$ is correct and complete. The next step is then to try and improve upon it. Let us look for patterns occurring in both sides of the same rule and ponder whether they can be avoided. For instance, we observe that $[y\,|\,t]$ is used as a whole, in other words, y and t are not used separately in the second right-hand side. Therefore, it is worth trying to fold back and replace the pattern by a more general one, in this case: $s = [y\,|\,t]$.

$$\mathsf{last}([x]) \rightarrow x;$$
$$\mathsf{last}([x\,|\,s]) \rightarrow \mathsf{last}(s).$$

This transformation is correct because the case where s is empty has already been matched by the first pattern. Notice also that we indeed considered a definition as some data. (We should write more accurately *metadata* since definitions are not data processed by the program, but by the programmer.) In passing, last/1 is in tail form.

What if we had tried to find directly a definition in tail form? We might have recalled that such definitions often need an accumulator and we would have tried perhaps something along these lines:

$$\mathsf{last}_0(s) \rightarrow \mathsf{last}_1(s, 0).$$
$$\mathsf{last}_1([\,], y) \rightarrow y;$$
$$\mathsf{last}_1([x \,|\, s], y) \rightarrow \mathsf{last}_1(s, x).$$

The first observation may be about the function name last_1. Why not write the following, in accordance with the style up to now?

$$\mathsf{last}_0(s) \rightarrow \mathsf{last}_0(s, 0).$$
$$\mathsf{last}_0([\,], y) \rightarrow y;$$
$$\mathsf{last}_0([x \,|\, s], y) \rightarrow \mathsf{last}_0(s, x).$$

There would be no confusion between last_0/1 and last_0/2 because, each taking a different number of arguments, they are logically considered different. The reason why we recommend to distinguish the names and, in general, to use one name for only one function, is that this discipline enables the compiler to catch the error consisting in forgetting one argument. For instance, the program

$$\mathsf{last}_0(s) \rightarrow \mathsf{last}_0(s, 0).$$
$$\mathsf{last}_0([\,], y) \rightarrow y;$$
$$\mathsf{last}_0([x \,|\, s], y) \rightarrow \underline{\mathsf{last}_0(s)}.$$

contains an error that goes unreported, while

$$\mathsf{last}_0(s) \rightarrow \mathsf{last}_1(s, 0).$$
$$\mathsf{last}_1([\,], y) \rightarrow y;$$
$$\mathsf{last}_1([x \,|\, s], y) \rightarrow \underline{\mathsf{last}_1(s)}.$$

raises an error. However, for didactic purposes in this book, we will not always follow this recommendation of having unique function names. The possibility to use the same name for different functions which can be otherwise distinguished by the number of their arguments is called *overloading*. Overloading of functions in the programming language C++ is permitted, but the rules used to distinguish amongst the different functions sharing the same name is different than in Erlang, as it makes use of the number of parameters but also their static types.

Computing the call $last_0([1, 2, 3])$ with the original definition, we find that the three rules are covered until the correct result is found, that is 3. Because we recommended previously to make some litmus test and the argument is a stack, we try the empty stack and obtain the evaluation $last_0([]) \rightarrow last_1([], 0) \rightarrow 0$, which is unexpected, since this test ought to fail (see how $last/1$ is not defined for the empty stack). Can we fix this?

Let us simply change the left-hand side of $last_0/1$ so that only non-empty stacks are matched. We find here a case where more information on the structure of the input is needed and a variable is too general a pattern. We need instead

$$last_0([\underline{x \,|\, s}]) \rightarrow last_0([\underline{x \,|\, s}], 0).$$
$$last_0([], y) \rightarrow y;$$
$$last_0([x \,|\, s], y) \rightarrow last_0(s, x).$$

This emendation seems to go against an improvement we made earlier, when we replaced $[y \,|\, t]$ by s, but it does not: here we want to exclude some input, that is, we do not seek an equivalent function, whilst before the purpose was to simplify and obtain an equivalent function.

The definition of $last_0/1$ is correct and complete but a careful review should raise some doubts about its actual simplicity. For example, the initial value of the accumulator, given in the unique right-hand side of $last_0/1$ is 0, but this value is never used, because it is discarded immediately after in the second right-hand side of $last_0/2$. Indeed, we could write the equivalent definition:

$$last_1([x \,|\, s]) \rightarrow last_1([x \,|\, s], \underline{7}).$$
$$last_1([], y) \rightarrow y;$$
$$last_1([x \,|\, s], y) \rightarrow last_1(s, x).$$

The initial value of the accumulator here does not even need to be an integer, it could be of any type, like $[4, []]$. This is the sign that we should better give up this overly complicated definition, which is the product of a method that does not consider programs as data and is founded on the wrong assumption that definitions in tail form often require an accumulator: in general, they do not.

Take for example the polymorphic identity: $id(x) \rightarrow x$. It is trivially in tail form. In passing, being in tail form has nothing to do, in general, with recursion, despite the widespread and unfortunate locution 'tail-recursive function'. A recursive definition may only feature tail calls (at least one recursive, directly or indirectly), but a definition with only tail calls may not be recursive, like $id/1$.

2.2 Reversal

Involution   Sometimes a proof requires some lemma to be devised. Let us consider the definition of a function $\mathsf{rev_0}/1$ reversing a stack:

$$\mathsf{cat}([\,],t) \xrightarrow{\alpha} t; \qquad\qquad \mathsf{rev_0}([\,]) \xrightarrow{\gamma} [\,];$$
$$\mathsf{cat}([x\,|\,s],t) \xrightarrow{\beta} [x\,|\,\mathsf{cat}(s,t)]. \quad \mathsf{rev_0}([x\,|\,s]) \xrightarrow{\delta} \mathsf{cat}(\mathsf{rev_0}(s),[x]).$$

An evaluation is shown with abstract syntax trees in FIGURE 2.1. Let $\mathsf{Inv}(s)$ be the property $\mathsf{rev_0}(\mathsf{rev_0}(s)) \equiv s$, that is, the function $\mathsf{rev_0}/1$ is an *involution*.

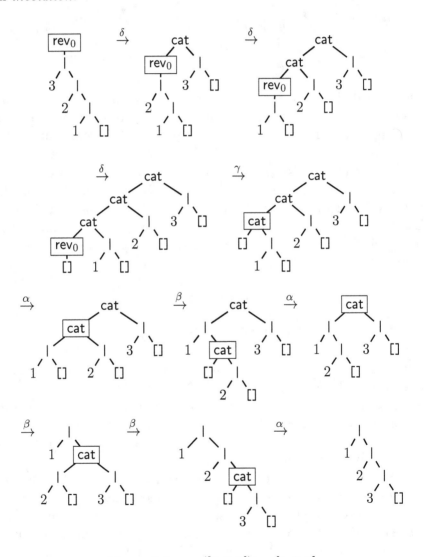

Figure 2.1: $\mathsf{rev_0}([3,2,1]) \twoheadrightarrow [1,2,3]$

In order to prove $\forall s \in S.\mathsf{Inv}(s)$, the induction principle on the structure of s requires that we establish

- the basis $\mathsf{Inv}([])$;
- the inductive step $\forall s \in S.\mathsf{Inv}(s) \Rightarrow \forall x \in T.\mathsf{Inv}([x\,|\,s])$.

The basis is quickly found (we underline the call being rewritten, when there is more than one):

$$\mathsf{rev_0}(\underline{\mathsf{rev_0}}([])) \overset{\gamma}{\to} \mathsf{rev_0}([]) \overset{\gamma}{\to} [].$$

The induction hypothesis is $\mathsf{Inv}(s)$ and we want to establish $\mathsf{Inv}([x\,|\,s])$, for any x. If we commence head-on with

$$\mathsf{rev_0}(\underline{\mathsf{rev_0}}([x\,|\,s])) \overset{\delta}{\to} \mathsf{rev_0}(\mathsf{cat}(\mathsf{rev_0}(s), [x])),$$

we are stuck. But the term to rewrite involves both $\mathsf{rev_0}/1$ and $\mathsf{cat}/2$, hence spurring us to conceive a lemma where the stumbling pattern $\mathsf{cat}(\mathsf{rev_0}(\dots), \dots)$ occurs and is equivalent to a simpler term.

Let $\mathsf{CatRev}(s, t)$ denote $\mathsf{cat}(\mathsf{rev_0}(t), \mathsf{rev_0}(s)) \equiv \mathsf{rev_0}(\mathsf{cat}(s, t))$. In order to prove it by induction on the structure of s, we need, for all t,

- the basis $\mathsf{CatRev}([], t)$;
- the inductive step $\forall s, t \in S.\mathsf{CatRev}(s, t) \Rightarrow \forall x \in T.\mathsf{CatRev}([x\,|\,s], t)$.

The former is almost within reach:

$$\mathsf{rev_0}(\mathsf{cat}([], t)) \overset{\alpha}{\to} \mathsf{rev_0}(t) \rightsquigarrow \mathsf{cat}(\mathsf{rev_0}(t), []) \overset{\gamma}{\leftarrow} \mathsf{cat}(\mathsf{rev_0}(t), \mathsf{rev_0}([])).$$

The missing part is filled by showing that $(\rightsquigarrow)$ is $\mathsf{CatNil}(s)$.

Let $\mathsf{CatNil}(s)$ be the property $\mathsf{cat}(s, []) \equiv s$. In order to prove it by induction on the structure of s, we have to prove

- the basis $\mathsf{CatNil}([])$;
- the inductive step $\forall s \in S.\mathsf{CatNil}(s) \Rightarrow \forall x \in T.\mathsf{CatNil}([x\,|\,s])$.

The former is easy: $\mathsf{cat}([], []) \overset{\alpha}{\to} []$. The latter is not complicated either: $\mathsf{cat}([x\,|\,s], []) \overset{\beta}{\to} [x\,|\,\mathsf{cat}(s, [])] \equiv [x\,|\,s]$, where the equivalence is none other than the induction hypothesis $\mathsf{CatNil}(s)$. $\square$

Assuming $\mathsf{CatRev}(s, t)$, we must establish $\forall x \in T.\mathsf{CatRev}([x\,|\,s], t)$:

$$
\begin{aligned}
\mathsf{cat}(\mathsf{rev_0}(t), \underline{\mathsf{rev_0}}([x\,|\,s])) \overset{\delta}{\to} \ & \mathsf{cat}(\mathsf{rev_0}(t), \mathsf{cat}(\mathsf{rev_0}(s), [x])) \\
\equiv \ & \mathsf{cat}(\mathsf{cat}(\mathsf{rev_0}(t), \mathsf{rev_0}(s)), [x]) && \mathsf{CatAssoc} \\
\equiv \ & \mathsf{cat}(\mathsf{rev_0}(\mathsf{cat}(s, t)), [x]) && \mathsf{CatRev}(s, t) \\
\overset{\delta}{\leftarrow} \ & \underline{\mathsf{rev_0}}([x\,|\,\mathsf{cat}(s, t)]) \\
\overset{\beta}{\leftarrow} \ & \mathsf{rev_0}(\underline{\mathsf{cat}}([x\,|\,s], t)). && \square
\end{aligned}
$$

Let us resume the proof of $\mathsf{Inv}([x\,|\,s])$:

$$
\begin{aligned}
\mathsf{rev}_0(\underline{\mathsf{rev}_0}([x\,|\,s])) &\xrightarrow{\delta} \mathsf{rev}_0(\mathsf{cat}(\mathsf{rev}_0(s),[x])) \\
&\equiv \mathsf{cat}(\mathsf{rev}_0([x]),\mathsf{rev}_0(\mathsf{rev}_0(s))) && \mathsf{CatRev}(\mathsf{rev}_0(s),[x]) \\
&\equiv \mathsf{cat}(\underline{\mathsf{rev}_0}([x]),s) && \mathsf{Inv}(s) \\
&\xrightarrow{\delta} \mathsf{cat}(\mathsf{cat}(\underline{\mathsf{rev}_0}([\,]),[x]),s) \\
&\xrightarrow{\gamma} \mathsf{cat}(\underline{\mathsf{cat}}([\,],[x]),s) \\
&\xrightarrow{\alpha} \mathsf{cat}([x],s) \\
&\xrightarrow{\beta} [x\,|\,\mathsf{cat}([\,],s)] \\
&\xrightarrow{\alpha} [x\,|\,s]. && \square
\end{aligned}
$$

Equivalence　We may have two definitions meant to describe the same function, which differ in complexity and/or efficiency. For instance, $\mathsf{rev}_0/1$ was given an intuitive definition, as we can clearly see in rule δ that the item x, which is the top of the input, is intended to be located at the bottom of the output. Unfortunately, this definition is computationally inefficient, that is, it leads to a great deal of rewrites relatively to the size of the input.

Let us assume that we also have an efficient definition for the stack reversal, named $\mathsf{rev}/1$, which depends upon an auxiliary function $\mathsf{rcat}/2$ (*reverse and (con)catenate*):

$$
\begin{aligned}
\mathsf{rev}(s) &\xrightarrow{\epsilon} \mathsf{rcat}(s,[\,]). \\
\mathsf{rcat}([\,],t) &\xrightarrow{\zeta} t; \\
\mathsf{rcat}([x\,|\,s],t) &\xrightarrow{\eta} \mathsf{rcat}(s,[x\,|\,t]).
\end{aligned}
\tag{2.2}
$$

An additional parameter introduced by $\mathsf{rcat}/2$ accumulates partial results, thus called an *accumulator*. We can see it at work in FIGURE 2.2.

Let us prove $\mathsf{EqRev}(s)\colon \mathsf{rev}_0(s) \equiv \mathsf{rev}(s)$ by structural induction on s:

- the basis $\mathsf{EqRev}([\,])$;

- the inductive step $\forall s \in S.\mathsf{EqRev}(s) \Rightarrow \forall x \in T.\mathsf{EqRev}([x\,|\,s])$.

$$
\begin{aligned}
\mathsf{rev}([3,2,1]) &\xrightarrow{\epsilon} \mathsf{rcat}([3,2,1],[\,]) \\
&\xrightarrow{\eta} \mathsf{rcat}([2,1],[3]) \\
&\xrightarrow{\eta} \mathsf{rcat}([1],[2,3]) \\
&\xrightarrow{\eta} \mathsf{rcat}([\,],[1,2,3]) \\
&\xrightarrow{\zeta} [1,2,3].
\end{aligned}
$$

Figure 2.2: $\mathsf{rev}([3,2,1]) \twoheadrightarrow [1,2,3]$

The former is easy:

$$\mathsf{rev}_0([]) \xrightarrow{\gamma} [] \xleftarrow{\zeta} \mathsf{rcat}([],[]) \xleftarrow{\epsilon} \mathsf{rev}([]).$$

For the latter, let us rewrite $\mathsf{rev}_0([x\,|\,s])$ and $\mathsf{rev}([x\,|\,s])$ so they converge:

$$
\begin{aligned}
\mathsf{rev}_0([x\,|\,s]) &\xrightarrow{\delta} \mathsf{cat}(\mathsf{rev}_0(s),[x]) \\
&\equiv \mathsf{cat}(\mathsf{rev}(s),[x]) && \mathsf{EqRev}(s) \\
&\rightsquigarrow \mathsf{rcat}(s,[x]) && \textit{To be determined.} \\
&\xleftarrow{\eta} \mathsf{rcat}([x\,|\,s],[]) \\
&\xleftarrow{\epsilon} \mathsf{rev}([x\,|\,s]).
\end{aligned}
$$

The missing part is filled by showing ($\rightsquigarrow$) to be ($\equiv$) as follows.

Let $\mathsf{RevCat}(s,t)$ be the property $\mathsf{rcat}(s,t) \equiv \mathsf{cat}(\mathsf{rev}(s),t)$. Induction on the structure of s requires the proofs of

- the basis $\forall t \in S.\mathsf{RevCat}([],t)$;

- the general case $\forall s,t \in S.\mathsf{RevCat}(s,t) \Rightarrow \forall x \in T.\mathsf{RevCat}([x\,|\,s],t)$.

First, for the establishment of the basis, we have:

$$
\begin{aligned}
\mathsf{rcat}([],t) &\xrightarrow{\zeta} t \\
&\xleftarrow{\alpha} \mathsf{cat}([],t) \\
&\xleftarrow{\zeta} \mathsf{cat}(\underline{\mathsf{rcat}([],[])},t) \\
&\xleftarrow{\epsilon} \mathsf{cat}(\underline{\mathsf{rev}([])},t).
\end{aligned}
$$

Next, let us assume $\mathsf{RevCat}(s,t)$ and prove $\forall x \in T.\mathsf{RevCat}([x\,|\,s],t)$:

$$
\begin{aligned}
\mathsf{rcat}([x\,|\,s],t) &\xrightarrow{\eta} \mathsf{rcat}(s,[x\,|\,t]) \\
&\equiv \mathsf{cat}(\mathsf{rev}(s),[x\,|\,t]) && \mathsf{RevCat}(s,[x\,|\,t]) \\
&\xleftarrow{\alpha} \mathsf{cat}(\mathsf{rev}(s),[x\,|\,\underline{\mathsf{cat}([],t)}]) \\
&\xleftarrow{\beta} \mathsf{cat}(\mathsf{rev}(s),\underline{\mathsf{cat}([x],t)}) \\
&\equiv \mathsf{cat}(\mathsf{cat}(\mathsf{rev}(s),[x]),t) && \mathsf{CatAssoc}(\mathsf{rev}(s),[x],t) \\
&\equiv \mathsf{cat}(\mathsf{rcat}(s,[x]),t) && \mathsf{RevCat}(s,[x]) \\
&\xleftarrow{\eta} \mathsf{cat}(\underline{\mathsf{rcat}([x\,|\,s],[])},t) \\
&\xleftarrow{\epsilon} \mathsf{cat}(\underline{\mathsf{rev}([x\,|\,s])},t).
\end{aligned}
$$

Finally, we proved $\forall s.\mathsf{EqRev}(s)$, that is, $\mathsf{rev}/1 = \mathsf{rev}_0/1$. $\qquad\qquad \square$

Cost The definition of $\mathsf{rev}_0/1$ directly leads to the recurrences

$$C_0^{\mathsf{rev}_0} = 1, \qquad C_{k+1}^{\mathsf{rev}_0} = 1 + C_k^{\mathsf{rev}_0} + C_k^{\mathsf{cat}} = C_k^{\mathsf{rev}_0} + k + 2,$$

because the length of $\mathsf{rev}_0(s)$ is k if the length of s is k, and we already know $C_k^{\mathsf{cat}} = k+1$ (page 8). We have

$$\sum_{k=0}^{n-1}(C_{k+1}^{\mathsf{revo}} - C_k^{\mathsf{revo}}) = C_n^{\mathsf{revo}} - C_0^{\mathsf{revo}} = \sum_{k=0}^{n-1}(k+2) = 2n + \sum_{k=0}^{n-1}k.$$

The remaining sum is a classic of algebra:

$$2 \cdot \sum_{k=0}^{n-1}k = \sum_{k=0}^{n-1}k + \sum_{k=0}^{n-1}k = \sum_{k=0}^{n-1}k + \sum_{k=0}^{n-1}(n - k - 1) = n(n-1).$$

Consequently,

$$\sum_{k=0}^{n-1}k = \frac{n(n-1)}{2}, \tag{2.3}$$

and we can finally conclude

$$C_n^{\mathsf{revo}} = \frac{1}{2}n^2 + \frac{3}{2}n + 1 \sim \frac{1}{2}n^2.$$

Another way to reach the result is to induce an *evaluation trace*. A trace is a composition of rewrite rules, noted using the mathematical convention for multiplication. From FIGURE 2.1 on page 38, we draw the trace $\mathcal{T}_n^{\mathsf{revo}}$ of the evaluation of $\mathsf{rev}_0(s)$, where n is the length of s:

$$\mathcal{T}_n^{\mathsf{revo}} := \delta^n \gamma \alpha (\beta \alpha) \dots (\beta^{n-1}\alpha) = \delta^n \gamma \prod_{k=0}^{n-1} \beta^k \alpha.$$

If we note $|\mathcal{T}_n^{\mathsf{revo}}|$ the length of $\mathcal{T}_n^{\mathsf{revo}}$, that is, the number of rule applications it contains, we expect to have the equations $|x| = 1$, for a rule x, and $|x \cdot y| = |x| + |y|$, for rules x and y. By definition of the cost:

$$C_n^{\mathsf{revo}} := |\mathcal{T}_n^{\mathsf{revo}}| = \left| \delta^n \gamma \prod_{k=0}^{n-1} \beta^k \alpha \right| = |\delta^n \gamma| + \sum_{k=0}^{n-1} |\beta^k \alpha|$$

$$= (n+1) + \sum_{k=0}^{n-1}(k+1) = (n+1) + \sum_{k=1}^{n+1}k = \frac{1}{2}n^2 + \frac{3}{2}n + 1.$$

The reason for this inefficiency can be seen in the fact that rule δ produces a series of calls to $\mathsf{cat}/2$ following the pattern

$$\mathsf{rev}_0(s) \twoheadrightarrow \mathsf{cat}(\mathsf{cat}(\dots \mathsf{cat}([], [x_n]), \dots, [x_2]), [x_1]), \tag{2.4}$$

where $s = [x_1, x_2, \ldots, x_n]$. The cost of all these calls to cat/2 is thus

$$1 + 2 + \cdots + (n-1) = \frac{1}{2}n(n-1) \sim \frac{1}{2}n^2,$$

because the cost of $\mathsf{cat}(s, t)$ is $1 + \mathsf{len}(s)$, where

$$\begin{aligned} \mathsf{len}([\,]) &\xrightarrow{a} 0; \\ \mathsf{len}([x \,|\, s]) &\xrightarrow{b} 1 + \mathsf{len}(s). \end{aligned} \tag{2.5}$$

The problem is not calling cat/2, but the fact that the calls are embedded in the most unfavourable configuration. Indeed, if we proved the associativity of cat/2 on page 14, to wit, $\mathsf{cat}(\mathsf{cat}(s, t), u) \equiv \mathsf{cat}(s, \mathsf{cat}(t, u))$, the cost of both sides differ.

Let $\mathcal{C}[\![f(x)]\!]$ be the cost of the call $f(x)$. Then

$$\begin{aligned} \mathcal{C}[\![\mathsf{cat}(\mathsf{cat}(s, t), u)]\!] &= (\mathsf{len}(s) + 1) + (\mathsf{len}(\mathsf{cat}(s, t)) + 1) \\ &= (\mathsf{len}(s) + 1) + (\mathsf{len}(s) + \mathsf{len}(t) + 1) \quad \mathsf{LenCat}(s, t) \\ &= 2 \cdot \mathsf{len}(s) + \mathsf{len}(t) + 2, \end{aligned}$$

assuming $\mathsf{LenCat}(s, t)$: $\mathsf{len}(\mathsf{cat}(s, t)) = \mathsf{len}(s) + \mathsf{len}(t)$. On the other hand:

$$\begin{aligned} \mathcal{C}[\![\mathsf{cat}(s, \mathsf{cat}(t, u))]\!] &= (\mathsf{len}(t) + 1) + (\mathsf{len}(s) + 1) \\ &= \mathsf{len}(s) + \mathsf{len}(t) + 2. \end{aligned}$$

From which we conclude:

$$\mathcal{C}[\![\mathsf{cat}(\mathsf{cat}(s, t), u)]\!] = \mathsf{len}(s) + \mathcal{C}[\![\mathsf{cat}(s, \mathsf{cat}(t, u))]\!]. \tag{2.6}$$

The items of s are being traversed twice, although one visit suffices.

Yet another way to determine the cost of revo/1 consists in first guessing that it is *quadratic*, that is, $C_n^{\mathsf{revo}} = an^2 + bn + c$, where a, b and c are unknowns. Since there are three coefficients, we only need three values of C_n^{revo} to determine them, for instance $n = 0, 1, 2$. Making some traces, we find $C_0^{\mathsf{revo}} = 1$, $C_1^{\mathsf{revo}} = 3$ and $C_2^{\mathsf{revo}} = 6$, so we solve

$$C_0^{\mathsf{revo}} = c = 1, \quad C_1^{\mathsf{revo}} = a + b + c = 3, \quad C_2^{\mathsf{revo}} = a \cdot 2^2 + b \cdot 2 + c = 6.$$

We draw $a = 1/2$, $b = 3/2$ and $c = 1$, that is $C_n^{\mathsf{revo}} = (n^2 + 3n + 2)/2$. Since the assumption about the quadratic behaviour could have been wrong, it is then important to try other values with the newly found formula, for instance $C_4^{\mathsf{revo}} = (4+1)(4+2)/2 = 15$, then compare with the cost of $\mathsf{revo}([1, 2, 3, 4])$, for example. Here, the contents of the stack is irrelevant, only its length matters.

After finding a formula for the cost using the empirical method above, it is necessary to prove it for all values of n. Since the initial equations are recurrent, the proof method of choice is *induction*.

Let $\mathsf{Quad}(n)$ be the property $C_n^{\mathsf{revo}} = (n^2 + 3n + 2)/2$. We already checked its validity for some small values, here, $n = 0, 1, 2$. Let us suppose it is valid for some value of n (induction hypothesis) and let us prove $\mathsf{Quad}(n + 1)$. We already know $C_{n+1}^{\mathsf{revo}} = C_n^{\mathsf{revo}} + n + 2$. The induction hypothesis implies

$$C_{n+1}^{\mathsf{revo}} = (n^2 + 3n + 2)/2 + n + 2 = ((n + 1)^2 + 3(n + 1) + 2)/2,$$

which is $\mathsf{Quad}(n + 1)$. Therefore, the induction principle says that the cost we found experimentally is always correct.

To draw the cost of $\mathsf{rev}/1$, it is sufficient to notice that the first argument of $\mathsf{rcat}/2$ strictly decreases at each rewrite, so an evaluation trace has the shape $\epsilon \eta^n \zeta$, so $C_n^{\mathsf{rev}} = n + 2$. The cost is *linear*, so $\mathsf{rev}/1$ must be used instead of $\mathsf{rev}_0/1$ in all contexts.

Exercises

1. Prove $\mathsf{CatNil}(s)$: $\mathsf{cat}(s, [\,]) \equiv s$.

2. Prove $\mathsf{LenRev}(s)$: $\mathsf{len}(\mathsf{rev}_0(s)) \equiv \mathsf{len}(s)$.

3. Prove $\mathsf{LenCat}(s, t)$: $\mathsf{len}(\mathsf{cat}(s, t)) \equiv \mathsf{len}(s) + \mathsf{len}(t)$.

4. What is wrong with the proof of involution of $\mathsf{rev}/1$ in section 3.4.9 of the book of Cousineau and Mauny (1998)?

2.3   Skipping

First occurrence   Let us suppose that $\mathsf{sfst}(s, x)$ (*skip the first occurrence*) evaluates in a stack identical to s but without the first occurrence of x, starting from the top. In particular, if x is absent in s, then the value of the call is identical to s. This is our *specification*. For instance, we expect the following evaluations:

$$\mathsf{sfst}([\,], 3) \twoheadrightarrow [\,];$$
$$\mathsf{sfst}([\,], [\,]) \twoheadrightarrow [\,];$$
$$\mathsf{sfst}([3, [\,]], [5, 2]) \twoheadrightarrow [3, [\,]];$$
$$\mathsf{sfst}([[\,], [1, 2], 4, [\,], 4], 4) \twoheadrightarrow [[\,], [1, 2], [\,], 4];$$
$$\mathsf{sfst}([4, [1, 2], [\,], [\,], 4], [\,]) \twoheadrightarrow [4, [1, 2], [\,], 4].$$

First attempt Let us try a direct approach. In particular, at this point, it is important *not* to seek a definition in tail form. Tail form must be considered as an optimisation and early optimisation is unsealing Pandora's jar. The first idea that may come to mind is to define an auxiliary function mem/2 such that the call mem(s, x) checks whether a given item x is in a given stack s, because that notion of membership is implicit in the wording of the specification. But two problems then arise. Firstly, what would be the result of such a function? Secondly, what would be the additional cost for using it? For the sake of the argument, let us follow this track and find out how where it leads. A stack can either be empty or not, so let us make two rules:

$$\mathsf{mem}([], x) \rightarrow \boxed{};$$
$$\mathsf{mem}([y\,|\,s], x) \rightarrow \boxed{}.$$

Note that we introduced a variable y, distinct from variable x. *Two different variables may or may not denote the same value, but two occurrences of the same variable always denote the same value.* Had we written instead

$$\mathsf{mem}([], x) \rightarrow \boxed{};$$
$$\mathsf{mem}([\underline{x}\,|\,s], x) \rightarrow \boxed{}.$$

one case would be missing, namely when the top of the stack is not the item sought for, for instance, mem($3, [4]$) would fail due to a match failure. Now, what is the first right-hand side? The first pattern matches only if the stack is empty. In particular, this means that the item is not in the stack, since, by definition, an empty stack is a stack containing no item. How do we express that? Since the original problem is silent on the matter, it is said to be *underspecified*. We may think that zero would be a token of choice to denote the absence of the item in the stack:

$$\mathsf{mem}([], x) \rightarrow 0;$$
$$\mathsf{mem}([y\,|\,s], x) \rightarrow \boxed{}.$$

But this would be a mistake because there is no natural and necessary relationship between the concept of emptiness and the number zero. Zero is best understood algebraically as the number noted 0 such that we have $0 + n = n + 0 = n$, for any number n. Then, let us try the empty stack:

$$\mathsf{mem}([], x) \rightarrow [];$$
$$\mathsf{mem}([y\,|\,s], x) \rightarrow \boxed{}.$$

The next step is to find a way to actually compare the value of x to the value of y. We can use the rule above about variables: two occurrences of the same variable mean that they hold the same value. Therefore

$$\mathsf{mem}([\,],x) \to [\,];$$
$$\mathsf{mem}([x\,|\,s],x) \to \boxed{}.$$

was not so bad, after all? Indeed, but we know now that a case is missing, so let us add it at the end, where $x \neq y$:

$$\mathsf{mem}([\,],x) \to [\,];$$
$$\mathsf{mem}([x\,|\,s],x) \to \boxed{};$$
$$\underline{\mathsf{mem}([y\,|\,s],x)} \to \boxed{}.$$

Now, what is the second right-hand side? It is evaluated if the item we were looking for is present at the top of the stack. How do we express that? We may think of ending with the item itself, the rationale being that if the result is the empty stack, then the item is not in the input stack, otherwise the result is the item itself:

$$\mathsf{mem}([\,],x) \to [\,];$$
$$\mathsf{mem}([x\,|\,s],x) \to x;$$
$$\mathsf{mem}([y\,|\,s],x) \to \boxed{}.$$

The last right-hand side is easier to guess since it deals with the case where the top of the stack (y) is not the item we seek (x), so a recursive call which ignores y should come to mind:

$$\mathsf{mem}([\,],x) \to [\,];$$
$$\mathsf{mem}([x\,|\,s],x) \to x;$$
$$\mathsf{mem}([y\,|\,s],x) \to \mathsf{mem}(s,x).$$

Some tests would increase the confidence that this definition is correct and complete with respect to the specification. Let us label the rules first:

$$\mathsf{mem}([\,],x) \overset{\varsigma}{\to} [\,];$$
$$\mathsf{mem}([x\,|\,s],x) \overset{\eta}{\to} x;$$
$$\mathsf{mem}([y\,|\,s],x) \overset{\theta}{\to} \mathsf{mem}(s,x).$$

Then we could try the following cases:

$$\mathsf{mem}([\,],3) \overset{\varsigma}{\to} [\,],$$
$$\mathsf{mem}([1],3) \overset{\theta}{\to} \mathsf{mem}([\,],3) \quad \overset{\varsigma}{\to} [\,],$$
$$\mathsf{mem}([1,3,2],3) \overset{\theta}{\to} \mathsf{mem}([3,2],3) \overset{\eta}{\to} 3.$$

The code seems to work: item x is in stack s if the result is x, otherwise it is $[\,]$. However, this function is not correct. The hidden and flawed assumption is 'items can not be stacks', in spite of the counter-examples given at the beginning for illustrating the expected behaviour of sfst/2. In particular, an item can be the empty stack and this situation leads to an ambiguity with our definition of mem/2:

$$\text{mem}([\,],[\,]) \xrightarrow{\varsigma} [\,] \xleftarrow{\eta} \text{mem}([[\,]],[\,]).$$

It is impossible to discriminate the two cases, the first one meaning absence of the item and the second presence, because they both end with the empty stack. In fact, we should have distinguished two data constructors to denote the outcomes 'the item was found' and 'the item was not found'. For example,

$$\begin{aligned}
\text{mem}([\,],x) &\xrightarrow{\varsigma} \text{false}(); \\
\text{mem}([x\,|\,s],x) &\xrightarrow{\eta} \text{true}(); \\
\text{mem}([y\,|\,s],x) &\xrightarrow{\theta} \text{mem}(s,x).
\end{aligned}$$

But, for now, let us backtrack and ask ourselves again whether using mem/2 is really a good idea.

A better approach Let us suppose that the input stack contains the item at the bottom. Using mem/2 to find it leads to a complete traversal of the input stack. Then another traversal from the beginning (the top of the stack) is needed to copy the stack without its last item, so, in total, two complete traversals are performed.

A better idea consists in *interleaving* these two passes into one because the problem stems from the fact that mem/2 forgets about the items which are not the item of interest, thus, when it is found or known to be absent, there is no way to build a copy to make the result. By interleaving, we mean that during the traversal, the concepts of membership and of copying are combined, instead of being used sequentially as two function calls. A similar situation was encountered in the design of a function reversing a stack: $\text{rev}_0/1$, which calls cat/2, is much slower than rev/1, which uses an auxiliary stack.

Here, our algorithm consists in memorising all visited items and, if the item is not found, the resulting stack is rebuilt from them; if found, the result is built from them *and* the remaining, unvisited, items. There are usually two ways to keep visited items: either in an accumulative parameter, called *accumulator*, or in the context of recursive calls. At this point, it is important to recall a cardinal guideline: *Do not try first to design a definition in tail form, but opt instead for a direct approach.* In some simple cases, a direct approach may actually be in tail form, but the point is methodological: *a priori* ignore all concerns about tail forms.

Accordingly, let us use the context of a recursive call to record the visited items. A stack being either empty or not, it is natural to start with

$$\mathsf{sfst}([\,], x) \rightarrow \boxed{};$$
$$\mathsf{sfst}([y\,|\,s], x) \rightarrow \boxed{}.$$

Then, just as we tried with mem/2, we must distinguish the case when x is the same as y:

$$\mathsf{sfst}([\,], x) \rightarrow \boxed{};$$
$$\underline{\mathsf{sfst}([x\,|\,s], x) \rightarrow \boxed{}};$$
$$\overline{\mathsf{sfst}([y\,|\,s], x)} \rightarrow \boxed{}.$$

This method is a *linear search*: the items in the stack are compared one by one to x, starting from the top, until the bottom or an item equal to x is reached. Since we know that the last rule deals with the case when $x \neq y$, we must memorise y and go on comparing x with the other items in s (if any). This is where the recursive call with a context, discussed above, is set as $[y\,|\,\_]$:

$$\mathsf{sfst}([\,], x) \rightarrow \boxed{};$$
$$\mathsf{sfst}([x\,|\,s], x) \rightarrow \boxed{};$$
$$\mathsf{sfst}([y\,|\,s], x) \rightarrow [y\,|\,\mathsf{sfst}(s, x)].$$

Very importantly, let us remark that the position of y in the result is the same as in the input (the top). The second rule corresponds to the case where the item we are looking for, namely x, is found to be the top of the current stack, which is a substack of the original input. A stack made of successive items from the beginning of a given stack is called a *prefix* of the latter. When a stack is a substack of another, that is, it is made of successive items including the last, it is called a *suffix*. We know that the x in $[x\,|\,s]$ is the first occurrence of x in the original stack (the one in the first call), because we wouldn't be dealing with this case *again*: the specification states that this first occurrence must be absent from the resulting stack; since it is now at the top of a suffix, we just need to end with s, *which we do not visit*:

$$\mathsf{sfst}([\,], x) \rightarrow \boxed{};$$
$$\mathsf{sfst}([x\,|\,s], x) \rightarrow \underline{s}\,;$$
$$\mathsf{sfst}([y\,|\,s], x) \rightarrow [y\,|\,\mathsf{sfst}(s, x)]\,.$$

The first rule handles the case where we traversed the whole original stack (up to []) without finding x. Thus the result is simply the empty stack because the empty stack without x is the empty stack:

$$\mathsf{sfst}([\,], x) \to [\,];$$
$$\mathsf{sfst}([x\,|\,s], x) \to s;$$
$$\mathsf{sfst}([y\,|\,s], x) \to [y\,|\,\mathsf{sfst}(s, x)].$$

Let us run some tests now and, in order avoid mistakes, it is handy to label the rules with some Greek letters:

$$\mathsf{sfst}([\,], x) \xrightarrow{\theta} [\,];$$
$$\mathsf{sfst}([x\,|\,s], x) \xrightarrow{\iota} s;$$
$$\mathsf{sfst}([y\,|\,s], x) \xrightarrow{\kappa} [y\,|\,\mathsf{sfst}(s, x)].$$

The item is absent in θ, the item is found in ι and the search continues with κ. Note that equality is implicitly meant in non-linear rules like ι; in other words, the cost of such equality test is 0 in our model. Also remark how important is for rule ι to be written before κ, otherwise ι would be useless (so-called *dead code*). Here is an example of a successful search:

$$\mathsf{sfst}([3, 0, 1, 2], 1) \xrightarrow{\kappa} [3\,|\,\mathsf{sfst}([0, 1, 2], 1)] \xrightarrow{\kappa} [3, 0\,|\,\mathsf{sfst}([1, 2], 1)] \xrightarrow{\iota} [3, 0, 2].$$

Now an example of an unsuccessful search:

$$\mathsf{sfst}([3, 0], 4) \xrightarrow{\kappa} [3\,|\,\mathsf{sfst}([0], 4)] \xrightarrow{\kappa} [3, 0\,|\,\mathsf{sfst}([\,], 4)] \xrightarrow{\theta} [3, 0].$$

More complicated examples, given on page 44, yield

$$
\begin{aligned}
\mathsf{sfst}([4, [1, 2], [\,], [\,], 4], [\,]) \ & \xrightarrow{\kappa}\ [4\,|\,\mathsf{sfst}([[1, 2], [\,], [\,], 4], [\,])] \\
& \xrightarrow{\kappa}\ [4\,|\,[[1, 2]\,|\,\mathsf{sfst}([[\,], [\,], 4], [\,])]] \\
& =\ [4, [1, 2]\,|\,\mathsf{sfst}([[\,], [\,], 4], [\,])] \\
& \xrightarrow{\iota}\ [4, [1, 2]\,|\,[[\,], 4]] \\
& =\ [4, [1, 2], [\,], 4].
\end{aligned}
$$

$$
\begin{aligned}
\mathsf{sfst}([3, [\,]], [5, 2]) \ & \xrightarrow{\kappa}\ [3\,|\,\mathsf{sfst}([[\,]], [5, 2])] \\
& \xrightarrow{\kappa}\ [3\,|\,[[\,]\,|\,\mathsf{sfst}([\,], [5, 2])]] \\
& =\ [3, [\,]\,|\,\mathsf{sfst}([\,], [5, 2])] \\
& \xrightarrow{\theta}\ [3, [\,]\,|\,[\,]] \\
& =\ [3, [\,]].
\end{aligned}
$$

Once we are convinced that our definition is correct and complete with respect to the specification, there is a little extra worth testing: we can check *what happens for inputs which are not expected by the specification.* Our specification says at one point that the second argument of $\mathsf{sfst}/2$ is a stack. What happens if we supply an integer instead? For example, we have $\mathsf{sfst}(3, [\,]) \nrightarrow$. We have a match failure, that is, the rewrites are stuck, so that our definition is not *robust*, in other words, it fails abruptly on unspecified inputs.

When programming in the small, as we do here, robustness is usually not a concern because we want to focus on learning a language by expressing simple algorithms, but when developing large applications, we must take care of making the code robust by catching and signalling errors. Notice that a program can be complete but not robust, because completeness is relative to what is specified behaviour (all valid inputs must be accepted and not lead to an error), whereas robustness is relative to what is left unspecified.

These considerations are germane to discussing the merits and weaknesses of scripting languages, whose semantics try hard to ignore errors by defaulting on special values (like the empty string) to keep running. In the setting of our abstract functional language, we can use a data constructor, that is, a function without evaluation rules, like error(), to signal an error or notify some piece of information about the arguments. For instance, here is the definition of a function which distinguishes between stacks and non-stack arguments:

$$\begin{aligned}
\mathsf{is\_a\_stack}([]) &\rightarrow \mathsf{yes}(); \\
\mathsf{is\_a\_stack}([x\,|\,s]) &\rightarrow \mathsf{yes}(); \\
\mathsf{is\_a\_stack}(s) &\rightarrow \mathsf{no}().
\end{aligned}$$

Data constructors come handy in signalling errors because they are like unique identifiers, therefore they cannot be confused with any other kind of data the function computes and so can be detected easily by the caller. Consider this robust version of **sfst/2** which discriminates errors:

$$\begin{aligned}
\mathsf{sfst}([], x) &\rightarrow []; \\
\mathsf{sfst}([x\,|\,s], x) &\rightarrow s; \\
\mathsf{sfst}([y\,|\,s], x) &\rightarrow [y\,|\,\mathsf{sfst}(s, x)]; \\
\mathsf{sfst}(s, x) &\rightarrow \mathsf{error}().
\end{aligned}$$

Then a function calling **sfst/2** can make the difference between a normal rewrite and an error by using a data constructor in a pattern:

$$\begin{aligned}
\mathsf{caller}(s, x) &\rightarrow \mathsf{check}(\mathsf{sfst}(s, x)). \\
\mathsf{check}(\mathsf{error}()) &\rightarrow \boxed{}; \\
\mathsf{check}(r) &\rightarrow \boxed{}.
\end{aligned}$$

Cost In general, the cost C_n^{sfst} of $\mathsf{sfst}(s, x)$, where n is the length of s, depends on x being present in s or not. In the latter case, the trace is $\kappa^n\theta$, so $C_n^{\mathsf{sfst}} = |\kappa^n\theta| = n + 1$. If the former, the cost depends on the position

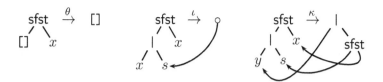

Figure 2.3: Directed acyclic graphs for sfst/2

of x in s. Let us set that the top of s is at position 0 and x occurs at position j. We then have $C_{n,j}^{\mathsf{sfst}} = |\kappa^j \iota| = j+1$. If we decide that position n (or greater) means absence, we can actually retain the last formula for both cases.

The minimum cost $\mathcal{B}_n^{\mathsf{sfst}}$ is then the minimum value of $C_{n,j}^{\mathsf{sfst}}$, for j ranging from 0 to n, therefore $\mathcal{B}_n^{\mathsf{sfst}} = C_{n,0}^{\mathsf{sfst}} = 1$, that is, when the item occurs at the top, and, dually, the maximum cost is $\mathcal{W}_n^{\mathsf{sfst}} = C_{n,n}^{\mathsf{sfst}} = n + 1$, that is, when the item is absent. The average cost $\mathcal{A}_n^{\mathsf{sfst}}$ of a successful search assumes that j can take all the positions in the stack:

$$\mathcal{A}_n^{\mathsf{sfst}} = \frac{1}{n}\sum_{j=0}^{n-1} C_{n,j}^{\mathsf{sfst}} = \frac{1}{n}\sum_{j=0}^{n-1}(j+1) = \frac{1}{n}\sum_{j=0}^{n} j = \frac{n+1}{2} \sim \frac{n}{2}, \quad \text{by (2.3)}.$$

Notice that rule κ implies the creation of a ($|$)-node, which we call *cons-node*, as shown in FIGURE 2.3. Hence, whilst the contents of the new stack is shared with the original stack, j nodes are newly allocated if x occurs at position j in s. The worst case happens when x is absent so the memory needed amounts to n nodes, all of which being useless because in this case $\mathsf{sfst}(s, x) \equiv s$. If we want to avoid this situation, another definition of sfst/2 has to be devised, one that discards all constructed nodes and allows us to reference the input when x is missing.

The crux of the matter is embodied in the construct $[y \,|\, \_]$ of rule κ, called the *context* of the call $\mathsf{sfst}(s, x)$, which we want if x is present, but not otherwise. To resolve this conflicting requirement, we opt for removing the context and store the information it contains (y) into an accumulator, in a new rule ξ derived from κ. We use the accumulator in a new rule ν derived from ι. The new sfst/2 is called sfst$_0$/2 and is shown in FIGURE 2.4. Of course, whilst in ι we just referenced s, the construction corresponding to the now missing context of κ must be performed by ν. Also, we must add another argument which refers to the original stack, so we can use it in a new rule μ, the pendant of θ.

Note the shapes of the right-hand sides: they are either a value (ζ and μ) or a function call whose arguments contain values. In other words, no function call has a context. This syntactic property of a definition is named *tail form*. Intuitively, the practical consequence of such a form is that terminating calls unfold until a value is reached and nothing else is left to be done: *the value of the last call is the value of the first call.* This kind of definition enables the sharing in rule μ, where u (the reference to the original stack) becomes the value, instead of $\mathsf{rev}(t)$.

Implementations of functional language often use this property to optimise the evaluation, as we shall see in the last part of this book. The downside of $\mathsf{sfst}_0/2$ with respect to $\mathsf{sfst}/2$ is the additional cost incurred by having to reverse t in rule ν, that is, the call $\mathsf{rcat}(t, s)$. More precisely, there are two complementary cases: either x is missing in s or x occurs in s. Let us assume that s contains n items and x is absent in s. The evaluation trace of the call $\mathsf{sfst}_0(s, x)$ is $\lambda \xi^n \mu$, so

$$C_n^{\mathsf{sfst}_0} = |\lambda \xi^n \mu| = |\lambda| + n|\xi| + |\mu| = n + 2.$$

Let us now assume that x occurs at position k in s, with the first item having position 0. The evaluation trace is then $\lambda \xi^k \nu \eta^k \zeta$, hence

$$C_{n,k}^{\mathsf{sfst}_0} = |\lambda \xi^k \nu \eta^k \zeta| = 2k + 3.$$

Clearly now,

$$
\begin{aligned}
\mathcal{B}_0^{\mathsf{sfst}_0} &= 2, \\
\mathcal{B}_n^{\mathsf{sfst}_0} &= \min_{0 \leqslant k < n} \{C_n^{\mathsf{sfst}_0}, C_{n,k}^{\mathsf{sfst}_0}\} = \min_{0 \leqslant k < n} \{n + 2, 2k + 3\} = 3, \\
\mathcal{W}_n^{\mathsf{sfst}_0} &= \max_{0 \leqslant k < n} \{n + 2, 2k + 3\} = 2n + 1,
\end{aligned}
$$

where the minimum cost occurs when the item is the top of the stack; the maximum cost happens when the sought item is last in the stack (at the bottom). Since calling $\mathsf{rcat}/2$ to reverse the visited items is the source of the extra cost, we might try to maintain the order of these items in FIGURE 2.5 on the facing page but using stack concatenation instead of pushing. The problem is that the last rule of $\mathsf{sfst}_2/4$ yields $\mathsf{cat}(\ldots \mathsf{cat}(\mathsf{cat}([\,], [x_1]), [x_2]) \ldots)$, whose cost we know to be quadratic as

$$
\begin{array}{ll}
\mathsf{rcat}([\,], t) \xrightarrow{\zeta} t; & \mathsf{sfst}([\,], x, t, u) \xrightarrow{\mu} u; \\
\mathsf{rcat}([x \,|\, s], t) \xrightarrow{\eta} \mathsf{rcat}(s, [x \,|\, t]). & \mathsf{sfst}([x \,|\, s], x, t, u) \xrightarrow{\nu} \mathsf{rcat}(t, s); \\
\mathsf{sfst}_0(s, x) \xrightarrow{\lambda} \mathsf{sfst}(s, x, [\,], s). & \mathsf{sfst}([y \,|\, s], x, t, u) \xrightarrow{\xi} \mathsf{sfst}(s, x, [y \,|\, t], u).
\end{array}
$$

Figure 2.4: Skipping the first occurrence with maximum sharing

in the rewrite (2.4) on page 42, from which we can quickly conclude that

$$\mathcal{W}_n^{\mathsf{sfst}_1} \sim \frac{1}{2}n^2.$$

Last occurrence Let us suppose that $\mathsf{slst}(s, x)$ (*skip the last occurrence*) evaluates in a stack identical to s but without the last occurrence of x. In particular, if x is absent in s, then the value of the call is identical to s. The first design that may come to mind is to see this problem as the dual problem of ignoring the first occurrence:

$$\mathsf{slst}_0(s, x) \xrightarrow{\pi} \mathsf{rev}(\mathsf{sfst}(\mathsf{rev}(s), x)). \qquad (2.7)$$

If x is missing in s, we have $C_n^{\mathsf{slst}_0} = 1 + C_n^{\mathsf{rev}} + \mathcal{W}_n^{\mathsf{sfst}} + C_n^{\mathsf{rev}} = 3n + 6$. If x occurs in s at position k, $C_{n,k}^{\mathsf{slst}_0} = 1 + C_n^{\mathsf{rev}} + C_{n,n-k-1}^{\mathsf{sfst}} + C_{n-1}^{\mathsf{rev}} = 3n - k + 4$. Therefore, we can derive the minimum and maximum costs:

$$\mathcal{B}_n^{\mathsf{slst}_0} = \min_{k<n}\{3n + 6, 3n - k + 4\} = 2n + 5,$$

when x is last in s, and

$$\mathcal{W}_n^{\mathsf{slst}_0} = \max_{k<n}\{3n + 6, 3n - k + 4\} = 3n + 6,$$

when x is missing in s. The mean cost when x is present is

$$\mathcal{A}_n^{\mathsf{slst}_0} = \frac{1}{n}\sum_{k=0}^{n-1} C_{n,k}^{\mathsf{slst}_0} = \frac{1}{n}\sum_{k=0}^{n-1}(3n - k + 4) = \frac{5n + 9}{2} \sim \frac{5}{2}n.$$

When x is present, the worst case is when it is the top of the stack: $\mathcal{W}_n^{\mathsf{slst}_0} = \max_{k<n}\{3n - k + 4\} = 3n + 4 \leqslant 3n + 6$.

In any case, the maximum cost is asymptotically equivalent to $3n$, that is, three complete traversals of s are performed, whilst the absence of x could be detected with one. Dually, the minimum cost is asymptotically equivalent to $2n$, accounting for two full traversals, whilst x being

$$\begin{aligned}
\mathsf{sfst}_1(s, x) &\to \mathsf{sfst}_2(s, x, [\,], s). \\
\mathsf{sfst}_2([\,], x, t, u) &\to u; \\
\mathsf{sfst}_2([x\,|\,s], x, t, u) &\to \mathsf{cat}(t, s); \\
\mathsf{sfst}_2([y\,|\,s], x, t, u) &\to \mathsf{sfst}_2(s, x, \mathsf{cat}(t, [y]), u).
\end{aligned}$$

Figure 2.5: Skipping the first occurrence (bad design)

$$\begin{array}{ll}
\mathsf{slst}([\,],x) \xrightarrow{\rho} [\,]; & \mathsf{slst}([\,],x,t) \xrightarrow{\upsilon} t; \\
\mathsf{slst}([x\,|\,s],x) \xrightarrow{\sigma} \mathsf{slst}(s,x,s); & \mathsf{slst}([x\,|\,s],x,t) \xrightarrow{\phi} [x\,|\,\mathsf{slst}(t,x)]; \\
\mathsf{slst}([y\,|\,s],x) \xrightarrow{\tau} [y\,|\,\mathsf{slst}(s,x)]. & \mathsf{slst}([y\,|\,s],x,t) \xrightarrow{\chi} \mathsf{slst}(s,x,t).
\end{array}$$

Figure 2.6: Skipping the last occurrence with slst/2

$$\begin{aligned}
\mathsf{slst}([2,7,0,7,1],7) \xrightarrow{\tau}\ & [2\,|\,\mathsf{slst}([7,0,7,1],7)] \\
\xrightarrow{\sigma}\ & [2\,|\,\mathsf{slst}([0,7,1],7,[0,7,1])] \\
\xrightarrow{\chi}\ & [2\,|\,\mathsf{slst}([7,1],7,[0,7,1])] \\
\xrightarrow{\phi}\ & [2,7\,|\,\mathsf{slst}([0,7,1],7)] \\
\xrightarrow{\tau}\ & [2,7,0\,|\,\mathsf{slst}([7,1],7)] \\
\xrightarrow{\sigma}\ & [2,7,0\,|\,\mathsf{slst}([1],7,[1])] \\
\xrightarrow{\chi}\ & [2,7,0\,|\,\mathsf{slst}([\,],7,[1])] \\
\xrightarrow{\upsilon}\ & [2,7,0\,|\,[1]] = [2,7,0,1].
\end{aligned}$$

Figure 2.7: $\mathsf{slst}([2,7,0,7,1],7) \twoheadrightarrow [2,7,0,1]$

the last item could be assessed with one. All this suggests that a better design is worth thinking about.

Consider FIGURE 2.6, where, with a linear search (rules ρ and τ), we find the first occurrence of x (rule σ), but, in order to check whether it is also the last, another linear search has to be run (χ). If it is successful (ϕ), we retain the occurrence find earlier (x) and resume another search; if it is unsuccessful (υ), the x found earlier was indeed the last occurrence. Notice how we have two mutually recursive functions, slst/2 and slst/3. The definition of the latter features a third parameter, t, which is a copy of the stack s when an occurrence of x was found by slst/2 (σ). This copy is used to resume (ϕ) the search from where the previous occurrence was found. This is necessary as y in rule χ must be discarded because we do not know at that point whether the previous x was the last. Consider FIGURE 2.7. If the item is missing, the linear search fails as usual with a cost of $|\tau^n \rho| = n+1$. Otherwise, let us name $0 \leqslant x_1 < x_2 < \cdots < x_p < n$ the positions of the p occurrences of x in s. The evaluation trace is

$$\tau^{x_1} \cdot \prod_{k=2}^{p} (\sigma \chi^{x_k - x_{k-1} - 1})(\phi \tau^{x_k - x_{k-1} - 1}) \cdot (\sigma \chi^{n - x_p - 1} \upsilon),$$

whose length is

$$x_1 + 2\sum_{k=2}^{p} (x_k - x_{k-1}) + (n - x_p + 1) = n + x_p - x_1 + 1.$$

In other words, if the position of the first occurrence is noted f and the position of the last is l, we find that

$$C^{\text{slst}}_{n,f,l} = n + l - f + 1.$$

We deduce that the minimum cost happens when $l - f + 1 = p$, that is, when all the occurrences are consecutive, so $\mathcal{B}^{\text{slst}}_{n,p} = n + p$. The maximum cost occurs when $f = 0$ and $l = n - 1$, that is, when there is at least two occurrences of x, one at the top and one at the bottom: $\mathcal{W}^{\text{slst}}_n = 2n$. We can check that when the stack is entirely made of x, minimum and maximum costs concur in $2n$. The average cost when x is present requires determining the cost for every possible pair (f, l), with $0 \leqslant f \leqslant l < n$:

$$\mathcal{A}^{\text{slst}}_n = \frac{2}{n(n+1)} \sum_{f=0}^{n-1}\sum_{l=f}^{n-1} C^{\text{slst}}_{n,f,l} = \frac{2}{n(n+1)} \sum_{f=0}^{n-1}\sum_{l=f}^{n-1} (n + l - f + 1)$$

$$= \frac{2}{n(n+1)} \sum_{f=0}^{n-1} \left((n - f + 1)(n - f) + \sum_{l=0}^{n-f-1} (l + f) \right)$$

$$= \frac{1}{n(n+1)} \sum_{f=0}^{n-1} (3n + 1 - f)(n - f)$$

$$= \frac{n(3n+1)}{n+1} - \frac{4n+1}{n(n+1)} \sum_{f=0}^{n-1} f + \frac{1}{n(n+1)} \sum_{f=0}^{n-1} f^2 = \frac{4n+2}{3} \sim \frac{4}{3}n,$$

where $\sum_{f=0}^{n-1} f = n(n-1)/2$ is equation (2.3), on page 42, and the sum of the successive squares is obtained as follows.

We use the *telescoping* or *difference* method on the series $(k^3)_{k>0}$. We start with the equality $(k+1)^3 = k^3 + 3k^2 + 3k + 1$, hence

$$(k+1)^3 - k^3 = 3k^2 + 3k + 1.$$

Then we can sum these differences, whose terms cancel out, leaving the first and the last:

$$(1+1)^3 - \boxed{1^3} = 3 \cdot 1^2 + 3 \cdot 1 + 1$$
$$+ \qquad (2+1)^3 - 2^3 = 3 \cdot 2^2 + 3 \cdot 2 + 1$$

$$+ \qquad \vdots$$

$$+ \qquad \boxed{(n+1)^3} - n^3 = 3n^2 + 3n + 1$$

$$\Rightarrow \qquad \boxed{(n+1)^3} - \boxed{1^3} = 3 \sum_{k=1}^{n} k^2 + 3 \sum_{k=1}^{n} k + n$$

$$n^3 + 3n^2 + 3n = 3\sum_{k=1}^{n} k^2 + 3 \cdot \frac{n(n+1)}{2} + n$$

$$\Leftrightarrow \qquad \sum_{k=1}^{n} k^2 = \frac{n(n+1)(2n+1)}{6}. \tag{2.8}$$

Exercises

1. Prove that $\mathsf{sfst}/2 = \mathsf{sfst}_0/2$.
2. Show that $\mathcal{B}_n^{\mathsf{sfsto}} = 3$, $\mathcal{W}_n^{\mathsf{sfsto}} = 2n+1$ and $\mathcal{A}_n^{\mathsf{sfsto}} = n+2$ (successful search).
3. Prove that $\mathsf{slst}/2 = \mathsf{slst}_0/2$.
4. Show that, in a worst case to be identified, $\mathsf{slst}_0(s, x)$ creates $3n$ useless nodes if s contains n items. Compare the memory usage of $\mathsf{slst}_0/2$ with that of $\mathsf{slst}/2$.

2.4 Flattening

Let us design a function $\mathsf{flat}/1$ such that the call $\mathsf{flat}(s)$, where s is a stack, is rewritten into a stack containing only the non-stack items found in s, in the same order. If s contains no stack, then $\mathsf{flat}(s) \equiv s$. Let us review some examples to grasp the concept:

$$\mathsf{flat}([]) \twoheadrightarrow []; \quad \mathsf{flat}([[], [[]]]) \twoheadrightarrow []; \quad \mathsf{flat}([[], [1, [2, []], 3], []]) \twoheadrightarrow [1, 2, 3].$$

First, let us focus on designing the left-hand sides of the rules, in order to ensure that our definition is *complete* (all valid inputs are matched). A stack is either empty or not and, in the latter case, the specific issue at hand appears clearly: we need to distinguish the items which are stacks themselves from those which are not. This is very simply achieved by ordering the patterns so that $[]$ and $[x \,|\, s]$ *as items* appear first:

$$\mathsf{flat}([]) \xrightarrow{\psi} \boxed{};$$
$$\mathsf{flat}([[] \,|\, t]) \xrightarrow{\omega} \boxed{};$$
$$\mathsf{flat}([[x \,|\, s] \,|\, t]) \xrightarrow{\gamma} \boxed{};$$
$$\mathsf{flat}([y \,|\, t]) \xrightarrow{\delta} \boxed{}.$$

We know that y in the last line is not a stack, otherwise the penultimate or antepenultimate pattern would have matched. Almost all the right-hand sides are easy to guess now:

$$\mathsf{flat}([]) \xrightarrow{\psi} [];$$
$$\mathsf{flat}([[] \,|\, t]) \xrightarrow{\omega} \mathsf{flat}(t);$$
$$\mathsf{flat}([[x \,|\, s] \,|\, t]) \xrightarrow{\gamma} \boxed{};$$
$$\mathsf{flat}([y \,|\, t]) \xrightarrow{\delta} [y \,|\, \mathsf{flat}(t)].$$

$$\begin{aligned}
\mathsf{flat_0}([]) &\xrightarrow{\psi} [];\\
\mathsf{flat_0}([[]\,|\,t]) &\xrightarrow{\omega} \mathsf{flat_0}(t);\\
\mathsf{flat_0}([[x\,|\,s]\,|\,t]) &\xrightarrow{\gamma} \mathsf{cat}(\mathsf{flat_0}([x\,|\,s]), \mathsf{flat_0}(t));\\
\mathsf{flat_0}([y\,|\,t]) &\xrightarrow{\delta} [y\,|\,\mathsf{flat_0}(t)].
\end{aligned}$$

Figure 2.8: Flattening a stack with $\mathsf{flat_0}/1$

The design of the remaining right-hand side can be guided by two slightly different principles. If we look back at the definitions of $\mathsf{rev_0}/1$ and $\mathsf{rev}/1$ in section 2.2, we see that the former was designed with the result in mind, as if the arrows would reach a value, which is then decomposed in terms of the variables of the corresponding left-hand side:

$$\begin{aligned}
\mathsf{rev_0}([]) &\to [];\\
\mathsf{rev_0}([x\,|\,s]) &\to \mathsf{cat}(\mathsf{rev_0}(s), [x]).
\end{aligned}$$

By contrast, $\mathsf{rev}/1$ relies on another function, $\mathsf{rcat}/2$, to accumulate partial results, as if each arrow covered a short distance, only contributing minimally to the final value:

$$\begin{aligned}
\mathsf{rev}(s) &\xrightarrow{\epsilon} \mathsf{rcat}(s, []).\\
\mathsf{rcat}([], t) &\xrightarrow{\zeta} t;\\
\mathsf{rcat}([x\,|\,s], t) &\xrightarrow{\eta} \mathsf{rcat}(s, [x\,|\,t]).
\end{aligned}$$

The first approach might be called *big-step design*, and the other *small-step design*. Another vantage point is to see that the former uses the context of the recursive call to build the value, whilst the latter relies exclusively on an argument (the accumulator) and is in tail form. For example, in section 2.3, we may find that the definition of $\mathsf{sfst}/2$ follows a big-step design, while $\mathsf{sfst_0}/2$ illustrates a small-step design.

Big-step design Abstractly, a big-step design means that the right-hand sides are made up of recursive calls on substructures, for instance, in the case of rule γ, the substructures of $[[x\,|\,s]\,|\,t]$ are x, s, t and $[x\,|\,s]$. By thinking how to make up the value by means of $\mathsf{flat}([x\,|\,s])$ and $\mathsf{flat}(t)$, we obtain a new version, $\mathsf{flat_0}/1$, in FIGURE 2.8.

Let us consider an example in FIGURE 2.9 on the next page, where the call to be rewritten next is underlined in case of ambiguity. Note that the call-by-value strategy (section 1.3) does not specify the order of evaluation of the arguments of a function call: in our example, we delayed the evaluation of $\mathsf{cat}([1], [2])$ after that of the calls to $\mathsf{flat_0}/1$.

$$\begin{aligned}
\mathsf{flat}_0([[\,], [[1], 2], 3]) &\xrightarrow{\omega} \mathsf{flat}_0([[[1], 2], 3]) \\
&\xrightarrow{\gamma} \mathsf{cat}(\underline{\mathsf{flat}_0}([[1], 2]), \mathsf{flat}_0([3])) \\
&\xrightarrow{\gamma} \mathsf{cat}(\mathsf{cat}(\underline{\mathsf{flat}_0}([1]), \mathsf{flat}_0([2])), \mathsf{flat}_0([3])) \\
&\xrightarrow{\delta} \mathsf{cat}(\mathsf{cat}([1 \,|\, \underline{\mathsf{flat}_0}([\,])], \mathsf{flat}_0([2])), \mathsf{flat}_0([3])) \\
&\xrightarrow{\psi} \mathsf{cat}(\mathsf{cat}([1], \underline{\mathsf{flat}_0}([2])), \mathsf{flat}_0([3])) \\
&\xrightarrow{\delta} \mathsf{cat}(\mathsf{cat}([1], [2 \,|\, \underline{\mathsf{flat}_0}([\,])]), \mathsf{flat}_0([3])) \\
&\xrightarrow{\psi} \mathsf{cat}(\mathsf{cat}([1], [2]), \underline{\mathsf{flat}_0}([3])) \\
&\xrightarrow{\delta} \mathsf{cat}(\mathsf{cat}([1], [2]), [3 \,|\, \underline{\mathsf{flat}_0}([\,])]) \\
&\xrightarrow{\psi} \mathsf{cat}(\mathsf{cat}([1], [2]), [3]) \\
&\twoheadrightarrow [1, 2, 3].
\end{aligned}$$

Figure 2.9: $\mathsf{flat}_0([[\,], [[1], 2], 3]) \twoheadrightarrow [1, 2, 3]$

When deriving complicated recurrences or traces, we may try instead counting the number of times each rule is used in any evaluation.

Calling $\mathsf{flat}_0/1$ yields

- using rule ω once for each empty stack originally in the input;
- using rule ψ once when the end of the input is reached *and* once for each empty stack t in rule γ;
- using rule δ once for each item which is not a stack;
- using rule γ once for each non-empty embedded stack;
- calling $\mathsf{cat}/2$ once for each non-empty embedded stack.

We now know the parameters which the cost depends upon:

1. the length of $\mathsf{flat}_0(s)$, noted n;
2. the number of non-empty stacks embedded in the input, say Γ;
3. the number of embedded empty stacks, denoted by Ω.

The dependence upon the size of the output, n, is an instance of *output-dependent cost*. We can reformulate the above analysis in the following terms: rule ψ is used $1 + \Gamma$ times, rule ω is used Ω times, rule γ is used Γ times, rule δ is used n times. So the cost due to the rules of $\mathsf{flat}_0/1$ alone is $1 + n + \Omega + 2\Gamma$. For instance, in the case of $\mathsf{flat}_0([[\,], [[1], 2], 3])$, we correctly find $1 + 3 + 1 + 2 \cdot 2 = 9 = |\omega\gamma^2(\delta\psi)^3|$.

As far as the costs of the calls to $\mathsf{cat}/2$ are concerned, their associativity was proved on page 14 and equation (2.6) on page 43 suggests that there are configurations of the input to $\mathsf{flat}_0/1$ that lead to greater costs, when the parameters n, Ω and Γ are fixed. A similar pattern of calls to $\mathsf{cat}/2$ with a quadratic cost is generated from the definition of

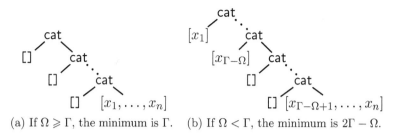

(a) If $\Omega \geqslant \Gamma$, the minimum is Γ.   (b) If $\Omega < \Gamma$, the minimum is $2\Gamma - \Omega$.

Figure 2.10: Minimum costs for the concatenations in $\mathsf{flat}_0/1$

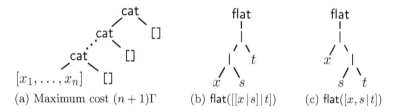

(a) Maximum cost $(n+1)\Gamma$ (b) $\mathsf{flat}([[x\,|\,s]\,|\,t])$ (c) $\mathsf{flat}([x, s\,|\,t])$

Figure 2.11: Maximum cost and right rotations

$\mathsf{rev}_0/1$, as seen in FIGURE 2.1 on page 38, after the first application of rule α. The right-hand side of rule γ is $\mathsf{cat}(\mathsf{flat}_0([x\,|\,s]), \mathsf{flat}_0(t))$ and it implies that the arguments of $\mathsf{cat}/2$ may be empty stacks.

Given Γ cat-nodes, n non-stack nodes $(x_1,\ \ldots,\ x_n)$, what are the abstract syntax trees with minimum and maximum costs? We found that the minimum cost for $\mathsf{cat}/2$ is achieved when all the cat-nodes make up the rightmost *branch* of the abstract syntax tree. (A branch is a series of nodes such that one is the parent of the next, from the root to a leaf.)

- If $\Omega \geqslant \Gamma$, the minimum configuration is shown in FIGURE 2.10a (at least one empty stack must be placed in any non-empty stack whose flattening results in an empty stack).

- Otherwise, the abstract syntax tree of minimum cost is found in FIGURE 2.10b, where all the available empty stacks (Ω) are used for the bottommost cat-nodes. We draw that the minimum cost is $\mathcal{B}_{n,\Omega,\Gamma}^{\mathsf{flat}_0} = 1 + n + \Omega + 3\Gamma + \min\{\Omega, \Gamma\}$.

The maximum cost in FIGURE 2.11a occurs for the symmetrical tree of FIGURE 2.10a. We have $\mathcal{W}_{n,\Omega,\Gamma}^{\mathsf{flat}_0} = \Omega + (n+3)(\Gamma+1) - 2$.

Small-step design   An alternative method for the flattening of a stack consists in lifting x in rule γ one level up amongst the embedded stacks, thus approaching little by little a flat stack. In terms of the abstract

$$\begin{aligned}
\mathsf{flat}([\,]) &\xrightarrow{\psi} [\,]; \\
\mathsf{flat}([[\,]\,|\,t]) &\xrightarrow{\omega} \mathsf{flat}(t); \\
\mathsf{flat}([[x\,|\,s]\,|\,t]) &\xrightarrow{\gamma} \mathsf{flat}([x, s\,|\,t]); \\
\mathsf{flat}([y\,|\,t]) &\xrightarrow{\delta} [y\,|\,\mathsf{flat}(t)].
\end{aligned}$$

Figure 2.12: Defining flat/1

$$\begin{aligned}
\mathsf{flat}([[\,], [[1], 2], 3]) &\xrightarrow{\omega} \mathsf{flat}([[[1], 2], 3]) \\
&\xrightarrow{\gamma} \mathsf{flat}([[1], [2], 3]) \\
&\xrightarrow{\gamma} \mathsf{flat}([1, [\,], [2], 3]) \\
&\xrightarrow{\delta} [1\,|\,\mathsf{flat}([[\,], [2], 3])] \\
&\xrightarrow{\omega} [1\,|\,\mathsf{flat}([[2], 3])] \\
&\xrightarrow{\gamma} [1\,|\,\mathsf{flat}([2, [\,], 3])] \\
&\xrightarrow{\delta} [1, 2\,|\,\mathsf{flat}([[\,], 3])] \\
&\xrightarrow{\omega} [1, 2\,|\,\mathsf{flat}([3])] \\
&\xrightarrow{\delta} [1, 2, 3\,|\,\mathsf{flat}([\,])] \\
&\xrightarrow{\psi} [1, 2, 3].
\end{aligned}$$

Figure 2.13: flat($[[\,], [[1], 2], 3]$) $\twoheadrightarrow [1, 2, 3]$

syntax trees, this operation is a *right rotation* of the tree associated with the argument, as shown in FIGURES 2.11b to 2.11c on the preceding page, where the new function is flat/1 and defined in FIGURE 2.12. Let us run the previous example of FIGURE 2.9 on page 58 again in FIGURE 2.13 with flat/1. The difference in cost with flat_0/1 resides in the number of times rule γ is used: once for each item in all the embedded stacks. Hence the cost is $1 + n + \Omega + \Gamma + L$, where L is the sum of the lengths of all the embedded stacks.

Comparison Consider the following costs:

$$\begin{aligned}
\mathcal{C}[\![\mathsf{flat}([[[[[1, 2]]]]])]\!] &= 12 < 23 = \mathcal{C}[\![\mathsf{flat}_0([[[[[1, 2]]]]])]\!]; \\
\mathcal{C}[\![\mathsf{flat}([[\,], [[1], 2], 3])]\!] &= 10 < 14 = \mathcal{C}[\![\mathsf{flat}_0([[\,], [[1], 2], 3])]\!]; \\
\mathcal{C}[\![\mathsf{flat}([[\,], [[1, [2]]], 3])]\!] &= 12 < 19 = \mathcal{C}[\![\mathsf{flat}_0([[\,], [[1, [2]]], 3])]\!]; \\
\mathcal{C}[\![\mathsf{flat}([[[\,], [\,], [[\,]]])]\!] &= 8 > 7 = \mathcal{C}[\![\mathsf{flat}_0([[[\,], [\,], [[\,]]])]\!].
\end{aligned}$$

Simple algebra shows that

$$\mathcal{C}^{\mathsf{flat}}_{n,\Omega,\Gamma} \leqslant \mathcal{B}^{\mathsf{flat}_0}_{n,\Omega,\Gamma} \Leftrightarrow \begin{cases} L \leqslant 3\Gamma - \Omega, & \text{if } \Omega \geqslant \Gamma; \\ L \leqslant 2\Gamma, & \text{otherwise.} \end{cases}$$

This criterion is impractical to check and it is inconclusive if the inequalities on the right-hand side fail. Things worsen if we settle for

$L \leqslant 2\Gamma \Rightarrow C_{n,\Omega,\Gamma}^{\mathsf{flat}} \leqslant C_{n,\Omega,\Gamma}^{\mathsf{flat}_0}$, because this condition is too strong when Ω is large. Let us examine what happens at the other extreme, when $\Omega = 0$. Considering an example like $[0, [1, [2]], 3, [4, 5, [6, 7], 8], 9]$, it may occur to us that if there are no empty stacks, the length of each stack is lower than or equal to the number of non-stack items in it and its embeddings (it is equal if there is no further embedded stack). Therefore, summing up all these inequalities, the following inequality ensues:

$$\Omega = 0 \Rightarrow C - L \geqslant 0, \tag{2.9}$$

where C is the cost of rewriting the calls to $\mathsf{cat}/2$ in $\mathsf{flat}_0/1$. Because $C_{n,\Omega,\Gamma}^{\mathsf{flat}_0} = (1 + n + \Omega + \Gamma) + (C + \Gamma)$ and $C_{n,\Omega,\Gamma}^{\mathsf{flat}} = (1 + n + \Omega + \Gamma) + L$,

$$C_{n,\Omega,\Gamma}^{\mathsf{flat}_0} - C_{n,\Omega,\Gamma}^{\mathsf{flat}} = (C - L) + \Gamma.$$

From equation (2.9), we deduce that, in the absence of empty stacks, we have the inequality $C_{n,\Omega,\Gamma}^{\mathsf{flat}_0} - C_{n,\Omega,\Gamma}^{\mathsf{flat}} \geqslant L$, that is, $\mathsf{flat}/1$ is faster.

Termination As we have seen with the simplified Ackermann's function (section 1.5, on page 13), termination follows from finding a well-founded order ($\succ$) on the recursive calls, which is entailed by the rewrite relation ($\rightarrow$), that is, $x \rightarrow y \Rightarrow x \succ y$. One well-founded order for stacks is the *immediate subterm order*, satisfying $[x \mid s] \succ s$ and $[x \mid s] \succ x$. Since big-step design uses recursive calls to subterms (section 1.5, on page 12), it eases termination proofs based on such an ordering.

For instance, let us recall the definition of $\mathsf{flat}_0/1$ in FIGURE 2.8 on page 57. Since $\mathsf{cat}/2$ is independent of $\mathsf{flat}_0/1$, we prove its termination in isolation by using the proper subterm order on its first argument. Assuming now that $\mathsf{cat}/2$ terminates, let us prove the termination of $\mathsf{flat}_0/1$. Because the recursive calls of $\mathsf{flat}_0/1$ contain only (stack) constructors, we can try to order their arguments (Arts and Giesl, 1996). Again, the same order works:

- $[y \mid t] \succ t$ by rule δ and rule ω when $y = [\,]$,
- $[[x \mid s] \mid t] \succ t$ and
- $[[x \mid s] \mid t] \succ [x \mid s]$ by rule γ.

Termination ensues. $\square$

Let us further recall the definition of $\mathsf{flat}/1$ in FIGURE 2.12 and prove its termination. Here, the order we used for $\mathsf{flat}_0/1$ fails:

$$[[x \mid s] \mid t] \not\succ [x, s \mid t] = [x \mid [s \mid t]].$$

We could try the more general *proper subterm order*, that is, the strict inclusion of a term into another, but, despite $[x\,|\,s] \succ x$, we have $t \not\succ [s\,|\,t]$. One way out is to define a *measure* on the stacks (Giesl, 1995a).

A measure $\mathcal{M}[\![\cdot]\!]$ is a map from terms to a well-ordered set $(A, \succ)$, which is *monotone* with respect to rewriting:

$$x \to y \Rightarrow \mathcal{M}[\![x]\!] \succ \mathcal{M}[\![y]\!].$$

Actually, we will only consider *dependency pairs* (Arts and Giesl, 2000), that is, pairs of calls whose first component is the left-hand side of a rule and the second components are the calls in the righ-hand side of same rule. This is easier than working with x and y in $x \to y$, as only subterms of y are considered. The pairs are:

- $(\mathsf{flat}([[\,]\,|\,t]), \mathsf{flat}(t))_\omega,$
- $(\mathsf{flat}([[x\,|\,s]\,|\,t]), \mathsf{flat}([x, s\,|\,t]))_\gamma$ and
- $(\mathsf{flat}([y\,|\,t]), \mathsf{flat}(t))_\delta$, with $y \notin S$.

We can actually drop the function names, as all the pairs involve $\mathsf{flat}/1$. A common class of measures are monotone embeddings into $(\mathbb{N}, >)$, so let us seek a measure satisfying:

- $\mathcal{M}[\![[[x\,|\,s]\,|\,t]]\!] > \mathcal{M}[\![[x, s\,|\,t]]\!]$;
- $\mathcal{M}[\![[y\,|\,t]]\!] > \mathcal{M}[\![t]\!]$, if $y \notin S$ or $y = [\,]$.

For instance, let us set the following *polynomial measure*:

- $\mathcal{M}[\![[x\,|\,s]]\!] := 1 + 2 \cdot \mathcal{M}[\![x]\!] + \mathcal{M}[\![s]\!]$;
- $\mathcal{M}[\![y]\!] := 0$, if $y \notin S$ or $y = [\,]$.

We have, for each stack,

- $\mathcal{M}[\![[[x\,|\,s]\,|\,t]]\!] = 3 + 4 \cdot \mathcal{M}[\![x]\!] + 2 \cdot \mathcal{M}[\![s]\!] + \mathcal{M}[\![t]\!]$,
- $\mathcal{M}[\![[x, s\,|\,t]]\!] = 2 + 2 \cdot \mathcal{M}[\![x]\!] + 2 \cdot \mathcal{M}[\![s]\!] + \mathcal{M}[\![t]\!]$.

Therefore $\mathcal{M}[\![[[x\,|\,s]\,|\,t]]\!] = \mathcal{M}[\![[x, s\,|\,t]]\!] + 1 + 2 \cdot \mathcal{M}[\![x]\!]$. Because $\mathcal{M}[\![x]\!] \in \mathbb{N}$, for all x, we have $\mathcal{M}[\![[[x\,|\,s]\,|\,t]]\!] > \mathcal{M}[\![[x, s\,|\,t]]\!]$. The second inequality yields faster: $\mathcal{M}[\![[y\,|\,t]]\!] = 1 + \mathcal{M}[\![t]\!] > \mathcal{M}[\![t]\!]$. This entails the termination of $\mathsf{flat}/1$.   □

Giesl (1997) tackled the termination of mutually recursive functions. Functional programs, as special cases of term-rewriting systems, have been considered by Giesl (1995b) and Giesl et al. (1998).

Exercises

1. Define gamma/1, lambda/1 and omega/1, which compute Γ, L and Ω, respectively.
2. Compare the costs of flat/1 and $\mathsf{flat}_1/1$ defined in FIGURE 2.14 (see ($\rightsquigarrow$)).

$$\mathsf{flat}_1([\,]) \to [\,];$$
$$\mathsf{flat}_1([[\,]\,|\,t]) \to \mathsf{flat}_1(t);$$
$$\mathsf{flat}_1([[x]\,|\,t]) \rightsquigarrow \mathsf{flat}_1([x\,|\,t]);$$
$$\mathsf{flat}_1([[x\,|\,s]\,|\,t]) \to \mathsf{flat}_1([x,s\,|\,t]);$$
$$\mathsf{flat}_1([y\,|\,t]) \to [y\,|\,\mathsf{flat}_1(t)].$$

Figure 2.14: Variant flattening

2.5 Queueing

Despite its didactic qualities, aggregate analysis (see page 10) is less frequently applied when the data structures are not directly connected to numeration. We propose to extend its scope by showing a compelling case study on *functional queues* (Burton, 1982, Okasaki, 1995, 1998b). A functional queue is a linear data structure that is used in functional languages, whose semantics force the programmer to model a *queue* with two stacks. Items can be pushed only on one stack and popped only on the other:

Push, Pop (top) $\longleftrightarrow$ | a | b | c | d | e |

A queue is like a stack where items are added, or *enqueued*, at one end, called *rear*, but taken out, or *dequeued*, at the other end, called *front*:

Enqueue (rear end) $\rightsquigarrow$ | a | b | c | d | e | $\rightsquigarrow$ Dequeue (front end).

Let us implement a queue with two stacks: one for enqueueing, called the *rear stack*, and one for dequeueing, called the *front stack*. The previous ideal queue is equivalent to the functional queue

Enqueue (rear) $\rightsquigarrow$ | a | b | c | | d | e | $\rightsquigarrow$ Dequeue (front).

Enqueueing is now pushing on the rear stack and dequeueing is popping on the front stack. In the latter case, if the front stack is empty and the rear stack is not, we swap the stacks and reverse the new front stack. Graphically, dequeueing in the configuration

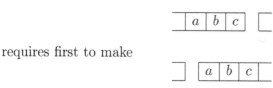

requires first to make

and then dequeue c.

Let us model a queue as we modelled the operation push by a function cons/2 without a definition, on page 6. We shall use the name q/2 and the call $q(r, f)$ denotes a functional queue with rear stack r and front stack f. Enqueueing is performed by the function enq/2:

$$enq(x, q(r, f)) \rightarrow q([x \,|\, r], f). \qquad (2.10)$$

Dequeueing requires the result to be a *pair* made of the dequeued item and the new queue without it. Actually, the new queue is the first component of the pair, to fit how the operation is depicted in the figures as a rightwards arrow. Let us call deq/1 the dequeueing function:

$$\begin{aligned} deq(q([x \,|\, r], [\,])) &\stackrel{\theta}{\rightarrow} deq(q([\,], rcat(r, [x]))); \\ deq(q(r, [x \,|\, f])) &\stackrel{\iota}{\rightarrow} (q(r, f), x). \end{aligned} \qquad (2.11)$$

See page 40 for the definition (2.2) of rcat/2. We shall say that the queue has size n if the total number of items in both stacks is n. The cost of enqueueing is $C_n^{enq} = 1$. The minimum cost for dequeueing is $\mathcal{B}_n^{deq} = 1$, by rule ι. The maximum cost is

$$\mathcal{W}_n^{deq} = |\theta \eta^{n-1} \zeta \iota| = 1 + (n-1) + 1 + 1 = n + 2. \qquad (2.12)$$

Let $\mathcal{S}_n$ be the cost of a sequence of n updates on a functional queue originally empty. A first attempt at assessing $\mathcal{S}_n$ consists in ignoring any dependence on previous operations and take the maximum individual cost. Since $C_k^{enq} \leqslant C_k^{deq}$, we consider a series of n dequeueings in their worst case, that is, with all the items located in the rear stack. Besides, after k updates, there may be at most k items in the queue, so

$$\mathcal{S}_n \leqslant \sum_{k=1}^{n-1} \mathcal{W}_k^{deq} = \sum_{k=1}^{n-1} (k+2) = \frac{1}{2}(n+4)(n-1) \sim \frac{1}{2}n^2. \qquad (2.13)$$

from equations (2.12) and (2.3).

Aggregate analysis Actually, this is overly pessimistic and even unrealistic. First, one cannot dequeue on an empty queue, therefore, at any time, the number of enqueueings since the beginning is always greater or equal than the number of dequeueings and the series must start with one enqueueing. Second, when dequeueing with the front being empty, the rear stack is reversed onto the front stack, so its items cannot be reversed again during the next dequeueing, whose cost will be 1. Moreover, as remarked above, $C_k^{enq} \leqslant C_k^{deq}$, so the worst case for a series of n operations occurs when the number of dequeueings is maximum, that is, when

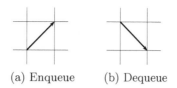

(a) Enqueue   (b) Dequeue

Figure 2.15: Graphical representations of operations on queues

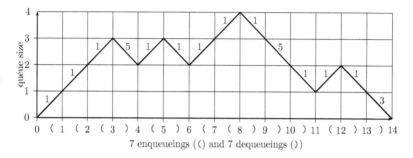

7 enqueueings (() and 7 dequeueings ())

Figure 2.16: Dyck path modelling queue operations (cost 24)

it is $\lfloor n/2 \rfloor$. If we denote by e the number of enqueueings and by d the number of dequeueings, we have the relationship $n = e + d$ and the two requisites for a worst case become $e = d$ (n even) or $e = d + 1$ (n odd). The former corresponds graphically to a *Dyck path* and the latter to a *Dyck meander*.

Dyck path Let us depict updates as in FIGURE 2.15. Textually, we represent an enqueueing as an opening parenthesis and a dequeueing as a closing parenthesis. For example, ((()()(())))()) can be represented in FIGURE 2.16 as a Dyck path. For a broken line to qualify as a Dyck path of length n, it has to start at the origin $(0,0)$, stay above the abscissa axis, and end at coordinates $(n,0)$. In terms of a *Dyck language*, an enqueueing is called a *rise* and a dequeueing is called a *fall*. A rise followed by a fall, that is, (), is called a *peak*. For instance, in FIGURE 2.16, there are four peaks. The number near each rise or fall is the cost incurred by the corresponding operation. The abscissa axis bears the ordinal of each operation.

When $e = d$, the line is a Dyck path of length $n = 2e = 2d$. In order to deduce the total cost in this case, we must find a *decomposition* of the path, by which we mean to identify patterns whose costs are easy to calculate and which make up any path, or to associate any path to another path whose cost is the same but easy to find. FIGURE 2.17 shows how the previous path is mapped to an equivalent path only made of a

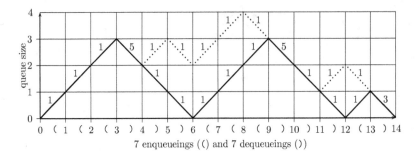

Figure 2.17: Dyck path equivalent to FIGURE 2.16

series of isosceles triangles whose bases belong to the abscissa axis. Let
us call them *mountains* and their series a *range*. The mapping is simple:
after the first series of falls, if we are back to the abscissa axis, we have
a mountain and we proceed with the rest of the path. Otherwise, the
next operation is a rise and we exchange it with the first fall after it.
This brings us down by 1 and the process resumes until the abscissas
are reached. We call this method *rescheduling* because it amounts, in
operational terms, to reordering subsequences of operations *a posteriori*.
For instance, FIGURE 2.18 on the next page displays the rescheduling of
FIGURE 2.16 on the preceding page. Note that two different paths can be
rescheduled into the same path. What makes FIGURE 2.18c equivalent
to FIGURE 2.18a is the invariance of the cost because all operations have
cost 1. This always holds because enqueueings always have cost 1 and the
dequeueings involved in a rescheduling have cost 1, because they found
the front stack non-empty after a peak. We proved that all paths are
equivalent to a range with the same cost, therefore, the maximum cost
can be found on ranges alone.

Let us note $e_1, e_2, \ldots, e_k$ the maximal subsequences of rises; for example, in FIGURE 2.17, we have $e_1 = 3$, $e_2 = 3$ and $e_3 = 1$. Of course,
$e = e_1 + e_2 + \cdots + e_k$. The fall making up the ith peak incurs the
cost $\mathcal{W}^{\text{deq}}_{e_i} = e_i + 2$, due to the front being empty because we started
the rises from the abscissa axis. The next $e_i - 1$ falls have all cost 1,
because the front is not empty. For the ith mountain, the cost is thus
$e_i + (e_i + 2) + (e_i - 1) = 3e_i + 1$. Then

$$\mathcal{S}_{e,k} = \sum_{i=1}^{k} (3e_i + 1) = 3e + k.$$

The maximum cost is obtained by maximising $\mathcal{S}_{e,k}$ for a given e:

$$\mathcal{W}_{e,e} := \max_{1 \leqslant k \leqslant e} \mathcal{S}_{e,k} = \mathcal{S}_{e,e} = 4e = 2n, \quad \text{with } n = e + d = 2e,$$

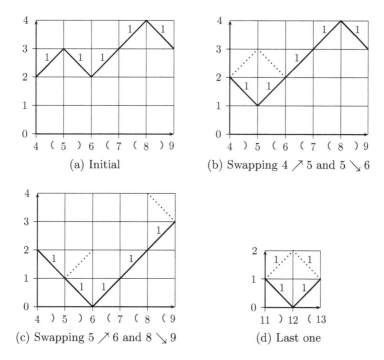

(a) Initial

(b) Swapping 4 ↗ 5 and 5 ↘ 6

(c) Swapping 5 ↗ 6 and 8 ↘ 9

(d) Last one

Figure 2.18: Rescheduling of FIGURE 2.16 into FIGURE 2.17

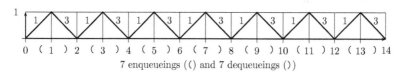

0 (1) 2 (3) 4 (5) 6 (7) 8 (9) 10 (11) 12 (13) 14

7 enqueueings (() and 7 dequeueings ())

Figure 2.19: Worst case when $e = d = 7$ (cost 28)

where $\mathcal{W}_{e,e}$ is the maximum cost when there are e enqueueings and $d = e$ dequeueings. In other words, the worst case when $e = d = 7$ is the saw-toothed Dyck path shown in FIGURE 2.19. Importantly, there are no other Dyck paths whose rescheduling lead to this worst case and the reason is that the reverse transformation from ranges to general Dyck paths works on dequeueings of cost 1 and the solution we found is the only one with no dequeueing equal to 1.

Dyck meander   Another worst case occurs if $e = d + 1$ and the line is then a Dyck meander whose extremity ends at ordinate $e - d = 1$. An example is given in FIGURE 2.20, where the last operation is a dequeueing. The dotted line delineates the result of applying the rescheduling we used on Dyck paths. Here, the last operation becomes an enqueueing. Another possibility is shown in FIGURE 2.21, where the last operation is left unchanged. The difference between the two examples lies in the fact that the original last dequeueing has, in the former case, a cost of 1 (thus is changed) and, in the latter case, a cost greater than 1 (thus is invariant). The third kind of Dyck meander is one ending with an enqueueing, but because this enqueueing must start from the abscissa axis, this is the same situation as the result of rescheduling a meander ending with a dequeueing with cost 1 (see dotted line in FIGURE 2.20 again). Therefore, we are left to compare the results of rescheduling meanders ending with a dequeueing, that is, we envisage two cases.

- If we have a range of $n-1$ operations followed by an enqueueing, the maximum cost of the range is the cost of a saw-toothed Dyck path, that is, $\mathcal{W}_{e-1,e-1} = 4(e-1) = 2n-2$, because $n = e + d = 2e - 1$, followed by an enqueueing, totalling $2n - 1$.

- Otherwise, we have a range of $n - 3$ operations followed by two rises and one fall (of cost 6). The cost is $\mathcal{W}_{e-2,e-2} + 6 = 2n$, which is marginally greater than the previous case.

Amortised cost The cost $\mathcal{S}_n$ of a series of n queue updates, starting on an empty queue, is tightly bounded as

$$n \leqslant \mathcal{S}_n \leqslant 2n,$$

where the lower bound is tight if all updates are enqueueings and the upper bound when a saw-toothed range is followed by one enqueueing or else two enqueueings and one dequeueing. By definition, the amortised cost of one operation is $\mathcal{S}_n/n$ and so lies between 1 and 2, which is less than the upper bound in inequality (2.13) could have lead us to believe.

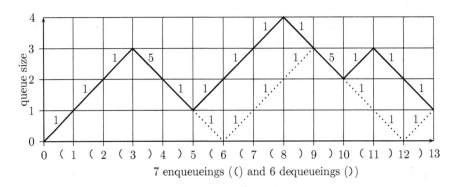

Figure 2.20: Dyck meander modelling queue operations (total cost 21)

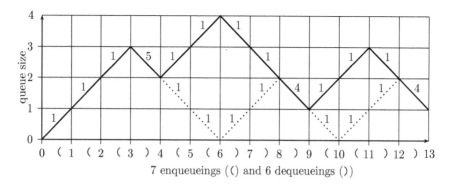

Figure 2.21: Dyck meander modelling queue operations (total cost 23)

Side note We can gain some more abstraction by using a dedicated constructor for the empty queue, nilq/0, and changing accordingly the definition of enq/2 in (2.10) on page 64 so it handles this case:

$$\mathsf{enq}(x, \mathsf{nilq}()) \to \mathsf{q}([x], []);$$
$$\mathsf{enq}(x, \mathsf{q}(r, f)) \to \mathsf{q}([x\,|\,r], f).$$

We can improve this a little by pushing x directly into the front stack:

$$\mathsf{enq}(x, \mathsf{nilq}()) \to \mathsf{q}([], [x]);$$
$$\mathsf{enq}(x, \mathsf{q}(r, f)) \to \mathsf{q}([x\,|\,r], f).$$

Exercises

1. Let $\mathsf{nxt}(q)$ be the next item to be dequeued from q:

   $$\mathsf{nxt}(\mathsf{q}([x\,|\,r], [])) \to \mathsf{nxt}(\mathsf{q}([], \mathsf{rcat}(r, [x])));$$
   $$\mathsf{nxt}(\mathsf{q}(r, [x\,|\,f])) \to x.$$

   Modify enq/2, deq/1 and nxt/1 in such a way that $C_n^{\mathsf{nxt}} = 1$, where n is the number of items in the queue.

2. Find $\mathcal{S}_n$ using the slightly different definition

   $$\mathsf{deq}(\mathsf{q}([x\,|\,r], [])) \to \mathsf{deq}(\mathsf{q}([], \mathsf{rev}([x\,|\,r])));$$
   $$\mathsf{deq}(\mathsf{q}(r, [x\,|\,f])) \to (\mathsf{q}(r, f), x).$$

2.6 Cutting

Let us consider the problem of cutting a stack s at the kth place. Obviously, the result is a pair of stacks. More precisely, let (t, u) be the value of $\mathsf{cut}(s, k)$, such that $\mathsf{cat}(t, u) \twoheadrightarrow s$ and t contains k items, that is to say, $\mathsf{len}(t) \twoheadrightarrow k$. In particular, if $k = 0$, then $t = []$; invalid inputs lead to unspecified behaviours. For instance, $\mathsf{cut}([4, 2], 0) \twoheadrightarrow ([], [4, 2])$ and $\mathsf{cut}([5, 3, 6, 0, 2], 3) \twoheadrightarrow ([5, 3, 6], [0, 2])$, but, for the sake of simplicity, nothing is said about $\mathsf{cut}([0], 7)$ and $\mathsf{cut}([0], -1)$. We derive two cases: $k = 0$ or else the stack is not empty. The former is easy to guess:

$$\mathsf{cut}(s, 0) \rightarrow ([], s); \qquad \mathsf{cut}([x \,|\, s], k) \rightarrow \boxed{}.$$

A big-step design uses some substructural recursive calls to set the structure of the value in the right-hand side. Because $\mathsf{cut}/2$ takes two arguments, we expect a lexicographic order (definition (1.8), page 13):

$$\mathsf{cut}(s_0, k_0) \succ \mathsf{cut}(s_1, k_1) :\Leftrightarrow s_0 \succ s_1 \text{ or } (s_0 = s_1 \text{ and } k_0 > k_1).$$

Using the proper subterm order (section 1.5, page 12) on stacks for $(\succ)$,

$$\mathsf{cut}([x \,|\, s], k) \succ \mathsf{cut}(s, j); \quad \mathsf{cut}([x \,|\, s], k) \succ \mathsf{cut}([x \,|\, s], j), \text{ if } k > j.$$

In the latter case, we can set $j = k - 1$, but the value of $\mathsf{cut}(s, j)$ needs to be projected into (t, u) so x is injected in and yields $([x \,|\, t], u)$. This can be achieved with an auxiliary function $\mathsf{push}/2$:

$$\mathsf{cut}(s, 0) \rightarrow ([], s); \qquad\qquad \mathsf{push}(x, (t, u)) \rightarrow ([x \,|\, t], u).$$
$$\mathsf{cut}([x \,|\, s], k) \rightarrow \mathsf{push}(x, \mathsf{cut}(s, k - 1)).$$

Inference systems When the value of a recursive call needs to be destructured, it is convenient to use an extension of our language to avoid creating auxiliary functions like $\mathsf{push}/2$:

$$\mathsf{cut}(s, 0) \rightarrow ([], s) \ \text{N}\textsc{il} \qquad \frac{\mathsf{cut}(s, k - 1) \twoheadrightarrow (t, u)}{\mathsf{cut}([x \,|\, s], k) \twoheadrightarrow ([x \,|\, t], u)} \ \textsc{Pref}$$

The new construct is called an *inference rule* because it means: 'For the value of $\mathsf{cut}([x \,|\, s], k)$ to be $([x \,|\, t], u)$, we infer that the value of $\mathsf{cut}(s, k-1)$ must be (t, u)'. This interpretation corresponds to an upwards reading of the rule $\textsc{Pref}$ (*prefix*). Just as we compose horizontally rewrite rules, we compose inference rules vertically, stacking them, as in

$$\frac{\dfrac{\dfrac{\mathsf{cut}([0, 2], 0) \rightarrow ([], [0, 2])}{\mathsf{cut}([6, 0, 2], 1) \twoheadrightarrow ([6], [0, 2])}}{\mathsf{cut}([3, 6, 0, 2], 2) \twoheadrightarrow ([3, 6], [0, 2])}}{\mathsf{cut}([5, 3, 6, 0, 2], 3) \twoheadrightarrow ([5, 3, 6], [0, 2])}$$

When determining the cost of $\mathsf{cut}(s, k)$, we take into account the hidden function $\mathsf{push}/2$, so $\mathcal{C}[\![\mathsf{cut}([5, 3, 6, 0, 2], 3)]\!] = 7$. In general, $\mathcal{C}_k^{\mathsf{cut}} = 2k + 1$.

Beyond simplifying programs, what makes this formalism interesting is that it enables two kinds of interpretation: logical and computational. The computational reading, called *inductive* in some contexts, has just been illustrated. The logical understanding considers inference rules as logical implications of the form $P_1 \wedge P_2 \wedge \ldots \wedge P_n \Rightarrow C$, written

$$\frac{P_1 \qquad P_2 \qquad \cdots \qquad P_n}{C}$$

The propositions P_i are called *premises* and C is the *conclusion*. In the case of PREF, there is only one premise. When premises are lacking, as in NIL, then C is called an *axiom* and no horizontal line is drawn. The composition of inference rules is a *derivation*. In the case of $\mathsf{cut}/2$, all derivations are isomorphic to a stack, whose top is the conclusion.

The logical reading of rule PREF is:

'If $\mathsf{cut}(s, k - 1) \twoheadrightarrow (t, u)$, then we have $\mathsf{cut}([x \,|\, s], k) \twoheadrightarrow ([x \,|\, t], u)$.'

This top-down reading qualifies as *deductive*. The previous derivation then can be regarded as the proof of the relation instance
$\mathsf{cut}([5, 3, 6, 0, 2], 3) \twoheadrightarrow ([5, 3, 6], [0, 2])$.

Induction on proofs   A single formalism with such a dual interpretation is powerful because a definition by means of inference rules enables the proof of theorems about a function by *induction on the structure of the proof.* As we have done previously, structural induction can be applied to stacks considered as a data type (objects). Since, in the case of $\mathsf{cut}/2$, derivations are stacks in themselves, so can induction be applied to their structure (as meta-objects).

Let us illustrate this elegant inductive technique with a proof of the *soundness* of $\mathsf{cut}/2$.

Soundness   The concept of soundness or *correctness* (McCarthy, 1962, Floyd, 1967, Hoare, 1971, Dijkstra, 1976) is a binary relationship, so we always ought to speak of the soundness of a program with respect to its *specification*. A specification is a logical description of the expected properties of the output of a program, given some assumptions on its input. In the case of $\mathsf{cut}(s, k)$, we already mentioned what to expect: the value must be a pair (t, u) such that the concatenation of t and u is s and the length of t is k.

Formally, let $\mathsf{CorCut}(s, k)$ be the proposition

If $cut(s, k) \twoheadrightarrow (t, u)$, then $cat(t, u) \twoheadrightarrow s$ and $len(t) \twoheadrightarrow k$,

where the function len/1 is defined in equation (2.5) on page 43.

Let us suppose the antecedent of the implication to be true, otherwise the theorem is vacuously true, so there exists a derivation Δ whose conclusion is $cut(s, k) \twoheadrightarrow (t, u)$. This derivation is a (meta) stack whose top is the conclusion in question, which makes it possible to reckon by induction on its structure, that is, we assume that CorCut holds for the immediate subderivation of Δ (the induction hypothesis) and then proceed to prove that CorCut holds for the entire derivation. This is the immediate subterm induction we use when reasoning on a stack as an object: we assume the theorem to hold for s and then prove it for $[x \mid s]$.

A case by case analysis on the kind of rule that can end Δ guides the proof. To avoid clashes between variables in the theorem and in the inference system, we will overline the latter ones, like $\overline{s}$, $\overline{t}$ etc. which may differ from s and t in CorCut.

- *Case where Δ ends with* NIL. There are no premises, as NIL is an axiom. In this case, we have to establish CorCut without induction. The matching of $cut(s, k) \twoheadrightarrow (t, u)$ against $cut(\overline{s}, 0) \rightarrow ([\,], \overline{s})$ yields $\overline{s} = s$, $0 = k$, $[\,] = t$ and $\overline{s} = u$. Therefore, $cat(t, u) = cat([\,], s) \xrightarrow{\alpha} s$, which proves half of the conjunction. Moreover $len(t) = len([\,]) \xrightarrow{a} 0$. This is consistent with $k = 0$, so $CorCut(s, 0)$ is true.

- *Case where Δ ends with* PREF. The shape of Δ is thus as follows:

$$\frac{\begin{array}{c}\vdots\\ \overline{cut(\overline{s}, \overline{k} - 1) \twoheadrightarrow (\overline{t}, \overline{u})}\end{array}}{cut([\overline{x} \mid \overline{s}], \overline{k}) \twoheadrightarrow ([\overline{x} \mid \overline{t}], \overline{u})} \ \text{PREF}$$

The matching of $cut(s, k) \twoheadrightarrow (t, u)$ against the conclusion yields $[\overline{x} \mid \overline{s}] = s$, $\overline{k} = k$, $[\overline{x} \mid \overline{t}] = t$ and $\overline{u} = u$. The induction hypothesis in this case is that the theorem holds for the subderivation, therefore $cat(\overline{t}, \overline{u}) \twoheadrightarrow \overline{s}$ and $len(\overline{t}) \twoheadrightarrow \overline{k} - 1$. The induction principle requires that we establish now $cat([\overline{x} \mid \overline{t}], \overline{u}) \twoheadrightarrow [\overline{x} \mid \overline{s}]$ and $len([\overline{x} \mid \overline{t}]) \twoheadrightarrow \overline{k}$. From the definition of cat/2 and part of the hypothesis, we easily deduce $cat([\overline{x} \mid \overline{t}], \overline{u}) \xrightarrow{\beta} [\overline{x} \mid cat(\overline{t}, \overline{u})] \twoheadrightarrow [\overline{x} \mid \overline{s}]$. Now the other part: $len([\overline{x} \mid \overline{t}]) \xrightarrow{b} 1 + len(\overline{t}) \twoheadrightarrow 1 + (\overline{k} - 1) = \overline{k}$.   □

Exercise   Write an equivalent definition of cut/2 in tail form.

2.7 Persistence

Persistence is a distinctive feature of purely functional languages, meaning that values are constants. Functions update a data structure by creating a new version of it, instead of modifying it in place and thereby erasing its history. We saw in section 1.3 on page 5 that subtrees common to both sides of the same rule are shared. Such a sharing is sound because of persistence: there is no logical way to tell apart a copied subtree from the original.

Maximum sharing An obvious source of sharing is the occurrence of a variable in the pattern of a rule and its right-hand side, as seen in FIGURE 1.4 on page 7 for instance. But this does not always lead to maximum sharing as the definition of red/1 (*reduce*) in FIGURE 2.22 shows. This function copies a stack without its consecutively repeated items. For example, we might have $red([4, 1, 2, 2, 2, 1, 1]) \twoheadrightarrow [4, 1, 2, 1]$.

A directed acyclic graph of the second rule is depicted in FIGURE 2.23a. In this picture, sharing is based on commonly occurring variables, but we can see that $[x \mid s]$ is not completely shared. Consider the same rule in FIGURE 2.23b with maximum sharing, where a whole subtree is shared.

$$red([\,]) \rightarrow [\,];$$
$$red([x, x \mid s]) \rightarrow red([x \mid s]);$$
$$red([x \mid s]) \rightarrow [x \mid red(s)].$$

Figure 2.22: Reducing

When discussing memory management, *we assume that sharing is maximum for each rule*, so, for instance, FIGURE 2.23b would be the default. But this property is not enough to insure that sharing is maximum between the arguments of a function call and its value. For example,

$$cp([\,]) \rightarrow [\,]; \qquad cp([x \mid s]) \rightarrow [x \mid cp(s)].$$

makes a copy of its argument, but the value of $cp(s)$ only shares its items with s, despite $cp(s) \equiv s$.

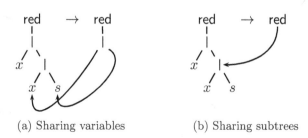

(a) Sharing variables   (b) Sharing subtrees

Figure 2.23: Directed acyclic graphs (DAG) of the second rule of red/1

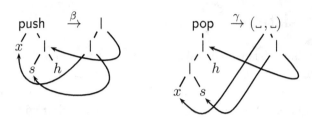

Figure 2.24: DAGs of push/2 and pop/1 with maximum sharing

Revision control   A simple idea to implement data structures enabling
backtracking consists in keeping all successive versions. A stack can be
used to keep such a record, called *history*, and backtracking is reduced
to linear search. For example, we may be interested in recording a series
of stacks, each one obtained from its predecessor by a push or a pop, like
the history $[[4, 2, 1], [2, 1], [3, 2, 1], [2, 1], [1], []]$, where the initial stack was
empty; next, 1 was pushed, followed by 2 and 3; then 3 was popped and
4 pushed instead. This way, the *last version* is the top of history, like
$[4, 2, 1]$ in our example. Furthermore, we want two successive versions
to share as much structure as possible. (We speak of 'version' instead
of 'state', because the latter applies when values can be not persistent.)
These requirements are at the heart of *revision control* software, used by
programmers to keep track of the evolution of their source code.

    As a simple case study, we shall continue with our example of re-
cording the different versions of a stack, while keeping in mind that the
technique described further applies to any data structure. We need to
write two functions, push/2 (different from the one defined in section 2.6)
and pop/1, which, instead of processing one stack, deal with a history of
stacks. Consider the following definitions:

$$\mathsf{push}(x, []) \stackrel{\alpha}{\rightarrow} [[x], []]; \qquad \mathsf{pop}([[x \,|\, s] \,|\, h]) \stackrel{\gamma}{\rightarrow} (x, [s, [x \,|\, s] \,|\, h]).$$
$$\mathsf{push}(x, [s \,|\, h]) \stackrel{\beta}{\rightarrow} [[x \,|\, s], s \,|\, h]. \quad \mathsf{top}([[x \,|\, s] \,|\, h]) \rightarrow x. \tag{2.14}$$

The corresponding directed acyclic graphs are found in FIGURE 2.24.
History $[[4, 2, 1], [2, 1], [3, 2, 1], [2, 1], [1], []]$ is displayed in FIGURE 2.25 as
a directed acyclic graph as well. It is obtained as the evaluation of

$$\mathsf{push}(4, \mathsf{pop}(\mathsf{push}(3, \mathsf{push}(2, \mathsf{push}(1, []))))). \tag{2.15}$$

    Let $\mathsf{ver}(k, h)$ evaluate in the kth previous version in the history h,
so $\mathsf{ver}(0, h)$ is the last version. As expected, ver/2 is just a linear search
with a countdown:

$$\mathsf{ver}(0, [s \,|\, h]) \rightarrow s; \qquad \mathsf{ver}(k, [s \,|\, h]) \rightarrow \mathsf{ver}(k - 1, h).$$

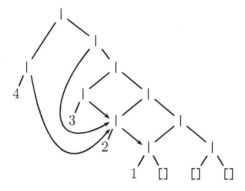

Figure 2.25: History $[[4, 2, 1], [2, 1], [3, 2, 1], [2, 1], [1], []]$

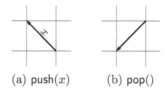

(a) push(x)   (b) pop()

Figure 2.26: Stack updates

Our encoding of history allows the last version to be easily modified, but not older ones. When a data structure allows every version in its history to be modified, it is said *fully persistent*; if only the last version can be replaced, it is said *partially persistent* (Mehlhorn and Tsakalidis, 1990).

Backtracking updates   In order to achieve full persistence, we should keep a history of updates, $\underline{push}(x)$ and $\underline{pop}()$, instead of successive, maximally overlapping versions. In the following, the underlining avoids confusion with the functions push/2 and pop/1. Instead of equation (2.15), we have now the history

$$[\underline{push}(4), \underline{pop}(), \underline{push}(3), \underline{push}(2), \underline{push}(1)].\qquad(2.16)$$

But not all series of $\underline{push}(x)$ and $\underline{pop}()$ are valid, as $[\underline{pop}(), \underline{pop}(), \underline{push}(x)]$ and $[\underline{pop}()]$. In order to characterise valid histories, let us consider a graphical representation of updates in FIGURE 2.26. This is the same model we used in section 2.5 where we studied queueing (see in particular FIGURE 2.15 on page 65), except that we choose here a leftwards orientation to mirror the notation for stacks, whose tops are laid out on the left of the page. Consider for instance the history in FIGURE 2.27 on the following page. It is clear that *a valid history is a line which never*

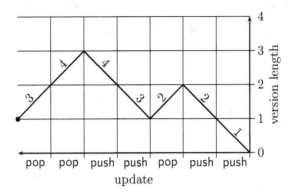

Figure 2.27: $[\underline{\mathsf{pop}}(), \underline{\mathsf{pop}}(), \underline{\mathsf{push}}(4), \underline{\mathsf{push}}(3), \underline{\mathsf{pop}}(), \underline{\mathsf{push}}(2), \underline{\mathsf{push}}(1)]$

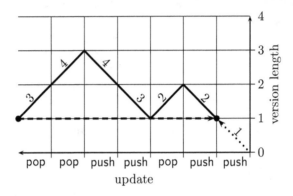

Figure 2.28: Finding the top of the last version

crosses the absissa axis.

Programming top/1 with a history of updates is more difficult because we must find the top item of the last version without constructing
it. The idea is to walk back the historical line and determine the last push
leading to a version whose length is equal to that of the last version. In
FIGURE 2.27, the last version is (•). If we draw a horizontal line from it
rightwards, the first push ending on the line is $\underline{\mathsf{push}}(1)$, so the top of the
last version is 1.

This thought experiment is depicted in FIGURE 2.28. Notice that we
do not need to determine the length of the last version: the difference of
length with the current version, while walking back, is enough.

Let $\mathsf{top}_0/1$ and $\mathsf{pop}_0/1$ be the equivalent of top/1 and pop/1 operating
on updates instead of versions. Their definitions are found in FIGURE 2.29
on the next page. An ancillary function $\mathsf{top}_0/2$ keeps track of the difference between the lengths of the last and current versions. We have found
the item when the difference is 0 and the current update is a push.

$$\begin{aligned}
&\text{pop}_0(h) \rightarrow [\underline{\text{pop}}()\,|\,h]. \quad \text{top}_0(0, [\underline{\text{push}}(x)\,|\,h]) \rightarrow x; \\
&\text{top}_0(h) \rightarrow \text{top}_0(0, h). \quad \text{top}_0(k, [\underline{\text{push}}(x)\,|\,h]) \rightarrow \text{top}_0(k-1, h); \\
&\qquad\qquad\qquad\qquad\quad \text{top}_0(k, [\underline{\text{pop}}()\,|\,h]) \rightarrow \text{top}_0(k+1, h).
\end{aligned}$$

Figure 2.29: The top and the rest of an history of updates

As previously, we want the call $\text{ver}_0(k, h)$ to evaluate in the kth previous version in h. Here, we need to walk back k updates in the past,

$$\text{ver}_0(0, h) \rightarrow \text{lst}_0(h); \qquad \text{ver}_0(k, [s\,|\,h]) \rightarrow \text{ver}_0(k-1, h).$$

and build the last version from the rest of the history with $\text{lst}_0/1$:

$$\text{lst}_0([\,]) \rightarrow [\,]; \quad \text{lst}_0([\underline{\text{push}}(x)\,|\,h]) \rightarrow [x\,|\,\text{lst}_0(h)]; \quad \frac{\text{lst}_0(h) \twoheadrightarrow [x\,|\,s]}{\text{lst}_0([\underline{\text{pop}}()\,|\,h]) \twoheadrightarrow s}.$$

Let $C_{k,n}^{\text{ver}_0}$ be the cost of the call $\text{ver}_0(k, h)$ and $C_n^{\text{lst}_0}$ the cost of $\text{lst}_0(h)$, where n is the length of h: $C_i^{\text{lst}_0} = i+1$ and $C_{k,n}^{\text{ver}_0} = (k+1)+C_{n-k}^{\text{lst}_0} = n+2$.

What is the total amount of memory allocated? More precisely, we want to know the number of pushes performed. The only rule of $\text{lst}_0/1$ featuring a push in its right-hand side is the second one, so the number of cons-nodes is the number of push updates. But this is a waste in certain cases, for example, when the version built is empty, like the history $[\text{pop}(), \underline{\text{push}}(6)]$. The optimal situation is to allocate only as much as the computed version actually contains.

We can achieve this memory optimality with $\text{lst}_1/1$ in FIG-URE 2.30 by retaining features of both $\text{top}_0/1$ and $\text{lst}_0/1$. We have $C_n^{\text{lst}_1} = C_n^{\text{lst}_0} = n+1$, and the number of cons-nodes created is now the length of the last version itself. This is an-

$$\begin{aligned}
&\text{lst}_1(h) \rightarrow \text{lst}_1(0, h). \\
&\text{lst}_1(0, [\underline{\text{push}}(x)\,|\,h]) \rightarrow [x\,|\,\text{lst}_1(0, h)]; \\
&\text{lst}_1(k, [\underline{\text{push}}(x)\,|\,h]) \rightarrow \text{lst}_1(k-1, h); \\
&\text{lst}_1(k, [\underline{\text{pop}}()\,|\,h]) \rightarrow \text{lst}_1(k+1, h); \\
&\text{lst}_1(k, [\,]) \rightarrow [\,].
\end{aligned}$$

Figure 2.30: Last version

other instance of an output-dependent cost, like $\text{flat}_0/1$ in section 2.4 on page 56. There is still room for improvement if the historical line meets the absissa axis, as there is no need to visit the updates *before* a pop resulting into an empty version; for instance, in FIGURE 2.31 on the next page, it is useless to go past $\underline{\text{push}}(3)$ to find the last version to be $[3]$. But, in order to detect whether the historical line meets the abscissa axis, we need to augment the history h with the length n of the last version, that

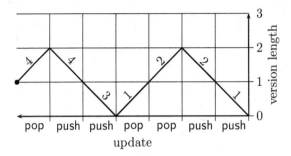

Figure 2.31: Last version [3] found in four steps

$$
\begin{aligned}
\mathsf{ver}_3(k, (n, h)) &\rightarrow \mathsf{ver}_3(k, n, h). \\
\mathsf{ver}_3(0, n, h) &\rightarrow \mathsf{lst}_3(0, n, h); \\
\mathsf{ver}_3(k, n, [\underline{\mathsf{pop}}()\,|\,h]) &\rightarrow \mathsf{ver}_3(k-1, n+1, h); \\
\mathsf{ver}_3(k, n, [\underline{\mathsf{push}}(x)\,|\,h]) &\rightarrow \mathsf{ver}_3(k-1, n-1, h). \\
\mathsf{lst}_3((n, h)) &\rightarrow \mathsf{lst}_3(0, n, h). \\
\mathsf{lst}_3(k, 0, h) &\rightarrow []; \\
\mathsf{lst}_3(0, n, [\underline{\mathsf{push}}(x)\,|\,h]) &\rightarrow [x\,|\,\mathsf{lst}_3(0, n-1, h)]; \\
\mathsf{lst}_3(k, n, [\underline{\mathsf{push}}(x)\,|\,h]) &\rightarrow \mathsf{lst}_3(k-1, n-1, h); \\
\mathsf{lst}_3(k, n, [\underline{\mathsf{pop}}()\,|\,h]) &\rightarrow \mathsf{lst}_3(k+1, n+1, h).
\end{aligned}
$$

Figure 2.32: Querying a version without pairs

is, work with (n, h), and modify **push/2** and **pop/1** accordingly:

$$
\begin{aligned}
\mathsf{push}_2(x, (n, h)) &\rightarrow (n+1, [\underline{\mathsf{push}}(x)\,|\,h]). \\
\mathsf{pop}_2((n, h)) &\rightarrow (n-1, [\underline{\mathsf{pop}}()\,|\,h]).
\end{aligned}
$$

We have to rewrite **ver/2** so it keeps track of the length of the last version:

$$
\begin{aligned}
\mathsf{ver}_2(0, (n, h)) &\rightarrow \mathsf{lst}_1(0, h); \\
\mathsf{ver}_2(k, (n, [\underline{\mathsf{pop}}()\,|\,h])) &\rightarrow \mathsf{ver}_2(k-1, (n+1, h)); \\
\mathsf{ver}_2(k, (n, [\underline{\mathsf{push}}(x)\,|\,h])) &\rightarrow \mathsf{ver}_2(k-1, (n-1, h)).
\end{aligned}
$$

We can reduce the memory footprint by separating the length n of the last version from the current history h, so no pairs are allocated, and we can stop when the current version is $[]$, as planned, in FIGURE 2.32.

One may wonder why bother pairing n and h just to separate them again, defeating the purpose of data abstraction. This example demonstrates that abstraction is desirable for callers, but called functions may break it due to pattern matching. We may also realise that the choice of a stack for storing updates is not the best in terms of memory usage. Instead, we can directly chain updates with an additional argument

$$\begin{aligned}
\text{ver}_4(k, (n, h)) &\to \text{ver}_4(k, n, h). \\
\text{ver}_4(0, n, h) &\to \text{lst}_4(0, n, h); \\
\text{ver}_4(k, n, \underline{\text{pop}}(h)) &\to \text{ver}_4(k - 1, n + 1, h); \\
\text{ver}_4(k, n, \underline{\text{push}}(x, h)) &\to \text{ver}_4(k - 1, n - 1, h). \\
\text{lst}_4((n, h)) &\to \text{lst}_4(0, n, h). \\
\text{lst}_4(k, 0, h) &\to [\,]; \\
\text{lst}_4(0, n, \underline{\text{push}}(x, h)) &\to [x \,|\, \text{lst}_4(0, n - 1, h)]; \\
\text{lst}_4(k, n, \underline{\text{push}}(x, h)) &\to \text{lst}_4(k - 1, n - 1, h); \\
\text{lst}_4(k, n, \underline{\text{pop}}(h)) &\to \text{lst}_4(k + 1, n + 1, h).
\end{aligned}$$

Figure 2.33: Querying a version without a stack

denoting the previous update, so, for instance, instead of equation (2.16):

$$(3, \underline{\text{push}}(4, \underline{\text{pop}}(\underline{\text{push}}(3, \underline{\text{push}}(2, \underline{\text{push}}(1, [\,]))))))\,.$$

This new encoding closely mirrors the call (2.15) on page 74 and saves n cons-nodes in a history of length n. See FIGURE 2.33.

$$\begin{aligned}
\text{push}_4(x, (n, h)) &\to (n+1, \underline{\text{push}}(x, h)). \\
\text{pop}_4((n, h)) &\to (n-1, \underline{\text{pop}}(h)).
\end{aligned}$$

There is now a minimum and maximum cost. The worst case is when the bottommost item of the last version is the first item pushed in the history, so $\text{lst}_4/3$ has to recur until the origin of time. In other words, the historical line never reaches the abscissa axis after the first push. We have same cost as before: $\mathcal{W}_n^{\text{lst}_4} = n+1$. The best case happens when the last version is empty. In this case, $\mathcal{B}_n^{\text{lst}_4} = 1$, and this is an occurrence of the kind of improvement we sought.

Full persistence   The update-based approach to history is fully persistent by enabling the modification of the past as follows: traverse history until the required moment, pop up the update at that point, push another one and simply put back the previously traversed updates, which must have been kept in some accumulator. But changing the past must not create a history with a non-constructible version in it, to wit, the historical line must not cross the absissa axis after the modification. If the change consists in replacing a pop by a push, there is no need to worry, as this will raise by 2 the end point of the line. It is the converse change that requires special attention, as this will lower by 2 the end point. The ± 2 offset comes from the vertical difference between the end

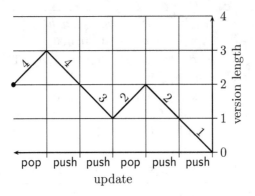

Figure 2.34: $\mathsf{pop}(\underline{\mathsf{push}}(4, \mathsf{push}(3, \mathsf{pop}(\underline{\mathsf{push}}(2, \underline{\mathsf{push}}(1, [])))))))$

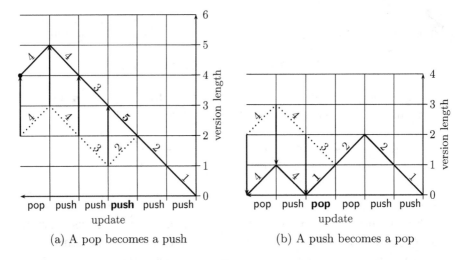

(a) A pop becomes a push   (b) A push becomes a pop

Figure 2.35: Changing updates

points of a push and a pop update of same origin, as can be easily seen in FIGURE 2.26 on page 75. As a consequence, in FIGURE 2.27, the last version has length 1, which implies that it is impossible to replace a push by a pop, anywhere in the past.

Let us consider the history in FIGURE 2.34. Let $\mathsf{chg}(k, u, (n, h))$ be the changed history, where k is the index of the update we want to change, indexing the last one at 0; u is the new update we want to set; n is the length of the last version of history h. The call

$$\mathsf{chg}(3, \underline{\mathsf{push}}(5), (2, \mathsf{pop}(\underline{\mathsf{push}}(4, \mathsf{push}(3, \mathsf{pop}(\underline{\mathsf{push}}(2, \mathsf{push}(1, []))))))))$$

results in $(4, \mathsf{pop}(\underline{\mathsf{push}}(4, \mathsf{push}(3, \underline{\mathsf{push}}(5, \mathsf{push}(2, \underline{\mathsf{push}}(1, []))))))))$.This call succeeds because in FIGURE 2.35a the new historical line does not cross the absissa axis. We can see in FIGURE 2.35b the result of the call

$$\mathsf{chg}(2, \underline{\mathsf{pop}}(), (2, \mathsf{pop}(\underline{\mathsf{push}}(4, \mathsf{push}(3, \mathsf{pop}(\underline{\mathsf{push}}(2, \mathsf{push}(1, []))))))))).$$

All these examples help in guessing the characteristic property for a replacement to be valid:

- the replacements of a pop by a push, a pop by a pop, a push by a push are always valid;
- the replacement of a push by a pop as update $k > 0$ is valid if and only if the historical line between updates 0 and $k - 1$ remains above or reaches without crossing the horizontal line of ordinate 2.

We can divide the algorithm in two phases. First, the update to be replaced must be found, but, the difference with $\mathsf{ver}_4/3$ is that we may need to know if the historical line before reaching the update lies above the horizontal line of ordinate 2. This is easy to check if we maintain across recursive calls the lowest ordinate reached by the line. The second phase substitute the update and checks if the resulting history is valid.

Let us implement the first phase. First, we project n and h out of (n, h) in order to save some memory, and the lowest ordinate is n, which we pass as an additional argument to another function $\mathsf{chg}/5$:

$$\mathsf{chg}(k, u, (n, h)) \rightarrow \mathsf{chg}(k, u, n, h, n).$$

Function $\mathsf{chg}/5$ traverses h while decrementing k, until $k = 0$, which means that the update to be changed has been found. At the same time, the length of the current version is computed (third argument) and compared to the previous lowest ordinate (the fifth argument), which is updated according to the outcome. We may try the following canvas:

$$
\begin{array}{ll}
\mathsf{chg}(0, u, n, h, m) \rightarrow \boxed{}; & \\
\mathsf{chg}(k, u, n, \underline{\mathsf{pop}}(h), m) \rightarrow \mathsf{chg}(k - 1, u, n + 1, h, m); & \\
\mathsf{chg}(k, u, n, \underline{\mathsf{push}}(x, h), m) \rightarrow \mathsf{chg}(k - 1, u, n - 1, h, m), & \text{if } m < n; \\
\mathsf{chg}(k, u, n, \underline{\mathsf{push}}(x, h), m) \rightarrow \mathsf{chg}(k - 1, u, n - 1, h, n - 1). &
\end{array}
$$

The problem is that we forget the history down to the update we are looking for. There are two methods to record it: either we use an accumulator and stick with a definition in tail form (small-step design), or we put back a visited update after returning from a recursive call (big-step design). The latter is faster, as there is no need to reverse the accumulator when we are done; the former allows us to share the history up to the update when it leaves history structurally invariant, at the cost of an extra parameter being the original history. This same dilemma

$$\mathsf{chg}(0, u, n, h, m) \rightarrow \mathsf{rep}(u, h, m) \quad \frac{\mathsf{chg}(k - 1, u, n + 1, h, m) \twoheadrightarrow (n', h')}{\mathsf{chg}(k, u, n, \underline{\mathsf{pop}}(h), m) \twoheadrightarrow (n', \underline{\mathsf{pop}}(h'))}$$

$$\frac{\mathsf{chg}(k - 1, u, n - 1, h, m) \twoheadrightarrow (n', h') \quad m < n}{\mathsf{chg}(k, u, n, \underline{\mathsf{push}}(x, h), m) \twoheadrightarrow (n', \underline{\mathsf{push}}(x, h'))}$$

$$\frac{\mathsf{chg}(k - 1, u, n - 1, h, n - 1) \twoheadrightarrow (n', h')}{\mathsf{chg}(k, u, n, \underline{\mathsf{push}}(x, h), m) \twoheadrightarrow (n', \underline{\mathsf{push}}(x, h'))}$$

Figure 2.36: Changing a past version (big-step design)

was encountered when we compared $\mathsf{sfst}/2$ and $\mathsf{sfst_0}/2$ in section 2.3 on page 44. Let us opt for a big-step design in FIGURE 2.36. Notice how the length n' of the new history is simply passed down the inference rules. It can simply be made out:

- replacing a pop by a pop or a push by a push leaves the original length invariant;
- replacing a pop by a push increases the original length by 2;
- replacing a push by a pop, assuming this is valid, decreases the original length by 2.

This task is up to the new function $\mathsf{rep}/3$ (*replace*), which implements the second phase. The design is to return a pair made of the differential in length d and the new history h':

$$\mathsf{rep}(\underline{\mathsf{pop}}(), \underline{\mathsf{pop}}(h), m) \rightarrow (0, \underline{\mathsf{pop}}(h));$$
$$\mathsf{rep}(\underline{\mathsf{push}}(x), \underline{\mathsf{push}}(y, h), m) \rightarrow (0, \underline{\mathsf{push}}(x, h));$$
$$\mathsf{rep}(\underline{\mathsf{push}}(x), \underline{\mathsf{pop}}(h), m) \rightarrow (2, \underline{\mathsf{push}}(x, h));$$
$$\mathsf{rep}(\underline{\mathsf{pop}}(), \underline{\mathsf{push}}(y, h), m) \rightarrow (-2, \underline{\mathsf{pop}}(h)).$$

This definition implies that we need to redefine $\mathsf{chg}/3$ as follows:

$$\frac{\mathsf{chg}(k, u, n, h, n) \twoheadrightarrow (d, h')}{\mathsf{chg}(k, u, (n, h)) \twoheadrightarrow (n + d, h')}.$$

2.8   Optimal sorting

Sorting is the process of rearranging a series of objects, called *keys*, to conform with a predefined order. According to Knuth (1998a), the first sorting algorithms were invented and automated as tabulating machines in the late nineteenth century, in order to support the establishment of the census of the United States of America.

Permutations We saw on page 9 that the average cost of a comparison-based sorting algorithm is defined as the arithmetic mean of the costs of sorting all permutations of a given length. A permutation of $(1, 2, \ldots, n)$ is another tuple $(a_1, a_2, \ldots, a_n)$ such that $a_i \in \{1, \ldots, n\}$ and $a_i \neq a_j$ for all $i \neq j$. For example, all the permutations of $(1, 2, 3)$ are

$$(1, 2, 3) \quad (1, 3, 2) \quad (2, 1, 3) \quad (2, 3, 1) \quad (3, 1, 2) \quad (3, 2, 1).$$

Given all the permutations of $(1, 2, \ldots, n-1)$, let us build inductively all the permutations of $(1, 2, \ldots, n)$. If $(a_1, a_2, \ldots, a_{n-1})$ is a permutation of $(1, 2, \ldots, n-1)$, then we can construct n permutations of $(1, 2, \ldots, n)$ by inserting n at all possible places in $(a_1, a_2, \ldots, a_{n-1})$:

$$(\boldsymbol{n}, a_1, a_2, \ldots, a_{n-1}) \quad (a_1, \boldsymbol{n}, a_2, \ldots, a_{n-1}) \quad \cdots \quad (a_1, a_2, \ldots, a_{n-1}, \boldsymbol{n}).$$

For example, it is obvious that all the permutations of $(1, 2)$ are $(1, 2)$ and $(2, 1)$. The method leads from $(1, 2)$ to $(\boldsymbol{3}, 1, 2)$, $(1, \boldsymbol{3}, 2)$ and $(1, 2, \boldsymbol{3})$; and from $(2, 1)$ to $(\boldsymbol{3}, 2, 1)$, $(2, \boldsymbol{3}, 1)$ and $(2, 1, \boldsymbol{3})$. If we name p_n the number of permutations on n elements, we then draw the recurrence $p_n = n \cdot p_{n-1}$, which, with $p_1 = 1$, leads to $p_n = n!$, for all $n > 0$, exactly as expected. If the n objects to permute are not $(1, 2, \ldots, n)$ but, for example, $(\mathsf{b}, \mathsf{d}, \mathsf{a}, \mathsf{c})$, simply associate each of them to their index in the tuple, for example, b is represented by 1, d by 2, a by 3 and c by 4, so the tuple is then associated to $(1, 2, 3, 4)$ and, for instance, the permutation $(4, 1, 2, 3)$ means $(\mathsf{c}, \mathsf{b}, \mathsf{d}, \mathsf{a})$.

Factorial We encountered the factorial function in the introduction and here again. There is a simple derivation enabling the characterisation of its asymptotic growth, proposed by Graham et al. (1994). We start by squaring the factorial and regrouping the factors as follows:

$$n!^2 = (1 \cdot 2 \cdot \ldots \cdot n)(n \cdot \ldots \cdot 2 \cdot 1) = \prod_{k=1}^{n} k(n + 1 - k).$$

The parabola $P(k) := k(n+1-k) = -k^2 + (n+1)k$ reaches its maximum where its derivative is zero: $P'(k_{\max}) = 0 \Leftrightarrow k_{\max} = (n+1)/2$. The corresponding ordinate is $P(k_{\max}) = ((n+1)/2)^2 = k_{\max}^2$. When k ranges from 1 to n, the minimal ordinate, n, is reached at abississas 1 and n, as shown in FIGURE 2.37 on the next page. Hence, $1 \leqslant k \leqslant k_{\max}$ implies

$$P(1) \leqslant P(k) \leqslant P(k_{\max}), \quad \text{that is,} \quad n \leqslant k(n + 1 - k) \leqslant \left(\frac{n + 1}{2}\right)^2.$$

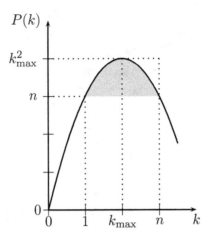

Figure 2.37: Parabola $P(k) := k(n + 1 - k)$

Multiplying the sides by varying k over the discrete interval $[1..n]$ yields

$$n^n = \prod_{k=1}^{n} n \leqslant n!^2 \leqslant \prod_{k=1}^{n} \left(\frac{n+1}{2}\right)^2 = \left(\frac{n+1}{2}\right)^{2n} \Rightarrow n^{n/2} \leqslant n! \leqslant \left(\frac{n+1}{2}\right)^n.$$

It is clear now that $n!$ is *exponential*, so it asymptotically outgrows any polynomial. Concretely, a function whose cost is proportional to a factorial is useless even for small inputs. For the cases where an equivalence is preferred, Stirling's formula states that

$$n! \sim n^n e^{-n} \sqrt{2\pi n}. \tag{2.17}$$

Enumerating all permutations   Let us write a program computing all the permutations of a given stack. We define the function perm/1 such that perm(s) is the stack of all permutations of the items in stack s. We implement the inductive method presented above, which worked by inserting a new object into all possible places of a shorter permutation.

$$\text{perm}([]) \xrightarrow{\alpha} [];\quad \text{perm}([x]) \xrightarrow{\beta} [[x]];\quad \text{perm}([x\,|\,s]) \xrightarrow{\gamma} \text{dist}(x, \text{perm}(s)).$$

The function dist/2 (*distribute*) is such that dist(x, s) is the stack of all stacks obtained by inserting the item x at all different places in stack s. Because such an insertion into a permutation of length n yields a permutation of length $n + 1$, we must join the new permutations to the previously found others of same length:

$$\text{dist}(x, []) \xrightarrow{\delta} [];\quad \text{dist}(x, [p\,|\,t]) \xrightarrow{\epsilon} \text{cat}(\text{ins}(x, p), \text{dist}(x, t)).$$

The call $\mathsf{ins}(x, p)$ computes the stack of permutations resulting from inserting x at all places in the permutation p. We thus derive

$$\mathsf{ins}(x, [\,]) \overset{\varsigma}{\to} [[x]]; \quad \mathsf{ins}(x, [j \,|\, s]) \overset{\eta}{\to} [[x, j \,|\, s] \,|\, \mathsf{push}(j, \mathsf{ins}(x, s))].$$

where the function $\mathsf{push}/2$ (not to be confused with the function of same name and arity in section 2.7) is such that any call $\mathsf{push}(x, t)$ pushes item x on all the permutations of the stack of permutations t. The order is left unchanged:

$$\mathsf{push}(x, [\,]) \overset{\theta}{\to} [\,]; \quad \mathsf{push}(x, [p \,|\, t]) \overset{\iota}{\to} [[x \,|\, p] \,|\, \mathsf{push}(x, t)].$$

Now we can compute all the permutations of $(4, 1, 2, 3)$ or $(\mathsf{c}, \mathsf{b}, \mathsf{d}, \mathsf{a})$ by calling $\mathsf{perm}([4, 1, 2, 3])$ or $\mathsf{perm}([\mathsf{c}, \mathsf{b}, \mathsf{d}, \mathsf{a}])$. Note that, after computing the permutations of length $n + 1$, the permutations of length n are not needed anymore, which would allow an implementation to reclaim the corresponding memory for further uses (a process called *garbage collection*). As far as the costs are concerned, the definition of $\mathsf{push}/2$ yields

$$C_0^{\mathsf{push}} \overset{\theta}{=} 1; \quad C_{n+1}^{\mathsf{push}} \overset{\iota}{=} 1 + C_n^{\mathsf{push}}, \quad \text{with } n \geqslant 0.$$

We easily deduce $C_n^{\mathsf{push}} = n + 1$. We know that the result of $\mathsf{ins}(x, p)$ is a stack of length $n + 1$ if p is a permutation of n objects into which we insert one more object x. Hence, the definition of $\mathsf{ins}/2$ leads to

$$C_0^{\mathsf{ins}} \overset{\varsigma}{=} 1; \quad C_{k+1}^{\mathsf{ins}} \overset{\eta}{=} 1 + C_{k+1}^{\mathsf{push}} + C_k^{\mathsf{ins}} = 3 + k + C_k^{\mathsf{ins}}, \quad \text{with } k \geqslant 0,$$

where C_k^{ins} is the cost of $\mathsf{ins}(x, p)$ with p of length k. By summing for all k from 0 to $n - 1$, for $n > 0$, on both sides we draw

$$\sum_{k=0}^{n-1} C_{k+1}^{\mathsf{ins}} = \sum_{k=0}^{n-1} 3 + \sum_{k=0}^{n-1} k + \sum_{k=0}^{n-1} C_k^{\mathsf{ins}}.$$

By cancelling identical terms in the sums (telescoping) $\sum_{k=0}^{n-1} C_{k+1}^{\mathsf{ins}}$ and $\sum_{k=0}^{n-1} C_k^{\mathsf{ins}}$, we draw

$$C_n^{\mathsf{ins}} = 3n + \frac{1}{2}n(n - 1) + C_0^{\mathsf{ins}} = \frac{1}{2}n^2 + \frac{5}{2}n + 1.$$

This last equation is actually valid even if $n = 0$. Let $C_{n!}^{\mathsf{dist}}$ be the cost for distributing an item among $n!$ permutations of length n. The definition of $\mathsf{dist}/2$ shows that it repeats calls to $\mathsf{cat}/2$ and $\mathsf{ins}/2$ whose arguments are always of length $n + 1$ and n, respectively, because all processed permutations here have the same length. We deduce, for $k \geqslant 0$, that

$$C_0^{\mathsf{dist}} \overset{\delta}{=} 1; \quad C_{k+1}^{\mathsf{dist}} \overset{\epsilon}{=} 1 + C_{n+1}^{\mathsf{cat}} + C_n^{\mathsf{ins}} + C_k^{\mathsf{dist}} = \frac{1}{2}n^2 + \frac{7}{2}n + 4 + C_k^{\mathsf{dist}},$$

since we already know that $C_n^{\text{cat}} = n+1$ and the value of C_n^{ins}. By summing both sides of the last equation for all k from 0 to $n! - 1$, we can eliminate most of the terms and find a non-recursive definition of $C_{n!}^{\text{dist}}$:

$$\sum_{k=0}^{n!-1} C_{k+1}^{\text{dist}} = \sum_{k=0}^{n!-1} \left(\frac{1}{2}n^2 + \frac{7}{2}n + 4 \right) + \sum_{k=0}^{n!-1} C_k^{\text{dist}},$$

$$C_{n!}^{\text{dist}} = \left(\frac{1}{2}n^2 + \frac{7}{2}n + 4 \right) n! + C_0^{\text{dist}} = \frac{1}{2}(n^2 + 7n + 8)n! + 1.$$

Let us finally compute the cost of $\mathsf{perm}(s)$, noted C_k^{perm}, where k is the length of the stack s. From rules α to γ, we deduce the following equations, where $k > 0$:

$$C_0^{\text{perm}} \overset{\alpha}{=} 1; \qquad C_1^{\text{perm}} \overset{\beta}{=} 1;$$

$$C_{k+1}^{\text{perm}} \overset{\gamma}{=} 1 + C_k^{\text{perm}} + C_{k!}^{\text{dist}} = \frac{1}{2}(k^2 + 7k + 8)k! + 2 + C_k^{\text{perm}}.$$

Again, summing both sides, most of the terms cancel out:

$$\sum_{k=1}^{n-1} C_{k+1}^{\text{perm}} = \frac{1}{2}\sum_{k=1}^{n-1} (k^2 + 7k + 8)k! + \sum_{k=1}^{n-1} 2 + \sum_{k=1}^{n-1} C_k^{\text{perm}},$$

$$C_n^{\text{perm}} = \frac{1}{2}\sum_{k=1}^{n-1} (k^2 + 7k + 8)k! + 2(n - 1) + C_1^{\text{perm}}$$

$$= \frac{1}{2}\sum_{k=1}^{n-1} ((k + 2)(k + 1) + 6 + 4k)k! + 2n - 1$$

$$= \frac{1}{2}\sum_{k=1}^{n-1} (k + 2)(k + 1)k! + 3\sum_{k=1}^{n-1} k! + 2\sum_{k=1}^{n-1} kk! + 2n - 1$$

$$= \frac{1}{2}\sum_{k=1}^{n-1} (k + 2)! + 3\sum_{k=1}^{n-1} k! + 2\sum_{k=1}^{n-1} kk! + 2n - 1$$

$$= \frac{1}{2}\sum_{k=3}^{n+1} k! + 3\sum_{k=1}^{n-1} k! + 2\sum_{k=1}^{n-1} kk! + 2n - 1$$

$$= \frac{1}{2}(n + 2)n! + \frac{7}{2}\sum_{k=1}^{n-1} k! + 2\sum_{k=1}^{n-1} kk! + 2n - \frac{5}{2}.$$

This last equation is actually valid even if $n = 1$. One sum has a simple closed form:

$$\sum_{k=1}^{n-1} kk! = \sum_{k=1}^{n-1} ((k + 1)! - k!) = \sum_{k=2}^{n} k! - \sum_{k=1}^{n-1} k! = n! - 1.$$

Resuming our previous derivation,

$$C_n^{\text{perm}} = \frac{1}{2}nn! + n! + \frac{7}{2}\sum_{k=1}^{n-1} k! + 2(n! - 1) + 2n - \frac{5}{2}$$

$$= \frac{1}{2}nn! + 3n! + 2n - \frac{9}{2} + \frac{7}{2}\sum_{k=1}^{n-1} k!, \quad \text{with } n > 0.$$

The remaining sum is called the *left factorial* (Kurepa, 1971) and is usually defined as

$$!n := \sum_{k=1}^{n-1} k!, \quad \text{with } n > 0.$$

Unfortunately, no closed expression of the left factorial is known. This is actually a common situation when determining the cost of relatively complex functions. The best course of action is then to study the asymptotic approximation of the cost. Obviously, $n! \leqslant !(n+1)$. Also,

$$!(n+1)-n! \leqslant (n-2)\cdot(n-2)!+(n-1)! \leqslant (n-1)\cdot(n-2)!+(n-1)! = 2(n-1)!$$

Therefore,

$$1 \leqslant \frac{!(n+1)}{n!} \leqslant \frac{n! + 2(n-1)!}{n!} = 1 + \frac{2}{n} \Rightarrow !n \sim (n-1)!$$

Also, $(n+1)! = (n+1)n!$, so $(n+1)!/(nn!) = 1+1/n$, hence $nn! \sim (n+1)!$. Consequently,

$$C_n^{\text{perm}} \sim \frac{1}{2}(n+1)! + 3n! + \frac{7}{2}(n-1)! + 2n - \frac{9}{2} \sim \frac{1}{2}(n+1)!$$

This is an unbearably slow program, as expected. We should not hope to compute C_{11}^{perm} easily and there is no way to improve significantly the cost because the number of permutations it computes is inherently exponential, so it would even suffice to spend only one function call per permutation to obtain an exponential cost. In other words, the memory necessary to hold the result has a size which is exponential in the size of the input, therefore, the cost is at least exponential, because at least one function call is necessary to allocate some memory. For a deep study on the enumeration of all permutations, refer to the survey of Knuth (2011).

Permutations and sorting Permutations are worth studying in detail because of their intimate relationship with sorting. A permutation can be thought of as scrambling originally ordered keys and a sorting permutation puts them back to their place. A slightly different notation for permutations is helpful here, one which shows the indexes together with the keys. For example, instead of writing $\pi_1 = (2, 4, 1, 5, 3)$, we write

$$\pi_1 = \begin{pmatrix} 1 & 2 & 3 & 4 & 5 \\ 2 & 4 & 1 & 5 & 3 \end{pmatrix}.$$

The first line is made of the ordered indexes and the second line contains the keys. In general, a permutation $\pi = (a_1, a_2, \ldots, a_n)$ is equivalent to

$$\pi = \begin{pmatrix} 1 & 2 & \ldots & n \\ \pi(1) & \pi(2) & \ldots & \pi(n) \end{pmatrix},$$

where $a_i = \pi(i)$, for all i from 1 to n. The following permutation π_s sorts the keys of π_1:

$$\pi_s = \begin{pmatrix} 1 & 2 & 3 & 4 & 5 \\ 3 & 1 & 5 & 2 & 4 \end{pmatrix}.$$

To see why, we define the composition of two permutations π_a and π_b:

$$\pi_b \circ \pi_a := \begin{pmatrix} 1 & 2 & \ldots & n \\ \pi_b(\pi_a(1)) & \pi_b(\pi_a(2)) & \ldots & \pi_b(\pi_a(n)) \end{pmatrix}.$$

Then $\pi_s \circ \pi_1 = \mathcal{I}$, where the *identity permutation* $\mathcal{I}$ is such that $\mathcal{I}(k) = k$, for all indexes k. In other words, $\pi_s = \pi_1^{-1}$, that is, *sorting a permutation consists in building its inverse*:

$$\begin{pmatrix} 1 & 2 & 3 & 4 & 5 \\ 3 & 1 & 5 & 2 & 4 \end{pmatrix} \circ \begin{pmatrix} 1 & 2 & 3 & 4 & 5 \\ 2 & 4 & 1 & 5 & 3 \end{pmatrix} = \begin{pmatrix} 1 & 2 & 3 & 4 & 5 \\ 1 & 2 & 3 & 4 & 5 \end{pmatrix}.$$

An alternative representation of permutations and their composition is based on considering them as bijections from an interval onto itself, denoted by *bipartite graphs*, also called *bigraphs*. Such graphs are made of two disjoint, ordered sets of vertices of same cardinal, the indexes and the keys, and the edges always go from an index to a key, without sharing the vertices with other edges. For example, permutation π_1 is shown in FIGURE 2.38a on the facing page and its inverse π_1^{-1} is displayed in FIGURE 2.38b on the next page. The composition of π_1^{-1} and π_1 is then obtained by identifying the key vertices of π_1 with the index vertices of π_1^{-1}, as shown in FIGURE 2.39a on the facing page. The identity permutation is obtained by replacing two adjacent edges by their transitive closure and erasing the intermediate vertices, as shown in FIGURE 2.39b page 89. Note that a permutation may equal its inverse:

$$\pi_3 = \begin{pmatrix} 1 & 2 & 3 & 4 & 5 \\ 3 & 4 & 1 & 2 & 5 \end{pmatrix}.$$

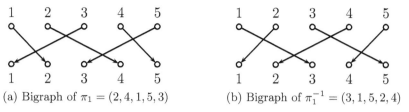

(a) Bigraph of $\pi_1 = (2, 4, 1, 5, 3)$ (b) Bigraph of $\pi_1^{-1} = (3, 1, 5, 2, 4)$

Figure 2.38: Permutation π_1 and its inverse π_1^{-1}

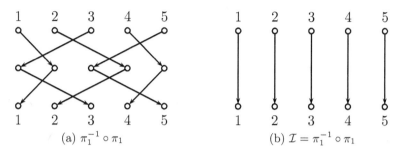

(a) $\pi_1^{-1} \circ \pi_1$ (b) $\mathcal{I} = \pi_1^{-1} \circ \pi_1$

Figure 2.39: Applying π_1 to π_1^{-1}.

In FIGURE 2.40 is shown that $\pi_3 \circ \pi_3 = \pi_3$, so π_3 is an *involution*.

Studying permutations and their basic properties helps understanding sorting algorithms, particularly their average cost. They also provide a way to quantify disorder. Given $(1, 3, 5, 2, 4)$, we can see that only the pairs of keys $(3, 2)$, $(5, 2)$ and $(5, 4)$ are out of order. In general, given $(a_1, a_2, \ldots, a_n)$, the pairs (a_i, a_j) such that $i < j$ and $a_i > a_j$ are called *inversions*. The more inversions, the greater the disorder. As expected, the identity permutation has no inversions and the previously studied permutation $\pi_1 = (2, 4, 1, 5, 3)$ has 4. When considering permutations as represented by bigraphs, an inversion corresponds to an intersection of two edges, more precisely, it is the pair made of the keys pointed at by two arrows. Therefore, the number of inversions is the number of edge

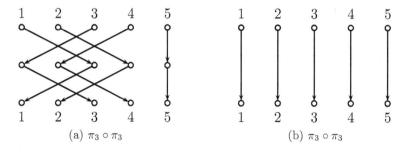

(a) $\pi_3 \circ \pi_3$ (b) $\pi_3 \circ \pi_3$

Figure 2.40: Involution π_3 sorts itself

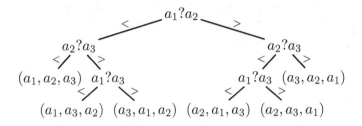

Figure 2.41: A comparison tree for sorting three keys

crossings, so, for instance, π_1^{-1} has 4 inversions. In fact, *the inverse of a permutation has the same number of inversions as the permutation itself.* This can be clearly seen when comparing the bigraphs of π_1 and π_1^{-1} in FIGURE 2.38 on the previous page: in order to deduce the bigraph of π_1^{-1} from the one corresponding to π_1, let us reverse each edge, that is, the direction in which the arrows are pointing, then swap the indexes and the keys, that is, exchange the two lines of vertices. Alternatively, we can imagine that we fold down the paper along the key line, then look through and reverse the arrows. Anyhow, the crossings are invariant. The horizontal symmetry is obvious in FIGURES 2.39a and 2.40a.

Minimax   After analysing the cost of a sorting algorithm based on comparisons, we will need to know how close it is to an optimal sorting algorithm. The first theoretical problem we examine is that of the best worst case, so called the *minimax*. FIGURE 2.41 features the tree of all possible comparisons for sorting three numbers. The *external nodes* are all the permutations of (a_1, a_2, a_3). The *internal nodes* are comparisons between two keys a_i and a_j, noted $a_i?a_j$. Note that leaves, in this setting, are internal nodes with two external nodes as children.

If $a_i < a_j$, then this property holds everywhere in the left subtree, otherwise $a_i > a_j$ holds in the right subtree. This tree is one possible amongst many: it corresponds to an algorithm which starts by comparing a_1 and a_2 and there are, of course, many other strategies. But it does not contain redundant comparisons: if a path from the root to a leaf includes $a_i < a_j$ and $a_j < a_k$, we do not expect the useless $a_i < a_k$. FIGURE 2.42 on the next page shows an excerpt of a comparison tree with such a useless comparison. The special external node $\bot$ corresponds to no permutation because the comparison $a_1 < a_3$ cannot fail as it is implied by transitivity of the previous comparisons on the path from the root. Therefore, *a comparison tree for n keys without redundancy has $n!$ external nodes.*

Because we are investigating minimum-comparison sorting, we shall

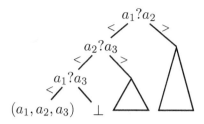

Figure 2.42: Useless $a_1 > a_3$

consider henceforth optimal comparison trees with $n!$ external nodes. Furthermore, amongst them, we want to determine the trees such that the maximum number of comparisons is minimal.

An *external path* is a path from the root to an external node. Let the *height* of a tree be the length (that is, the number of edges) of its longest external path. In FIGURE 2.41, the height is 3 and there are 4 external paths of length 3, like $(a_1 < a_2) \rightarrow (a_2 > a_3) \rightarrow (a_1 > a_3) \rightarrow (a_3, a_1, a_2)$.

The maximality constraint means that we must consider the height of the comparison tree because the number of internal nodes (comparisons) along the maximum external paths is an upper bound for the number of comparisons needed for sorting *all* the permutations.

The minimality constraint in the problem statement above then signifies that *we want a lower bound on the height of a comparison tree with $n!$ external nodes.*

A *perfect binary tree* is a binary tree whose internal nodes have children which are either two internal nodes or two external nodes. If such a tree has height h, then it has 2^h external nodes. For instance, FIGURE 2.43 shows the case where the height h is 3 and there are indeed $2^h = 8$ external nodes, figured as squares. Since, by definition, minimum-comparison trees have $n!$ external nodes and height $S(n)$, they must contain fewer external nodes than a perfect binary tree of identical height, that is, $n! \leqslant 2^{S(n)}$, therefore

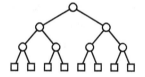

Figure 2.43: Perfect binary tree of height 3

$$\lceil \lg n! \rceil \leqslant S(n),$$

where $\lceil x \rceil$ *(ceiling of x)* is the least integer greater than or equal to x. To deduce a good lower bound on $S(n)$, we need the following theorem.

Theorem 1 (Sum and integral). *Let $f \colon [a, b] \rightarrow \mathbb{R}$ be an integrable, monotonically increasing function. Then*

$$\sum_{k=a}^{b-1} f(k) \leqslant \int_a^b f(x)\, dx \leqslant \sum_{k=a+1}^{b} f(k). \qquad \Box$$

Let us take $a := 1$, $b := n$ and $f(x) := \lg x$. The theorem implies

$$n \lg n - \frac{n}{\ln 2} + \frac{1}{\ln 2} = \int_1^n \lg x \, dx \leqslant \sum_{k=2}^n \lg k = \lg n! \leqslant S(n).$$

A more powerful but more complex approach in real analysis, known as Euler-Maclaurin summation, yields Stirling's formula (Sedgewick and Flajolet, 1996, chap. 4), which is a very precise lower bound for $\lg n!$:

$$\left(n + \frac{1}{2}\right) \lg n - \frac{n}{\ln 2} + \lg \sqrt{2\pi} < \lg n! \leqslant S(n). \qquad (2.18)$$

Minimean We investigate here the best mean case, or *minimean*. Let us call the sum of the lengths of all the external paths the *external path length of the tree*. Then, the average number of comparisons is the mean external path length. In FIGURE 2.41 on page 90, this is $(2 + 3 + 3 + 3 + 3 + 2)/3! = 8/3$. Our problem here therefore consists in determining the shape of the optimal comparison trees of minimum external path length.

These trees have their external nodes on one or two successive levels and are thus *almost perfect*. Let us consider a binary tree where this is not the case, so the topmost external nodes are located at level l and the bottommost at level L, with $L \geqslant l+2$. If we exchange a leaf at level $L-1$ with an external node at level l, the external path length is decreased by $(l + 2L) - (2(l+1) + (L-1)) = L - l - 1 \geqslant 1$. Repeating these exchanges yields the expected shape.

The external paths are made up of p paths ending at the penultimate level $h - 1$ and q paths ending at the bottommost level h. (The root has level 0.) Let us find two equations whose solutions are p and q.

- From the minimax problem, we know that an optimal comparison tree for n keys has $n!$ external nodes: $p + q = n!$.

- If we replace the external nodes at level $h - 1$ by leaves, the level h becomes full with 2^h external nodes: $2p + q = 2^h$.

We now have two linear equations satisfied by p and q, whose solutions are $p = 2^h - n!$ and $q = 2n! - 2^h$. Furthermore, we can now express the minimal external path length as follows: $(h - 1)p + hq = (h + 1)n! - 2^h$. Finally, we need to determine the height h of the tree in terms of $n!$. This can be done by remarking that, by contruction, the last level may be incomplete, so $0 < q \leqslant 2^h$, or, equivalently, $h = \lceil \lg n! \rceil$. We conclude that the minimum external path length is

$$(\lceil \lg n! \rceil + 1)n! - 2^{\lceil \lg n! \rceil}.$$

Let $M(n)$ be the minimum average number of comparisons of an optimal sorting algorithm. We have

$$M(n) = \lceil \lg n! \rceil + 1 - \frac{1}{n!} 2^{\lceil \lg n! \rceil}.$$

We have $\lceil \lg n! \rceil = \lg n! + x$, with $0 \leqslant x < 1$, therefore, if we set the function $\theta(x) := 1 + x - 2^x$, we draw

$$M(n) = \lg n! + \theta(x).$$

We have $\max_{0 \leqslant x < 1} \theta(x) = 1 - (1 + \ln \ln 2)/\ln 2 \simeq 0.08607$, therefore,

$$\lg n! \leqslant M(n) < \lg n! + 0.09. \tag{2.19}$$

Chapter 3

Insertion Sort

If we have a stack of totally ordered, distinct keys, it is easy to insert one more key so the stack remains ordered by comparing it with the first on top, then, if necessary, with the second, the third etc. For example, inserting 1 into $[3, 5]$ requires comparing 1 with 3 and results in $[1, 3, 5]$, without relating 1 to 5. The algorithm called *insertion sort* (Knuth, 1998a) consists in inserting thusly keys one by one in a stack originally empty. The playful analogy is that of sorting a hand in a card game: each card, from left to right, is moved leftwards until it reaches its place.

3.1 Straight insertion

Let $\mathsf{ins}(s, x)$ (not to be confused with the function of same name and arity in section 2.8) be the increasingly ordered stack resulting from the straight insertion of x into the stack s. Function $\mathsf{ins}/2$ can be defined assuming a minimum and a maximum function, $\mathsf{min}/2$ and $\mathsf{max}/2$:

$$\mathsf{ins}(x, [\,]) \to [x];$$
$$\mathsf{ins}(x, [y\,|\,s]) \to [\mathsf{min}(x, y)\,|\,\mathsf{ins}(\mathsf{max}(x, y), s)].$$

Temporarily, let us restrict ourselves to sorting natural numbers in increasing order. We need to provide definitions to calculate the minimum and maximum:

$$\mathsf{max}(0, y) \to y; \qquad\qquad \mathsf{min}(0, y) \to 0;$$
$$\mathsf{max}(x, 0) \to x; \qquad\qquad \mathsf{min}(x, 0) \to 0;$$
$$\mathsf{max}(x, y) \to 1 + \mathsf{max}(x - 1, y - 1). \quad \mathsf{min}(x, y) \to 1 + \mathsf{min}(x - 1, y - 1).$$

While this approach fits in our functional language, it is both inefficient and bulky, hence it is worth extending our language so rewrite rules are

$$\begin{aligned}
\mathsf{isrt}([3,1,2]) &\overset{\nu}{\rightarrow} \mathsf{ins}(\mathsf{isrt}([1,2]),3) \\
&\overset{\nu}{\rightarrow} \mathsf{ins}(\mathsf{ins}(\mathsf{isrt}([2]),1),3) \\
&\overset{\nu}{\rightarrow} \mathsf{ins}(\mathsf{ins}(\mathsf{ins}(\mathsf{isrt}([\,]),2),1),3) \\
&\overset{\mu}{\rightarrow} \mathsf{ins}(\mathsf{ins}(\mathsf{ins}([\,],2),1),3) \\
&\overset{\lambda}{\rightarrow} \mathsf{ins}(\mathsf{ins}([2],1),3) \\
&\overset{\lambda}{\rightarrow} \mathsf{ins}([1,2],3) \\
&\overset{\kappa}{\rightarrow} [1\,|\,\mathsf{ins}([2],3)] \\
&\overset{\kappa}{\rightarrow} [1,2\,|\,\mathsf{ins}([\,],3)] \\
&\overset{\lambda}{\rightarrow} [1,2,3].
\end{aligned}$$

Figure 3.1: $\mathsf{isrt}([3,1,2]) \twoheadrightarrow [1,2,3]$

selected by pattern matching only if some optional associated comparison holds. We can then define $\mathsf{isrt}/1$ (*insertion sort*) and redefine $\mathsf{ins}/2$ as

$$\mathsf{ins}([y\,|\,s],x) \overset{\kappa}{\rightarrow} [y\,|\,\mathsf{ins}(s,x)], \text{ if } x \succ y; \qquad \mathsf{isrt}([\,]) \overset{\mu}{\rightarrow} [\,];$$
$$\mathsf{ins}(s,x) \overset{\lambda}{\rightarrow} [x\,|\,s]. \qquad\qquad \mathsf{isrt}([x\,|\,s]) \overset{\nu}{\rightarrow} \mathsf{ins}(\mathsf{isrt}(s),x).$$

Let us consider a short example in FIGURE 3.1.

Let C_n^{isrt} be the cost of sorting by straight insertion n keys, and C_i^{ins} the cost of inserting one key in a stack of length i. We directly derive from the functional program the following recurrences:

$$C_0^{\mathsf{isrt}} \overset{\mu}{=} 1; \qquad C_{i+1}^{\mathsf{isrt}} \overset{\nu}{=} 1 + C_i^{\mathsf{ins}} + C_i^{\mathsf{isrt}}.$$

The latter equation assumes that the length of $\mathsf{isrt}(s)$ is the same as s and the length of $\mathsf{ins}(s,x)$ is the same as $[x\,|\,s]$. We deduce

$$C_n^{\mathsf{isrt}} = 1 + n + \sum_{i=0}^{n-1} C_i^{\mathsf{ins}}. \qquad (3.1)$$

A look up at the definition of $\mathsf{ins}/2$ reveals that C_i^{ins} cannot be expressed only in terms of i because it depends on the relative order of all the keys. Instead, we resort to the minimum, maximum and average costs.

Minimum cost   The best case does not exert rule κ, which is recursive, whilst λ rewrites to a value. In other words, in rule ν, each key x to be inserted in a non-empty, sorted stack $\mathsf{isrt}(s)$ would be lower than or equal to the top of the stack. This rule also inserts the keys in reverse order:

$$\mathsf{isrt}([x_1,\ldots,x_n]) \twoheadrightarrow \mathsf{ins}(\mathsf{ins}(\ldots(\mathsf{ins}([\,],x_n)\ldots),x_2),x_1). \qquad (3.2)$$

As a consequence, *the minimum cost results from the input stack being already increasingly sorted,* that is, the keys in the result are increasing, but may be repeated. Then $\mathcal{B}_n^{\text{ins}} = |\lambda| = 1$ and equation (3.1) implies that straight insertion sort has a linear cost in the best case:

$$\mathcal{B}_n^{\text{isrt}} = 2n + 1 \sim 2n.$$

Maximum cost   The worst case must exert rule κ as much as possible, which implies that *the worst case happens when the input is a stack decreasingly sorted.* We have

$$\mathcal{W}_n^{\text{ins}} = |\kappa^n \lambda| = n + 1.$$

Substituting maximum costs in equation (3.1) then implies that straight insertion sort has a quadratic cost in the worst case:

$$\mathcal{W}_n^{\text{isrt}} = \frac{1}{2}n^2 + \frac{3}{2}n + 1 \sim \frac{1}{2}n^2.$$

Another way is to take the length of the longest trace:

$$\mathcal{W}_n^{\text{isrt}} = \left| \nu^n \mu \prod_{i=0}^{n-1} \kappa^i \lambda \right| = |\nu^n \mu| + \sum_{i=0}^{n-1} |\kappa^i \lambda| = \frac{1}{2}n^2 + \frac{3}{2}n + 1.$$

This cost should not be surprising because isrt/1 and rev_0/1, in section 2.2, yield the same kind of partial rewrite, as seen by comparing (3.2), on the preceding page, and (2.4) on page 42, and also $\mathcal{C}_n^{\text{cat}} = \mathcal{W}_n^{\text{ins}}$, where n is the size of their first argument. Hence $\mathcal{W}_n^{\text{isrt}} = \mathcal{W}_n^{\text{rev}_0}$.

Average cost   The average cost obeys equation (3.1) because all permutations $(x_1, \ldots, x_n)$ are equally likely, hence

$$\mathcal{A}_n^{\text{isrt}} = 1 + n + \sum_{i=0}^{n-1} \mathcal{A}_i^{\text{ins}}. \qquad (3.3)$$

Without loss of generality, $\mathcal{A}_i^{\text{ins}}$ is the cost of inserting the key $i + 1$ into all permutations of $(1, \ldots, i)$, divided by $i + 1$. (This is how the set of permutations of a given length is inductively built on page 83.) The partial evaluation (3.2) on page 96 has length $|\nu^n \mu| = n + 1$. The trace for inserting in an empty stack is μ. If the stack has length i, inserting on top has trace λ; just after the first key, $\kappa\lambda$ etc. until after the last key, $\kappa^i \lambda$. Therefore, the average cost for inserting one key is, for $i \geqslant 0$,

$$\mathcal{A}_i^{\text{ins}} = \frac{1}{i+1} \sum_{j=0}^{i} |\kappa^j \lambda| = \frac{i}{2} + 1. \qquad (3.4)$$

The average cost for inserting n keys in an empty stack is therefore $\sum_{i=0}^{n-1} \mathcal{A}_i^{\mathsf{ins}} = \frac{1}{4}n^2 + \frac{3}{4}n$. Finally, from equation (3.3), the average cost of sorting n keys by straight insertion is

$$\mathcal{A}_n^{\mathsf{isrt}} = \frac{1}{4}n^2 + \frac{7}{4}n + 1.$$

Assessment Despite the average cost being asymptotically equivalent to 50% of the maximum cost, it is nevertheless quadratic. On a positive note, straight insertion is quite efficient when the data is short or nearly sorted (Cook and Kim, 1980). It is a typical example of an *adaptive sorting algorithm* (Estivill-Castro and Wood, 1992, Moffat and Petersson, 1992). The natural measure of sortedness for insertion sort is the number of inversions. Indeed, the partial evaluation (3.2), on page 96 shows that the keys are inserted in reverse order. Thus, in rule κ, we know that the key x was originally before y, but $x \succ y$. Therefore, one application of *rule κ removes one inversion from the input*. As a corollary, the average number of inversions in a random permutation of n objects is

$$\sum_{j=0}^{n-1} \frac{1}{j+1} \sum_{i=0}^{j} |\kappa^i| = \sum_{j=0}^{n-1} \frac{1}{j+1} \cdot \frac{j(j+1)}{2} = \frac{1}{2} \sum_{j=0}^{n-1} j = \frac{n(n-1)}{4}.$$

Exercises

1. A sorting algorithm that preserves the relative order of equal keys is said *stable*. Is isrt/1 stable?

2. Prove $\mathsf{len}([x \,|\, s]) \equiv \mathsf{len}(\mathsf{ins}(x, s))$.

3. Prove $\mathsf{len}(s) \equiv \mathsf{len}(\mathsf{isrt}(s))$.

4. Traditionally, textbooks about the analysis of algorithms assess the cost of sorting procedures by counting the comparisons, not the function calls. Doing so allows one to compare with the same measure different sorting algorithms as long as they perform comparisons, even if they are implemented in different programming languages. (There are sorting techniques that do not rely on comparisons.) Let $\overline{\mathcal{B}}_n^{\mathsf{isrt}}$, $\overline{\mathcal{W}}_n^{\mathsf{isrt}}$ and $\overline{\mathcal{A}}_n^{\mathsf{isrt}}$ be the minimum, maximum and average numbers of comparisons needed to sort by straight insertion a stack of length n. Establish that

$$\overline{\mathcal{B}}_n^{\mathsf{isrt}} = n - 1; \quad \overline{\mathcal{W}}_n^{\mathsf{isrt}} = \frac{1}{2}n(n-1); \quad \overline{\mathcal{A}}_n^{\mathsf{isrt}} = \frac{1}{4}n^2 + \frac{3}{4}n - H_n,$$

where $H_n := \sum_{k=1}^{n} 1/k$ is the nth *harmonic number* and, by convention, $H_0 := 0$. *Hint:* The use of rule λ implies a comparison if, and only if, s is not empty.

Ordered stacks As we did for the proof of the soundness of cut/2 on page 71, we need to express the characteristic properties we expect on the output of isrt/1, and relate them to some assumptions on the input, first informally, then formally. We would say that 'The stack isrt(s) is totally, increasingly ordered and contains all the keys in s, but no more'. This captures all what is expected from any sorting program.

Let us name Ord(s) the proposition 'The stack s is sorted increasingly'. To define formally this concept, let us use *inductive logic definitions*. We employed this technique to formally define stacks, on page 6, in a way that generates a simple well-founded order used by structural induction, to wit, $[x \,|\, s] \succ x$ and $[x \,|\, s] \succ s$. Here, we similarly propose that, for Ord(s) to hold, Ord(t) must hold with $s \succ t$. We defined cut/2 in section 2.6, on page 69, using the same technique and relying on inference rules. All three cases, namely, data structure, proposition and function, are instances of inductive definitions. Let us constructively define Ord by the axioms ORD_0 and ORD_1, and the inference rule ORD_2:

$$\text{Ord}([]) \ \text{ORD}_0 \qquad \text{Ord}([x]) \ \text{ORD}_1 \qquad \frac{x \prec y \qquad \text{Ord}([y\,|\,s])}{\text{Ord}([x,y\,|\,s])} \ \text{ORD}_2$$

Note that this system is parameterised by the well-founded order ($\prec$) on the keys such that $x \prec y :\Leftrightarrow y \succ x$. Rule ORD_2 could equivalently be $(x \prec y \wedge \text{Ord}([y\,|\,s])) \Rightarrow \text{Ord}([x,y\,|\,s])$ or $x \prec y \Rightarrow (\text{Ord}([y\,|\,s]) \Rightarrow \text{Ord}([x,y\,|\,s]))$ or $x \prec y \Rightarrow \text{Ord}([y\,|\,s]) \Rightarrow \text{Ord}([x,y\,|\,s])$. Because the set of ordered stacks is exactly generated by this system, if the statement $\text{Ord}([x,y\,|\,s])$ holds, then, necessarily, ORD_2 has been used to produce it, hence $x \prec y$ and $\text{Ord}([y\,|\,s])$ are true as well. This usage of an inductive definition is called an *inversion lemma* and can be understood as inferring necessary conditions for a putative formula, or as *case analysis on inductive definitions*.

Equivalent stacks The second part of our informal definition above was: 'The stack isrt(s) contains all the keys in s, but no more'. In order to provide a general criterion matching this concept, we should abstract it as: 'The stack s contains all the keys in the stack t, but no more'. Permutations allow us to clarify the meaning with a mathematical phrasing: 'Stacks s and t are permutations of each other,' which we note $s \approx t$ and

$$\frac{\dfrac{[1,2] \approx [2,1] \; \text{Swap}}{[3,1,2] \approx [3,2,1]} \; \text{Push} \qquad \dfrac{[3,2,1] \approx [2,3,1] \; \text{Swap}}{}}{[3,1,2] \approx [2,3,1]} \; \text{Trans}$$

(a) Extended tree

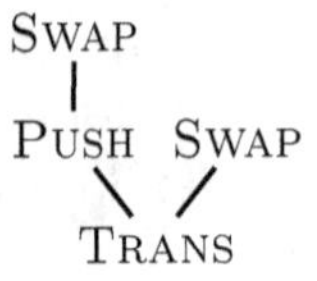

$$\begin{array}{c} \text{Swap} \\ | \\ \text{Push} \quad \text{Swap} \\ \diagdown \quad \diagup \\ \text{Trans} \end{array}$$

(b) Pruned tree

Figure 3.2: Proof tree of $[3,1,2] \approx [2,3,1]$

$t \approx s$. Since the role of s do not differ in any way from that of t, we expect the relation $(\approx)$ to be symmetric: $s \approx t \Rightarrow t \approx s$. Moreover, we expect it to be *transitive* as well: $s \approx u$ and $u \approx t$ imply $s \approx t$. Also, we want $(\approx)$ to be *reflexive*, that is, $s \approx s$. By definition, a binary relation which is reflexive, symmetric and transitive is an *equivalence relation*.

The relation $(\approx)$ can be defined in different ways. The idea here consists in defining a permutation as a series of *transpositions*, namely, exchanges of adjacent keys. This approach is likely to work here because insertion can be thought of as adding a key on top of a stack and then performing a series of transpositions until the total order is restored.

$$[] \approx [] \; \text{Pnil} \qquad [x,y\,|\,s] \approx [y,x\,|\,s] \; \text{Swap}$$

$$\frac{s \approx t}{[x\,|\,s] \approx [x\,|\,t]} \; \text{Push} \qquad \frac{s \approx u \qquad u \approx t}{s \approx t} \; \text{Trans}$$

We recognise Pnil and Swap as axioms, the latter being synonymous with transposition. Rule Trans is transitivity and offers an example with two premises, so a derivation using it becomes a *binary tree*, as shown in Figure 3.2. As an exception to the convention about tree layouts, proof trees have their root at the bottom of the figure.

We must now prove the *reflexivity* of $(\approx)$, namely Refl(s): $s \approx s$, by induction on the structure of the proof. The difference with the proof of the soundness of cut/2, on page 71, is that, due to Trans having two premises, the induction hypothesis applies to both of them. Also, the theorem is not explicitly an implication. First, we start by proving Refl on the axioms (the leaves of the proof trees) and proceed with the induction on the proper inference rules, to wit, reflexivity is conserved while moving towards the root of the proof tree.

- Axiom Pnil proves Refl($[]$). Axiom Swap proves Refl($[x,x\,|\,s]$).

- Let us assume now that Refl holds for the premise in Push, namely, $s = t$. Clearly, the conclusion implies Refl($[x\,|\,s]$).

- Let us assume that Refl holds for the *two* antecedents in PUSH, that is, $s = u = t$. The conclusion leads to $\mathsf{Refl}(s)$. □

Let us prove the *symmetry* of $(\approx)$ using the same technique. Let $\mathsf{Sym}(s,t)\colon s \approx t \Rightarrow t \approx s$. We deal with an implication here, so let us suppose that $s \approx t$, that is, we have a proof tree Δ whose root is $s \approx t$, and let us establish $t \approx s$. In the following, we overline variables from the inference system.

- If Δ ends with PNIL, then $[] = s = t$, which trivially implies $t \approx s$.

- If Δ ends with SWAP, then $[\overline{x}, \overline{y} \,|\, \overline{s}] = s$ and $[\overline{y}, \overline{x} \,|\, \overline{s}] = t$, so $t \approx s$.

- If Δ ends with PUSH, then $[\overline{x} \,|\, \overline{s}] = s$ and $[\overline{x} \,|\, \overline{t}] = t$. The induction hypothesis applies to the premise, $\overline{s} \approx \overline{t}$, hence $\overline{t} \approx \overline{s}$ holds. An application of PUSH with the latter premise implies $[\overline{x} \,|\, \overline{t}] \approx [\overline{x} \,|\, \overline{s}]$, that is, $t \approx s$.

- If Δ ends with TRANS, then the induction hypothesis applies to its premises and we deduce $u \approx s$ and $t \approx u$, which can be premises for TRANS itself and lead to $t \approx s$. □

Soundness   Let us now turn our attention to our main objective, which we may call $\mathsf{lsrt}(s)\colon \mathsf{Ord}(\mathsf{isrt}(s)) \wedge \mathsf{isrt}(s) \approx s$. Let us tackle its proof by structural induction on s.

- The basis is $\mathsf{lsrt}([])$ and it is showed to hold twofold. First, we have $\mathsf{isrt}([]) \overset{\mu}{\hookrightarrow} []$ and $\mathsf{Ord}([])$ is axiom $\mathrm{ORD_0}$. The other conjunct holds as well since $\mathsf{isrt}([]) \approx [] \Leftrightarrow [] \approx []$, which is axiom PNIL.

- Let us assume $\mathsf{lsrt}(s)$ and establish $\mathsf{lsrt}([x \,|\, s])$. In other words, let us assume $\mathsf{Ord}(\mathsf{isrt}(s))$ and $\mathsf{isrt}(s) \approx s$. We have

$$\mathsf{isrt}([x \,|\, s]) \overset{\nu}{\hookrightarrow} \mathsf{ins}(\mathsf{isrt}(s), x). \tag{3.5}$$

Since we want $\mathsf{Ord}(\mathsf{isrt}([x \,|\, s]))$, assuming $\mathsf{Ord}(\mathsf{isrt}(s))$, we realise that we need the lemma $\mathsf{Ord}(s) \Rightarrow \mathsf{Ord}(\mathsf{ins}(s, x))$, which we may name $\mathsf{InsOrd}(s)$. To prove the conjunct $\mathsf{isrt}([x \,|\, s]) \approx [x \,|\, s]$, assuming $\mathsf{isrt}(s) \approx s$, we need the lemma $\mathsf{InsCmp}(s)\colon \mathsf{ins}(s, x) \approx [x \,|\, s]$. In particular, $\mathsf{InsCmp}(\mathsf{isrt}(s))$ is $\mathsf{ins}(\mathsf{isrt}(s), x) \approx [x \,|\, \mathsf{isrt}(s)]$. We have

  - Rule PUSH and the induction hypothesis $\mathsf{isrt}(s) \approx s$ imply $[x \,|\, \mathsf{isrt}(s)] \approx [x \,|\, s]$.
  - By the transitivity of $(\approx)$, we draw $\mathsf{ins}(\mathsf{isrt}(s), x) \approx [x \,|\, s]$,
  - by rewrite (3.5), $\mathsf{isrt}([x \,|\, s]) \approx [x \,|\, s]$ and $\mathsf{lsrt}([x \,|\, s])$ follow.

By the induction principle, we conclude $\forall s \in S.\mathsf{lsrt}(s)$. □

Insertion adds a key   To complete the previous proof, we prove the lemma $\mathsf{InsCmp}(s)$: $\mathsf{ins}(s, x) \approx [x\,|\,s]$ by structural induction on s.

- The basis $\mathsf{InsCmp}([\,])$ stands because $\mathsf{ins}([\,], x) \overset{\lambda}{\to} [x] \approx [x]$, by composing rules PNIL and PUSH.
- Let us assume $\mathsf{InsCmp}(s)$ and deduce $\mathsf{InsCmp}([y\,|\,s])$, that is,

$$\mathsf{ins}(s, x) \approx [x\,|\,s] \Rightarrow \mathsf{ins}([y\,|\,s], x) \approx [x, y\,|\,s].$$

There are two cases to analyse.

- – If $y \succ x$, then $\mathsf{ins}([y\,|\,s], x) \overset{\lambda}{\to} [x, y\,|\,s] \approx [x, y\,|\,s]$, by rule SWAP.
- – Otherwise, $x \succ y$ and $\mathsf{ins}([y\,|\,s], x) \overset{\kappa}{\to} [y\,|\,\mathsf{ins}(s, x)]$.
    - * We deduce $[y\,|\,\mathsf{ins}(s, x)] \approx [y, x\,|\,s]$ by using the induction hypothesis as the premise of rule PUSH.
    - * Furthermore, SWAP yields $[y, x\,|\,s] \approx [x, y\,|\,s]$.
    - * Transitivity of ($\approx$) applied to the two last statements leads to $\mathsf{ins}([y\,|\,s], x) \approx [x, y\,|\,s]$.

    Note that we do not need to assume that s is sorted: what matters here is that $\mathsf{ins}/2$ loses no key it inserts, but misplacement is irrelevant.   □

Insertion preserves order   To complete the soundness proof, we must prove the lemma $\mathsf{InsOrd}(s)$: $\mathsf{Ord}(s) \Rightarrow \mathsf{Ord}(\mathsf{ins}(s, x))$ by induction on the structure of s, meaning that insertion preserves order.

- The basis $\mathsf{InsOrd}([\,])$ is easy to check: ORD$_0$ states $\mathsf{Ord}([\,])$; we have the rewrite $\mathsf{ins}([\,], x) \overset{\lambda}{\to} [x]$ and ORD$_1$ is $\mathsf{Ord}([x])$.
- Let us prove $\mathsf{InsOrd}(s) \Rightarrow \mathsf{InsOrd}([x\,|\,s])$ by assuming

(H_0) $\mathsf{Ord}(s)$, (H_1) $\mathsf{Ord}(\mathsf{ins}(s, x))$, (H_2) $\mathsf{Ord}([y\,|\,s])$,

and deriving $\mathsf{Ord}(\mathsf{ins}([y\,|\,s], x))$.

Two cases arise from comparing x to y:

- – If $y \succ x$, then H_2 implies $\mathsf{Ord}([x, y\,|\,s])$, by rule ORD$_2$. Since $\mathsf{ins}([y\,|\,s], x) \overset{\lambda}{\to} [x, y\,|\,s]$, we have $\mathsf{Ord}(\mathsf{ins}([y\,|\,s], x))$.
- – Otherwise, $x \succ y$ and we derive

$$\mathsf{ins}([y\,|\,s], x) \overset{\kappa}{\to} [y\,|\,\mathsf{ins}(s, x)]. \tag{3.6}$$

Here, things get more complicated because we need to consider the structure of s.

- * If $s = [\,]$, then $[y\,|\,\mathsf{ins}(s, x)] \overset{\lambda}{\to} [y, x]$. Furthermore, $x \succ y$, ORD$_1$ and ORD$_2$ imply $\mathsf{Ord}([y, x])$, so $\mathsf{Ord}(\mathsf{ins}([y\,|\,s], x))$.

* Else, there exists a key z and a stack t such that $s = [z\,|\,t]$.
  · If $z \succ x$, then

$$[y\,|\,\mathsf{ins}(s, x)] = [y\,|\,\mathsf{ins}([z\,|\,t], x)] \overset{\lambda}{\to} [y, x, z\,|\,t] = [y, x\,|\,s].$$
(3.7)

H_0 is $\mathsf{Ord}([z\,|\,t])$, which, with $z \succ x$ and rule ORD_2, implies $\mathsf{Ord}([x, z\,|\,t])$. Since $x \succ y$, another application of ORD_2 yields $\mathsf{Ord}([y, x, z\,|\,t])$, that is, $\mathsf{Ord}([y, x\,|\,s])$. This and rewrite (3.7) entail that $\mathsf{Ord}([y\,|\,\mathsf{ins}(s, x)])$. Finally, due to rewrite (3.6), $\mathsf{Ord}(\mathsf{ins}([y\,|\,s], x))$ holds.
  · The last remaining case to examine is when $x \succ z$:

$$[y\,|\,\mathsf{ins}(s, x)] = [y\,|\,\mathsf{ins}([z\,|\,t], x)] \overset{\kappa}{\to} [y, z\,|\,\mathsf{ins}(t, x)].$$ (3.8)

Hypothesis H_2 is $\mathsf{Ord}([y, z\,|\,t])$, which, by means of the inversion lemma of rule ORD_2, leads to $y \succ z$. By the last rewrite, hypothesis H_1 is equivalent to $\mathsf{Ord}([z\,|\,\mathsf{ins}(t, x)])$, which, with $y \succ z$, enables the use of rule ORD_2 again, leading to $\mathsf{Ord}([y, z\,|\,\mathsf{ins}(t, x)])$. Rewrite (3.8) then yields $\mathsf{Ord}([y\,|\,\mathsf{ins}(s, x)])$, which, together with rewrite (3.6) yields $\mathsf{Ord}(\mathsf{ins}([y\,|\,s], x))$. □

Assessment Perhaps the most striking feature of the soundness proof is its length. More precisely, two aspects may give rise to questions. First, since the program is four lines long and the specification (the S_i and P_j) consists in a total of seven cases, it may be unclear how the proof raises our confidence in the program. Second, the proof itself is rather long, which leads us to wonder whether any error is hiding in it. The first concern can be addressed by noting that the two parts of the specification are disjoint and thus as easy to comprehend as the program. Moreover, specifications, being logical and not necessarily computable, are likely to be more abstract and composable than programs, so a larger proof may reuse them in different instances. For example, the predicate lsrt can easily be abstracted (higher-order) over the sorting function as $\mathsf{lsrt}(f, s) \colon \mathsf{Ord}(f(s)) \wedge f(s) \approx s$ and thus applies to many sorting algorithms, with the caveat that ($\approx$) is probably not always suitably defined by transpositions. The second concern can be completely taken care of by relying on a *proof assistant*, like Coq (Bertot and Castéran, 2004). For instance, the formal specification of ($\approx$) and the automatic proofs (by means of `eauto`) of its reflexivity and symmetry consists in the following script, where `x::s` stands for $[x\,|\,s]$, (`->`) is ($\Rightarrow$), `perm s t` is $s \approx t$ and `List` is synonymous with stack:

```
Set Implicit Arguments.
Require Import List.
Variable A: Type.

Inductive perm: list A -> list A -> Prop :=
  Pnil  : perm nil nil
| Push  : forall x s t, perm s t -> perm (x::s) (x::t)
| Swap  : forall x y s, perm (x::y::s) (y::x::s)
| Trans : forall s t u, perm s u -> perm u t -> perm s t.

Hint Constructors perm.

Lemma reflexivity: forall s, perm s s.
Proof. induction s; eauto. Qed.

Lemma symmetry: forall s t, perm s t -> perm t s.
Proof. induction 1; eauto. Qed.
```

Termination   Informally, what soundness means is that, if some program terminates, then the result is what was expected. This property is called *partial correctness* when it is relevant to distinguish it from *total correctness*, which is partial correctness and termination. Let us prove the termination of isrt/1 by the method of dependency pairs (section 2.4, page 61). The pairs to order are the following: $(\mathsf{ins}([y\,|\,s],x),\mathsf{ins}(s,x))_\kappa$, $(\mathsf{isrt}([x\,|\,s]),\mathsf{isrt}(s))_\nu$ and $(\mathsf{isrt}([x\,|\,s]),\mathsf{ins}(\mathsf{isrt}(s),x))_\nu$. By using the proper subterm relation on the first parameter of ins/2, we order the first pair:

$$\mathsf{ins}([y\,|\,s],x) \succ \mathsf{ins}(s,x) \Leftrightarrow [y\,|\,s] \succ s.$$

This is enough to prove that ins/2 terminates. The second pair is similarly oriented:

$$\mathsf{isrt}([x\,|\,s]) \succ \mathsf{isrt}(s) \Leftrightarrow [x\,|\,s] \succ s.$$

The third pair is not worth considering after all, because we already know that ins/2 terminates, so the second pair is enough to entail the termination of isrt/1. In other words, since ins/2 terminates, it can be considered, as far as termination analysis is concerned, as a data constructor, so the third pair becomes useless:

$$\mathsf{isrt}([x\,|\,s]) \succ \underline{\mathsf{ins}}(\mathsf{isrt}(s),x) \Leftrightarrow \mathsf{isrt}([x\,|\,s]) \succ \mathsf{isrt}(s) \Leftrightarrow [x\,|\,s] \succ s,$$

where $\underline{\mathsf{ins}}$/2 stands for ins/2 considered as a constructor. (We have used this notation in FIGURE 2.33 on page 79.)   □

3.2 2-way insertion

Let us recall the definition of sorting by straight insertion:

$$\mathsf{ins}([y\,|\,s], x) \xrightarrow{\kappa} [y\,|\,\mathsf{ins}(s, x)], \text{ if } y \succ x; \qquad \mathsf{isrt}([]) \xrightarrow{\mu} [];$$
$$\mathsf{ins}(s, x) \xrightarrow{\lambda} [x\,|\,s]. \qquad \mathsf{isrt}([x\,|\,s]) \xrightarrow{\nu} \mathsf{ins}(\mathsf{isrt}(s), x).$$

The reason why ins/2 is called straight insertion is because keys are compared in one direction only: from the top of the stack towards its bottom. We may wonder what would happen if we could move up or down, *starting from the previously inserted key.* Conceptually, this is like having a finger pointing at the last inserted key and the next insertion resuming from that point, up or down the stack. Let us call it *two-way insertion* and name i2w/1 the sorting function based upon it. The stack with finger can be simulated by having two stacks, t and u, such that $\mathsf{rcat}(t, u)$ stands for the currently sorted stack, corresponding to $\mathsf{isrt}(s)$ in rule ν. (In section 2.5, on page 63, we used two stacks to simulate a queue.) Let us call $\mathsf{rcat}(t, u)$ the *simulated stack*; stack t is a *reversed prefix* of the simulated stack and stack u is a *suffix*. For example, a finger pointing at 5 in the simulated stack $[0, 2, 4, 5, 7, 8, 9]$ would be represented by $[4, 2, 0]$ and $[5, 7, 8, 9]$. The reversing of the first stack is best visually understood by drawing it with the top facing the *right* side of the page:

$$t = \boxed{0 \mid 2 \mid 4 \mid } \qquad \overset{\downarrow}{\boxed{5 \mid 7 \mid 8 \mid 9}} = u$$

Given some key x, it is straightly inserted either in t (minding it is sorted in reverse order) or in u. If we want to insert 1, we should pop 4 and push it on the right stack, same for 2 and then push 1 on the right stack, as, by convention, the finger always points to the top of the right stack, where the last inserted key is:

$$\boxed{0 \mid } \qquad \overset{\downarrow}{\boxed{1 \mid 2 \mid 4 \mid 5 \mid 7 \mid 8 \mid 9}}$$

Let i2w(s) (*insertion going two ways*) be the sorted stack corresponding to stack s. Let i2w(s, t, u) be the sorted stack containing all the keys from s, t and u, where s is a suffix of the original (probably unsorted) stack and $\mathsf{rcat}(t, u)$ is the current simulated stack, that is, t is the left stack (reversed prefix) and u the right stack (suffix). The function i2w/1 is defined in FIGURE 3.3 on the following page. Rule ξ introduces the two stacks used for insertion. Rules π and ρ could be replaced by i2w([], t, u) $\rightarrow$ rcat(t, u), but we opted for a self-contained definition. Rule σ is used to move keys from the right stack to the left

$$
\begin{aligned}
\text{i2w}(s) &\xrightarrow{\xi} \text{i2w}(s,[],[]). \\
\text{i2w}([],[],u) &\xrightarrow{\pi} u; \\
\text{i2w}([],[y\,|\,t],u) &\xrightarrow{\rho} \text{i2w}([],t,[y\,|\,u]); \\
\text{i2w}([x\,|\,s],t,[z\,|\,u]) &\xrightarrow{\sigma} \text{i2w}([x\,|\,s],[z\,|\,t],u), \quad \text{if } x \succ z; \\
\text{i2w}([x\,|\,s],[y\,|\,t],u) &\xrightarrow{\tau} \text{i2w}([x\,|\,s],t,[y\,|\,u]), \quad \text{if } y \succ x; \\
\text{i2w}([x\,|\,s],t,u) &\xrightarrow{\upsilon} \text{i2w}(s,t,[x\,|\,u]).
\end{aligned}
$$

Figure 3.3: Sorting with 2-way insertion i2w/1

$$
\begin{aligned}
\text{i2w}([2,3,1,4]) &\xrightarrow{\xi} \text{i2w}([2,3,1,4],[],[]) \\
&\xrightarrow{\upsilon} \text{i2w}([3,1,4],[],[2]) \\
&\xrightarrow{\sigma} \text{i2w}([3,1,4],[2],[]) \\
&\xrightarrow{\upsilon} \text{i2w}([1,4],[2],[3]) \\
&\xrightarrow{\tau} \text{i2w}([1,4],[],[2,3]) \\
&\xrightarrow{\upsilon} \text{i2w}([4],[],[1,2,3]) \\
&\xrightarrow{\sigma} \text{i2w}([4],[1],[2,3]) \\
&\xrightarrow{\sigma} \text{i2w}([4],[2,1],[3]) \\
&\xrightarrow{\sigma} \text{i2w}([4],[3,2,1],[]) \\
&\xrightarrow{\upsilon} \text{i2w}([],[3,2,1],[4]) \\
&\xrightarrow{\rho} \text{i2w}([],[2,1],[3,4]) \\
&\xrightarrow{\rho} \text{i2w}([],[1],[2,3,4]) \\
&\xrightarrow{\rho} \text{i2w}([],[],[1,2,3,4]) \\
&\xrightarrow{\pi} [1,2,3,4].
\end{aligned}
$$

Figure 3.4: i2w($[2,3,1,4]$) $\twoheadrightarrow [1,2,3,4]$

stack. Rule τ moves them the other way. Rule υ performs the insertion itself, namely, on top of the right stack. FIGURE 3.4 shows the evaluation of i2w($[2,3,1,4]$), whose trace is then $(\xi)(\upsilon)(\sigma\upsilon)(\tau\upsilon)(\sigma^3\upsilon)(\rho^3\pi)$. The number of times rule ρ is used is the number of keys on the left stack after there are no more keys to sort. Rule π is used once.

Extremal costs Let us find the minimum and maximum costs for an input stack of n keys. The best case will exert minimally rules σ and τ, and this minimum number of calls turns out to be zero when the two comparisons are false. The first key inserted does not use rules σ and τ, but only rule υ, so, right after, the reversed prefix is empty and the suffix contains this key. If we want to insert the second key without moving the first key, and go straight to use rule υ, the second key must be smaller than the first. Based on the same argument, the third key must be smaller than the second etc. In the end, this means that *the input, in the best case, is a stack sorted non-increasingly*. The last steps consisting in the reversal of the prefix, such prefix being empty, we do not even use rule ρ at all – only rule π once. In other words, the evaluation trace is $\zeta\epsilon^n\alpha$ and, if we note $\mathcal{B}_n^{\text{i2w}}$ the cost when the stack contains n keys in non-increasing order, then we have

$$\mathcal{B}_n^{\text{i2w}} = |\zeta\epsilon^n\alpha| = n + 2.$$

Let us assume that the input stack is noted $[x_0, x_1, \ldots, x_{n-1}]$ and $x \prec y$ means $y \succ x$. The worst case must exert maximally rules σ and τ, on the one hand, and rules π and ρ, on the other hand. Let us focus first on maximising the use of σ and τ. Since x_0 is the first key, it is always pushed on the suffix stack by rule v. The second key, x_1, in order to travel the furthest, has to be inserted below x_0. By doing so, rule σ is used once and then v, therefore, as a result, x_0 is on the left (the reversed prefix) and x_1 on the right (the suffix). In other words: we have $[x_0]$ and $[x_1]$. Because of this symmetry, in pursuit of the worst case, we can now move either x_0 or x_1 to the facing stack, that is, choose either to set $x_2 \prec x_0$ or $x_1 \prec x_2$.

- If $x_2 \prec x_0$, rule τ is used once, then rule v. As a result, we have the configuration $[]$ and $[x_2, x_0, x_1]$. This translates as $x_2 \prec x_0 \prec x_1$. The fourth key, x_3, must be inserted at the bottom of the right stack, which must be first reversed on top of the left stack by rule σ: we then obtain $[x_1, x_0, x_2]$ and $[x_3]$, that is, $x_2 \prec x_0 \prec x_1 \prec x_3$. Finally, the left stack is reversed on top of the second by rule ρ and rule π is last. The evaluation trace is $(\xi)(v)(\sigma v)(\tau v)(\sigma^3 v)(\rho^3 \pi)$, whose length is 14.

- If $x_1 \prec x_2$, we would have $[x_1, x_0]$ and $[x_2]$, then the stacks $[]$ and $[x_3, x_0, x_1, x_2]$, that is, $x_3 \prec x_0 \prec x_1 \prec x_2$. The complete evaluation trace is $(\xi)(v)(\sigma v)(\sigma v)(\tau^2 v)(\pi)$. The length of this trace is 10, which is shorter than the previous trace.

As a conclusion, the choice $x_2 \prec x_0$ leads to a worse case. But what if the input stack contains an odd number n of keys? To guess what happens, let us insert x_4 assuming either $x_1 \prec x_2$ or $x_2 \prec x_0$.

- If $x_2 \prec x_0$, we move all the keys out of the left stack, yielding the configuration $[x_4]$ and $[x_2, x_0, x_1, x_3]$, so $x_4 \prec x_2 \prec x_0 \prec x_1 \prec x_3$, corresponding to the trace

$$(\xi)(v)(\sigma v)(\tau v)(\sigma^3 v)(\tau^3 v)(\rho\pi),$$

whose length is 16.

- If $x_1 \prec x_2$, we want to insert x_4 at the bottom of the right stack, thus obtaining $[x_2, x_1, x_0, x_3]$ and $[x_4]$: $x_3 \prec x_0 \prec x_1 \prec x_2 \prec x_4$, corresponding to the trace

$$(\xi)(\upsilon)(\sigma\upsilon)(\sigma\upsilon)(\tau^2\upsilon)(\sigma^4\upsilon)(\rho^4\pi),$$

whose length is 19. It is perhaps better visualised by means of oriented edges, revealing a spiral in FIGURE 3.5.

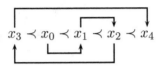

Figure 3.5: Worst case for i2w/1 if $n = 5$ ($x_1 \prec x_2$)

Therefore, it seems that when the number of keys is odd, having $x_1 \prec x_2$ leads to the maximum cost, whilst $x_2 \prec x_0$ leads to the maximum cost when the number of keys is even. Let us determine these costs for any n and find out which is the greater.

Let us note $\mathcal{W}_{2p+1}^{x_1 \prec x_2}$ the former cost and $\mathcal{W}_{2p}^{x_2 \prec x_0}$ the latter.

- If $n = 2p + 1$ and $x_1 \prec x_2$, then the evaluation trace is

$$(\xi)(\upsilon)(\sigma\upsilon)(\sigma\upsilon)(\tau^2\upsilon)(\sigma^4\upsilon)(\tau^4\upsilon)\ldots(\sigma^{2p-2}\upsilon)(\tau^{2p-2}\upsilon)(\sigma^{2p}\upsilon)(\rho^{2p}\pi),$$

as a partial evaluation with $p = 3$ suggests:

$$
\begin{aligned}
\mathsf{i2w}([x_0, x_1, x_2, x_3, x_4, x_5, x_6]) &\xrightarrow{\xi} \mathsf{i2w}([\,], [\,], [x_0, x_1, x_2, x_3, x_4, x_5, x_6]) \\
&\xrightarrow{\upsilon} \mathsf{i2w}([\,], [x_0], [x_1, x_2, x_3, x_4, x_5, x_6]) \\
&\xrightarrow{\sigma} \mathsf{i2w}([x_0], [\,], [x_1, x_2, x_3, x_4, x_5, x_6]) \\
&\xrightarrow{\upsilon} \mathsf{i2w}([x_0], [x_1], [x_2, x_3, x_4, x_5, x_6]) \\
&\xrightarrow{\sigma} \mathsf{i2w}([x_1, x_0], [\,], [x_2, x_3, x_4, x_5, x_6]) \\
&\xrightarrow{\tau^2} \mathsf{i2w}([x_1, x_0], [x_2], [x_3, x_4, x_5, x_6]) \\
&\twoheadrightarrow \mathsf{i2w}([\,], [x_0, x_1, x_2], [x_3, x_4, x_5, x_6]) \\
&\xrightarrow{\upsilon}_{\sigma^4} \mathsf{i2w}([\,], [x_3, x_0, x_1, x_2], [x_4, x_5, x_6]) \\
&\twoheadrightarrow \mathsf{i2w}([x_2, x_1, x_0, x_3], [\,], [x_4, x_5, x_6]) \\
&\xrightarrow{\upsilon}_{\tau^4} \mathsf{i2w}([x_2, x_1, x_0, x_3], [x_4], [x_5, x_6]) \\
&\twoheadrightarrow \mathsf{i2w}([\,], [x_3, x_0, x_1, x_2, x_4], [x_5, x_6]) \\
&\xrightarrow{\upsilon}_{\sigma^6} \mathsf{i2w}([\,], [x_5, x_3, x_0, x_1, x_2, x_4], [x_6]) \\
&\twoheadrightarrow \mathsf{i2w}([x_4, x_2, x_1, x_0, x_3, x_5], [\,], [x_6]) \\
&\xrightarrow{\upsilon} \mathsf{i2w}([x_4, x_2, x_1, x_0, x_3, x_5], [x_6], [\,]).
\end{aligned}
$$

If we omit rules ξ, υ, π and ρ, we can see a pattern emerge from the subtrace $(\sigma^2\tau^2)(\sigma^4\tau^4)(\sigma^6\tau^6)\ldots(\sigma^{2p-2}\tau^{2p-2})(\sigma^{2p})$. Rule υ is used

n times because it inserts the key in the right place. So the total
cost is

$$W_{2p+1}^{x_1 \prec x_2} = |\xi| + |v^{2p+1}| + \sum_{k=1}^{p-1}\left(|\sigma^{2k}| + |\tau^{2k}|\right) + |\sigma^{2p}| + |\rho^{2p}\pi|$$

$$= 1 + (2p+1) + \sum_{k=1}^{p-1} 2(2k) + (2p) + (2p+1)$$

$$= 2p^2 + 4p + 3.$$

- If $n = 2p$ and $x_2 \prec x_0$, then the evaluation trace is

$$(\xi)(v)(\sigma v)(\tau v)(\sigma^3 v)(\tau^3 v)\dots(\sigma^{2p-1}v)(\rho^{2p-1}\pi),$$

as the following partial evaluation with $p = 3$ suggests (first difference with the previous case is in boldface type):

$$
\begin{aligned}
\mathsf{i2w}([x_0, x_1, x_2, x_3, x_4, x_5]) &\to \mathsf{i2w}([\,], [\,], [x_0, x_1, x_2, x_3, x_4, x_5]) \\
&\xrightarrow{v} \mathsf{i2w}([\,], [x_0], [x_1, x_2, x_3, x_4, x_5]) \\
&\xrightarrow{\sigma} \mathsf{i2w}([x_0], [\,], [x_1, x_2, x_3, x_4, x_5]) \\
&\xrightarrow{v} \mathsf{i2w}([x_0], [x_1], [x_2, x_3, x_4, x_5]) \\
&\xrightarrow{\tau} \mathsf{i2w}([\,], [\boldsymbol{x_0, x_1}], [\boldsymbol{x_2, x_3, x_4, x_5}]) \\
&\xrightarrow{v}{\sigma^3} \mathsf{i2w}([\,], [x_2, x_0, x_1], [x_3, x_4, x_5]) \\
&\twoheadrightarrow \mathsf{i2w}([x_1, x_0, x_2], [\,], [x_3, x_4, x_5]) \\
&\xrightarrow{v}{\tau^3} \mathsf{i2w}([x_1, x_0, x_2], [x_3], [x_4, x_5]) \\
&\twoheadrightarrow \mathsf{i2w}([\,], [x_2, x_0, x_1, x_3], [x_4, x_5]) \\
&\xrightarrow{v}{\sigma^5} \mathsf{i2w}([\,], [x_4, x_2, x_0, x_1, x_3], [x_5]) \\
&\twoheadrightarrow \mathsf{i2w}([x_3, x_1, x_0, x_2, x_4], [\,], [x_5]) \\
&\xrightarrow{v} \mathsf{i2w}([x_3, x_1, x_0, x_2, x_4], [x_5], [\,])
\end{aligned}
$$

If we omit rules ξ, v, π and ρ, we can see a pattern emerge from
the subtrace $(\sigma^1\tau^1)(\sigma^3\tau^3)(\sigma^5\tau^5)\dots(\sigma^{2p-3}\tau^{2p-3})(\sigma^{2p-1})$. Rule v is
used n times because it inserts the key in the right place. So the
total cost is

$$W_{2p}^{x_2 \prec x_0} = |\xi| + |v^{2p}| + \sum_{k=1}^{p-1}\left(|\sigma^{2k-1}| + |\tau^{2k-1}|\right) + |\sigma^{2p-1}| + |\rho^{2p-1}\pi|$$

$$= 1 + (2p) + \sum_{k=1}^{p-1} 2(2k-1) + (2p-1) + ((2p-1)+1)$$

$$= 2p^2 + 2p + 2.$$

These formulas hold for all $p \geqslant 0$. We can now conclude this discussion
about the worst case of i2w/1:

- If $n = 2p$, the worst case happens when the keys satisfy the total order $x_{2p} \prec x_{2p-2} \prec \cdots \prec x_0 \prec x_1 \prec x_3 \prec \cdots \prec x_{2p-3} \prec x_{2p-1}$ and $\mathcal{W}_{2p}^{\text{i2w}} = 2p^2 + 2p + 2$, that is, $\mathcal{W}_n^{\text{i2w}} = n^2/2 + n + 2$.

- If $n = 2p+1$, the worst case happens when the keys satisfy the order $x_{2p-1} \prec x_{2p-3} \prec \cdots \prec x_3 \prec x_0 \prec x_1 \prec x_2 \prec \cdots \prec x_{2p-2} \prec x_{2p}$ and $\mathcal{W}_{2p+1}^{\text{i2w}} = 2p^2 + 4p + 3$, that is, $\mathcal{W}_n^{\text{i2w}} = n^2/2 + n + 3/2$.

The first case yields the maximum cost:

$$\mathcal{W}_n^{\text{i2w}} = \frac{1}{2}n^2 + n + 2 = \mathcal{W}_n^{\text{isrt}} - n + 1 \sim \mathcal{W}_n^{\text{isrt}} \sim \frac{1}{2}n^2.$$

Average cost   Let $\mathcal{A}_n^{\text{i2w}}$ be the average cost of the call i2w(s), where the stack s has length n. We are going to use the same assumption as with $\mathcal{A}_n^{\text{isrt}}$, namely, we look for the cost for sorting all permutations of $(1, 2, \ldots, n)$, divided by $n!$. The insertions are illustrated by the *evaluation tree* in FIGURE 3.6, where the keys a, b and c are inserted in this order in a stack originally empty, with all possible total orders. Note how all permutations are attained exactly once at the external nodes (see page 90).

For example, $[a, b, c]$ and $[c, b, a]$ are external nodes. The total cost is the *external path length* of the tree, that is, the sum of the lengths of the paths from the root to all the external nodes, which is the same as the sum of the lengths of all possible traces: $|\xi\upsilon\sigma\upsilon\sigma\upsilon\rho^2\pi| + |\xi\upsilon\sigma\upsilon\tau\upsilon\pi| + |\xi\upsilon\sigma\upsilon^2\rho\pi| + |\xi\upsilon^2\sigma^2\upsilon\rho^2\pi| + |\xi\upsilon^2\sigma\upsilon\rho\pi| + |\xi\upsilon^3\pi| = 44$, so the average cost of sorting 3 keys is $44/3! = 22/3$.

Given a left stack of p keys and a right stack of q keys, let us characterise all the possible traces for the insertion of one more key, stopping before another key is inserted or the final stack is made. In the left stack, an insertion is possible after the first key, after the second etc. until after the last. After the kth key, with $1 \leqslant k \leqslant p$, the trace is thus $\tau^k\upsilon$. In the right stack, an insertion is possible on top, after the first key, after the second etc. until after the last. After the kth key, with $0 \leqslant k \leqslant q$, the trace is hence $\sigma^k\upsilon$. All the possible traces are thus

$$\sum_{k=1}^{p} \tau^k \upsilon + \sum_{k=0}^{q} \sigma^k \upsilon,$$

whose cumulated lengths amount to

$$C_{p,q} := \sum_{k=1}^{p} |\tau^k \upsilon| + \sum_{k=0}^{q} |\sigma^k \upsilon| = (p + q + 1) + \frac{1}{2}p(p+1) + \frac{1}{2}q(q+1).$$

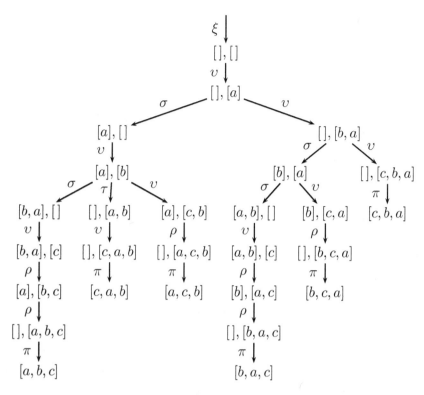

Figure 3.6: Sorting $[a, b, c]$ (first argument of i2w/3 hidden)

There are $p + q + 1$ insertion loci, so the average cost of one insertion in the configuration (p, q) is

$$A_{p,q} := \frac{C_{p,q}}{p + q + 1} = 1 + \frac{p^2 + q^2 + p + q}{2p + 2q + 2}. \tag{3.9}$$

By letting $k := p + q$, we can re-express this cost as

$$A_{k-q,q} = \frac{1}{k + 1} q^2 - \frac{k}{k + 1} q + \frac{k + 2}{2}.$$

The left stack is reversed after the last insertion, so the subsequent traces are $\rho^{p-k}\pi$, with $1 \leqslant k \leqslant p$, if the last insertion took place on the left, otherwise $\rho^{p+k}\pi$, with $0 \leqslant k \leqslant q$, that is, $\rho^0\pi$, $\rho^1\pi$, $\ldots$, $\rho^{p+q}\pi$. In other words, after an insertion, all possible configurations are uniquely realised (only the right stack being empty is invalid, due to rule v). As a consequence, we can average the average costs of inserting one key over all the partitions of k into $p + q$, with $q \neq 0$, so the average cost of inserting one key in a simulated stack of k keys is

$$\mathcal{A}_0 := 1; \quad \mathcal{A}_k := \frac{1}{k} \sum_{p+q=k} \mathcal{A}_{p,q} = \frac{1}{k} \sum_{q=1}^{k} \mathcal{A}_{k-q,q} = \frac{1}{3}k + \frac{7}{6},$$

minding that $\sum_{q=1}^{k} q^2 = k(k+1)(2k+1)/6$ (see equation (2.8) on page 56). The cost of the final reversal is also averaged over all possible configurations, here of $n > 0$ keys:

$$\mathcal{A}_n^{\curvearrowleft} = \frac{1}{n} \sum_{k=0}^{n-1} |\rho^k \pi| = \frac{n+1}{2}.$$

Finally, we know that all traces start with ξ, then proceed with all the insertions and conclude with a reversal. This means that the average cost $\mathcal{A}_n^{\mathsf{i2w}}$ of sorting n keys is defined by the following equations:

$$\mathcal{A}_0^{\mathsf{i2w}} = 2; \quad \mathcal{A}_n^{\mathsf{i2w}} = 1 + \sum_{k=0}^{n-1} \mathcal{A}_k + \mathcal{A}_n^{\curvearrowleft} = \frac{1}{6}n^2 + \frac{3}{2}n + \frac{4}{3} \sim \frac{1}{6}n^2.$$

We can check that $\mathcal{A}_3^{\mathsf{i2w}} = 22/3$, as expected. As a conclusion, in average, sorting with 2-way insertions is faster than with straight insertions, but the cost is still asymptotically quadratic.

Exercises

1. When designing i2w/3, we chose to always push the key to be inserted on top of the right stack in rule v. Let us modify slightly this strategy and push instead onto the left stack when it is empty. See rule ($\rightsquigarrow$) in FIGURE 3.7. Prove that the average cost satisfies now the equation

$$\mathcal{A}_n^{\mathsf{i2w_1}} = \mathcal{A}_n^{\mathsf{i2w}} - H_n + 2.$$

$$\mathsf{i2w_1}(s) \rightarrow \mathsf{i2w_1}(s, [\,], [\,]).$$
$$\mathsf{i2w_1}([\,], [\,], u) \rightarrow u;$$
$$\mathsf{i2w_1}([\,], [y\,|\,t], u) \rightarrow \mathsf{i2w_1}([\,], t, [y\,|\,u]);$$
$$\mathsf{i2w_1}([x\,|\,s], t, [z\,|\,u]) \rightarrow \mathsf{i2w_1}([x\,|\,s], [z\,|\,t], u), \quad \text{if } x \succ z;$$
$$\mathsf{i2w_1}([x\,|\,s], [\,], u) \rightsquigarrow \mathsf{i2w_1}(s, [x], u);$$
$$\mathsf{i2w_1}([x\,|\,s], [y\,|\,t], u) \rightarrow \mathsf{i2w_1}([x\,|\,s], t, [y\,|\,u]), \quad \text{if } y \succ x;$$
$$\mathsf{i2w_1}([x\,|\,s], t, u) \rightarrow \mathsf{i2w_1}(s, t, [x\,|\,u]).$$

Figure 3.7: Variation i2w$_1$/1 on i2w/1 (see ($\rightsquigarrow$))

Hint: Write down the examples similar to the ones in FIGURE 3.6 on page 111, determine the average path length and observe that the difference with i2w/1 is that the configuration with an empty left stack is replaced with a configuration with a singleton left stack, to wit, $\mathcal{A}_{0,k}$ is replaced with $\mathcal{A}_{1,k-1}$ in the definition of $\mathcal{A}_k$.

2. In rule v of i2w/3, the key x is pushed on the right stack. Consider in FIGURE 3.8 (rule ($\rightsquigarrow$)) the variant where it is pushed on the left stack instead. Show very simply that the average cost satisfies

$$\mathcal{A}_n^{\text{i2w2}} = \mathcal{A}_n^{\text{i2w}} + 1.$$

$$
\begin{array}{l}
\text{i2w}_2(s) \rightarrow \text{i2w}_2(s, [\,], [\,]). \\
\text{i2w}_2([\,], [\,], u) \rightarrow u; \\
\text{i2w}_2([\,], [y\,|\,t], u) \rightarrow \text{i2w}_2([\,], t, [y\,|\,u]); \\
\text{i2w}_2([x\,|\,s], t, [z\,|\,u]) \rightarrow \text{i2w}_2([x\,|\,s], [z\,|\,t], u), \quad \text{if } x \succ z; \\
\text{i2w}_2([x\,|\,s], [y\,|\,t], u) \rightarrow \text{i2w}_2([x\,|\,s], t, [y\,|\,u]), \quad \text{if } y \succ x; \\
\text{i2w}_2([x\,|\,s], t, u) \rightsquigarrow \text{i2w}_2(s, [x\,|\,t], u).
\end{array}
$$

Figure 3.8: Variation i2w$_2$/1 on i2w/1 (see ($\rightsquigarrow$))

3.3 Balanced 2-way insertion

When sorting with 2-way insertions, keys are inserted from whence the finger is on the simulated stack. We could maintain the finger at the middle of the stack, leading to what we call *balanced 2-way insertions*. The adjective 'balanced' refers to the shape of the comparison tree.

Our best effort to keep the two stacks about the same length must lead to two cases: either (*a*) they are exactly of the same length, or (*b*) one of them, say the right one, contains one more key. Let us envisage how to maintain this invariant through insertions. Let us suppose we are in case (*b*). Then, if the key has to be inserted in the left stack, the resulting stacks will have equal lengths, which means case (*a*); otherwise, we move the top of the right stack to the top of the left stack, in addition to the insertion itself, and we are back to case (*a*) as well. If we are in case (*a*) and the insertion takes place in the right stack, no rebalancing has to be done; otherwise, the top of the left stack is moved to the top of the right: in both events, we are in case (*b*). What if the key has to be inserted at the finger position? If the two stacks have same length, that is, case (*a*),

$$\begin{array}{rcl}
\mathsf{i2wb}(s) & \overset{\xi}{\to} & \mathsf{i2wb}(s, [\,], [\,], 0). \\
\mathsf{i2wb}([\,], [\,], u, d) & \overset{\pi}{\to} & u; \\
\mathsf{i2wb}([\,], [y \,|\, t], u, d) & \overset{\rho}{\to} & \mathsf{i2wb}([\,], t, [y \,|\, u], d); \\
\mathsf{i2wb}([x \,|\, s], t, [z \,|\, u], 0) & \overset{\sigma}{\to} & \mathsf{i2wb}(s, t, [z \,|\, \mathsf{iup}(u, x)], 1), \quad \text{if } x \succ z; \\
\mathsf{i2wb}([x \,|\, s], [y \,|\, t], u, 0) & \overset{\tau}{\to} & \mathsf{i2wb}(s, \mathsf{idn}(t, x), [y \,|\, u], 1), \quad \text{if } y \succ x; \\
\mathsf{i2wb}([x \,|\, s], t, u, 0) & \overset{\upsilon}{\to} & \mathsf{i2wb}(s, t, [x \,|\, u], 1); \\
\mathsf{i2wb}([x \,|\, s], t, [z \,|\, u], 1) & \overset{\phi}{\to} & \mathsf{i2wb}(s, [z \,|\, t], \mathsf{iup}(u, x), 0), \quad \text{if } x \succ z; \\
\mathsf{i2wb}([x \,|\, s], [y \,|\, t], u, 1) & \overset{\chi}{\to} & \mathsf{i2wb}(s, [y \,|\, \mathsf{idn}(t, x)], u, 0), \quad \text{if } y \succ x; \\
\mathsf{i2wb}([x \,|\, s], t, u, 1) & \overset{\psi}{\to} & \mathsf{i2wb}(s, [x \,|\, t], u, 0).
\end{array}$$

Figure 3.9: Balanced 2-way insertion

we push the key on top of the right one and go back to case (b); otherwise, it means that the right stack exceeds the left by one, that is, case (b), so it is best to push it on the left stack: as a result, the stacks end having equal lengths and we are back to case (a).

To program this algorithm, we need a variant idn/2 (*insert downwardly*) of ins/2 because the left stack is sorted decreasingly. Let us rename ins/2 into iup/2 (*insert upwardly*).

$$\begin{array}{ll}
\mathsf{iup}([y \,|\, s], x) \overset{\kappa_0}{\to} [y \,|\, \mathsf{iup}(s, x)], \text{ if } y \succ x; & \mathsf{iup}(s, x) \overset{\lambda_0}{\to} [x \,|\, s]. \\
\mathsf{idn}([y \,|\, s], x) \overset{\kappa_1}{\to} [y \,|\, \mathsf{idn}(s, x)], \text{ if } x \succ y; & \mathsf{idn}(s, x) \overset{\lambda_1}{\to} [x \,|\, s].
\end{array}$$

Furthermore, we need an additional parameter that represents the difference in length between the two stacks: 0 if they have the same length and 1 if the right contains one more key. Let us call the new function i2wb/1, whose definition is displayed in FIGURE 3.9. In FIGURE 3.10 on the facing page are shown all the possible traces and outcomes of sorting $[a, b, c]$. Note that the tree is not perfect, but balanced, as some arrows correspond to two rewrites. The *internal path length* of the tree is 43, that is the sum of the lengths of the paths from the root to each internal node, so the average cost is $43/6$.

Minimum cost   Let us continue by finding what is the minimum cost of i2wb/1. Let us assume that we have the input $[x_0, x_1, x_2, x_3, x_4]$ and we want it to minimise the rewrites, which means not to use rules σ, τ, ϕ and χ; also, the usage of rule ρ should be minimum. The latter rule is not an issue because it reverses the left stack and, by design, the right stack has the same length as the left, or exceeds it at most by one key. A simple diagram with the two stacks initially empty suffices to convince us that

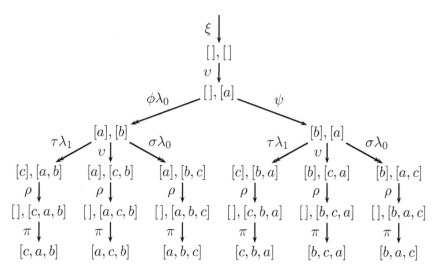

Figure 3.10: Sorting $[a, b, c]$ by balanced 2-way insertions

the keys must go alternatively to the right and then to the left, leading, for example, to $[x_3, x_1]$ and $[x_4, x_2, x_0]$. This is perhaps better visualised by means of oriented edges revealing a whirlpool in FIGURE 3.11, to be contrasted with the spiral in FIGURE 3.5 on page 108 for i2w/1.

The rule definining i2w/1 has to be used first. Then each key is inserted, alternatively by means of rule v and ψ. Finally, the left stack is reversed by rules π and ρ, so the question hinges on determining the length of the left stack in the best case. By design, if the total number of keys is even, then the two stacks will end up containing, before using rule ρ, exactly half of them, because the stacks have the same length. If the total is odd, the left stack contains the integral part of this number halved.

Technically, let us note $\mathcal{B}_n^{i2wb}$ the cost of any call i2wb(s), where the stack s contains n keys. If $p \geqslant 0$, then

$$\mathcal{B}_{2p}^{i2wb} = 1 + 2p + p = 3p + 1,$$
$$\mathcal{B}_{2p+1}^{i2wb} = 1 + (2p + 1) + p = 3p + 2.$$

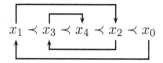

Figure 3.11: Best case for i2wb/1 if $n = 5$

Another, more compact, way to put it is:

$$\mathcal{B}_n^{\text{i2wb}} = 1 + n + \lfloor n/2 \rfloor \sim \frac{3}{2}n.$$

The equivalence is correct because $n/2 - 1 < \lfloor n/2 \rfloor \leqslant n/2$.

Exercise   The worst case occurs when insertions are repeatedly performed at the bottom of the longest stack. Find $\mathcal{W}_n^{\text{i2wb}}$ and characterise the worst case.

Average cost   Let us consider the average cost when $n = 2p$. Then

$$\mathcal{A}_{2p}^{\text{i2wb}} = 1 + \sum_{k=0}^{2p-1} \mathcal{A}_k + \mathcal{A}_p^{\frown}, \tag{3.10}$$

where $\mathcal{A}_k$ is the average cost of inserting a key into a simulated stack of k keys and $\mathcal{A}_p^{\frown}$ is the cost of reversing p keys from left to right. The variable p in $\mathcal{A}_p^{\frown}$ is correct since there are $\lfloor n/2 \rfloor$ keys in the left stack after all insertions are over. Clearly,

$$\mathcal{A}_p^{\frown} = p + 1.$$

The determination of $\mathcal{A}_k$ requires the consideration of only two cases: k is even or not. When analysing the average cost of i2w/1, there were much more configurations to take into account because not all the insertions lead to balanced stacks. If k is even, then there exists an integer j such that $k = 2j$ and

$$\mathcal{A}_{2j} = \mathcal{A}_{j,j},$$

where $\mathcal{A}_{j,j}$ is the average number of rewrites to insert a random number into a configuration of two stacks of length j. We already computed $\mathcal{A}_{p,q}$ in equation (3.9) on page 111. Consequently,

$$\mathcal{A}_{2j} = \frac{j^2 + 3j + 1}{2j + 1} = \frac{1}{2}j - \frac{1}{4} \cdot \frac{1}{2j + 1} + \frac{5}{4}.$$

The case $k = 2j + 1$ is similarly derived: $\mathcal{A}_{2j+1} = (j + 3)/2$. Hence equation (3.10) becomes:

$$\mathcal{A}_{2p}^{\text{i2wb}} = 1 + \sum_{k=0}^{2p-1} \mathcal{A}_k + (p + 1) = 2 + p + \sum_{j=0}^{p-1} (\mathcal{A}_{2j} + \mathcal{A}_{2j+1})$$

$$= \frac{1}{2}p^2 + \frac{13}{4}p + 2 - \frac{1}{4} \sum_{j=0}^{p-1} \frac{1}{2j + 1}. \tag{3.11}$$

We need to find the value of this sum. Let $H_n := \sum_{k=1}^{n} 1/k$ be the nth *harmonic number*. Then

$$H_{2p} = \sum_{j=0}^{p-1} \frac{1}{2j+1} + \sum_{j=1}^{p} \frac{1}{2j} = \sum_{j=0}^{p-1} \frac{1}{2j+1} + \frac{1}{2} H_p.$$

We can now replace our sum by harmonic numbers in equation (3.11):

$$\mathcal{A}_{2p}^{\text{i2wb}} = \frac{1}{2} p^2 + \frac{13}{4} p - \frac{1}{4} H_{2p} + \frac{1}{8} H_p + 2.$$

The remaining case is to find $\mathcal{A}_{2p+1}^{\text{i2wb}}$, which, by the same reckoning, is

$$\mathcal{A}_{2p+1}^{\text{i2wb}} = 1 + \sum_{k=0}^{2p} \mathcal{A}_k + \mathcal{A}_p^{\frown}.$$

Let us reuse previous calculations:

$$\mathcal{A}_{2p+1}^{\text{i2wb}} = \mathcal{A}_{2p}^{\text{i2wb}} + \mathcal{A}_{2p} = \frac{1}{2} p^2 + \frac{15}{4} p - \frac{1}{4} H_{2p+1} + \frac{1}{8} H_p + \frac{13}{4}.$$

We have $1 + x < e^x$, for all real $x \neq 0$. In particular, $x = 1/i$, for $i > 0$ integer, leads to $1 + 1/i < e^{1/i}$. Both sides being positive, we deduce

$$\prod_{i=1}^{n} \left(1 + \frac{1}{i} \right) < \prod_{i=1}^{n} e^{1/i} \Leftrightarrow n + 1 < \exp(H_n).$$

Finally, $\ln(n+1) < H_n$. An upper bound of H_n can be similarly derived by replacing x by $-1/i$:

$$\ln(n+1) < H_n < 1 + \ln n. \tag{3.12}$$

We can now express the bounds on $\mathcal{A}_n^{\text{i2wb}}$ without H_n:

$$\ln(p+1) - 2\ln(2p) + 14 < 8 \cdot \mathcal{A}_{2p}^{\text{i2wb}} - 4p^2 - 26p$$
$$< \ln p - 2\ln(2p+1) + 17;$$
$$\ln(p+1) - 2\ln(2p+1) + 24 < 8 \cdot \mathcal{A}_{2p+1}^{\text{i2wb}} - 4p^2 - 30p$$
$$< \ln p - 2\ln(2p+2) + 27.$$

Setting $n = 2p$ and $n = 2p+1$ leads to the respective bounds

$$-2\ln n + \ln(n+2) + 4 < \varphi(n) < -2\ln(n+1) + \ln n + 7,$$
$$-2\ln n + \ln(n+1) < \varphi(n) < -2\ln(n+1) + \ln(n-1) + 3,$$

where $\varphi(n) := 8 \cdot \mathcal{A}_n^{\text{i2wb}} - n^2 - 13n - 10 + \ln 2$. We retain the minimum of the lower bounds and the maximum of the upper bounds of $\varphi(n)$ so,

$$\ln(n+1) - 2\ln n < \varphi(n) < -2\ln(n+1) + \ln n + 7.$$

We can weaken the bounds a little bit with $\ln n < \ln(n+1)$ and simplify:

$$0 < 8 \cdot \mathcal{A}_n^{\text{i2wb}} - n^2 - 13n + \ln 2n - 10 < 7.$$

Therefore, for all $n > 0$, there exists ϵ_n such that $0 < \epsilon_n < 7/8$ and

$$\mathcal{A}_n^{\text{i2wb}} = \frac{1}{8}(n^2 + 13n - \ln 2n + 10) + \epsilon_n. \tag{3.13}$$

Chapter 4

Merge Sort

Knuth (1996) reports that the first computer program, designed in 1945 by the mathematician John von Neumann, was a sorting algorithm, nowadays called *merge sort*. It is amongst the most widely taught sorting algorithms because it illustrates the important solving strategy known as '*divide and conquer*': the input is split, each non-trivial part is recursively processed and the partial solutions are finally combined to form the complete solution. While merge sort is not difficult to program, finding its cost requires advanced mathematical knowledge. Most textbooks (Graham et al., 1994, Cormen et al., 2009) show how to find the order of growth of an upper bound of the cost (expressed by means of Bachmann's notation $\mathcal{O}$) from recurrences it satisfies, but the general case is often not presented in the main chapters, or not at all, because a precise asymptotic solution requires skills in *analytic combinatorics* (Flajolet and Sedgewick, 2001, 2009, Flajolet and Golin, 1994, Hwang, 1998, Chen et al., 1999). Moreover, there are several variants of merge sort (Knuth, 1998a, Golin and Sedgewick, 1993) and often the only one introduced, called *top-down*, is illustrated on arrays. We show in this chapter that stacks, as a purely functional data structure (Okasaki, 1998b), are suitable both for a top-down and a *bottom-up* approach of merge sort (Panny and Prodinger, 1995).

4.1 Merging

John von Neumann did not actually described merge sort, but its basic operation, *merging*, which he named *meshing*. Merging consists in combining two ordered stacks of keys into one ordered stack. Without loss of generality, we shall be only interested in sorting keys in increasing order. For instance, merging $[10, 12, 17]$ and $[13, 14, 16]$ results in

$$\begin{aligned}
&\mathsf{mrg}([\,], t) \xrightarrow{\theta} t; \\
&\mathsf{mrg}(s, [\,]) \xrightarrow{\iota} s; \\
&\mathsf{mrg}([x\,|\,s], [y\,|\,t]) \xrightarrow{\kappa} [y\,|\,\mathsf{mrg}([x\,|\,s], t)], \text{ if } x \succ y; \\
&\mathsf{mrg}([x\,|\,s], t) \xrightarrow{\lambda} [x\,|\,\mathsf{mrg}(s, t)].
\end{aligned}$$

Figure 4.1: Merging two stacks

$[10, 12, 13, 14, 16, 17]$. One way to achieve this consists in comparing the two smallest keys, output the smallest and repeat the procedure until one of the stacks becomes empty, in which case the other is wholly appended. We have (compared keys underlined):

$$\begin{cases} \underline{10}\ 12\ 17 \\ \underline{13}\ 14\ 16 \end{cases} \to 10 \begin{cases} \underline{12}\ 17 \\ \underline{13}\ 14\ 16 \end{cases} \to 10\ 12 \begin{cases} \underline{17} \\ \underline{13}\ 14\ 16 \end{cases} \to 10\ 12\ 13 \begin{cases} 17 \\ \underline{14}\ 16 \end{cases}$$

The function $\mathsf{mrg}/2$ (*merge*) in FIGURE 4.1 implements this scheme. Rule ι is not necessary but is retained because it allows the cost to be symmetric, just as $\mathsf{mrg}/2$ is: $\mathcal{C}^{\mathrm{mrg}}_{m,n} = \mathcal{C}^{\mathrm{mrg}}_{n,m}$ and $\mathsf{mrg}(s, t) \equiv \mathsf{mrg}(t, s)$, where m and n are the lengths of s and t. This property enables easier cost calculations and faster computations. Note that in the definition of $\mathsf{cat}/2$ (equation (1.3) on page 7), we do not include a similar rule, $\mathsf{cat}(s, [\,]) \to s$, because, despite the gain in speed, the function is asymmetric and cost calculations are simplified when using $\mathcal{C}^{\mathrm{cat}}_n$ rather than $\mathcal{C}^{\mathrm{cat}}_{m,n}$. FIGURE 4.2 shows a trace for $\mathsf{mrg}/2$. Rules κ and λ involve a comparison, while θ and ι do not and end the evaluations; therefore, if $\overline{\mathcal{C}}^{\mathrm{mrg}}_{m,n}$ is the number of comparisons to merge with $\mathsf{mrg}/2$ two stacks of lengths m and n, we have

$$\mathcal{C}^{\mathrm{mrg}}_{m,n} = \overline{\mathcal{C}}^{\mathrm{mrg}}_{m,n} + 1. \tag{4.1}$$

$$\begin{aligned}
\mathsf{mrg}([3, 4, 7], [1, 2, 5, 6]) &\xrightarrow{\kappa} [1\,|\,\mathsf{mrg}([3, 4, 7], [2, 5, 6])] \\
&\xrightarrow{\kappa} [1, 2\,|\,\mathsf{mrg}([3, 4, 7], [5, 6])] \\
&\xrightarrow{\lambda} [1, 2, 3\,|\,\mathsf{mrg}([4, 7], [5, 6])] \\
&\xrightarrow{\lambda} [1, 2, 3, 4\,|\,\mathsf{mrg}([7], [5, 6])] \\
&\xrightarrow{\kappa} [1, 2, 3, 4, 5\,|\,\mathsf{mrg}([7], [6])] \\
&\xrightarrow{\kappa} [1, 2, 3, 4, 5, 6\,|\,\mathsf{mrg}([7], [\,])] \\
&\xrightarrow{\iota} [1, 2, 3, 4, 5, 6, 7].
\end{aligned}$$

Figure 4.2: $\mathsf{mrg}([3, 4, 7], [1, 2, 5, 6]) \twoheadrightarrow [1, 2, 3, 4, 5, 6, 7]$

In order to gain some generality, we shall study $\overline{\mathcal{C}}_{m,n}^{\mathrm{mrg}}$. Graphically, we represent a key from one stack as a *white node* (∘) and a key from the other as a *black node* (•). Nodes of these kinds are printed in a horizontal line, the leftmost being the smallest. Comparisons are always performed between black and white nodes and are represented as *edges* in

$$(4.2)$$

An incoming arrow means that the node is smaller than the other end of the edge, so all edges point leftwards and the number of comparisons is the number of nodes with an incoming edge.

Minimum cost There are two consecutive white nodes without any edges at the right end, which suggests that the more keys from one stack we have at the end of the result, the fewer comparisons we needed for merging: the minimum number is achieved when *the shorter stack comes first in the result*. Consider the following example (the number of comparisons is the number of black nodes):

The minimum number of comparisons $\overline{\mathcal{B}}_{m,n}^{\mathrm{mrg}}$ when merging stacks of size m and n is

$$\overline{\mathcal{B}}_{m,n}^{\mathrm{mrg}} = \min\{m, n\}. \tag{4.3}$$

Maximum cost We can see that we can increase the number of comparisons with respect to $m + n$ by removing, in (4.2), those rightmost nodes in the result *that are not compared*, as can be seen in

This maximises comparisons because all nodes, but the last, are the destination of an edge. The maximum number of comparisons $\overline{\mathcal{W}}_{m,n}^{\mathrm{mrg}}$ is

$$\overline{\mathcal{W}}_{m,n}^{\mathrm{mrg}} = m + n - 1. \tag{4.4}$$

Interchanging the two rightmost nodes in the previous example leaves $m + n - 1$ invariant:

so the maximum number of comparisons occurs when *the last two keys of the result come from two stacks*.

Average cost   Let us seek the average number of comparisons in all distinct mergers of two stacks of lengths m and n. Consider FIGURE 4.3, with $m = 3$ white nodes and $n = 2$ black nodes which are interleaved in all possible manners. Note how the figure is structured. The first column lists the configurations where the rightmost black node is the last of the result. The second column lists the cases where the rightmost black node is the penultimate node of the result. The third column is divided in two groups itself, the first of which lists the cases where the rightmost black node is the antepenultimate. The total number of comparisons is 35 and the number of configurations is 10, thus the average number of comparisons is $35/10 = 7/2$. Let us devise a method to find this ratio for any m and n. First, the number of configurations: how many ways are there to combine m white nodes and n black nodes? This is the same as asking how many ways there are to paint in black n nodes picked amongst $m + n$ white nodes. More abstractly, this is equivalent to wonder how many ways there are to choose n objects amongst $m + n$. This number is called a *binomial coefficient* and noted $\binom{m+n}{n}$. For example, let us consider the set $\{a, b, c, d, e\}$ and the *combinations* of 3 objects taken from it are

$$\{a, b, c\}, \{a, b, d\}, \{a, b, e\}, \{a, c, d\}, \{a, c, e\}, \{a, d, e\},$$
$$\{b, c, d\}, \{b, c, e\}, \{b, d, e\},$$
$$\{c, d, e\}.$$

This enumeration establishes that $\binom{5}{3} = 10$. Notice that we use mathematical sets, therefore the order of the elements or their repetition are not meaningful. It is not difficult to count the combinations if we recall how we counted the permutations, on page 83. Let us determine $\binom{r}{k}$. We can pick the first object amongst r, the second amongst $r-1$ etc. until we pick the rth object amongst $r-k+1$, so there are $r(r-1)\ldots(r-k+1)$ choices. But these arrangements contain duplicates, for example, we may form $\{a, b, c\}$ and $\{b, a, c\}$, which are to be considered identical combinations because order does not matter. Therefore, we must divide the number

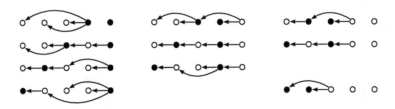

Figure 4.3: All possible mergers with $m = 3$ ($\circ$) and $n = 2$ ($\bullet$)

we just obtained by the number of redundant arrangements, which is the number of permutations of k objects, that is, $k!$. In the end:

$$\binom{r}{k} := \frac{r(r-1)\ldots(r-k+1)}{k!} = \frac{r!}{k!(r-k)!}.$$

We can check now that in FIGURE 4.3 on the facing page, we must have 10 cases: $\binom{5}{2} = 5!/(2!3!) = 10$. The symmetry of the problem means that merging a stack of m keys with a stack of n leads to exactly the same results as merging a stack of n keys with a stack of m keys:

$$\binom{m+n}{n} = \binom{m+n}{m}.$$

This can also be easily proved by means of the definition:

$$\binom{m+n}{n} := \frac{(m+n)!}{n!(m+n-n)!} = \frac{(m+n)!}{m!n!} =: \binom{m+n}{m}.$$

The total number $K(m,n)$ of comparisons needed to merge m and n keys in all possible manners with our algorithm is the number of nodes with incoming edges. Let $\overline{K}(m,n)$ be the total number of nodes *without* incoming edges, circled in FIGURE 4.4. This figure has been obtained by moving the third column of FIGURE 4.3 on the preceding page below the second column and by removing the edges. Since, for each merger, there are $m+n$ nodes and each has an incoming edge or not, and because there are $\binom{m+n}{n}$ mergers, we have

$$K(m,n) + \overline{K}(m,n) = (m+n)\binom{m+n}{n}. \tag{4.5}$$

It is simple to characterise the circled nodes: they make up the longest, rightmost contiguous series of nodes of the same colour. Since there are

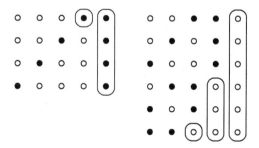

Figure 4.4: Counting vertically

only two colours, the problem of determining the total number $W(m, n)$ of white circled nodes is symmetric to the determination of the total number $B(m, n)$ of black circled nodes, that is,

$$B(m, n) = W(n, m).$$

Therefore,

$$\overline{K}(m, n) = W(m, n) + B(m, n) = W(m, n) + W(n, m). \qquad (4.6)$$

From equations (4.5) and (4.6), we draw

$$K(m, n) = (m + n)\binom{m + n}{n} - W(m, n) - W(n, m). \qquad (4.7)$$

We can decompose $W(m, n)$ by counting the circled white nodes *vertically*. In FIGURE 4.4, $W(3, 2)$ is the sum of the numbers of mergers with at least one, two and three ending circled white nodes: $W(3, 2) = 1 + 3 + 6 = 10$. The first column yields $B(3, 2) = 1 + 4 = 5$. In general, the number of mergers with one ending circled white node is the number of ways to combine n black nodes with $m - 1$ white nodes: $\binom{n+m-1}{n}$. The number of mergers with at least two ending white nodes is $\binom{n+m-2}{n}$, etc.

$$W(m, n) = \binom{n + m - 1}{n} + \binom{n + m - 2}{n} + \cdots + \binom{n + 0}{n} = \sum_{j=0}^{m-1} \binom{n + j}{n}.$$

This sum can actually be simplified, more precisely, it has a closed form, but in order to understand its underpinnings, we need firstly to develop our intuition about combinations. By computing combinations $\binom{r}{k}$ for small values of r and k using the definition, we can fill a table traditionally known as *Pascal's triangle* and displayed in FIGURE 4.5 on the facing page. Note how we set the convention $\binom{r}{k} = 0$ if $k > r$. Pascal's triangle features many interesting properties relative to the sum of some of its values. For instance, if we choose a number in the triangle and look at the one on its right, then the one below the latter is their sum. For the sake of illustration, let us extract from FIGURE 4.5 on the next page the lines $r = 7$ and $r = 8$:

| | 7 | 1 | 7 | 21 | 35 | 35 | 21 | 7 | 1 | 0 | 0 |
| | 8 | 1 | 8 | 28 | 56 | 70 | 56 | 28 | 8 | 1 | 0 |

We surrounded two examples of the additive property of combinations we discussed: $21 + 35 = 56$ and $21 + 7 = 28$. We would then bet that

$$\binom{r - 1}{k - 1} + \binom{r - 1}{k} = \binom{r}{k}.$$

$\binom{r}{k}$

$\binom{r}{k}$	k									
r		0	1	2	3	4	5	6	7	8	9
	0	1	0	0	0	0	0	0	0	0	0
	1	1	1	0	0	0	0	0	0	0	0
	2	1	2	1	0	0	0	0	0	0	0
	3	1	3	3	1	0	0	0	0	0	0
	4	1	4	6	4	1	0	0	0	0	0
	5	1	5	10	10	5	1	0	0	0	0
	6	1	6	15	20	15	6	1	0	0	0
	7	1	7	21	35	35	21	7	1	0	0
	8	1	8	28	56	70	56	28	8	1	0
	9	1	9	36	84	126	126	84	36	9	1

Figure 4.5: The corner of Pascal's triangle (in boldface type)

This is actually not difficult to prove if we go back to the definition:

$$\binom{r}{k} := \frac{r!}{k!(r-k)!} = \frac{r}{k} \cdot \frac{(r-1)!}{(k-1)!((r-1)-(k-1))!} = \frac{r}{k}\binom{r-1}{k-1}.$$

$$\binom{r}{k} := \frac{r!}{k!(r-k)!} = \frac{r}{r-k} \cdot \frac{(r-1)!}{k!((r-1)-k)!} = \frac{r}{r-k}\binom{r-1}{k}.$$

The first equality is valid if $k > 0$ and the second if $r \neq k$. We can now replace $\binom{r-1}{k-1}$ and $\binom{r-1}{k}$ in terms of $\binom{r}{k}$ in the sum

$$\binom{r-1}{k-1} + \binom{r-1}{k} = \frac{k}{r}\binom{r}{k} + \frac{r-k}{r}\binom{r}{k} = \binom{r}{k}.$$

The sum is valid if $r > 0$. There is direct proof of the formula by enumerative combinatorics without algebra. Let us suppose that we *already* have all the subsets of k keys chosen among r. By definition, there are $\binom{r}{k}$ of them. We choose to distinguish an arbitrary key amongst r and we want to group the subsets in two sets: on one side, all the combinations containing this particular key, on the other side, all the combinations without it. The former subset has cardinal $\binom{r-1}{k-1}$ because its combinations are built from the fixed key and further completed by choosing $k - 1$ remaining keys amongst $r - 1$. The latter subset is made of $\binom{r-1}{k}$ combinations which are made from $r - 1$ keys, of which k have to be selected because we ignore the distinguished key. This yields the same additive formula. Now, let us return to our pending sum

$$W(m,n) = \sum_{j=0}^{m-1} \binom{n+j}{n}.$$

1	0
5	1
15	6
35	21
	56

In terms of navigation across Pascal's triangle, we understand that this sum operates on numbers in the same column. More precisely, it starts from the diagonal with the number $\binom{n}{n} = 1$ and goes down until a total of m numbers have been added. So let us choose a simple example and fetch two adjacent columns were the sum is small. On the left is an excerpt for $n = 4$ (the left column is the fifth in Pascal's triangle) and $m = 4$ (height of the left column). Interestingly, the sum of left column, which is the sum under study, equals the number at the bottom of the second column: $1 + 5 + 15 + 35 = 56$. By checking other columns, we may feel justified to think that this is a general pattern. Before attempting a general proof, let us see how it may work on our particular example. Let us start from the bottom of the second column, that is, 56, and use the addition formula in reverse, that is, express 56 as the sum of the numbers in the row above it: $56 = 35 + 21$. We would like to keep 35 because it is part of the equality to prove. So let us apply the addition formula again to 21 and draw $21 = 15 + 6$. Let us keep 15 and resume the same procedure on 6 so $6 = 5 + 1$. Finally, $1 = 1 + 0$. We just checked $56 = 35 + (15 + (5 + (1 + 0)))$, which is exactly what we wanted. Because we want the number corresponding to 35 in our example to be $\binom{n+m-1}{n}$, we have the derivation

$$\binom{n+m}{n+1} = \binom{n+m-1}{n} + \binom{n+m-1}{n+1}$$

$$= \binom{n+m-1}{n} + \left[\binom{n+m-2}{n} + \binom{n+m-2}{n+1}\right]$$

$$= \binom{n+m-1}{n} + \binom{n+m-2}{n} + \cdots + \left[\binom{n}{n} + \binom{n}{n+1}\right],$$

$$\binom{n+m}{n+1} = \sum_{j=0}^{m-1} \binom{n+j}{n} = W(m,n). \tag{4.8}$$

Now, we can replace this closed form in equation (4.7) on page 124 so

$$K(m,n) = (m+n)\binom{m+n}{n} - \binom{m+n}{n+1} - \binom{m+n}{m+1}.$$

By definition, the average number of comparisons $\overline{\mathcal{A}}_{m,n}^{\mathrm{mrg}}$ is the ratio of $K(m,n)$ by $\binom{m+n}{n}$, therefore

$$\overline{\mathcal{A}}_{m,n}^{\mathrm{mrg}} = m + n - \frac{m}{n+1} - \frac{n}{m+1} = \frac{mn}{m+1} + \frac{mn}{n+1}. \tag{4.9}$$

Since we necessarily expect $\overline{\mathcal{B}}_{m,n}^{\mathrm{mrg}} \leqslant \overline{\mathcal{A}}_{m,n}^{\mathrm{mrg}} \leqslant \overline{W}_{m,n}^{\mathrm{mrg}}$, we may wonder if and when the bounds are tight. For the upper bound to be tight, we need

(m, n) to satisfy the equation $m^2 + n^2 - mn = 1$, whose only natural solutions are $(0, 1)$, $(1, 0)$ and $(1, 1)$. For the lower bound to be tight, we must have $mn/(m + 1) + mn/(n + 1) = \min\{m, n\}$, whose only natural solutions are $(0, n)$, $(m, 0)$ and $(1, 1)$. Furthermore, the cases $(m, 1)$ and $(1, n)$ may suggest that merging one key with others is equivalent to inserting that key amongst the others, as we did with straight insertion in section 3.1 on page 95. In other words, we expect the theorem

$$\mathsf{ins}(x, s) \equiv \mathsf{mrg}([x], s). \tag{4.10}$$

Therefore, *insertion is a special case of merging.* Nevertheless, the average costs are not exactly the same. First, we have $\mathcal{A}_{m,n}^{\mathrm{mrg}} = \overline{\mathcal{A}}_{m,n}^{\mathrm{mrg}} + 1$, because we need to account for using once either rule θ or ι in FIGURE 4.1 on page 120, as we already acknowledged by equation (4.1). Then, equations (3.4) on page 97 and (4.9) yield

$$\mathcal{A}_{1,n}^{\mathrm{mrg}} = \frac{1}{2}n + 2 - \frac{1}{n+1} \quad \text{and} \quad \mathcal{A}_n^{\mathrm{ins}} = \frac{1}{2}n + 1.$$

Asymptotically, they are equivalent:

$$\mathcal{A}_{1,n}^{\mathrm{mrg}} \sim \mathcal{A}_n^{\mathrm{ins}}.$$

But mrg/2 is slightly slower in average than ins/2 in this special case:

$$\mathcal{A}_{1,n}^{\mathrm{mrg}} - \mathcal{A}_n^{\mathrm{ins}} = 1 - \frac{1}{n+1} < 1 \quad \text{and} \quad \mathcal{A}_{1,n}^{\mathrm{mrg}} - \mathcal{A}_n^{\mathrm{ins}} \sim 1.$$

Also, it may be interesting to see what happens when $m = n$, that is, when the two stacks to be merged have the same length:

$$\mathcal{A}_{n,n}^{\mathrm{mrg}} = 2n - 1 + \frac{2}{n+1} = \mathcal{W}_{n,n}^{\mathrm{mrg}} - 1 + \frac{2}{n+1} \sim 2n. \tag{4.11}$$

In other words, the average cost of merging two stacks of identical length is asymptotically the total number of keys being merged, which is the worst case.

Termination   The termination of mrg/2 in FIGURE 4.1 on page 120 is easy to prove by considering a lexicographic order (page 13) on pairs of stacks which are, in turn, partially ordered by the immediate subterm relation (page 12), or, more restrictively, the *immediate substack relation*, that is, $[x \,|\, s] \succ s$. The dependency pairs of rules κ and λ are ordered by $([x \,|\, s], [y \,|\, t]) \succ ([x \,|\, s], t)$ and $([x \,|\, s], t) \succ (s, t)$. $\square$

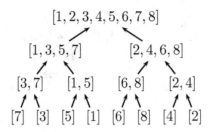

Figure 4.6: Sorting $[7, 3, 5, 1, 6, 8, 4, 2]$

4.2   Sorting 2^n keys

Merging can be used to sort *one* stack of keys as follows. The initial
stack of keys is split in two, then the two pieces are split again etc.
until singletons remain. These are then merged pairwise etc. until only
one stack remains, which is inductively sorted, since a singleton stack is a
sorted stack on its own and $\mathsf{mrg}(s, t)$ is sorted if s and t are. The previous
scheme leaves open the choice of a splitting strategy and, perhaps, the
most intuitive way is to cut in two halves, which works well in the case
of 2^p keys. We will see in later sections how to deal with the general
case and with a different splitting strategy. For now, let us consider in
FIGURE 4.6 all the mergers and their relative order to sort the stack
$[7, 3, 5, 1, 6, 8, 4, 2]$. We name this structure a *merge tree*, because each
node of the tree is a sorted stack, either a singleton or the merger of its
two children. The root logically holds the result. The merge tree is best
understood from a bottom-up, level by level examination. Let us note
$\mathcal{C}_p^{\bowtie}$ the number of comparisons to sort 2^p keys and consider a merge tree
with 2^{p+1} leaves. It is made of two immediate subtrees with 2^p leaves
and the root holds 2^{p+1} keys. Therefore

$$\mathcal{C}_0^{\bowtie} = 0, \quad \mathcal{C}_{p+1}^{\bowtie} = 2 \cdot \mathcal{C}_p^{\bowtie} + \overline{\mathcal{C}}_{2^p, 2^p}^{\mathrm{mrg}}.$$

Unrolling the recursion, we arrive at

$$\mathcal{C}_{p+1}^{\bowtie} = 2^p \sum_{k=0}^{p} \frac{1}{2^k} \overline{\mathcal{C}}_{2^k, 2^k}^{\mathrm{mrg}}. \tag{4.12}$$

Minimum cost   When the given stack is already sorted, either in increasing or decreasing order, the number of comparisons is minimum. In
fact, given a minimum-comparison merge tree, any exchange of two subtrees whose roots are merged leaves the number of comparisons invariant.
This happens because the merge tree is built bottom-up and the number

of comparisons is a symmetric function. Let us note $\mathcal{B}_p^{\bowtie}$ the minimum number of comparisons to sort 2^p keys. From equations (4.12) and (4.3),

$$\mathcal{B}_p^{\bowtie} = 2^{p-1} \sum_{k=0}^{p-1} \frac{1}{2^k} \overline{B}_{2^k,2^k}^{\mathrm{mrg}} = p2^{p-1}. \tag{4.13}$$

Maximum cost Just as with the best case, constructing a maximum-comparison merge sort is achieved by making worst cases for all the sub-trees, for example, $[7, 3, 5, 1, 4, 8, 6, 2]$. Let $\mathcal{W}_p^{\bowtie}$ be the maximum number of comparisons for sorting 2^p keys. From equations (4.12) and (4.4),

$$\mathcal{W}_p^{\bowtie} = 2^{p-1} \sum_{k=0}^{p-1} \frac{1}{2^k} \overline{W}_{2^k,2^k}^{\mathrm{mrg}} = (p-1)2^p + 1. \tag{4.14}$$

Average cost For a given stack, all permutations of which are equally likely, the average cost of sorting it by merging is obtained by considering the average costs of all the subtrees of the merge tree: all the permutations of the keys are considered for a given length. Therefore, equation (4.12) is satisfied by $\overline{A}_{2^k,2^k}^{\mathrm{mrg}}$ and $\mathcal{A}_p^{\bowtie}$, that is, the average number of comparisons for sorting 2^p keys. Equations (4.11) and (4.1) yield

$$\overline{A}_{n,n}^{\mathrm{mrg}} = 2n - 2 + \frac{2}{n+1}.$$

Together with equation (4.12), we further draw, for $p > 0$,

$$\mathcal{A}_p^{\bowtie} = 2^{p-1} \sum_{k=0}^{p-1} \frac{1}{2^k} \overline{A}_{2^k,2^k}^{\mathrm{mrg}} = 2^p \sum_{k=0}^{p-1} \frac{1}{2^k} \left(2^k - 1 + \frac{1}{2^k + 1} \right)$$

$$= 2^p \left(p - \sum_{k=0}^{p-1} \frac{1}{2^k} + \sum_{k=0}^{p-1} \frac{1}{2^k(2^k + 1)} \right)$$

$$= 2^p \left(p - \sum_{k=0}^{p-1} \frac{1}{2^k} + \sum_{k=0}^{p-1} \left(\frac{1}{2^k} - \frac{1}{2^k + 1} \right) \right) = p2^p - 2^p \sum_{k=0}^{p-1} \frac{1}{2^k + 1}$$

$$= p2^p - 2^p \sum_{k \geqslant 0} \frac{1}{2^k + 1} + 2^p \sum_{k \geqslant p} \frac{1}{2^k + 1} = (p - \alpha)2^p + \sum_{k \geqslant 0} \frac{1}{2^k + 2^{-p}},$$

$$\tag{4.15}$$

where $\alpha := \sum_{k \geqslant 0} \frac{1}{2^k + 1} \simeq 1.264500$ is irrational (Borwein, 1992). Since $0 < 2^{-p} < 1$, we have $1/(2^k + 1) < 1/(2^k + 2^{-p}) < 1/2^k$ and we conclude

$$(p - \alpha)2^p + \alpha < A_p^{\bowtie} < (p - \alpha)2^p + 2. \tag{4.16}$$

The uniform convergence of the series $\sum_{k \geqslant 0} \frac{1}{2^k + 2^{-p}}$ allows us to interchange the limits on k and p and deduce that $A_p^{\bowtie} - (p - \alpha)2^p - 2 \to 0^-$, as $p \to \infty$. In other words, $A_p^{\bowtie}$ is best approximated by its upper bound, for sufficiently large values of p.

4.3   Top-down merge sort

When generalising the fifty-fifty splitting rule to an arbitrary number of keys, thus obtaining stacks of lengths $\lfloor n/2 \rfloor$ and $\lceil n/2 \rceil$, we obtain the variant of merge sort called *top-down*. The corresponding program is shown in FIGURE 4.7. Note that the call $\mathsf{cutr}(s, t, u)$ reverses the first half of t on top of s if $s = t$. The technique consists in starting with $s = [\,]$ and projecting the keys of t one by one and those of u two by two, so when $\mathsf{cutr}(s, t, [\,])$ or $\mathsf{cutr}(s, t, [y])$ are reached, we know that t is the second half of the original stack and s is the reversed first half (of length $\lfloor n/2 \rfloor$ if n is the length of the original stack). In the first rule of $\mathsf{tms}/1$, we saved one recursive call to $\mathsf{cutr}/3$ and some memory by calling $\mathsf{cutr}([x], [y \,|\, t], t)$ instead of $\mathsf{cutr}([\,], [x, y \,|\, t], [x, y \,|\, t])$. Moreover, this way, the second rule implements the two base cases, $\mathsf{tms}([\,])$ and $\mathsf{tms}([y])$. Furthermore, notice that, in the second rule of $\mathsf{cutr}/2$, if $u = [\,]$, then the length of the original stack is even and if $u = [a]$, then it is odd. One possible drawback of $\mathsf{tms}/1$ is that the sort is *unstable*, that is, the relative order of equal keys is not invariant.

$$
\begin{aligned}
\mathsf{tms}([x, y \,|\, t]) &\to \mathsf{cutr}([x], [y \,|\, t], t); \\
\mathsf{tms}(t) &\to t.
\end{aligned}
$$

$$
\begin{aligned}
\mathsf{cutr}(s, [y \,|\, t], [a, b \,|\, u]) &\to \mathsf{cutr}([y \,|\, s], t, u); \\
\mathsf{cutr}(s, t, u) &\to \mathsf{mrg}(\mathsf{tms}(s), \mathsf{tms}(t)).
\end{aligned}
$$

$$
\begin{aligned}
\mathsf{mrg}([\,], t) &\to t; \\
\mathsf{mrg}(s, [\,]) &\to s; \\
\mathsf{mrg}([x \,|\, s], [y \,|\, t]) &\to [y \,|\, \mathsf{mrg}([x \,|\, s], t)], \text{ if } x \succ y; \\
\mathsf{mrg}([x \,|\, s], t) &\to [x \,|\, \mathsf{mrg}(s, t)].
\end{aligned}
$$

Figure 4.7: Top-down merge sort with $\mathsf{tms}/1$

Since all comparisons are performed by $\mathsf{mrg}/2$, the definition of $\mathsf{tms}/1$ implies that the number of comparisons satisfies

$$\overline{C}_0^{\mathsf{tms}} = \overline{C}_1^{\mathsf{tms}} = 0, \qquad \overline{C}_n^{\mathsf{tms}} = \overline{C}_{\lfloor n/2 \rfloor}^{\mathsf{tms}} + \overline{C}_{\lceil n/2 \rceil}^{\mathsf{tms}} + \overline{C}_{\lfloor n/2 \rfloor, \lceil n/2 \rceil}^{\mathsf{mrg}}. \qquad (4.17)$$

Minimum cost The minimum number of comparisons satisfies

$$\underline{\mathcal{B}}_0^{\mathsf{tms}} = \underline{\mathcal{B}}_1^{\mathsf{tms}} = 0, \ \underline{\mathcal{B}}_n^{\mathsf{tms}} = \underline{\mathcal{B}}_{\lfloor n/2 \rfloor}^{\mathsf{tms}} + \underline{\mathcal{B}}_{\lceil n/2 \rceil}^{\mathsf{tms}} + \underline{\mathcal{B}}_{\lfloor n/2 \rfloor, \lceil n/2 \rceil}^{\mathsf{mrg}}.$$

We have $\underline{\mathcal{B}}_n^{\mathsf{tms}} = \underline{\mathcal{B}}_{\lfloor n/2 \rfloor}^{\mathsf{tms}} + \underline{\mathcal{B}}_{\lceil n/2 \rceil}^{\mathsf{tms}} + \lfloor n/2 \rfloor$, using equation (4.3) on page 121. In particular

$$\underline{\mathcal{B}}_{2p}^{\mathsf{tms}} = 2 \cdot \underline{\mathcal{B}}_p^{\mathsf{tms}} + p, \quad \underline{\mathcal{B}}_{2p+1}^{\mathsf{tms}} = \underline{\mathcal{B}}_p^{\mathsf{tms}} + \underline{\mathcal{B}}_{p+1}^{\mathsf{tms}} + p.$$

2^0	1
2^1	10
	11
2^2	100
	101
	110
	111
2^3	1000
	1001
	1010
	1011
	1100
	1101
	1110
	1111
$\vdots$	$\vdots$
$2^{\lfloor \lg n \rfloor}$	$\ldots$
	$\vdots$
	n

Figure 4.8

Let us introduce the difference of two successive terms, $\Delta_n := \underline{\mathcal{B}}_{n+1}^{\mathsf{tms}} - \underline{\mathcal{B}}_n^{\mathsf{tms}}$, so $\Delta_0 = 0$, and find some constraints on it. Because of the floor and ceiling functions of $n/2$, we consider two complementary cases.

- $\Delta_{2p} = \underline{\mathcal{B}}_{2p+1}^{\mathsf{tms}} - \underline{\mathcal{B}}_{2p}^{\mathsf{tms}} = \underline{\mathcal{B}}_{p+1}^{\mathsf{tms}} - \underline{\mathcal{B}}_p^{\mathsf{tms}} = \Delta_p.$

- $\Delta_{2p+1} = \underline{\mathcal{B}}_{p+1}^{\mathsf{tms}} - \underline{\mathcal{B}}_p^{\mathsf{tms}} + 1 = \Delta_p + 1.$

We already met Δ_n under the name ν_n in equation (1.7) on page 11. Let us define it recursively:

$$\nu_0 := 0, \quad \nu_{2n} := \nu_n, \quad \nu_{2n+1} := \nu_n + 1. \qquad (4.18)$$

This definition becomes obvious when we consider the binary representations of $2n$ and $2n + 1$. Notice that ν is a deceptively simple function: it is periodic because $\nu_1 = \nu_{2p} = 1$, but $\nu_{2p-1} = p$. Resuming our argument: $\underline{\mathcal{B}}_{n+1}^{\mathsf{tms}} = \underline{\mathcal{B}}_n^{\mathsf{tms}} + \nu_n$, and summing on both sides yields

$$\underline{\mathcal{B}}_n^{\mathsf{tms}} = \sum_{k=0}^{n-1} \nu_k. \qquad (4.19)$$

Trollope (1968) first found a closed form for $\sum_{k=0}^{n-1} \nu_k$, whose demonstration was later simplified by Delange (1975), who extended the analysis with Fourier series. Stolarsky (1977) provided many references on the subject. In equation (4.13), we have $\underline{\mathcal{B}}_{2p}^{\mathsf{tms}} = \frac{1}{2} p 2^p$, that is, $\underline{\mathcal{B}}_n^{\mathsf{tms}} = \frac{1}{2} n \lg n$ when $n = 2^p$. This should prompt us to look, like McIlroy (1974), for

Bits of n				n
0	0	$\ldots$	0	0
$\vdots$	$\overline{\mathcal{B}}^{\text{tms}}_{2^p}$			$\vdots$
0	1	$\ldots$	1	$2^p - 1$
1	0	$\ldots$	0	2^p
$\vdots$	$\overline{\mathcal{B}}^{\text{tms}}_i$			$\vdots$
1		$\ldots$		$2^p + i - 1$
				$2^p + i$

Figure 4.9: $\overline{\mathcal{B}}^{\text{tms}}_{2^p+i} = \overline{\mathcal{B}}^{\text{tms}}_{2^p} + \overline{\mathcal{B}}^{\text{tms}}_i + i$

an additional linear term in the general case, that is, the greatest real constants a and b such that, for $n \geqslant 2$,

$$\mathsf{Low}(n) \colon \frac{1}{2} n \lg n + an + b \leqslant \overline{\mathcal{B}}^{\text{tms}}_n. \tag{4.20}$$

The base case is $\mathsf{Low}(2)$: $2a + b \leqslant 0$. The most obvious way to structure the inductive argument is to follow the definition of $\overline{\mathcal{B}}^{\text{tms}}_n$ when $n = 2p$ and $n = 2p + 1$, but a bound on $\overline{\mathcal{B}}^{\text{tms}}_{2p+1}$ would rely on bounds on $\overline{\mathcal{B}}^{\text{tms}}_p$ and $\overline{\mathcal{B}}^{\text{tms}}_{p+1}$, compounding imprecision. Instead, if we could have at least one exact value from which to inductively build the bound, we would gain accuracy. Therefore, we may expect a better bound if we can find a decomposition of $\overline{\mathcal{B}}^{\text{tms}}_{2^p+i}$, where $0 < i \leqslant 2^p$, in terms of $\overline{\mathcal{B}}^{\text{tms}}_{2^p}$ (exact) and $\overline{\mathcal{B}}^{\text{tms}}_i$. This is easy if we count the 1-bits in FIGURE 4.9, which is the same as the table in FIGURE 4.8, where $n = 2^p + i$. (Keep in mind that $\overline{\mathcal{B}}^{\text{tms}}_n$ is the sum of the bits up to $n - 1$, as seen in equation (4.19).) We find:

$$\overline{\mathcal{B}}^{\text{tms}}_{2^p+i} = \overline{\mathcal{B}}^{\text{tms}}_{2^p} + \overline{\mathcal{B}}^{\text{tms}}_i + i. \tag{4.21}$$

(The term i is the sum of the leftmost bits.) Therefore, let us assume $\mathsf{Low}(n)$, for all $1 \leqslant n \leqslant 2^p$, and prove $\mathsf{Low}(2^p + i)$, for all $0 < i \leqslant 2^p$. The induction principle entails then that $\mathsf{Low}(n)$ holds for all $n \geqslant 2$. The inductive step $\mathsf{Low}(2^p + i)$ should give us the opportunity to maximise the constants a and b. Let $m = 2^p$. Using $\overline{\mathcal{B}}^{\text{tms}}_{2^p} = \frac{1}{2} p 2^p$ and the inductive hypothesis $\mathsf{Low}(i)$, we have

$$\frac{1}{2} m \lg m + \left(\frac{1}{2} i \lg i + ai + b \right) + i \leqslant \overline{\mathcal{B}}^{\text{tms}}_m + \overline{\mathcal{B}}^{\text{tms}}_i + i = \overline{\mathcal{B}}^{\text{tms}}_{m+i}. \tag{4.22}$$

We need now to find a and b such that the inductive step $\mathsf{L}(m + i)$ holds as well, that is, $\frac{1}{2}(m + i) \lg(m + i) + a(m + i) + b \leqslant \mathcal{B}_{m+i}$. Using (4.22), this inequality is implied by

$$\frac{1}{2}(m+i)\lg(m+i) + a(m+i) + b \leqslant \frac{1}{2}m\lg m + \left(\frac{1}{2}i\lg i + ai + b\right) + i.$$

We can already notice that this inequality is equivalent to

$$\frac{1}{2}m\lg(m+i) + \frac{1}{2}i\lg(m+i) + am \leqslant \frac{1}{2}m\lg m + \frac{1}{2}i\lg i + i. \quad (4.23)$$

But $\frac{1}{2}m\lg m < \frac{1}{2}m\lg(m+i)$ and $\frac{1}{2}i\lg i < \frac{1}{2}i\lg(m+i)$, therefore the constant a we are seeking must satisfy $am \leqslant i$ for all $0 < i < m$, hence we expect a to be strictly negative.

We extend i over the real numbers by defining $i = x2^p = xm$, where x is a real number such that $0 < x \leqslant 1$. By replacing i by xm in inequality (4.23), we obtain

$$\frac{1}{2}(1+x)\lg(1+x) + a \leqslant \frac{1}{2}x\lg x + x.$$

Let $\Phi(x) := \frac{1}{2}x\lg x - \frac{1}{2}(1+x)\lg(1+x) + x$. Then, the previous inequality is equivalent to $a \leqslant \Phi(x)$. The function Φ can be continuously extended at 0, as $\lim_{x\to 0} x\lg x = 0$, and it is differentiable on the interval $]0,1]$:

$$\frac{d\Phi}{dx} = \frac{1}{2}\lg\frac{4x}{x+1}. \quad (4.24)$$

The root of $d\Phi/dx = 0$ is $1/3$, and the derivative is negative before, and positive after. Therefore, $a_{\max} := \min_{0\leqslant x\leqslant 1}\Phi(x) = \Phi(\frac{1}{3}) = -\frac{1}{2}\lg\frac{4}{3}$. The base case was $b \leqslant -2a$, therefore $b_{\max} := -2a_{\max} = \lg\frac{4}{3}$. Finally,

$$\frac{1}{2}n\lg n - \left(\frac{1}{2}\lg\frac{4}{3}\right)n + \lg\frac{4}{3} \leqslant \overline{B}_n^{\text{tms}}, \quad (4.25)$$

where $\frac{1}{2}\lg\frac{4}{3} \simeq 0.2075$ and $\lg\frac{4}{3} \simeq 0.415$. Importantly, the lower bound is tight if $x = 1/3$, that is, when $2^p + i = 2^p + x2^p = (1+1/3)2^p = 2^{p+2}/3$, or, in general, $2^k/3$. The nearest integers are $\lfloor 2^k/3 \rfloor$ and $\lceil 2^k/3 \rceil$, so we must find out which one minimises $\overline{B}_n^{\text{tms}} - \frac{1}{2}n\lg(\frac{3}{4}n)$, because we have $\frac{1}{2}n\lg n - (\frac{1}{2}\lg\frac{4}{3})n = \frac{1}{2}n\lg(\frac{3}{4}n)$. We start with the following theorems.

Lemma 1. *Integers of the form $4^p - 1$ are divisible by 3.*

Proof. Let $\text{Div}(p)$ be the proposition to prove. Trivially, $\text{Div}(1)$ is true. Let us assume $\text{Div}(p)$ and proceed to establish $\text{Div}(p+1)$. The former means that there exists an integer q such that $4^p - 1 = 3q$. Therefore, $4^{p+1} - 1 = 3(4q+1)$, which means that $\text{Div}(p+1)$ holds. The induction principle then entails that the lemma holds for all integers p. □

Theorem 2. We have $\overline{\mathcal{B}}^{\text{tms}}_{1+\phi_k} - \overline{\mathcal{B}}^{\text{tms}}_{\phi_k} = \lfloor k/2 \rfloor$, where $\phi_k := \lfloor 2^k/3 \rfloor$.

Proof. Let $\phi_k := \lfloor 2^k/3 \rfloor$. Either k is even or odd.

- If $k = 2m$, then $2^k/3 = (4^m - 1)/3 + 1/3$. Since $1/3 < 1$ and, by lemma 1, $(4^m - 1)/3$ is an integer, we have $2^k/3 = \lfloor 2^k/3 \rfloor + 1/3$ and

$$\lfloor 2^k/3 \rfloor = (4^m - 1)/3 = 4^{m-1} + 4^{m-2} + \cdots + 1$$
$$= 2^{2m-2} + 2^{2m-4} + \cdots + 1$$
$$= (1010\ldots 01)_2.$$

  Hence $\nu_{\phi_{2m}} = m$. We know that $\overline{\mathcal{B}}^{\text{tms}}_{m+1} = \overline{\mathcal{B}}^{\text{tms}}_{m} + \nu_m$, therefore $\overline{\mathcal{B}}^{\text{tms}}_{1+\phi_{2m}} - \overline{\mathcal{B}}^{\text{tms}}_{\phi_{2m}} = m$, or, equivalently, $\overline{\mathcal{B}}^{\text{tms}}_{1+\phi_k} - \overline{\mathcal{B}}^{\text{tms}}_{\phi_k} = \lfloor k/2 \rfloor$.

- If $k = 2m + 1$, then $2^k/3 = 2(4^m - 1)/3 + 2/3$. Since $2/3 < 1$ and, by lemma 1, $(4^m - 1)/3$ is an integer, we have

$$2^k/3 = \lfloor 2^k/3 \rfloor + 2/3 = \lceil 2^k/3 \rceil - 1/3$$

  and

$$\lfloor 2^k/3 \rfloor = 2(4^m - 1)/3$$
$$= 2^{2m-1} + 2^{2m-3} + \cdots + 2$$
$$= (1010\ldots 10)_2;$$

  so $\nu_{\phi_{2m+1}} = m$. From $\overline{\mathcal{B}}^{\text{tms}}_{m+1} = \overline{\mathcal{B}}^{\text{tms}}_{m} + \nu_m$, we can deduce that: $\overline{\mathcal{B}}^{\text{tms}}_{1+\phi_{2m+1}} - \overline{\mathcal{B}}^{\text{tms}}_{\phi_{2m+1}} = m$, or, equivalently, $\overline{\mathcal{B}}^{\text{tms}}_{1+\phi_k} - \overline{\mathcal{B}}^{\text{tms}}_{\phi_k} = \lfloor k/2 \rfloor$. □

Let $Q(x) := \frac{1}{2} x \lg(\frac{3}{4} x)$ and let us proceed to compare $\overline{\mathcal{B}}^{\text{tms}}_{\phi_k} - Q(\phi_k)$ with $\overline{\mathcal{B}}^{\text{tms}}_{1+\phi_k} - Q(1 + \phi_k)$ by making two cases depending upon the parity of k. If the former difference is smaller, then $p = \phi_k$ is the integer which minimises $\overline{\mathcal{B}}^{\text{tms}}_{p} - \frac{1}{2} p \lg(\frac{3}{4} p)$; otherwise, it is $p = 1 + \phi_k$.

- If $k = 2m + 2$, then $\phi_{2m+2} = 2^{2m} + \phi_{2m}$ (see proof of theorem 2). From equation (4.21), we draw

$$\overline{\mathcal{B}}^{\text{tms}}_{\phi_{2m+2}} = \overline{\mathcal{B}}^{\text{tms}}_{2^{2m}} + \overline{\mathcal{B}}^{\text{tms}}_{\phi_{2m}} + \phi_{2m} = \overline{\mathcal{B}}^{\text{tms}}_{\phi_{2m}} - m 4^m + \phi_{2m}.$$

  Summing both sides from $m = 0$ to $m = n - 1$ yields

$$\overline{\mathcal{B}}^{\text{tms}}_{\phi_{2n}} = \overline{\mathcal{B}}^{\text{tms}}_{\phi_0} + S_n + \sum_{m=0}^{n-1} \phi_{2m}, \text{ where } S_n := \sum_{m=0}^{n-1} m 4^m.$$

We need now to make out a closed form for S_n. We have

$$S_n + n4^n = \sum_{m=1}^{n} m4^m = \sum_{m=0}^{n-1} (m+1)4^{m+1} = 4 \cdot S_n + 4 \sum_{m=0}^{n-1} 4^m.$$

Since $\sum_{m=0}^{n-1} 4^m = (4^n - 1)/3$, we draw $9 \cdot S_n = (3n-4)4^n + 4$. On the other hand, $9 \sum_{m=0}^{n-1} \phi_{2m} = 4^n - 3n - 1$. Finally, remarking that $\phi_0 = 0$ and $\overline{B}_0^{\text{tms}} = 0$, we gather that

$$\overline{B}_{\phi_{2n}}^{\text{tms}} = (n-1)\phi_{2n}. \tag{4.26}$$

Let us now work out

$$Q(\phi_{2n}) = \frac{1}{2}\phi_{2n}(2(n-1)+\lg(1-1/4^n)) = \overline{B}_{\phi_{2n}}^{\text{tms}} + \frac{1}{2}\phi_{2n}\lg(1-1/4^n),$$

with an application of (4.26). If we let $f(x) := (1-x)\ln(1-1/x)$, then $\overline{B}_{\phi_{2n}}^{\text{tms}} - Q(\phi_{2n}) = f(4^n)/(6\ln 2)$. Elementary analysis shows that $3\ln(3/4) \leqslant f(x) < 1$, for $x \geqslant 4$, that is,

$$1 - \frac{1}{2}\lg 3 \leqslant \overline{B}_{\phi_{2n}}^{\text{tms}} - Q(\phi_{2n}) < \frac{1}{6\ln 2}, \text{ if } n \geqslant 1.$$

This means that

$$0.2075 < \overline{B}_{\phi_{2n}}^{\text{tms}} - Q(\phi_{2n}) < 0.2405. \tag{4.27}$$

Now, from theorem 2 and equation (4.26), we have

$$\overline{B}_{1+\phi_{2n}}^{\text{tms}} = (1 + \phi_{2n})(n-1) + 1. \tag{4.28}$$

Furthermore,

$$Q(1 + \phi_{2n}) = \frac{1}{2}(1 + \phi_{2n})(2(n-1) + \lg(1 + 1/2^{2n-1}))$$

$$= \overline{B}_{1+\phi_{2n}}^{\text{tms}} - 1 + \frac{1}{6}(4^n + 2)\lg(1 + 2/4^n),$$

the last step using (4.28). If $g(x) := 1 - \frac{1}{6}(x+2)\lg(1+2/4^n)$, then $\overline{B}_{1+\phi_{2n}}^{\text{tms}} - Q(1+\phi_{2n}) = g(4^n)$. Some elementary analysis entails the inequality $2 - \lg 3 \leqslant g(x) < 1 - 1/(3\ln 2)$, when $x \geqslant 4$, that is, $2 - \lg 3 \leqslant g(4^n) < 1 - 1/(3\ln 2)$, for $n \geqslant 1$. Approximately,

$$0.4150 < \overline{B}_{1+\phi_{2n}}^{\text{tms}} - Q(1 + \phi_{2n}) < 0.5192. \tag{4.29}$$

Comparing (4.27) and (4.29) shows that $p = \phi_{2n} = (1010\ldots 01)_2$ minimises $\overline{B}_p^{\text{tms}} - \frac{1}{2}p\lg(\frac{3}{4}p)$.

- If $k = 2m+1$, then $\phi_{2m+1} = 2^{2m-1}+\phi_{2m-1}$ (see proof of theorem 2). From equation (4.21), we draw

$$\overline{B}^{\text{tms}}_{\phi_{2m+1}} = \overline{B}^{\text{tms}}_{2^{2m-1}} + \overline{B}^{\text{tms}}_{\phi_{2m-1}} + \phi_{2m-1}$$

$$= \overline{B}^{\text{tms}}_{\phi_{2m-1}} - (2m-1)4^{m-1} + \phi_{2m-1}.$$

Summing both sides from $m = 1$ to $m = n - 1$ and multiplying by 9 yields $9\overline{B}^{\text{tms}}_{\phi_{2n+1}} = S_{n+1}/2 - 3(4^n - 1) + \sum_{m=0}^{n-1} \phi_{2m+1}$, which simplifies into

$$\overline{B}^{\text{tms}}_{\phi_{2n+1}} = \frac{1}{2}\phi_{2n+1}(2n-1). \tag{4.30}$$

We have

$$Q(\phi_{2n+1}) = \frac{1}{2}\phi_{2n+1}(2n-1+\lg(1-1/4^n))$$

$$= \overline{B}^{\text{tms}}_{\phi_{2n+1}} + \frac{1}{2}\phi_{2n+1}\lg(1-1/4^n),$$

where the last equality follows from (4.30). If, as we did for $Q(\phi_{2n})$, we let $f(x) := (1-x)\ln(1-1/x)$, then we have

$$\overline{B}^{\text{tms}}_{\phi_{2n+1}} - Q(\phi_{2n+1}) = f(4^n)/(3\ln 2).$$

We know $3\ln(3/4) \leqslant f(x) < 1$, for $x \geqslant 4$, therefore

$$\lg 3 - 2 \leqslant \overline{B}^{\text{tms}}_{\phi_{2n+1}} - Q(\phi_{2n+1}) < \frac{1}{3\ln 2}, \text{ if } n \geqslant 1.$$

Hence

$$0.4150 < \overline{B}^{\text{tms}}_{\phi_{2n+1}} - Q(\phi_{2n+1}) < 0.4809. \tag{4.31}$$

Now, from theorem 2 and equation (4.30), we deduce

$$\overline{B}^{\text{tms}}_{1+\phi_{2n+1}} = \frac{1}{2}(1+\phi_{2n+1})(2n-1) + \frac{1}{2}. \tag{4.32}$$

Moreover,

$$Q(1+\phi_{2n+1}) = \frac{1}{2}(1+\phi_{2n+1})(2n-1+\lg(1+1/2^{2n+1}))$$

$$= \overline{B}^{\text{tms}}_{1+\phi_{2n+1}} - \frac{1}{2} + \frac{1}{6}(1+2^{2n+1})\lg(1+1/2^{2n+1}),$$

from (4.32). We deduce $\overline{B}^{\text{tms}}_{1+\phi_{2n+1}} - Q(1+\phi_{2n+1}) = h(2^{2n+1})$, by letting $h(x) := \frac{1}{2} - \frac{1}{6}(1+x)\lg(1+1/x)$. Elementary analysis shows that $5 - 3\lg 3 \leqslant h(x) < 1/2 - 1/(6\ln 2)$, for $x \geqslant 8$, that is to say,

$$5 - 3\lg 3 \leqslant \overline{B}^{\text{tms}}_{1+\phi_{2n+1}} - Q(1+\phi_{2n+1}) < \frac{1}{2} - \frac{1}{6\ln 2}, \text{ if } n \geqslant 1.$$

So

$$0.2450 < \overline{B}^{\text{tms}}_{1+\phi_{2n+1}} - Q(1 + \phi_{2n+1}) < 0.2596. \qquad (4.33)$$

From (4.31) and (4.33), $p = 1 + \phi_{2m+1} = (1010\ldots 1011)_2$ minimises $\overline{B}^{\text{tms}}_p - \frac{1}{2}p \lg p$.

Finally, we conclude that the lower bound in (4.25) is tight if $n = 2$ (from the base case) and is otherwise the sharpest when $n = (1010\ldots 01)_2$ or $n = (1010\ldots 1011)_2$. As a whole, these values constitute the *Jacobsthal sequence*, defined as

$$J_0 = 0; \quad J_1 = 1; \quad J_{n+2} = J_{n+1} + 2J_n, \text{ for } n \geqslant 0. \qquad (4.34)$$

Let us use now the same inductive approach to find a good upper bound to $\overline{B}^{\text{tms}}_n$. In other words, we want to minimise the real constants a' and b' such that, for $n \geqslant 2$,

$$\overline{B}^{\text{tms}}_n \leqslant \frac{1}{2}n \lg n + a'n + b'.$$

The only difference with the search for the lower bound is that inequalities are reversed, so we want

$$\Phi(x) \leqslant a', \text{ where } \Phi(x) := \frac{1}{2}x \lg x - \frac{1}{2}(1 + x) \lg(1 + x) + x.$$

Here, we need to find the maximum of Φ on the closed interval $[0, 1]$. The two positive roots of Φ are 0 and 1, and Φ is negative between them (see equation (4.24)). Therefore $a'_{\min} := \max_{0 \leqslant x \leqslant 1} \Phi(x) = \Phi(0) = \Phi(1) = 0$. From the base case, we have $b'_{\min} = -2a_{\min} = 0$. Therefore, we have the bounds

$$\frac{1}{2}n \lg n - \left(\frac{1}{2}\lg\frac{4}{3}\right)n + \lg\frac{4}{3} \leqslant \overline{B}^{\text{tms}}_n \leqslant \frac{1}{2}n \lg n. \qquad (4.35)$$

The upper bound is clearly tight when $n = 2^p$ because of equation (4.13). It is also very obvious now that we have $\overline{B}^{\text{tms}}_n \sim \frac{1}{2}n \lg n$, but if we were only interested in this asymptotic result, Bush (1940) gave a very simple counting argument on the bits in FIGURE 4.8 on page 131. Delange (1975) investigated $\overline{B}^{\text{tms}}_n$ by means of advanced real analysis and showed that $\overline{B}^{\text{tms}}_n = \frac{1}{2}n \lg n + F_0(\lg n) \cdot n$, where F_0 is a continuous, nowhere differentiable function of period 1, and whose Fourier series shows the mean value to be approximately -0.145599.

Maximum cost   The maximum number of comparisons satisfies

$$\overline{\mathcal{W}}_0^{\text{tms}} = \overline{\mathcal{W}}_1^{\text{tms}} = 0, \qquad \overline{\mathcal{W}}_n^{\text{tms}} = \overline{\mathcal{W}}_{\lfloor n/2 \rfloor}^{\text{tms}} + \overline{\mathcal{W}}_{\lceil n/2 \rceil}^{\text{tms}} + \overline{\mathcal{W}}_{\lfloor n/2 \rfloor, \lceil n/2 \rceil}^{\text{mrg}}.$$

Equation (4.4) on page 121 yields $\overline{\mathcal{W}}_n^{\text{tms}} = \overline{\mathcal{W}}_{\lfloor n/2 \rfloor}^{\text{tms}} + \overline{\mathcal{W}}_{\lceil n/2 \rceil}^{\text{tms}} + n - 1$ and

$$\overline{\mathcal{W}}_0^{\text{tms}} = \overline{\mathcal{W}}_1^{\text{tms}} = 0; \quad \overline{\mathcal{W}}_{2p}^{\text{tms}} = 2\overline{\mathcal{W}}_p^{\text{tms}} + 2p - 1, \quad \overline{\mathcal{W}}_{2p+1}^{\text{tms}} = \overline{\mathcal{W}}_p^{\text{tms}} + \overline{\mathcal{W}}_{p+1}^{\text{tms}} + 2p.$$

Let the difference of two successive terms be $\Delta_n := \mathcal{W}_{n+1} - \mathcal{W}_n$. If we know Δ_n, we know $\mathcal{W}_n$ because

$$\sum_{k=1}^{n-1} \Delta_k = \sum_{k=1}^{n-1} \mathcal{W}_{k+1} - \sum_{k=1}^{n-1} \mathcal{W}_k = \mathcal{W}_n - \mathcal{W}_1 = \mathcal{W}_n.$$

We remark that

- if $n = 2p$, then $\Delta_{2p} = \Delta_p + 1$,

- else $n = 2p + 1$ and $\mathcal{W}_{2p+2} = 2 \cdot \mathcal{W}_{p+1} + 2p + 1$, so $\Delta_{2p+1} = \Delta_p + 1$.

In summary, $\Delta_0 = 0$ and $\Delta_n = \Delta_{\lfloor n/2 \rfloor} + 1$. If we start unravelling the recurrence, we get $\Delta_n = \Delta_{\lfloor \lfloor n/2 \rfloor / 2 \rfloor} + 2$, so we must simplify $\lfloor \lfloor \lfloor \ldots \rfloor / 2 \rfloor / 2 \rfloor$.

Theorem 3 (Floors and Fractions). *Let x be a real number and q a natural number. Then $\lfloor \lfloor x \rfloor / q \rfloor = \lfloor x/q \rfloor$.*

Proof. The equality is equivalent to the conjunction of the two complementary inequalities $\lfloor \lfloor x \rfloor / q \rfloor \leqslant \lfloor x/q \rfloor$ and $\lfloor x/q \rfloor \leqslant \lfloor \lfloor x \rfloor / q \rfloor$. The former is straightforward because it is a consequence of $\lfloor x \rfloor \leqslant x$. In the latter, because both sides of the inequality are integers, $\lfloor x/q \rfloor \leqslant \lfloor \lfloor x \rfloor / q \rfloor$ is equivalent to stating that $p \leqslant \lfloor x/q \rfloor \Rightarrow p \leqslant \lfloor \lfloor x \rfloor / q \rfloor$, for any integer p. An obvious lemma is that if i is an integer and y a real number, $i \leqslant \lfloor y \rfloor \Leftrightarrow i \leqslant y$, so the original inequality is equivalent to $p \leqslant x/q \Rightarrow p \leqslant \lfloor x \rfloor / q$, which is trivially equivalent to $pq \leqslant x \Rightarrow pq \leqslant \lfloor x \rfloor$. Since pq is an integer, this implication is true from the same lemma. $\qquad \square$

Using theorem 3, we deduce $\Delta_n = m$, with m being the smallest natural number such that $\lfloor n/2^m \rfloor = 0$. In other words, m is the number of bits in the binary notation of n, which is found in equation (1.6) to be $\Delta_n = \lfloor \lg n \rfloor + 1$. Since we already know that $\mathcal{W}_n = \sum_{k=1}^{n-1} \Delta_k$, we conclude, with (1.4), that

$$\mathcal{W}_n = \sum_{k=1}^{n-1} (\lfloor \lg k \rfloor + 1). \tag{4.36}$$

Whilst the minimum cost is the number of 1-bits up to $n-1$, we find now that the maximum cost is the total number of bits up to $n-1$. Informally, this leads us to bet that $\overline{\mathcal{W}}_n^{\text{tms}} \sim 2 \cdot \overline{\mathcal{B}}_n^{\text{tms}} \sim n \lg n$, since we would expect the number of 0-bits and 1-bits to be the same in average. Consider again the bit table in FIGURE 4.8 on page 131. The greatest power of 2 smaller than n is $2^{\lfloor \lg n \rfloor}$ because it is the binary number $(10\ldots0)_2$ having the same number of bits as n; it thus appears in the same section of the table as n. The trick consists in counting the bits in *columns*, from top to bottom, and leftwards. In the rightmost column, we find n bits. In the second column, from the right, we find $n-2^1+1$ bits. The third from the right contains $n-2^2+1$ bits etc. until the leftmost column containing $n-2^{\lfloor \lg n \rfloor}+1$ bits. The total number of bits in the table is

$$\sum_{k=1}^{n}(\lfloor \lg k \rfloor + 1) = \sum_{k=0}^{\lfloor \lg n \rfloor}(n - 2^k + 1) = (n+1)(\lfloor \lg n \rfloor + 1) - 2^{\lfloor \lg n \rfloor + 1} + 1.$$

Let express the binary representation of n: $n := (b_{m-1}\ldots b_0)_2$, then $2^{m-1} \leqslant n \leqslant 2^m - 1$ and $2^{m-1} < 2^{m-1} + 1 \leqslant n+1 \leqslant 2^m$, so we have $m - 1 < \lg(n+1) \leqslant m$, that is, $m = \lceil \lg(n+1) \rceil$, which, with equation (1.6) on page 11, establishes that

$$1 + \lfloor \lg n \rfloor = \lceil \lg(n+1) \rceil.$$

As a consequence, equation (4.36) can be rewritten as

$$\overline{\mathcal{W}}_0^{\text{tms}} = \overline{\mathcal{W}}_1^{\text{tms}} = 0, \qquad \overline{\mathcal{W}}_n^{\text{tms}} = n \lceil \lg n \rceil - 2^{\lceil \lg n \rceil} + 1. \qquad (4.37)$$

This equation is subtler than it seems, due to the periodicity hidden in $2^{\lceil \lg n \rceil}$. Depending on whether $n = 2^p$ or not, two cases arise:

- if $n = 2^p$, then $\overline{\mathcal{W}}_n^{\text{tms}} = n \lg n - n + 1$;
- otherwise, we have $\lceil \lg n \rceil = \lfloor \lg n \rfloor + 1 = \lg n - \{\lg n\} + 1$ and then $\overline{\mathcal{W}}_n^{\text{tms}} = n \lg n + \theta(1 - \{\lg n\}) \cdot n + 1$, with $\theta(x) := x - 2^x$ and $\{x\} := x - \lfloor x \rfloor$ is the *fractional part* of x ($0 \leqslant \{x\} < 1$). The derivative $\theta'(x) = 1 - 2^x \ln 2$ has one root: $\theta'(x_0) = 0$, that is $x_0 = -\lg \ln 2$, and it is positive before x_0, and negative after. Concordantly, $\max_{0 < x \leqslant 1} \theta(x) = \theta(x_0) = -(1 + \ln \ln 2)/\ln 2 \simeq -0.9139$, and $\min_{0 < x \leqslant 1} \theta(x) = \theta(1) = -1$. By injectivity, $\theta(1) = \theta(1 - \{\lg n\})$ implies $\{\lg n\} = 0$, that is, $n = 2^p$ (first case).

Hence $\overline{\mathcal{W}}_n^{\text{tms}} = n \lg n + A(\lg n) \cdot n + 1$, where $A(x) := 1 - \{x\} - 2^{1-\{x\}}$ is a periodic function, since $A(x) = A(\{x\})$, such that $-1 \leqslant A(x) < -0.91$. Further analysis of $A(x)$ requires Fourier series or complex analysis; its mean value is about -0.942695. Read Flajolet and Golin (1994), as well as Panny and Prodinger (1995).

$$n \lg n - n + 1 \leqslant \overline{\mathcal{W}}_n^{\text{tms}} < n \lg n - 0.91n + 1. \tag{4.38}$$

The lower bound is attained when $n = 2^p$. The upper bound is most accurate when $\{\lg n\} = 1 + \lg \ln 2$, that is, when n is the nearest integer to $2^p \ln 2$ (take the binary expansion of $\ln 2$, shift the point p times to the right and round). Obviously, $\overline{\mathcal{W}}_n^{\text{tms}} \sim n \lg n$.

Average cost   Let $\overline{\mathcal{A}}_n^{\text{tms}}$ be the average number of comparisons to sort n keys top-down. All permutations of the input stack being equally likely, equation (4.17) becomes

$$\overline{\mathcal{A}}_0^{\text{tms}} = \overline{\mathcal{A}}_1^{\text{tms}} = 0, \qquad \overline{\mathcal{A}}_n^{\text{tms}} = \overline{\mathcal{A}}_{\lfloor n/2 \rfloor}^{\text{tms}} + \overline{\mathcal{A}}_{\lceil n/2 \rceil}^{\text{tms}} + \overline{\mathcal{A}}_{\lfloor n/2 \rfloor, \lceil n/2 \rceil}^{\text{mrg}},$$

which, with equation (4.9), in turn implies

$$\overline{\mathcal{A}}_n^{\text{tms}} = \overline{\mathcal{A}}_{\lfloor n/2 \rfloor}^{\text{tms}} + \overline{\mathcal{A}}_{\lceil n/2 \rceil}^{\text{tms}} + n - \frac{\lfloor n/2 \rfloor}{\lceil n/2 \rceil + 1} - \frac{\lceil n/2 \rceil}{\lfloor n/2 \rfloor + 1}.$$

If we proceed as we did for the extremal costs, we get

$$\overline{\mathcal{A}}_{2p}^{\text{tms}} = 2 \cdot \overline{\mathcal{A}}_p^{\text{tms}} + 2p - 2 + \frac{2}{p+1}, \quad \overline{\mathcal{A}}_{2p+1}^{\text{tms}} = \overline{\mathcal{A}}_p^{\text{tms}} + \overline{\mathcal{A}}_{p+1}^{\text{tms}} + 2p - 1 + \frac{2}{p+2}.$$

These recurrences are a bit tricky. Setting $\Delta_n := \overline{\mathcal{A}}_{n+1}^{\text{tms}} - \overline{\mathcal{A}}_n^{\text{tms}}$ yields

$$\Delta_{2p+1} = \Delta_{2p} + \frac{2}{(p+1)(p+2)}.$$

Contrary to the difference equations derived for the extremal costs, this one is not helpful, so we should try an inductive approach, as we did for finding bounds on $\overline{\mathcal{B}}_n^{\text{tms}}$. Inequations (4.16) on page 130 are equivalent to $n \lg n - \alpha n + \alpha < \overline{\mathcal{A}}_n^{\text{tms}} < n \lg n - \alpha n + 2$, where $n = 2^p$, and this suggests us to also look for bounds of the form $n \lg n + an + b$ when $n \neq 2^p$.

   Let us start with the lower bound and set to maximise the real constants a and b in

$$\mathsf{H}(n) \colon n \lg n + an + b \leqslant \overline{\mathcal{A}}_n^{\text{tms}}, \text{ for } n \geqslant 2.$$

Since $\mathsf{H}(2p)$ depends on $\mathsf{H}(p)$, and $\mathsf{H}(2p+1)$ depends on $\mathsf{H}(p)$ and $\mathsf{H}(p+1)$, the property $\mathsf{H}(n)$, for any $n > 1$, transitively depends on $\mathsf{H}(2)$ alone, because we are iterating divisions by 2. If we write $\mathsf{H}(n) \rightsquigarrow \mathsf{H}(m)$ to mean

'H(n) depends on H(m)', we have, for example, $H(2^3) \rightsquigarrow H(2^2) \rightsquigarrow H(2^1)$; $H(7) \rightsquigarrow H(3) \rightsquigarrow H(2)$ and $H(7) \rightsquigarrow H(4) \rightsquigarrow H(2)$. $H(2)$ is equivalent to

$$2a + b + 1 \leqslant 0. \tag{4.39}$$

Because the definition of $\overline{\mathcal{A}}_n^{\mathrm{tms}}$ depends on the parity of n, the inductive step will be twofold. Let us assume H(m) for $m < 2p$, in particular, we suppose H(p), which, with the expression of $\overline{\mathcal{A}}_{2p}^{\mathrm{tms}}$ above, entails

$$(2p \lg p + 2ap + 2b) + 2p - 2 + \frac{2}{p+1} \leqslant \overline{\mathcal{A}}_{2p}^{\mathrm{tms}}.$$

We want H($2p$): $2p \lg(2p) + 2ap + b = 2p \lg p + 2ap + 2p + b \leqslant \overline{\mathcal{A}}_{2p}^{\mathrm{tms}}$, which holds if the following condition does:

$$2p \lg p + 2ap + 2p + b \leqslant 2p \lg p + 2ap + 2b + 2p - 2 + \frac{2}{p+1},$$

which is equivalent to

$$2 - \frac{2}{p+1} = \frac{2p}{p+1} \leqslant b.$$

Let $\Phi(p) := 2p/(p+1)$. This function is strictly increasing for $p > 0$ and $\Phi(p) \to 2^-$, as $p \to +\infty$.

The other inductive step deals with the odd values of n. We assume H(m) for all $m < 2p + 1$, in particular, we suppose H(p) and H($p+1$), which, with the expression of $\overline{\mathcal{A}}_{2p+1}^{\mathrm{tms}}$ above, implies

$$(p \lg p + ap + b) + ((p+1) \lg(p+1) + a(p+1) + b) + 2p - 1 + \frac{2}{p+2} \leqslant \overline{\mathcal{A}}_{2p+1}^{\mathrm{tms}},$$

which may be simplified slightly into

$$p \lg p + (p+1) \lg(p+1) + a(2p+1) + 2b + 2p - 1 + \frac{2}{p+2} \leqslant \overline{\mathcal{A}}_{2p+1}^{\mathrm{tms}}.$$

We want to prove H($2p + 1$): $(2p+1) \lg(2p+1) + a(2p+1) + b \leqslant \mathcal{A}_{2p+1}$, which is thus implied by

$$(2p+1) \lg(2p+1) \leqslant p \lg p + (p+1) \lg(p+1) + b + 2p - 1 + \frac{2}{p+2}. \tag{4.40}$$

Let $\Psi(p) := (2p+1) \lg(2p+1) - (p+1) \lg(p+1) - p \lg p - 2p + 1 - 2/(p+2)$. Then (4.40) is equivalent to $\Psi(p) \leqslant b$. Furthermore,

$$\frac{d\Psi}{dp}(p) = \frac{2}{(p+2)^2} + \lg\left(1 + \frac{1}{4p(p+1)}\right).$$

Clearly, $d\Psi/dp > 0$, for all $p > 0$, so $\Psi(p)$ is strictly increasing for $p > 0$. Let us find $\lim_{p \to +\infty} \Psi(p)$ by rewriting $\Psi(p)$ as follows:

$$\Psi(p) = 2 - \frac{2}{p+2} + (2p+1)\lg(p+1/2) - (p+1)\lg(p+1) - p\lg p$$

$$= 2 - \frac{2}{p+2} + p\left(\lg(p+1/2)^2 - \lg(p+1) - \lg p\right) + \lg(p+1/2)$$

$$\quad - \lg(p+1)$$

$$= 2 - \frac{2}{p+2} + p\lg\left(1 + \frac{1}{4p(p+1)}\right) + \lg\frac{p+1/2}{p+1}.$$

The limit of $x\ln(1+1/x^2)$ as $x \to +\infty$ can be found by changing x into $1/y$ and considering the limit as $y \to 0^+$, which is shown by l'Hôpital's rule to be 0. This result can be extended to apply to the large term in $\Psi(p)$ and, since all the other variable terms converge to 0, we can conclude that $\Psi(p) \to 2^-$, as $p \to +\infty$.

Because we need to satisfy the conditions $\Psi(p) \leqslant b$ and $\Phi(p) \leqslant b$ for both inductive steps to hold, we have to compare $\Psi(p)$ and $\Phi(p)$, when p is a natural number: we have $\Phi(1) < \Psi(1)$ and $\Phi(2) < \Psi(2)$, but also $\Psi(p) < \Phi(p)$, if $p \geqslant 3$. Therefore, for b not to depend on p, we need it to be greater than 2, the smallest upper bound of Φ and Ψ. Inequality (4.39) means that we need to minimise b in order to maximise a (which is the priority), so we settle for the limit: $b_{\min} = 2$, and the same inequality entails $a \leqslant -3/2$, hence $a_{\max} = -3/2$. The principle of complete induction finally establishes that, for $n \geqslant 2$,

$$n\lg n - \frac{3}{2}n + 2 < \overline{\mathcal{A}}_n^{\mathsf{tms}}. \tag{4.41}$$

This bound is not very good, but it was easy to obtain. We may recall the lower bound when $n = 2^p$, in (4.16) on page 130: $n\lg n - \alpha n + \alpha < \overline{\mathcal{A}}_n^{\mathsf{tms}}$, where $\alpha \simeq 1.264499$. In fact, Flajolet and Golin (1994) proved

$$n\lg n - \alpha n < \overline{\mathcal{A}}_n^{\mathsf{tms}}. \tag{4.42}$$

Asymptotically, that bound is, up to the linear term, the same as for the case $n = 2^p$. Our inductive method cannot reach this nice result because it yields sufficient conditions that are too strong, in particular, we found no obvious way to get the decomposition $\overline{\mathcal{A}}_{2^p+i}^{\mathsf{tms}} = \overline{\mathcal{A}}_{2^p}^{\mathsf{tms}} + \overline{\mathcal{A}}_i^{\mathsf{tms}} + \dots$

Now, let us find the smallest real constants a' and b' such that for $n \geqslant 2$, $\overline{\mathcal{A}}_n^{\mathsf{tms}} \leqslant n\lg n + a'n + b'$. The base case of $H(n)$ in (4.39) is here reversed: $2a' + b' + 1 \geqslant 0$. Hence, in order to minimise a', we need to maximise b'. Furthermore, the conditions on b' from the inductive steps are reversed as well with respect to b: $b' \leqslant \Phi(p)$ and $b' \leqslant \Psi(p)$. The base case is $\mathsf{H}(2)$, that is, $p = 1$, and we saw earlier that $\Phi(1) \leqslant \Psi(1)$, thus we must have $b' \leqslant \Phi(1) = 1$. The maximum value is thus $b'_{\max} = 1$. Finally, this implies that $a' \geqslant -1$, thus $a'_{\min} = -1$.

Gathering the bounds, we hence established that

$$n \lg n - \frac{3}{2}n + 2 < \overline{\mathcal{A}}_n^{\mathsf{tms}} < n \lg n - n + 1.$$

Trivially, we have $\overline{\mathcal{A}}_n^{\mathsf{tms}} \sim n \lg n \sim \overline{\mathcal{W}}_n^{\mathsf{tms}} \sim 2 \cdot \overline{\mathcal{B}}_n^{\mathsf{tms}}$. Flajolet and Golin (1994) proved, using complex analysis the following very strong result:

$$\overline{\mathcal{A}}_n^{\mathsf{tms}} = n \lg n + B(\lg n) \cdot n + \mathcal{O}(1),$$

where B is continuous, non-differentiable, periodic with period 1, of mean value -1.2481520. The notation $\mathcal{O}(1)$ is an instance of Bachmann's notation for an unknown positive constant. The maximum value of $B(x)$ is approximately -1.24075, so

$$\overline{\mathcal{A}}_n^{\mathsf{tms}} = n \lg n - (1.25 \pm 0.01) \cdot n + \mathcal{O}(1).$$

4.4 Bottom-up merge sort

Instead of cutting a stack of n keys in two halves, we could split into $2^{\lceil \lg n \rceil - 1}$ and $n - 2^{\lceil \lg n \rceil - 1}$ keys, where the first number represents the highest power of 2 strictly smaller than n. For instance, if $n = 11 = 2^3 + 2^1 + 2^0$, we would split into $2^3 = 8$ and $2^1 + 2^0 = 3$. Of course, if $n = 2^p$, this strategy, called *bottom-up*, coincides with that of top-down merge sort, which, in terms of cost, is expressed as $\overline{\mathcal{C}}_{2^p}^{\mathsf{bms}} = \overline{\mathcal{C}}_{2^p}^{\mathsf{tms}} = \mathcal{C}_p^{\bowtie}$, where bms/1 implements *bottom-up merge sort*. The difference between top-down and bottom-up merge sort can be easily seen in the FIGURE 4.10. In all generality,

$$\overline{\mathcal{C}}_0^{\mathsf{bms}} = \overline{\mathcal{C}}_1^{\mathsf{bms}} = 0, \quad \overline{\mathcal{C}}_n^{\mathsf{bms}} = \overline{\mathcal{C}}_{2^{\lceil \lg n \rceil - 1}}^{\mathsf{bms}} + \overline{\mathcal{C}}_{n - 2^{\lceil \lg n \rceil - 1}}^{\mathsf{bms}} + \overline{\mathcal{C}}_{2^{\lceil \lg n \rceil - 1}, n - 2^{\lceil \lg n \rceil - 1}}^{\mathsf{mrg}}.$$

$$(4.43)$$

FIGURE 4.11a on the next page shows the merge tree of seven keys being sorted in that fashion. Note how the bottommost singleton $[4]$ is merged with $[2, 6]$, a stack twice as long. The imbalance in length is further propagated upwards. The general case is better suggested by retaining at each node only the length of the associated stack, as shown in FIGURE 4.11b on the following page.

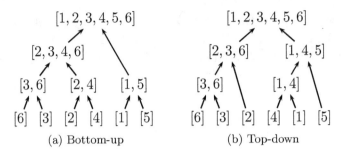

Figure 4.10: Comparing merge sorts of $[6, 3, 2, 4, 1, 5]$

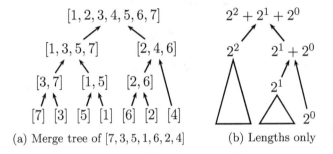

Figure 4.11: Sorting seven keys

Minimum cost   Let $\overline{\mathcal{B}}_n^{\text{bms}}$ be the minimum cost for sorting n keys, bottom-up. Let $n = 2^p + i$, with $0 < i < 2^p$. Then, from equation (4.43) and (4.3) on page 121, we deduce

$$\overline{\mathcal{B}}_{2^p+i}^{\text{bms}} = \overline{\mathcal{B}}_{2^p}^{\text{bms}} + \overline{\mathcal{B}}_i^{\text{bms}} + i,$$

which we recognise as an instance of the following functional equations: $f(0) = f(1) = 0$, $f(2) = 1$ and $f(2^p + i) = f(2^p) + f(i) + i$, where $f = \overline{\mathcal{B}}^{\text{tms}}$ as seen in equation (4.21) on page 132. Therefore,

$$\overline{\mathcal{B}}_n^{\text{bms}} = \overline{\mathcal{B}}_n^{\text{tms}} = \sum_{k=0}^{n-1} \nu_k. \qquad (4.44)$$

We can thus reuse the bounds on $\overline{\mathcal{B}}_n^{\text{tms}}$:

$$\frac{1}{2} n \lg n - \left(\frac{1}{2} \lg \frac{4}{3} \right) n + \lg \frac{4}{3} \leqslant \overline{\mathcal{B}}_n^{\text{bms}} \leqslant \frac{1}{2} n \lg n. \qquad (4.45)$$

The lower bound is tight for $n = 2$ and most accurate when n is a Jacobsthal number (see equations (4.34) on page 137). The upper bound is tight when $n = 2^p$.

Maximum cost Let $\overline{W}_n^{\text{bms}}$ be the maximum cost for sorting n keys, bottom-up. Let $n = 2^p + i$, with $0 < i < 2^p$. Then, from equation (4.43), on page 143, and (4.4) on page 121, we deduce

$$\overline{W}_{2^p+i}^{\text{bms}} = \overline{W}_{2^p}^{\text{bms}} + \overline{W}_i^{\text{bms}} + 2^p + i - 1. \tag{4.46}$$

Let us search a lower bound of $\overline{W}_n^{\text{bms}}$ by induction based on that equation. Let us find the greatest real constants a and b such that, for $n \geqslant 2$,

$$n \lg n + an + b \leqslant \overline{W}_n^{\text{bms}}.$$

The base case is $n = 2$, that is, $b \leqslant -2a - 1$. Let us assume the bound holds for $n = i$ and let us recall equation (4.14) on page 129, which here takes the guise of $\overline{W}_{2^p}^{\text{bms}} = p2^p - 2^p + 1$. Then (4.46) yields

$$(p2^p - 2^p + 1) + (i \lg i + ai + b) + 2^p + i - 1 \leqslant \overline{W}_{2^p+i}^{\text{bms}},$$

which is equivalent to $p2^p + i \lg i + i + ai + b \leqslant \overline{W}_{2^p+i}^{\text{bms}}$. We want to prove the bound holds for $n = 2^p + i$, that is, $(2^p + i) \lg(2^p + i) + a(2^p + i) + b \leqslant \overline{W}_{2^p+i}^{\text{bms}}$. Clearly, this is true if the following stronger constraint holds:

$$(2^p + i) \lg(2^p + i) + a(2^p + i) + b \leqslant p2^p + i \lg i + i + ai + b.$$

It is equivalent to $a2^p \leqslant p2^p - (2^p + i) \lg(2^p + i) + i \lg i + i$. Let us extend i over the real numbers by defining $i = x2^p$, where x is a real number such that $0 < x \leqslant 1$. Then, the running inequality is equivalent to

$$a \leqslant \Phi(x), \text{ where } \Phi(x) := x \lg x - (1 + x) \lg(1 + x) + x.$$

The function Φ can be continuously extended at 0, as $\lim_{x \to 0} x \lg x = 0$, and it is differentiable on the closed interval $[0, 1]$:

$$\frac{d\Phi}{dx} = \lg \frac{2x}{x + 1}.$$

The root of $d\Phi/dx = 0$ is 1, the derivative is negative before, and positive after; so Φ decreases until $x = 1$: $a_{\max} := \min_{0 \leqslant x \leqslant 1} \Phi(x) = \Phi(1) = -1$. From the base case, $b_{\max} := -2a_{\max} - 1 = 1$. Therefore, we have

$$n \lg n - n + 1 \leqslant \overline{W}_n^{\text{bms}}.$$

The bound is tight when $x = 1$, that is, $i = 2^p$, hence $n = 2^{p+1}$.

Let us find the smallest real constants a' and b' such that, for $n \geqslant 2$,

$$\overline{W}_n^{\text{bms}} \leqslant n \lg n + a'n + b'.$$

The difference with the lower bound is that the inequalities are reversed
and we minimise the unknowns, instead of maximising them. Thus, the
base case here is $b' \geqslant -2a-1$ and the condition for induction is $a' \geqslant \Phi(x)$.
We know the behaviour of Φ, so $a'_{min} := \max_{0 \leqslant x \leqslant 1} \Phi(x) = \Phi(0) = 0$, and
$b'_{min} := -2a'_{min} - 1 = -1$. As a conclusion,

$$n \lg n - n + 1 \leqslant \overline{\mathcal{W}}_n^{\text{bms}} < n \lg n - 1. \tag{4.47}$$

Because $\Phi(x)$ was extended at $x = 0$, the upper bound is best approched
when $i = 1$, the smallest possible integer value, that is, when $n = 2^p + 1$
(the most unbalanced merger: stacks of size 2^p and 1). A deeper study
by Panny and Prodinger (1995), based on Fourier analysis, confirms that
the linear terms of these bounds cannot be improved and shows the mean
value of the coefficient of the linear term to be, approximately, -0.70057.

Alternative expression   While we already bounded $\overline{\mathcal{W}}_n^{\text{bms}}$ tightly, we
may learn something more about it by expressing it differently from
its definition, in a way more suitable to elementary computations as
well. In all generality, let us set $n := 2^{e_r} + \cdots + 2^{e_1} + 2^{e_0} > 0$, with
$e_r > \cdots > e_1 > e_0 \geqslant 0$ and $r \geqslant 0$. We used this decomposition in
equation (1.6) on page 11. Let us con-
sider in FIGURE 4.12 the tree of all the
mergers when we only retain the stacks
lengths. The triangles are subtrees made
of *balanced mergers*, that is, mergers performed on stacks of same length, for which
we already found the number of comparisons. The lengths of the *unbalanced mergers* are found in the nodes from the root
$2^{e_r} + \cdots + 2^{e_0}$ down to $2^{e_1} + 2^{e_0}$. In FIGURE 4.13 on the next page are

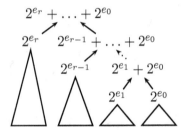

Figure 4.12: $\sum_{j=0}^{r} 2^{e_j}$ keys

shown the maximum-cost trees for n even and $n + 1$. The boxed expressions are not found in the opposite tree, therefore, the sum in each tree
of the non-boxed terms is identical.

- *If n is even*, in FIGURE 4.13a on the facing page, this sum is $\overline{\mathcal{W}}_n^{\text{bms}} -$
  r. It equals $\overline{\mathcal{W}}_{n+1}^{\text{bms}} - 2^{e_0} - \overline{\mathcal{W}}_{2^0}^{\text{bms}}$ in FIGURE 4.13b on the next page.
  Equating both counts yields

$$\overline{\mathcal{W}}_n^{\text{bms}} - r = \overline{\mathcal{W}}_{n+1}^{\text{bms}} - 2^{e_0} - \overline{\mathcal{W}}_{2^0}^{\text{bms}}. \tag{4.48}$$

Let us explicit that e_0 is a function of n (it is the highest power of 2
dividing n): $e_0 := \rho_n$. Furthermore, we already know $\nu_n = r + 1$
and $\overline{\mathcal{W}}_1^{\text{bms}} = 0$. Setting $n = 2k$ in equation (4.48) is equivalent to

$$\overline{\mathcal{W}}_{2k+1}^{\text{bms}} = \overline{\mathcal{W}}_{2k}^{\text{bms}} + 2^{\rho_{2k}} + \nu_{2k} - 1. \tag{4.49}$$

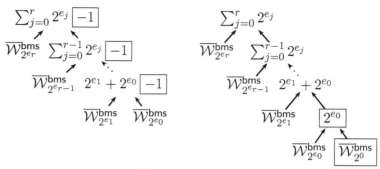

(a) The sum of the nodes is $\overline{\mathcal{W}}_n^{\text{bms}}$ (b) The sum of the nodes is $\overline{\mathcal{W}}_{n+1}^{\text{bms}}$

Figure 4.13: Maximum-cost trees for n even and $n + 1$

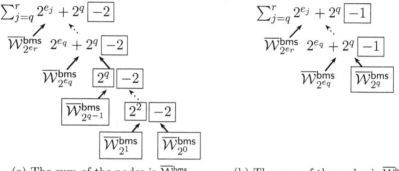

(a) The sum of the nodes is $\overline{\mathcal{W}}_n^{\text{bms}}$ (b) The sum of the nodes is $\overline{\mathcal{W}}_{n+1}^{\text{bms}}$

Figure 4.14: Maximum-cost trees for n odd and $n + 1$

The function ρ_n is the *ruler function* (Graham et al., 1994, Knuth, 2011), which satisfies, for $n > 0$, the recurrences

$$\rho_1 = 0, \qquad \rho_{2n} = \rho_n + 1, \qquad \rho_{2n+1} = 0, \qquad (4.50)$$

which are easily guessed from the binary notation of n as ρ_n simply counts the number of trailing zeros. This enables us to slightly simplify equation (4.49) into

$$\overline{\mathcal{W}}_{2k+1}^{\text{bms}} = \overline{\mathcal{W}}_{2k}^{\text{bms}} + 2 \cdot 2^{\rho_k} + \nu_k - 1. \qquad (4.51)$$

- *If n is odd,* we make FIGURE 4.14a, where the non-boxed expressions sum

$$\overline{\mathcal{W}}_n^{\text{bms}} - \sum_{k=0}^{q-1} \overline{\mathcal{W}}_{2k}^{\text{bms}} - \sum_{k=2}^{q} 2^k + 2((q-1) + (r - q + 1))$$

$$= \overline{\mathcal{W}}_n^{\mathsf{bms}} - \sum_{k=0}^{q-1}((k-1)2^k + 1) - \sum_{k=2}^{q} 2^k + 2r$$

$$= \overline{\mathcal{W}}_n^{\mathsf{bms}} - (q-1)2^q - q + 2r + 1,$$

using equation (4.14) and $\sum_{k=0}^{q-1} k2^k = (q-2)2^q + 2$. Indeed, let $S_q := \sum_{k=0}^{q-1} k2^{k-1}$. Then

$$S_q + q2^{q-1} = \sum_{k=1}^{q} k2^{k-1} = \sum_{k=0}^{q-1}(k+1)2^k$$

$$= \sum_{k=0}^{q-1} k2^k + \sum_{k=0}^{q-1} 2^k = 2 \cdot S_{q-1} + 2^q - 1,$$

hence

$$S_q = \sum_{k=1}^{q-1} k2^{k-1} = (q-2)2^{q-1} + 1. \tag{4.52}$$

The same sum in FIGURE 4.14b equals

$$\overline{\mathcal{W}}_{n+1}^{\mathsf{bms}} - \overline{\mathcal{W}}_{2^q}^{\mathsf{bms}} + (r - q + 1) = \overline{\mathcal{W}}_{n+1}^{\mathsf{bms}} - (q-1)2^q - q + r.$$

Equating the two quantities and simplifying yields

$$\overline{\mathcal{W}}_{n+1}^{\mathsf{bms}} = \overline{\mathcal{W}}_n^{\mathsf{bms}} + r + 1 = \overline{\mathcal{W}}_n^{\mathsf{bms}} + \nu_n.$$

Recalling the recurrences (4.18) on page 131 and setting $n = 2k-1$, this equation is simplified into

$$\overline{\mathcal{W}}_{2k}^{\mathsf{bms}} = \overline{\mathcal{W}}_{2k-1}^{\mathsf{bms}} + \nu_{k-1} + 1. \tag{4.53}$$

From equations (4.53) and (4.51), we deduce

$$\overline{\mathcal{W}}_{2k+1}^{\mathsf{bms}} = \overline{\mathcal{W}}_{2k-1}^{\mathsf{bms}} + 2 \cdot 2^{\rho_k} + \nu_{k-1} + \nu_k, \quad \overline{\mathcal{W}}_{2k+2}^{\mathsf{bms}} = \overline{\mathcal{W}}_{2k}^{\mathsf{bms}} + 2 \cdot 2^{\rho_k} + 2\nu_k.$$

These equations allow us to compute the values of $\overline{\mathcal{W}}_n^{\mathsf{bms}}$ only with elementary operations. Furthermore, summing on all sides yields

$$\overline{\mathcal{W}}_{2p+1}^{\mathsf{bms}} = \overline{\mathcal{W}}_1^{\mathsf{bms}} + 2\sum_{k=1}^{p} 2^{\rho_k} + \sum_{k=1}^{p} \nu_{k-1} + \sum_{k=1}^{p} \nu_k = 2\sum_{k=1}^{p} 2^{\rho_k} + 2\sum_{k=1}^{p-1} \nu_k + \nu_p. \tag{4.54}$$

$$\overline{\mathcal{W}}_{2p}^{\mathsf{bms}} = \overline{\mathcal{W}}_2^{\mathsf{bms}} + 2\sum_{k=1}^{p-1} 2^{\rho_k} + 2\sum_{k=1}^{p-1} \nu_k = 1 + 2\sum_{k=1}^{p-1} 2^{\rho_k} + 2\sum_{k=1}^{p-1} \nu_k. \tag{4.55}$$

These expressions involve two interesting number-theoretic functions, $\sum_{k=1}^{p-1} 2^{\rho_k}$ and $\sum_{k=1}^{p-1} \nu_k$, the latter being $\overline{\mathcal{B}}_p^{\mathsf{bms}}$, as found in equation (4.44).

Average cost Let $\overline{\mathcal{A}}_n^{\text{bms}}$ be the average number of comparisons to sort n keys bottom-up. All permutations of the input stack being equally likely, equation (4.43) on page 143 becomes $\overline{\mathcal{A}}_0^{\text{bms}} = \overline{\mathcal{A}}_1^{\text{bms}} = 0$ and

$$\overline{\mathcal{A}}_n^{\text{bms}} = \overline{\mathcal{A}}_{2^{\lceil \lg n \rceil -1}}^{\text{bms}} + \overline{\mathcal{A}}_{n-2^{\lceil \lg n \rceil -1}}^{\text{bms}} + \overline{\mathcal{A}}_{2^{\lceil \lg n \rceil -1}, n-2^{\lceil \lg n \rceil -1}}^{\text{mrg}},$$

which, with equation (4.9), in turn implies $\overline{\mathcal{A}}_0^{\text{bms}} = \overline{\mathcal{A}}_1^{\text{bms}} = 0$ and

$$\overline{\mathcal{A}}_n^{\text{bms}} = \overline{\mathcal{A}}_{2^{\lceil \lg n \rceil -1}}^{\text{bms}} + \overline{\mathcal{A}}_{n-2^{\lceil \lg n \rceil -1}}^{\text{bms}} + n - \frac{2^{\lceil \lg n \rceil -1}}{n - 2^{\lceil \lg n \rceil -1} + 1} - \frac{n - 2^{\lceil \lg n \rceil -1}}{2^{\lceil \lg n \rceil -1} + 1}.$$

This definition is quite daunting, so let us turn to induction to find bounds, as we did for $\overline{\mathcal{B}}_n^{\text{tms}}$ in inequality (4.20) on page 132. Let us start with the lower bound and set to maximise the real constants a and b in

$$\mathsf{H}(n): n \lg n + an + b \leqslant \overline{\mathcal{A}}_n^{\text{bms}}, \text{ for } n \geqslant 2.$$

The base case for induction is $\mathsf{H}(2)$:

$$2a + b + 1 \leqslant 0. \tag{4.56}$$

Let us assume now $\mathsf{H}(n)$ for all $2 \leqslant n \leqslant 2^p$, and let us prove $\mathsf{H}(2^p + i)$, for all $0 < i \leqslant 2^p$. The induction principle entails then that $\mathsf{H}(n)$ holds for any $n \geqslant 2$. If $n = 2^p + i$, then $\lceil \lg n \rceil - 1 = p$, so

$$\overline{\mathcal{A}}_{2^p+i}^{\text{bms}} = \overline{\mathcal{A}}_{2^p}^{\text{bms}} + \overline{\mathcal{A}}_i^{\text{bms}} + 2^p + i - \frac{2^p}{i+1} - \frac{i}{2^p+1}. \tag{4.57}$$

By hypothesis, $\mathsf{H}(i)$ holds, that is, $i \lg i + ai + b \leqslant \overline{\mathcal{A}}_i^{\text{bms}}$, but, instead of using $\mathsf{H}(2^p)$, we will use the exact value in equation (4.15) on page 129, where $\alpha := \sum_{k \geqslant 0} 1/(2^k + 1)$. From equation (4.57), we derive

$$(p-\alpha)2^p + \sum_{k \geqslant 0} \frac{1}{2^k + 2^{-p}} + (i \lg i + ai + b) + 2^p + i - \frac{2^p}{i+1} - \frac{i}{2^p+1} < \overline{\mathcal{A}}_{2^p+i}^{\text{bms}}.$$

We want to prove $\mathsf{H}(2^p + i): (2^p + i) \lg(2^p + i) + a(2^p + i) + b \leqslant \overline{\mathcal{A}}_{2^p+i}^{\text{bms}}$, which is thus implied by

$$(2^p + i) \lg(2^p + i) + a2^p \leqslant (p - \alpha + 1)2^p - \frac{2^p}{i+1} + i \lg i + i - \frac{i}{2^p+1} + c_p,$$

where $c_p := \sum_{k \geqslant 0} 1/(2^k + 2^{-p})$. Let

$$\Psi(p, i) := p - \alpha + 1 - \frac{1}{i+1} + \frac{i}{2^p+1} - \frac{1}{2^p}((2^p + i) \lg(2^p + i) - i \lg i - c_p).$$

Then the sufficient condition above is equivalent to $a \leqslant \Psi(p, i)$. To study the behaviour of $\Psi(p, i)$, let us fix p and let i range over the real interval $]0, 2^p]$. The partial derivative of Ψ with respect to i is

$$\frac{\partial \Psi}{\partial i}(p, i) = \frac{1}{2^p + 1} + \frac{1}{(i+1)^2} - \frac{1}{2^p} \lg\left(\frac{2^p}{i} + 1\right).$$

Let us also determine the second derivative with respect to i:

$$\frac{\partial^2 \Psi}{\partial i^2}(p, i) = \frac{1}{(2^p + i)i \ln 2} - \frac{2}{(i+1)^3},$$

where $\ln x$ is the natural logarithm of x. Let the cubic polynomial

$$K_p(i) := i^3 + (3 - 2\ln 2)i^2 + (3 - 2^{p+1}\ln 2)i + 1.$$

Then $\partial^2\Psi/\partial i^2 = 0 \Leftrightarrow K_p(i) = 0$ and the sign of $\partial^2\Psi/\partial i^2$ is the sign of $K_p(i)$. In general, a cubic equation has the form

$$ax^3 + bx^2 + cx + d = 0, \text{ with } a \neq 0.$$

A classic result about the nature of the roots is as follows. Let the *discriminant* of the cubic be $\Delta := 18abcd - 4b^3d + b^2c^2 - 4ac^3 - 27a^2d^2$.

1. If $\Delta > 0$, the equation has three distinct real roots;

2. if $\Delta = 0$, the equation has a multiple root and all its roots are real;

3. if $\Delta < 0$, the equation has one real root and two nonreal complex conjugate roots.

Let us resume now our discussion. Let the cubic polynomial

$$\Delta(x) := (4\ln 2)x^3 - (9 - 2\ln 2)(3 + 2\ln 2)x^2 + 12(9 - 2\ln 29)x - 4(27 - 8\ln 2).$$

Then the discriminant of $K_p(i) = 0$ is $\Delta(2^{p+1}) \cdot \ln^2 2$. The discriminant of $\Delta(x) = 0$ is negative, thus $\Delta(x)$ has one real root $x_0 \simeq 8.64872$. Because the coefficient of x^3 is positive, $\Delta(x)$ is negative if $x < x_0$ and positive if $x > x_0$.

1. Since $p \geqslant 3$ implies $2^{p+1} > x_0$, the discriminant of $K_p(i) = 0$ is positive, which means that $K_p(i)$ has three distinct real roots if $p \geqslant 3$, and so does $\partial^2\Psi/\partial i^2$.

2. Otherwise, $K_p(i)$ has one real root if $0 \leqslant p \leqslant 2$.

Before we study these two cases in detail, we need a small reminder about cubic polynomials. Let ρ_0, ρ_1 and ρ_2 be the roots of the polynomial $P(x) = ax^3 + bx^2 + cx + d$. So $P(x) = a(x - \rho_0)(x - \rho_1)(x - \rho_2) = ax^3 - a(\rho_0 + \rho_1 + \rho_2)x^2 + a(\rho_0\rho_1 + \rho_0\rho_2 + \rho_1\rho_2)x - a(\rho_0\rho_1\rho_2)$, so $\rho_0\rho_1\rho_2 = -d/a$.

1. Let $p \in \{0, 1, 2\}$. We just found that $K_p(i)$ has one real root, say ρ_0, and two nonreal conjugate roots, say ρ_1 and $\rho_2 = \overline{\rho_1}$. Then $\rho_0\rho_1\rho_2 = \rho_0|\rho_1|^2 = -1$, so $\rho_0 < 0$. Since the coefficient of x^3 is positive, this entails that $K_p(i) > 0$ if $i > 0$, which is true for $\partial^2\Psi/\partial i^2$ as well: $i > 0$ implies $\partial^2\Psi/\partial i^2 > 0$, therefore $\partial\Psi/\partial i$ increases. Since

$$\frac{\partial\Psi}{\partial i}(p, i) \xrightarrow[i \to 0^+]{} -\infty < 0, \text{ and } \left.\frac{\partial\Psi}{\partial i}(p, i)\right|_{i=2^p} = -\frac{1}{2^p(2^p + 1)^2} < 0,$$

we deduce that $\partial\Psi/\partial i < 0$ if $i > 0$, which means that $\Psi(p, i)$ decreases when $i \in {]0, 2^p]}$. Since we are looking to minimise $\Psi(p, i)$, we have $\min_{0 < i \leqslant 2^p} \Psi(p, i) = \Psi(p, 2^p)$.

2. If $p \geqslant 3$, then $K_p(i)$ has three real roots. Here, the product of the roots of $K_p(i)$ is -1, so at most two of them are positive. Since we have $K_p(0) = 1 > 0$, $K_p(1) < 0$ and $\lim_{i \to +\infty} K_p(i) > 0$, we see that $K_p(i)$ has one root in ${]0, 1[}$ and one in ${]1, +\infty[}$, and so does $\partial^2\Psi/\partial i^2$. Furthermore, $\partial\Psi/\partial i|_{i=1} > 0$ and $\partial\Psi/\partial i|_{i=2^p} < 0$, therefore, from the intermediate theorem, there exists a real $i_p \in {]1, 2^p[}$ such that $\partial\Psi/\partial i|_{i=i_p} = 0$, and we know that it is unique because $\partial\Psi^2/\partial i^2$ changes sign only once in ${]1, +\infty[}$. This also means that $\Psi(p, i)$ increases if i increases on $[1, i_p[$, reaches its maximum when $i = i_p$, and then decreases on ${]i_p, 2^p]}$. Since $\lim_{i \to 0^+} \Psi(p, i) = -\infty$ and we are searching for a lower bound of $\Psi(p, i)$, we need to know which of $i = 1$ or $i = 2^p$ minimises $\Psi(p, i)$: actually, we have $\Psi(p, 1) \geqslant \Psi(p, 2^p)$, so we conclude $\min_{0 < i \leqslant 2^p} \Psi(p, i) = \Psi(p, 2^p)$.

In any case, we need to minimise $\Psi(p, 2^p)$. We have:

$$\Psi(p, 2^p) = -\frac{1}{2^p + 1} - \sum_{k=0}^{p} \frac{1}{2^k + 1}.$$

We check that $\Psi(p, 2^p) > \Psi(p + 1, 2^{p+1})$, so the function decreases for integer points and $a_{max} = \min_{p > 0} \Psi(p, 2^p) = \lim_{p \to \infty} \Psi(p, 2^p) = -\alpha^+$. From inequation (4.56), we draw $b_{max} = -2a_{max} - 1 = 2\alpha - 1 \simeq 1.52899$. In total, by the principle of induction, we have established, for $n \geqslant 2$,

$$n \lg n - \alpha n + 2\alpha - 1 < \overline{A}_n^{\mathrm{bms}}.$$

This bound is better than for the average cost of top-down merge sort, inequation (4.41) on page 142, because there, we had to decompose n into even and odd values, not $n = 2^p + i$ which allowed us here to use the exact value of $\overline{\mathcal{A}}_{2^p}^{\text{bms}}$. It is even slightly better than (4.16) on page 130, which is quite a nice surprise.

We need now to work out an upper bound using the same technique. In other words, we want to minimise the real constants a' and b' in $\overline{\mathcal{A}}_n^{\text{bms}} \leqslant n \lg n + a'n + b'$, for $n \geqslant 2$. The difference with the lower bound is that the inequations are reversed: $a' \geqslant \Psi(p, i)$ and $b' \geqslant -2a' - 1$. We revisit the two cases above:

1. If $0 \leqslant p \leqslant 2$, then $\max_{0 < i \leqslant 2^p} \Psi(p, i) = \Psi(p, 1)$. We easily check that $\max_{0 \leqslant p \leqslant 2} \Psi(p, 1) = \Psi(0, 1) = 1 - \alpha$.

2. If $p \geqslant 3$, we need to express i_p as a function of p, but it is hard to solve the equation $\partial\Psi/\partial i|_{i=i_p} = 0$, even approximately.

Before giving up, we could try to differentiate Ψ with respect to p, instead of i. Indeed, $(p, i, \Psi(p, i))$ defines a surface in space, and by privileging p over i, we are slicing the surface along planes perpendicular to the i axis. Sometimes, slicing in one direction instead of another makes the analysis easier. The problem here is to differentiate c_p. We can work our way round with the bound $c_p < 2$ from (4.16) on page 130 and define

$$\Phi(p, i) := p - \alpha + 1 - \frac{1}{i+1} + \frac{i}{2^p + 1} - \frac{1}{2^p}((2^p + i)\lg(2^p + i) - i\lg i - 2).$$

Now we have $\Psi(p, i) < \Phi(p, i)$ and, instead of $\Psi(p, i) \leqslant a'$, we can impose the stronger constraint $\Phi(p, i) \leqslant a'$ and cross our fingers. In FIGURE 4.15 on the facing page, are outlined $\Phi(p, 1)$, $\Phi(p, 2)$ and $\Phi(p, 3)$. (The starting point for each curve is marked by a white disk.) Differentiating with respect to p yields

$$\frac{\partial\Phi}{\partial p}(p, i) = \frac{i}{2^p}\ln\left(\frac{2^p}{i} + 1\right) - \frac{\ln 2}{2^{p-1}} - \frac{i2^p \ln 2}{(2^p + 1)^2}.$$

To study the sign of $\partial\Phi(p, i)/\partial p$ when p varies, let us define

$$\varphi(x, i) := \frac{x}{i\ln 2} \cdot \frac{\partial\Phi}{\partial p}(p, i)\bigg|_{p=\lg x}.$$

Because $x \geqslant 1$ implies $x/i\ln 2 > 0$ and $\lg x \geqslant 0$, the sign of $\varphi(x, i)$ when $x \geqslant 1$ varies is the same as the sign of $\partial\Phi(p, i)/\partial p$ when $p \geqslant 0$ varies, bearing in mind that $x = 2^p$. We have

$$\varphi(x, i) = \lg\left(\frac{x}{i} + 1\right) - \left(\frac{x}{x+1}\right)^2 - \frac{2}{i},$$

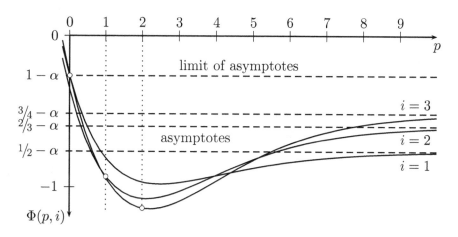

Figure 4.15: $\Phi(p,1)$, $\Phi(p,2)$ and $\Phi(p,3)$

$$\frac{\partial\varphi}{\partial x}(x,i) = \frac{1}{(x+i)\ln 2} - \frac{2x}{(x+1)^3}.$$

This should remind us of a familiar sight:

$$\frac{\partial\varphi}{\partial x}(x,i) = x \cdot \frac{\partial^2\Psi}{\partial x^2}(p,x)\Big|_{p=\lg i}.$$

When $x \geqslant 1$ varies, the sign of $\partial\varphi(x,i)/\partial x$ is the same as the sign of $\partial^2\Psi(p,x)/\partial x^2\big|_{p=\lg i}$, so we can reuse the previous discussion on the roots of $K_p(i)$, while taking care to replace i by x, and 2^p by i:

1. If $i \in \{1,2,3,4\}$, then $\partial\varphi(x,i)/\partial x > 0$ when $x > 0$.

2. If $i \geqslant 5$, then $\partial\varphi(x,i)/\partial x > 0$ when $x \geqslant 1$.

In both cases, $\varphi(x,i)$ increases when $x \geqslant 1$, which, with the facts that $\lim_{x\to 0+}\varphi(x,i) = -\infty < 0$ and $\lim_{x\to\infty}\varphi(x,i) = +\infty > 0$, entails that there exists a unique root $\rho > 0$ such that $\varphi(x,i) < 0$ if $x < \rho$, and $\varphi(x,i) > 0$ if $x > \rho$, and the same holds for $\partial\Phi/\partial p$ (with a different root). Concordantly, $\Phi(p,i)$ is decreasing down to its minimum, and increasing afterwards. (See again FIGURE 4.15.)

Moreover $\overline{\lim}_{p\to\infty}\Phi(p,i) = i/(i+1) - \alpha < 1 - \alpha = \Phi(0,1)$, so the curves have asymptotes. Since we are searching for the maximum, we deduce: $a'_{\min} = \max_{0<i\leqslant 2^p}\Phi(p,i) = 1 - \alpha \simeq -0.2645$, and the constant is $b'_{\min} = -2a'_{\min} - 1 = 2\alpha - 3 \simeq -0.471$. In sum, we found, for $n \geqslant 2$,

$$n\lg n - \alpha n + (2\alpha - 1) < \overline{A}_n^{\mathsf{bms}} < n\lg n - (\alpha - 1)n - (3 - 2\alpha). \quad (4.58)$$

The lower bound is most accurate when $n = 2^p$. To interpret the values of n for which the upper bound is most accurate, we need another glance at FIGURE 4.15 on the preceding page. We have $i/(i+1) - \alpha \to 1 - \alpha$, as $p \to \infty$, but this does not tell us anything about p. Unfortunately, as noted earlier, for a given p, we cannot characterise explicitly i_p, which is the value of i maximising $\Phi(p, i)$ (in the planes perpendicular to this page). Anyway, the linear terms of these bounds cannot be improved upon. This means that the additional number of comparisons incurred by sorting $n = 2^p + i$ keys instead of 2^p is at most n. As with top-down merge sort, more advanced mathematics by Panny and Prodinger (1995) show that $\overline{\mathcal{A}}_n^{\mathsf{bms}} = n \lg n + B^*(\lg n) \cdot n$, where B^* is a continuous, non-differentiable, periodic function whose average value is approximately -0.965. Obviously, we have $\overline{\mathcal{A}}_n^{\mathsf{bms}} \sim n \lg n \sim \overline{\mathcal{W}}_n^{\mathsf{bms}} \sim 2 \cdot \overline{\mathcal{B}}_n^{\mathsf{bms}}$.

Program   We managed to analyse the number of comparisons to sort by merging because the whole process can easily be depicted as a tree. It is time to provide a program whose traces conform to these merge trees. In FIGURE 4.16 on the next page is shown the definitions of the main sorting function bms/1 and several auxiliaries.

- The call solo(s) is a stack containing singletons with all the keys of s in the same order. In other words, it is the leaves of the merge tree.

- The call all(u) is a stack containing stacks which are the result of merging adjacent stacks in u. In other words, it is the level just above u in the merge tree.

- The call all(solo(s)) is the sorted stack corresponding to the stack of singletons solo(s). In other words, starting with the leaves, it keeps building levels up by calling mrg/2 until the root of the merge tree is reached.

What is beautiful about this program is that there is no need for two distinct phases, first building the perfect merge trees and then performing the unbalanced mergers with the roots of these: it is possible to achieve the same effect by interleaving rightwards and upwards constructions.

Additional cost   In order to determine the cost $\mathcal{C}_n^{\mathsf{bms}}$ we need to add to the number of comparisons the number of rewrite steps that do not involve comparisons, that is, other than by rules κ and λ.

- Rules θ and ι are used once to conclude each merger. Let $\overline{\mathcal{C}}_n^{\kappa}$ be the number of comparisons to perform the unbalanced mergers when

$$
\begin{aligned}
&\mathsf{bms}([]) \xrightarrow{\mu} []; && \mathsf{solo}([]) \xrightarrow{\xi} []; \\
&\mathsf{bms}(s) \xrightarrow{\nu} \mathsf{all}(\mathsf{solo}(s)). && \mathsf{solo}([x\,|\,s]) \xrightarrow{\pi} [[x]\,|\,\mathsf{solo}(s)]. \\[2mm]
&\mathsf{all}([s]) \xrightarrow{\rho} s; && \mathsf{nxt}([s,t\,|\,u]) \xrightarrow{\tau} [\mathsf{mrg}(s,t)\,|\,\mathsf{nxt}(u)]; \\
&\mathsf{all}(s) \xrightarrow{\sigma} \mathsf{all}(\mathsf{nxt}(s)). && \mathsf{nxt}(u) \xrightarrow{v} u.
\end{aligned}
$$

$$
\begin{aligned}
\mathsf{mrg}([],t) &\xrightarrow{\theta} t; \\
\mathsf{mrg}(s,[]) &\xrightarrow{\iota} s; \\
\mathsf{mrg}([x\,|\,s],[y\,|\,t]) &\xrightarrow{\kappa} [y\,|\,\mathsf{mrg}([x\,|\,s],t)], \text{ if } x \succ y; \\
\mathsf{mrg}([x\,|\,s],t) &\xrightarrow{\lambda} [x\,|\,\mathsf{mrg}(s,t)].
\end{aligned}
$$

Figure 4.16: Sorting by bottom-up mergers with bms/1

there are n keys to sort. Looking back at FIGURE 4.12 on page 146, we see that

$$
\overline{C}_n^{\times} := \sum_{i=1}^{r} \overline{C}_{2^{e_i},2^{e_{i-1}}+\cdots+2^{e_0}}^{\mathrm{mrg}}. \tag{4.59}
$$

The total number of comparisons is the sum of the numbers of comparisons of the balanced and unbalanced mergers:

$$
\overline{C}_n^{\mathrm{bms}} = \sum_{i=0}^{r} C_{e_i}^{\bowtie} + \overline{C}_n^{\times} = \sum_{i=0}^{r} \overline{C}_{2^{e_i}}^{\mathrm{bms}} + \sum_{i=1}^{r} \overline{C}_{2^{e_i},2^{e_{i-1}}+\cdots+2^{e_0}}^{\mathrm{mrg}}. \tag{4.60}
$$

To find the number of mergers, let us set $\overline{C}_{m,n}^{\mathrm{mrg}} = 1$ in equation (4.12) on page 128, yielding $\overline{C}_{2^p}^{\mathrm{bms}} = 2^p - 1$. By plugging this result in equation (4.60), we draw $\overline{C}_n^{\mathrm{bms}} = n-1$. In other words, rules θ and ι are used $n - 1$ times in total.

- In rule τ, one call $\mathsf{nxt}([s,t\,|\,u])$ corresponds to one call $\mathsf{mrg}(s,t)$, one for each merger. Therefore, τ is used $n - 1$ times.

- Rule v is used once for each level in the merge tree, except the root, with u either empty or a singleton. Let $\Lambda(j)$ be the number of nodes at level j, where $j = 0$ represents the level of the leaves. Then, the number z we are looking for is the greatest natural satisfying the equation $\Lambda(z) = 1$, at the root. Function $\mathsf{nxt}/1$ implies

$$
\Lambda(j+1) = \lceil \Lambda(j)/2 \rceil, \text{ with } \Lambda(0) = n.
$$

This recurrence is equivalent to the closed form $\Lambda(j) = \lceil n/2^j \rceil$, as a consequence of the following theorem.

Theorem 4 (Ceilings and Fractions). *Let x be a real number and q a natural number. Then $\lceil \lceil x \rceil / q \rceil = \lceil x/q \rceil$.*

Proof. The equality is equivalent to the conjunction of the two complementary inequalities $\lceil \lceil x \rceil / q \rceil \geqslant \lceil x/q \rceil$ and $\lceil \lceil x \rceil / q \rceil \leqslant \lceil x/q \rceil$. The former is direct: $\lceil x \rceil \geqslant x \Rightarrow \lceil x \rceil / q \geqslant x/q \Rightarrow \lceil \lceil x \rceil / q \rceil \geqslant \lceil x/q \rceil$. Since both sides of the inequality are integers, $\lceil \lceil x \rceil / q \rceil \leqslant \lceil x/q \rceil$ is equivalent to state that $p \leqslant \lceil \lceil x \rceil / q \rceil \Rightarrow p \leqslant \lceil x/q \rceil$, for any integer p. An obvious lemma is that if i is an integer and y a real number, $i \leqslant \lceil y \rceil \Leftrightarrow i \leqslant y$, so the original inequality is equivalent to $p \leqslant \lceil x \rceil / q \Rightarrow p \leqslant x/q$, for any integer p, which is $pq \leqslant \lceil x \rceil \Rightarrow pq \leqslant x$. The lemma yields this implication, achieving the proof.　□

To find z, we express n in binary: $n := \sum_{k=0}^{m-1} b_k 2^k = (b_{m-1} \ldots b_0)_2$, where $b_k \in \{0, 1\}$ and $b_{m-1} = 1$. It is easy to derive a formula for b_i. We have

$$\frac{n}{2^{i+1}} = \frac{1}{2^{i+1}} \sum_{k=0}^{m-1} b_k 2^k = \frac{1}{2^{i+1}} \sum_{k=0}^{i} b_k 2^k + (b_{m-1} \ldots b_{i+1})_2. \quad (4.61)$$

We prove that $\lfloor n/2^{i+1} \rfloor = (b_{m-1} \ldots b_{i+1})_2$ as follows:

$$\sum_{k=0}^{i} 2^k < 2^{i+1} \Rightarrow 0 \leqslant \sum_{k=0}^{i} b_k 2^k < 2^{i+1} \Leftrightarrow 0 \leqslant \frac{1}{2^{i+1}} \sum_{k=0}^{i} b_k 2^k < 1.$$

This and equation (4.61) imply that

$$\left\lceil \frac{n}{2^i} \right\rceil = (b_{m-1} \ldots b_i)_2 + \begin{cases} 0, & \text{if } (b_{i-1} \ldots b_0)_2 = 0; \\ 1, & \text{otherwise.} \end{cases}$$

Therefore, $\lceil n/2^z \rceil = 1$ is equivalent to $z = m - 1$ if $n = 2^{m-1}$, and $z = m$ otherwise. Equation (1.6) on page 11 states $m = \lfloor \lg n \rfloor + 1$, thus $z = \lfloor \lg n \rfloor$ if n is a power of 2, and $z = \lfloor \lg n \rfloor + 1$ otherwise. More simply, this means that $z = \lceil \lg n \rceil$.

- Rule ρ is used once, at the root. Rule σ is used z times.

- The trace of $\mathsf{solo}(s)$ is $\pi^n \xi$ if s contains n keys, so $C_n^{\mathsf{solo}} = n + 1$.

- The contribution to the total cost of rules μ and ν is simply 1.

In total, $C_n^{\mathsf{bms}} = \overline{C}_n^{\mathsf{bms}} + 3n + 2\lceil \lg n \rceil + 1$ and $C_n^{\mathsf{bms}} \sim \overline{C}_n^{\mathsf{bms}}$.

$$\mathsf{bms}_0(s) \to \mathsf{all}(\mathsf{duo}(s)).$$

$$\mathsf{duo}([x, y \,|\, s]) \to [[y, x] \,|\, \mathsf{duo}(s)], \qquad \text{if } x \succ y;$$
$$\mathsf{duo}([x, y \,|\, s]) \to [[x, y] \,|\, \mathsf{duo}(s)];$$
$$\mathsf{duo}(s) \to [s].$$

$$\mathsf{all}([s]) \to s;$$
$$\mathsf{all}(s) \to \mathsf{all}(\mathsf{nxt}(s)).$$

$$\mathsf{nxt}([s, t \,|\, u]) \to [\mathsf{mrg}(s, t) \,|\, \mathsf{nxt}(u)];$$
$$\mathsf{nxt}(u) \to u.$$

$$\mathsf{mrg}([\,], t) \to t;$$
$$\mathsf{mrg}(s, [\,]) \to s;$$
$$\mathsf{mrg}([x \,|\, s], [y \,|\, t]) \to [y \,|\, \mathsf{mrg}([x \,|\, s], t)], \quad \text{if } x \succ y;$$
$$\mathsf{mrg}([x \,|\, s], t) \to [x \,|\, \mathsf{mrg}(s, t)].$$

Figure 4.17: Faster bottom-up merge sort with $\mathsf{bms}_0/1$

Improvement It is easy to improve upon bms/1 by directly building the second level of the merge tree *without using mrg/2*. Consider the program in FIGURE 4.17, where solo/1 has been replaced by duo/1. The number of comparisons is unchanged, but the cost, measured as the number of rewrites, is slightly smaller. The added cost of $\mathsf{duo}(s)$ is $\lfloor n/2 \rfloor + 1$, where n is the length of s. On the other hand, we save the cost of $\mathsf{solo}(s)$. The first rewrite by rule σ is not performed, as well as the subsequent call $\mathsf{nxt}(s)$, to wit, $\lfloor n/2 \rfloor$ calls to mrg/2 on pairs of singletons by κ or λ, plus one rewrite by θ or ι for the last singleton or the empty stack, totalling $\lfloor n/2 \rfloor C_{1,1}^{\mathrm{mrg}} + 1 = 2\lfloor n/2 \rfloor + 1$. In the end, the total cost is decreased by

$$((n+1) + 1 + (2\lfloor n/2 \rfloor + 1)) - (\lfloor n/2 \rfloor + 1) = n + \lfloor n/2 \rfloor + 2.$$

Hence, $\mathcal{C}_n^{\mathsf{bms}_0} = \overline{\mathcal{C}}_n^{\mathsf{bms}} + \lceil 3n/2 \rceil + 2\lceil \lg n \rceil - 1$, for $n > 0$, and $\mathcal{C}_0^{\mathsf{bms}_0} = 3$. Asymptotically, we have $\mathcal{C}_n^{\mathsf{bms}_0} \sim \overline{\mathcal{C}}_n^{\mathsf{bms}}$.

4.5 Comparison

In this section we gather our findings about top-down and bottom-up merge sort for an easier comparison, and we also present new results which relate the costs of both algorithms.

Minimum cost   The minimum cost of both variants of merge sort is the same: $\overline{\mathcal{B}}_n^{\mathrm{tms}} = \overline{\mathcal{B}}_n^{\mathrm{bms}}$ and

$$\frac{1}{2} n \lg n - \left(\frac{1}{2} \lg \frac{4}{3} \right) n + \lg \frac{4}{3} \leqslant \overline{\mathcal{B}}_n^{\mathrm{tms}} \leqslant \frac{1}{2} n \lg n.$$

The lower bound is tight for $n = 2$ and most accurate when n is a Jacobsthal number (see (4.34) on page 137). The upper bound is tight when $n = 2^p$. These results may not be intuitive *a priori*.

Maximum cost   In the previous sections, we found the following bounds:

$$n \lg n - n + 1 \leqslant \overline{\mathcal{W}}_n^{\mathrm{tms}} < n \lg n - 0.91 n + 1;$$
$$n \lg n - n + 1 \leqslant \overline{\mathcal{W}}_n^{\mathrm{bms}} < n \lg n - 1.$$

In both cases, the lower bound is tight if, and only if, $n = 2^p$. The upper bound of top-down merge sort is most accurate when n is the nearest integer to $2^p \ln 2$. The upper bound of bottom-up merge sort is most accurate if $n = 2^p + 1$.

It is interesting to bound $\overline{\mathcal{W}}_n^{\mathrm{bms}}$ in term of $\overline{\mathcal{W}}_n^{\mathrm{tms}}$, shedding further light on the relationship between these two variants of merge sort. We already noted $\overline{\mathcal{C}}_{2^p}^{\mathrm{bms}} = \overline{\mathcal{C}}_{2^p}^{\mathrm{tms}}$, so $\overline{\mathcal{W}}_{2^p}^{\mathrm{bms}} = \overline{\mathcal{W}}_{2^p}^{\mathrm{tms}}$. Furthermore, we have $\overline{\mathcal{W}}_{2^p}^{\mathrm{bms}} = \overline{\mathcal{W}}_{2^p-1}^{\mathrm{bms}} + p$, thus $\overline{\mathcal{W}}_{2^p-1}^{\mathrm{bms}} = \overline{\mathcal{W}}_{2^p-1}^{\mathrm{tms}}$. Another interesting value is $\overline{\mathcal{W}}_{2^p+1}^{\mathrm{tms}} = (p-1)2^p + p + 2$, so $\overline{\mathcal{W}}_{2^p+1}^{\mathrm{bms}} - \overline{\mathcal{W}}_{2^p+1}^{\mathrm{tms}} = 2^p - p - 1$. This leads us to conjecture the following tight bounds in relationship with top-down merge sort:

$$\overline{\mathcal{W}}_n^{\mathrm{tms}} \leqslant \overline{\mathcal{W}}_n^{\mathrm{bms}} \leqslant \overline{\mathcal{W}}_n^{\mathrm{tms}} + n - \lceil \lg n \rceil - 1.$$

We will prove these inequalities by means of mathematical induction on n and, in the process, we will discover when they become equalities. First, let us deduce from the general recurrence for the cost of bottom-up merge sort the recurrence for the maximum cost:

$$\overline{\mathcal{W}}_0^{\mathrm{bms}} = \overline{\mathcal{W}}_1^{\mathrm{bms}} = 0; \quad \overline{\mathcal{W}}_n^{\mathrm{bms}} = \overline{\mathcal{W}}_{2^{\lceil \lg n \rceil - 1}}^{\mathrm{bms}} + \overline{\mathcal{W}}_{n-2^{\lceil \lg n \rceil - 1}}^{\mathrm{bms}} + n - 1. \quad (4.62)$$

Also, we easily check that, for all $p \geqslant 0$,

$$\overline{\mathcal{W}}_{2^p}^{\mathrm{tms}} = \overline{\mathcal{W}}_{2^p}^{\mathrm{bms}}. \qquad (4.63)$$

Lower bound   Let us prove, for all $n \geqslant 0$,

$$\mathsf{W}_L(n) \colon \overline{\mathcal{W}}_n^{\mathrm{tms}} \leqslant \overline{\mathcal{W}}_n^{\mathrm{bms}}. \qquad (4.64)$$

From (4.63), it is clear that $W_L(2^0)$ holds. Let the induction hypothesis be $\forall m \leqslant 2^p . W_L(m)$. The induction principle requires that we prove $W_L(2^p + i)$, for all $0 < i < 2^p$. Note that we leave aside the case when $i = 2^p$, because $W_L(2^{p+1})$ is already true from (4.63).

Equations (4.62) and (4.63) yield

$$\overline{W}^{\text{bms}}_{2^p+i} = \overline{W}^{\text{bms}}_{2^p} + \overline{W}^{\text{bms}}_i + 2^p + i - 1$$
$$= \overline{W}^{\text{tms}}_{2^p} + \overline{W}^{\text{bms}}_i + 2^p + i - 1 \geqslant \overline{W}^{\text{tms}}_{2^p} + \overline{W}^{\text{tms}}_i + 2^p + i - 1,$$

the inequality being the instance $W_L(i)$ of the induction hypothesis. Consequently, if the inequality

$$\overline{W}^{\text{tms}}_{2^p} + \overline{W}^{\text{tms}}_i + 2^p + i - 1 \geqslant \overline{W}^{\text{tms}}_{2^p+i} \tag{4.65}$$

holds, the result $W_L(2^p + i)$ ensues. Let us try to prove it.

Let $n = 2^p + i$. Then $p = \lfloor \lg n \rfloor$ and $\lceil \lg n \rceil = \lfloor \lg n \rfloor + 1$. Equation (4.37) on page 139 entails

$$\overline{W}^{\text{tms}}_{2^p+i} = (2^p + i)(p + 1) - 2^{p+1} + 1 = ((p - 1)2^p + 1) + (p + 1)i$$
$$= \overline{W}^{\text{tms}}_{2^p} + (p + 1)i.$$

Therefore, inequation (4.65) is equivalent to $pi \leqslant \overline{W}^{\text{tms}}_i + 2^p - 1$. Using equation (4.37), this inequality in turn is equivalent to

$$(p - \lceil \lg i \rceil)i \leqslant 2^p - 2^{\lceil \lg i \rceil}. \tag{4.66}$$

To prove it, we have two complementary cases to analyse:

- $i = 2^q$, with $0 \leqslant q < p$. Then $\lg i = q$ and equation (4.66) is equivalent to $(p - q)2^q \leqslant 2^p - 2^q$, that is

$$p - q \leqslant 2^{p-q} - 1. \tag{4.67}$$

  Let $f(x) := 2^x - x - 1$, with $x > 0$. We have $f(0) = f(1) = 0$ and $f(x) > 0$ for $x > 1$, so the inequality (4.67) holds and is tight if, and only if, $x = 1$, that is, $q = p - 1$.

- $i = 2^q + j$, with $0 \leqslant q < p$ and $0 < j < 2^q$. Then we have the equalities $\lfloor \lg i \rfloor = q = \lceil \lg i \rceil - 1$ and inequation (4.66) is then equivalent to the inequality $(p - q - 1)i \leqslant 2^p - 2^{q+1}$, that is to say,

$$(p - q + 1)2^q + (p - q - 1)j \leqslant 2^p. \tag{4.68}$$

  Since $p - q - 1 \geqslant 0$ and $j < 2^q$, we have $(p - q - 1)j \leqslant (p - q - 1)2^q$ (tight if $q = p - 1$). Hence

$$(p - q + 1)2^q + (p - q - 1)j \leqslant (p - q)2^{q+1}.$$

Inequation (4.68) is entailed if $2(p-q) \leqslant 2^{p-q}$. Let $g(x) := 2^x - 2x$, with $x > 0$. We have $g(1) = g(2) = 0$ and $f(x) > 0$ for $x > 2$. Thus, inequality (4.68) holds and is tight if, and only if, $x = 1$, that is, $q = p - 1$ (case $x = 2$ implies $i \leqslant 2^{p-1}$, which cannot be tight). $\square$

Let us find now the shape of n when $\mathsf{W}_L(n)$ is tight. We proved above that, if $q = p - 1$, that is, the binary notation of n starts with two 1-bits, formally written as $(11(0+1)^*)_2$, then the following inequality holds:

$$\overline{\mathcal{W}}^{\text{tms}}_{2^p+i} = \overline{\mathcal{W}}^{\text{tms}}_{2^p} + \overline{\mathcal{W}}^{\text{tms}}_i + 2^p + i - 1 \leqslant \overline{\mathcal{W}}^{\text{tms}}_{2^p} + \overline{\mathcal{W}}^{\text{bms}}_i + 2^p + i - 1 = \overline{\mathcal{W}}^{\text{bms}}_{2^p+i}.$$

This inequality is tight: $\overline{\mathcal{W}}^{\text{tms}}_{2^p+i} = \overline{\mathcal{W}}^{\text{bms}}_{2^p+i} \Leftrightarrow \overline{\mathcal{W}}^{\text{tms}}_i = \overline{\mathcal{W}}^{\text{bms}}_i$.

Using the case analysis above, if $i = 2^q + j$, we have $\overline{\mathcal{W}}^{\text{tms}}_{2^p+i} = \overline{\mathcal{W}}^{\text{bms}}_{2^p+i}$, if, and only if, $\overline{\mathcal{W}}^{\text{tms}}_{2^{p-1}+j} = \overline{\mathcal{W}}^{\text{bms}}_{2^{p-1}+j}$. These equivalences can be repeated, yielding two strictly decreasing sequences of positive integers, that is, $2^p + i > 2^{p-1} + j > 2^{p-2} + k > \dots$ and $i > j > k > \dots$ The end of the latter recursive descent is simply 0, which means that the former stops at a power of 2, for which we know equation (4.63). In other words, the binary representation of n is made of a series of one or more 1-bits (from 2^p, 2^{p-1}, 2^{p-2}, $\dots$), possibly followed by successive 0-bits, which we formally write $n = (1^+0^*)_2$, that is, n is the difference between two powers of 2. Moreover, recalling that $\overline{\mathcal{W}}^{\text{bms}}_{2^q} = \overline{\mathcal{W}}^{\text{tms}}_{2^q}$, we have established

$$\boxed{\overline{\mathcal{W}}^{\text{bms}}_n = \overline{\mathcal{W}}^{\text{tms}}_n \Leftrightarrow n = 2^q \text{ or } n = 2^p - 2^q, \text{with } p > q \geqslant 0.}$$

Note that if $n = 2^p - 1$, the number of unbalanced mergers, bottom-up, is maximum, and the maximum costs are the same in both variants.

Upper bound If $n = 2^p + 1$, then $p = \lfloor \lg n \rfloor = \lceil \lg n \rceil - 1$. Furthermore, definition (4.62) entails $\overline{\mathcal{W}}^{\text{bms}}_{2^p+1} = p2^p + 1$ and definition (4.37) on page 139 $\overline{\mathcal{W}}^{\text{tms}}_{2^p+1} = (p-1)2^p + p + 2$, so $\overline{\mathcal{W}}^{\text{bms}}_{2^p+i} - \overline{\mathcal{W}}^{\text{tms}}_{2^p+i} = 2^p - p - 1$. In terms of n, this means that $\overline{\mathcal{W}}^{\text{bms}}_n - \overline{\mathcal{W}}^{\text{tms}}_n = n - \lceil \lg n \rceil - 1$, if $n = 2^p + 1$. We want to prove that this difference is maximum:

$$\mathsf{W}_U(n) \colon \overline{\mathcal{W}}^{\text{bms}}_n \leqslant \overline{\mathcal{W}}^{\text{tms}}_n + n - \lceil \lg n \rceil - 1. \tag{4.69}$$

Notice how equation (4.63) entails $\mathsf{W}_U(2^0)$. Consequently, let the induction hypothesis be $\forall m \leqslant 2^p . \mathsf{W}_U(m)$ and let us prove that $\mathsf{W}_U(2^p + i)$, for all $0 < i < 2^p$.

Let $n = 2^p + i$. Equations (4.62) and (4.63) yield

$$\overline{\mathcal{W}}^{\text{bms}}_{2^p+i} = \overline{\mathcal{W}}^{\text{bms}}_{2^p} + \overline{\mathcal{W}}^{\text{bms}}_i + 2^p + i - 1 = \overline{\mathcal{W}}^{\text{tms}}_{2^p} + \overline{\mathcal{W}}^{\text{bms}}_i + 2^p + i - 1$$
$$\leqslant \overline{\mathcal{W}}^{\text{tms}}_{2^p} + \overline{\mathcal{W}}^{\text{tms}}_i + 2^p + 2i - \lceil \lg i \rceil - 2,$$

where the inequality is the instance $\mathsf{W}_U(i)$ of the induction hypothesis. Furthermore, $n - \lceil \lg n \rceil - 1 = 2^p + i - p - 2$. Therefore, if

$$\overline{\mathcal{W}}_{2^p}^{\mathsf{tms}} + \overline{\mathcal{W}}_i^{\mathsf{tms}} + 2^p + 2i - \lceil \lg i \rceil - 2 \leqslant \overline{\mathcal{W}}_{2^p+i}^{\mathsf{tms}} + 2^p + i - p - 2,$$

then $\mathsf{W}_U(2^p + i)$ would ensue. Using equation (4.37), we deduce

$$\overline{\mathcal{W}}_i^{\mathsf{tms}} = i\lceil \lg i \rceil - 2^{\lceil \lg i \rceil} + 1,$$
$$\overline{\mathcal{W}}_{2^p}^{\mathsf{tms}} = (p-1)2^p + 1,$$
$$\overline{\mathcal{W}}_{2^p+i}^{\mathsf{tms}} = \overline{\mathcal{W}}_{2^p}^{\mathsf{tms}} + (p+1)i.$$

The unproven inequality becomes $\overline{\mathcal{W}}_i^{\mathsf{tms}} + i - \lceil \lg i \rceil \leqslant (p+1)i - p$, or

$$1 \leqslant (i-1)(p - \lceil \lg i \rceil) + 2^{\lceil \lg i \rceil}. \tag{4.70}$$

We have two complementary cases to consider:

- $i = 2^q$, with $0 \leqslant q < p$. Then $\lg i = q$ and inequation (4.70) is equivalent to $(p - q + 1)(2^q - 1) \geqslant 0$. Since $0 \leqslant q < p$ implies $p - q + 1 > 1$ and $2^q \geqslant 1$, the inequality is proved, the bound being tight if, and only if, $q = 0$.

- $i = 2^q + j$, with $0 \leqslant q < p$ and $0 < j < 2^q$. Then we have $\lfloor \lg i \rfloor = q = \lceil \lg i \rceil - 1$ and inequation (4.70) is then equivalent to $1 \leqslant (2^q + j - 1)(p - q) + 2^q$, or

$$1 \leqslant (p - q + 1)2^q + (p - q - 1)(j - 1). \tag{4.71}$$

  From $q < p$ we deduce $p - q + 1 \geqslant 2$ and $p - q - 1 \geqslant 0$; we also have $2^q \geqslant 1$ and $j \geqslant 1$. Consequently, $(p - q + 1)2^q \geqslant 2$ and $(p - q - 1)(j - 1) \geqslant 0$, hence inequation (4.71) holds, but the bound is never tight. □

As a side-effect, we proved that if $i = 1$, that is, $n = 2^p + 1$, then we have the following inequation:

$$\overline{\mathcal{W}}_{2^p+1}^{\mathsf{bms}} = \overline{\mathcal{W}}_{2^p}^{\mathsf{tms}} + \overline{\mathcal{W}}_1^{\mathsf{bms}} + 2^p \leqslant \overline{\mathcal{W}}_{2^p}^{\mathsf{tms}} + \overline{\mathcal{W}}_1^{\mathsf{tms}} + 2^p = \overline{\mathcal{W}}_{2^p+1}^{\mathsf{tms}} + 2^p - p - 1.$$

But, since $\overline{\mathcal{W}}_1^{\mathsf{tms}} = \overline{\mathcal{W}}_1^{\mathsf{bms}} = 0$, the inequality is actually an equality.

$$\boxed{\overline{\mathcal{W}}_n^{\mathsf{bms}} = \overline{\mathcal{W}}_n^{\mathsf{tms}} + n - \lceil \lg n \rceil - 1 \Leftrightarrow n = 1 \text{ or } n = 2^p + 1, \text{with } p \geqslant 0.}$$

Program   Although we will present the programming language Erlang in part III, here is how to compute efficiently the maximum costs:

```
-module(max).
-compile(nowarn_export_all).
-compile(export_all).

ceiling(X) when X > trunc(X) -> trunc(X) + 1;
ceiling(X)                   -> trunc(X).

log2(X) -> math:log(X)/math:log(2).

exp2(0) -> 1;
exp2(N) -> E=exp2(N div 2), (1 + N rem 2)*(E*E).

rho(1) -> 0;
rho(N) -> case N rem 2 of
               0 -> rho(N div 2) + 1;
               1 -> 0
          end.

nu(0) -> 0;
nu(N) -> nu(N div 2) + N rem 2.

bms(0) -> 0;
bms(1) -> 0;
bms(N) -> K = N div 2,
          case N rem 2 of
              0 -> bms(N-1) + nu(K-1) + 1;
              1 -> bms(N-2) + 2*exp2(rho(K)) + nu(K-1) + nu(K)
          end.

tms(0) -> 0; tms(1) -> 0;
tms(N) -> L = ceiling(log2(N)), N*L - exp2(L) + 1.
```

Note how we efficiently computed the binary exponentiation 2^n by means of the recurrent equations

$$2^0 = 1, \quad 2^{2m} = (2^m)^2, \quad 2^{2m+1} = 2(2^m)^2.$$

The cost C_n^{exp2} thus satisfies $C_0^{\text{exp2}} = 1$ and $C_n^{\text{exp2}} = 1 + C_{\lfloor n/2 \rfloor}^{\text{exp2}}$, if $n > 0$. Therefore, if $n > 0$, it is 1 plus the number of bits of n, that is to say, $C_n^{\text{exp2}} = \lfloor \lg n \rfloor + 2$, else $C_0^{\text{exp2}} = 1$.

Average cost   In sum, we established, for $n \geqslant 2$,

$$n \lg n - \frac{3}{2}n + 2 < \overline{\mathcal{A}}_n^{\mathsf{tms}} < n \lg n - n + 1,$$

$$n \lg n - \alpha n + (2\alpha - 1) < \overline{\mathcal{A}}_n^{\mathsf{bms}} < n \lg n - (\alpha - 1)n - (3 - 2\alpha),$$

where $\alpha \simeq 1.2645$, $2\alpha - 1 \simeq 1.52899$ and $3 - 2\alpha \simeq 0.471$. For top-down merge sort, the nature of n for the bounds to be most accurate was not conclusively found by our inductive method. For bottom-up merge sort, the lower bound is most accurate when $n = 2^p$, but we could not determine the values of n that make the upper bound most accurate.

The previous inequalities on $\overline{\mathcal{A}}_n^{\mathsf{bms}}$ do not allow us to compare the average costs of the two variants of merge sort we have studied. Here, we prove that top-down merge sort performs fewer key comparisons than bottom-up merge sort in average. Since we already proved that this is true as well in the worst case (see (4.64) on page 158), and that their minimum costs are equal (see (4.44) on page 144), this will be the last nail in the coffin of the bottom-up variant, before its rebirth in section 4.6 on page 168. We want to prove by induction

$$\overline{\mathcal{A}}_n^{\mathsf{tms}} \leqslant \overline{\mathcal{A}}_n^{\mathsf{bms}}.$$

We already now that the bound is tight when $n = 2^p$, so let us check the inequality for $n = 2$ and let us assume that it holds up to 2^p and proceed to establish that it also holds for $2^p + i$, with $0 < i \leqslant 2^p$, thus reaching our goal. Let us recall equation (4.57) on page 149:

$$\overline{\mathcal{A}}_{2^p+i}^{\mathsf{bms}} = \overline{\mathcal{A}}_{2^p}^{\mathsf{bms}} + \overline{\mathcal{A}}_i^{\mathsf{bms}} + 2^p + i - \frac{2^p}{i+1} - \frac{i}{2^p+1}.$$

Since $\overline{\mathcal{A}}_{2^p}^{\mathsf{bms}} = \overline{\mathcal{A}}_{2^p}^{\mathsf{tms}}$ and, by hypothesis, $\overline{\mathcal{A}}_i^{\mathsf{tms}} \leqslant \overline{\mathcal{A}}_i^{\mathsf{bms}}$, we have

$$\overline{\mathcal{A}}_{2^p+i}^{\mathsf{bms}} \geqslant \overline{\mathcal{A}}_{2^p}^{\mathsf{tms}} + \overline{\mathcal{A}}_i^{\mathsf{tms}} + 2^p + i - \frac{2^p}{i+1} - \frac{i}{2^p+1}. \qquad (4.72)$$

If we could show the right-hand side to be greater than or equal to $\overline{\mathcal{A}}_{2^p+i}^{\mathsf{tms}}$, we would win. Let us actually generalise this sufficient condition and express it as the following lemma:

$$\mathsf{T}(m, n)\colon \overline{\mathcal{A}}_{m+n}^{\mathsf{tms}} \leqslant \overline{\mathcal{A}}_m^{\mathsf{tms}} + \overline{\mathcal{A}}_n^{\mathsf{tms}} + m + n - \frac{m}{n+1} - \frac{n}{m+1}.$$

Let us use a lexicographic ordering on the pairs (m, n) of natural numbers m and n (see definition (1.8) on page 13). The base case, $(0, 0)$, is easily seen to hold. We observe that the statement to be proved is symmetric, $\mathsf{T}(m, n) \Leftrightarrow \mathsf{T}(n, m)$, hence we only need to make three cases: $(2p, 2q)$, $(2p, 2q + 1)$ and $(2p + 1, 2q + 1)$.

1. $(m, n) = (2p, 2q)$. In this case,

   - $\overline{A}_{m+n}^{\text{tms}} = \overline{A}_{2(p+q)}^{\text{tms}} = 2\overline{A}_{p+q}^{\text{tms}} + 2(p+q) - 2 + 2/(p+q+1)$;
   - $\overline{A}_m^{\text{tms}} = \overline{A}_{2p}^{\text{tms}} = 2\overline{A}_p^{\text{tms}} + 2p - 2 + 2/(p+1)$;
   - $\overline{A}_n^{\text{tms}} = \overline{A}_{2q}^{\text{tms}} = 2\overline{A}_q^{\text{tms}} + 2q - 2 + 2/(q+1)$.

Then, the right-hand side of $\mathsf{T}(m, n)$ is

$$r := 2\left(\overline{A}_p^{\text{tms}} + \overline{A}_q^{\text{tms}} + 2(p+q) - 2 + \tfrac{1}{p+1} + \tfrac{1}{q+1} - \tfrac{p}{2q+1} - \tfrac{q}{2p+1}\right).$$

The induction hypothesis $\mathsf{T}(p, q)$ is

$$\overline{A}_{p+q}^{\text{tms}} \leqslant \overline{A}_p^{\text{tms}} + \overline{A}_q^{\text{tms}} + p + q - \frac{p}{q+1} - \frac{q}{p+1}.$$

Therefore, $r/2 \geqslant \overline{A}_{p+q}^{\text{tms}} + p + q - 2 + \tfrac{q+1}{p+1} + \tfrac{p+1}{q+1} - \tfrac{p}{2q+1} - \tfrac{q}{2p+1}$. If the right-hand side is greater than or equal to $\overline{A}_{m+n}^{\text{tms}}/2$, then $\mathsf{T}(m, n)$ is proved. In other words, we need to prove

$$\frac{p+1}{q+1} + \frac{q+1}{p+1} \geqslant 1 + \frac{p}{2q+1} + \frac{q}{2p+1} + \frac{1}{p+q+1}.$$

We expand everything in order to get rid of the fractions; we then observe that we can factorise pq and the remaining bivariate polynomial is 0 if $p = q$ (the inequality is tight), which means that we can factorise by $p - q$ (actually, twice). In the end, this inequation is equivalent to $pq(p-q)^2(2p+2q+3) \geqslant 0$, with $p, q \geqslant 0$, which means that $\mathsf{T}(m, n)$ holds.

2. $(m, n) = (2p, 2q + 1)$. In this case,

   - $\overline{A}_{m+n}^{\text{tms}} = \overline{A}_{2(p+q)+1}^{\text{tms}} = \overline{A}_{p+q}^{\text{tms}} + \overline{A}_{p+q+1}^{\text{tms}} + 2(p+q) - 1 + \tfrac{2}{p+q+2}$;
   - $\overline{A}_m^{\text{tms}} = \overline{A}_{2p}^{\text{tms}} = 2\overline{A}_p^{\text{tms}} + 2p - 2 + 2/(p+1)$;
   - $\overline{A}_n^{\text{tms}} = \overline{A}_{2q+1}^{\text{tms}} = \overline{A}_q^{\text{tms}} + \overline{A}_{q+1}^{\text{tms}} + 2q - 1 + 2/(q+2)$.

Then, the right-hand side of $\mathsf{T}(m, n)$ is

$$r := 2\overline{A}_p^{\text{tms}} + \overline{A}_q^{\text{tms}} + \overline{A}_{q+1}^{\text{tms}} + 4(p+q) - 2 + \tfrac{2}{p+1} + \tfrac{2}{q+2} - \tfrac{p}{q+1} - \tfrac{2q+1}{2p+1}.$$

The induction hypotheses $\mathsf{T}(p, q)$ and $\mathsf{T}(p, q + 1)$ are

   - $\overline{A}_{p+q}^{\text{tms}} \leqslant \overline{A}_p^{\text{tms}} + \overline{A}_q^{\text{tms}} + p + q - \tfrac{p}{q+1} - \tfrac{q}{p+1}$;
   - $\overline{A}_{p+(q+1)}^{\text{tms}} \leqslant \overline{A}_p^{\text{tms}} + \overline{A}_{q+1}^{\text{tms}} + p + (q+1) - \tfrac{p}{q+2} - \tfrac{q+1}{p+1}$.

Thus, $r \geqslant \overline{\mathcal{A}}^{\text{tms}}_{p+q} + \overline{\mathcal{A}}^{\text{tms}}_{p+q+1} + 2(p+q) - 3 + \frac{2q+3}{p+1} + \frac{p+2}{q+2} - \frac{2q+1}{2p+1}$. If the right-hand side is greater than or equal to $\overline{\mathcal{A}}^{\text{tms}}_{m+n}$, then $\mathsf{T}(m,n)$ is proved. In other words, we need to prove

$$\frac{2q+3}{p+1} + \frac{p+2}{q+2} \geqslant 2 + \frac{2q+1}{2p+1} + \frac{2}{p+q+2}.$$

By expanding and getting rid of the fractions, we obtain a bivariate polynomial with the trivial factors p and $p - q$ (because if $p = q$, the inequality is tight). After that, a computer algebra system can finish the factorisation and the inequality is found to be equivalent to $p(p-q)(p-q-1)(2p+2q+5) \geqslant 0$, therefore $\mathsf{T}(m,n)$ holds.

3. $(m,n) = (2p+1, 2q+1)$. In this case,

- $\overline{\mathcal{A}}^{\text{tms}}_{m+n} = \overline{\mathcal{A}}^{\text{tms}}_{2(p+q+1)} = 2\overline{\mathcal{A}}^{\text{tms}}_{p+q+1} + 2(p+q) + 2/(p+q+2)$;
- $\overline{\mathcal{A}}^{\text{tms}}_n = \overline{\mathcal{A}}^{\text{tms}}_{2p+1} = \overline{\mathcal{A}}^{\text{tms}}_p + \overline{\mathcal{A}}^{\text{tms}}_{p+1} + 2p - 1 + 2/(p+2)$;
- $\overline{\mathcal{A}}^{\text{tms}}_n = \overline{\mathcal{A}}^{\text{tms}}_{2q+1} = \overline{\mathcal{A}}^{\text{tms}}_q + \overline{\mathcal{A}}^{\text{tms}}_{q+1} + 2q - 1 + 2/(q+2)$.

Then, the right-hand side of $\mathsf{T}(m,n)$ is

$$r := \overline{\mathcal{A}}^{\text{tms}}_p + \overline{\mathcal{A}}^{\text{tms}}_q + \overline{\mathcal{A}}^{\text{tms}}_{p+1} + \overline{\mathcal{A}}^{\text{tms}}_{q+1} + 4(p+q) + \frac{2}{p+2} + \frac{2}{q+2} - \frac{2p+1}{2q+2} - \frac{2q+1}{2p+2}.$$

The (symmetric) induction hypotheses $\mathsf{T}(p, q+1)$ and $\mathsf{T}(p+1, q)$:

- $\overline{\mathcal{A}}^{\text{tms}}_{p+(q+1)} \leqslant \overline{\mathcal{A}}^{\text{tms}}_p + \overline{\mathcal{A}}^{\text{tms}}_{q+1} + p + q + 1 - \frac{p}{q+2} - \frac{q+1}{p+1}$;
- $\overline{\mathcal{A}}^{\text{tms}}_{(p+1)+q} \leqslant \overline{\mathcal{A}}^{\text{tms}}_{p+1} + \overline{\mathcal{A}}^{\text{tms}}_q + p + q + 1 - \frac{p+1}{q+1} - \frac{q}{p+2}$.

Thus, $r \geqslant 2\overline{\mathcal{A}}^{\text{tms}}_{p+q+1} + 2(p+q) - 2 + \frac{q+1}{p+1} + \frac{q}{p+2} + \frac{p+1}{q+1} + \frac{p}{q+2} + \frac{2}{p+2} + \frac{2}{q+2} - \frac{2p+1}{2q+2} - \frac{2q+1}{2p+2}$. If the right-hand side is greater than or equal to $\overline{\mathcal{A}}^{\text{tms}}_{m+n}$, then $\mathsf{T}(m,n)$ is proved. In other words, we need to prove

$$\frac{q+1}{p+1} + \frac{q+2}{p+2} + \frac{p+2}{q+2} + \frac{p+1}{q+1} \geqslant 2 + \frac{2p+1}{2q+2} + \frac{2q+1}{2p+2} + \frac{2}{p+q+2}.$$

After expansion to form a positive polynomial, we note that the inequality is tight if $p = q$, so the polynomial has a factor $p - q$. After division, another factor $p - q$ is clear. The inequality is thus equivalent to $(p-q)^2(2p^2(q+1) + p(2q^2 + 9q + 8) + 2(q+2)^2) \geqslant 0$, so $\mathsf{T}(m,n)$ holds in this case as well.

In total, $\mathsf{T}(m,n)$ holds in each case, therefore the lemma is true for all m and n. By applying the lemma to (4.72), we prove the theorem $\overline{\mathcal{A}}^{\text{tms}}_n \leqslant \overline{\mathcal{A}}^{\text{bms}}_n$, for all n. Collecting all the cases where the bound is tight shows what we would expect: $m = n$, $m = n+1$ or $n = m+1$. For (4.72), this means $i = 2^p$ or $i = 2^p - 1$. In other words,

$$\boxed{\overline{\mathcal{A}}^{\text{tms}}_n = \overline{\mathcal{A}}^{\text{bms}}_n \Leftrightarrow n = 2^p \text{ or } n = 2^p - 1, \text{ with } p \geqslant 0.}$$

Program In Erlang, we would implement as follows the computation
of the average costs of top-down and bottom-up merge sort:

```
-module(mean).
-compile(nowarn_export_all).
-compile(export_all).
-compile({no_auto_import,[floor/1]}).

floor(X) when X < trunc(X)    -> trunc(X) - 1;
floor(X)                      -> trunc(X).

ceiling(X) when X > trunc(X) -> trunc(X) + 1;
ceiling(X)                   -> trunc(X).

log2(X) -> math:log(X)/math:log(2).
exp2(0) -> 1;
exp2(N) -> E=exp2(N div 2), (1 + N rem 2)*(E*E).

mrg(M,N) -> M + N - M/(N+1) - N/(M+1).
bms0(N) -> bms(N) + N + ceiling(N/2) + 2*ceiling(log2(N)) - 1.

bms(0) -> 0;
bms(1) -> 0;
bms(N) -> E=exp2(ceiling(log2(N))-1),
          bms(E) + bms(N-E) + mrg(E,N-E).

tms(0) -> 0;
tms(1) -> 0;
tms(N) -> F=floor(N/2), C=ceiling(N/2),
          tms(F) + tms(C) + mrg(C,F).

h(0) -> 0;
h(N) -> 1/N + h(N-1).

i2wb(N) -> P = N div 2,
           case N rem 2 of
             0 -> P*P/2 + 13*P/4 + h(P)/8 - h(N)/4 + 2;
             1 -> P*P/2 + 15*P/4 + h(P)/8 - h(N)/4 + 13/4
           end.
```

Merging vs. inserting Let us compare insertion sort and bottom-
up merge sort in their fastest variant. We found in equation (3.13) on

page 118 the average cost of balanced 2-way insertion sort:

$$\mathcal{A}_n^{\mathsf{i2wb}} = \frac{1}{8}(n^2 + 13n - \ln 2n + 10) + \epsilon_n, \text{ with } 0 < \epsilon_n < \frac{7}{8}.$$

We also just found that the cost in addition to comparisons is $\lceil 3n/2 \rceil + 2\lceil \lg n \rceil - 1$ for $\mathsf{bms_0/1}$, and $\overline{\mathcal{C}}_n^{\mathsf{bms_0}} = \overline{\mathcal{C}}_n^{\mathsf{bms}}$. Moreover, we found bounds on $\overline{\mathcal{A}}_n^{\mathsf{bms}}$ in (4.58) on page 153, the upper one being excellent. Therefore

$$\mathcal{A}_n^{\mathsf{bms_0}} < (n \lg n - (\alpha - 1)n - (3 - 2\alpha)) + (\lceil 3n/2 \rceil + 2\lceil \lg n \rceil - 1)$$
$$< (n + 2) \lg n + 1.236n + 1.529;$$
$$\mathcal{A}_n^{\mathsf{bms_0}} > (n \lg n - 1.35n + 1.69) + (\lceil 3n/2 \rceil + 2\lceil \lg n \rceil - 1)$$
$$> (n + 2) \lg n + 0.152n + 0.69;$$

$$(n^2 + 13n - \ln 2n + 10)/8 < \mathcal{A}_n^{\mathsf{i2wb}} < (n^2 + 13n - \ln 2n + 17)/8.$$

where $\alpha \simeq 1.2645$ and $\lceil x \rceil < x + 1$. Hence,

$$(n + 2) \lg n + 1.236n + 1.529 < (n^2 + 13n - \ln 2n + 10)/8$$

implies $\mathcal{A}_n^{\mathsf{bms_0}} < \mathcal{A}_n^{\mathsf{i2wb}}$, and also

$$(n^2 + 13n - \ln 2n + 17)/8 < (n + 2) \lg n + 0.152n + 0.69$$

implies $\mathcal{A}_n^{\mathsf{i2wb}} < \mathcal{A}_n^{\mathsf{bms_0}}$. With the help of a computer algebra system, we find that

1. $\mathcal{A}_n^{\mathsf{i2wb}} < \mathcal{A}_n^{\mathsf{bms_0}}$ if $3 \leqslant n \leqslant 29$,

2. $\mathcal{A}_n^{\mathsf{bms_0}} < \mathcal{A}_n^{\mathsf{i2wb}}$ if $43 \leqslant n$.

For the case $n = 2$, we find: $\mathcal{A}_2^{\mathsf{i2wb}} = 11/2 > 5 = \mathcal{A}_2^{\mathsf{bms_0}}$. If we set aside this peculiar case, we may conclude that insertion sort is faster, in average, for stacks of less than 30 keys, and the opposite is true for stacks of at least 43 keys.

In-between, we do not know, but we can compute efficiently the average costs and use dichotomy on the interval from 30 to 43. By using the Erlang program above, we quickly find that insertion sort is first beaten by bottom-up merge sort at $n = 36$. This suggests to drop $\mathsf{duo/1}$ in favour of a function that constructs chunks of 35 keys from the original stack, then sorts them using balanced 2-way insertions and, finally, if there are more than 35 keys, starts merging those sorted stacks. This improvement amounts to not constructing the first 35 levels in the merge tree but, instead, build the 35th level by insertions.

Despite the previous analysis, we should be aware that it relies on a measure based on the number of function calls, which assumes that each function call is indeed performed by the run-time system (no inlining), that all context switchings have the same duration, that other operations take a negligible time in comparison, that cache, jump predictions and instruction pipelining have no effect etc. Even using the same compiler on the same machine does not exempt from careful benchmarking.

4.6   Online merge sort

Sorting algorithms can be distinguished depending on whether they operate on the whole stack of keys, or key by key. The former are said *off-line*, as keys are not sorted while they are coming in, and the latter are called *online*, as the sorting process can be temporally interleaved with the input process. Bottom-up merge sort is an off-line algorithm, but it can be easily modified to become online by remarking that balanced mergers can be repeated whenever a new key arrives, and the unbalanced mergers are performed only when the sorted stack is required.

More precisely, consider again FIGURE 4.12 on page 146 without the unbalanced mergers. The addition of another key (at the right) yields two cases: if n is even, that is, $e_0 > 0$, then nothing is done as the key becomes a singleton, sorted stack of length 2^0; otherwise, a cascade of mergers between stacks of identical lengths 2^{e_i}, with $e_i = i$, is triggered until $e_j > j$. This is exactly the binary addition of 1 to n, except that mergers, instead of bitwise additions, are performed as long as a carry is issued and propagated.

To our knowledge, only Okasaki (1998a) mentions this variant; he shows that it can be efficiently implemented with purely functional data structures, just as the off-line version. (Notice that his context is nevertheless different from ours as he relies on lazy evaluation and amortised analysis.) Online merge sort is used in the standard library of the proof assistant Coq (Bertot and Castéran, 2004).

Our code is shown in FIGURE 4.18. We use zero() to represent a 0-bit in the binary notation of the number of currently sorted keys. Dually, the call one(s) denotes a 1-bit, where the stack s holds a number of sorted keys equal to the associated power of two in the binary notation. Each call to one/1 corresponds to a subtree in FIGURE 4.12 on page 146. For instance, [one([4]), zero(), one([3, 6, 7, 9])] corresponds to the binary number $(101)_2$, hence the stack holds $1 \cdot 2^2 + 0 \cdot 2^1 + 1 \cdot 2^0 = 5$ keys in total. Keep in mind that the bits are reversed in the stack, as the subsequent processing of key 5 would yield [zero(), one([4, 5]), one([3, 6, 7, 9])].

$$\mathsf{oms}(s) \xrightarrow{\phi} \mathsf{unb}(\mathsf{sum}(s,[\,]),[\,]).$$

$$\mathsf{sum}([\,],t) \xrightarrow{\chi} t;$$
$$\mathsf{sum}([x\,|\,s],t) \xrightarrow{\psi} \mathsf{sum}(s,\mathsf{add}([x],t)).$$

$$\mathsf{add}(s,[\,]) \xrightarrow{\omega} [\mathsf{one}(s)];$$
$$\mathsf{add}(s,[\mathsf{zero}()\,|\,t]) \xrightarrow{\gamma} [\mathsf{one}(s)\,|\,t];$$
$$\mathsf{add}(s,[\mathsf{one}(u)\,|\,t]) \xrightarrow{\delta} [\mathsf{zero}()\,|\,\mathsf{add}(\mathsf{mrg}(s,u),t)].$$

$$\mathsf{unb}([\,],u) \xrightarrow{\mu} u;$$
$$\mathsf{unb}([\mathsf{zero}()\,|\,s],u) \xrightarrow{\nu} \mathsf{unb}(s,u);$$
$$\mathsf{unb}([\mathsf{one}(t)\,|\,s],u) \xrightarrow{\xi} \mathsf{unb}(s,\mathsf{mrg}(t,u)).$$

$$\mathsf{mrg}([\,],t) \xrightarrow{\theta} t;$$
$$\mathsf{mrg}(s,[\,]) \xrightarrow{\iota} s;$$
$$\mathsf{mrg}([x\,|\,s],[y\,|\,t]) \xrightarrow{\kappa} [y\,|\,\mathsf{mrg}([x\,|\,s],t)], \text{ if } x \succ y;$$
$$\mathsf{mrg}([x\,|\,s],t) \xrightarrow{\lambda} [x\,|\,\mathsf{mrg}(s,t)].$$

Figure 4.18: Online merge sort with oms/1

Note that the program in FIGURE 4.18 does not capture the normal use case of online merge sort, as, in practice, the argument s of the call $\mathsf{oms}(s)$ would not be known in its entirety, so $\mathsf{add}/2$ would only be called whenever a key becomes available. In the following analysis, however, we are interested in the number of comparisons of a sequence of updates by $\mathsf{sum}/2$ (a framework we used in section 2.5), followed by a series of unbalanced mergers by $\mathsf{unb}/2$ (*unbalanced*) in order to obtain a sorted stack; therefore, our program is suitable because we do want to assess $\overline{\mathcal{C}}_n^{\mathsf{oms}}$.

Let us note $\overline{\mathcal{C}}_n^{\mathsf{add}}$ the number of comparisons to add a new key to a current stack of length n and recall that $\overline{\mathcal{C}}_{m,n}^{\mathsf{mrg}}$ is the number of comparisons to merge two stacks of lengths m and n by calling $\mathsf{mrg}/2$. If n is even, then there are no comparisons, as this is similar to adding 1 to a binary sequence $(\Xi 0)_2$, where Ξ is an arbitrary bit string. Otherwise, a series of balanced mergers of size 2^i are performed, as this is dual to adding 1 to $(\Xi 011 \ldots 1)_2$, where Ξ is arbitrary. Therefore

$$\overline{\mathcal{C}}_{2j}^{\mathsf{add}} = 0, \qquad \overline{\mathcal{C}}_{2j-1}^{\mathsf{add}} = \sum_{i=0}^{\rho_{2j}} \overline{\mathcal{C}}_{2^i,2^i}^{\mathsf{mrg}},$$

where ρ_n is the highest power of 2 dividing n (ruler function). Let $\overline{\mathcal{C}}_n^{\mathsf{sum}}$

be the number of comparisons to add n keys to the empty stack $[\,]$. That is to say, we have the following:

$$\overline{C}_n^{\mathsf{sum}} = \sum_{k=0}^{n-1} \overline{C}_k^{\mathsf{add}}.$$

$$\overline{C}_{2p}^{\mathsf{sum}} = \overline{C}_{2p+1}^{\mathsf{sum}} = \sum_{k=1}^{2p-1} \overline{C}_k^{\mathsf{add}} = \sum_{j=1}^{p} \overline{C}_{2j-1}^{\mathsf{add}} = \sum_{j=1}^{p} \sum_{i=0}^{1+\rho_j} \overline{C}_{2^i,2^i}^{\mathsf{mrg}}. \qquad (4.73)$$

From (4.59), the number of comparisons of the unbalanced mergers is

$$\overline{C}_n^{\mathsf{unb}} = \overline{C}_n^{\ltimes} = \sum_{i=1}^{r} \overline{C}_{2^{e_i},2^{e_i-1}+\cdots+2^{e_0}}^{\mathsf{mrg}}. \qquad (4.74)$$

Let $\overline{C}_n^{\mathsf{oms}}$ the number of comparisons to sort n keys online. We have

$$\overline{C}_n^{\mathsf{oms}} = \overline{C}_n^{\mathsf{sum}} + \overline{C}_n^{\mathsf{unb}}. \qquad (4.75)$$

Minimum cost   Replacing $\mathcal{C}$ by $\mathcal{B}$ in equation (4.73), we obtain the equations for the minimum number of comparisons, allowing us to simplify $\overline{\mathcal{B}}_n^{\mathsf{sum}}$ with the help of equation (4.3) on page 121:

$$\overline{\mathcal{B}}_{2p}^{\mathsf{sum}} = \overline{\mathcal{B}}_{2p+1}^{\mathsf{sum}} = \sum_{j=1}^{p} \sum_{i=0}^{1+\rho_j} \overline{\mathcal{B}}_{2^i,2^i}^{\mathsf{mrg}} = \sum_{j=1}^{p} \sum_{i=0}^{1+\rho_j} 2^i = 4 \sum_{j=1}^{p} 2^{\rho_j} - p. \qquad (4.76)$$

Let $T_p := \sum_{j=1}^{p} 2^{\rho_j}$. The recurrences on the ruler function (4.50) on page 147 help us in finding a recurrence for T_p as follows:

$$T_{2q} = \sum_{k=0}^{q-1} 2^{\rho_{2k+1}} + \sum_{k=1}^{q} 2^{\rho_{2k}} = q + 2 \cdot T_q,$$

$$T_{2q+1} = \sum_{j=1}^{2q+1} 2^{\rho_j} = 1 + T_{2q} = (q+1) + 2 \cdot T_q.$$

Equivalently, $T_p = 2 \cdot T_{\lfloor p/2 \rfloor} + \lceil p/2 \rceil = 2 \cdot T_{\lfloor p/2 \rfloor} + p - \lfloor p/2 \rfloor$. Therefore, unravelling a few terms of the recurrence quickly reveals the equation

$$2 \cdot T_p = 2p + \sum_{j=1}^{\lfloor \lg p \rfloor} \left\lfloor \frac{p}{2^j} \right\rfloor 2^j,$$

using Theorem 3 on page 138. By definition, $\{x\} := x - \lfloor x \rfloor$, thus

$$2 \cdot T_p = p \lfloor \lg p \rfloor + 2p - \sum_{j=1}^{\lfloor \lg p \rfloor} \left\{ \frac{p}{2^j} \right\} 2^j.$$

Using $0 \leqslant \{x\} < 1$, we obtain the bounds

$$p\lfloor \lg p \rfloor + 2p - 2^{\lfloor \lg p \rfloor + 1} + 2 < 2 \cdot T_p \leqslant p\lfloor \lg p \rfloor + 2p.$$

Furthermore, $x - 1 < \lfloor x \rfloor \leqslant x$ and $\lfloor x \rfloor = x - \{x\}$, therefore

$$p(\lg p - \{\lg p\}) + 2p - 2^{\lg p - \{\lg p\} + 1} + 2 < 2 \cdot T_p \leqslant p \lg p + 2p,$$
$$p \lg p + 2p + 2 - p \cdot \theta_L(\{\lg p\}) < 2 \cdot T_p \leqslant p \lg p + 2p,$$

with $\theta_L(x) := x + 2^{1-x}$. Since $\max_{0 \leqslant x < 1} \theta_L(x) = \theta_L(0) = 2$, we conclude:

$$p \lg p + 2 < 2 \cdot T_p \leqslant p \lg p + 2p.$$

The upper bound is tight if $p = 2^q$. Applying these bounds to the definition of $\overline{B}_{2p}^{\mathsf{sum}}$ in (4.76) yields

$$2p \lg p - p + 4 < \overline{B}_{2p}^{\mathsf{sum}} \leqslant 2p \lg p + 3p. \tag{4.77}$$

Consequently, $\overline{B}_{2p}^{\mathsf{sum}} = \overline{B}_{2p+1}^{\mathsf{sum}} \sim 2p \lg p$, hence $\overline{B}_n^{\mathsf{sum}} \sim n \lg n$.

Equation (4.3) and (4.74) imply $\overline{B}_n^{\mathsf{unb}} = \sum_{i=1}^{r} \min\{2^{e_i}, 2^{e_{i-1}} + \cdots + 2^{e_0}\}$. Let us commence by noting that

$$\sum_{j=0}^{i} 2^{e_j} \leqslant \sum_{j=0}^{e_i} 2^j = 2 \cdot 2^{e_i} - 1.$$

This is equivalent to a given binary number being always lower than or equal to the number with the same number of bits all set to 1, for example, $(10110111)_2 \leqslant (11111111)_2$. By definition of e_i, we have $e_{i-1} + 1 \leqslant e_i$, so

$$\sum_{j=0}^{i-1} 2^{e_j} \leqslant 2^{e_{i-1}+1} - 1 \leqslant 2^{e_i} - 1 < 2^{e_i}$$

and $\min\{2^{e_i}, 2^{e_{i-1}} + \cdots + 2^{e_0}\} = 2^{e_{i-1}} + \cdots + 2^{e_0}$. We have now

$$\overline{B}_n^{\mathsf{unb}} = \sum_{i=1}^{r} \sum_{j=0}^{i-1} 2^{e_j} < n. \tag{4.78}$$

Trivially, $0 < \overline{B}_n^{\mathsf{unb}}$, so equation (4.75) entails $\overline{B}_n^{\mathsf{oms}} \sim n \lg n \sim 2 \cdot \overline{B}_n^{\mathsf{bms}}$.

Maximum cost   Replacing $\mathcal{C}$ by $\mathcal{W}$ in equation (4.73) on page 170, we obtain equations for the maximum number of comparisons, which we can simplify with the help of equation (4.4) on page 121 into

$$\overline{\mathcal{W}}^{\mathsf{sum}}_{2p} = \overline{\mathcal{W}}^{\mathsf{sum}}_{2p+1} = \sum_{j=1}^{p}\sum_{i=0}^{1+\rho_j} \overline{\mathcal{W}}^{\mathsf{mrg}}_{2^i,2^i} = 8\sum_{j=1}^{p} 2^{\rho_j} - \sum_{j=1}^{p}\rho_j - 4p. \qquad (4.79)$$

We can reach a closed form for $\sum_{j=1}^{p}\rho_j$ if we think of the carry propagation and the number of 1-bits when adding 1 to a binary number (since j ranges over successive integers). This amounts to finding a relationship between ρ_j, ρ_{j+1}, ν_j and ν_{j+1}.

- Let us assume that $2n+1 = (\Xi 0 1^a)_2$, where Ξ is an arbitrary bit string and $(1^a)_2$ is a 1-bit string of length a. Then $\nu_{2n+1} = \nu_\Xi + a$ and $\rho_{2n+1} = 0$.

- Otherwise, $2n+2 = (\Xi 1 0^a)_2$, so $\nu_{2n+2} = \nu_\Xi + 1$ and $\rho_{2n+2} = a$. Now, we can relate ρ and ν by means of a:

$$\rho_{2n+2} = \nu_{2n+1} - \nu_\Xi = \nu_{2n+1} - (\nu_{2n+2} - 1) = 1 + \nu_{2n+1} - \nu_{2n+2}.$$

We can check now that the same pattern also works for ρ_{2n+1} by simply using the definitions of ρ and ν: $\rho_{2n+1} = 1 + \nu_{2n} - \nu_{2n+1}$.

This achieves to establish, for any integer $n > 0$, that $\rho_n = 1 + \nu_{n-1} - \nu_n$. Summing on both sides yields

$$\sum_{j=1}^{p}\rho_j = p - \nu_p.$$

Interestingly, we already met $p - \nu_p$ in equation (1.7), on page 11. We can now further simplify (4.79) as follows:

$$\overline{\mathcal{W}}^{\mathsf{sum}}_{2p} = \overline{\mathcal{W}}^{\mathsf{sum}}_{2p+1} = 8\sum_{j=1}^{p} 2^{\rho_j} - 5p - \nu_p = 2\cdot \overline{\mathcal{B}}^{\mathsf{sum}}_{2p} - 3p - \nu_p.$$

Reusing the bounds on $\overline{\mathcal{B}}^{\mathsf{sum}}_{2p}$ in (4.77) leads to $\overline{\mathcal{W}}^{\mathsf{sum}}_{2p} = \overline{\mathcal{W}}^{\mathsf{sum}}_{2p+1} \sim 4p\lg p$. Equations (4.4) and (4.74) and inequation (4.78) imply

$$\overline{\mathcal{W}}^{\mathsf{unb}}_{n} = \sum_{i=1}^{r}\sum_{j=0}^{i} 2^{e_j} - \nu_n + 1 = \overline{\mathcal{B}}^{\mathsf{unb}}_{n} + n - \rho_n - \nu_n + 1 < 2n+1.$$

Therefore, $\overline{\mathcal{W}}^{\mathsf{oms}}_{n} \sim 2n\lg n \sim 2\cdot \overline{\mathcal{W}}^{\mathsf{bms}}_{n}$.

Additional cost Let us account now for all the rewrites in the evaluation of a call $\mathsf{oms}(s)$. Let C_n^{oms} be this number. We already know the contribution due to the comparisons, $\overline{C}_n^{\mathsf{oms}}$, either in rule κ or λ, so let us assess $C_n^{\mathsf{oms}} - \overline{C}_n^{\mathsf{oms}}$:

- Rule ϕ is used once.

- Rules χ and ψ are involved in the subtrace $\psi^n\chi$, hence are used $n+1$ times.

- Rules ω, γ and δ are used $F(n) = 2n - \nu_n$ times, as seen in equation (1.7). We also must account for the rules θ and ι requested by the calls $\mathsf{mrg}(s, u)$ in rule δ. Each 1-bit in the binary notations of the numbers from 1 to $n-1$ triggers such a call, that is, $\sum_{k=1}^{n-1} \nu_k$.

- Rules ν and ξ are used for each bit in the binary notation of n and rule μ is used once, making up $\lfloor \lg n \rfloor + 2$ calls. We also need to add the number of calls $\mathsf{mrg}(t, u)$ in rule ξ, witnessing the application of rules θ and ι. This is the number of 1-bits in n, totalling ν_n.

In total, we have $C_n^{\mathsf{oms}} - \overline{C}_n^{\mathsf{oms}} = 3n + \lfloor \lg n \rfloor + \sum_{k=1}^{n-1} \nu_k + 2$. Equation (4.44) on page 144 entails $C_n^{\mathsf{oms}} = \overline{C}_n^{\mathsf{oms}} + 3n + \lfloor \lg n \rfloor + \overline{B}_n^{\mathsf{bms}} + 2$. Bounds (4.35) on page 137 imply $\overline{B}_n^{\mathsf{bms}} \sim \frac{1}{2} n \lg n$, thus $C_n^{\mathsf{oms}} \sim \overline{C}_n^{\mathsf{oms}}$.

Exercises

1. Prove $\mathsf{mrg}(s, t) \equiv \mathsf{mrg}(t, s)$.
2. Prove that $\mathsf{mrg}(s, t)$ is a sorted stack if s and t are sorted.
3. Prove that all the keys of s and t are in $\mathsf{mrg}(s, t)$.
4. Prove the termination of $\mathsf{bms}/1$, $\mathsf{oms}/1$ and $\mathsf{tms}/1$.
5. Is $\mathsf{bms}/1$ stable? What about $\mathsf{tms}/1$?
6. Find $C_n^{\mathsf{tms}} - \overline{C}_n^{\mathsf{tms}}$. *Hint:* mind equation (1.7) on page 11.
7. Page 155, we found that the number of mergers of $\mathsf{bms}(s)$ is $n-1$ if n is the number of keys in s. Show that $\mathsf{tms}(s)$ performs the same number of mergers. (*Hint:* Consider equation (4.17) on page 131.)
8. Find a counting argument on the table of FIGURE 4.8 on page 131 showing that

$$\sum_{k=1}^{p-1} 2^{\rho_k} = \sum_{i=0}^{\lceil \lg p \rceil - 1} \left\lceil \frac{p - 2^i}{2^{i+1}} \right\rceil 2^i.$$

9. Compare the number of $(|)$-nodes created by $\mathsf{bms}/1$ and $\mathsf{tms}/1$.

Chapter 5

Word Factoring

Let us call *alphabet* a non-empty, finite set of symbols, called *letters* and set in a sans-serif type, for example a, b etc. A *word* is a finite series of letters, like word; in particular, a letter is a word, as in English. We denote repetition of a letter or word with an exponent, for instance, $a^3 = aaa$. Just as letters can be joined to make up words, so can words: the word $u \cdot v$ is made of the letters of word u followed by the letters of word v, for instance, if $u = back$ and $v = up$, then $u \cdot v = backup$. This operation is associative: $(u \cdot v) \cdot w = u \cdot (v \cdot w)$. As a shorthand, the operator may be omitted: $(uv)w = u(vw)$. Concatenation on words behave like a non-commutative product, so it has a neutral element ε, called the *empty word*: $u \cdot \varepsilon = \varepsilon \cdot u = u$.

A word x is a *factor* of a word y if there exists two words u and v such that $y = uxv$. The word x is a *prefix* of y, noted $x \trianglelefteq y$, if $u = \varepsilon$, that is, if $y = xv$. Moreover, it is a *proper prefix*, noted $x \triangleleft y$, if $v \neq \varepsilon$. Given $y = uxv$, the word x is a *suffix* of y if $v = \varepsilon$. Furthermore, it is a *proper suffix* if $u \neq \varepsilon$. Let a be any letter and x, y any word, then the prefix relation is easy to define by an inference system as

$$\varepsilon \trianglelefteq y \qquad \frac{x \trianglelefteq y}{a \cdot x \trianglelefteq a \cdot y}$$

The purpose being to write a functional program for factoring, we need to translate words and operations on them into terms of the language. A letter is translated into a constant data constructor; for example, a becomes $a()$. A word of more than one letter is mapped to a stack of mapped letters, such as hi in $[h(), i()]$. The concatenation of a letter and a word is translated as a push, like a $\cdot$ bed becomes $[a(), b(), e(), d()]$. The concatenation of two words is associated to stack concatenation, so ab $\cdot$ cd leads to $cat([a(), b()], [c(), d()])$.

As usual, the translation of the inference system defining ($\lhd$) into a function pre/2 requires that the cases corresponding to the axioms evaluate in true() and the cases left unspecified ($\ntriangleleft$) evaluate in false():

$$\text{pre}([\,], y) \to \text{true}(); \quad \text{pre}([a\,|\,x], [a\,|\,y]) \to \text{pre}(x, y); \quad \text{pre}(x, y) \to \text{false}().$$

The inference system is now a formal specification for the program.

A letter in a word can be uniquely characterised by a natural number, called *index*, assuming that the first letter has index 0 (Dijkstra, 1982). If $x = $ top, then the letter at index 0 is written $x[0] = $ t and the one at index 2 is $x[2] = $ p. A factor x of y can be identified by the index of $x[0]$ in y. The end of the factor can also be given; for example, $x = $ sit is a factor of $y = $ curiousity at index 6, written $y[6, 8] = x$, meaning $y[6] = x[0]$, $y[7] = x[1]$ and $y[8] = x[2]$. Given two words p and t, determining whether p is a factor of t is called *factoring p in t*.

Factor matching is common in text editing, although it is usually better known as *exact string matching* in the academic field of *stringology* or *text algorithmics* (Charras and Lecroq, 2004, Crochemore et al., 2007) (Cormen et al., 2009, §32). Because of the asymmetric nature of factoring, the word p is called the *pattern* and the word t is the *text*.

5.1   Naïve factoring

In section 2.3, on page 44, we introduced the linear search, that is, the stepwise search for the occurrence of an item in a stack. We can generalise it to search for a series of items occurring consecutively in a stack, that is, to solve the factoring problem. This approach is qualified as being naïve because it is a simple extension of a simple idea and it is implied that it is not the most efficient.

Everything starts with $p[0]$ and $t[0]$ being compared, then, assuming $p[0] = t[0]$, letters $p[1]$ and $t[1]$ are, in turn, compared etc. until one of the words is exhausted or a mismatch occurs. Assuming that p is shorter than t, the former case means that p is a prefix of t. In the latter case, p is shifted so $p[0]$ is aligned with $t[1]$ and the comparisons are resumed from there. If p cannot be shifted anymore because its end would surpass the end of t, then it is not a factor. The essence of this procedure is summed up in FIGURE 5.1 on the next page, where $p[i] \neq t[j]$ (the letters a and b are not relevant in themselves).

FIGURE 5.2 on the facing page shows an abstract program implementing this scheme. The call $\text{loc}_0(p, t)$ evaluates in absent() if the pattern p is not a factor of the text t, otherwise in factor(k), where k is the index in t where p occurs first. Conceptually, this design consists in combining

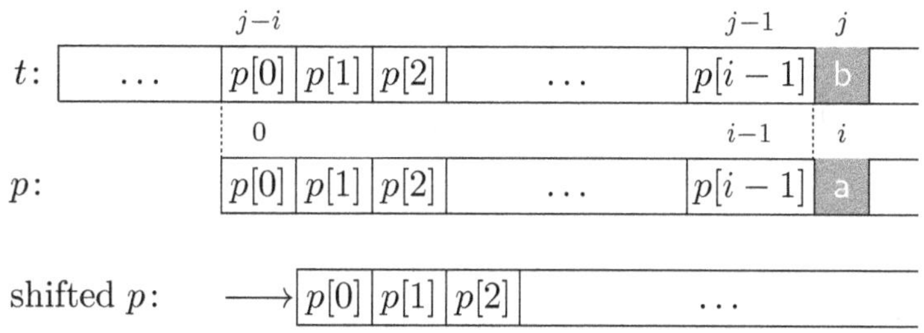

Figure 5.1: Naïvely matching pattern p against text t (failure in grey)

$$\text{loc}_0(p, t) \rightarrow \text{loc}_0(p, t, 0).$$

$$\text{pre}([], t) \rightarrow \text{true}();$$
$$\text{pre}([a \,|\, p], [a \,|\, t]) \rightarrow \text{pre}(p, t);$$
$$\text{pre}(p, t) \rightarrow \text{false}().$$

$$\text{loc}_0([x \,|\, p], [], j) \rightarrow \text{absent}();$$

$$\frac{\text{pre}(p, t) \twoheadrightarrow \text{true}()}{\text{loc}_0(p, t, j) \rightarrow \text{factor}(j)};$$

$$\frac{\text{pre}(p, [a \,|\, t]) \twoheadrightarrow \text{false}()}{\text{loc}_0(p, [a \,|\, t], j) \rightarrow \text{loc}_0(p, t, j + 1)}.$$

Figure 5.2: Naïve factoring with $\text{loc}_0/2$

a linear search for the first letter of the pattern and a prefix check for the rest of the pattern and text. It is important to verify whether the invariants implicit in general do not break in the presence of limit cases. For instance, in stack processing, set the different stacks to be empty and interpret the result of single rewrites and entire evaluations. We have $\text{pre}([], t) \twoheadrightarrow \text{true}()$, because $t = \varepsilon \cdot t$. Accordingly, $\text{loc}_0([], t) \twoheadrightarrow \text{factor}(0)$.

Refinements   While this program composition is intuitive, it is too long. We may remark that, after a call to $\text{pre}/2$ evaluates in $\text{true}()$, the interpretation ends with $\text{factor}(j)$. Dually, a value $\text{false}()$ is followed by the call $\text{loc}_0(p, t, j + 1)$. Therefore, instead of calling $\text{pre}/2$ and then inspecting the resulting value to decide what to do next, we could have $\text{pre}/2$ take the lead. This entails that it needs to receive additional arguments to be able to end with $\text{factor}(j)$ or resume with $\text{loc}_0(p, t, j + 1)$, as expected. The corresponding code is shown in FIGURE 5.3.

Further examination reveals that we can merge $\text{loc}_1/3$ and $\text{pre}_1/5$ into

$$\mathsf{loc}_1(p, t) \to \mathsf{loc}_1(p, t, 0).$$

$$\mathsf{loc}_1([a \,|\, p], [\,], j) \to \mathsf{absent}();$$
$$\mathsf{loc}_1(p, t, j) \to \mathsf{pre}_1(p, t, p, t, j).$$

$$\mathsf{pre}_1([\,], t, p', t', j) \to \mathsf{factor}(j);$$
$$\mathsf{pre}_1([a \,|\, p], [a \,|\, t], p', t', j) \to \mathsf{pre}_1(p, t, p', t', j);$$
$$\mathsf{pre}_1(p, t, p', [a \,|\, t'], j) \to \mathsf{loc}_1(p', t', j + 1).$$

Figure 5.3: Refinement of FIGURE 5.2 on the preceding page

pre/5 in FIGURE 5.4. This kind of progressive design, where a program is transformed into a guided series of equivalent programs is called a *refinement*. Here, each refinement is more efficient than the preceding, but less legible than the original, so each step must be cautiously checked.

$$\mathsf{loc}(p, t) \xrightarrow{\pi} \mathsf{pre}(p, t, p, t, 0).$$

$$\mathsf{pre}([\,], t, p', t', j) \xrightarrow{\rho} \mathsf{factor}(j);$$
$$\mathsf{pre}(p, [\,], p', t', j) \xrightarrow{\sigma} \mathsf{absent}();$$
$$\mathsf{pre}([a \,|\, p], [a \,|\, t], p', t', j) \xrightarrow{\tau} \mathsf{pre}(p, t, p', t', j);$$
$$\mathsf{pre}(p, t, p', [b \,|\, t'], j) \xrightarrow{\upsilon} \mathsf{pre}(p', t', p', t', j + 1).$$

Figure 5.4: Refinement of FIGURE 5.3

Termination   We want to show that the index in the text always increases, whether a comparison fails or not, so we choose a lexicographic order on the dependency pairs of **pre/5** made of the fourth and second arguments (definition (1.8) on page 13), where $s \succ t$ if t is the immediate substack of s. The third rule satisfies $(t', [a \,|\, t]) \succ (t', t)$. The fourth rule is also ordered, because $([b \,|\, t'], t) \succ (t', t')$. $\square$

Completeness   Note how, in rule σ, the pattern p can not be empty because the rules are ordered and that case would always match rule ρ. The completeness of the definition of **pre/5** deserves some attention and we need to justify why the call $\mathsf{pre}([a \,|\, p], [b \,|\, t], p', [\,], j)$, with $a \neq b$, cannot happen. Perhaps surprisingly, a more general statement is easier to establish:

$$\mathsf{loc}(p, t) \twoheadrightarrow \mathsf{pre}(p_0, t_0, p_0', t_0', j) \text{ implies } t_0' \succcurlyeq t_0,$$

where ($\succcurlyeq$) is the reflexive substack relation. Let us prove this property by *induction on the length of the derivation*. More precisely, we want to establish the proposition

$$\mathsf{Comp}(n)\colon \mathsf{loc}(p, t) \xrightarrow{n} \mathsf{pre}(p_0, t_0, p_0', t_0', j) \Rightarrow t_0' \succcurlyeq t_0.$$

- The basis $\mathsf{Comp}(0)$ is easy to prove without induction by means of rule $\pi\colon \mathsf{loc}(p, t) \xrightarrow{\pi} \mathsf{pre}(p, t, p, t, 0)$ and $t \succcurlyeq t$ trivially holds.

- The induction hypothesis is $\mathsf{Comp}(n)$ and we want to show that, under this assumption, $\mathsf{Comp}(n + 1)$ holds as well. In other words, let us suppose that $\mathsf{loc}(p, t) \xrightarrow{n} \mathsf{pre}(p_0, t_0, p_0', t_0', j)$ implies $t_0' \succcurlyeq t_0$ and we want to prove that $\mathsf{pre}(p_0, t_0, p_0', t_0', j) \rightarrow \mathsf{pre}(p_1, t_1, p_1', t_1', k)$ implies $t_1' \succcurlyeq t_1$. This rewrite can only be by means of τ or υ.

  - If τ, the induction hypothesis on the left-hand side entails $t' \succcurlyeq [a \mid t]$, so $t' \succcurlyeq t$ in the right-hand side;
  - otherwise, the right-hand side of υ trivially satisfies $t' \succcurlyeq t'$.

In summary, $\mathsf{Comp}(0)$ is true and $\mathsf{Comp}(n) \Rightarrow \mathsf{Comp}(n + 1)$. Therefore, the induction principle yields $\forall n.\mathsf{Comp}(n)$, which, in turn, entails our formulation with ($\twoheadrightarrow$). Note how, in this case, this proof technique reduces to mathematical induction on n. □

Cost In the following cost analysis, let m be the length of the pattern p and n be the length of the text t. Moreover, as it is common with search algorithms, we discriminate on p being a factor of t or not.

Minimum cost If $m \leqslant n$, the best case happens when the pattern is a prefix of the text, so the evaluation trace is $\pi\tau^m\rho$ and $\mathcal{B}_{m,n}^{\mathsf{loc}} = m + 2$. If $m > n$, the minimum cost is $\mathcal{B}_{m,n}^{\mathsf{loc}} = |\pi\tau^n\sigma| = n + 2$. We can gather these two cases in one formula:

$$\mathcal{B}_{m,n}^{\mathsf{loc}} = \min\{m, n\} + 2.$$

Maximum cost To find the maximum cost, let us investigate the cases where the pattern is a factor of the text and when it is not.

- *The text contains the pattern.* The discovery of the pattern must be delayed as much as possible, therefore the worst case is when w is a suffix of t and every mismatch involves the last letter of the pattern. An example is $p = \mathsf{a}^{m-1}\mathsf{b}$ and $t = \mathsf{a}^{n-1}\mathsf{b}$. The evaluation trace corresponding to this case is $\pi(\tau^{m-1}v)^{n-m}\tau^m\rho$, whose length is $mn - m^2 + m + 2$.

- *The text does not contain the pattern.* The pattern is not the prefix of any suffix of the text. The most delayed comparison failure should occur at the last letter of the pattern, like $p = \mathsf{a}^{m-1}\mathsf{b}$ and $t = \mathsf{a}^n$. The cost is $|\pi(\tau^{m-1}v)^{n-m+1}\tau^{m-1}\sigma| = mn - m^2 + 2m + 1$.

Therefore, the maximum cost is $\mathcal{W}^{\mathsf{loc}}_{m,n} = mn - m^2 + 2m + 1$, when the pattern is not a factor of the text and $m \geqslant 1$. The previous analysis suggests an improvement for that case, but would make the case when the text contains the pattern the worst: just after rule τ, let us add

$$\mathsf{pre}([a], [b], p', t', j) \to \mathsf{absent}();$$

Average cost Let us suppose that $0 < m \leqslant n$ and that the letters of p and t are chosen from the same alphabet, whose cardinal is $\breve{a} > 1$. Naïve factoring consists in matching a pattern against the prefixes of the suffixes of a text, by decreasing lengths. Let $\overline{\mathcal{A}}^{\breve{a}}_m$ be the average number of letter comparisons for comparing two words of length m over the alphabet $\breve{a}$. TTrehrefore, the average number $\overline{\mathcal{A}}^{\mathsf{loc}}_{m,n}$ of comparisons for the naïve factoring algorithm is

$$\overline{\mathcal{A}}^{\mathsf{loc}}_{m,n} = (n - m + 1)\overline{\mathcal{A}}^{\breve{a}}_m + \overline{\mathcal{A}}^{\breve{a}}_{m-1}, \tag{5.1}$$

because there are $n - m + 1$ suffixes of length at least m and 1 suffix of length $m - 1$, against which the pattern is matched.

The determination of $\overline{\mathcal{A}}^{\breve{a}}_m$ is achieved by fixing the pattern p and letting the text t vary over all possible letters. There are $\breve{a}^m$ comparisons between $p[0]$ and $t[0]$, as much as there are different texts; if $p[0] = t[0]$, there are $\breve{a}^{m-1}$ comparisons between $p[1]$ and $t[1]$, as much as there are different $t[1, m - 1]$ etc. In total, there are

$$\breve{a}^m + \breve{a}^{m-1} + \cdots + \breve{a} = \breve{a}(\breve{a}^m - 1)/(\breve{a} - 1)$$

comparisons. There are $\breve{a}^m$ possible texts, hence the average is

$$\overline{\mathcal{A}}^{\breve{a}}_m = \frac{\breve{a}(\breve{a}^m - 1)}{\breve{a}^m(\breve{a} - 1)} = \frac{\breve{a}}{\breve{a} - 1}\left(1 - \frac{1}{\breve{a}^m}\right) < \frac{\breve{a}}{\breve{a} - 1} \leqslant 2.$$

Since $\overline{\mathcal{A}}^{\breve{a}}_1 = 1$, we draw the following bounds from equation (5.1):

$$n - m + 2 \leqslant \overline{\mathcal{A}}^{\mathsf{loc}}_{m,n} < 2(n - m + 2) \leqslant 2n + 4.$$

Naïve factoring is thus efficient in average, but its hypothesis is unlikely to apply to random English texts. Moreover, notice how the average cost gets down as the alphabet grows since $\lim_{\breve{a}\to\infty} \overline{\mathcal{A}}^{\breve{a}}_m = 1$.

5.2 Morris-Pratt algorithm

In case of mismatch, the naïve algorithm resumes comparing the first letters of p without using the information of the partial success, to wit, we know $p[0, i-1] = t[j-i, j-1]$ and $p[i] \neq t[j]$ (see FIGURE 5.1 on page 177). The attempt at matching p with $t[j-i+1, j-1]$ could reuse $t[j-i+1, j-1] = p[1, i-1]$, in other words, $p[0, i-2]$ is compared to $p[1, i-1]$, i.e. the pattern p is compared to a part of itself. If we know an index k such that $p[0, k-1] = p[i-k, i-1]$, that is, $p[0, k-1]$ is a *border* of $p[0, i-1]$ (also known as a *side*), then we can resume by comparing $t[j]$ with $p[k]$. Clearly, the greater k, the more comparisons are skipped, so we want to find the *maximum borders* of the prefixes of p.

Border The border of a non-empty word y is a proper prefix of y which is also a suffix. For example, the word abacaba has three borders: ε, a and aba. The last one is the maximum border and we write $\mathfrak{B}(\underline{\text{abacaba}}) = \text{aba}$. Another example is $\mathfrak{B}(\text{abac}) = \varepsilon$, simply because we have abac $= \varepsilon$abacε. Note that maximum borders can overlap; consider, for example, $\mathfrak{B}(\underline{\text{aaaa}}) = \mathfrak{B}(\text{a\underline{aaa}}) = \text{aaa}$.

The speed-up brought by Morris and Pratt to the naïve search is depicted in FIGURE 5.5. Notice that, contrary to naïve factoring, letters in the text are compared in a strictly increasing order (never having to backtrack). Consider the complete run in FIGURE 5.6 on the next page where, in the end, p is not found to be a factor of t. As usual, letters on a grey background correspond to mismatches. It is clear that $\mathfrak{B}(a) = \varepsilon$, for all letters a.

We now have the choice of finding either $\mathfrak{B}(ay)$ or $\mathfrak{B}(ya)$, where y is a non-empty word. Since we are interested in knowing the maximum borders of all the prefixes of a given pattern, the latter is more suitable ($y \lhd ya$). The idea is to recursively consider $\mathfrak{B}(y) \cdot a$: if it is a prefix of y, then $\mathfrak{B}(ya) = \mathfrak{B}(y) \cdot a$; otherwise, we seek the maximum border of the

Figure 5.5: Morris-Pratt algorithm (failure in grey)

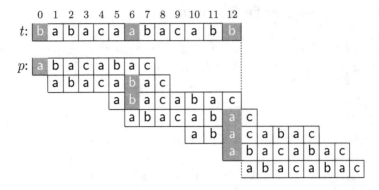

Figure 5.6: Morris-Pratt algorithm at work (no match found)

maximum border of y, namely, $\mathfrak{B}^2(y) \cdot a$ etc. until $\mathfrak{B}^q(y) \cdot a$ is a prefix of y or else $\mathfrak{B}^q(y) = \varepsilon$. For example, $\mathfrak{B}(y \cdot a) = \mathfrak{B}^3(y) \cdot a$ in FIGURE 5.7.

Formally, for all words $y \neq \varepsilon$ and any letter a,

$$\mathfrak{B}(a) := \varepsilon; \qquad \mathfrak{B}(y \cdot a) := \begin{cases} \mathfrak{B}(y) \cdot a, & \text{if } \mathfrak{B}(y) \cdot a \trianglelefteq y; \\ \mathfrak{B}(\mathfrak{B}(y) \cdot a), & \text{otherwise.} \end{cases} \tag{5.2}$$

Consider the following examples where y and $\mathfrak{B}(y)$ are given:

$y = \text{abaabb},\quad \mathfrak{B}(y) = \varepsilon,\quad \mathfrak{B}(y \cdot b) = \mathfrak{B}(\mathfrak{B}(y) \cdot b) = \mathfrak{B}(b) = \varepsilon;$

$y = \text{baaaba},\quad \mathfrak{B}(y) = \text{ba},\quad \mathfrak{B}(y \cdot a) = \mathfrak{B}(y) \cdot a = \text{baa};$

$y = \text{abbbab},\quad \mathfrak{B}(y) = \text{ab},\quad \mathfrak{B}(y \cdot a) = \mathfrak{B}(\mathfrak{B}(y) \cdot a) = \mathfrak{B}^2(y) \cdot a = \text{a}.$

Failure function   Let us note $\|y\|$ the length of a word y. For a given word x, let us define a function $\mathfrak{F}_x$ on all its prefixes as

$$\mathfrak{F}_x(\|y\|) := \|\mathfrak{B}(y)\|, \quad \text{for all } x \text{ and } y \neq \varepsilon \text{ such that } y \trianglelefteq x. \tag{5.3}$$

$$y \cdot a = \boxed{\mathfrak{B}(y) \;|\; \text{a?}} \quad \dots \quad \boxed{\mathfrak{B}(y) \;|\; \text{a}}$$

$$\mathfrak{B}(y) \cdot a = \boxed{\mathfrak{B}^2(y) \;|\; \text{a?}} \quad \dots \quad \boxed{\mathfrak{B}^2(y) \;|\; \text{a}}$$

$$\mathfrak{B}^2(y) \cdot a = \boxed{\mathfrak{B}^3(y) \;|\; \text{a}} \quad \dots \quad \boxed{\mathfrak{B}^3(y) \;|\; \text{a}}$$

Figure 5.7: $\mathfrak{B}(y \cdot a) = \mathfrak{B}(\mathfrak{B}(y) \cdot a) = \mathfrak{B}(\mathfrak{B}^2(y) \cdot a) = \mathfrak{B}^3(y) \cdot a.$

x	a	b	a	c	a	b	a	c
i	0	1	2	3	4	5	6	7
$\mathfrak{F}_x(i)$	−1	0	0	1	0	1	2	3

Figure 5.8: Failure function of abacabac

For reasons which will be clear soon, this function is called the *failure function* of x. An equivalent definition is

$$\mathfrak{F}_x(i) = \|\mathfrak{B}(x[0, i-1])\|, \quad \text{for all } x \text{ and } i \text{ such that } 0 < i \leqslant \|x\|.$$

For example, FIGURE 5.8 shows the table of the maximum borders for the prefixes of the word abacabac. In FIGURE 5.5 on page 181, the length of the maximum border is k, so $k = \mathfrak{F}_p(i)$ and $p[\mathfrak{F}_p(i)]$ is the first letter to be compared with $t[j]$ after the shift. Also, the figure assumes that $i > 0$, so the border in question is defined. Equations (5.2) on the preceding page defining the maximum border can be unfolded as follows:

$$\mathfrak{B}(ya) = \mathfrak{B}(\mathfrak{B}(y) \cdot a), \qquad \mathfrak{B}(y) \cdot a \ntrianglelefteq y;$$
$$\mathfrak{B}(\mathfrak{B}(y) \cdot a) = \mathfrak{B}(\mathfrak{B}^2(y) \cdot a), \qquad \mathfrak{B}^2(y) \cdot a \ntrianglelefteq \mathfrak{B}(y);$$
$$\vdots \qquad\qquad\qquad \vdots$$
$$\mathfrak{B}(\mathfrak{B}^{p-1}(y) \cdot a) = \mathfrak{B}(\mathfrak{B}^p(y) \cdot a), \qquad \mathfrak{B}^p(y) \cdot a \ntrianglelefteq \mathfrak{B}^{p-1}(y);$$

and $\varepsilon \notin \{y, \mathfrak{B}(y), \ldots, \mathfrak{B}^{p-1}(y)\}$. By transitivity, the equations entail $\mathfrak{B}(ya) = \mathfrak{B}(\mathfrak{B}^p(y) \cdot a)$. Two cases are possible: either $\mathfrak{B}^p(y) = \varepsilon$, so $\mathfrak{B}(ya) = \mathfrak{B}(a) = \varepsilon$, or the unfolding resumes until we find the smallest $q > p$ such that $\mathfrak{B}(\mathfrak{B}^{q-1}(y) \cdot a) = \mathfrak{B}(\mathfrak{B}^q(y) \cdot a)$ with $\mathfrak{B}^q(y) \cdot a \trianglelefteq \mathfrak{B}^{q-1}(y)$. Because a border is a proper prefix, that is to say, $\mathfrak{B}(y) \triangleleft y$, we have $\mathfrak{B}^2(y) = \mathfrak{B}(\mathfrak{B}(y)) \triangleleft \mathfrak{B}(y)$, so $\mathfrak{B}^q(y) \cdot a \trianglelefteq \mathfrak{B}^{q-1}(y) \triangleleft \cdots \triangleleft \mathfrak{B}(y) \triangleleft y$. Therefore $\mathfrak{B}^q(y) \cdot a \trianglelefteq y$, since $q > 0$, and $\mathfrak{B}(ya) = \mathfrak{B}^q(y) \cdot a$. This line of reasoning establishes that

$$\mathfrak{B}(ya) = \begin{cases} \mathfrak{B}^q(y) \cdot a, & \text{if } \mathfrak{B}^q(y) \cdot a \trianglelefteq y; \\ \varepsilon, & \text{otherwise}; \end{cases}$$

with the additional constraint that q must be as small as possible. This form of the definition of $\mathfrak{B}$ is simpler because it does not contain an embedded call like $\mathfrak{B}(\mathfrak{B}(y) \cdot a)$. We can now take the lengths of each sides of the equations, leading to

$$\|\mathfrak{B}(ya)\| = \begin{cases} \|\mathfrak{B}^q(y) \cdot a\| = 1 + \|\mathfrak{B}^q(y)\|, & \text{if } \mathfrak{B}^q(y) \cdot a \trianglelefteq y; \\ \|\varepsilon\| = 0, & \text{otherwise}. \end{cases}$$

If $ya \lhd x$, then $\|\mathfrak{B}(ya)\| = \mathfrak{F}_x(\|ya\|) = \mathfrak{F}_x(\|y\| + 1)$. Let $i := \|y\| > 0$.

$$\mathfrak{F}_x(i+1) = \begin{cases} 1 + \|\mathfrak{B}^q(y)\|, & \text{if } \mathfrak{B}^q(y) \cdot a \lhd y; \\ 0, & \text{otherwise.} \end{cases}$$

We need to work on $\|\mathfrak{B}^q(y)\|$ now. From the definition of $\mathfrak{F}$ by equation (5.3) on page 182, we deduce

$$\mathfrak{F}_x^q(\|y\|) = \|\mathfrak{B}^q(y)\|, \quad \text{with } y \lhd x, \tag{5.4}$$

which we can prove by complete induction on q. Let us call this property $\mathsf{P}(q)$. Trivially, we have $\mathsf{P}(0)$. Let us suppose $\mathsf{P}(n)$ for all $n \leqslant q$: this is the induction hypothesis. Let us suppose $y \lhd x$ and prove now $\mathsf{P}(q+1)$:

$$\mathfrak{F}_x^{q+1}(\|y\|) = \mathfrak{F}_x^q(\mathfrak{F}_x(\|y\|)) = \mathfrak{F}_x^q(\|\mathfrak{B}(y)\|) \doteq \|\mathfrak{B}^q(\mathfrak{B}(y))\| = \|\mathfrak{B}^{q+1}(y)\|,$$

where ($\doteq$) is a valid application of the induction hypothesis because $\mathfrak{B}(y) \lhd y \lhd x$. This proves $\mathsf{P}(q+1)$ and the induction principle entails that $\mathsf{P}(n)$ holds for all $n \geqslant 0$. Therefore, equation (5.4) allows us to refine our definition of $\mathfrak{F}_x(i+1)$ as follows, with $i > 0$:

$$\mathfrak{F}_x(i+1) = \begin{cases} 1 + \mathfrak{F}_x^q(i), & \text{if } \mathfrak{B}^q(y) \cdot a \lhd y; \\ 0, & \text{otherwise.} \end{cases}$$

There is one part of the definition (5.2) on page 182 that we did not use: $\mathfrak{B}(a) := \varepsilon$. It implies $\mathfrak{F}_x(1) = \mathfrak{F}_x(\|a\|) = \|\mathfrak{B}(a)\| = \|\varepsilon\| = 0$ and, since the definition of $\mathfrak{F}$ implies $\mathfrak{F}_x(1) = 1 + \mathfrak{F}_x(0)$, so $\mathfrak{F}_x(0) = -1$. Property '$\mathfrak{B}^q(y) \cdot a \lhd y$ and $ya \lhd x$ and $\|y\| = i$' implies any of the equalities $y[\|\mathfrak{B}^q(y)\|] = a \Leftrightarrow y[\mathfrak{F}_x^q(i)] = a \Leftrightarrow x[\mathfrak{F}_x^q(i)] = x[\|y\|] \Leftrightarrow x[\mathfrak{F}_x^q(i)] = x[i]$. We now know

$$\mathfrak{F}_x(0) = -1 \quad \text{and} \quad \mathfrak{F}_x(i+1) = \begin{cases} 1 + \mathfrak{F}_x^q(i), & \text{if } x[\mathfrak{F}_x^q(i)] = x[i]; \\ 0, & \text{otherwise;} \end{cases}$$

where q is the smallest nonzero natural satisfying the condition. This can be further simplified into

$$\mathfrak{F}_x(0) = -1 \quad \text{and} \quad \mathfrak{F}_x(i+1) = 1 + \mathfrak{F}_x^q(i),$$

where $i \geqslant 0$ and $q > 0$ is the smallest natural such that $\mathfrak{F}_x^q(i) = -1$ or $x[\mathfrak{F}_x^q(i)] = x[i]$.

$$\mathsf{fail}_0(x, 0) \to -1; \quad \mathsf{fail}_0(x, i) \to 1 + \mathsf{fp}(x, \mathsf{nth}(x, i-1), \mathsf{fail}_0(x, i-1)).$$
$$\mathsf{nth}([a \,|\, x], 0) \to a; \quad \mathsf{nth}([a \,|\, x], i) \to \mathsf{nth}(x, i-1).$$
$$\mathsf{fp}(x, a, -1) \to -1; \quad \frac{\mathsf{nth}(x, k) \twoheadrightarrow a}{\mathsf{fp}(x, a, k) \twoheadrightarrow k}; \quad \mathsf{fp}(x, a, k) \to \mathsf{fp}(x, a, \mathsf{fail}_0(x, k)).$$

Figure 5.9: The failure function $\mathfrak{F}$ as $\mathsf{fail}_0/2$

Preprocessing The function call $\mathsf{fail}_0(x, i)$, defined in FIGURE 5.9, implements $\mathfrak{F}_x(i)$. The function $\mathsf{fp}/3$ (*fixed point*) computes $\mathfrak{F}_x^q(i-1)$, starting with $\mathsf{fail}_0(x, i-1)$ and $\mathsf{nth}(x, i-1)$, which denotes $x[i-1]$ and is needed to check the condition $x[\mathfrak{F}_x^q(i-1)] = x[i-1]$. The equality test $\mathfrak{F}_x^q(i-1) = -1$ is performed by the first rule of $\mathsf{fp}/3$.

The algorithm of Morris and Pratt requires that $\mathfrak{F}_x(i)$ be computed for all indexes i of the pattern x and, since it depends on the values of some calls $\mathfrak{F}_x(j)$, with $j < i$, it is more efficient to compute $\mathfrak{F}_x(i)$ for increasing values of i and store them, so they can be reused instead of being recomputed. This technique is called *memoisation* (not to be confused with memorisation). In this instance, the evaluation of $\mathfrak{F}_x(i)$ relies on the memo $[(x[i-1], \mathfrak{F}_x(i-1)), (x[i-2], \mathfrak{F}_x(i-2)), \dots, (x[0], \mathfrak{F}_x(0))]$. The memoising version of $\mathsf{fail}_0/2$ is named $\mathsf{fail}/2$ in FIGURE 5.10. Here, we work with the memo p, which is a reversed prefix, instead of x, so we need to know its length i in order to know how many letters must be discarded by $\mathsf{suf}/2$ (*suffix*): $\mathsf{suf}(x, i-k-1)$ instead of $\mathsf{fail}_0(x, k)$. Thanks to the memo, $\mathsf{fp}/4$ does not need to call $\mathsf{fail}/2$, just to look in p with $\mathsf{suf}/2$. Note that, as a small improvement, we also moved the increment: instead of $1 + \mathsf{fp}(\dots)$ and $\cdots \twoheadrightarrow k$, we do now $\mathsf{fp}(\dots)$ and $\cdots \twoheadrightarrow k+1$.

Let us name $\mathsf{pp}/1$ (*preprocessing*) the function computing the stack $[(x[0], \mathfrak{F}_x(0)), (x[1], \mathfrak{F}_x(1)), \dots, (x[m-1], \mathfrak{F}_x(m-1))]$ for a pattern x of

$$\mathsf{fail}(p, 0) \to -1; \quad \mathsf{fail}([(a, k) \,|\, p], i) \to \mathsf{fp}(p, a, k, i-1).$$
$$\mathsf{fp}(p, a, -1, i) \to 0; \quad \frac{\mathsf{suf}(p, i-k-1) \twoheadrightarrow [(a, k') \,|\, p']}{\mathsf{fp}(p, a, k, i) \twoheadrightarrow k+1};$$
$$\frac{\mathsf{suf}(p, i-k-1) \twoheadrightarrow [(b, k') \,|\, p']}{\mathsf{fp}(p, a, k, i) \twoheadrightarrow \mathsf{fp}(p', a, k', k)}.$$
$$\mathsf{suf}(p, 0) \to p; \quad \mathsf{suf}([a \,|\, p], i) \to \mathsf{suf}(p, i-1).$$

Figure 5.10: The failure function with memoisation

$$\mathsf{pp}(x) \to \mathsf{pp}(x, [\,], 0).$$

$$\mathsf{pp}([\,], p, i) \to \mathsf{rev}(p);$$
$$\mathsf{pp}([a \,|\, x], p, i) \to \mathsf{pp}(x, [(a, \mathsf{fail}(p, i)) \,|\, p], i + 1).$$

Figure 5.11: Preprocessing of a pattern y by $\mathsf{pp}/1$

length m. Its definition is shown in FIGURE 5.11, where $\mathsf{rev}/1$ is the reversal function (definition (2.2) on page 40), and $\mathsf{pp}/1$ simply calls the failure function $\mathsf{fail}/2$ for each new index i on the current memo p and creates a new memo by pairing the failure index with the current letter and pushing on the current memo $([(a, \mathsf{fail}(p, i)) \,|\, p])$. The stack reversal at the end is necessary because the memo contains the letters in reversed order with respect to the pattern. For example, the example in FIGURE 5.8 on page 183 leads to the evaluation

$$\mathsf{pp}(x) \twoheadrightarrow [(\mathsf{a}, -1), (\mathsf{b}, 0), (\mathsf{a}, 0), (\mathsf{c}, 1), (\mathsf{a}, 0), (\mathsf{b}, 1), (\mathsf{a}, 2), (\mathsf{c}, 3)],$$

where $x = \mathsf{abacabac}$. If $x = \mathsf{ababaca}$, then

$$\mathsf{pp}(x) \twoheadrightarrow [(\mathsf{a}, -1), (\mathsf{b}, 0), (\mathsf{a}, 0), (\mathsf{b}, 1), (\mathsf{a}, 2), (\mathsf{c}, 3), (\mathsf{a}, 0)].$$

Minimum cost   It is clear from the definition (5.2) on page 182 that the determination of the maximum border of a non-empty word requires finding the maximum borders of some or all proper prefixes, so, if the word contains n letters, at least $n - 1$ comparisons are needed, as the border of the first letter alone needs no comparison. This lower bound is tight, as the following reasoning shows. Let us call *positive comparison* a successful prefix test, as found in the definition of $\mathfrak{B}$, in other words: $\mathfrak{B}(y) \cdot a \trianglelefteq y$. Dually, a *negative comparison* is a failed prefix test. In order to minimise the number of calls to evaluate $\mathfrak{B}(ya)$, we may notice that a positive comparison only entails the evaluation of $\mathfrak{B}(y)$, whilst a negative comparison requires two: $\mathfrak{B}(\mathfrak{B}(y) \cdot a)$. Therefore, the first idea may be to assume that only positive comparisons occur:

$$\mathfrak{B}(x) \overset{n-2}{=} \mathfrak{B}(x[0, n-2]) \cdot x[n-1] \overset{n-1}{=} \cdots \overset{0}{=} \mathfrak{B}(x[0]) \cdot x[1, n-1] = x[1, n-1],$$

where $(\overset{i}{=})$ implies $\mathfrak{B}(x[0, i]) \cdot x[i+1] \trianglelefteq x[0, i]$, for $0 \leqslant i \leqslant n - 2$. Firstly, $i = 0$ and the corresponding positive comparison yields $x[0] = x[1]$. Unfolding the other comparisons yields $x[0] = x[1] = \cdots = x[n-1]$, so a best case is $x = a^n$, for any letter a.

But there is another case, because the outermost call to $\mathcal{B}$ after a negative comparison does not imply a comparison if its argument is a single letter:

$$\mathcal{B}(x) \stackrel{n-2}{=} \mathcal{B}(\mathcal{B}(x[0, n-2]) \cdot x[n-1])$$
$$\stackrel{n-3}{=} \mathcal{B}(\mathcal{B}(\mathcal{B}(x[0, n-3]) \cdot x[n-2]) \cdot x[n-1])$$
$$\vdots$$
$$\stackrel{0}{=} \mathcal{B}(\mathcal{B}(\dots \mathcal{B}(\mathcal{B}(x[0]) \cdot x[1]) \dots) \cdot x[n-1])$$
$$\stackrel{\cdot}{=} \mathcal{B}(\mathcal{B}(\dots \mathcal{B}(\mathcal{B}(x[1]) \cdot x[2]) \dots) \cdot x[n-1])$$
$$\vdots$$
$$\stackrel{\cdot}{=} \mathcal{B}(x[n-1]) = \varepsilon.$$

where $(\stackrel{i}{=})$ implies $\mathcal{B}(x[0, i]) \cdot x[i+1] \not\trianglelefteq x[0, i]$, for $0 \leqslant i \leqslant n-2$ and $(\stackrel{\cdot}{=})$ involves no comparisons. Starting with $i = 0$ yields $x[1] \neq x[0]$, then $i = 1$ leads to $x[2] \neq x[0]$ etc. so the consequences of all these negative comparisons are $x[0] \neq x[i]$, for $1 \leqslant i \leqslant n-2$. The number of negative comparisons is $n-1$, thus is minimal, but the shape of the word is different than previously, as the first letter must differ from all the following. Let $\overline{B}_n^{\mathsf{pp}}$ be the minimum number of comparisons involved in the evaluation of $\mathsf{pp}(x)$, where the length of the pattern x is n. It is the same as the number of comparisons to evaluate $\mathcal{B}(x[0, n-2])$ when $x[0, n-2]$ is a best case. Therefore, $\overline{B}_n^{\mathsf{pp}} = n-2$.

Maximum cost   The determination of the maximum border of a word implies finding the maximum borders of some or all proper prefixes, so, if we want to maximise the number of comparisons, we may want to compute as many borders as possible. In order to do so, evaluating $\mathcal{B}(x)$ would lead to finding the maximum border of a factor of length $n-1$, where n is the length of x. The best case $x = a^n$ shows that we have $\mathcal{B}(x) = x[1, n-1]$, which is fitting, except we would like $\mathcal{B}(x[1, n-1])$. In other words, to obtain the maximum cost, we add the constraint that the first comparison must be negative:

$$\mathcal{B}(x) \stackrel{n-1}{=} \mathcal{B}(\mathcal{B}(x[0, n-2]) \cdot x[n-1])$$
$$\stackrel{n-2}{=} \mathcal{B}(\mathcal{B}(x[0, n-3]) \cdot x[n-2, n-1])$$
$$\vdots$$
$$\stackrel{1}{=} \mathcal{B}(\mathcal{B}(x[0]) \cdot x[1, n-1]) = \mathcal{B}(x[1, n-1]),$$

where $(\stackrel{n-1}{=})$ supposes $\mathcal{B}(x[0, n-2]) \cdot x[n-1] \not\trianglelefteq x[0, n-2]$, and $(\stackrel{i}{=})$, with $1 \leqslant i \leqslant n-2$, corresponds to $\mathcal{B}(x[0, i]) \cdot x[i+1] \trianglelefteq x[0, i]$. These constraints imply $x[0] = x[1] = \dots = x[n-2] \neq x[n-1]$, that is to say,

$x = a^{n-1}b$, with $a \neq b$. Up to now, the number of comparisons is $n - 1$, as in the minimal case, but the evaluation continues as follows:

$$\mathcal{B}(a^i b) \overset{i}{\doteq} \mathcal{B}(\mathcal{B}(a^i) \cdot b) \doteq \mathcal{B}(\mathcal{B}(a^{i-1}) \cdot ab) \doteq \cdots \doteq \mathcal{B}(a^{i-1}b),$$

for $1 \leqslant i \leqslant n - 2$ and ($\overset{i}{\doteq}$) entails the negative comparisons $\mathcal{B}(a^i) \cdot b \not\trianglelefteq a^i$ and the positive comparisons ($\doteq$), which we do not count because we have in mind to find $\overline{\mathcal{W}}_n^{\mathsf{pp}}$, so repeated evaluations of the same border do not entail repeated comparisons thanks to memoisation. Thus, we have $n - 2$ negative comparisons until $\mathcal{B}(b) = \varepsilon$, which, with the $n - 1$ earlier positive comparisons, sum up $2n - 3$. Since $\overline{\mathcal{W}}_n^{\mathsf{pp}}$ is the number of comparisons to compute $\mathcal{B}(x[0, n - 2])$ without repetitions, we have

$$\overline{\mathcal{W}}_n^{\mathsf{pp}} = 2(n - 1) - 3 = 2n - 5.$$

Search   We found above that $n - 2 \leqslant \mathcal{C}_n^{\mathsf{pp}} \leqslant 2n - 5$, where the bounds are tight if $n \geqslant 3$. To make use of the value of $\mathsf{pp}(p)$, we could start by modifying the linear search in section 5.1, in particular the program in FIGURE 5.4 on page 178, while keeping an eye on FIGURE 5.5 on page 181. The result is displayed in FIGURE 5.12. Note how the first argument of $\mathsf{mp}/5$, p, is the working copy and the third, p', is the original which remains invariant (it is used to reset p after a letter mismatch). Indexes i, j and k are the same as in FIGURE 5.5 on page 181. The latter is none other than the value computed by the failure function; variables i and j are incremented each time a letter in the pattern is successfully matched against a letter in the text (third rule of $\mathsf{mp}/5$) and j is also incremented each time there is a mismatch of the first letter of the pattern (fourth rule of $\mathsf{mp}/5$).

$$\frac{\mathsf{pp}(p) \twoheadrightarrow p'}{\mathsf{mp}(p, t) \twoheadrightarrow \mathsf{mp}(p', t, p', 0, 0)}.$$

$$\mathsf{mp}([\,], t, p', i, j) \rightarrow \mathsf{factor}(j - i);$$
$$\mathsf{mp}(p, [\,], p', i, j) \rightarrow \mathsf{absent}();$$
$$\mathsf{mp}([(a, k) \,|\, p], [a \,|\, t], p', i, j) \rightarrow \mathsf{mp}(p, t, p', i + 1, j + 1);$$
$$\mathsf{mp}([(a, -1) \,|\, p], [b \,|\, t], p', 0, j) \rightarrow \mathsf{mp}(p', t, p', 0, j + 1);$$
$$\mathsf{mp}([(a, k) \,|\, p], t, p', i, j) \rightarrow \mathsf{mp}(\mathsf{suf}(p', k), t, p', k, j).$$

Figure 5.12: Morris-Pratt algorithm (search phase)

Minimum cost   Let $\overline{\mathcal{B}}_{m,n}^{\mathsf{mp}/5}$ be the minimum number of comparisons performed during the evaluation of $\mathsf{mp}/5$, where m is the length of the pattern and n is the length of the text. Just as with naïve factoring, the best case is when the pattern is a prefix of the text, so $\overline{\mathcal{B}}_{m,n}^{\mathsf{mp}/5} = m$. Taking into account the preprocessing stage, the minimum number of comparisons $\overline{\mathcal{B}}_{m,n}^{\mathsf{mp}}$ of $\mathsf{mp}/2$ is

$$\overline{\mathcal{B}}_{m,n}^{\mathsf{mp}} = \overline{\mathcal{B}}_m^{\mathsf{pp}} + \overline{\mathcal{B}}_{m,n}^{\mathsf{mp}/5} = (m-2) + m = 2m - 2.$$

Maximum cost Since the Morris-Pratt algorithm only reads the text forwards, the worst case must maximise the number of times the letters of the text t are compared with a letter in the pattern p. Therefore, the first letter of the pattern cannot differ from all the letters of the text, otherwise each letter of the text would be compared exactly once. Let us assume the exact opposite: $p[0] = t[i]$, with $i \geqslant 0$. But this would also imply one comparison per letter in the text. The way to force the pattern to shift as little as possible is to further impose $p[1] \neq t[i]$, for $i > 0$. In short, this means that $ab \trianglelefteq p$, with letters a and b such that $a \neq b$ and $t = a^n$. A simple drawing is enough to reveal that this configuration leads to the maximum number of comparisons $\overline{\mathcal{W}}_{m,n}^{\mathsf{mp}/5} = 2n - 1$, as each letter in the text is compared twice, except the first, which is compared once. Taking into account the preprocessing stage, the maximum number of comparisons $\overline{\mathcal{W}}_{m,n}^{\mathsf{mp}}$ of $\mathsf{mp}/2$ satisfies

$$\overline{\mathcal{W}}_{m,n}^{\mathsf{mp}} = \overline{\mathcal{W}}_m^{\mathsf{pp}} + \overline{\mathcal{B}}_{m,n}^{\mathsf{mp}/5} = (2m - 5) + (2n - 1) = 2(n + m - 3).$$

Metaprogramming The previous study leads to programs for the preprocessing and search phases that somewhat obscure the main idea supporting the algorithm of Morris and Pratt, to wit, the use of the maximum borders of the proper prefixes of the pattern and the forward-only reading of the text. The reason for that somewhat unfortunate situation is that, for efficiency imperatives, we have to memoise the values of the failure function and, instead of working with the original pattern, we proceed with a version of it augmented with these values. Also, the utilisation of stacks for modelling the pattern slows down and obfuscates the reading of the letters and the shifts.

If the pattern is fixed, a more legible approach is available, consisting in the modification of the preprocessing stage so that a dedicated program is output. This kind of taylored method, where a program is the result of the execution of another, is called *metaprogramming*. Of course, it is an option only if the time needed to output, compile and execute a program is amortised in the long run, which implies for the problem at hand that the pattern and the text are expected to be significantly long or that the search is likely to be repeated with the same pattern on other texts (or the remainder of the same text after an occurrence of the pattern has been found).

There is a graphical way to represent the contents of the table in FIGURE 5.8 on page 183 called a *deterministic finite automaton*, and it is shown in FIGURE 5.14. We will here only describe informally such automata; for a full treatment, see Perrin (1990), Hopcroft et al. (2003), Sakarovitch (2003). Consider that the circles, called *states*, contain the values of i from the table. The edges, called *transitions*, between two states are of two kinds: either solid and carrying a letter, called *label*, or dotted and going backwards. The sequence of states throughout solid edges make the word $x = \mathsf{abacabac}$. The rightmost state is distinguished by a double circling because it marks the end of x. There is a back edge between state i and j only if $\mathfrak{F}_x(i) = j$. The leftmost state has an incoming, solid edge without a source and a dotted, outgoing edge. The former simply denotes the beginning of the word and the latter corresponds to the special value $\mathfrak{F}_x(0) = -1$. What matters for us is that the intuitive support brought by an automaton also can be implemented intuitively, with each state corresponding to one function and

$$\mathsf{mp}_0(t) \to \mathsf{zero}(t, 0).$$

$$\mathsf{zero}([\mathsf{a}()\,|\,t], j) \to \mathsf{one}(t, j+1);$$
$$\mathsf{zero}([\mathsf{a}\,|\,t], j) \to \mathsf{zero}(t, j+1);$$
$$\mathsf{zero}([\,], j) \to \mathsf{absent}().$$

$$\mathsf{one}([\mathsf{b}()\,|\,t], j) \to \mathsf{two}(t, j+1);$$
$$\mathsf{one}(t, j) \to \mathsf{zero}(t, j).$$

$$\mathsf{two}([\mathsf{a}()\,|\,t], j) \to \mathsf{three}(t, j+1);$$
$$\mathsf{two}(t, j) \to \mathsf{zero}(t, j).$$

$$\mathsf{three}([\mathsf{c}()\,|\,t], j) \to \mathsf{four}(t, j+1);$$
$$\mathsf{three}(t, j) \to \mathsf{one}(t, j).$$

$$\mathsf{four}([\mathsf{a}()\,|\,t], j) \to \mathsf{five}(t, j+1);$$
$$\mathsf{four}(t, j) \to \mathsf{zero}(t, j).$$

$$\mathsf{five}([\mathsf{b}()\,|\,t], j) \to \mathsf{six}(t, j+1);$$
$$\mathsf{five}(t, j) \to \mathsf{one}(t, j).$$

$$\mathsf{six}([\mathsf{a}()\,|\,t], j) \to \mathsf{seven}(t, j+1);$$
$$\mathsf{six}(t, j) \to \mathsf{two}(t, j).$$

$$\mathsf{seven}([\mathsf{c}()\,|\,t], j) \to \mathsf{factor}(j-6);$$
$$\mathsf{seven}(t, j) \to \mathsf{three}(t, j).$$

Figure 5.13: Factoring abacabac

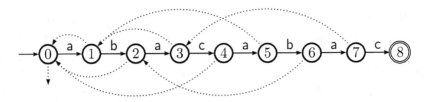

Figure 5.14: Morris-Pratt automaton for the pattern abacabac

the outgoing transitions associated with different rules of the definition of the state function. The example abacabac is shown in FIGURE 5.13. The automaton states, 0, 1, through 7, correspond to the functions zero/2, one/2 etc. through seven/2. Notice how $mp_0/1$ sets the index to 0 when initialising the first state, that is, calling zero/2. The index j plays the same role as in FIGURE 5.5 on page 181. The first rule of each function corresponds to a rightwards transition in the automaton in FIGURE 5.14 on the facing page and the second rule is a backwards transition, that is, a failure, except in zero/2, where it means that the pattern is shifted by one letter. The function zero/2 has a third rule handling the case when the pattern is absent in the text. We could add a similar rule to the other functions, as an optimisation, but we opt for brevity and let successive failure rules bring us back to zero/2. The first rule of seven/2 is special as well, because it is used when the pattern has been found. Note the index $j - 6$, clearly showing that the length of the pattern is part of the program, which is hence a metaprogram.

Knuth's variant In FIGURE 5.5 on page 181, if $a = $ a, then the sliding would immediately lead to a comparison failure. Hence let us compare $p[\mathfrak{F}_p(i)]$ to $t[j]$ only if $p[\mathfrak{F}_p(i)] \neq p[i]$. Else, we consider the maximum border of the maximum border etc. until we find the smallest q such that $p[\mathfrak{F}_p^q(i)] \neq p[i]$. This is an improvement by Knuth et al. (1977). There is an updated reprint by Knuth (2010) and a treatment based on automata theory by Crochemore et al. (2007), in its section 2.6. See also an interesting derivation of the program by algebraic refinements in the book by Bird (2010). In terms of the search automaton, when a failure occurs at state i on the letter a, we follow the back edge to state $\mathfrak{F}_x(i)$, but, if the normal transition is a again, we follow another back edge etc. until there is a transition different from a or we have to shift the pattern. The improvement proposed by Knuth consists in replacing all these successive failure transitions by only one. For example, the automaton in FIGURE 5.15 is Knuth's optimisation of the one in FIGURE 5.14.

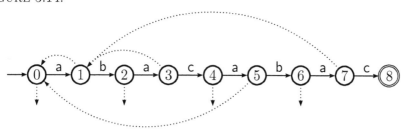

Figure 5.15: Knuth-Morris-Pratt automaton for the pattern abacabac

Exercises

1. Find $A^{loc}_{m,n}$.

2. Prove that pp/1 and mp/2 terminate.

3. Prove loc/2 = mp/2 (correctness of the algorithm of Morris and Pratt).

4. Find B^{pp}_m and W^{pp}_m. (Mind the cost of suf/2.)

5. Find $B^{mp}_{m,n}$ and $W^{mp}_{m,n}$.

6. Find a simple modification to avoid calling rev/1 in FIGURE 5.11 on page 186.

7. Modify fail/2 so that mp/2 implements the Knuth-Morris-Pratt algorithm. Study the best and worst cases of this variant and show that $\overline{W^{pp}_m} = 2m - 6$, for $m \geqslant 3$.

8. Write the metaprogram corresponding to the automaton in FIGURE 5.15 on the previous page.

9. Write a function rlw/2 (*remove the last word*) such that rlw(w, t) is rewritten into the text t if the word w is absent, otherwise into t without the last occurrence of t in it.

Part II

Arborescent Structures

Chapter 6

Catalan Trees

In part I, we dealt with linear structures, like stacks and queues, but, to really understand programs operating on such structures, we needed the concept of tree. This is why we introduced very early on abstract syntax trees, directed acyclic graphs (e.g., FIGURE 1.4 on page 7), comparison trees (e.g., FIGURE 2.41 on page 90), binary trees (e.g., FIGURE 2.43 on page 91), proof trees (e.g., FIGURE 3.2a on page 100), evaluation trees (e.g., FIGURE 3.6 on page 111) and merge trees (e.g., FIGURE 4.6 on page 128). Those trees were meta-objects, or concepts, used to understand the linear structure at hand.

In this chapter, we take a more abstract point of view and we consider the general class of *Catalan trees*, or general trees. We will study them as mathematical objects with the aim to transfer our results to the trees used as data structures to implement algorithms. In particular, we will be interested in measuring, counting them, and determining some average parameters relative to their shape, the reason being that knowing what a random tree looks like will tell us something about the cost of traversing it in different ways.

Catalan trees are a special kind of graph, that is, an object made of *nodes* (also called *vertices*) connected by *edges*, without orientation (only the connection matters). What makes Catalan trees is the distinction of a node, called the *root*, and the absence of cycles, that is, closed paths made of nodes successively connected. Catalan trees are often called *ordered trees*, or *planted plane trees*, in graph theory, and *unranked trees*, *n-ary trees*, or *rose trees* in programming theory. An example is given in FIGURE 6.1. Note how the root is the topmost node and has four subtrees, whose

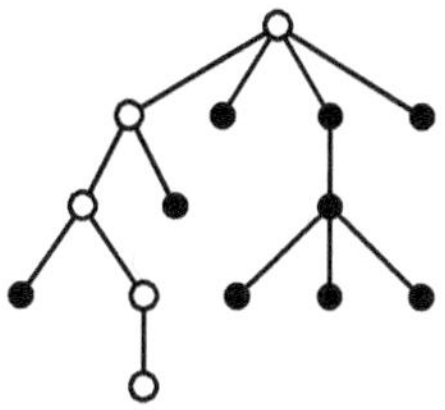

Figure 6.1: Catalan tree of height 4

root are called *children*, given in order. The nodes drawn as white disks
(○) make up a maximal path starting from the root (the number of nodes
along it is maximal). The ending node has no children; there are actually 8 such nodes in total, called the *leaves*. The number of edges connecting white disks is the *height* of the Catalan tree (there may be several
maximal paths of same length), so the given example has height 4.

Programmers implement Catalan trees as a data structure, *e.g.*, using XML, in which case some information is stored in the nodes and its
retrieval may – in the worst case – require the reaching of a leaf. The
maximum cost of a search is thus proportional to the height of the tree
and the determination of the average height becomes relevant when performing a series of random searches (Vitter and Flajolet, 1990). For this
kind of analysis, we need first to find the number of Catalan trees with
a given size. There are two common measures for the size: either we
quantify the trees by their number of nodes or we count the edges. In
fact, using one or the other is a matter of convenience or style: there are
n edges if there are $n+1$ nodes, simply because each node, save the root,
has one parent. It is often the case that formulas about Catalan trees
are a bit simpler when using the number of edges, so this will be our
measure of size in this chapter.

6.1   Enumeration

In most textbooks (Sedgewick and
Flajolet, 1996, § 5.1 & 5.2), it
is shown how to find the number
of Catalan trees with n edges by
leveraging some extremely powerful mathematical method known
as *generating functions* (Graham
et al., 1994, chap. 7). Instead, here,
for didactical purposes, we decided
to use a more intuitive technique in

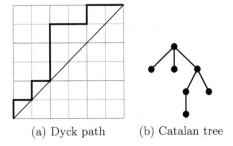

(a) Dyck path   (b) Catalan tree

Figure 6.2: Bijection

enumerative combinatorics which consists in constructing a one-to-one
correspondence between two finite sets, so the cardinal of one set is the
cardinal of the other. In other words, we are going to relate bijectively, on
the one hand, Catalan trees, and, on the other hand, other combinatorial
objects which are relatively easy to count.

The objects most suitable for our purpose are *monotonic lattice paths*
in a square grid (Mohanty, 1979, Humphreys, 2010). These paths are
made up of steps oriented upwards (↑), called *rises*, and steps rightwards

($\rightarrow$), called *falls*, starting at the bottom left corner $(0,0)$. *Dyck paths* of length $2n$ are paths ending at (n, n) which stay above the diagonal, or touch it. We want to show that *there exists a bijection between Dyck paths of length $2n$ and Catalan trees with n edges.*

To understand that bijection, we need first to present a particular kind of *traversal*, or *walk*, of Catalan trees. Let us imagine that a tree is a map where nodes represent towns and edges roads. A complete traversal of the tree consists then in starting our trip at the root and, following edges, to visit all the nodes. (It is allowed to visit several times the same nodes, since there are no cycles.) Of course, there are many ways to achieve this tour and the one we envisage here is called a *preorder traversal*. At every node, we take the leftmost unvisited edge and visit the subtree in preorder; when back at the node, we repeat the choice with the remaining unvisited children. For more clarity, we show in FIGURE 6.3 the *preorder numbering* of FIGURE 6.2b, where the order in which a node is visited first is shown instead of a black disk ($\bullet$).

Figure 6.3

The first part of the bijection is an injection from Catalan trees with n edges to Dyck paths of length $2n$. By traversing the tree in preorder, we associate one rise to an edge on the way down, and a fall to the same edge on the way up. Obviously, there are $2n$ steps in the Dyck path. The surjection simply consists in reversing the process by reading the Dyck path step by step, rightwards, and build the corresponding tree. Now, we need to count the number of Dyck paths of length $2n$, which we know now is also the number of Catalan trees with n edges.

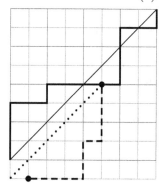

Figure 6.4: Reflection of a prefix w.r.t. $y = x - 1$

The total number of monotonic paths of length $2n$ is the number of choices of n rises amongst $2n$ steps, that is, $\binom{2n}{n}$. We need now to subtract the number of paths that start with a rise and cross the diagonal. Such a path is shown in FIGURE 6.4, drawn as a bold continuous line. The first point reached below the diagonal is used to plot a dotted line parallel to the diagonal. All the steps from that point back to $(0,0)$ are then changed into their counterpart: a rise by a fall and vice-versa. The resulting segment is drawn as a dashed line. This operation is called a *reflection* (Renault, 2008). The crux of the matter is that we can reflect each monotonic path crossing the diagonal into a distinct path from $(1, -1)$ to (n, n). Furthermore, all reflected paths can be reflected when they reach the dotted line back into their original counterpart. In other words, the reflection is bijective. (Another intuitive and visual approach to the same result has been published by Callan (1995).) Consequently, there are as many monotonic paths from $(0,0)$ to (n,n) that cross the diagonal as there are monotonic paths from $(1,-1)$ to (n,n). The latter are readily enumerated: $\binom{2n}{n-1}$. As a conclusion, the number of Dyck paths of length $2n$ is

$$
C_n = \binom{2n}{n} - \binom{2n}{n-1} = \binom{2n}{n} - \frac{(2n)!}{(n-1)!(n+1)!}
$$
$$
= \binom{2n}{n} - \frac{n}{n+1} \cdot \frac{(2n)!}{n!n!} = \binom{2n}{n} - \frac{n}{n+1}\binom{2n}{n} = \frac{1}{n+1}\binom{2n}{n}.
$$

The numbers C_n are called *Catalan numbers*. Using Stirling's formula, seen in equation (2.17) on page 84, we find that the number of Catalan trees with n edges is

$$
C_n = \frac{1}{n+1}\binom{2n}{n} \sim \frac{4^n}{n\sqrt{\pi n}}. \tag{6.1}
$$

6.2 Average path length

The *path length* of a Catalan tree is the sum of the lengths of the paths from the root. We have seen this concept in the context of binary trees, where it was declined in two variants, *internal path length* (page 114) and *external path length* (page 92), depending on the end node being internal or external. In the case of Catalan trees, the pertinent distinction between nodes is to be a *leaf* (that is, a node without subtrees) or not, but some authors nevertheless speak of external path length when referring to the distances to the leaves, and of internal path length for the non-leaf nodes, hence we must bear in mind whether the context is the Catalan trees or the binary trees.

In order to study the average path length of Catalan trees, and some related parameters, we may follow Dershowitz and Zaks (1981) by finding first the average number of nodes of degree d at level l in a Catalan tree with n edges. The *degree of a node* is the number of its children and its *level* is its distance to the root counted in edges and the root is at level 0.

The first step of our method for finding the average path length consists in finding an alternative bijection between Catalan trees and Dyck paths. In FIGURE 6.2b, we see a Catalan tree equivalent to the Dyck path in FIGURE 6.2a, built from the preorder traversal of that tree. FIGURE 6.5b shows the same tree, where the contents of the nodes is their degree. The preorder traversal (of the degrees) is $[3,0,0,2,1,0,0]$. Since the last degree is always 0 (a leaf), we remove it and settle for

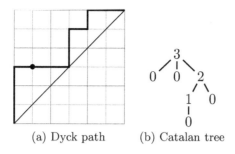

(a) Dyck path   (b) Catalan tree

Figure 6.5: Degree-based bijection

$[3, 0, 0, 2, 1, 0]$. Another equivalent Dyck path is obtained by mapping the degrees of that list into as many occurrences of rises ($\uparrow$) and one fall ($\rightarrow$), so, for instance, 3 is mapped to ($\uparrow, \uparrow, \uparrow, \rightarrow$) and 0 to ($\rightarrow$). In the end, $[3, 0, 0, 2, 1, 0]$ is mapped into $[\uparrow, \uparrow, \uparrow, \rightarrow, \rightarrow, \rightarrow, \uparrow, \uparrow, \rightarrow, \uparrow, \rightarrow, \rightarrow]$, which corresponds to the Dyck path in FIGURE 6.5a. It is easy to convince ourself that we can reconstruct the tree from the Dyck path, so we indeed have a bijection.

The reason for this new bijection is that we need to find the average number of Catalan trees whose root has a given degree. This number will help us in finding the average path length, following an idea of Ruskey (1983). From the bijection, it is clear that the number of trees whose root has degree $r = 3$ is the number of Dyck paths made of the segment from $(0, 0)$ to $(0, r)$, followed by one fall (see the dot at $(1, r)$ in FIGURE 6.5a), and then all monotonic paths above the diagonal until the upper right corner (n, n). Therefore, we need to determine the number of such paths.

We have seen in section 6.4 on page 204 the bijective reflection of paths and the counting principle of inclusion and exclusion. Let us add to our tools one more bijection which proves often useful: the *reversal*. It simply consists in reversing the order of the steps making up a path. Consider for example FIGURE 6.6a. Of course, the composition of two bijections being a bijection, the composition of a reversal and a reflection is bijective, hence the monotonic paths above the diagonal from $(1, r)$ to (n, n) are in bijection with the monotonic paths above the diagonal from $(0, 0)$ to $(n - r, n - 1)$. For example, FIGURE 6.6b shows the reversal and reflection of the Dyck path of FIGURE 6.5a after the point $(1, 3)$, distinguished by the black disk ($\bullet$).

Recalling that Catalan trees with n edges are in bijection with Dyck paths of length $2n$ (section 6.1 on page 196), we now know that the number of Catalan trees with n edges and whose root has degree r is the number of monotonic paths above the diagonal from the point $(0, 0)$ to $(n - r, n - 1)$. We can find this number using the same technique we used

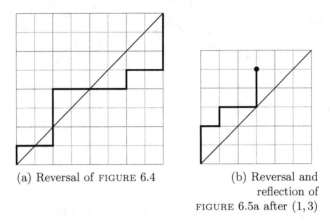

(a) Reversal of FIGURE 6.4   (b) Reversal and
                                                         reflection of
                                                    FIGURE 6.5a after $(1,3)$

Figure 6.6: Reversals and reflections

for the total number C_n of Dyck paths. The principle of inclusion and exclusion says that we should count the total number of paths with same extremities and retract the number of paths that cross the diagonal. The former is $\binom{2n-r-1}{n-1}$, which enumerates the ways to interleave $n-1$ rises ($\uparrow$) and $n-r$ falls ($\rightarrow$). The latter number is the same as the number of monotonic paths from $(1,-1)$ to $(n-r, n-1)$, as shown by reflecting the paths up to their first crossing, that is, $\binom{2n-r-1}{n}$; in other words, that is the number of interleavings of n rises with $n-r-1$ falls. Finally, imitating the derivation of equation (6.1), the number $\mathcal{R}_n(r)$ of trees with n edges and root of degree r is

$$\mathcal{R}_n(r) = \binom{2n-r-1}{n-1} - \binom{2n-r-1}{n} = \frac{r}{2n-r}\binom{2n-r}{n}.$$

Let $\mathcal{N}_n(l, d)$ be the number of nodes in the set of all Catalan trees with n edges, which are at level l and have degree d. This number is the next step in determining the average path length because Ruskey (1983) found a neat bijection to relate it to $\mathcal{R}_n(r)$ by the following equation:

$$\mathcal{N}_n(l, d) = \mathcal{R}_{n+l}(2l + d).$$

In FIGURE 6.7a is shown the general pattern of a Catalan tree with node ($\bullet$) of level d and degree d. The double edges denote a set of edges, so the $\mathcal{L}_i$, $\mathcal{R}_i$ and $\mathcal{B}_i$ actually represent forests. In FIGURE 6.7b we see a Catalan tree in bijection with the former, from which it is made by lifting the node of interest ($\bullet$) to become the root, the forests $\mathcal{L}_i$ with their respective parents are attached below it, then the $\mathcal{B}_i$, and, finally, the $\mathcal{R}_i$ for which new parents are needed (inside a dashed frame in the figure). Clearly, the new root is of degree $2l + d$ and there are $n + l$ edges. Importantly, the

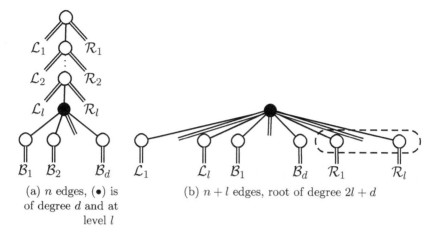

(a) n edges, ($\bullet$) is of degree d and at level l (b) $n + l$ edges, root of degree $2l + d$

Figure 6.7: Bijection

transformation can be inverted for any tree (it is injective and surjective), so it is indeed a bijection. We deduce

$$\mathcal{N}_n(l, d) = \frac{2l + d}{2n - d}\binom{2n - d}{n + l} = \binom{2n - d - 1}{n + l - 1} - \binom{2n - d - 1}{n + l},$$

where the last step follows from expressing the binomial coefficient in terms of the factorial function. In particular, this entails that the total number of nodes at level l in all Catalan trees with n edges is

$$\sum_{d=0}^{n} \mathcal{N}_n(l, d) = \sum_{d=0}^{n}\binom{2n - d - 1}{n + l - 1} - \sum_{d=0}^{n}\binom{2n - d - 1}{n + l}.$$

Let us consider the first sum:

$$\sum_{d=0}^{n}\binom{2n - d - 1}{n + l - 1} = \sum_{i=n-1}^{2n-1}\binom{i}{n + l - 1} = \sum_{i=n+l-1}^{2n-1}\binom{i}{n + l - 1}.$$

We can now make use of the identity (4.8) on page 126, which is equivalent to $\sum_{i=j}^{k}\binom{i}{j} = \binom{k+1}{j+1}$, so $j = n + l - 1$ and $k = 2n - 1$ yields

$$\sum_{d=0}^{n}\binom{2n - d - 1}{n + l - 1} = \binom{2n}{n + l}.$$

Furthermore, replacing l by $l + 1$ gives $\sum_{d=0}^{n}\binom{2n-d-1}{n+l} = \binom{2n}{n+l+1}$, so the total number of nodes at level l in all Catalan trees with n edges is

$$\sum_{d=0}^{n} \mathcal{N}_n(l, d) = \binom{2n}{n + l} - \binom{2n}{n + l + 1} = \frac{2l + 1}{2n + 1}\binom{2n + 1}{n - l}. \tag{6.2}$$

Let $\mathbb{E}[P_n]$ be the *average path length* of a Catalan tree with n edges. We have, by definition:

$$\mathbb{E}[P_n] := \frac{1}{C_n} \cdot \sum_{l=0}^{n} l \sum_{d=0}^{n} \mathcal{N}_n(l, d),$$

because there are C_n trees and the double summation is the sum of the path lengths of all the trees. If we average again by the number of nodes, *i.e.*, $n+1$, we obtain the average level of a node in a random Catalan tree and beware that some authors take this as the definition of the average path length. Alternatively, if we pick distinct Catalan trees with n edges at random and then pick random, distinct nodes in them, $\mathbb{E}[P_n]/(n+1)$ is the limit of the average cost of reaching the nodes in question from the root. Using equations (6.2) and (6.1) on page 198, we get

$$\mathbb{E}[P_n] \cdot C_n = \sum_{l=0}^{n} l \left[\binom{2n}{n+l} - \binom{2n}{n+l+1} \right]$$

$$= \sum_{l=1}^{n} l \binom{2n}{n+l} - \sum_{l=0}^{n-1} l \binom{2n}{n+l+1}$$

$$= \sum_{l=1}^{n} l \binom{2n}{n+l} - \sum_{l=1}^{n} (l-1) \binom{2n}{n+l}$$

$$= \sum_{l=1}^{n} \binom{2n}{n+l} = \sum_{i=n+1}^{2n} \binom{2n}{i}.$$

The remaining summation is easy to crack because it is the sum of one half of an even row in Pascal's triangle. We see in FIGURE 4.5 on page 125 that the first half equals the second half, only the central element remaining (there is an odd number of entries in an even row). This is readily proven as follows:

$$\sum_{j=0}^{n-1} \binom{2n}{j} = \sum_{j=0}^{n-1} \binom{2n}{2n-j} = \sum_{i=n+1}^{2n} \binom{2n}{i}.$$

Therefore

$$\sum_{i=0}^{2n} \binom{2n}{i} = 2 \cdot \sum_{i=n+1}^{2n} \binom{2n}{i} + \binom{2n}{n},$$

and we can continue as follows:

$$\frac{\mathbb{E}[P_n]}{n+1} = \frac{1}{2} \binom{2n}{n}^{-1} \left[\sum_{i=0}^{2n} \binom{2n}{i} - \binom{2n}{n} \right] = \frac{1}{2} \left[\binom{2n}{n}^{-1} \sum_{i=0}^{2n} \binom{2n}{i} - 1 \right].$$

The remaining sum is perhaps the most famous combinatorial identity because it is a corollary of the venerable *binomial theorem*, which states that, for all real numbers x and y, and all positive integers n, we have the following equality:

$$(x + y)^n = \sum_{k=0}^{n} \binom{n}{k} x^{n-k} y^k.$$

The truth of this statement can be seen by the following reckoning. Since, by definition, $(x+y)^n = \underbrace{(x + y)(x + y) \ldots (x + y)}_{n \text{ times}}$, each term in the expansion of $(x + y)^n$ has the form $x^{n-k} y^k$, for some k ranging from 0 to n, included. The coefficient of $x^{n-k} y^k$ for a given k is simply the number of ways to choose k variables y from the n factors of $(x + y)^n$, the x variables coming from the remaining $n - k$ factors.

Setting $x = y = 1$ yields the identity $2^n = \sum_{k=0}^{n} \binom{n}{k}$, which finally unlocks our last step:

$$E[P_n] = \frac{n + 1}{2} \left[4^n \binom{2n}{n}^{-1} - 1 \right]. \tag{6.3}$$

Recalling (6.1) on page 198, we obtain the asymptotic expansion:

$$E[P_n] \sim \frac{1}{2} n \sqrt{\pi n}. \tag{6.4}$$

Note that this equivalence also holds if n denotes a number of nodes, instead of edges. The exact formula for the average path length of Catalan trees with n nodes is $E[P_{n-1}]$ because there are then $n - 1$ edges.

For some applications, it may be useful to know the external and internal path lengths, which are, respectively, the path lengths up to the leaves and to inner nodes (not to be confused with the external and internal path lengths of binary trees). Let $E[E_n]$ be the former and $E[I_n]$ the latter. We have

$$E[E_n] \cdot C_n := \sum_{l=0}^{n} l \cdot \mathcal{N}_n(l, 0) = \sum_{l=0}^{n} l \left[\binom{2n - 1}{n + l - 1} - \binom{2n - 1}{n + l} \right]$$

$$= \sum_{l=0}^{n-1} (l + 1) \binom{2n - 1}{n + l} - \sum_{l=0}^{n-1} l \binom{2n - 1}{n + l} = \sum_{l=0}^{n-1} \binom{2n - 1}{n + l}$$

$$= \sum_{i=n}^{2n-1} \binom{2n - 1}{i} = \frac{1}{2} \sum_{j=0}^{2n-1} \binom{2n - 1}{j} = 4^{n-1},$$

where the penultimate step follows from the fact that an odd row in Pascal's triangle contains an even number of coefficients and the two halves have equal sums. We conclude:

$$\mathbb{E}[E_n] = (n+1)4^{n-1}\binom{2n}{n}^{-1} \sim \frac{1}{4}n\sqrt{\pi n}. \tag{6.5}$$

The derivation of $\mathbb{E}[I_n]$ is easy because

$$\mathbb{E}[P_n] = \mathbb{E}[E_n] + \mathbb{E}[I_n]. \tag{6.6}$$

From (6.3) and (6.5), we express $\mathbb{E}[P_n]$ in terms of $\mathbb{E}[E_n]$:

$$\mathbb{E}[P_n] = 2\mathbb{E}[E_n] - \frac{n+1}{2},$$

then, replacing it in (6.6), we finally draw

$$\mathbb{E}[I_n] = \mathbb{E}[E_n] - \frac{n+1}{2},$$

and

$$\mathbb{E}[I_n] = (n+1)4^{n-1}\binom{2n}{n}^{-1} - \frac{n+1}{2} \sim \frac{1}{4}n\sqrt{\pi n}. \tag{6.7}$$

Finally, formulas (6.3), (6.5) and (6.7) entail

$$\mathbb{E}[I_n] \sim \mathbb{E}[E_n] \sim \frac{1}{2}\mathbb{E}[P_n].$$

6.3   Average number of leaves

The degree-based bijection we introduced in FIGURE 6.5 on page 199 implies that there are $(n+1)/2$ leaves in average in a random Catalan tree with n edges. Indeed, a leaf is a corner in the ordinary lattice path, and it is *not* a corner in the degree-based lattice path, that is, an internal node (non-leaf), therefore, leaves and non-leaves are equinumerous and, since their total number is $n+1$, the average number of leaves is $(n+1)/2$.

For further reading, we recommend the papers by Dershowitz and Zaks (1980, 1981, 1990).

6.4   Average height

As mentioned earlier, the *height* of a tree is the number of edges on a maximal path from the root to a leaf, that is, a node without subtrees; for example, we can follow down and count the edges connecting the

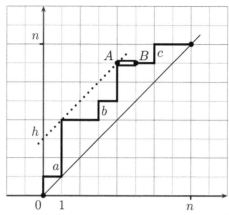

Figure 6.8: A Dyck path of length $2n$ and height h

nodes ($\circ$) in FIGURE 6.1 on page 195. Accordingly, a tree reduced to a single leaf has height 0.

We begin with the key observation that a Catalan tree with n edges and height h is in bijection with a Dyck path of length $2n$ and height h (see FIGURE 6.2 on page 196). This simple fact allows us to reason on the height of the Dyck paths and transfer the result back to Catalan trees. Indeed, we have already seen the correspondence between lattice paths and Catalan trees, in which a rise reaching the lth diagonal corresponds to a node at level l in the tree, counting levels from root level 0. A simple bijection between paths will show that for every node on level l of a tree of height h and size n, there is a corresponding node on either level $h - l + 1$ or $h - l$ in another tree of same height and size (Dershowitz and Rinderknecht, 2015).

Consider the Dyck path in FIGURE 6.8, in bijection with a tree with $n = 8$ edges and height $h = 3$. Let us find the last (rightmost) point on the path where it reaches its full height (the dotted line of equation $y = x + h$), which we call the *apex* of the path (marked A in the figure). The immediately following fall leads to B and it is drawn with a double line. Let us rotate the segment from $(0, 0)$ to A, and the segment from B to (n, n) by 180°. The invariant fall (A, B) now connects the rotated segments. This way, what was the apex becomes the origin and vice-versa, making this a height-preserving bijection between paths. See FIGURE 6.9 on the next page.

The point is that every rise to level l in FIGURE 6.8, representing a node on level l in the corresponding Catalan tree, ends up reaching level $h - l + 1$ or $h - l$ in FIGURE 6.9, depending on whether it was to the left (segment before A) or right (segment after B) of the apex. In the

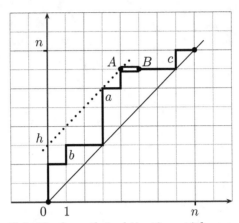

Figure 6.9: Dyck path in bijection with FIGURE 6.8

example in the figure, the rise a reaches level 1, and its counterpart after the transformation rises to level $3 - 1 + 1 = 3$; the rise b reached level 2 and still does so after because $3 - 2 + 1 = 2$; the rise c also reached level 2, but because it was to the right of the apex, it reaches now level $3 - 2 = 1$. It follows from this bijection that *the average height is within one of twice the average level of a node, that is, the average path length.* Equation (6.3) is equivalent to

$$2\frac{\mathbb{E}[P_n]}{n+1} = 4^n \binom{2n}{n}^{-1} - 1.$$

If $\mathbb{E}[H_n]$ is the average height of a Catalan tree with n edges, we then have, recalling (6.4),

$$\mathbb{E}[H_n] \sim 2\frac{\mathbb{E}[P_n]}{n+1} \sim \sqrt{\pi n}.$$

Chapter 7

Binary Trees

In this chapter, we focus on the binary tree as a data structure in itself, redefining it on the way and introducing related classical algorithms and measures.

FIGURE 7.1 displays a binary tree as an example. Nodes are of two kinds: internal (∘ and •) or external (□). The characteristic feature of a binary tree is that internal nodes are downwardly connected to two nodes, called *children*, whilst external nodes have no such links. The root is the topmost internal node, represented with a circle and a diameter. *Leaves* are internal nodes whose children are two external nodes; they are depicted as black discs.

Internal nodes are usually associated with some kind of information, whilst external nodes are not, like the one shown in FIGURE 7.3a on the next page: this is the default representation we use in the present book. Sometimes, in order to draw more attention to the internal nodes, the external nodes may be omitted, as in FIGURE 7.3b on the following page. Moreover, only

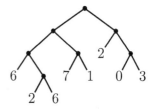

Figure 7.2: A leaf tree

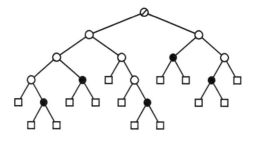

Figure 7.1: A binary tree

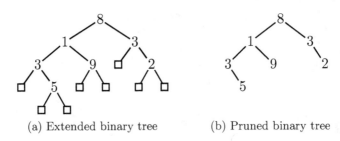

(a) Extended binary tree   (b) Pruned binary tree

Figure 7.3: Two representations of a binary tree

the leaves might then carry information, in which case the tree is a *leaf tree*, as in FIGURE 7.2 on the previous page. Another variant sees all nodes carrying some piece of data, as was the case with comparison trees (refer for example to FIGURE 2.41 on page 90, where external nodes contain permutations and internal nodes hold comparisons of keys).

As seen in the study of sorting algorithms optimal in average, on page 90, an *external path* is a path from the root to an external node and the *height* of a tree is the length of the maximum external paths. For example, the height of the binary tree in FIGURE 7.1 on the preceding page is 5 and there are two external paths of maximum length. A path from the root to an internal node is an *internal path*. The *internal path length of a tree* is the sum of the lengths of all its internal paths. We already have met the *external path length of a tree*, on page 110, which is the sum of the lengths of all its external paths. (The length of a path is the number of its edges.)

Warning   Some authors use a different nomenclature for the definition of the leaves and height. It is also common to stumble upon the concept of *depth* of a tree, coming from graph theory and which can be mistaken for its height, the former counting the number of nodes on a maximum path. Confusing depth and height leads to an off-by-one error in formulas.

Theorem 5 (Internal and external nodes). *A binary tree with n internal nodes has $n + 1$ external nodes.*

Proof. Let e be the number of external nodes to be determined. We can count the edges in two complementary ways. Top-down, we see that each internal node has exactly two children, so $l = 2n$, where l is the number of edges. Bottom-up, we see that each node has exactly one parent, except the root, which as none. Therefore, $l = (n + e) - 1$. Identifying the two values of l yields $e = n + 1$.   □

Data structure There are many ways to represent a binary tree as a data structure. First, we can remark that, just as a stack can be empty or not, there are two kinds of nodes, internal or external, and the empty tree can be identified to an external node. Therefore, we only need two data constructors, say ext/0 for external nodes, and int/3 for internal nodes. The latter applies to three arguments because two children are expected, as well as some information. The order of these arguments may differ. Because we may see an internal node to stand, horizontally, between its subtrees t_1 and t_2, we may prefer to write $int(t_1, x, t_2)$. Alternatively, we may consider that an internal node lies, vertically, before its subtrees, in which case we might prefer to write $int(x, t_1, t_2)$. The latter makes typing or handwriting small trees easier, in particular for testing purposes. For example, the binary tree of FIGURE 7.3a on the facing page formally corresponds to $int(8, t_1, int(3, ext(), ext(2, ext(), ext())))$, where $t_1 = int(1, ext(3, ext(), int(5, ext(), ext())), ext(9, ext(), ext()))$. We will use henceforth the convention $int(x, t_1, t_2)$, sometimes called *prefix notation*.

The *size* of a binary tree is the number of its internal nodes. It is the most common measure used on trees when expressing costs of functions. As a warm-up exercise, let us write a program computing the size of a given binary tree:

$$size(ext()) \rightarrow 0; \quad size(int(x, t_1, t_2)) \rightarrow 1 + size(t_1) + size(t_2). \quad (7.1)$$

Notice the similarity with computing the length of a stack:

$$len(nil()) \rightarrow 0; \quad len(cons(x, s)) \rightarrow 1 + len(s).$$

The difference lies in that two recursive calls are needed to visit all the nodes of a binary tree, instead of one for a stack. This bidimensional topology gives rise to many kinds of visits, called *walks* or *traversals*.

7.1 Traversals

In this section, we present the classic traversals of binary trees, which are distinguished by the order in which the data stored in the internal nodes is pushed onto a stack originally empty.

Preorder A *preorder* traversal of a non-empty binary tree consists in having in a stack the root (recursively, it is the current internal node), followed by the nodes in preorder of the left subtree and, finally, the nodes in preorder of the right subtree. (For the sake of brevity, we will identify the contents of the nodes with the nodes themselves, when there is no ambiguity.) For example, the (contents of the) nodes in preorder of the tree in FIGURE 7.3a on page 208 are $[8, 1, 3, 5, 9, 3, 2]$. Because this method first visits the children of a node before its sibling (two internal nodes are *siblings* if they have the same parent), it is a *depth-first* traversal. A simple program is

$$\mathsf{pre_0}(\mathsf{ext}()) \xrightarrow{\gamma} [\,];$$
$$\mathsf{pre_0}(\mathsf{int}(x, t_1, t_2)) \xrightarrow{\delta} [x \,|\, \mathsf{cat}(\mathsf{pre_0}(t_1), \mathsf{pre_0}(t_2))]. \tag{7.2}$$

We used the concatenation on stacks provided by $\mathsf{cat}/2$, defined in (1.3) on page 7, to order the values of the subtrees. We know that the cost of $\mathsf{cat}/2$ is linear in the size of its first argument: $C_p^{\mathsf{cat}} := C[\![\mathsf{cat}(s, t)]\!] = p + 1$, where p is the length of s. Let $C_n^{\mathsf{pre_0}}$ be the cost of $\mathsf{pre_0}(t)$, where n is the number of internal nodes of t. From the definition of $\mathsf{pre_0}/1$, we deduce

$$C_0^{\mathsf{pre_0}} = 1; \quad C_{n+1}^{\mathsf{pre_0}} = 1 + C_p^{\mathsf{pre_0}} + C_{n-p}^{\mathsf{pre_0}} + C_p^{\mathsf{cat}},$$

where p is the size of t_1. So $C_{n+1}^{\mathsf{pre_0}} = C_p^{\mathsf{pre_0}} + C_{n-p}^{\mathsf{pre_0}} + p + 2$. This recurrence belongs to a class that is an instance of the *divide and conquer* principle because it springs from strategies which consists in splitting the input (here, of size $n + 1$), recursively applying the relevant solving strategy to the smaller parts (here, of sizes p and $n - p$) and finally combining the solutions of the parts into a solution of the partition. The extra cost incurred by combining smaller solutions (here, $p + 2$) is called the *toll* and the closed form and asymptotic behaviour of the solution to the recurrence crucially depends upon its kind.

In another context (see page 57), we, idiosyncratically, called this strategy *big-step design* because we wanted a convenient way to contrast it with another sort of modelling which we called *small-step design*. As a consequence, we already have seen instances of 'divide and conquer', for example, in the case of merge sort in chapter 4 on page 119, which often epitomises the concept itself.

The maximum cost $W_k^{\mathsf{pre_0}}$ satisfies the extremal recurrence

$$W_0^{\mathsf{pre_0}} = 1; \quad W_{k+1}^{\mathsf{pre_0}} = 2 + \max_{0 \leqslant p \leqslant k} \{W_p^{\mathsf{pre_0}} + W_{k-p}^{\mathsf{pre_0}} + p\}. \tag{7.3}$$

Instead of attacking frontally these equations, we can guess a possible solution and check it. Here, we could try to consistently choose $p = k$, prompted by the idea that maximising the toll at each node of the tree will perhaps lead to a total maximum (*eager solving*). Thus, we envisage

$$W_0^{\mathsf{pre_0}} = 1; \quad W_{k+1}^{\mathsf{pre_0}} = W_k^{\mathsf{pre_0}} + k + 3. \tag{7.4}$$

Summing both sides from $k = 0$ to $k = n - 1$ and simplifying yields

$$W_n^{\mathsf{pre}_0} = \frac{1}{2}(n^2 + 5n + 2) \sim \frac{1}{2}n^2.$$

At this point, we check whether this closed form satisfies equation (7.3). We have $2(W_p^{\mathsf{pre}_0} + W_{n-p}^{\mathsf{pre}_0} + p + 2) = 2p^2 + 2(1 - n)p + n^2 + 5n + 8$. This is the equation of a parabola whose minimum occurs at $p = (n - 1)/2$ and maximum at $p = n$, over the interval $[0, n]$. The maximum, whose value is $n^2 + 7n + 8$, equals $2 \cdot W_{n+1}^{\mathsf{pre}_0}$, so the closed form satisfies the extremal recurrence.

What does a binary tree maximising the cost of $\mathsf{pre}_0/1$ look like? The toll $k + 3$ in (7.4) is a consequence of taking the maximum cost of $\mathsf{cat}/2$ at each node, which means that all the internal nodes being concatenated come from the left subtrees, the left subtree of the left subtree etc. so these nodes are concatenated again and again while going up (that is, returning from the recursive calls), leading to a quadratic cost. The shape of such a tree is shown in FIGURE 7.4a.

Dually, the minimum cost $B_k^{\mathsf{pre}_0}$ satisfies the extremal recurrence

$$B_0^{\mathsf{pre}_0} = 1; \quad B_{k+1}^{\mathsf{pre}_0} = 2 + \min_{0 \leqslant p \leqslant k} \{B_p^{\mathsf{pre}_0} + B_{k-p}^{\mathsf{pre}_0} + p\}.$$

Along the same line as before, but on the opposite direction, we may try to minimise the toll by choosing $p = 0$, which means that all external nodes, but one, are left subtrees. Consequently, we have

$$B_0^{\mathsf{pre}_0} = 1; \quad B_{k+1}^{\mathsf{pre}_0} = B_k^{\mathsf{pre}_0} + 3. \tag{7.5}$$

Summing both sides from $k = 0$ to $k = n - 1$ and simplifying yields

$$B_n^{\mathsf{pre}_0} = 3n + 1 \sim 3n.$$

It is easy to check that this is indeed a solution to (7.5). The shape of the corresponding tree is shown in FIGURE 7.4b. Note that both extremal trees are isomorphic to a stack (that is, the abstract syntax tree of a stack)

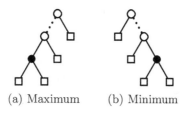

(a) Maximum   (b) Minimum

Figure 7.4: Extremal trees for $C_n^{\mathsf{pre}_0}$

$$\boxed{\begin{array}{c} \mathsf{pre}_1(t) \rightarrow \mathsf{flat}(\mathsf{pre}_2(t)). \\[1em] \mathsf{pre}_2(\mathsf{ext}()) \rightarrow []; \\ \mathsf{pre}_2(\mathsf{int}(x, t_1, t_2)) \rightarrow [x, \mathsf{pre}_2(t_1) \,|\, \mathsf{pre}_2(t_2)]. \end{array}}$$

Figure 7.5: Preorder traversal using flat/1

and, as such, are instances of *degenerate trees*. Also, the maximum cost of $\mathsf{pre}_0/1$ is quadratic, which calls for some improvement.

Another big-step design we may come up with consists in not using cat/2 and calling instead flat/1, defined in FIGURE 2.12 on page 60, *once at the end*. FIGURE 7.5 shows that new version of the preorder traversal, named $\mathsf{pre}_1/1$. The cost of $\mathsf{pre}_2(t)$ is now reduced to $2n+1$ (see theorem 5 on page 208). On page 60, the cost of $\mathsf{flat}(s)$ was $1+n+\Omega+\Gamma+L$, where n is the length of $\mathsf{flat}(s)$, Ω is the number of empty stacks in s, Γ is the number of non-empty stacks and L is the sum of the lengths of the embedded stacks. The value of Ω is $n+1$ because this is the number of external nodes. The value of Γ is $n-1$, because each internal node yields a non-empty stack by the second rule of $\mathsf{pre}_2/1$ and the root is excluded because we only count embedded stacks. The value of L is $3(n-1)$ because those stacks have length 3 by the same rule. In the end, $\mathcal{C}[\![\mathsf{flat}(s)]\!] = 6n - 2$, where $\mathsf{pre}_2(t) \twoheadrightarrow s$ and n is the size of t. Finally, we must account for the rule defining $\mathsf{pre}_1/1$ and assess afresh the cost incurred by the empty tree:

$$C_0^{\mathsf{pre}_1} = 3; \quad C_n^{\mathsf{pre}_1} = 1 + (2n+1) + (6n-2) = 8n, \text{ when } n > 0.$$

Despite a significant improvement in the cost and the lack of extreme cases, we should try a small-step design before giving up. The underlying principle in this kind of approach is to do as little as possible in each rule. Looking back at $\mathsf{pre}_0/1$, it is clear that the root is correctly placed, but, without resorting to $\mathsf{pre}_3(t_1)$ and $\mathsf{pre}_3(t_2)$ in the following canvas, what can be done further?

$$\mathsf{pre}_3(\mathsf{ext}()) \rightarrow []; \quad \mathsf{pre}_3(\mathsf{int}(x, t_1, t_2)) \rightarrow [x \,|\, \underline{\qquad\qquad}].$$

The way forth is to think in terms of forests, instead of single trees, because a forest is a stack of trees and, as such, can also be used to accumulate trees. This is a common technique when processing trees. See FIGURE 7.6 on the next page. Empty trees in the forest are skipped in rule γ. In rule δ, the subtrees t_1 and t_2 are now simply pushed back onto the forest f, for later processing. This way, there is no need to compute

$$\mathsf{pre}_3(t) \xrightarrow{\alpha} \mathsf{pre}_4([t]).$$

$$\mathsf{pre}_4([]) \xrightarrow{\beta} [];$$
$$\mathsf{pre}_4([\mathsf{ext}() \,|\, f]) \xrightarrow{\gamma} \mathsf{pre}_4(f);$$
$$\mathsf{pre}_4([\mathsf{int}(x, t_1, t_2) \,|\, f]) \xrightarrow{\delta} [x \,|\, \mathsf{pre}_4([t_1, t_2 \,|\, f])].$$

Figure 7.6: Efficient preorder traversal with a forest

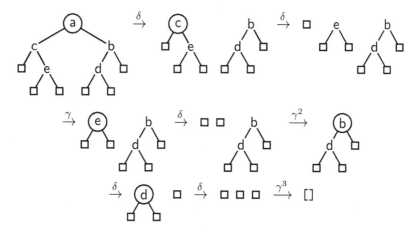

Figure 7.7: A preorder traversal with $\mathsf{pre}_4/1$

$\mathsf{pre}_4(t_1)$ or $\mathsf{pre}_4(t_2)$ immediately. This method is slightly different from using an accumulator which contains, at every moment, a partial result or a reversed partial result. Here, no parameter is added but, instead, a stack replaces the original parameter, and it does not contain partial results, but pieces of the original tree from which to pick internal nodes easily (the root of the first tree) in the expected order. An example is given in FIGURE 7.7, where the forest is the argument of $\mathsf{pre}_4/1$ and the circle nodes are the current value of x in rule δ of FIGURE 7.6.

The cost of $\mathsf{pre}_3(t)$, where the size of t is n, is simple:

- rule α is used once;
- rule β is used once;
- rule γ is used once for each external node, that is, $n + 1$ times;
- rule δ is used once for each internal node, so n times, by definition.

In total, $C_n^{\mathsf{pre}_3} = 2n + 3 \sim 2n$, which is a notable improvement. The keen reader may remark that we could further reduce the cost by not visiting the external nodes, as shown in FIGURE 7.8. We then have

$$C_n^{\mathsf{pre}_5} = C_n^{\mathsf{pre}_3} - (n + 1) = n + 2.$$

$$\mathsf{pre}_5(t) \rightarrow \mathsf{pre}_6([t]).$$

$$\mathsf{pre}_6([\,]) \rightarrow [\,];$$
$$\mathsf{pre}_6([\mathsf{ext}()\,|\,f]) \rightarrow \mathsf{pre}_6(f);$$
$$\mathsf{pre}_6([\mathsf{int}(x,\mathsf{ext}(),\mathsf{ext}())\,|\,f]) \rightarrow [x\,|\,\mathsf{pre}_6(f)];$$
$$\mathsf{pre}_6([\mathsf{int}(x,\mathsf{ext}(),t_2)\,|\,f]) \rightarrow [x\,|\,\mathsf{pre}_6([t_2\,|\,f])];$$
$$\mathsf{pre}_6([\mathsf{int}(x,t_1,\mathsf{ext}())\,|\,f]) \rightarrow [x\,|\,\mathsf{pre}_6([t_1\,|\,f])];$$
$$\mathsf{pre}_6([\mathsf{int}(x,t_1,t_2)\,|\,f]) \rightarrow [x\,|\,\mathsf{pre}_6([t_1,t_2\,|\,f])].$$

Figure 7.8: Lengthy definition of a preorder traversal

Despite the gain, the optimised program is significantly longer and the right-hand sides of the new rules are partial evaluations of rule δ. The measure of the input we use for calculating the costs does not include the abstract time needed to select the rule to apply but it is likely, though, that the more patterns, the higher this hidden penalty. In this book, we prefer to visit the external nodes unless there is a logical reason not to do so, if only for the sake of conciseness.

The total number of cons-nodes created by the rules α and δ is the total number of nodes, $2n + 1$, but if we want to know how many there can be at any time, we need to consider how the shape of the original tree influences the rules γ and δ. In the best case, t_1 in δ is $\mathsf{ext}()$ and will be eliminated next by rule γ without additional creation of nodes. In the worst case, t_1 maximises the number of internal nodes on its left branch. Therefore, these two configurations correspond to the extremal cases for the cost of $\mathsf{pre}_0/1$ in FIGURE 7.4 on page 211. In the worst case, all the $2n + 1$ nodes of the tree will be in the stack at one point, whilst, in the best case, only two will be. The question of the average stack size will be considered later in this text in relation with the average height.

The distinction between big-step design (or 'divide and conquer') and small-step design is not always a clear cut and is mainly intended to be a didactical means. In particular, we should not assume that there are only two possible kinds of design for every given task. To bring further clarity to the subject, let us use an heterogeneous approach to design another version, $\mathsf{pre}/1$, which computes efficiently the preorder traversal of a given binary tree. Looking back at $\mathsf{pre}_0/1$, we can identify the source of the inefficiency in the fact that, in the worst case,

$$\mathsf{pre}_0(t) \twoheadrightarrow [x_1\,|\,\mathsf{cat}([x_2\,|\,\mathsf{cat}(\ldots\mathsf{cat}([x_n\,|\,\mathsf{cat}([\,],[\,])],[\,])\ldots)])]$$

where $t = \mathsf{int}(x_1,\mathsf{int}(x_2,\ldots,\mathsf{int}(x_n,\mathsf{ext}(),\mathsf{ext}()),\ldots,\mathsf{ext}()),\mathsf{ext}())$ is the tree in FIGURE 7.4a on page 211. We met this kind of partial rewrite

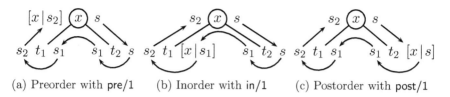

(a) Preorder with pre/1   (b) Inorder with in/1   (c) Postorder with post/1

Figure 7.9: Efficient classic traversals

in formula (2.4) on page 42 and (3.2) on page 96, and we found that it leads to a quadratic cost. Whilst the use of cat/2 in itself is not the issue, but rather the accumulation of calls to cat/2 as their first argument, let us nevertheless seek out a definition not relying on concatenation at all. This means that we want to build the preorder stack by using exclusively pushes. Therefore, we must add an auxiliary parameter, originally set to the empty stack, on which the contents of the nodes are pushed in the proper order: $pre(t) \rightarrow pre(t, [])$. Now, we should wonder what the interpretation of this accumulator is when considering the pattern $pre(t, s)$.

Let us have a look at the internal node $t = int(x, t_1, t_2)$ in FIGURE 7.9a. The arrows evince the traversal in the tree and connect different stages of the preorder stack: a downwards arrow points to the argument of a recursive call on the corresponding child; an upward arrow points to the result of the call on the parent.

For instance, the subtree t_2 corresponds to the recursive call $pre(t_2, s)$ whose value is named s_1. Likewise, we have $pre(t_1, s_1) \twoheadrightarrow s_2$, which is therefore equivalent to $pre(t_1, pre(t_2, s)) \twoheadrightarrow s_2$. Finally, the root is associated with the evaluation $pre(t, s) \twoheadrightarrow [x \,|\, s_2]$, which is none other than the equivalence $pre(t, s) \equiv [x \,|\, pre(t_1, pre(t_2, s))]$. The rule for external nodes is not shown and simply consists in letting the stack invariant. Finally we have the functional program in FIGURE 7.10.

We now understand that, given $pre(t, s)$, the nodes in the stack s are the nodes that follow, in preorder, the nodes in the subtree t. The cost

$$pre(t) \xrightarrow{\theta} pre(t, []).$$

$$pre(ext(), s) \xrightarrow{\iota} s;$$
$$pre(int(x, t_1, t_2), s) \xrightarrow{\kappa} [x \,|\, pre(t_1, pre(t_2, s))].$$

Figure 7.10: Cost and memory efficient preorder

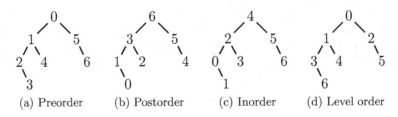

(a) Preorder   (b) Postorder   (c) Inorder   (d) Level order

Figure 7.11: Classic numberings of a pruned binary tree

is extremely simple:

$$C_n^{\text{pre}} = 1 + (n + 1) + n = 2n + 2. \tag{7.6}$$

(Keep in mind that there are $n + 1$ external nodes when there are n internal nodes.)

This variant is to be preferred over $\text{pre}_3/1$ because its memory usage is lower: rule δ in FIGURE 7.6 on page 213 pushes t_1 and t_2, thus allocates two cons-nodes per internal node, totalling $2n$ supplementary nodes. By contrast, $\text{pre}/1$ creates none, but allocates n call-nodes pre (one per internal node), so the advantage stands, albeit moot. Note that $\text{pre}_3/1$ is in tail form, but not $\text{pre}/2$.

Preorder numbering FIGURE 7.11a shows a binary tree whose internal nodes have been replaced by their rank in preorder, with the smallest number, 0, at the root. In particular, the preorder traversal of that tree yields $[0, 1, 2, 3, 4, 5, 6]$. Producing such a tree from some initial tree is a *preorder numbering*. A complete example is shown in FIGURE 7.12, where the preorder numbers are exponents to the internal nodes. Note how these numbers increase along downwards paths.

Their generation can be tackled in two phases: first, we need to understand how to produce the right number for a given node; second, we need to use these numbers to build a tree. The scheme for the former is shown on internal nodes in FIGURE 7.13a on the facing page. A num-

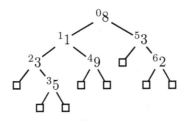

Figure 7.12: Preorder numbers as exponents

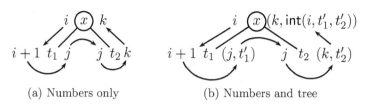

(a) Numbers only   (b) Numbers and tree

Figure 7.13: Preorder numbering in two phases

ber on the left side of a node indexes it, for example node x is indexed
with i: these numbers descend in the tree. A number on the right side of
a node is the smallest number not used in the numbering of the subtrees
attached to that node: these numbers ascend and may be used for the
numbering of another subtree. For instance, j is the smallest integer not
numbering the nodes of the subtree t_1. External nodes do not change
their incoming number and are not depicted.

The second and final design phase consists in the construction of the
tree made of these numbers and it is pictured in FIGURE 7.13b. Conceptually, it is the completion of the first phase in the sense that upwards
arrows, which denote values of recursive calls on subtrees, now point
at pairs whose first component is the number we found earlier and the
second component is a numbered tree. As usual with recursive definitions,
we assume that the recursive calls on substructures are correct (that is,
they yield the expected values) and we infer the value of the call on the
whole structure at hand, here $(k, \mathsf{int}(i, t_1', t_2'))$.

The function npre/1 (*number in preorder*) in FIGURE 7.14 implements
this algorithm, using a function npre/2 such that $\mathsf{npre}(i, t) \twoheadrightarrow (j, t')$,
where t' is the preorder numbering of t, with root i, and j is the smallest
integer not found in t' (in other words, $j - i$ is the size of t and t'). This
function is the one illustrated in FIGURE 7.13b. By the way, we should
perhaps recall that inference systems, first seen on page 70, can be eliminated by the introduction of auxiliary functions (one for each premise).

$$
\frac{\mathsf{npre}(0, t) \twoheadrightarrow (i, t')}{\mathsf{npre}(t) \twoheadrightarrow t'} \, . \qquad \mathsf{npre}(i, \mathsf{ext}()) \to (i, \mathsf{ext}());
$$

$$
\frac{\mathsf{npre}(i + 1, t_1) \twoheadrightarrow (j, t_1') \qquad \mathsf{npre}(j, t_2) \twoheadrightarrow (k, t_2')}{\mathsf{npre}(i, \mathsf{int}(x, t_1, t_2)) \twoheadrightarrow (k, \mathsf{int}(i, t_1', t_2'))} \, .
$$

Figure 7.14: Preorder numbering

$$\mathsf{npre}(t) \rightarrow \mathsf{snd}(\mathsf{npre}(0, t)).$$

$$\mathsf{snd}((x, y)) \rightarrow y.$$

$$\mathsf{npre}(i, \mathsf{ext}()) \rightarrow (i, \mathsf{ext}());$$
$$\mathsf{npre}(i, \mathsf{int}(x, t_1, t_2)) \rightarrow \mathsf{t}_1(\mathsf{npre}(i + 1, t_1), i, t_2).$$

$$\mathsf{t}_1((j, t_1'), i, t_2) \rightarrow \mathsf{t}_2(\mathsf{npre}(j, t_2), i, t_1').$$

$$\mathsf{t}_2((k, t_2'), i, t_1') \rightarrow (k, \mathsf{int}(i, t_1', t_2')).$$

Figure 7.15: Version of npre/1 without inference rules

In this instance, we could equivalently write the program in FIGURE 7.15.

Termination   It is easy to prove the termination of pre/2 because the technique used for proving the termination of Ackermann's function on page 13 is pertinent in the current context as well. We define a lexicographic order on the calls to pre/2 (dependency pairs) as follows:

$$\mathsf{pre}(t, s) \succ \mathsf{pre}(t', s') :\Leftrightarrow t \succ_B t' \text{ or } (t = t' \text{ and } s \succ_S s'), \quad (7.7)$$

where B is the set of all binary trees, S is the set of all stacks, $t \succ_B t'$ means that the tree t' is an immediate subtree of t, and $s \succ_S s'$ means that the stack s' is an immediate substack of s (page 12). From the definition in FIGURE 7.10 on page 215, we see that rule θ maintains termination if pre/2 terminates; rule ι terminates; finally, rule κ rewrites a call into smaller calls, according to ($\succ$):

$$\mathsf{pre}(\mathsf{int}(x, t_1, t_2), s) \succ \mathsf{pre}(t_2, s),$$
$$\mathsf{pre}(\mathsf{int}(x, t_1, t_2), s) \succ \mathsf{pre}(t_1, u), \text{ for all } u,$$

in particular if $\mathsf{pre}(t_2, s) \twoheadrightarrow u$. As a consequence, pre/1 terminates on all possible inputs.   □

Equivalence   To see how structural induction can be used to prove properties on binary trees, we will consider a simple statement we made earlier, formally expressed as $\mathsf{Pre}(t): \mathsf{pre}_0(t) \equiv \mathsf{pre}(t)$. We need to prove

- the basis $\mathsf{Pre}(\mathsf{ext}())$;

- the inductive step $\forall t_1.\mathsf{Pre}(t_1) \Rightarrow \forall t_2.\mathsf{Pre}(t_2) \Rightarrow \forall x.\mathsf{Pre}(\mathsf{int}(x, t_1, t_2))$.

The basis is easy because

$$\mathsf{pre}_0(\mathsf{ext}()) \xrightarrow{\gamma} [] \xleftarrow{\iota} \mathsf{pre}(\mathsf{ext}(), []) \xleftarrow{\theta} \mathsf{pre}(\mathsf{ext}()).$$

See definition of $\mathsf{pre}_0/1$ at equation (7.2) on page 210. It is useful here to recall the definition of $\mathsf{cat}/2$:

$$\mathsf{cat}([], t) \xrightarrow{\alpha} t; \qquad \mathsf{cat}([x\,|\,s], t) \xrightarrow{\beta} [x\,|\,\mathsf{cat}(s, t)].$$

In order to discover how to use the two induction hypotheses $\mathsf{Pre}(t_1)$ and $\mathsf{Pre}(t_2)$, let us start from one side of the equivalence we wish to establish, for example, the left-hand side, and rewrite it until we reach the other side or get stuck. Let $t := \mathsf{int}(x, t_1, t_2)$, then

$$
\begin{aligned}
\mathsf{pre}_0(t) &= \mathsf{pre}_0(\mathsf{int}(x, t_1, t_2)) \\
&\xrightarrow{\delta} [x\,|\,\mathsf{cat}(\mathsf{pre}_0(t_1), \mathsf{pre}_0(t_2))] \\
&\equiv [x\,|\,\mathsf{cat}(\mathsf{pre}(t_1), \mathsf{pre}_0(t_2))] && \mathsf{Pre}(t_1) \\
&\equiv [x\,|\,\mathsf{cat}(\mathsf{pre}(t_1), \mathsf{pre}(t_2))] && \mathsf{Pre}(t_2) \\
&\xrightarrow{\theta} [x\,|\,\mathsf{cat}(\mathsf{pre}(t_1, []), \mathsf{pre}(t_2))] \\
&\xrightarrow{\theta} [x\,|\,\mathsf{cat}(\mathsf{pre}(t_1, []), \mathsf{pre}(t_2, []))].
\end{aligned}
$$

At this point, we start rewriting the other side, until we get stuck as well:

$$\mathsf{pre}(t) = \mathsf{pre}(\mathsf{int}(x, t_1, t_2)) \xrightarrow{\theta} \mathsf{pre}(\mathsf{int}(x, t_1, t_2), []) \xrightarrow{\kappa} [x\,|\,\mathsf{pre}(t_1, \mathsf{pre}(t_2, []))].$$

Comparing the two stuck expressions suggests a subgoal to reach.

Let $\mathsf{CatPre}(t, s)$: $\mathsf{cat}(\mathsf{pre}(t, []), s) \equiv \mathsf{pre}(t, s)$. When a predicate depends upon two parameters, we have different options to ponder: either we need lexicographic induction, or simple induction on one of the variables. It is best to use a lexicographic ordering on pairs and, if we realise afterwards that only one component was needed, we can rewrite the proof with a simple induction on that component. Let us then define

$$(t, s) \succ_{B \times S} (t', s') :\Leftrightarrow t \succ_B t' \text{ or } (t = t' \text{ and } s \succ_S s').$$

This is conceptually the same order as the one on the calls to $\mathsf{pre}/1$, in definition (7.7). If we find out later that immediate subterm relations are too restrictive, we would choose here general subterm relations, which means, in the case of binary trees, that a tree is a subtree of another. The minimum element for the lexicographic order we just defined is $(\mathsf{ext}(), [])$.

The well-founded induction principle then requires that we establish

- the basis $\mathsf{CatPre}(\mathsf{ext}(), [])$;

$$
\begin{aligned}
\mathsf{cat}(\mathsf{pre}(t,[\,]),s) &= \mathsf{cat}(\underline{\mathsf{pre}}(\mathsf{int}(x,t_1,t_2),[\,]),s) \\
&\overset{\kappa}{\to} \underline{\mathsf{cat}}([x\,|\,\mathsf{pre}(t_1,\mathsf{pre}(t_2,[\,]))],s) \\
&\overset{\beta}{\to} [x\,|\,\mathsf{cat}(\mathsf{pre}(t_1,\mathsf{pre}(t_2,[\,])),s)] \\
&\equiv_0 [x\,|\,\mathsf{cat}(\mathsf{cat}(\mathsf{pre}(t_1,[\,]),\mathsf{pre}(t_2,[\,])),s)] \\
&\equiv_1 [x\,|\,\mathsf{cat}(\mathsf{pre}(t_1,[\,]),\mathsf{cat}(\mathsf{pre}(t_2,[\,]),s))] \\
&\equiv_2 [x\,|\,\mathsf{cat}(\mathsf{pre}(t_1,[\,]),\mathsf{pre}(t_2,s))] \\
&\equiv_3 [x\,|\,\mathsf{pre}(t_1,\mathsf{pre}(t_2,s))] \\
&\overset{\kappa}{\leftarrow} \mathsf{pre}(\mathsf{int}(x,t_1,t_2),s) \\
&= \mathsf{pre}(t,s). \qquad\qquad\qquad \square
\end{aligned}
$$

Figure 7.16: Proof of $\mathsf{CatPre}(t)$: $\mathsf{cat}(\mathsf{pre}(t,[\,]),s) \equiv \mathsf{pre}(t,s)$

- $\forall t,s.(\forall t',s'.(t,s) \succ_{B\times S} (t',s') \Rightarrow \mathsf{CatPre}(t',s')) \Rightarrow \mathsf{CatPre}(t,s)$.

The basis is easy:

$$
\mathsf{cat}(\underline{\mathsf{pre}}(\mathsf{ext}(),[\,]),[\,]) \overset{\iota}{\to} \mathsf{cat}([\,],[\,]) \overset{\alpha}{\to} [\,] \overset{\iota}{\leftarrow} \mathsf{pre}(\mathsf{ext}(),[\,]).
$$

We then assume $\forall t',s'.(t,s) \succ_{B\times S} (t',s') \Rightarrow \mathsf{CatPre}(t',s')$, which is the induction hypothesis, and proceed to rewrite the left-hand side after letting $t := \mathsf{int}(x,t_1,t_2)$. See FIGURE 7.16, where

- ($\equiv_0$) is the instance $\mathsf{CatPre}(t_1,\mathsf{pre}(t_2,[\,]))$ of the induction hypothesis because $(t,s) \succ_{B\times S} (t_1,s')$, for all stacks s', in particular when $\mathsf{pre}(t_2,[\,]) \twoheadrightarrow s'$;

- ($\equiv_1$) is an application of the lemma on the associativity of stack concatenation (page 14), that is: $\mathsf{CatAssoc}(\mathsf{pre}(t_1,[\,]),\mathsf{pre}(t_2,[\,]),s)$;

- ($\equiv_2$) is the instance $\mathsf{CatPre}(t_2,s)$ of the induction hypothesis because $(t,s) \succ_{B\times S} (t_2,s)$;

- ($\equiv_3$) is the instance $\mathsf{CatPre}(t_1,\mathsf{pre}(t_2,s))$ of the induction hypothesis because $(t,s) \succ_{B\times S} (t_1,s')$, for all stacks s', in particular when $s' = \mathsf{pre}(t_2,s)$.

We can resume conclusively in FIGURE 7.17 on the next page. $\square$

Flattening revisited In section 2.4 on page 56, we defined two functions for flattening stacks (see FIGURE 2.8 on page 57 and FIGURE 2.12 on page 60). With the understanding of preorder traversals, it may occur to us that the flattening of a stack is equivalent to the preorder traversal of a binary leaf tree (see FIGURE 7.2 on page 207 for an example) which

$$\begin{aligned}
\mathsf{pre}_0(t) \;&=\; \mathsf{pre}_0(\mathsf{int}(x,t_1,t_2))\\
&\xrightarrow{\delta}\; [x\,|\,\mathsf{cat}(\mathsf{pre}_0(t_1),\mathsf{pre}_0(t_2))]\\
&\equiv\; [x\,|\,\mathsf{cat}(\underline{\mathsf{pre}(t_1)},\mathsf{pre}_0(t_2))] && \mathsf{Pre}(t_1)\\
&\equiv\; [x\,|\,\mathsf{cat}(\underline{\mathsf{pre}(t_1)},\underline{\mathsf{pre}(t_2)})] && \mathsf{Pre}(t_2)\\
&\xrightarrow{\theta}\; [x\,|\,\mathsf{cat}(\underline{\mathsf{pre}(t_1,[\,])},\mathsf{pre}(t_2))]\\
&\xrightarrow{\theta}\; [x\,|\,\mathsf{cat}(\mathsf{pre}(t_1,[\,]),\underline{\mathsf{pre}(t_2,[\,])})]\\
&\equiv\; [x\,|\,\underline{\mathsf{pre}(t_1,\mathsf{pre}(t_2,[\,]))}] && \mathsf{CatPre}(t_1,\mathsf{pre}(t_2,[\,]))\\
&\xleftarrow{\kappa}\; \mathsf{pre}(\mathsf{int}(x,t_1,t_2),[\,])\\
&\xleftarrow{\theta}\; \mathsf{pre}(\mathsf{int}(x,t_1,t_2))\\
&=\; \mathsf{pre}(t). && \square
\end{aligned}$$

Figure 7.17: Proof of $\mathsf{Pre}(t)$: $\mathsf{pre}_0(t) \equiv \mathsf{pre}(t)$

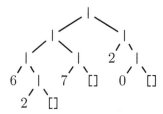

Figure 7.18: Embedded stacks as a leaf tree

ignores empty stacks. The key is to see a stack, possibly containing other stacks, as a leaf tree, as shown for example in FIGURE 7.18, where the internal nodes (|) are cons-nodes.

The first step consists in defining inductively the set of the binary leaf trees as the smallest set L generated by the deductive (downwards) reading of the inference system

$$\mathsf{leaf}(x) \in L \qquad \frac{t_1 \in L \qquad t_2 \in L}{\mathsf{fork}(t_1,t_2) \in L}.$$

In other words, a leaf containing the piece of data x is noted $\mathsf{leaf}(x)$ and the other internal nodes are *forks*, written $\mathsf{fork}(t_1,t_2)$, with t_1 and t_2 being binary leaf trees themselves. The second step requires a modification of $\mathsf{pre}/1$, defined in FIGURE 7.10 on page 215, so it processes binary leaf trees. The new function, $\mathsf{lpre}/1$, is shown in FIGURE 7.19 on the following page. The final step is the translation of $\mathsf{lpre}/1$ and $\mathsf{lpre}/2$ into $\mathsf{flat}_2/1$ and $\mathsf{flat}_2/2$, respectively, in FIGURE 7.20 on the next page. The key is to see that $\mathsf{fork}(t_1,t_2)$ becomes $[t_1\,|\,t_2]$, and $\mathsf{leaf}(x)$, when x is not an empty

$$\mathsf{lpre}(t) \rightarrow \mathsf{lpre}(t, [\,]).$$

$$\mathsf{lpre}(\mathsf{leaf}(x), s) \rightarrow [x \,|\, s];$$
$$\mathsf{lpre}(\mathsf{fork}(t_1, t_2), s) \rightarrow \mathsf{lpre}(t_1, \mathsf{lpre}(t_2, s)).$$

Figure 7.19: Preorder on binary leaf trees

$$\mathsf{flat}_2(t) \rightarrow \mathsf{flat}_2(t, [\,]).$$

$$\mathsf{flat}_2([\,], s) \rightarrow s;$$
$$\mathsf{flat}_2([t_1 \,|\, t_2], s) \rightarrow \mathsf{flat}_2(t_1, \mathsf{flat}_2(t_2, s));$$
$$\mathsf{flat}_2(x, s) \rightarrow [x \,|\, s].$$

Figure 7.20: Flattening like lpre/1

stack, becomes x as the *last* pattern. The case $\mathsf{leaf}([\,])$ becomes $[\,]$ as the first pattern.

The cost of pre/1 was found to be $\mathcal{C}_n^{\mathsf{pre}} = 2n + 2$ in equation (7.6) on page 216, where n was the number of internal nodes. Here, n is the length of $\mathsf{flat}_2(t)$, namely, the number of non-stack leaves in the leaf tree. With this definition, the number of cons-nodes is $n + \Omega + \Gamma$, where Ω is the number of embedded empty stacks and Γ is the number of embedded non-empty stacks, so $S := 1 + \Omega + \Gamma$ is the total number of stacks. Consequently, $\mathcal{C}_n^{\mathsf{flat}_2} = 2(n + S)$. For example,

$$\mathsf{flat}_2([1, [[\,], [2, 3]], [[4]], 5]) \xrightarrow{22} [1, 2, 3, 4, 5],$$

because $n = 5$ and $S = 6$. (The latter is the number of opening square brackets.) When $S = 1$, that is, the stack is flat, then $\mathcal{C}_n^{\mathsf{pre}} = \mathcal{C}_n^{\mathsf{flat}_2}$, otherwise $\mathcal{C}_n^{\mathsf{pre}} < \mathcal{C}_n^{\mathsf{flat}_2}$.

Inorder   The *inorder* (or *symmetric*) traversal of a non-empty binary tree consists in having in a stack the nodes of the left subtree in inorder, followed by the root and then the nodes of the right subtree in inorder. For example, the nodes in inorder of the tree in FIGURE 7.3a on page 208 are $[3, 5, 1, 9, 8, 3, 2]$. Clearly, it is a depth-first traversal, like a preorder, because children are visited before siblings. According to our findings about pre/1 in FIGURE 7.10 on page 215, we understand that we should structure our program to follow the strategy depicted in FIGURE 7.9b on page 215, where the only difference with FIGURE 7.9a is the moment when

$$\mathsf{in}(t) \xrightarrow{\xi} \mathsf{in}(t, []).$$

$$\mathsf{in}(\mathsf{ext}(), s) \xrightarrow{\pi} s;$$
$$\mathsf{in}(\mathsf{int}(x, t_1, t_2), s) \xrightarrow{\rho} \mathsf{in}(t_1, [x \,|\, \mathsf{in}(t_2, s)]).$$

Figure 7.21: Inorder traversal

$$\frac{\mathsf{nin}(0, t) \twoheadrightarrow (i, t')}{\mathsf{nin}(t) \twoheadrightarrow t'} . \qquad \mathsf{nin}(i, \mathsf{ext}()) \to (i, \mathsf{ext}());$$

$$\frac{\mathsf{nin}(i, t_1) \twoheadrightarrow (j, t'_1) \qquad \mathsf{nin}(j + 1, t_2) \twoheadrightarrow (k, t'_2)}{\mathsf{nin}(i, \mathsf{int}(x, t_1, t_2)) \twoheadrightarrow (k, \mathsf{int}(j, t'_1, t'_2))} .$$

Figure 7.22: Inorder numbering

the root x is pushed on the accumulator: between the inorder traversals of the subtrees t_1 and t_2. The implicit rewrites in FIGURE 7.9b are

$$\mathsf{in}(t_2, s) \twoheadrightarrow s_1,$$
$$\mathsf{in}(t_1, [x \,|\, s_1]) \twoheadrightarrow s_2,$$
$$\mathsf{in}(t, s) \twoheadrightarrow s_2,$$

where $t = \mathsf{int}(x, t_1, t_2)$. Eliminating the intermediary variables s_1 and s_2 we obtain the equivalence

$$\mathsf{in}(t_1, [x \,|\, \mathsf{in}(t_2, s)]) \equiv \mathsf{in}(t, s).$$

The case of the external node is the same as for preorder. This reasoning yields the function defined in FIGURE 7.21, whose cost is the same as for preorder:

$$C_n^{\mathsf{in}} = C_n^{\mathsf{pre}} = 2n + 2.$$

FIGURE 7.11c on page 216 gives the example of a binary tree which is the result of an *inorder numbering*. The inorder traversal of that tree yields $[0, 1, 2, 3, 4, 5, 6]$. Inorder numberings have an interesting property: given any internal node, all the nodes in its left subtree have smaller numbers, and all nodes in its right subtree have greater numbers. Let $\mathsf{nin}/1$ be a function computing the inorder numbering of a given tree in FIGURE 7.22, where j, at the root, is the smallest number greater than any number in t_1.

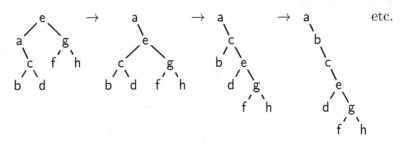

Figure 7.23: Composing right-rotations, top-down

$$\mathsf{in}_1(\mathsf{ext}()) \xrightarrow{\alpha} [\,];$$
$$\mathsf{in}_1(\mathsf{int}(y, \mathsf{int}(x, t_1, t_2), t_3)) \xrightarrow{\beta} \mathsf{in}_1(\mathsf{int}(x, t_1, \mathsf{int}(y, t_2, t_3)));$$
$$\mathsf{in}_1(\mathsf{int}(y, \mathsf{ext}(), t_3)) \xrightarrow{\gamma} [y \,|\, \mathsf{in}_1(t_3)].$$

Figure 7.24: Inorder traversal by right rotations

Flattening revisited   The design of flat/1 in FIGURE 2.12 on page 60 may suggest a new approach to inorder traversals. By composing right rotations as defined in FIGURES 2.11b to 2.11c on page 59 (the converse is, of course, a *left rotation*), the node to be visited first in inorder can be brought to be the root of a tree whose left subtree is empty. Recursively, the right subtree is then processed, in a top-down fashion. This algorithm is sound because *inorder traversals are invariant through rotations*, which is formally expressed as follows.

$\mathsf{Rot}(x, y, t_1, t_2, t_3)\colon \mathsf{in}(\mathsf{int}(y, \mathsf{int}(x, t_1, t_2), t_3)) \equiv \mathsf{in}(\mathsf{int}(x, t_1, \mathsf{int}(y, t_2, t_3))).$

In FIGURE 7.23, we show how a binary tree becomes a right-leaning, degenerate tree, isomorphic to a stack, by repeatedly applying right rotations, top-down. Dually, we could compose left rotations and obtain a left-leaning, degenerate tree, whose inorder traversal is also equal to the inorder traversal of the original tree. The function $\mathsf{in}_1/1$ based on right rotations is given in FIGURE 7.24. Note how, in rule γ, we push the root y in the result as soon as we can, which would not be possible had we used left rotations instead, and thus we do *not* build the whole rotated tree, as in FIGURE 7.23.

The cost $\mathcal{C}_n^{\mathsf{in}_1}$ depends on the topology of the tree at hand. Firstly, let us note that rule α is used only once, on the rightmost external node. Secondly, if the tree to be traversed is already a right-leaning degenerate tree, rule β is not used and rule γ is used n times. Clearly, this is the best case and

$$\mathcal{B}_n^{\mathsf{in}_1} = n + 1.$$

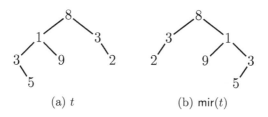

(a) t (b) mir(t)

Figure 7.25: Mirroring a binary tree

Thirdly, we should remark that a right rotation brings exactly one more node (named x in $\mathsf{Rot}(x, y, t_1, t_2, t_3)$) into the *rightmost branch*, that is, the series of nodes starting with the root and reached using repeatedly right edges (for instance, in the initial tree in FIGURE 7.23 on the preceding page, the rightmost branch is $[\mathsf{e}, \mathsf{g}, \mathsf{h}]$). Therefore, if we want to maximise the use of rule β, we must have an initial tree whose right subtree is empty, so the left subtree contains $n - 1$ nodes (the root belongs, by definition, to the rightmost branch): this yields that

$$\mathcal{W}_n^{\mathsf{in}_1} = (n - 1) + (n + 1) = 2n.$$

Exercise   Prove $\forall x, y, t_1, t_2, t_3.\mathsf{Rot}(x, y, t_1, t_2, t_3)$.

Mirroring   Let us define a function $\mathsf{mir}/1$ (*mirror*) such that $\mathsf{mir}(t)$ is the symmetric of the binary tree t with respect to an exterior vertical line. An example is given in FIGURE 7.25. It is easy to define this function:

$$\mathsf{mir}(\mathsf{ext}()) \overset{\sigma}{\rightarrow} \mathsf{ext}(); \quad \mathsf{mir}(\mathsf{int}(x, t_1, t_2)) \overset{\tau}{\rightarrow} \mathsf{int}(x, \mathsf{mir}(t_2), \mathsf{mir}(t_1)).$$

From the previous example, it is quite simple to postulate the property

$$\mathsf{InMir}(t): \mathsf{in}(\mathsf{mir}(t)) \equiv \mathsf{rev}(\mathsf{in}(t)),$$

where $\mathsf{rev}/1$ reverses its stack argument (see definition (2.2) on page 40). This property is useful because the left-hand side of the equivalence is more costly than the right-hand side:

$$\mathcal{C}[\![\mathsf{in}(\mathsf{mir}(t))]\!] = \mathcal{C}_n^{\mathsf{mir}} + \mathcal{C}_n^{\mathsf{in}} = (2n + 1) + (2n + 2) = 4n + 3,$$

to be compared with $\mathcal{C}[\![\mathsf{rev}(\mathsf{in}(t))]\!] = \mathcal{C}_n^{\mathsf{in}} + \mathcal{C}_n^{\mathsf{rev}} = (2n+2)+(n+2) = 3n+4$.

Structural induction on the immediate subtrees requires that we establish

- the basis $\mathsf{InMir}(\mathsf{ext}())$;

- the step $\forall t_1.\mathsf{InMir}(t_1) \Rightarrow \forall t_2.\mathsf{InMir}(t_2) \Rightarrow \forall x.\mathsf{InMir}(\mathsf{int}(x, t_1, t_2))$.

The former results from

$$\text{in}(\underline{\text{mir}}(\text{ext}())) \xrightarrow{\sigma} \text{in}(\text{ext}())$$
$$\xrightarrow{\xi} \text{in}(\text{ext}(), [])$$
$$\xrightarrow{\pi} []$$
$$\xleftarrow{\varsigma} \text{rcat}([], [])$$
$$\xleftarrow{\epsilon} \text{rev}([])$$
$$\xleftarrow{\pi} \text{rev}(\underline{\text{in}}(\text{ext}(), []))$$
$$\xleftarrow{\xi} \text{rev}(\underline{\text{in}}(\text{ext}())).$$

Let us assume $\textsf{InMir}(t_1)$ and $\textsf{InMir}(t_2)$ and let $t := \text{int}(x, t_1, t_2)$, for any x. We rewrite the left-hand side of the equivalence to be proved until we reach the right-hand side or we get stuck:

$$\begin{aligned}
\text{in}(\text{mir}(t)) =\ & \text{in}(\underline{\text{mir}}(\text{int}(x, t_1, t_2))) \\
\xrightarrow{\tau}\ & \underline{\text{in}}(\text{int}(x, \text{mir}(t_2), \text{mir}(t_1))) \\
\xrightarrow{\xi}\ & \underline{\text{in}}(\text{int}(x, \text{mir}(t_2), \text{mir}(t_1)), []) \\
\xrightarrow{\rho}\ & \text{in}(\text{mir}(t_2), [x \mid \text{in}(\text{mir}(t_1), [])]) \\
\xleftarrow{\varsigma}\ & \text{in}(\text{mir}(t_2), [x \mid \underline{\text{in}}(\text{mir}(t_1))]) \\
\equiv\ & \text{in}(\text{mir}(t_2), [x \mid \text{rev}(\underline{\text{in}}(t_1))]) \qquad\qquad \textsf{InMir}(t_1) \\
\xrightarrow{\xi}\ & \text{in}(\text{mir}(t_2), [x \mid \underline{\text{rev}}(\text{in}(t_1, []))]) \\
\xrightarrow{\epsilon}\ & \text{in}(\text{mir}(t_2), [x \mid \text{rcat}(\text{in}(t_1, []), [])]).
\end{aligned}$$

We cannot use the induction hypothesis $\textsf{InMir}(t_2)$ to get rid of $\text{mir}(t_2)$. Close examination of the terms suggests to *weaken* the property and overload $\textsf{InMir}$ with a new definition:

$$\textsf{InMir}(t, s): \text{in}(\text{mir}(t), s) \equiv \text{rcat}(\text{in}(t, []), s).$$

We have $\textsf{InMir}(t, []) \Leftrightarrow \textsf{InMir}(t)$. Now, we rewrite as follows:

$$\begin{aligned}
\text{in}(\text{mir}(t), s) =\ & \text{in}(\underline{\text{mir}}(\text{int}(x, t_1, t_2)), s) \\
\xrightarrow{\tau}\ & \underline{\text{in}}(\text{int}(x, \text{mir}(t_2), \text{mir}(t_1)), s) \\
\xrightarrow{\rho}\ & \text{in}(\text{mir}(t_2), [x \mid \text{in}(\text{mir}(t_1), s)]) \\
\equiv\ & \text{in}(\text{mir}(t_2), [x \mid \text{rcat}(\text{in}(t_1, []), s)]) \qquad \textsf{InMir}(t_1, s) \\
\equiv_0\ & \text{rcat}(\text{in}(t_2, []), [x \mid \text{rcat}(\text{in}(t_1, []), s)]) \\
\xleftarrow{\eta}\ & \underline{\text{rcat}}([x \mid \text{in}(t_2, [])], \text{rcat}(\text{in}(t_1, []), s)),
\end{aligned}$$

where $(\equiv_0)$ is $\textsf{InMir}(t_2, [x \mid \text{rcat}(\text{in}(t_1, []), s)])$. The right-hand side now:

$$\text{rcat}(\text{in}(t, []), s) = \text{rcat}(\underline{\text{in}}(\text{int}(x, t_1, t_2), []), s) \xrightarrow{\rho} \text{rcat}(\text{in}(t_1, [x \mid \text{in}(t_2, [])]), s).$$

The two stuck expressions share the subterm $[x \mid \text{in}(t_2, [])]$. The main difference is that the former expression contains two calls to $\text{rcat}/2$, instead of one in the latter. Can we find a way to have only one call in the former too? We need to find an expression equivalent to $\mathsf{rcat}(s, \mathsf{rcat}(t, u))$, whose shape is $\mathsf{rcat}(v, w)$, where v and w contain no call to $\mathsf{rcat}/2$. Some examples quickly suggest

$$\mathsf{Rcat}(s, t, u): \mathsf{rcat}(s, \mathsf{rcat}(t, u)) \equiv \mathsf{rcat}(\mathsf{cat}(t, s), u).$$

We actually do not need induction if we recall what we already proved:

- $\mathsf{CatRev}(s, t): \mathsf{cat}(\mathsf{rev}_0(t), \mathsf{rev}_0(s)) \equiv \mathsf{rev}_0(\mathsf{cat}(s, t))$;
- $\mathsf{EqRev}(s): \mathsf{rev}_0(s) \equiv \mathsf{rev}(s)$;
- $\mathsf{CatAssoc}(s, t, u): \mathsf{cat}(s, \mathsf{cat}(t, u)) \equiv \mathsf{cat}(\mathsf{cat}(s, t), u)$;
- $\mathsf{RevCat}(s, t): \mathsf{rcat}(s, t) \equiv \mathsf{cat}(\mathsf{rev}(s), t)$.

Then, we have the equivalences

$$
\begin{aligned}
\mathsf{rcat}(s, \mathsf{rcat}(t, u)) &\equiv \mathsf{rcat}(s, \mathsf{cat}(\mathsf{rev}(t), u)) && \mathsf{RevCat}(t, u) \\
&\equiv \mathsf{rcat}(s, \mathsf{cat}(\mathsf{rev}_0(t), u)) && \mathsf{EqRev}(t) \\
&\equiv \mathsf{cat}(\mathsf{rev}(s), \mathsf{cat}(\mathsf{rev}_0(t), u)) && \mathsf{RevCat}(s, \mathsf{cat}(\mathsf{rev}_0(t), u)) \\
&\equiv \mathsf{cat}(\mathsf{rev}_0(s), \mathsf{cat}(\mathsf{rev}_0(t), u)) && \mathsf{EqRev}(s) \\
&\equiv \mathsf{cat}(\mathsf{cat}(\mathsf{rev}_0(s), \mathsf{rev}_0(t)), u) && \mathsf{CatAssoc}(\mathsf{rev}(s), \mathsf{rev}(t), u) \\
&\equiv \mathsf{cat}(\mathsf{rev}_0(\mathsf{cat}(t, s)), u) && \mathsf{CatRev}(s, t) \\
&\equiv \mathsf{cat}(\mathsf{rev}(\mathsf{cat}(t, s)), u) && \mathsf{EqRev}(\mathsf{cat}(t, s)) \\
&\equiv \mathsf{rcat}(\mathsf{cat}(t, s), u) && \mathsf{RevCat}(\mathsf{cat}(t, s), u)
\end{aligned}
$$

Let us resume rewriting the first stuck expression:

$$
\begin{aligned}
\mathsf{in}(\mathsf{mir}(t), s) &\equiv_0 \mathsf{rcat}([x \,|\, \mathsf{in}(t_2, [\,])], \mathsf{rcat}(\mathsf{in}(t_1, [\,]), s)) \\
&\equiv_1 \mathsf{rcat}(\mathsf{cat}(\mathsf{in}(t_1, [\,]), [x \,|\, \mathsf{in}(t_2, [\,])]), s),
\end{aligned}
$$

where $(\equiv_0)$ is a short-hand for the previous derivation and $(\equiv_1)$ is the instance $\mathsf{Rcat}([x \,|\, \mathsf{in}(t_2, [\,])], \mathsf{in}(t_1, [\,]), s)$. Another comparison of the stuck expressions reveals that we need to prove $\mathsf{cat}(\mathsf{in}(t, [\,]), s) \equiv \mathsf{in}(t, s)$. This equivalence is likely to be true, as it is similar to $\mathsf{CatPre}(t, s)$. Assuming this lemma, we conclude the proof. $\qquad\square$

Exercises

1. Prove the missing lemma $\mathsf{CatIn}(t, s): \mathsf{cat}(\mathsf{in}(t, [\,]), s) \equiv \mathsf{in}(t, s)$.

2. Define a function which builds a binary tree from its preorder and inorder traversals, assuming that its internal nodes are all distinct. Make sure its cost is linear in the number of internal nodes. Compare your solution with that of Mu and Bird (2003).

$$\mathsf{post}(t) \overset{\lambda}{\twoheadrightarrow} \mathsf{post}(t, []).$$

$$\mathsf{post}(\mathsf{ext}(), s) \overset{\mu}{\twoheadrightarrow} s;$$
$$\mathsf{post}(\mathsf{int}(x, t_1, t_2), s) \overset{\nu}{\twoheadrightarrow} \mathsf{post}(t_1, \mathsf{post}(t_2, [x \,|\, s])).$$

Figure 7.26: Postorder traversal

$$\frac{\mathsf{npost}(0, t) \twoheadrightarrow (i, t')}{\mathsf{npost}(t) \twoheadrightarrow t'} \,. \qquad \mathsf{npost}(i, \mathsf{ext}()) \to (i, \mathsf{ext}());$$

$$\frac{\mathsf{npost}(i, t_1) \twoheadrightarrow (j, t'_1) \qquad \mathsf{npost}(j, t_2) \twoheadrightarrow (k, t'_2)}{\mathsf{npost}(i, \mathsf{int}(x, t_1, t_2)) \to (k+1, \mathsf{int}(k, t'_1, t'_2))} \,.$$

Figure 7.27: Postorder numbering

Postorder   A *postorder* traversal of a non-empty binary tree consists in storing in a stack the nodes of the right subtree in postorder, followed by the nodes of the left subtree in postorder, and, in turn, by the root. For example, the nodes in postorder of the tree in FIGURE 7.3a on page 208 are $[5, 3, 9, 1, 2, 3, 8]$. Clearly, it is a depth-first traversal, like a preorder, but, unlike a preorder, it saves the root last in the resulting stack. This approach is summarised for internal nodes in FIGURE 7.9c on page 215. The difference with pre/1 and in/1 lies in the moment when the root is pushed in the accumulator. The function definition is given in FIGURE 7.26. The meaning of the stack s in the call $\mathsf{post}(t, s)$ is the same as in $\mathsf{pre}(t, s)$, modulo ordering: s is made of the contents, in postorder, of the nodes that follow, in postorder, the nodes of the subtree t. The cost is familiar as well:

$$C_n^{\mathsf{post}} = C_n^{\mathsf{in}} = C_n^{\mathsf{pre}} = 2n + 2.$$

An example of *postorder numbering* is shown in FIGURE 7.11b on page 216, so the postorder traversal of that tree yields $[0, 1, 2, 3, 4, 5, 6]$. Notice how the numbers increase along upwards paths. FIGURE 7.27 shows the program to number a binary tree in postorder. The root is numbered with the number coming up from the right subtree, following the pattern of a postorder traversal.

A proof   Let $\mathsf{PreMir}(t) \colon \mathsf{pre}(\mathsf{mir}(t)) \equiv \mathsf{rev}(\mathsf{post}(t))$. Previous experience with proving $\mathsf{InMir}(t)$ leads us to weaken (generalise) the property in order to facilitate the proof: Let

$$\mathsf{PreMir}(t, s)\colon \mathsf{pre}(\mathsf{mir}(t), s) \equiv \mathsf{rcat}(\mathsf{post}(t, [\,]), s).$$

Clearly, $\mathsf{PreMir}(t, [\,]) \Leftrightarrow \mathsf{PreMir}(t)$. Let us then define

$$(t, s) \succ_{B \times S} (t', s') :\Leftrightarrow t \succ_B t' \text{ or } (t = t' \text{ and } s \succ_S s').$$

This is conceptually the same order as the one on the calls to $\mathsf{pre}/1$, in definition (7.7) on page 218. The minimum element for this lexicographic order is $(\mathsf{ext}(), [\,])$. Well-founded induction then requires that we prove

- the basis $\mathsf{PreMir}(\mathsf{ext}(), [\,])$;
- $\forall t, s.(\forall t', s'.(t, s) \succ_{B \times S} (t', s') \Rightarrow \mathsf{PreMir}(t', s')) \Rightarrow \mathsf{PreMir}(t, s)$.

The basis is proved as follows:

$$\mathsf{pre}(\underline{\mathsf{mir}(\mathsf{ext}())}, [\,]) \xrightarrow{\sigma} \mathsf{pre}(\mathsf{ext}(), [\,])$$
$$\xrightarrow{\iota} [\,]$$
$$\xleftarrow{\varsigma} \mathsf{rcat}([\,], [\,])$$
$$\xleftarrow{\mu} \mathsf{rcat}(\underline{\mathsf{post}}(\mathsf{ext}(), [\,]), [\,]).$$

Let $t := \mathsf{int}(x, t_1, t_2)$. In FIGURE 7.28 on the following page, we have the rewrites of the left-hand side, where

- ($\equiv_0$) is $\mathsf{PreMir}(t_1, s)$, an instance of the induction hypothesis;
- ($\equiv_1$) is $\mathsf{PreMir}(t_2, \mathsf{rcat}(\mathsf{post}(t_1, [\,]), s))$, as inductive hypothesis;
- ($\equiv_2$) is $\mathsf{Rcat}(\mathsf{post}(t_2, [\,]), \mathsf{post}(t_1, [\,]), s)$;
- ($\equiv_3$) is $\mathsf{Rcat}([x], \mathsf{cat}(\mathsf{post}(t_1, [\,]), \mathsf{post}(t_2, [\,])), s)$;
- ($\equiv_4$) is $\mathsf{CatAssoc}(\mathsf{post}(t_1, [\,]), \mathsf{post}(t_2, [\,]), [x])$;
- ($\equiv_5$) is $\mathsf{CatPost}(t_2, [x])$ if $\mathsf{CatPost}(t, s)\colon \mathsf{cat}(\mathsf{post}(t), s) \equiv \mathsf{post}(t, s)$;
- ($\equiv_6$) is $\mathsf{CatPost}(t_1, \mathsf{post}(t_2, [x]))$.

Then $\mathsf{CatPost}(t, s) \Rightarrow \mathsf{PreMir}(t, s) \Rightarrow \mathsf{pre}(\mathsf{mir}(t)) \equiv \mathsf{rev}(\mathsf{post}(t))$. □

Duality   The dual theorem $\mathsf{PostMir}(t)\colon \mathsf{post}(\mathsf{mir}(t)) \equiv \mathsf{rev}(\mathsf{pre}(t))$ can be proved in at least two ways: either we design a new proof in the spirit of the proof of $\mathsf{PreMir}(t)$, or we take advantage of the fact that the theorem is an equivalence and we produce equivalent but simpler theorems. Let us do the latter and start by considering $\mathsf{PreMir}(\mathsf{mir}(t))$ and proceed by finding equivalent expressions on both sides of the equivalence, until we reach $\mathsf{PostMir}(t)$:

$$\mathsf{pre}(\mathsf{mir}(\mathsf{mir}(t))) \equiv \mathsf{rev}(\mathsf{post}(\mathsf{mir}(t))) \qquad\qquad \mathsf{PreMir}(\mathsf{mir}(t))$$
$$\mathsf{pre}(t) \equiv \mathsf{rev}(\mathsf{post}(\mathsf{mir}(t))) \qquad\qquad \mathsf{InvMir}(t)$$
$$\mathsf{rev}(\mathsf{pre}(t)) \equiv \mathsf{rev}(\mathsf{rev}(\mathsf{post}(\mathsf{mir}(t))))$$
$$\mathsf{rev}(\mathsf{pre}(t)) \equiv \mathsf{post}(\mathsf{mir}(t)) \qquad\qquad \mathsf{InvRev}(\mathsf{post}(\mathsf{mir}(t)))$$

where $\mathsf{InvMir}(t)\colon \mathsf{mir}(\mathsf{mir}(t)) \equiv t$ and $\mathsf{InvRev}(s) :\Leftrightarrow \mathsf{Inv}(s) \wedge \mathsf{EqRev}(s)$. □

$$\begin{aligned}
\mathsf{pre}(\mathsf{mir}(t), s) &= \mathsf{pre}(\underline{\mathsf{mir}(\mathsf{int}(x, t_1, t_2))}, s) \\
&\overset{\tau}{\to} \mathsf{pre}(\mathsf{int}(x, \mathsf{mir}(t_2), \mathsf{mir}(t_1)), s) \\
&\overset{\kappa}{\to} \overline{[x \,|\, \mathsf{pre}(\mathsf{mir}(t_2), \mathsf{pre}(\mathsf{mir}(t_1), s))]} \\
&\equiv_0 [x \,|\, \mathsf{pre}(\mathsf{mir}(t_2), \mathsf{rcat}(\mathsf{post}(t_1, [\,]), s))] \\
&\equiv_1 [x \,|\, \mathsf{rcat}(\mathsf{post}(t_2, [\,]), \mathsf{rcat}(\mathsf{post}(t_1, [\,]), s))] \\
&\equiv_2 [x \,|\, \mathsf{rcat}(\mathsf{cat}(\mathsf{post}(t_1, [\,]), \mathsf{post}(t_2, [\,])), s)] \\
&\overset{\varsigma}{\leftarrow} \mathsf{rcat}([\,], [x \,|\, \mathsf{rcat}(\mathsf{cat}(\mathsf{post}(t_1, [\,]), \mathsf{post}(t_2, [\,])), s)]) \\
&\overset{\eta}{\leftarrow} \mathsf{rcat}([x], \mathsf{rcat}(\mathsf{cat}(\mathsf{post}(t_1, [\,]), \mathsf{post}(t_2, [\,])), s)) \\
&\equiv_3 \mathsf{rcat}(\mathsf{cat}(\mathsf{cat}(\mathsf{post}(t_1, [\,]), \mathsf{post}(t_2, [\,])), [x]), s) \\
&\equiv_4 \mathsf{rcat}(\mathsf{cat}(\mathsf{post}(t_1, [\,]), \mathsf{cat}(\mathsf{post}(t_2, [\,]), [x])), s) \\
&\equiv_5 \mathsf{rcat}(\mathsf{cat}(\mathsf{post}(t_1, [\,]), \mathsf{post}(t_2, [x])), s) \\
&\equiv_6 \mathsf{rcat}(\mathsf{post}(t_1, \mathsf{post}(t_2, [x])), s) \\
&\overset{\nu}{\leftarrow} \mathsf{rcat}(\mathsf{post}(\mathsf{int}(x, t_1, t_2), [\,]), s) \\
&= \mathsf{rcat}(\mathsf{post}(t, [\,]), s). \qquad\qquad \square
\end{aligned}$$

Figure 7.28: Proof of $\mathsf{pre}(\mathsf{mir}(t), s) \equiv \mathsf{rcat}(\mathsf{post}(t, [\,]), s)$

Exercises

1. Prove the lemma $\mathsf{CatPost}(t, s)$: $\mathsf{cat}(\mathsf{post}(t, [\,]), s) \equiv \mathsf{post}(t, s)$.

2. Use $\mathsf{rev}_0/1$ instead of $\mathsf{rev}/1$ in $\mathsf{InMir}(t)$ and $\mathsf{PreMir}(t)$. Are the proofs easier?

3. Prove the missing lemma $\mathsf{InvMir}(t)$: $\mathsf{mir}(\mathsf{mir}(t)) \equiv t$.

4. Can you build a binary tree from its postorder and inorder traversals, assuming that its internal nodes are all distinct?

Level order   The *level l* in a tree is a stack of nodes in preorder whose internal path lengths are l. In particular, the root is the only node at level 0. In the tree of FIGURE 7.3a on page 208, $[3, 9, 2]$ is level 2. To understand the preorder condition, we need to consider the preorder numbering of the tree, shown in FIGURE 7.12 on page 216 with preorder numbers as left exponents to the contents. This way, there is no more ambiguity when referring to nodes. For instance, $[3, 9, 2]$ was in fact ambiguous because there are two nodes whose associated data is 3. We meant that $[^2 3, {}^4 9, {}^6 2]$ is the level 2 because these nodes all have internal path lengths 2 *and* have increasing preorders $(2, 4, 6)$.

$$\mathsf{bf_0}(t) \to \mathsf{bf_1}([t]). \quad \mathsf{bf_1}([\,]) \to [\,]; \qquad \frac{\mathsf{def}(f) \twoheadrightarrow (r, f')}{\mathsf{bf_1}(f) \twoheadrightarrow \mathsf{cat}(r, \mathsf{bf_1}(f'))}.$$

Figure 7.29: Level order $\mathsf{bf_0}/1$

A *level-order* traversal consists in making a stack with the nodes of all the levels by increasing path lengths. For instance, the level order of the tree in FIGURE 7.3a on page 208 is $[8, 1, 3, 3, 9, 2, 5]$. Because this method visits the sibling of a node before its children, it is said *breadth-first*.

In FIGURE 7.11d on page 216 is shown the *level-order numbering* of the tree in FIGURE 7.12 on page 216, more often called *breadth numbering*. (Mind the common misspellings 'bread numbering' and 'breath numbering'.) Notice how the numbers increase along downwards path between nodes, as in a preorder numbering.

We may now realise that the notion of level in a tree is not straightforward. The reason is simple: the nodes in a level are not siblings, except in level 1, so, in general, we cannot expect to build a level of a tree $\mathsf{int}(x, t_1, t_2)$ by means of levels in t_1 and t_2 alone, that is, with a big-step design. As a consequence, a small-step approach is called for, standing in contrast, for example, with $\mathsf{size}/1$ in (7.1) on page 209.

Let $\mathsf{bf_0}/1$ (*breadth-first*) be the function such that $\mathsf{bf_0}(t)$ is the stack of nodes of t in level order. It is partially defined in FIGURE 7.29. If we imagine that we cut off the root of a binary tree, we obtain the immediate subtrees. If, in turn, we cut down these trees, we obtain more subtrees. This suggests that we should better work on general forests instead of trees, one or two at a time.

The cutting function is $\mathsf{def}/1$ (*deforest*), defined in FIGURE 7.30, such that $\mathsf{def}(f)$, where f represents a forest, evaluates in a pair (r, f'), where r are the roots in preorder of the trees in f, and f' is the immediate subforest of f. (Beware, the word deforestation is used by scholars of functional languages with a different meaning, but it will do for us, as we already encountered a function $\mathsf{cut}/2$.) Note how, in FIGURE 7.30, the inference rule augments the partial level r with the root x, and

$$\mathsf{def}([\,]) \to ([\,], [\,]); \quad \mathsf{def}([\mathsf{ext}() \,|\, f]) \to \mathsf{def}(f);$$
$$\frac{\mathsf{def}(f) \twoheadrightarrow (r, f')}{\mathsf{def}([\mathsf{int}(x, t_1, t_2) \,|\, f]) \twoheadrightarrow ([x \,|\, r], [t_1, t_2 \,|\, f'])}.$$

Figure 7.30: Deforestation

how t_2 is pushed before t_1 onto the rest of the immediate forest of f, to be processed later by $\mathsf{bf}_0/1$. Instead of building the stack of levels $[[8], [1, 3], [3, 9, 2], [5]]$, we actually flatten step by step simply by calling $\mathsf{cat}/2$ in rule μ. If we really want the levels, we would write $[r \mid \mathsf{bf}_1(f')]$ instead of $\mathsf{cat}(r, \mathsf{bf}_1(f'))$, which, by the way, reduces the cost.

The underlying concept here is that of the *traversal of a forest*. Except in inorder, all the traversals we have discussed naturally carry over to binary forests: the preorder traversal of a forest consists in the preorder traversal of the first tree in the forest, followed by the preorder traversal of the rest of the forest. Same logic for postorder and level order. This uniformity stems from the fact that all these traversals are performed rightwards, to wit, a left child is visited just before its sibling. The notion of height of a tree also extends naturally to a forest: the height of a forest is the maximum height of each individual tree. The reason why this is simple is because height is a purely vertical view of a tree, thus independent of the siblings' order.

To assess now the cost $C_{n,h}^{\mathsf{bf}_0}$ of the call $\mathsf{bf}_0(t)$, where n is the size of the binary tree t and h is its height, it is convenient to work with *extended levels*. An extended level is a level where external nodes are included (they are not implicitly numbered in preorder because external nodes are indistinguishable). For example, the extended level 2 of the tree in FIGURE 7.12 on page 216 is $[^2 3, {}^4 9, \square, {}^6 2]$. If it is needed to draw a contrast with the other kind of level, we may call the latter *pruned levels*, which is consistent with our terminology in FIGURE 7.3 on page 208. Note that there is always one more extended level than pruned levels, made entirely of external nodes. (We avoided writing that these are the highest nodes, as the trouble with the term 'height' is that it really makes sense if the trees are laid out with the root at the bottom of the page. That is perhaps why some authors prefer the less confusing concept of *depth*, in use in graph theory. For a survey of the different manners of drawing trees, see Knuth (1997) in its section 2.3.) In other words, $l_h = 0$, where l_i is the number of internal nodes on the extended level i.

- Rule ι is used once;
- rule κ is used once;
- rules λ and μ are used once for each extended level of the original tree; these amount to $2(h + 1)$ calls;
- the cost of $\mathsf{cat}(r, \mathsf{loc}_1(f'))$ is the length of the level r, plus one, thus the cumulative cost of concatenation is $\sum_{i=0}^{h} C_{l_i}^{\mathsf{cat}} = n + h + 1$;
- rule ϵ is used once per extended level, that is, $h + 1$ times;
- rule ζ is used once per external node, that is, $n + 1$ times;
- rules η and θ are used once per internal node, that is, $2n$ times.

Gathering these enumerations, we find that

$$C_{n,h}^{\text{bfo}} = 4n + 4h + 7.$$

By definition, the minimum cost is $\mathcal{B}_n^{\text{bfo}} = \min_h C_{n,h}^{\text{bfo}}$. The height is minimum when the binary tree is *perfect*, that is, when all levels are full (see FIGURE 2.43 on page 91). In this case, $l_i = 2^i$, for $0 \leqslant i \leqslant h-1$, and, by extension, there are 2^h external nodes. Theorem 5 on page 208 yields the equation $n+1 = 2^h$, so $h = \lg(n+1)$, and $\mathcal{B}_n^{\text{bfo}} = 4n + 4\lg(n+1) + 7 \sim 4n$.

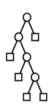

The maximum cost is obtained by maximising the height, while keeping the size constant. This happens for degenerate trees, as the ones shown in FIGURE 7.4 on page 211 and FIGURE 7.31. Here, $h = n$ and the cost is $\mathcal{W}_n^{\text{bfo}} = 8n + 7 \sim 8n$.

Figure 7.31: Zigzag

By contrast, we found programs that perform preorder, postorder and inorder traversals in $2n+2$ function calls. It is possible to reduce the cost by using a different design, based on pre$_3$/1 in FIGURE 7.6 on page 213. The difference is that, instead of using a stack to store subtrees to be traversed later, we use a queue, a linear data structure introduced in section 2.5. Consider in FIGURE 7.32 the algorithm at work on the same example found in FIGURE 7.7 on page 213. Keep in mind that trees are dequeued on the right side of the forest and enqueued on the left. (Some authors prefer the other way.) The root of the next tree to be dequeued is circled.

In order to compare with pre$_4$/1 in FIGURE 7.6 on page 213, we write $x \prec q$ instead of enq(x, q), and $q \succ x$ instead of (q, x). The empty queue is noted $\ominus$. More importantly, we will allow these expressions in the patterns of bf$_2$/1, which performs a level-order traversal in FIGURE 7.33. The difference in data structure (accumulator) has already been mentioned:

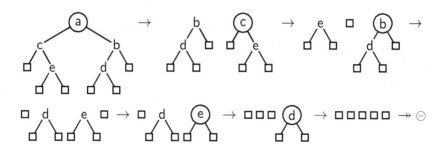

Figure 7.32: A level-order traversal with a queue

$$\mathsf{bf}_1(t) \to \mathsf{bf}_2(t \prec \ominus).$$

$$\mathsf{bf}_2(\ominus) \to [\,];$$
$$\mathsf{bf}_2(q \succ \mathsf{ext}()) \to \mathsf{bf}_2(q);$$
$$\mathsf{bf}_2(q \succ \mathsf{int}(x, t_1, t_2)) \to [x \,|\, \mathsf{bf}_2(t_2 \prec t_1 \prec q)].$$

Figure 7.33: Abstract level-order traversal with a queue

$$\mathsf{bf}_3(t) \to \mathsf{bf}_4(\mathsf{enq}(t, \mathsf{q}([\,], [\,]))). \qquad \mathsf{bf}_4(\mathsf{q}([\,], [\,])) \to [\,];$$

$$\frac{\mathsf{deq}(q) \twoheadrightarrow (q', \mathsf{ext}())}{\mathsf{bf}_4(q) \twoheadrightarrow \mathsf{bf}_4(q')} ; \qquad \frac{\mathsf{deq}(q) \twoheadrightarrow (q', \mathsf{int}(x, t_1, t_2))}{\mathsf{bf}_4(q) \twoheadrightarrow [x \,|\, \mathsf{bf}_4(\mathsf{enq}(t_2, \mathsf{enq}(t_1, q')))]} .$$

Figure 7.34: Refinement of FIGURE 7.33

$\mathsf{pre}_4/1$ uses a stack and $\mathsf{bf}_2/1$ a queue, but, as far as algorithms are concerned, they differ only in the relative order in which t_1 and t_2 are added to the accumulator.

In section 2.5, we saw how to implement a queue with two stacks as $\mathsf{q}(r, f)$: the rear stack r, where items are pushed (logically enqueued), and the front stack f, from whence items are popped (logically dequeued). Also, we defined enqueueing by $\mathsf{enq}/2$ in (2.10), on page 64, and dequeueing with $\mathsf{deq}/1$ in (2.11). This allows us to refine the definition of $\mathsf{bf}_2/1$ into $\mathsf{bf}_3/1$ in FIGURE 7.34.

We can specialise the program further, so we save some memory by not using the constructor $\mathsf{q}/2$ and remembering that its first argument is the rear and the second is the front. Moreover, instead of calling $\mathsf{deq}/1$ and $\mathsf{enq}/2$, we can expand their definitions and merge them with the definition at hand. The result is shown in FIGURE 7.35 on the next page. Recall that $\mathsf{rcat}/2$ (*reverse and concatenate*) is defined in equation (2.2) on page 40. Note that $\mathsf{bf}_4(\mathsf{enq}(t, \mathsf{q}([\,], [\,])))$ has been optimised in $\mathsf{bf}([\,], [t])$ in order to save a stack reversal. The definition of $\mathsf{bf}/1$ can be considered the most *concrete* of the refinements, the more *abstract* program being the original definition of $\mathsf{bf}_1/1$. The former is shorter than $\mathsf{bf}_0/1$, but the real gain is the cost. Let n be the size of the binary tree at hand and h its height. Rules are applied as follows:

- rule ν is used once;
- rule ξ is used once;

$$\mathsf{bf}(t) \xrightarrow{\nu} \mathsf{bf}([\,], [t]).$$

$$\mathsf{bf}([\,], [\,]) \xrightarrow{\xi} [\,];$$
$$\mathsf{bf}([t\,|\,r], [\,]) \xrightarrow{\pi} \mathsf{bf}([\,], \mathsf{rcat}(r, [t]));$$
$$\mathsf{bf}(r, [\mathsf{ext}()\,|\,f]) \xrightarrow{\rho} \mathsf{bf}(r, f);$$
$$\mathsf{bf}(r, [\mathsf{int}(x, t_1, t_2)\,|\,f]) \xrightarrow{\sigma} [x\,|\,\mathsf{bf}([t_2, t_1\,|\,r], f)].$$

Figure 7.35: Refinement of FIGURE 7.34 on the preceding page

- rule π is used once per level, except the first one (the root), hence, in total h times;
- all levels but the first (the root) are reversed by **rev/1**, accounting $\sum_{i=1}^{h} C_{e_i}^{\mathsf{rev}} = \sum_{i=1}^{h}(e_i+2) = (n-1)+(n+1)+2h = 2n+2h$, where e_i is the number of nodes on the extended level i;
- rule ρ is used once per external node, that is, $n+1$;
- rule σ is used once per internal node, so n times.

Gathering all these enumerations yields the formula

$$C_{n,h}^{\mathsf{bf}} = 4n + 3h + 3.$$

As with **bf$_0$/1**, the minimum cost happens here when $h = \lg(n+1)$, so

$$\mathcal{B}_n^{\mathsf{bf}} = 4n + 3\lg(n+1) + 3 \sim 4n.$$

The maximum cost occurs when $h = n$, so

$$\mathcal{W}_n^{\mathsf{bf}} = 7n + 3 \sim 7n.$$

We can now compare **bf$_0$/1** and **bf/1**: $C_{n,h}^{\mathsf{bf}} < C_{n,h}^{\mathsf{bf}_0}$ and the difference in cost is most observable in their worst cases, which are both degenerate trees. Therefore **bf/1** is preferable in any case.

Termination With the aim to prove the termination of **bf/2**, we re-use the lexicographic order on pairs of stacks, based on the immediate substack order $(\succ_S)$ that proved the termination of **mrg/2** on page 127:

$$(s, t) \succ_{S^2} (s', t') :\Leftrightarrow s \succ_S s' \text{ or } (s = s' \text{ and } t \succ_S t').$$

Unfortunately, $(\succ_{S^2})$ fails to monotonically order (with respect to the rewrite relation) the left-hand side and right-hand side of rule σ, because of $(r, [\mathsf{int}(x, t_1, t_2)\,|\,f]) \not\succ_{S^2} ([t_2, t_1\,|\,r], f)$. Another approach consists in defining a well-founded order on the number of nodes in a pair of forests:

$$(r, f) \succ_{S^2} (r', f') :\Leftrightarrow \dim(r) + \dim(f) > \dim(r') + \dim(f'),$$

with

$$\mathsf{dim}([]) \to []; \qquad \mathsf{dim}([t\,|\,f]) \to \mathsf{size}(t) + \mathsf{dim}(f).$$

where $\mathsf{size}/1$ is defined in (7.1) on page 209. This is a kind of polynomial measure on dependency pairs, as exemplified with $\mathsf{flat}/1$ on page 61. Here, $\mathcal{M}[\![\mathsf{bf}(s,t)]\!] := \mathsf{dim}(s) + \mathsf{dim}(t)$. Unfortunately, this order monotonically fails on rule π, because $(r, []) \not\succ_{S^2} ([], \mathsf{rev}(r))$.

The conundrum can be lifted if we visualise the complete set of traces of $\mathsf{bf}/2$ in a compact manner. If we assume that $\mathsf{rev}/1$ is a constructor, the right-hand sides either contain no call or exactly one recursive call. The traces of calls to such definitions are nicely represented as finite automata. An example of a deterministic finite automaton (DFA) was given in FIGURE 5.14 on page 190. Here, a transition is a rewrite rule and a state corresponds to an abstraction of the input. In the case of $\mathsf{bf}/2$, the input is a pair of stacks. Let us decide for the moment that we will only take into account whether a stack is empty or not, yielding four states. Let '$|$' denote an arbitrary non-empty stack. Examining the definitions of $\mathsf{bf}/1$ and $\mathsf{bf}/2$ in FIGURE 7.35 on the previous page, we see that

- rule ξ applies to the state $([], [])$ only;
- rule π applies to the state $(|, [])$, and leads to a state $([], |)$;
- rule ρ applies to the states $([], |)$ and $(|, |)$, and leads to any state;
- rule σ applies to the states $([], |)$ and $(|, |)$, and leads to the states $(|, [])$ and $(|, |)$.

In FIGURE 7.36a, we gather all this connectivity into a finite automaton. Note that, by definition, the initial state has an incoming edge ν without

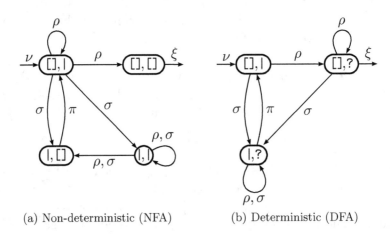

(a) Non-deterministic (NFA)　　　　(b) Deterministic (DFA)

Figure 7.36: Traces of $\mathsf{bf}/2$ as finite automata

source and the final state has an outgoing edge ξ without destination. A trace is any sequence of transitions from the initial state $([\,],|)$ to the final state $([\,],[\,])$, for example, $\nu\rho^p\sigma^q\pi\rho\xi$, with $p \geqslant 0$ and $q \geqslant 2$. This automaton is called a *non-deterministic finite automaton* (NFA) because a state may have more than one outgoing transition with the same label (consider the initial state and the two transitions labelled σ, for example).

It is always possible to construct a *deterministic finite automaton* (DFA) equivalent to a given non-deterministic finite automaton (Perrin, 1990, Hopcroft et al., 2003). The outgoing transitions of each state of the former have a unique label. Equivalence means that the sets of traces of each automaton are the same. If '?' denotes a stack, empty or not, FIGURE 7.36b on the preceding page shows an equivalent DFA for the traces of bf/1 and bf/2.

As we observed earlier, using the well-founded order $(\succ_{S^2})$ based on the sizes of the stacks, all transitions $x \to y$ in the DFA satisfy $x \succ_{S^2} y$, except π, for which $x =_{S^2} y$ holds (the total number of nodes is invariant). We can nevertheless conclude that bf/2 terminates because the only way to have non-termination would be the existence of a π-*circuit*, that is, a series of successive transitions from a state to itself all labelled with π, along which the number of nodes remains identical. In fact, all traces have π followed by ρ or σ.

Yet another spin on this matter would be to prove, by examining all rules in isolation and all compositions of two rules, that

$$x \to y \Rightarrow x \succcurlyeq_{S^2} y \quad \text{and} \quad x \xrightarrow{2} y \Rightarrow x \succ_{S^2} y.$$

Consequently, if $n > 0$, then $x \xrightarrow{2n} y$ entails $x \succ_{S^2} y$, because $(\succ_{S^2})$ is transitive. Furthermore, if $x \xrightarrow{2n} y \to z$, then $x \succ_{S^2} y \succcurlyeq_{S^2} z$, hence $x \succ_{S^2} z$. In the end, $x \xrightarrow{n} y$ implies $x \succ_{S^2} y$, for all $n > 1$. □

Breadth-first numbering As mentioned earlier, FIGURE 7.11d on page 216 shows an example of breadth-first numbering. This problem has received notable attention (Jones and Gibbons, 1993, Gibbons and Jones, 1998, Okasaki, 2000) because functional programmers usually feel a bit challenged by this problem. A good approach consists in modifying the function $bf_1/2$ in FIGURE 7.33 on page 234 so that it builds a tree instead of a stack. We do so by enqueueing immediate subtrees, so they are recursively numbered when they are dequeued, and by incrementing a counter, initialised with 0, every time a non-empty tree has been dequeued.

Consider $bfn_1/1$ and $bfn_2/2$ (*breadth-first numbering*) in FIGURE 7.37 on the following page, and compare them with the definitions in FIG-

$$\frac{\mathsf{bfn}_2(0, t \prec \ominus) \twoheadrightarrow \ominus \succ t'}{\mathsf{bfn}_1(t) \twoheadrightarrow t'}.$$

$$\mathsf{bfn}_2(i, \ominus) \to \ominus; \qquad \mathsf{bfn}_2(i, q \succ \mathsf{ext}()) \to \mathsf{ext}() \prec \mathsf{bfn}_2(i, q);$$

$$\frac{\mathsf{bfn}_2(i+1, t_2 \prec t_1 \prec q) \twoheadrightarrow q' \succ t'_1 \succ t'_2}{\mathsf{bfn}_2(i, q \succ \mathsf{int}(x, t_1, t_2)) \twoheadrightarrow \mathsf{int}(i, t'_1, t'_2) \prec q'}.$$

Figure 7.37: Abstract breadth-first numbering

URE 7.33 on page 234. In particular, notice how, in contrast with $\mathsf{bf}_1/2$, external nodes are enqueued instead of being discarded, because they are later needed to make the numbered tree.

In FIGURE 7.38 on the facing page is shown an example, where the numbers on the left represent the values of i (the first argument of $\mathsf{bf}_2/2$), the downward rewrites define the successive states of the working queue (the second argument of $\mathsf{bf}_2/2$), and the upward rewrites show the successive states of the resulting queue (right-hand side of $\mathsf{bf}_2/2$). Recall that trees are enqueued on the left and dequeued on the right (other authors may use the opposite convention, as Okasaki (2000)) and pay attention to the fact that, in the vertical rewrites on the left, t_1 is enqueued first whilst, on the right, t'_2 is dequeued first, which appears when contrasting $t_2 \prec t_1 \prec q = t_2 \prec (t_1 \prec q)$ and $q' \succ t'_1 \succ t'_2 = (q' \succ t'_1) \succ t'_2$.

We can refine $\mathsf{bfn}_1/1$ and $\mathsf{bfn}_2/2$ by introducing explicitly the function calls for enqueueing and dequeueing, as shown in FIGURE 7.39 on page 240, which could be contrasted with FIGURE 7.34 on page 234.

Exercises

1. How would you proceed to prove the correctness of $\mathsf{bfn}/1$?
2. Find the cost C_n^{bfn} of $\mathsf{bfn}(t)$, where n is the size of t.

7.2   Classic shapes

In this section, we briefly review some particular binary trees which are useful in assessing the extremal costs of many algorithms.

Perfection   We already mentioned what a *perfect binary tree* is in the context of optimal sorting (see FIGURE 2.43 on page 91). One way to define such trees is to say that all their external nodes belong to the

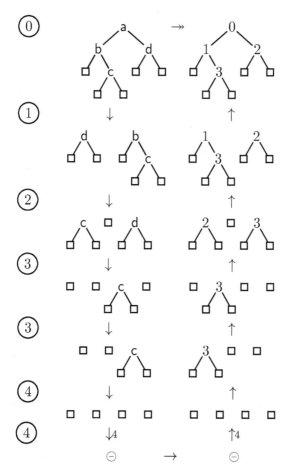

Figure 7.38: Example of breadth-first numbering

same level or, equivalently, the immediate subtrees of any node have same level or, equivalently, the immediate subtrees of any node have same height. (The height of an external node is 0.) The definition of per/1 (*perfection*) is shown in FIGURE 7.40 on the following page. If the tree t is perfect, we also know its height h: $\mathsf{per}(t) \twoheadrightarrow \mathsf{true}(h)$. Note that the rules are ordered, so the last one may only apply when the previous ones have not been matched. A refinement without inference rules is shown in FIGURE 7.41 on the next page, where $\mathsf{per}_0(t_1)$ is evaluated before $\mathsf{per}_0(t_2)$ since $\mathsf{t}(\mathsf{per}_0(t_1), \mathsf{per}_0(t_2))$ is inefficient if $\mathsf{per}_0(t_1) \twoheadrightarrow \mathsf{false}()$.

Completeness A binary tree is *complete* if the children of every internal node are either two external nodes or two internal nodes themselves. An example is provided in FIGURE 7.42 on page 241. Recursively, a given tree is complete if, and only if, its immediate subtrees

$$\frac{\mathsf{deq}(\mathsf{bfn}(0,\mathsf{q}([],[t]))) \twoheadrightarrow (\mathsf{q}([],[]),t')}{\mathsf{bfn}_3(t) \twoheadrightarrow t'}.$$

$$\mathsf{bfn}_4(i,\mathsf{q}([],[])) \to \mathsf{q}([],[]);\qquad \frac{\mathsf{deq}(q) \twoheadrightarrow (q',\mathsf{ext}())}{\mathsf{bfn}_4(i,q) \twoheadrightarrow \mathsf{enq}(\mathsf{ext}(),\mathsf{bfn}_4(i,q'))};$$

$$\frac{\mathsf{deq}(q) \twoheadrightarrow (q_1,\mathsf{int}(x,t_1,t_2))}{\mathsf{deq}(\mathsf{bfn}_4(i+1,\mathsf{enq}(t_2,\mathsf{enq}(t_1,q_1)))) \twoheadrightarrow (q_2,t_2') \qquad \mathsf{deq}(q_2) \twoheadrightarrow (q',t_1')}{\mathsf{bfn}_4(i,q) \twoheadrightarrow \mathsf{enq}(\mathsf{int}(i,t_1',t_2'),q')}$$

Figure 7.39: Refinement of FIGURE 7.37 on page 238

$$\mathsf{per}(\mathsf{ext}()) \to \mathsf{true}(0);\qquad \frac{\mathsf{per}(t_1) \twoheadrightarrow \mathsf{true}(h) \qquad \mathsf{per}(t_2) \twoheadrightarrow \mathsf{true}(h)}{\mathsf{per}(\mathsf{int}(x,t_1,t_2)) \to \mathsf{true}(h+1)};$$

$$\mathsf{per}(t) \to \mathsf{false}().$$

Figure 7.40: Abstract checking of perfection

are complete. This is the same rule we used for perfection. In other words, perfection and completeness are propagated fron the bottom up. Therefore, we need to decide what to say about the external nodes, in particular, the empty tree. If we decide that the latter is complete, then $\mathsf{int}(x,\mathsf{ext}(),\mathsf{int}(y,\mathsf{ext}(),\mathsf{ext}()))$ would, incorrectly, be deemed complete. If not, leaves $\mathsf{int}(x,\mathsf{ext}(),\mathsf{ext}())$ would, incorrectly, be found to be incomplete. Thus, we can choose either option and handle the problematic case separately; for example, we may choose that external nodes are incomplete trees, but leaves are complete trees. The program is shown in

$$\mathsf{per}_0(\mathsf{ext}()) \to \mathsf{true}(0);$$
$$\mathsf{per}_0(\mathsf{int}(x,t_1,t_2)) \to \mathsf{t}_1(\mathsf{per}_0(t_1),t_2).$$

$$\mathsf{t}_1(\mathsf{false}(),t_2) \to \mathsf{false}();$$
$$\mathsf{t}_1(h,t_2) \to \mathsf{t}_2(h,\mathsf{per}_0(t_2)).$$

$$\mathsf{t}_2(\mathsf{true}(h),\mathsf{true}(h)) \to \mathsf{true}(h+1);$$
$$\mathsf{t}_2(h,x) \to \mathsf{false}().$$

Figure 7.41: Refinement of FIGURE 7.40

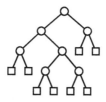

Figure 7.42: A complete tree

$$comp(int(x, ext(), ext())) \rightarrow true();$$

$$\frac{comp(t_1) \twoheadrightarrow true() \qquad comp(t_2) \twoheadrightarrow true()}{comp(int(x, t_1, t_2)) \twoheadrightarrow true()}; \quad comp(t) \rightarrow false().$$

Figure 7.43: Checking completeness

FIGURE 7.43. The last rule applies either if $t = ext()$ or $t = int(x, t_1, t_2)$, with t_1 or t_2 incomplete.

Balance The last interesting kind of binary trees is the *balanced trees*. There are two sorts of criteria to define balance: either height or size (Nievergelt and Reingold, 1972, Hirai and Yamamoto, 2011). In the latter case, siblings are roots of trees with similar sizes; in the former case, they have similar height. The usual criterion being height, we will use it in the following. Depending on the algorithm, what 'similar' means may vary.

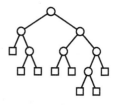

Figure 7.44

For example, we may decide that two trees whose heights differ at most by 1 have similar heights. See FIGURE 7.44 for an instance. Let us start with a definition of the height of a binary tree and then modify it to obtain a function checking the balance:

$$height(ext()) \rightarrow 0;$$
$$height(int(x, t_1, t_2)) \rightarrow 1 + \max\{height(t_1), height(t_2)\}.$$

The modification is shown in FIGURE 7.45 on the next page, where the inference rule of $bal_0/1$ is needed to check the condition $|h_1 - h_2| \leqslant 1$. Note that a perfect tree is balanced ($h_1 = h_2$).

7.3   Tree encodings

In general, many binary trees yield the same preorder, postorder or inorder traversal, so it is not possible to rebuild the original tree from one traversal alone. The problem of uniquely representing a binary tree by a

$$\mathsf{bal}_0(\mathsf{ext}()) \to \mathsf{true}(0);$$

$$\frac{\mathsf{bal}_0(t_1) \twoheadrightarrow \mathsf{true}(h_1) \quad \mathsf{bal}_0(t_2) \twoheadrightarrow \mathsf{true}(h_2) \quad |h_1 - h_2| \leqslant 1}{\mathsf{bal}_0(\mathsf{int}(x, t_1, t_2)) \twoheadrightarrow \mathsf{true}(1 + \max\{h_1, h_2\})} ;$$

$$\mathsf{bal}_0(t) \to \mathsf{false}().$$

Figure 7.45: Checking balance

$$\mathsf{epost}(t) \to \mathsf{epost}(t, [\,]).$$

$$\mathsf{epost}(\mathsf{ext}(), s) \to [\mathsf{ext}() \,|\, s];$$
$$\mathsf{epost}(\mathsf{int}(x, t_1, t_2), s) \to \mathsf{epost}(t_1, \mathsf{epost}(t_2, [x \,|\, s])).$$

Figure 7.46: Postorder encoding

linear structure is called *tree encoding* (Mäkinen, 1991) and is related to the problem of generating all binary trees of a given size (Knuth, 2011, 7.2.1.6). One simple approach consists in extending a traversal with the external nodes; this way, enough information from the binary tree is retained in the encoding, allowing us to unambiguously go back to the original tree.

The encoding function epost/1 (*extended postorder*) in FIGURE 7.46, is a simple modification of post/1 in FIGURE 7.26 on page 228. For example, the tree in FIGURE 7.11b on page 216 yields the following encoding: $[\square, \square, \square, 0, 1, \square, \square, 2, 3, \square, \square, \square, 4, 5, 6]$, where $\square$ stands for ext(). Since a binary tree with n internal nodes has $n + 1$ external nodes (see theorem 5 on page 208), the cost is straightforward to find:

$$C_n^{\mathsf{epost}} = 2n + 2.$$

We already noticed that the postorder of the nodes increases along upwards paths, which corresponds to the order in which a tree is built: from the external nodes up to the root. Therefore, all we have to do is to identify the growing subtrees by putting the unused numbers and subtrees in an auxiliary stack: when the contents of a root (anything different from ext()) appears in the original stack, we can make an internal node with the two first subtrees in the auxiliary stack. The definition of post2b/1 (*extended postorder to binary tree*) is given in FIGURE 7.47 on the facing page. Variable f stands for *forest*, which is how stacks of trees

$$\mathsf{post2b}(s) \to \mathsf{post2b}([\,], s).$$

$$\mathsf{post2b}([t], [\,]) \to t;$$
$$\mathsf{post2b}(f, [\mathsf{ext}()\,|\,s]) \to \mathsf{post2b}([\mathsf{ext}()\,|\,f], s);$$
$$\mathsf{post2b}([t_2, t_1\,|\,f], [x\,|\,s]) \to \mathsf{post2b}([\mathsf{int}(x, t_1, t_2)\,|\,f], s).$$

Figure 7.47: Postorder decoding

$$\mathsf{epre}(t) \to \mathsf{epre}(t, [\,]).$$

$$\mathsf{epre}(\mathsf{ext}(), s) \to [\mathsf{ext}()\,|\,s];$$
$$\mathsf{epre}(\mathsf{int}(x, t_1, t_2), s) \to [x\,|\,\mathsf{epre}(t_1, \mathsf{epre}(t_2, s))].$$

Figure 7.48: Preorder encoding

are usually called in computing science. Note that a problem would arise if the original tree contains trees because, in that case, an external node contained in an internal node would confuse $\mathsf{post2b/1}$. The cost is easy to assess because a postorder encoding must have length $2n+1$, which is the total number of nodes of a binary with n internal nodes. Therefore,

$$\mathcal{C}_n^{\mathsf{post2b}} = 2n + 3.$$

The expected theorem is, of course,

$$\mathsf{post2b}(\mathsf{epost}(t)) \equiv t. \qquad (7.8)$$

Considering preorder now, the encoding function $\mathsf{epre/1}$ (*extended preorder*) in FIGURE 7.48 is a simple modification of $\mathsf{pre/1}$ in FIGURE 7.10 on page 215. The cost is as simple as a postorder encoding:

$$\mathcal{C}_n^{\mathsf{epre}} = 2n + 2.$$

Working out the inverse function, from preorder encodings back to binary trees, is a little trickier than for postorder traversals, because the preorder numbers increase downwards in the trees, which is the opposite direction in which trees grow (programmers have trees grow from the leaves to the root). One solution consists in recalling the relationship $\mathsf{PreMir}(t)$ between preorder and postorder we proved earlier on page 228:

$$\mathsf{pre}(\mathsf{mir}(t)) \equiv \mathsf{rev}(\mathsf{post}(t)).$$

$$\boxed{\begin{array}{c} \mathsf{pre2b}(s) \to \mathsf{pre2b}([\,], \mathsf{rev}(s)). \\[1.5em] \mathsf{pre2b}([t], [\,]) \to t; \\ \mathsf{pre2b}(f, [\mathsf{ext}()\,|\,s]) \to \mathsf{pre2b}([\mathsf{ext}()\,|\,f], s); \\ \mathsf{pre2b}([t_1, t_2\,|\,f], [x\,|\,s]) \to \mathsf{pre2b}([\mathsf{int}(x, t_1, t_2)\,|\,f], s). \end{array}}$$

Figure 7.49: Preorder decoding

We should extend the proof of this theorem so we have

$$\mathsf{epre}(\mathsf{mir}(t)) \equiv \mathsf{rev}(\mathsf{epost}(t)). \qquad (7.9)$$

In section 2.2, we proved $\mathsf{Inv}(s)$ and $\mathsf{EqRev}(s)$, that is to say, the involution of $\mathsf{rev}/1$:

$$\mathsf{rev}(\mathsf{rev}(s)) \equiv t. \qquad (7.10)$$

Property (7.10) and (7.9) yield

$$\mathsf{rev}(\mathsf{epre}(\mathsf{mir}(t))) \equiv \mathsf{rev}(\mathsf{rev}(\mathsf{epost}(t))) \equiv \mathsf{epost}(t).$$

Applying (7.8), we obtain

$$\mathsf{post2b}(\mathsf{rev}(\mathsf{epre}(\mathsf{mir}(t)))) \equiv \mathsf{post2b}(\mathsf{epost}(t)) \equiv t.$$

From exercise 3 on page 230, we have $\mathsf{mir}(\mathsf{mir}(t)) \equiv t$, therefore

$$\mathsf{post2b}(\mathsf{rev}(\mathsf{epre}(t))) \equiv \mathsf{mir}(t) \quad \text{hence} \quad \mathsf{mir}(\mathsf{post2b}(\mathsf{rev}(\mathsf{epre}(t)))) \equiv t.$$

Because we want the encoding followed by the decoding to be the identity, $\mathsf{pre2b}(\mathsf{epre}(t)) \equiv t$, we have $\mathsf{pre2b}(\mathsf{epre}(t)) \equiv \mathsf{mir}(\mathsf{post2b}(\mathsf{rev}(\mathsf{epre}(t))))$, that is, setting the stack $s := \mathsf{epre}(t)$,

$$\mathsf{pre2b}(s) \equiv \mathsf{mir}(\mathsf{post2b}(\mathsf{rev}(s))).$$

We obtain $\mathsf{pre2b}/1$ by modifying $\mathsf{post2b}/1$ in FIGURE 7.49. The difference between $\mathsf{pre2b}/2$ and $\mathsf{post2b}/2$ lies in their last pattern, that is, $\mathsf{post2b}([t_2, t_1\,|\,f], [x\,|\,s])$ versus $\mathsf{pre2b}([t_1, t_2\,|\,f], [x\,|\,s])$, which implements the fusion of $\mathsf{mir}/1$ and $\mathsf{post2b}/1$.

Unfortunately, the cost of $\mathsf{pre2b}(t)$ is greater than the cost of $\mathsf{post2b}(t)$ because of the stack reversal $\mathsf{rev}(s)$ at the start:

$$\mathcal{C}_n^{\mathsf{pre2b}} = 2n + 3 + \mathcal{C}_n^{\mathsf{rev}} = 3n + 5.$$

The design of $\mathsf{pre2b}/1$ is based on small steps with an accumulator. A more direct approach would extract the left subtree and then the right

$$\frac{\mathsf{pre2b}_1(s) \twoheadrightarrow (t, [\,])}{\mathsf{pre2b}_0(s) \twoheadrightarrow t}. \qquad \mathsf{pre2b}_1([\mathsf{ext}()\,|\,s]) \rightarrow (\mathsf{ext}(), s);$$

$$\frac{\mathsf{pre2b}_1(s) \twoheadrightarrow (t_1, s_1) \qquad \mathsf{pre2b}_1(s_1) \twoheadrightarrow (t_2, s_2)}{\mathsf{pre2b}_1([x\,|\,s]) \twoheadrightarrow (\mathsf{int}(x, t_1, t_2), s_2)}.$$

Figure 7.50: Another preorder decoding

subtree from the rest of the encoding. In other words, the new version $\mathsf{pre2b}_1(s)$ would return a tree build from a prefix of the encoding s, paired with the rest of the encoding.

The definition is displayed in FIGURE 7.50. Notice the absence of any adventitious concept, contrary to $\mathsf{pre2b}/1$, which relies on the reversal of a stack and a theorem about mirror trees and postorders. To wit, $\mathsf{pre2b}_0/1$ is conceptually simpler, although its cost is greater than that of $\mathsf{pre2b}/1$ because we count the number of function calls after the inference rules are translated into the core functional language (so two more calls matching (t_1, s_1) and (t_2, s_2) are implicit).

Tree encodings show that it is possible to compactly represent binary trees, as long as we do not care for the contents of the internal nodes. For instance, we mentioned that the tree in FIGURE 7.11b on page 216 yields the extended postorder traversal $[\square, \square, \square, 0, 1, \square, \square, 2, 3, \square, \square, \square, 4, 5, 6]$. If we only want to retain the shape of the tree, we could replace the contents of the internal nodes by 0 and the external nodes by 1, yielding the encoding $[1, 1, 1, 0, 0, 1, 1, 0, 0, 1, 1, 1, 0, 0, 0]$. A binary tree of size n can be uniquely represented by a binary number of $2n+1$ bits. In fact, we can discard the first bit because the first two bits are always 1, so $2n$ bits are actually enough. For an extended preorder traversal, we choose to map external nodes to 0 and internal nodes to 1, so, the tree in FIGURE 7.11a on page 216 yields $[0, 1, 2, \square, 3, \square, \square, 4, \square, \square, 5, \square, 6, \square, \square]$, which corresponds to the binary number $(111010010010100)_2$. We can also discard the rightmost bit, since the last two bits are always 0.

7.4 Random traversals

Some applications require a tree traversal to depend on the interaction with a user or another piece of software, that is, the tree is supplemented with the notion of a current node so the next node to be visited can be chosen amongst any of the children, the parent or even the siblings.

This interactivity stands in contrast with preorder, inorder and postorder, where the visit order is predetermined and cannot be changed during the traversal.

Normally, the visit of a functional data structure starts always at the same location, for example, in the case of a stack, it is the top item and, in the case of a tree, the access point is the root. Sometimes, updating a data structure with an online algorithm (see page 9 and section 4.6 on page 168) requires to keep a direct access 'inside' the data structure, usually where the last update was performed, or nearby, in view of a better amortised (see page 9) or average cost (see 2-way insertion in section 3.2 on page 105).

Let us call the current node the *slider*, also called the *focus*. A *zipper* on a binary tree is made of a subtree, whose root is the slider, and a *path* from it up to the root. That path is the reification, in reverse order, of the recursive calls that led to the subtree (the *call stack*), together with the subtrees left unvisited on the way down. Put in more abstract terms, a zipper is made of a linear context (a rooted path) and a substructure (at the end of that path), whose handle is the focus. In one move, it is possible to visit the children in any order, the parent or the sibling. Consider FIGURE 7.51 where the slider is the node d. The substructure is

Figure 7.51

$$s := \mathsf{int}(\mathsf{d}(), \mathsf{int}(\mathsf{e}(), \mathsf{ext}(), \mathsf{ext}()), \mathsf{int}(\mathsf{f}(), \mathsf{ext}(), \mathsf{ext}())).$$

To define rooted paths for the zipper, we need three data constructors: one denoting the empty path, $\mathsf{top}()$, one denoting a turn to the left, $\mathsf{left}(x, t, p)$, where x is a node on the path, t is the right subtree of x, and p is the rest of the path up to the root, and one constructor denoting a turn to the right, $\mathsf{right}(x, t, p)$, where t is the left subtree of x.

Resuming our example above, the zipper is then the pair (p, s), with the path p being $\mathsf{right}(\mathsf{b}(), \mathsf{int}(\mathsf{c}(), \mathsf{ext}(), \mathsf{ext}()), p_1)$, meaning that the node b has an unvisited left child c (or, equivalently, we turned right when going down), and where $p_1 := \mathsf{left}(\mathsf{a}(), \mathsf{int}(\mathsf{g}(), \mathsf{ext}(), \mathsf{ext}()), \mathsf{top}())$, meaning that the node a has an unvisited right child g, and that it is the root of the whole tree, due to $\mathsf{top}()$. Note that since b is the first in the path up, it is the parent of the slider d.

At the beginning, the original tree t is injected into a zipper $(\mathsf{top}(), t)$. Then, the operations we want for traversing a binary tree on demand are $\mathsf{up}/1$ (go to the parent), $\mathsf{left}/1$ (go to the left child), $\mathsf{right}/1$ (go to the right child) and $\mathsf{sibling}/1$ (go to the sibling). All take a zipper as input and all calls evaluate into a zipper. After any of these steps is performed,

$$\begin{aligned}
\mathsf{up}((\mathsf{left}(x, t_2, p), t_1)) &\rightarrow (p, \mathsf{int}(x, t_1, t_2)); \\
\mathsf{up}((\mathsf{right}(x, t_1, p), t_2)) &\rightarrow (p, \mathsf{int}(x, t_1, t_2)).
\end{aligned}$$

$$\mathsf{left}((p, \mathsf{int}(x, t_1, t_2))) \rightarrow (\mathsf{left}(x, t_2, p), t_1).$$

$$\mathsf{right}((p, \mathsf{int}(x, t_1, t_2))) \rightarrow (\mathsf{right}(x, t_1, p), t_2).$$

$$\begin{aligned}
\mathsf{sibling}((\mathsf{left}(x, t_2, p), t_1)) &\rightarrow (\mathsf{right}(x, t_1, p), t_2); \\
\mathsf{sibling}((\mathsf{right}(x, t_1, p), t_2)) &\rightarrow (\mathsf{left}(x, t_2, p), t_1).
\end{aligned}$$

Figure 7.52: Basic steps in a binary tree

a new zipper is assembled as the value of the call. See FIGURE 7.52 for the program. Beyond random traversals of a binary tree, this technique, which is an instance of *Huet's zipper* (Huet, 1997, 2003), also allows local editing. This simply translates as the replacement of the current tree by another:

$$\mathsf{graft}(t', (p, t)) \rightarrow (p, t').$$

If we only want to change the slider, we would use

$$\mathsf{slider}(x', (p, \mathsf{int}(x, t_1, t_2))) \rightarrow (p, \mathsf{int}(x', t_1, t_2)).$$

If we want to go up to the root and extract the new tree:

$$\mathsf{zip}((\mathsf{top}(), t)) \rightarrow t; \quad \mathsf{zip}(z) \rightarrow \mathsf{zip}(\mathsf{up}(z)).$$

We do not need a zipper to perform a preorder, inorder or postorder traversal, because it is primarily designed to open down and close up paths from the root of a tree, in the manner of a zipper in a cloth. Nevertheless, if we retain one aspect of its design, namely, the accumulation of unvisited nodes and subtrees, we can define the classic traversals in tail form, that is, by means of a definition where the right-hand sides either are a value or a function call whose arguments are not function calls themselves. Such definitions are equivalent to loops in imperative languages and may be a target for some compilers (Appel, 1992).

We show a preorder traversal following this design in FIGURE 7.53 on the following page, where, in $\mathsf{pre}_8(s, f, t)$, the stack s is expected to collect the visited nodes in preorder, the stack f (forest) is the accumulator of unvisited parts of the original tree and t is the current subtree to be traversed. The cost is simple:

$$C_n^{\mathsf{pre}_7} = 3n + 2.$$

$$\mathsf{pre}_7(t) \rightarrow \mathsf{pre}_8([\,],[\,],t).$$

$$\mathsf{pre}_8(s,[\,],\mathsf{ext}()) \rightarrow s;$$
$$\mathsf{pre}_8(s,[\mathsf{int}(x,t_1,\mathsf{ext}())\,|\,f],\mathsf{ext}()) \rightarrow \mathsf{pre}_8(s,[x\,|\,f],t_1);$$
$$\mathsf{pre}_8(s,[x\,|\,f],\mathsf{ext}()) \rightarrow \mathsf{pre}_8([x\,|\,s],f,\mathsf{ext}());$$
$$\mathsf{pre}_8(s,f,\mathsf{int}(x,t_1,t_2)) \rightarrow \mathsf{pre}_8(s,[\mathsf{int}(x,t_1,\mathsf{ext}())\,|\,f],t_2).$$

Figure 7.53: Preorder in tail form

7.5   Enumeration

Many publications (Knuth, 1997, § 2.3.4.4) (Sedgewick and Flajolet, 1996, § 5.1) show how to find the number of binary trees of size n using an advanced mathematical tool called *generating functions* (Graham et al., 1994, chap. 7). Instead, for didactical purposes, we opt for a more intuitive technique in enumerative combinatorics which consists in constructing a one-to-one correspondence between two finite sets, so the cardinal of one is the cardinal of the other. In other words, we are going to relate bijectively, on the one hand, binary trees, and, on the other hand, other combinatorial objects which are relatively easy to count, for a given size.

We actually know the appropriate objects in the instance of *Dyck paths*, introduced in section 2.5 about queueing. A Dyck path is a broken line in a grid from the point $(0,0)$ to $(2n,0)$, made up of the two kinds of segments shown in FIGURE 7.54, such that it remains above the abscissa axis or reaches it. Consider again the example given in FIGURE 2.16 on page 65, without taking into account the individual costs associated to each step. Following the same convention as in chapter 5, we would say here that a *Dyck word* is a finite word over the alphabet made of the letters r (rise) and f (fall), such that all its prefixes contain more letters r than f, or an equal number. This condition is equivalent to the geometrical characterisation 'above the abscissa axis or reaches it'. For

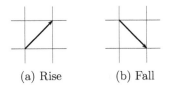

(a) Rise   (b) Fall

Figure 7.54: Basic steps in a grid

instance, rff is not a Dyck word because the prefix rff (actually, the whole word) contains more falls than rises, so the associated path ends below the axis. The Dyck word corresponding to the Dyck path in FIGURE 2.16 on page 65 is rrrfrfrrfffrff. Conceptually, there is no difference between a Dyck path and a Dyck word, we use the former when a geometrical framework is more intuitive and the latter when symbolic reasoning and programming are expected.

First, let us map injectively binary trees to Dyck words, in other words, we want to traverse any tree and produce a Dyck word which is not the mapping of another tree. Since, by definition, non-empty binary trees are made of an internal node connected to two binary subtrees, we may wonder how to split a Dyck word into three parts: one corresponding to the root of the tree and two corresponding to the immediate subtrees.

Since any Dyck word starts with a rise and ends with a fall, we may ask what is the word in-between. In general, it is not a Dyck word; for example, chopping off the ends of rfrrff yields frrf. Instead, we seek a decomposition of Dyck words into Dyck words. If the Dyck word has exactly one *return*, that is, one fall leading to the abscissa axis, then cutting out the first rise and that unique return (which must be the last fall) yields another Dyck word. For instance, rrfrrfff = r · rfrrff · f.

Such words are called *prime*, because any Dyck word can be uniquely decomposed as the concatenation of such words (whence the reference to prime factorisation in elementary number theory): for all non-empty Dyck words d, there exists $n > 0$ unique prime Dyck words p_i such that $d = p_1 \cdot p_2 \cdots p_n$.

This naturally yields the *arch decomposition*, whose name stems from an architectural analogy: for all Dyck words d, there exists $n > 0$ Dyck words d_i and returns f_i such that

$$d = (r \cdot d_1 \cdot f_1) \cdots (r \cdot d_n \cdot f_n).$$

For more details, see Panayotopoulos and Sapounakis (1995), Lothaire (2005), Flajolet and Sedgewick (2009).

Unfortunately, this analysis is not suitable as it stands, because n may be greater than 2, precluding any analogy with binary trees. The solution is simple enough: let us keep the first prime factor $r \cdot d_1 \cdot f_1$ and *not* factorise the suffix, which is a Dyck word. To wit, for all non-empty Dyck words d, there exists one return f_1 and two Dyck subwords d_1 and d_2 (possibly empty) such that we have

$$d = (r \cdot d_1 \cdot f_1) \cdot d_2.$$

This is the *first return decomposition*, also known as *quadratic decomposition* – also possible is $d = d_1 \cdot (r \cdot d_2 \cdot f_1)$. For example, the Dyck

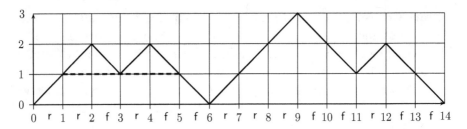

Figure 7.55: Quadratic decomposition of a Dyck path

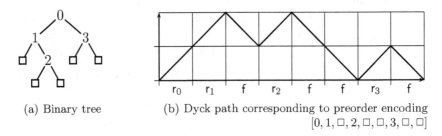

(a) Binary tree   (b) Dyck path corresponding to preorder encoding
$$[0, 1, \Box, 2, \Box, \Box, 3, \Box, \Box]$$

Figure 7.56: Bijection between a binary tree and a Dyck path

word rrfrffrrrffrff, shown in FIGURE 7.55 admits the quadratic decomposition r · rfrf · f · rrrffrff. This decomposition is unique because the prime factorisation is unique.

Given a tree $\mathsf{int}(x, t_1, t_2)$, the rise and fall explicitly distinguished in the quadratic decomposition are to be conceived as a pair which is the mapping of x, while d_1 is the mapping of t_1 and d_2 is the mapping of t_2. More precisely, the value of x is not relevant here, only the existence of an internal node, and a fork in a leaf tree would be mapped just as well. Formally, if $\delta(t)$ is the Dyck word mapped from the binary tree t, then we expect the following equations to hold:

$$\delta(\mathsf{ext}()) = \varepsilon; \quad \delta(\mathsf{int}(x, t_1, t_2)) = r_x \cdot \delta(t_1) \cdot f \cdot \delta(t_2). \quad (7.11)$$

Note that we attached the node contents x to the rise, so we do not lose information. For example, the tree in FIGURE 7.56a would formally be

$$t := \mathsf{int}(0, \mathsf{int}(1, \mathsf{ext}(), \mathsf{int}(2, \mathsf{ext}(), \mathsf{ext}())), \mathsf{int}(3, \mathsf{ext}(), \mathsf{ext}()),$$

and mapped into the Dyck path in FIGURE 7.56b as follows:

$$\begin{aligned}
\delta(t) &= r_0 \cdot \delta(\mathsf{int}(1, \mathsf{ext}(), \mathsf{int}(2, \mathsf{ext}(), \mathsf{ext}()))) \cdot f \cdot \delta(\mathsf{int}(3, \mathsf{ext}(), \mathsf{ext}())) \\
&= r_0 \cdot (r_1 \cdot \delta(\mathsf{ext}()) \cdot f \cdot \delta(\mathsf{int}(2, \mathsf{ext}(), \mathsf{ext}()))) \cdot f \cdot \delta(\mathsf{int}(3, \mathsf{ext}(), \mathsf{ext}())) \\
&= r_0 r_1 \varepsilon \cdot f \cdot (r_2 \cdot \delta(\mathsf{ext}()) \cdot f \cdot \delta(\mathsf{ext}())) \cdot f \cdot (r_3 \cdot \delta(\mathsf{ext}()) \cdot f \cdot \delta(\mathsf{ext}())) \\
&= r_0 r_1 f \cdot (r_2 \cdot \varepsilon \cdot f \cdot \varepsilon) \cdot f \cdot (r_3 \cdot \varepsilon \cdot f \cdot \varepsilon) = r_0 \cdot r_1 \cdot f \cdot r_2 \cdot f \cdot f \cdot r_3 \cdot f.
\end{aligned}$$

$$\mathsf{dpre}(t) \to \mathsf{dpre}(t, [\,]).$$

$$\mathsf{dpre}(\mathsf{ext}(), s) \to s;$$
$$\mathsf{dpre}(\mathsf{int}(x, t_1, t_2), s) \to [\mathsf{r}(x) \,|\, \mathsf{dpre}(t_1, [\mathsf{f}() \,|\, \mathsf{dpre}(t_2, s)])].$$

Figure 7.57: Mapping in preorder a binary tree to a Dyck path

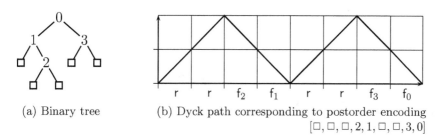

(a) Binary tree

(b) Dyck path corresponding to postorder encoding
$[\square, \square, \square, 2, 1, \square, \square, 3, 0]$

Figure 7.58: Bijection between a binary tree and a Dyck path

Notice that if we replace the rises by their associated contents (in subscript) and the falls by $\square$, we obtain $[0, 1, \square, 2, \square, \square, 3, \square]$, which is the preorder encoding of the tree without its last $\square$. We could then modify epre/2 in FIGURE 7.48 on page 243 to map a binary tree to a Dyck path, but we would have to remove the last item from the resulting stack, so it is more efficient to directly implement δ as function dpre/1 (*Dyck path as preorder*) in FIGURE 7.57. If the size of the binary tree is n, then the length of the Dyck path is $2n$ and

$$C_n^{\mathsf{dpre}} = 2n + 2.$$

This mapping is clearly reversible, as we already solved the problem of decoding a tree in preorder in FIGURES 7.49 and 7.50 on page 245, and we understand now that the reversed mapping is based on the quadratic ('first return') decomposition of the path.

If we are concerned about efficiency, though, we may recall that using a postorder encoding yields a more efficient decoding, as we saw in FIGURES 7.46 and 7.47 no page 242, therefore a faster reverse mapping. To create a Dyck path based on a postorder, we map external nodes to rises and internal nodes to falls (with associated contents), and then remove the first rise. See FIGURE 7.58b for the Dyck path obtained from the postorder traversal of the same previous tree. Of course, just as we did with the preorder mapping, we are not going to make the postorder encoding, but instead go directly from the binary tree to the Dyck path, as shown in FIGURE 7.59 on the next page. Note that we push r() and

$$\text{dpost}(t) \rightarrow \text{dpost}(t, [\,]).$$

$$\text{dpost}(\text{ext}(), s) \rightarrow s;$$
$$\text{dpost}(\text{int}(x, t_1, t_2), s) \rightarrow \text{dpost}(t_1, [\text{r}() \,|\, \text{dpost}(t_2, [\text{f}(x) \,|\, s])]).$$

Figure 7.59: Mapping in postorder a binary tree to a Dyck path

$$\text{d2b}(s) \rightarrow \text{d2b}([\text{ext}()], s).$$

$$\text{d2b}([t], [\,]) \rightarrow t;$$
$$\text{d2b}(f, [\text{r}() \,|\, s]) \rightarrow \text{d2b}([\text{ext}() \,|\, f], s);$$
$$\text{d2b}([t_2, t_1 \,|\, f], [\text{f}(x) \,|\, s]) \rightarrow \text{d2b}([\text{int}(x, t_1, t_2) \,|\, f], s).$$

Figure 7.60: Mapping a Dyck path to a binary tree in postorder

$\text{f}(x)$ in the same rule, so we do not have to remove the first rise at the end. (We use a similar optimisation with $\text{dpre}/2$ in FIGURE 7.57 on the preceding page.) In structural terms, the inverse of this postorder mapping corresponds to a decomposition $d = d_1 \cdot (\text{r} \cdot d_2 \cdot \text{f}_1)$, which we mentioned earlier in passing as an alternative to the 'first return' decomposition.

The mapping from Dyck paths encoded in postorder to binary trees is a simple variation on $\text{post2b}/1$ and $\text{post2b}/2$ in FIGURE 7.47 on page 243: simply make the auxiliary stack be $[\text{ext}()]$ at the beginning. The definition is named $\text{d2b}/1$ and shown in FIGURE 7.60. The cost is

$$C_n^{\text{d2b}} = 2n + 2.$$

Whether we choose a preorder or a postorder mapping, as a consequence of the established bijections, we know that there are as many binary trees of size n as Dyck paths of length $2n$. We already know, from chapter 6, and equation (6.1) on page 198, that there are C_n paths:

$$C_n = \frac{1}{n+1} \binom{2n}{n} \sim \frac{4^n}{n\sqrt{\pi n}}.$$

Other encodings of binary trees were found by Knuth (1997) (section 2.3.3) and Sedgewick and Flajolet (1996) (section 5.11).

Average path length Most of the usual average parameters of binary trees, like average internal path length, average height and width, are quite difficult to derive and require mathematical tools which are beyond the scope of this book.

The *internal path length* $I(t)$ of a binary tree t is the sum of the path lengths from the root to every internal node. We already saw the concept of external path length $E(t)$, that is, the sum of the path lengths from the root to every internal node, in section 2.8 on page 82 about optimal sorting, where we showed that the binary tree with minimum average external path length has all its external nodes on two successive levels. The relation between these two path lengths is quite simple because the binary structure yields an equation depending only on the size n:

$$E_n = I_n + 2n. \tag{7.12}$$

Indeed, let $\text{int}(x, t_1, t_2)$ be a tree with n internal nodes. Then we have

$$I(\text{ext}()) = 0, \quad I(\text{int}(x, t_1, t_2)) = I(t_1) + I(t_2) + n - 1, \tag{7.13}$$

because each path in t_1 and t_2 is extended with one more edge back to the root x, and there are $n - 1$ such paths by definition. On the other hand,

$$E(\text{ext}()) = 0, \quad E(\text{int}(x, t_1, t_2)) = E(t_1) + E(t_2) + n + 1, \tag{7.14}$$

because the paths in t_1 and t_2 are extended by one more step to the root x and there are $n + 1$ such paths, from theorem 5 on page 208. Subtracting equation (7.13) from (7.14) yields

$$E(\text{ext}()) - I(\text{ext}()) = 0,$$
$$E(\text{int}(x, t_1, t_2)) - I(\text{int}(x, t_1, t_2)) = (E(t_1) - I(t_1)) + (E(t_2) - I(t_2)) + 2.$$

In other words, each internal node adds 2 to the difference between the external and internal path lengths from it. Since the difference is 0 at the external nodes, we get equation (7.12) for the tree of size n. Unfortunately, almost anything else is quite hard to prove. For instance, the *average internal path length* $\mathbb{E}[I_n]$ has been shown to be

$$\mathbb{E}[I_n] = \frac{4^n}{C_n} - 3n - 1 \sim n\sqrt{\pi n}$$

by Knuth (1997), in exercise 5 of section 2.3.4.5, and Sedgewick and Flajolet (1996), in Theorem 5.3 of section 5.6. Using equation (7.12), we deduce $\mathbb{E}[E_n] = \mathbb{E}[I_n] + 2n$, implying that the cost for traversing a random binary tree of size n from the root to a random external node is $\mathbb{E}[E_n]/(n + 1) \sim \sqrt{\pi n}$. Moreover, the value $\mathbb{E}[I_n]/n$ can be understood as the average level of a random internal node.

Average height   The average height h_n of a binary tree of size n is even more difficult to obtain and was studied by Flajolet and Odlyzko (1981), Brown and Shubert (1984), Flajolet and Odlyzko (1984), Odlyzko (1984):

$$h_n \sim 2\sqrt{\pi n}.$$

In the case for Catalan trees, to wit, trees whose internal nodes may have any number of children, the analysis of the average height has been carried out by Dasarathy and Yang (1980), Dershowitz and Zaks (1981), Kemp (1984) in section 5.1.1, Dershowitz and Zaks (1990), Knuth et al. (2000) and Sedgewick and Flajolet (1996), in section 5.9.

Average width   The *width* of a binary tree is the length of its largest extended level. It can be shown that the *average width* w_n of a binary tree of size n satisfies

$$w_n \sim \sqrt{\pi n} \sim \frac{1}{2} h_n.$$

In particular, this result implies that the average size of the stack needed to perform the preorder traversal with $\mathsf{pre_4/2}$ in FIGURE 7.6 on page 213 is twice the average size of the queue needed to perform a level-order traversal with $\mathsf{bf/1}$ in FIGURE 7.35 on page 235. This is not obvious, as the two stacks used to simulate the queue do not always hold a complete level.

For Catalan trees, a bijective correspondence with binary trees and the transfer of some average parameters has been nicely presented by Dasarathy and Yang (1980).

Exercises

1. Prove $\mathsf{post2b}(\mathsf{epost}(t)) \equiv t$.

2. Prove $\mathsf{pre2b}(\mathsf{epre}(t)) \equiv t$.

3. Prove $\mathsf{epre}(\mathsf{mir}(t)) \equiv \mathsf{rev}(\mathsf{epost}(t))$.

4. Define the encoding of a tree based on its inorder traversal.

Chapter 8

Binary Search Trees

Searching for an internal node in a binary tree can be costly because, in the worst case, the whole tree must be traversed, for example, in preorder or level-order. To improve upon this, two situations are desirable: the binary tree should be as balanced as possible and the choice of visiting the left or right subtree should be taken only upon examining the contents in the root, called *key*.

The simplest solution consists in satisfying the latter condition and later see how it fits the former. A *binary search tree* (Mahmoud, 1992) $\mathsf{bst}(x, t_1, t_2)$ is a binary tree such that the key x is greater than the keys in t_1 and smaller than the keys in t_2. (The external node $\mathsf{ext}()$ is a trivial search tree.) The comparison function depends on the nature of the keys, but has to be *total*, that is, any key can be compared to any other key. An example is given in FIGURE 8.1. An immediate consequence of the definition is that the inorder traversal of a binary search tree yields an increasingly sorted stack, for example, $[3, 5, 11, 13, 17, 29]$ from the tree in FIGURE 8.1.

Figure 8.1

This property enables checking simply that a binary tree is a search tree: perform an inorder traversal and then check the order of the resulting stack. The corresponding function, $\mathsf{bst}_0/1$, is legible in FIGURE 8.2 on the following page, where $\mathsf{in}_2/2$ is just a redefinition of $\mathsf{in}/2$ in FIGURE 7.21 on page 223. Thus, the cost of $\mathsf{in}_2(t)$, when t has size n, is $C_n^{\mathsf{in}_2} = C_n^{\mathsf{in}} = 2n + 2$. The worst case for $\mathsf{ord}/1$ occurs when the stack is sorted increasingly, so the maximum cost is $\mathcal{W}_n^{\mathsf{ord}} = n$, if $n > 0$. The best case is manifest when the first key is greater than the second, so the minimum cost is $\mathcal{B}_n^{\mathsf{ord}} = 1$. Summing up:

$$\mathcal{B}_n^{\mathsf{bst}_0} = 1 + (2n + 2) + 1 = 2n + 4;$$
$$\mathcal{W}_n^{\mathsf{bst}_0} = 1 + (2n + 2) + n = 3n + 3.$$

255

$$\mathsf{bst}_0(t) \rightarrow \mathsf{ord}(\mathsf{in}_2(t, [\,])).$$

$$\mathsf{in}_2(\mathsf{ext}(), s) \rightarrow s;$$
$$\mathsf{in}_2(\mathsf{bst}(x, t_1, t_2), s) \rightarrow \mathsf{in}_2(t_1, [x \,|\, \mathsf{in}_2(t_2, s)]).$$

$$\mathsf{ord}([x, y \,|\, s]) \rightarrow \mathsf{ord}([y \,|\, s]), \text{ if } y \succ x;$$
$$\mathsf{ord}([x, y \,|\, s]) \rightarrow \mathsf{false}();$$
$$\mathsf{ord}(s) \rightarrow \mathsf{true}().$$

Figure 8.2: Naïvely checking a binary search tree

$$\mathsf{bst}(t) \rightarrow \mathsf{norm}(\mathsf{bst}_1(t, \mathsf{infty}())).$$

$$\mathsf{bst}_1(\mathsf{ext}(), m) \rightarrow m;$$
$$\mathsf{bst}_1(\mathsf{bst}(x, t_1, t_2), m) \rightarrow \mathsf{cmp}(x, t_1, \mathsf{bst}_1(t_2, m)).$$

$$\mathsf{cmp}(x, t_1, \mathsf{infty}()) \rightarrow \mathsf{bst}_1(t_1, x);$$
$$\mathsf{cmp}(x, t_1, m) \rightarrow \mathsf{bst}_1(t_1, x), \text{ if } m \succ x;$$
$$\mathsf{cmp}(x, t_1, m) \rightarrow \mathsf{false}().$$

$$\mathsf{norm}(\mathsf{false}()) \rightarrow \mathsf{false}();$$
$$\mathsf{norm}(m) \rightarrow \mathsf{true}().$$

Figure 8.3: Checking a binary search tree

A better design consists in not constructing the inorder stack and only *keeping the smallest key so far*, assuming the traversal is from right to left, and compare it with the current key. But this is a problem at the beginning, as we have not visited any node yet. A common trick to deal with exceptional values is to use a *sentinel*, which is a dummy. Here, we would like to set the sentinel to $+\infty$, as any key would be smaller, in particular the largest key, which is *unknown*. (Would it be known, we could use it as a sentinel.) It is actually easy to model this infinite value in our functional language: let us simply use a constant data constructor infty/0 (*infinity*) and make sure that we handle its comparison separately from the others. Actually, infty() is compared only once, with the largest key, but we will not try to optimise this, lest the design is obscured.

The program is displayed in FIGURE 8.3. The parameter m stands for the *minimum* key so far. The sole purpose of norm/1 is to get rid of the smallest key m in the tree and instead terminate with true(), but, if the tree is not empty, we could as well end with $\mathsf{true}(m)$, or even $\mathsf{false}(x)$, if more information were deemed useful.

In the worst case, the original tree is a binary search tree, hence it has to be traversed in its entirety. If there are n internal nodes, the maximum cost is

$$\mathcal{W}_n^{\mathsf{bst}} = 1 + 2n + (n+1) + 1 = 3n + 3,$$

because each internal node triggers one call to $\mathsf{bst}_1/2$ and, in turn, one call to $\mathsf{cmp}/3$; also, all the $n+1$ external nodes are visited. Consequently, $\mathcal{W}_n^{\mathsf{bsto}} = \mathcal{W}_n^{\mathsf{bst}}$, if $n > 0$, which is not an improvement. Nevertheless, here, we do not build a stack with all the keys, which is a definite gain in terms of memory allocation.

Memory is not the only advantage, though, as the minimum cost of $\mathsf{bst}/1$ is lower than for $\mathsf{bst}_0/1$. Indeed, the best case for both occurs when the tree is not a binary search tree, but this is discovered the sooner in $\mathsf{bst}/1$ at the second comparison, because the first one always succeeds by design ($+\infty \succ x$). Obviously, for the second comparison to occur as soon as possible, we need the first comparison to happen as soon as possible too. Two configurations work:

$$\mathsf{bst}(\mathsf{bst}(x, t_1, \mathsf{bst}(y, \mathsf{ext}(), \mathsf{ext}()))) \xrightarrow{8} \mathsf{false}(),$$
$$\mathsf{bst}(\mathsf{bst}(y, \mathsf{bst}(x, t_1, \mathsf{ext}()), \mathsf{ext}())) \xrightarrow{8} \mathsf{false}(),$$

where $x \succcurlyeq y$. (The second tree is the left rotation of the first. We have seen on page 224 that inorder traversals are invariant through rotations.) The minimum cost in both cases is

$$\mathcal{B}_n^{\mathsf{bst}} = 8,$$

to be contrasted with the linear cost $\mathcal{B}_n^{\mathsf{bsto}} = 2n + 4$ due to the inevitable complete inorder traversal.

8.1 Search

We now must find out whether searching for a key is faster than with an ordinary binary tree, which was our initial motivation. Given the search tree $\mathsf{bst}(x, t_1, t_2)$, if the key y we are searching for is such that $y \succ x$, then we search recursively for it in t_2; otherwise, if $x \succ y$, we look in t_1; finally, if $y = x$, we just found it at the root of the given tree. The definition of $\mathsf{mem}/2$ (*membership*) is shown in FIGURE 8.4 on the following page. The crucial point is that we may not need to visit all the nodes. More precisely, if all nodes are visited, then the tree is degenerate, to wit, it is isomorphic to a stack, like the trees in FIGURE 7.4 on page 211

$$\boxed{\begin{aligned}
&\mathsf{mem}(y, \mathsf{ext}()) \rightarrow \mathsf{false}(); \\
&\mathsf{mem}(x, \mathsf{bst}(x, t_1, t_2)) \rightarrow \mathsf{true}(); \\
&\mathsf{mem}(y, \mathsf{bst}(x, t_1, t_2)) \rightarrow \mathsf{mem}(y, t_1), \text{ if } x \succ y; \\
&\mathsf{mem}(y, \mathsf{bst}(x, t_1, t_2)) \rightarrow \mathsf{mem}(y, t_2).
\end{aligned}}$$

Figure 8.4: Searching in a binary search tree

and FIGURE 7.31 on page 233. Clearly, the minimum cost of a successful search occurs when the key is at the root, so $\mathcal{B}_{n(+)}^{\mathsf{mem}} = 1$, and the minimum cost of an unsuccessful search happens when the root has an external node as a child and $\mathsf{mem}/2$ visits it: $\mathcal{B}_{n(-)}^{\mathsf{mem}} = 2$. The maximum cost of a successful search occurs when the tree is degenerate and the key we are looking for is at the only leaf, so $\mathcal{W}_{n(+)}^{\mathsf{mem}} = n$, and the maximum cost of an unsuccessful search happens when visiting one of the children of the leaf of a degenerate tree: $\mathcal{W}_{n(-)}^{\mathsf{mem}} = n + 1$. Therefore,

$$\mathcal{B}_n^{\mathsf{mem}} = 1 \quad \text{and} \quad \mathcal{W}_n^{\mathsf{mem}} = n + 1.$$

These extremal costs are the same as for a linear search by $\mathsf{ls}/2$:

$$\mathsf{ls}(x, []) \rightarrow \mathsf{false}(); \quad \mathsf{ls}(x, [x \,|\, s]) \rightarrow \mathsf{true}(); \quad \mathsf{ls}(x, [y \,|\, s]) \rightarrow \mathsf{ls}(x, s).$$

The cost of a successful linear search is $C_{n,k}^{\mathsf{ls}} = k$, if the sought key is at position k, where the first key is at position 1. Therefore, the average cost of a successful linear search, assuming that each distinct key is equally likely to be sought is

$$\mathcal{A}_n^{\mathsf{ls}} = \frac{1}{n} \sum_{k=1}^{n} C_{n,k}^{\mathsf{ls}} = \frac{n+1}{2}.$$

This raises the question of the average cost of $\mathsf{mem}/2$.

Average cost   It is clear from the definition that a search path starts at the root and either ends at an internal node in case of success, or at an external node in case of failure; moreover, each node on these paths corresponds to one function call. Therefore, the average cost of $\mathsf{mem}/2$ is directly related to the average internal and external path lengths. To clearly see how, let us consider a binary search tree of size n containing distinct keys. The total cost of searching all of these keys is $n + I_n$, where I_n is the internal path length (we add n to I_n because we count the nodes on the paths, not the edges, as one internal node is associated with one function call). In other words, a random key chosen amongst those in a given tree of size n is found by mem/2 with an average cost of $1 + I_n/n$. Dually, the total cost of reaching all the external nodes of a given binary search tree is $(n + 1) + E_n$, where E_n is the external path length (there are $n+1$ external nodes in a tree with n internal nodes; see theorem 5 on page 208). In other words, the average cost of a failed search by mem/2 is $1 + E_n/(n + 1)$.

At this point, we should realise that we are dealing with a double randomness, or, equivalently, an average of averages. Indeed, the previous discussion assumed the search tree was given, but the key was random. The general case is when both are chosen randomly, that is, when the previous results are averaged over all possible trees of the same size n. Let $\mathcal{A}^{\text{mem}}_{n(+)}$ be the average cost of the successful search of a random key in a random tree of size n (any of the n keys being sought with same probability); moreover, let $\mathcal{A}^{\text{mem}}_{n(-)}$ be the average cost of the unsuccessful search of a random key in a random tree (any of the $n+1$ intervals whose end points are the n keys being equally likely to be searched). Then

$$\mathcal{A}^{\text{mem}}_{n(+)} = 1 + \frac{1}{n}\mathbb{E}[I_n] \quad \text{and} \quad \mathcal{A}^{\text{mem}}_{n(-)} = 1 + \frac{1}{n+1}\mathbb{E}[E_n], \qquad (8.1)$$

where $\mathbb{E}[I_n]$ and $\mathbb{E}[E_n]$ are, respectively, the average (or *expected*) internal path length and the average external path length. Reusing equation (7.12), page 253 ($E_n = I_n + 2n$), we deduce $\mathbb{E}[E_n] = \mathbb{E}[I_n] + 2n$ and we can now relate the average costs of searching by eliminating the average path lengths:

$$\mathcal{A}^{\text{mem}}_{n(+)} = \left(1 + \frac{1}{n}\right)\mathcal{A}^{\text{mem}}_{n(-)} - \frac{1}{n} - 2. \qquad (8.2)$$

Importantly, this equation holds for all binary search trees, *independently of how they are built*. In the next section, we shall envisage two methods for making search trees and we will be able to determine $\mathcal{A}^{\text{mem}}_{n(+)}$ and $\mathcal{A}^{\text{mem}}_{n(-)}$ with the help of equation (8.2).

But before that, we could perhaps notice that in FIGURE 8.4 on the facing page we did not follow the order of the comparisons as we wrote it down. In the case of a successful search, the comparison $y = x$ holds exactly once, at the very end; therefore, checking it before the others, as we did in the second rule in FIGURE 8.4 on the preceding page, means that it fails for every key on the search path, except for the last. If we measure the cost as the number of function calls, we would not care, but, if we are interested in minimising the number of comparisons involved in a search, it is best to move that rule *after* the other inequality tests, as in FIGURE 8.5 on the following page. (We assume that an equality is

$$
\begin{array}{l}
\mathsf{mem}_0(y, \mathsf{bst}(x, t_1, t_2)) \rightarrow \mathsf{mem}_0(y, t_1), \text{ if } x \succ y; \\
\mathsf{mem}_0(y, \mathsf{bst}(x, t_1, t_2)) \rightarrow \mathsf{mem}_0(y, t_2), \text{ if } y \succ x; \\
\quad\quad\mathsf{mem}_0(y, \mathsf{ext}()) \rightarrow \mathsf{false}(); \\
\quad\quad\mathsf{mem}_0(y, t) \rightarrow \mathsf{true}().
\end{array}
$$

Figure 8.5: Searching with fewer 2-way comparisons

checked as fast as an inequality.) With $\mathsf{mem}_0/2$, the number of comparisons for each search path is different because of the asymmetry between left and right: visiting t_1 yields one comparison ($x \succ y$), whilst t_2 begets two comparisons ($x \not\succ y$ and $y \succ x$). Moreover, we also moved the pattern for the external node after the rules with comparisons, because each search path contains exactly one external node at the end, so it is likely more efficient to check it last. By the way, all textbooks we are aware of suppose that exactly one atomic comparison with three possible outcomes (*3-way comparison*) occurs, despite the programs they provide clearly employing the *2-way comparisons* ($=$) and ($\succ$). This widespread blind spot renders the theoretical analysis based on the number of comparisons less pertinent, because most high-level programming languages simply do not feature native 3-way comparisons.

Andersson's variant   Andersson (1991) proposed a variant for searching which fully acknowledges the use of 2-way comparisons and reduces their number to a minimum, at the expense of more function calls. The design consists in threading a candidate key while descending in the tree and always ending a search at an external node: if the candidate then equals the sought key, the search is successful, otherwise it is not. Therefore, the cost in terms of function calls of an unsuccessful search is the same as with $\mathsf{mem}/2$ or $\mathsf{mem}_0/2$, and the ending external node is the same, but the cost for a successful search is higher. Nevertheless, the advantage is that *equality is not tested on the way down*, only when the external node is reached, so only one comparison per node is required. The program is shown in FIGURE 8.6 on the next page. The candidate is the third argument to $\mathsf{mem}_2/2$ and its first instance is the root of the tree itself, as seen in the first rule of $\mathsf{mem}_1/2$. The only conceptual difference with $\mathsf{mem}_0/2$ is how a successful search is acknowledged: if, somewhere along the search path, $x = y$, then x becomes the candidate and it will be threaded down to an external node where $x = x$ is checked.

The worst case happens when the tree is degenerate and $\mathsf{mem}_1/2$ performs $n + 1$ 2-way comparisons, which we write as $\overline{\mathcal{W}}_n^{\mathsf{mem}_1} = n + 1$,

$$\begin{aligned}
&\mathsf{mem}_1(y, \mathsf{bst}(x, t_1, t_2)) \to \mathsf{mem}_2(y, \mathsf{bst}(x, t_1, t_2), x);\\
&\qquad \mathsf{mem}_1(y, \mathsf{ext}()) \to \mathsf{false}().
\end{aligned}$$

$$\begin{aligned}
&\mathsf{mem}_2(y, \mathsf{bst}(x, t_1, t_2), c) \to \mathsf{mem}_2(y, t_1, c), \text{ if } x \succ y;\\
&\mathsf{mem}_2(y, \mathsf{bst}(x, t_1, t_2), c) \to \mathsf{mem}_2(y, t_2, x);\\
&\qquad \mathsf{mem}_2(y, \mathsf{ext}(), y) \to \mathsf{true}();\\
&\qquad \mathsf{mem}_2(y, \mathsf{ext}(), c) \to \mathsf{false}().
\end{aligned}$$

Figure 8.6: Andersson's search (key candidate)

after the notations we used in the analysis of merge sort, back in chapter 4 on page 119.

In the case of $\mathsf{mem}_0/2$, the recursive call to the right subtree incurs twice as much comparisons as in the left subtree, thus the worst case is a right-leaning degenerate tree, like in FIGURE 7.4b on page 211, and all internal nodes are visited: $\overline{\mathcal{W}}_n^{\mathsf{mem}_0} = 2n$.

In the case of $\mathsf{mem}/2$, the number of comparisons is symmetric because equality is tested first, so the worst case is a degenerate tree in which an unsuccessful search leads to the visit of all internal nodes and one external node: $\overline{\mathcal{W}}_n^{\mathsf{mem}} = 2n + 1$. Asymptotically, we have

$$\overline{\mathcal{W}}_n^{\mathsf{mem}} \sim \overline{\mathcal{W}}_n^{\mathsf{mem}_0} \sim 2 \cdot \overline{\mathcal{W}}_n^{\mathsf{mem}_1}.$$

In the case of Andersson's search, there is no difference between the cost, in terms of function calls, of a successful search and an unsuccessful one, so, for $n > 0$, we have

$$\mathcal{A}_n^{\mathsf{mem}_3} = 1 + \mathcal{A}_n^{\mathsf{mem}_2} \quad \text{and} \quad \mathcal{A}_n^{\mathsf{mem}_2} = \mathcal{A}_{n(-)}^{\mathsf{mem}}. \tag{8.3}$$

Choosing between $\mathsf{mem}_0/2$ and $\mathsf{mem}_1/2$ depends on the compiler or interpreter of the programming language chosen for the implementation. If a 2-way comparison is slower than an indirection (following a pointer, or, at the assembly level, jumping unconditionally), it is probably best to opt for Andersson's variant. But the final judgement requires a benchmark.

As a last note, we may simplify Andersson's program by getting rid of the initial emptiness test in $\mathsf{mem}_1/2$. What we need to do is simply have a candidate be the subtree whose root is the candidate in the original program. See FIGURE 8.7 on the following page, where the maximum costs are $\overline{\mathcal{W}}_n^{\mathsf{mem}_3} = \overline{\mathcal{W}}_n^{\mathsf{mem}_1} = n + 1$. This version may be preferred only if the programming language used for the implementation features $aliases$ in patterns or, equivalently, if the compiler can detect that the term $\mathsf{bst}(x, t_1, t_2)$ can be shared instead of being duplicated in the second

$$\mathsf{mem}_3(y, t) \rightarrow \mathsf{mem}_4(y, t, t).$$

$$\mathsf{mem}_4(y, \mathsf{bst}(x, t_1, t_2), t) \rightarrow \mathsf{mem}_4(y, t_1, t), \text{ if } x \succ y;$$
$$\mathsf{mem}_4(y, \mathsf{bst}(x, t_1, t_2), t) \rightarrow \mathsf{mem}_4(y, t_2, \mathsf{bst}(x, t_1, t_2));$$
$$\mathsf{mem}_4(y, \mathsf{ext}(), \mathsf{bst}(y, t_1, t_2)) \rightarrow \mathsf{true}();$$
$$\mathsf{mem}_4(y, \mathsf{ext}(), t) \rightarrow \mathsf{false}().$$

Figure 8.7: Andersson's search (tree candidate)

rule of $\mathsf{mem}_4/3$ (here, we assume that sharing is implicit and maximum within a rule). For additional information on Andersson's variant, read Spuler (1992).

8.2 Insertion

Leaf insertion   Since all unsuccessful searches end at an external node, it is extremely tempting to start the insertion of a unique key by a (failing) search and then grow a leaf with the new key at the external node we reached. FIGURE 8.8 displays the program for $\mathsf{insl}/2$ (*insert a leaf*). Note that it allows duplicates in the binary search tree, which hinders the cost analysis (Burge, 1976, Archibald and Clément, 2006, Pasanen, 2010). FIGURE 8.9 shows a variant which maintains the unicity of the keys, based on the definition of $\mathsf{mem}_0/2$ in FIGURE 8.5 on page 260. Alternatively, we can reuse Andersson's lookup, as shown in FIGURE 8.10 on the facing page.

$$\mathsf{insl}(y, \mathsf{bst}(x, t_1, t_2)) \xrightarrow{\tau} \mathsf{bst}(x, \mathsf{insl}(y, t_1), t_2), \text{ if } x \succ y;$$
$$\mathsf{insl}(y, \mathsf{bst}(x, t_1, t_2)) \xrightarrow{\upsilon} \mathsf{bst}(x, t_1, \mathsf{insl}(y, t_2));$$
$$\mathsf{insl}(y, \mathsf{ext}()) \xrightarrow{\phi} \mathsf{bst}(y, \mathsf{ext}(), \mathsf{ext}()).$$

Figure 8.8: Leaf insertion with possible duplicates

$$\mathsf{insl}_0(y, \mathsf{bst}(x, t_1, t_2)) \rightarrow \mathsf{bst}(x, \mathsf{insl}_0(y, t_1), t_2), \text{ if } x \succ y;$$
$$\mathsf{insl}_0(y, \mathsf{bst}(x, t_1, t_2)) \rightarrow \mathsf{bst}(x, t_1, \mathsf{insl}_0(y, t_2)), \text{ if } y \succ x;$$
$$\mathsf{insl}_0(y, \mathsf{ext}()) \rightarrow \mathsf{bst}(y, \mathsf{ext}(), \mathsf{ext}());$$
$$\mathsf{insl}_0(y, t) \rightarrow t.$$

Figure 8.9: Leaf insertion without duplicates

$$\mathsf{insl}_1(y, t) \to \mathsf{insl}_2(y, t, t).$$

$$\mathsf{insl}_2(y, \mathsf{bst}(x, t_1, t_2), t) \to \mathsf{bst}(x, \mathsf{insl}_2(y, t_1, t), t_2), \text{ if } x \succ y;$$
$$\mathsf{insl}_2(y, \mathsf{bst}(x, t_1, t_2), t) \to \mathsf{bst}(x, t_1, \mathsf{insl}_2(y, t_2, \mathsf{bst}(x, t_1, t_2)));$$
$$\mathsf{insl}_2(y, \mathsf{ext}(), \mathsf{bst}(y, t_1, t_2)) \to \mathsf{ext}();$$
$$\mathsf{insl}_2(y, \mathsf{ext}(), t) \to \mathsf{bst}(y, \mathsf{ext}(), \mathsf{ext}()).$$

Figure 8.10: Andersson's insertion

Average cost In order to carry out the average case analysis of leaf insertion, we must assume that all inserted keys are distinct; equivalently, we consider all the search trees resulting from the insertion into originally empty trees of all the keys of each permutation of $(1, 2, \ldots, n)$. Because the number of permutations is greater than the number of binary trees of same size, to wit, $n! > C_n$ if $n > 2$ (see equation (6.1) on page 198), we expect some tree shapes to correspond to many permutations. As we will see in the section about the average height, degenerate and wildly unbalanced trees are rare in average (Fill, 1996), making binary search trees a good random data structure as long as only leaf insertions are performed. Because we assume the unicity of the inserted keys, we shall only consider insl/2 in the following. (Andersson's insertion is only worth using if duplicate keys are possible inputs that must be detected, leaving the search tree invariant.)

Let us define a function mkl/1 (*make leaves*) in FIGURE 8.11 which builds a binary search tree by inserting as leaves all the keys in a given stack. Note that we could also define a function mklR/1 (*make leaves in reverse order*) such that $\mathsf{mklR}(s) \equiv \mathsf{mkl}(\mathsf{rev}(s))$ in a compact manner:

$$\mathsf{mklR}([]) \to \mathsf{ext}(); \quad \mathsf{mklR}([x \,|\, s]) \to \mathsf{insl}(x, \mathsf{mklR}(s)). \tag{8.4}$$

The cost of $\mathsf{insl}(x, t)$ depends on x and the shape of t, but, because all shapes are obtained by $\mathsf{mkl}(s) \twoheadrightarrow t$ for a given length of s, and all external nodes of t are equally likely to grow a leaf containing x, the average cost

$$\mathsf{mkl}(s) \xrightarrow{\xi} \mathsf{mkl}(s, \mathsf{ext}()). \qquad \mathsf{mkl}([], t) \xrightarrow{\psi} t;$$
$$\mathsf{mkl}([x \,|\, s], t) \xrightarrow{\omega} \mathsf{mkl}(s, \mathsf{insl}(x, t)).$$

Figure 8.11: Making a binary search tree with leaf insertions

$\mathcal{A}_k^{\mathsf{insl}}$ of $\mathsf{insl}(x, t)$ only depends on the size k of the trees:

$$\mathcal{A}_n^{\mathsf{mkl}} = 2 + \sum_{k=0}^{n-1} \mathcal{A}_k^{\mathsf{insl}}. \tag{8.5}$$

One salient feature of leaf insertion is that internal nodes do not move, hence the internal path length of the nodes is invariant and the cost of searching all keys in a tree of size n is the cost of inserting them in the first place. We already noticed that the former cost is, in average, $n + \mathbb{E}[I_n]$; the latter cost is $\sum_{k=0}^{n-1} \mathcal{A}_k^{\mathsf{insl}}$. From equation (8.5) then comes

$$n + \mathbb{E}[I_n] = \mathcal{A}_n^{\mathsf{mkl}} - 2 \tag{8.6}$$

(The subtraction of 2 is to account for rules ξ and ψ, which perform no insertion.) The cost of a leaf insertion is that of an unsuccessful search:

$$\mathcal{A}_k^{\mathsf{insl}} = \mathcal{A}_{k(-)}^{\mathsf{mem}}. \tag{8.7}$$

Recalling equation (8.1) on page 259, equations (8.5), (8.6) and (8.7):

$$\mathcal{A}_{n(+)}^{\mathsf{mem}} = 1 + \frac{1}{n}\mathbb{E}[I_n] = \frac{1}{n}(\mathcal{A}_n^{\mathsf{mkl}} - 2) = \frac{1}{n}\sum_{k=0}^{n-1}\mathcal{A}_k^{\mathsf{insl}} = \frac{1}{n}\sum_{k=0}^{n-1}\mathcal{A}_{k(-)}^{\mathsf{mem}}.$$

Finally, using equation (8.2) on page 259, we deduce

$$\frac{1}{n}\sum_{k=0}^{n-1}\mathcal{A}_{k(-)}^{\mathsf{mem}} = \left(1 + \frac{1}{n}\right)\mathcal{A}_{n(-)}^{\mathsf{mem}} - \frac{1}{n} - 2.$$

Equivalently,

$$2n + 1 + \sum_{k=0}^{n-1}\mathcal{A}_{k(-)}^{\mathsf{mem}} = (n+1)\mathcal{A}_{n(-)}^{\mathsf{mem}}.$$

This recurrence is easy to solve if we subtract its instance when $n - 1$:

$$2 + \mathcal{A}_{n-1(-)}^{\mathsf{mem}} = (n+1)\mathcal{A}_{n(-)}^{\mathsf{mem}} - n\mathcal{A}_{n-1(-)}^{\mathsf{mem}}.$$

Noting that $\mathcal{A}_{0(-)}^{\mathsf{mem}} = 1$, the equation becomes

$$\mathcal{A}_{0(-)}^{\mathsf{mem}} = 1, \quad \mathcal{A}_{n(-)}^{\mathsf{mem}} = \mathcal{A}_{n-1(-)}^{\mathsf{mem}} + \frac{2}{n+1},$$

thus

$$\mathcal{A}_{n(-)}^{\mathsf{mem}} = 1 + 2\sum_{k=2}^{n+1}\frac{1}{k} = 2H_{n+1} - 1, \tag{8.8}$$

where $H_n := \sum_{k=1}^{n} 1/k$ is the nth harmonic number. Replacing $\mathcal{A}_{n(-)}^{\text{mem}}$ back into equation (8.2) and using $H_{n+1} = H_n + 1/(n+1)$ yields

$$\mathcal{A}_{n(+)}^{\text{mem}} = 2\left(1 + \frac{1}{n}\right) H_n - 3. \tag{8.9}$$

From inequations (3.12) on page 117 and equations (8.8) and (8.9):

$$\mathcal{A}_n^{\text{insl}} \sim \mathcal{A}_{n(-)}^{\text{mem}} \sim \mathcal{A}_{n(+)}^{\text{mem}} \sim 2\ln n.$$

We obtain more information about the relative asymptotic behaviours of $\mathcal{A}_{n(-)}^{\text{mem}}$ and $\mathcal{A}_{n(+)}^{\text{mem}}$ by looking at their difference instead of their ratio:

$$\mathcal{A}_{n(-)}^{\text{mem}} - \mathcal{A}_{n(+)}^{\text{mem}} = \frac{2}{n}(n + 1 - H_{n+1}) \sim 2 \quad \text{and} \quad 1 \leqslant \mathcal{A}_{n(-)}^{\text{mem}} - \mathcal{A}_{n(+)}^{\text{mem}} < 2.$$

The average difference between an unsuccessful search and a successful one tends slowly to 2 for large values of n, which may not be intuitive. We can use this result to compare the average difference of the costs of a successful search with mem/2 and mem3/2 (Andersson). Recalling equation (8.3) on page 261, we draw $1 + \mathcal{A}_{n(-)}^{\text{mem}} = \mathcal{A}_{n(+)}^{\text{mem3}}$. The previous result now yields

$$\mathcal{A}_{n(+)}^{\text{mem3}} - \mathcal{A}_{n(+)}^{\text{mem}} \sim 3.$$

Therefore, the extra cost of Andersson's variant in case of a successful search is asymptotically 3, in average.

Furthermore, replacing $\mathcal{A}_{n(-)}^{\text{mem}}$ and $\mathcal{A}_{n(+)}^{\text{mem}}$ into equations (8.1) leads to

$$\mathbb{E}[I_n] = 2(n + 1)H_n - 4n \quad \text{and} \quad \mathbb{E}[E_n] = 2(n + 1)H_n - 2n. \tag{8.10}$$

Thus $\mathbb{E}[I_n] \sim \mathbb{E}[E_n] \sim 2n\ln n$. Note how easier it is to find $\mathbb{E}[I_n]$ for binary search trees, compared to simple binary trees.

If we are interested in slightly more theoretical results, we may like to know the average number of comparisons involved in a search and an insertion. A glance back at FIGURE 8.4 on page 258 uncovers that two 2-way comparisons are done when going down and one 2-way comparison (equality) is checked when finding the key, otherwise none:

$$\overline{\mathcal{A}}_{n(+)}^{\text{mem}} = 1 + \frac{2}{n}\mathbb{E}[I_n] \quad \text{and} \quad \overline{\mathcal{A}}_{n(-)}^{\text{mem}} = \frac{2}{n+1}\mathbb{E}[E_n]. \tag{8.11}$$

Reusing equations (8.10), we conclude that

$$\overline{\mathcal{A}}_{n(+)}^{\text{mem}} = 4\left(1 + \frac{1}{n}\right) H_n - 7 \quad \text{and} \quad \overline{\mathcal{A}}_{n(-)}^{\text{mem}} = 4H_n + \frac{4}{n+1} - 4. \tag{8.12}$$

Clearly, we have $\overline{\mathcal{A}}_{n(+)}^{\mathsf{mem}} \sim \overline{\mathcal{A}}_{n(-)}^{\mathsf{mem}} \sim 4\ln n$. Furthermore,

$$\overline{\mathcal{A}}_{n(-)}^{\mathsf{mem}} - \overline{\mathcal{A}}_{n(+)}^{\mathsf{mem}} = \frac{4}{n+1} - \frac{4}{n}H_n + 3 \sim 3 \quad\text{and}\quad 1 \leqslant \overline{\mathcal{A}}_{n(-)}^{\mathsf{mem}} - \overline{\mathcal{A}}_{n(+)}^{\mathsf{mem}} < 3.$$

The average costs for Andersson's search and insertions are easy to deduce as well, from equation (8.3) on page 261 and (8.8) on page 264: $\mathcal{A}_n^{\mathsf{mem3}} = 2H_{n+1} \sim 2\ln n$. A glimpse back at FIGURE 8.7 on page 262 brings to the fore that one 2-way comparison $(x \succ y)$ is performed when descending in the tree and one more when stopping at an external node, whether the search is successful or not:

$$\overline{\mathcal{A}}_n^{\mathsf{mem3}} = \frac{1}{n+1}\mathbb{E}[E_n] = 2H_n + \frac{2}{n+1} - 2 \sim 2\ln n.$$

We can now finally compare the average number of comparisons between mem/2 and mem$_3$/2 (Andersson):

$$\overline{\mathcal{A}}_{n(+)}^{\mathsf{mem}} - \overline{\mathcal{A}}_n^{\mathsf{mem3}} = 2\left(1 + \frac{2}{n}\right)H_n - \frac{2}{n+1} - 5 \sim 2\ln n,$$

$$\overline{\mathcal{A}}_{n(-)}^{\mathsf{mem}} - \overline{\mathcal{A}}_n^{\mathsf{mem3}} = 2H_n + \frac{2}{n+1} - 2 \sim 2\ln n.$$

As far as leaf insertion itself is concerned, insl/2 behaves as mem$_3$/2, except that no comparison occurs at the external nodes. Also, from equations (8.7) and (8.8), we finish the average case analysis of insl/2:

$$\overline{\mathcal{A}}_n^{\mathsf{insl}} = \overline{\mathcal{A}}_n^{\mathsf{mem3}} - 1 = 2H_n + \frac{2}{n+1} - 3 \quad\text{and}\quad \mathcal{A}_n^{\mathsf{insl}} = 2H_{n+1} - 1.$$

Finally, from equation (8.6) and (8.10), we deduce

$$\mathcal{A}_n^{\mathsf{mkl}} = n + \mathbb{E}[I_n] + 2 = 2(n+1)H_n - n + 2 \sim 2n\ln n. \qquad (8.13)$$

Amortised cost   The worst case for leaf insertion occurs when the search tree is degenerate and the key to be inserted becomes the deepest leaf. If the tree has size n, then $n+1$ calls are performed, as seen in FIGURE 8.8 on page 262, so $\mathcal{W}_n^{\mathsf{insl}} = n+1$ and $\overline{\mathcal{W}}_n^{\mathsf{insl}} = n$. In the case of Andersson's insertion in FIGURE 8.10 on page 263, the worst case is identical but there is a supplementary call to set the candidate key, so $\mathcal{W}_n^{\mathsf{insl_1}} = n+2$. Moreover, the number of comparisons is symmetric and equals 1 per internal node, so $\overline{\mathcal{W}}_n^{\mathsf{insl_1}} = n$ and any degenerate tree is the worst configuration.

The best case for leaf insertion with insl/2 and insl$_1$/2 happens when the key has to be inserted as the left or right child of the root, to wit, the root is the minimum or maximum key in inorder, so $\mathcal{B}_n^{\mathsf{insl}} = 2$ and $\mathcal{B}_n^{\mathsf{insl}_1} = 3$. As far as comparisons are concerned: $\overline{\mathcal{B}}_n^{\mathsf{insl}} = 1$ and $\overline{\mathcal{B}}_n^{\mathsf{insl}_1} = 2$.

While turning our attention to the extremal costs of mkl/1 and mkr/1, we need to realise that we cannot simply sum minimum or maximum costs of insl/2 because, as mentioned earlier, the call $\mathsf{insl}(x, t)$ depends on x and the shape of t. For instance, after three keys have been inserted into an empty tree, the root has no more empty children, so the best case we determined previously is not pertinent anymore.

Let $\overline{\mathcal{B}}_n^{\mathsf{mkl}}$ be the minimum number of comparisons needed to construct a binary search tree of size n using leaf insertions. If we want to minimise the cost at each insertion, then the path length for each new node must be as small as possible and this is achieved if the tree continuously grows as a perfect or almost perfect tree. The former is a tree whose external nodes all belong to the same level, a configuration we have seen on page 238 (the tree fits tightly inside an isosceles triangle); the latter is a tree whose external nodes lie on two consecutive levels and we have seen this kind of tree in the paragraph devoted to comparison trees and the minimean of sorting on page 92.

Let us assume first that the tree is perfect, with size n and height h. The height is the length, counted in number of edges, of the longest path from the root to an external node. The total path length for a level k made only of internal nodes is $k2^k$. Therefore, summing all levels yields

$$\overline{\mathcal{B}}_n^{\mathsf{mkl}} = \sum_{k=1}^{h-1} k2^k = (h-2)2^h + 2, \qquad (8.14)$$

by reusing equation (4.52) on page 148. Moreover, summing the number of internal nodes by levels: $n = \sum_{k=0}^{h-1} 2^k = 2^h - 1$, hence $h = \lg(n+1)$, which we can replace in equation (8.14) to obtain

$$\overline{\mathcal{B}}_n^{\mathsf{mkl}} = (n+1)\lg(n+1) - 2n.$$

We proved $1 + \lfloor \lg n \rfloor = \lceil \lg(n+1) \rceil$ when establishing the maximum number of comparisons of top-down merge sort in equation (4.37) on page 139, so we can proceed conclusively:

$$\overline{\mathcal{B}}_n^{\mathsf{mkl}} = (n+1)\lfloor \lg n \rfloor - n + 1. \qquad (8.15)$$

Let us assume now that the tree is almost perfect, with the penultimate level $h-1$ containing $q \neq 0$ internal nodes, so

$$\overline{\mathcal{B}}_n^{\mathsf{mkl}} = \sum_{k=1}^{h-2} k2^k + (h-1)q = (h-3)2^{h-1} + 2 + (h-1)q. \qquad (8.16)$$

Moreover, the total number n of internal nodes, when summed level by level, satisfies $n = \sum_{k=0}^{h-2} 2^k + q = 2^{h-1} - 1 + q$, hence $q = n - 2^{h-1} + 1$. By definition, we have $0 < q \leqslant 2^{h-1}$, hence $0 < n - 2^{h-1} + 1 \leqslant 2^{h-1}$, which yields $h - 1 < \lg(n+1) \leqslant h$, then $h = \lceil \lg(n+1) \rceil = \lfloor \lg n \rfloor + 1$, whence $q = n - 2^{\lfloor \lg n \rfloor} + 1$. We can now substitute h and q by their newly found values in terms of n back into equation (8.16):

$$\overline{B}_n^{\mathsf{mkl}} = (n+1)\lfloor \lg n \rfloor - 2^{\lfloor \lg n \rfloor} + 2. \tag{8.17}$$

Comparing equations (8.15) and (8.17), we see that the number of comparisons is minimised when the tree is perfect, so $n = 2^p - 1$. The asymptotic approximation of $\overline{B}_n^{\mathsf{mkl}}$ is not difficult to find, as long as we avoid the pitfall $2^{\lfloor \lg n \rfloor} \sim n$. Indeed, consider the function $x(p) := 2^p - 1$ ranging over the positive integers. First, let us notice that, for all $p > 0$,

$$2^{p-1} \leqslant 2^p - 1 < 2^p \Rightarrow p - 1 \leqslant \lg(2^p - 1) < p \Rightarrow \lfloor \lg(2^p - 1) \rfloor = p - 1.$$

Therefore, $2^{\lfloor \lg(x(p)) \rfloor} = 2^{p-1} = (x(p)+1)/2 \sim x(p)/2 \nsim x(p)$, which proves that $2^{\lfloor \lg(n) \rfloor} \nsim n$ when $n = 2^p - 1 \to \infty$. Instead, in the case of equation (8.15), let us use the standard inequalities $x - 1 < \lfloor x \rfloor \leqslant x$:

$$(n+1)\lg n - 2n < \overline{B}_n^{\mathsf{mkl}} \leqslant (n+1)\lg n - n + 1.$$

In the case of equation (8.17), let us use the definition of the fractional part $\{x\} := x - \lfloor x \rfloor$. Obviously, $0 \leqslant \{x\} < 1$. Then

$$\overline{B}_n^{\mathsf{mkl}} = (n+1)\lg n - n \cdot \theta(\{\lg n\}) + 2 - \{\lg n\},$$

where $\theta(x) := 1 + 2^{-x}$. Let us minimise and maximise the linear term: we have $\min_{0 \leqslant x < 1} \theta(x) = \theta(1) = 3/2$ and $\max_{0 \leqslant x < 1} \theta(x) = \theta(0) = 2$. Keeping in mind that $x = \{\lg n\}$, we have

$$(n+1)\lg n - 2n + 2 < \overline{B}_n^{\mathsf{mkl}} < (n+1)\lg n - \frac{3}{2}n + 1.$$

In any case, it is now clearly established that $\overline{B}_n^{\mathsf{mkl}} \sim n \lg n$.

Let $\overline{W}_n^{\mathsf{mkl}}$ be the maximum number of comparisons to build a binary search tree of size n by leaf insertions. If we maximise each insertion, we need to grow a degenerate tree and insert at one external node of maximal path length:

$$\overline{W}_n^{\mathsf{mkl}} = \sum_{k=1}^{n-1} k = \frac{n(n-1)}{2} \sim \frac{1}{2}n^2.$$

$$\text{rotr}(\text{bst}(y, \text{bst}(x, t_1, t_2), t_3)) \overset{\epsilon}{\to} \text{bst}(x, t_1, \text{bst}(y, t_2, t_3)).$$
$$\text{rotl}(\text{bst}(x, t_1, \text{bst}(y, t_2, t_3))) \overset{\zeta}{\to} \text{bst}(y, \text{bst}(x, t_1, t_2), t_3).$$

Figure 8.12: Right (ϵ) and left (ζ) rotations

Root insertion If recently inserted keys are looked up, the cost is relatively high because these keys are leaves or close to a leaf. In this scenario, instead of inserting a key as a leaf, it is better to insert it as a root (Stephenson, 1980). The idea is to perform a leaf insertion and, on the way back to the root (that is to say, after the recursive calls are evaluated, one after the other), we perform rotations to bring the inserted node up to the root. More precisely, if the node was inserted in a left subtree, then a right rotation brings it one level up, otherwise a left rotation has the same effect. The composition of these rotations brings the leaf to the root. Right rotation, rotr/1 (*rotate right*) and left rotation, rotl/1 (*rotate left*), were discussed in section 7.1 on page 224 and are defined in FIGURE 8.12. Obviously, they commute and are inverses of each other:

$$\text{rotl}(\text{rotr}(t)) \equiv \text{rotr}(\text{rotl}(t)) \equiv t.$$

Moreover, and less trivially, they preserve inorder traversals:

$$\text{in}_3(\text{rotl}(t)) \equiv \text{in}_3(\text{rotr}(t)) \equiv \text{in}_3(t),$$

where $\text{in}_3/1$ computes the inorder traversal of a tree: $\text{in}_3(t) \to \text{in}_2(t, [\,])$, with $\text{in}_2/2$ being defined in FIGURE 8.2 on page 256. This theorem is inherently connected to $\text{Rot}(x, y, t_1, t_2, t_3)$, on page 224, and it is easy to prove, without recourse to induction. First, we could remark that if $\text{in}_3(t) \equiv \text{in}_3(\text{rotl}(t))$, then, replacing t by $\text{rotr}(t)$ yields the equivalence

$$\text{in}_3(\text{rotr}(t)) \equiv \text{in}_3(\text{rotl}(\text{rotr}(t))) \equiv \text{in}_3(t),$$

so we only need to prove $\text{in}_3(\text{rotl}(t)) \equiv \text{in}_3(t)$. Since the left-hand side is larger, we should try to rewrite it into the right-hand side. Because a left rotation requires the tree to have the shape $t = \text{bst}(x, t_1, \text{bst}(y, t_2, t_3))$, we have the rewrites of FIGURE 8.13 on the following page. If we rotate subtrees, as we did, for example, in FIGURE 7.23 on page 224, the same theorem implies that the inorder traversal of the whole tree is invariant.

A corollary is that rotations keep invariant the property of being a binary search tree (FIGURE 8.3 on page 256):

$$\text{bst}(\text{rotl}(t)) \equiv \text{bst}(\text{rotr}(t)) \equiv \text{bst}(t).$$

$$
\begin{aligned}
\underline{\mathsf{in}_3}(\mathsf{rotl}(t)) &\to \mathsf{in}_2(\mathsf{rotl}(t), [\,]) \\
&= \mathsf{in}_2(\underline{\mathsf{rotl}}(\mathsf{bst}(x, t_1, \mathsf{bst}(y, t_2, t_3))), [\,]) \\
&\overset{\epsilon}{\to} \underline{\mathsf{in}_2}(\mathsf{bst}(y, \mathsf{bst}(x, t_1, t_2), t_3), [\,]) \\
&\to \mathsf{in}_2(\mathsf{bst}(x, t_1, t_2), [y \,|\, \mathsf{in}_2(t_3, [\,])]) \\
&\equiv \mathsf{in}_2(t_1, [x \,|\, \mathsf{in}_2(t_2, [y \,|\, \mathsf{in}_2(t_3, [\,])])]) \\
&\leftarrow \mathsf{in}_2(t_1, [x \,|\, \underline{\mathsf{in}_2}(\mathsf{bst}(y, t_2, t_3), [\,])]) \\
&\leftarrow \underline{\mathsf{in}_2}(\mathsf{bst}(x, t_1, \mathsf{bst}(y, t_2, t_3)), [\,]) \\
&= \mathsf{in}_2(t, [\,]) \\
&\leftarrow \mathsf{in}_3(t). \qquad\qquad \square
\end{aligned}
$$

Figure 8.13: Proof of $\mathsf{in}_3(\mathsf{rotl}(t)) \equiv \mathsf{in}_3(t)$

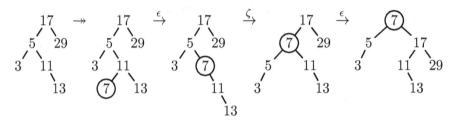

Figure 8.14: Root insertion of 7 into FIGURE 8.1 on page 255

Indeed, assuming that $\mathsf{bst}/1$ is the specification of $\mathsf{bst}_0/1$ in FIGURE 8.2 on page 256, and that the latter is correct, that is, $\mathsf{bst}(t) \equiv \mathsf{bst}_0(t)$, it is quite easy to prove our theorem, with the help of the previous theorem $\mathsf{in}_3(\mathsf{rotl}(t)) \equiv \mathsf{in}_3(t)$, which is equivalent to $\mathsf{in}_2(\mathsf{rotl}(t), [\,]) \equiv \mathsf{in}_2(t, [\,])$, and noticing that it is sufficient to prove $\mathsf{bst}_0(\mathsf{rotl}(t)) \equiv \mathsf{bst}_0(t)$. We conclude:

$$
\mathsf{bst}_0(\mathsf{rotl}(t)) \equiv \mathsf{ord}(\mathsf{in}_2(\mathsf{rotl}(t), [\,])) \equiv \mathsf{ord}(\mathsf{in}_2(t, [\,])) \leftarrow \mathsf{bst}_0(t).
$$

Let us consider now an example of root insertion in FIGURE 8.14, where the tree of FIGURE 8.1 on page 255 is augmented with 7. Remark that the transitive closure $(\twoheadrightarrow)$ captures the preliminary leaf insertion, $(\overset{\epsilon}{\to})$ is a right rotation and $(\overset{\varsigma}{\to})$ is a left rotation. It is now a simple matter to modify the definition of $\mathsf{insl}/2$ so it becomes root insertion as $\mathsf{insr}/2$, in FIGURE 8.15 on the facing page. Note that we can avoid creating the temporary internal nodes $\mathsf{bst}(x, \ldots, t_2)$ and $\mathsf{bst}(x, t_1, \ldots)$ by modifying $\mathsf{rotl}/1$ and $\mathsf{rotr}/1$ so that they take three arguments ($\mathsf{rotl}_0/3$ and $\mathsf{rotr}_0/3$), as shown along the new version $\mathsf{insr}_0/2$ in FIGURE 8.16.

Comparing leaf and root insertions A comparison between leaf and root insertions reveals interesting facts. For instance, because leaf

$$\begin{aligned}
\mathsf{insr}(y, \mathsf{bst}(x, t_1, t_2)) &\xrightarrow{\eta} \mathsf{rotr}(\mathsf{bst}(x, \mathsf{insr}(y, t_1), t_2)), \text{ if } x \succ y; \\
\mathsf{insr}(y, \mathsf{bst}(x, t_1, t_2)) &\xrightarrow{\theta} \mathsf{rotl}(\mathsf{bst}(x, t_1, \mathsf{insr}(y, t_2))); \\
\mathsf{insr}(y, \mathsf{ext}()) &\xrightarrow{\iota} \mathsf{bst}(y, \mathsf{ext}(), \mathsf{ext}()).
\end{aligned}$$

Figure 8.15: Root insertion with possible duplicates

$$\begin{aligned}
\mathsf{insr}_0(y, \mathsf{bst}(x, t_1, t_2)) &\rightarrow \mathsf{rotr}_0(x, \mathsf{insr}_0(y, t_1), t_2), \text{ if } x \succ y; \\
\mathsf{insr}_0(y, \mathsf{bst}(x, t_1, t_2)) &\rightarrow \mathsf{rotl}_0(x, t_1, \mathsf{insr}_0(y, t_2)); \\
\mathsf{insr}_0(y, \mathsf{ext}()) &\rightarrow \mathsf{bst}(y, \mathsf{ext}(), \mathsf{ext}()).
\end{aligned}$$

$$\begin{aligned}
\mathsf{rotr}_0(y, \mathsf{bst}(x, t_1, t_2), t_3) &\rightarrow \mathsf{bst}(x, t_1, \mathsf{bst}(y, t_2, t_3)). \\
\mathsf{rotl}_0(x, t_1, \mathsf{bst}(y, t_2, t_3)) &\rightarrow \mathsf{bst}(y, \mathsf{bst}(x, t_1, t_2), t_3).
\end{aligned}$$

Figure 8.16: Root insertion with possible duplicates (bis)

insertion does not displace any node, making the same tree from two permutations of the keys bears the same cost, for example, $(1, 3, 2, 4)$ and $(1, 3, 4, 2)$. On the other hand, as noted by Geldenhuys and der Merwe (2009), making the same search tree using different root insertions may yield different costs, like $(1, 2, 4, 3)$ and $(1, 4, 2, 3)$. They also prove that all the trees of a given size can either be created by leaf or root insertions because we have

$$\mathsf{RootLeaf}(s)\colon \mathsf{mkr}(s) \equiv \mathsf{mkl}(\mathsf{rev}(s)), \tag{8.18}$$

where $\mathsf{mkr}/1$ (*make roots*) is easily defined in FIGURE 8.17. Notice that this is equivalent to claim that $\mathsf{mkr}(s) \equiv \mathsf{mklR}(s)$, where $\mathsf{mklR}/1$ is defined in equation (8.4) on page 263. It is worth proving $\mathsf{RootLeaf}(s)$ here because, contrary to Geldenhuys and der Merwe (2009), we want to use structural induction to exactly follow the syntax of the function definitions, instead of induction on sizes, an adventitious concept, and we want to avoid using ellipses when describing the data. Furthermore, our logical framework is not separated from our actual function definitions (the abstract program): the rewrites themselves, that is, the computa-

$$\mathsf{mkr}(s) \xrightarrow{\kappa} \mathsf{mkr}(s, \mathsf{ext}()). \qquad \mathsf{mkr}([], t) \xrightarrow{\lambda} t; \\
\mathsf{mkr}([x \,|\, s], t) \xrightarrow{\mu} \mathsf{mkr}(s, \mathsf{insr}(x, t)).$$

Figure 8.17: Making a binary search tree with root insertions

tional steps, give birth to a logical interpretation as classes of equivalent terms.

We start by remarking that $\mathsf{RootLeaf}(s)$ is equivalent to

$$\mathsf{RootLeaf}_0(s)\colon \mathsf{mkr}(s) \equiv \mathsf{mkl}(\mathsf{rev}_0(s)),$$

where $\mathsf{rev}_0/1$ is defined at the start of section 2.2 on page 38, where we prove $\mathsf{EqRev}(s)\colon \mathsf{rev}_0(s) \equiv \mathsf{rev}(s)$. It is often a good idea to use $\mathsf{rev}_0/1$ in inductive proofs because of rule δ defining $\mathsf{rev}_0([x \mid s])$ directly in terms of $\mathsf{rev}_0(s)$. Let us recall the relevant definitions:

$$\mathsf{cat}([], t) \xrightarrow{\alpha} t; \qquad\qquad \mathsf{rev}_0([]) \xrightarrow{\gamma} [];$$
$$\mathsf{cat}([x \mid s], t) \xrightarrow{\beta} [x \mid \mathsf{cat}(s, t)]. \quad \mathsf{rev}_0([x \mid s]) \xrightarrow{\delta} \mathsf{cat}(\mathsf{rev}_0(s), [x]).$$

Of course, $\mathsf{rev}_0/1$ is worthless as a program because of its quadratic cost, which cannot compete with the linear cost of $\mathsf{rev}/1$, but, as far as theorem proving is concerned, it is a valuable specification and lemma $\mathsf{EqRev}(s)$ allows us to transfer any equivalence depending upon $\mathsf{rev}_0/1$ into an equivalence employing $\mathsf{rev}/1$.

Let us proceed by induction on the structure of the stack s. First, we need to prove directly (without induction) $\mathsf{RootLeaf}_0([])$. We have

$$\mathsf{mkr}([]) \xrightarrow{\kappa} \mathsf{mkr}([], \mathsf{ext}()) \xrightarrow{\lambda} \mathsf{ext}() \xleftarrow{\psi} \mathsf{mkl}([], \mathsf{ext}()) \xleftarrow{\xi} \mathsf{mkl}([]) \xleftarrow{\gamma} \mathsf{mkl}(\underline{\mathsf{rev}_0}([])).$$

Second, we set the inductive hypothesis to be $\mathsf{RootLeaf}_0(s)$ and we proceed to prove $\mathsf{RootLeaf}_0([x \mid s])$, for any x. Since the right-hand side is larger, we start rewriting it and whenever we feel astray, we rewrite the other side, aiming at their convergence. On the way, there will be steps, in the form of equivalences, which constitute lemmas (subgoals) that will need demonstration later.

$$
\begin{aligned}
\mathsf{mkl}(\underline{\mathsf{rev}_0}([x \mid s])) \xrightarrow{\delta}\ & \mathsf{mkl}(\mathsf{cat}(\mathsf{rev}_0(s), [x])) \\
\equiv\ & \mathsf{mkl}(\mathsf{cat}(\mathsf{rev}_0(s), [x]), \mathsf{ext}()) \\
\equiv_0\ & \mathsf{mkl}([x], \mathsf{mkl}(\mathsf{rev}_0(s), \mathsf{ext}())) && \text{Lemma} \\
\equiv\ & \mathsf{mkl}([], \mathsf{insl}(x, \mathsf{mkl}(\mathsf{rev}_0(s), \mathsf{ext}()))) \\
\equiv\ & \mathsf{insl}(x, \mathsf{mkl}(\mathsf{rev}_0(s), \mathsf{ext}())) \\
\equiv\ & \mathsf{insl}(x, \mathsf{mkl}(\mathsf{rev}_0(s))) \\
\equiv\ & \mathsf{insl}(x, \underline{\mathsf{mkr}}(s)) && \mathsf{RootLeaf}_0(s) \\
\xrightarrow{\xi}\ & \mathsf{insl}(x, \mathsf{mkr}(s, \mathsf{ext}())) \\
\equiv_1\ & \mathsf{mkr}(s, \underline{\mathsf{insl}}(x, \mathsf{ext}())) && \text{Lemma} \\
\xrightarrow{\phi}\ & \mathsf{mkr}(s, \mathsf{bst}(x, \mathsf{ext}(), \mathsf{ext}())) \\
\xleftarrow{\iota}\ & \mathsf{mkr}(s, \underline{\mathsf{insr}}(x, \mathsf{ext}())) \\
\xleftarrow{\mu}\ & \underline{\mathsf{mkr}}([x \mid s], \mathsf{ext}()) \\
\xleftarrow{\kappa}\ & \mathsf{mkr}([x \mid s]). && \square
\end{aligned}
$$

Now, we have to prove the two lemmas that we identified with our proof sketch. The first one, in the instance of ($\equiv_0$), looks like a corollary of $\mathsf{MklCat}(u, v, t)$: $\mathsf{mkl}(\mathsf{cat}(u, v), t) \equiv_0 \mathsf{mkl}(v, \mathsf{mkl}(u, t))$. The first action to be undertaken when facing a new proposition is to try to disprove it by some pertinent or tricky choice of variables. In this case, though, the truth of this lemma can be intuitively ascertained without effort, which gives us more confidence for working out a formal proof, instead of dispensing with one. It is enough to reason by induction on the structure of the stack u. First, we verify $\mathsf{MklCat}([], v, t)$:

$$\mathsf{mkl}(\underline{\mathsf{cat}([], v)}, t) \xrightarrow{\alpha} \mathsf{mkl}(v, t) \xleftarrow{\psi} \underline{\mathsf{mkl}(v, \mathsf{mkl}([], t))}.$$

Second, we assume $\mathsf{MklCat}(u, v, t)$, for all v and t, which is thus the inductive hypothesis, and we prove $\mathsf{MklCat}([x \,|\, u], v, t)$:

$$
\begin{aligned}
\mathsf{mkl}(\underline{\mathsf{cat}([x \,|\, u], v)}, t) &\xrightarrow{\beta} \mathsf{mkl}([x \,|\, \mathsf{cat}(u, v)], t) \\
&\equiv \mathsf{mkl}(\mathsf{cat}(u, v), \mathsf{insl}(x, t)) \\
&\equiv_0 \mathsf{mkl}(v, \mathsf{mkl}(u, \mathsf{insl}(x, t))) \quad \mathsf{MklCat}(u, v, \mathsf{inst}(x, t)) \\
&\xleftarrow{\omega} \mathsf{mkl}(v, \underline{\mathsf{mkl}([x \,|\, u], t)}). \qquad\qquad\qquad\qquad \square
\end{aligned}
$$

Let us formally define the second lemma whose instance we identified as ($\equiv_1$) in the proof of $\mathsf{RootLeaf}_0(s)$. Let

$$\mathsf{MkrInsr}(x, s, t): \mathsf{insl}(x, \mathsf{mkr}(s, t)) \equiv_1 \mathsf{mkr}(s, \mathsf{insl}(x, t)).$$

This proposition, despite its pleasurable symbolic symmetry, is not trivial and may require some examples to be better grasped. It means that a leaf insertion can be performed before or after a series of root insertions, yielding in both cases the same tree. We approach the proof by induction on the structure of the stack s only. (The other parameters are unlikely to be inductively relevant because x is a key, so we can assume nothing about its internal structure, if any, and t is the second parameter of both $\mathsf{mkr}/2$ and $\mathsf{insl}/2$, so we do not know anything about its shape nor contents.) We start, as usual, with a verification (A verification, by definition, does not involve the use of any inductive argument.) of the basis $\mathsf{MklInsr}(x, [], t)$:

$$\mathsf{insl}(x, \underline{\mathsf{mkr}([], t)}) \xrightarrow{\lambda} \mathsf{insl}(x, t) \equiv \mathsf{mkr}([], \mathsf{insl}(x, t)).$$

We now assume $\mathsf{MkrInsr}(x, s, t)$ for all x and t, and we try to prove $\mathsf{MkrInsr}(x, [y \,|\, s], t)$, for all keys y, by rewriting both sides of the equivalence and aiming at the same term:

$$
\begin{aligned}
\mathsf{insl}(x, \underline{\mathsf{mkr}([y \,|\, s], t)}) &\xrightarrow{\mu} \mathsf{insl}(x, \mathsf{mkr}(s, \mathsf{insr}(y, t))) \\
&\equiv_1 \mathsf{mkr}(s, \mathsf{insl}(x, \mathsf{insr}(y, t))) \quad \mathsf{MkrInsr}(x, s, \mathsf{insr}(y, t)) \\
&\equiv_2 \mathsf{mkr}(s, \mathsf{insr}(y, \mathsf{insl}(x, t))) \qquad\qquad\qquad \text{Lemma} \\
&\equiv \mathsf{mkr}([y \,|\, s], \mathsf{insl}(x, t)). \qquad\qquad\qquad\qquad\quad \square
\end{aligned}
$$

Note that we have found that we need a lemma in the guise of its instance $(\equiv_2)$, which states that a root insertion commutes with a leaf insertion. This is not obvious and probably needs to be seen on some examples to be believed. The process of inductive demonstration itself has brought us to the important concept on which our initial proposition hinges. Let the lemma in question be formally defined as follows:

$$\mathsf{Ins}(x, y, t)\colon \mathsf{insl}(x, \mathsf{insr}(y, t)) \equiv_2 \mathsf{insr}(y, \mathsf{insl}(x, t)).$$

We will use induction on the structure of the tree t, because the other variables are keys, hence are atomic. The verification of $\mathsf{Ins}(x, y, \mathsf{ext}())$, the basis, happens to be rather lengthy, compared to earlier related proofs:

$$\mathsf{insl}(x, \underline{\mathsf{insr}(y, \mathsf{ext}())}) \xrightarrow{\iota} \mathsf{insl}(x, \mathsf{bst}(y, \mathsf{ext}(), \mathsf{ext}())) \quad \otimes$$

The symbol $\otimes$ is a tag from which different rewrites are possible, depending on some condition, and we will need to resume from that mark. Here, two cases present themselves to us: either $x \succ y$ or $y \succ x$. We have

- If $x \succ y$, then

$$
\begin{aligned}
\otimes &\xrightarrow{\upsilon} \mathsf{bst}(y, \mathsf{ext}(), \underline{\mathsf{insl}(x, \mathsf{ext}())}) && x \succ y \\
&\xrightarrow{\phi} \mathsf{bst}(y, \mathsf{ext}(), \mathsf{bst}(x, \mathsf{ext}(), \mathsf{ext}())) \\
&\xleftarrow{\epsilon} \underline{\mathsf{rotr}(\mathsf{bst}(x, \mathsf{bst}(y, \mathsf{ext}(), \mathsf{ext}()), \mathsf{ext}()))} \\
&\xleftarrow{\iota} \mathsf{rotr}(\mathsf{bst}(x, \underline{\mathsf{insr}(y, \mathsf{ext}())}, \mathsf{ext}())) \\
&\xleftarrow{\eta} \underline{\mathsf{insr}(y, \mathsf{bst}(x, \mathsf{ext}(), \mathsf{ext}()))} && x \succ y \\
&\xleftarrow{\phi} \mathsf{insr}(y, \underline{\mathsf{insl}(x, \mathsf{ext}())}).
\end{aligned}
$$

- If $y \succ x$, then

$$
\begin{aligned}
\otimes &\xrightarrow{\tau} \mathsf{bst}(y, \underline{\mathsf{insl}(x, \mathsf{ext}())}, \mathsf{ext}()) && y \succ x \\
&\xrightarrow{\phi} \mathsf{bst}(y, \mathsf{bst}(x, \mathsf{ext}(), \mathsf{ext}()), \mathsf{ext}()) \\
&\xleftarrow{\xi} \underline{\mathsf{rotl}(\mathsf{bst}(x, \mathsf{ext}(), \mathsf{bst}(y, \mathsf{ext}(), \mathsf{ext}())))} \\
&\xleftarrow{\iota} \mathsf{rotl}(\mathsf{bst}(x, \mathsf{ext}(), \underline{\mathsf{insr}(y, \mathsf{ext}())})) \\
&\xleftarrow{\theta} \underline{\mathsf{insr}(y, \mathsf{bst}(x, \mathsf{ext}(), \mathsf{ext}()))} && y \succ x \\
&\xleftarrow{\phi} \mathsf{insr}(y, \underline{\mathsf{insl}(x, \mathsf{ext}())}).
\end{aligned}
$$

Now, let us assume $\mathsf{Ins}(x, y, t_1)$ and $\mathsf{Ins}(x, y, t_2)$ and proceed to prove $\mathsf{Ins}(x, y, t)$, with $t = \mathsf{bst}(a, t_1, t_2)$, for all keys a. We start arbitrarily with the right-hand side as follows:

$$\mathsf{insr}(y, \mathsf{insl}(x, t)) = \mathsf{insr}(y, \mathsf{insl}(x, \mathsf{bst}(a, t_1, t_2))) \quad \otimes$$

Two cases arise: either $a \succ x$ or $x \succ a$.

- If $a \succ x$, then $\otimes \overset{\tau}{\rightarrow} \mathsf{insr}(y, \mathsf{bst}(a, \mathsf{insl}(x, t_1), t_2)) \otimes$. Two subcases manifest: either $a \succ y$ or $y \succ a$.

  - If $a \succ y$, then

$$
\begin{aligned}
\otimes &\equiv \ \mathsf{rotr}(\mathsf{bst}(a, \mathsf{insr}(y, \mathsf{insl}(x, t_1)), t_2)) && a \succ y \\
&\equiv_2 \mathsf{rotr}(\mathsf{bst}(a, \mathsf{insl}(x, \mathsf{insr}(y, t_1)), t_2)) && \mathsf{Ins}(x, y, t_1) \\
&\equiv \ \mathsf{rotr}(\mathsf{insl}(x, \mathsf{bst}(a, \mathsf{insr}(y, t_1), t_2))) \\
&\equiv \ \mathsf{rotr}(\mathsf{insl}(x, \mathsf{rotl}(\mathsf{rotr}(\mathsf{bst}(a, \mathsf{insr}(y, t_1), t_2))))) \\
&\overset{\eta}{\leftarrow} \mathsf{rotr}(\mathsf{insl}(x, \mathsf{rotl}(\underline{\mathsf{insr}(y, \mathsf{bst}(a, t_1, t_2))}))) \\
&= \ \mathsf{rotr}(\mathsf{insl}(x, \mathsf{rotl}(\mathsf{insr}(y, t)))) && t = \mathsf{bst}(a, t_1, t_2) \\
&\equiv_3 \mathsf{rotr}(\mathsf{rotl}(\mathsf{insl}(x, \mathsf{insr}(y, t)))) && \text{Lemma} \\
&\equiv \ \mathsf{insl}(x, \mathsf{insr}(y, t)). && \mathsf{rotr}(\mathsf{rotl}(z)) \equiv z
\end{aligned}
$$

What makes this case of the proof work is that $a \succ x$ and $a \succ y$ allow us to move the calls to the rotations down into the term so that they are composed on the subtree t_1, enabling the application of the inductive hypothesis $\mathsf{Ins}(x, y, t_1)$. Then we bring back up the commuted calls, using the fact that composing a left and right rotation, and vice-versa, is the identity. Note how, in the process, we found a new lemma we need to prove later in the instance of ($\equiv_3$). The interpretation of this subgoal is that left rotation and leaf insertion commute, shedding more light on the matter.

  - If $y \succ a$, then

$$
\begin{aligned}
\otimes &\overset{\theta}{\rightarrow} \mathsf{rotl}(\mathsf{bst}(a, \mathsf{insl}(x, t_1), \mathsf{insr}(y, t_2))) && y \succ a \\
&\equiv \ \mathsf{rotl}(\mathsf{insl}(x, \mathsf{bst}(a, t_1, \mathsf{insr}(y, t_2)))) \\
&\equiv \ \mathsf{rotl}(\mathsf{insl}(x, \mathsf{rotr}(\mathsf{rotl}(\mathsf{bst}(a, t_1, \mathsf{insr}(y, t_2)))))) \\
&\overset{\theta}{\leftarrow} \mathsf{rotl}(\mathsf{insl}(x, \mathsf{rotr}(\underline{\mathsf{insr}(y, \mathsf{bst}(a, t_1, t_2))}))) \\
&= \ \mathsf{rotl}(\mathsf{insl}(x, \mathsf{rotr}(\mathsf{insr}(y, t)))) && t = \mathsf{bst}(a, t_1, t_2) \\
&\equiv_4 \mathsf{rotl}(\mathsf{rotr}(\mathsf{insl}(x, \mathsf{insr}(y, t)))) && \text{Lemma} \\
&\equiv \ \mathsf{insl}(x, \mathsf{insr}(y, t)). && \mathsf{rotl}(\mathsf{rotr}(z)) \equiv z
\end{aligned}
$$

Here, there was no need for the inductive hypothesis, because $a \succ x$ and $y \succ a$ imply $y \succ x$, hence the leaf and root insertions are not composed and apply to two different subtrees, t_1 and t_2. All we have to do then is to get them up in the same order we got them down (as in a queue). We discovered another subgoal that needs proving later, in the instance of ($\equiv_4$), and which is the dual of ($\equiv_3$) because it states that right rotation and leaf insertion commute. Together, they mean that rotations commute with leaf insertion.

- If $x \succ a$, then $\otimes \xrightarrow{\upsilon} \mathsf{insr}(y, \mathsf{bst}(a, t_1, \mathsf{insl}(y, t_2))) \otimes$. Two subcases become apparent: either $a \succ y$ or $y \succ a$.

    - If $a \succ y$, then

$$
\begin{aligned}
\otimes \equiv\ & \mathsf{rotr}(\mathsf{bst}(a, \mathsf{bst}(a, \mathsf{insr}(y, t_1), \mathsf{insl}(x, t_2)))) && a \succ y \\
\equiv\ & \mathsf{rotr}(\mathsf{insl}(x, \mathsf{bst}(a, \mathsf{insr}(y, t_1), t_2))) \\
\equiv\ & \mathsf{rotr}(\mathsf{insl}(x, \mathsf{rotl}(\mathsf{rotr}(\mathsf{bst}(a, \mathsf{insr}(y, t_1), t_2))))) \\
\xleftarrow{\eta}\ & \mathsf{rotr}(\mathsf{insl}(x, \mathsf{rotl}(\underline{\mathsf{insr}}(y, \mathsf{bst}(a, t_1, t_2))))) \\
=\ & \mathsf{rotr}(\mathsf{insl}(x, \mathsf{rotl}(\mathsf{insr}(y, t)))) && t = \mathsf{bst}(a, t_1, t_2) \\
\equiv_3\ & \mathsf{rotr}(\mathsf{rotl}(\mathsf{insl}(x, \mathsf{insr}(y, t)))) \\
\equiv\ & \mathsf{insl}(x, \mathsf{insr}(y, t)). && \mathsf{rotr}(\mathsf{rotl}(z)) \equiv z
\end{aligned}
$$

      This subcase is similar to the previous one in the sense that the insertions apply to different subtrees, thus there is no need for the inductive hypothesis. The difference is that, here, ($\equiv_3$) is required in stead of ($\equiv_4$).

    - If $y \succ a$, then

$$
\begin{aligned}
\otimes \equiv\ & \mathsf{rotl}(\mathsf{bst}(a, t_1, \mathsf{insr}(y, \mathsf{insl}(x, t_2)))) \\
\equiv_2\ & \mathsf{rotl}(\mathsf{bst}(a, t_1, \mathsf{insl}(x, \mathsf{insr}(y, t_2)))) && \mathsf{Ins}(x, y, t_2) \\
\equiv\ & \mathsf{rotl}(\mathsf{insl}(x, \mathsf{bst}(a, t_1, \mathsf{insr}(y, t_2)))) \\
\equiv_3\ & \mathsf{insl}(x, \mathsf{rotl}(\mathsf{bst}(a, t_1, \mathsf{insr}(y, t_2)))) \\
\xleftarrow{\theta}\ & \mathsf{insl}(x, \underline{\mathsf{insr}}(y, \mathsf{bst}(a, t_1, t_2))) \\
=\ & \mathsf{insl}(x, \mathsf{insr}(y, t)). && t = \mathsf{bst}(a, t_1, t_2)
\end{aligned}
$$

      This is the last subcase. It is similar to the first one, because the insertions are composed, albeit on t_2 instead of t_1, therefore calling for the inductive hypothesis to be applied. Then, insertions are brought up in the same order they were moved down, $e.g.$, insl/2 was pushed down before insr/2 and is lifted up before insr/2.   □

We now have to prove two remaining lemmas, dual of each other and meaning together that rotations commute with leaf insertions. Let us consider the first:

$$\mathsf{insl}(x, \mathsf{rotl}(t)) \equiv_3 \mathsf{rotl}(\mathsf{insl}(x, t)).$$

Implicitly, this proposition makes sense only if $t = \mathsf{bst}(a, t_1, \mathsf{bst}(b, t_2, t_3))$ is a binary search tree, which implies $b \succ a$. The proof is technical in nature, which means that it requires many cases and does not bring new insights, which the lack of induction underlies. We start as follows:

$$
\begin{aligned}
\mathsf{insl}(x, \mathsf{rotl}(t)) =\ & \mathsf{insl}(x, \underline{\mathsf{rotl}}(\mathsf{bst}(a, t_1, \mathsf{bst}(b, t_2, t_3)))) \\
\xrightarrow{\varsigma}\ & \mathsf{insl}(x, \mathsf{bst}(b, \mathsf{bst}(a, t_1, t_2), t_3)) \quad \otimes
\end{aligned}
$$

Two cases arise: either $b \succ x$ or $x \succ b$.

- If $b \succ x$, then $\otimes \xrightarrow{\tau}$ bst$(b, \text{insl}(x, \text{bst}(a, t_1, t_2)), t_3) \otimes$. Two subcases surface: either $a \succ x$ or $x \succ a$.

  - If $a \succ x$, then
  $$
  \begin{aligned}
  \otimes &\xrightarrow{\tau} \text{bst}(b, \text{bst}(a, \text{insl}(x, t_1), t_2), t_3) \\
  &\equiv \text{rotl}(\text{bst}(a, \text{insl}(x, t_1), \text{bst}(b, t_2, t_3))) \\
  &\xleftarrow{\tau} \text{rotl}(\underline{\text{insl}}(x, \text{bst}(a, t_1, \text{bst}(b, t_2, t_3)))) \\
  &= \text{rotl}(\text{insl}(x, t)).
  \end{aligned}
  $$

  - If $x \succ a$, then
  $$
  \begin{aligned}
  \otimes &\xrightarrow{\upsilon} \text{bst}(b, \text{bst}(a, t_1, \text{insl}(x, t_2)), t_3) \\
  &\equiv \text{rotl}(\text{bst}(a, t_1, \text{bst}(b, \text{insl}(x, t_2), t_3))) \\
  &\xleftarrow{\tau} \text{rotl}(\text{bst}(a, t_1, \underline{\text{insl}}(x, \text{bst}(b, t_2, t_3)))) \\
  &\xleftarrow{\upsilon} \text{rotl}(\underline{\text{insl}}(x, \text{bst}(a, t_1, \text{bst}(b, t_2, t_3)))) \\
  &= \text{rotl}(\text{insl}(x, t)).
  \end{aligned}
  $$

- If $x \succ b$, then the assumption $b \succ a$ implies $x \succ a$. We have
$$
\begin{aligned}
\otimes &\xrightarrow{\upsilon} \text{bst}(b, \text{bst}(a, t_1, t_2), \text{insl}(x, t_3)) \\
&\equiv \text{rotl}(\text{bst}(a, t_1, \text{bst}(b, t_2, \text{insl}(x, t_3)))) \\
&\xleftarrow{\upsilon} \text{rotl}(\text{bst}(a, t_1, \underline{\text{insl}}(x, \text{bst}(b, t_2, t_3)))) \qquad x \succ b \\
&\xleftarrow{\upsilon} \text{rotl}(\underline{\text{insl}}(x, \text{bst}(a, t_1, \text{bst}(b, t_2, t_3)))) \qquad x \succ a \\
&= \text{rotl}(\text{insl}(x, t)). \qquad\qquad\qquad\qquad\qquad \square
\end{aligned}
$$

The last remaining lemma is $\text{insl}(x, \text{rotr}(t)) \equiv_4 \text{rotr}(\text{insl}(x, t))$. In fact, it is a simple algebraic matter to show that it is equivalent to $\text{insl}(x, \text{rotl}(t)) \equiv_3 \text{rotl}(\text{insl}(x, t))$. Indeed, we have the following equivalent equations:

$$
\begin{aligned}
\text{insl}(x, \text{rotl}(t)) &\equiv_3 \text{rotl}(\text{insl}(x, t)) \\
\text{insl}(x, \text{rotl}(\text{rotr}(t))) &\equiv \text{rotl}(\text{insl}(x, \text{rotr}(t))) \\
\text{insl}(x, t) &\equiv \text{rotl}(\text{insl}(x, \text{rotr}(t))) \\
\text{rotr}(\text{insl}(x, t)) &\equiv \text{rotr}(\text{rotl}(\text{insl}(x, \text{rotr}(t)))) \\
\text{rotr}(\text{insl}(x, t)) &\equiv_4 \text{insl}(x, \text{rotr}(t)). \qquad \square
\end{aligned}
$$

Average cost The average number of comparisons of root insertion is the same as with leaf insertion, because rotations do not involve any comparison:

$$
\overline{A}_n^{\text{insr}} = \overline{A}_n^{\text{insro}} = \overline{A}_n^{\text{insl}} = 2H_n + \frac{2}{n+1} - 3 \sim 2\ln n.
$$

Rotations double the cost of a step down in the tree, though, and we have, recalling equations (8.11) and (8.12) on page 265,

$$A_n^{\mathsf{insr}} = 1 + \frac{2}{n+1}\mathbb{E}[E_n] = 1 + \overline{A}_{n(-)}^{\mathsf{mem}} = 4H_n + \frac{4}{n+1} - 3 \sim 4\ln n.$$

As a consequence of theorem (8.18) on page 271, all permutations of a given size yield the same set of binary search trees under mkl/1 and mkr/1. Therefore, inserting another key will incur the same average number of comparisons by insl/1 and insr/1 since $\overline{A}_n^{\mathsf{insr}} = \overline{A}_n^{\mathsf{insro}} = \overline{A}_n^{\mathsf{insl}}$. By induction on the size, we conclude that the average number of comparisons for mkl/1 and mkr/1 is the same:

$$\overline{A}_n^{\mathsf{mkr}} = \overline{A}_n^{\mathsf{mkl}} = \mathbb{E}[I_n] = 2(n+1)H_n - 4n.$$

Considering that the only difference between insl/1 and insr/1 is the additional cost of one rotation per edge down, we quickly realise, by recalling equations (8.13) and (8.10), that

$$A_n^{\mathsf{mkr}} = A_n^{\mathsf{mkl}} + \mathbb{E}[I_n] = n + 2 \cdot \mathbb{E}[I_n] + 2 = 4(n+1)H_n - 7n + 2.$$

Amortised cost   Since the first phase of root insertion is a leaf insertion, the previous analyses of the extremal costs of insl/2 and $\mathsf{insl}_1/2$ apply as well to insr/2. Let us consider now the amortised costs of insr/2, namely, the extremal costs of mkr/1.

Let $\overline{B}_n^{\mathsf{mkr}}$ the minimum number of comparisons to build a binary search tree of size n using root insertions. We saw that the best case with leaf insertion (insl/2) happens when the key is inserted as a child of the root. While this cannot lead to the best amortised cost (mkl/1), it yields the best amortised cost when using root insertions (mkr/1) because the newly inserted key becomes the root with exactly one rotation (a left rotation if it was the right child, and a right rotation if it was the left child of the root), leaving the spot empty again for another efficient insertion (insr/2). In the end, the search tree is degenerate, in fact, there are exactly two minimum-cost trees, whose shapes are those of FIGURE 7.4 on page 211. Interestingly, these trees correspond to maximum-cost trees built using leaf insertions. The first key is not compared, so we have

$$\overline{B}_n^{\mathsf{mkr}} = n - 1 \sim \overline{B}_n^{\mathsf{mkl}} / \lg n.$$

Perhaps surprisingly, it turns out that finding the maximum number of comparisons $\overline{W}_n^{\mathsf{mkr}}$ to make a search tree of size n with mkr/1, that is to say, the maximum amortised number of comparisons of insr/2, happens to be substantially more challenging than making out its average or minimum cost. Geldenhuys and der Merwe (2009) show that

$$\overline{\mathcal{W}}_n^{\mathsf{mkr}} = \frac{1}{4}n^2 + n - 2 - c,$$

where $c = 0$ for n even, and $c = {}^1\!/_4$ for n odd. This implies in turn:

$$\overline{\mathcal{W}}_n^{\mathsf{mkr}} = \frac{1}{2}\overline{\mathcal{W}}_n^{\mathsf{mkl}} + \frac{5}{4}n - 2 - c \sim \frac{1}{2}\overline{\mathcal{W}}_n^{\mathsf{mkl}}.$$

Exercises

1. Prove $\mathsf{bst}_0(t) \equiv \mathsf{bst}(t)$. See definitions of $\mathsf{bst}_0/1$ and $\mathsf{bst}/1$, respectively, in FIGURE 8.2 on page 256 and FIGURE 8.3 on page 256.

2. Prove $\mathsf{mem}(y, t) \equiv \mathsf{mem}_3(y, t)$, that is to say, the correctness of Andersson's search. See definitions of $\mathsf{mem}/2$ and $\mathsf{mem}_3/2$, respectively, in FIGURE 8.4 on page 258 and FIGURE 8.7 on page 262.

3. Prove $\mathsf{insr}(x, t) \equiv \mathsf{bst}(x, t_1, t_2)$. In other words, root insertion is really doing what it says it does.

4. Prove $\mathsf{mklR}(s) \equiv \mathsf{mkl}(\mathsf{rev}(s))$.

5. Prove $\mathsf{bst}(t) \equiv \mathsf{true}() \Rightarrow \mathsf{mkl}(\mathsf{pre}(t)) \equiv t$. See definition of $\mathsf{pre}/1$ in FIGURE 7.10 on page 215. Is the converse true as well?

8.3 Deletion

The removal of a key in a binary search tree is a bit tricky, in contrast with leaf insertion. Of course, 'removal' is a convenient figure of speech in the context of functional programming, where data structures are persistent, hence removal means that we have to rebuild a new search tree without the key in question. As with insertion, we could simply start with a search for the key: if absent, there is nothing else to be done, otherwise we replace the key with its immediate successor or predecessor in inorder, that is, the minimum of the right subtree or the maximum of the left subtree.

The definitions for these two phases are found in FIGURE 8.18 on the following page. We have $\mathsf{min}(t_2) \twoheadrightarrow (m, t'_2)$, where m is the minimum key of the tree t_2 and t'_2 is the reconstruction of t_2 without m; in other

$$\begin{aligned}
\mathsf{del}(y, \mathsf{bst}(x, t_1, t_2)) &\to \mathsf{bst}(x, \mathsf{del}(y, t_1), t_2), \text{ if } x \succ y; \\
\mathsf{del}(y, \mathsf{bst}(x, t_1, t_2)) &\to \mathsf{bst}(x, t_1, \mathsf{del}(y, t_2)), \text{ if } y \succ x; \\
\mathsf{del}(y, \mathsf{bst}(x, t_1, t_2)) &\to \mathsf{aux}_0(x, t_1, \mathsf{min}(t_2)); \\
\mathsf{del}(y, \mathsf{ext}()) &\to \mathsf{ext}().
\end{aligned}$$

$$\begin{aligned}
\mathsf{min}(\mathsf{bst}(x, \mathsf{ext}(), t_2)) &\to (x, t_2); \\
\mathsf{min}(\mathsf{bst}(x, t_1, t_2)) &\to \mathsf{aux}_1(x, \mathsf{min}(t_1), t_2).
\end{aligned}$$

$$\mathsf{aux}_1(x, (m, t_1'), t_2) \to (m, \mathsf{bst}(x, t_1', t_2)).$$

$$\mathsf{aux}_0(x, t_1, (m, t_2')) \to \mathsf{bst}(m, t_1, t_2').$$

Figure 8.18: Deletion of a key in a binary search tree

words, the leftmost internal node of t_2 contains the key m and that node has been replaced by an external node. The call to $\mathsf{aux}_0/3$ simply substitutes the key x to be deleted by its immediate successor m. The purpose of the auxiliary function $\mathsf{aux}_1/3$ is to rebuild the tree in which the minimum has been removed. Note that the pattern of the third rule is not $\mathsf{del}(y, \mathsf{bst}(y, t_1, t_2))$, because we already know that $x = y$ and we want to avoid a useless equality test.

Of course, we could also have taken the maximum of the left subtree, and this arbitrary asymmetry seems to be the cause of the imbalance, in average, of the trees obtained by arbitrarily composing insertions and deletions. In other words, the distribution of shapes of the trees thus produced differs from the distribution for the trees of same size but built only by insertions. Surprisingly, perhaps, it has been proved that the shape of the trees made by n insertions followed by m deletions ($n \geq m$) *do* have the same distribution as for the trees built by $n - m$ insertions! Those phenomena are difficult to understand and examples are needed to see them at play (Panny, 2010, Eppinger, 1983, Culberson and Munro, 1989, Culberson and Evans, 1994, Knuth, 1998b, Heyer, 2009).

Another kind of asymmetry is that deletion is much more complicated to program than insertion. This fact has lead some researchers to propose a common framework for insertion and deletion (Andersson, 1991, Hinze, 2002). In particular, when Andersson's search with a tree candidate is modified into deletion, the program is quite short if the programming language is imperative.

Another approach to deletion consists in marking the targeted nodes as deleted without actually removing them. They are still needed for fu-

$$
\begin{aligned}
&\mathsf{del}_0(y, \mathsf{bst}(x, t_1, t_2)) \rightarrowtail \mathsf{bst}(x, \mathsf{del}_0(y, t_1), t_2), \text{ if } x \succ y; \\
&\mathsf{del}_0(y, \mathsf{bst}(x, t_1, t_2)) \rightarrowtail \mathsf{bst}(x, t_1, \mathsf{del}_0(y, t_2)), \text{ if } y \succ x; \\
&\mathsf{del}_0(y, \mathsf{bst}(x, t_1, t_2)) \rightarrowtail \mathsf{del}(x, t_1, t_2); \\
&\mathsf{del}_0(y, \mathsf{del}(x, t_1, t_2)) \rightarrowtail \mathsf{del}(x, \mathsf{del}_0(y, t_1), t_2), \text{ if } x \succ y; \\
&\mathsf{del}_0(y, \mathsf{del}(x, t_1, t_2)) \rightarrowtail \mathsf{del}(x, t_1, \mathsf{del}_0(y, t_2)), \text{ if } y \succ x; \\
&\mathsf{del}_0(y, t) \rightarrowtail t.
\end{aligned}
$$

Figure 8.19: Lazy deletion of a key in a binary search tree

ture comparisons but they are not to be considered part of the collection of keys implemented by the search tree. We then have lazy deletion. It requires two kinds of internal nodes, bst/3 and del/3. This alternative design is shown in FIGURE 8.19. Note that the insertion of a key which happens to have been lazily deleted does not need to be performed at an external node: the constructor del/3 would simply be changed into bst/3, the mark of normal internal nodes.

Exercise Define the usual insertions on this new kind of search tree.

8.4 Average parameters

The average height h_n of a binary search tree of size n has been intensively studied (Devroye, 1986, 1987, Mahmoud, 1992, Knessl and Szpankowski, 2002), but the methods, mostly of analytic nature, are beyond the scope of this book. Reed (2003) proved that

$$
h_n = \alpha \ln n - \frac{3\alpha}{2\alpha - 2} \ln \ln n + \mathcal{O}(1),
$$

where α is the unique solution on $[2, +\infty[$ to the equation

$$
\alpha \ln(2e/\alpha) = 1,
$$

an approximation being $\alpha \simeq 4.31107$, and $\mathcal{O}(1)$ is an unknown function whose absolute value is bounded from above by an unknown constant. Particularly noteworthy is a rough logarithmic upper bound by Aslam (2001), expressed in a probabilistic model and republished by Cormen et al. (2009) in section 12.4.

Chauvin et al. (2001) studied the average width of binary search trees.

Part III

Implementation

Chapter 9

Translation to Erlang

Translating our toy functional language to Erlang happens to be very easy
a task. Section 1.6 in the introduction already provided an example. Besides the need for module headers, some lexical conventions are needed,
as well as a knowledge about how the compiler handles data sharing.
Furthermore, we explain in terms of the memory model in section 9.1
how the concepts of *control stack* and *heap* emerge, as well as an important optimisation technique implemented by most compilers of functional
languages: *tail call optimisation* (also known as *last call optimisation*).

Lexis and syntax   In Erlang, stacks are called *lists*. Nevertheless, we
shall keep using 'stack' to retain a uniform reading throughout this book.

The first letter of variables is set in uppercase, for instance, *data* is
translated as Data, and x becomes X.

Constant data constructors are set without their pair of parentheses,
for example, absent() is translated as absent. If arguments are present,
a tuple must be used. Tuples in Erlang are written with curly brackets,
to distinguish them from the parentheses of function calls, so (x, y) is
translated as {X,Y}. Then, one(s) becomes {one,S} in Erlang if one/1
is a constructor, otherwise one(S), if one/1 is a function. In Erlang, a
constant constructor is called an *atom*.

When a variable in a pattern is unused in the right-hand side, it may
be replaced by an underscore, so

$$\mathsf{len}([\,]) \to 0; \qquad \mathsf{len}([x\,|\,s]) \to 1 + \mathsf{len}(s).$$

may be translated in Erlang as

```
len(   []) -> 0;
len([_|S]) -> 1 + len(S).
```

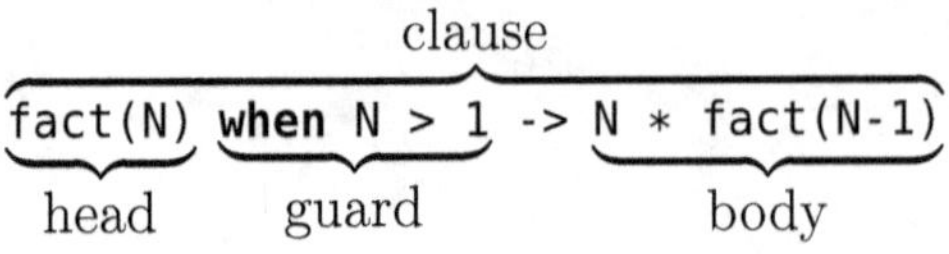

clause

$$\overbrace{\underbrace{\texttt{fact(N)}}_{\text{head}}\ \underbrace{\textbf{when}\ \texttt{N > 1}}_{\text{guard}}\ \texttt{->}\ \underbrace{\texttt{N * fact(N-1)}}_{\text{body}}}$$

Figure 9.1: Structure of a clause in Erlang

Insofar syntax is concerned, we must translate the conditional rewrite rules using the keyword **when** and lay the condition on the left-hand side. For instance, consider again straight insertion in section 3.1:

$$\mathsf{ins}([y\,|\,s], x) \to [y\,|\,\mathsf{ins}(s, x)], \text{ if } x \succ y; \qquad \mathsf{ins}(s, x) \to [x\,|\,s].$$

This definition is translated in Erlang as

```
ins([Y|S],X) when X > Y -> [Y|ins(S,X)];
ins(    S,X)            -> [X|S].
```

Note that, in Erlang, X > Y implies that X and Y are integers or atoms (which are ordered alphabetically). In Erlang, a rewrite rule is called a *clause*. Its left-hand side is called the *head* and the right-hand side the *body*. A condition on a clause is called a *guard*. As a side note, the lexical conventions, syntax and vocabulary of Erlang have been drawn indirectly from the Prolog programming language (Sterling and Shapiro, 1994, Bratko, 2000). The structure of a clause in Erlang is summed up in FIGURE 9.1.

A comment is introduced by % and extends till the end of the line.

Inference systems   The translation of programs defined by means of an inference system consists either in refining it so the new version does not contain any inference rule (see for example FIGURE 7.40 on page 240 and FIGURE 7.41), and then translate into Erlang, or else in using directly an Erlang construct called **case**, which is a general conditional expression. Consider again FIGURE 7.40 on page 240. A direct translation to Erlang yields

```
per(ext)              -> 0;
per({int,_,T1,T2}) -> case per(T1) of
                   false -> false;
                       H -> case per(T2) of
                           H -> H + 1;
                           _ -> false
                       end
               end.
```

Notice that we translated the inference rule in two cases, not one, because it would be inefficient to compute both per(T1) and per(T2) if per(T1) evaluates in false. Moreover, a variable in a pattern in a case can be bound to a value defined before (in OCaml, for example, it cannot), so **case** per(T2) **of** H -> ... implicitly implies that H has the same value as the H of **case** per(T1) **of** ...; H -> ...

Consider another example in FIGURE 7.43 on page 241. It is translated as follows:

```
comp({int,_,ext,ext}) -> true;
comp({int,_,T1,T2})    -> case comp(T1) of
                            false -> false;
                              _ -> comp(T2)
                          end;
comp(ext)               -> false.
```

The call comp(t_2) could evaluate in false(), leading to select the rule comp(t) $\rightarrow$ false(). This backtracking is not possible in Erlang: once the head of a clause has been successfully matched, the remaining heads will not be considered. By factoring the call comp(t_1), we can solve this problem and the inference rule becomes just one case.

The function in FIGURE 7.50 on page 245 becomes

```
pre2b0(S) -> case pre2b1(S) of {T,[]} -> T end.

pre2b1([ext|S]) -> {ext,S};
pre2b1([X|S])   ->
  case pre2b1(S) of
    {T1,S1} -> case pre2b1(S1) of
                 {T2,S2} -> {{int,X,T1,T2},S2}
               end
  end.
```

Here, we have a situation with case constructs which cannot fail on the one case they check. (It is said *irrefutable*.) Erlang provides a shorter syntax for this usage as follows:

```
pre2b0(S) -> {T,[]}=pre2b1(S), T.

pre2b1([ext|S]) -> {ext,S};
pre2b1([X|S])   -> {T1,S1}=pre2b1(S),
                   {T2,S2}=pre2b1(S1),
                   {{int,X,T1,T2},S2}.
```

Let us consider an example where inference rules are not used, but we realise that some functions act simply as a conditional expressions. We can see this in FIGURE 8.3 on page 256, with functions norm/1 and cmp/3:

```
bst(T) -> case bst(T,infty) of
            false -> false;
            _     -> true
         end.


bst(ext,M)            -> M;
bst({bst,X,T1,T2},M) -> case bst(T2,M) of
                          infty -> bst(T1,X);
                          N when N > X -> bst(T1,X);
                          _ -> false
                        end.
```

Note how we had to rename one variable *m* into N, to avoid the unwanted binding with M before. Would the definition of bst/1 in FIGURE 8.3 be shorter had we used inference rules?

Factoring a word in a text using the Morris-Pratt algorithm yielded a definition with some inference rules in FIGURES 5.10 to 5.12 on pages 185–188. Including the solution to Exercise 6 on page 192, we translate in Erlang as follows:

```
fail(          _,0) -> -1;
fail([{A,K}|P],I) -> fp(P,A,K,I-1).


fp(_,_,-1,_) -> 0;
fp(P,A, K,I) -> case suf(P,I-K-1) of
                  [{A,_}|_] -> K + 1;
                  [{_,J}|Q] -> fp(Q,A,J,K)
                end.


suf(    P,0) -> P;
suf([_|P],I) -> suf(P,I-1).


mp(P,T) -> PP=pp(P), mp(PP,T,PP,0,0).


mp(          [],    _, _,I,J) -> {factor,J-I};
mp(          _,    [], _,_,_) -> absent;
mp( [{A,_}|P],[A|T],PP,I,J) -> mp(P,T,PP,I+1,J+1);
mp([{_,-1}|_],[_|T],PP,0,J) -> mp(PP,T,PP,0,J+1);
mp( [{_,K}|_],    T,PP,_,J) -> mp(suf(PP,K),T,PP,K,J).
```

```
pp(X) -> pp(X,[],0).
```

```
pp(   [],_,_) -> [];
pp([A|X],P,I) -> U={A,fail(P,I)}, [U|pp(X,[U|P],I+1)].
```

The Erlang shell   The pieces of source code up to now are not complete Erlang programs for an Erlang program to be self-contained needs to be a *module*. A module is a unit of compilation containing a collection of function definitions. The module name must be the basename of the file containing the module. For instance, the following module named `math1`,

```
-module(math1).                    % Drop the file extension .erl
-export([fact/1]).
fact(1)             -> 1;
fact(N) when N > 1 -> N * fact(N-1).
```

must be written in a file named `math1.erl`. The -export line lists the names of the functions which can be called from outside the module, that is, either from another module or from the Erlang *shell*. A shell is an application which reads commands entered by some user, interprets them, prints a result or an error message and waits for further commands.

   In order to test some examples with `fact/1`, we first have to launch the Erlang shell. Depending on the operating system, the programming environment may vary greatly. Here, we shall assume a command-line interface, like the ones available in a terminal for the Unix operating systems and its derivatives. The Erlang shell is an application which allows us to interactively compile modules and call functions from them. Its name is likely to be `erl`. Here is the start of a session with the shell:

```
$ erl
Erlang R14B04 (erts-5.8.5) [source] [smp:4:4] [rq:4]
[async-threads:0] [hipe] [kernel-poll:false]

Eshell V5.8.5  (abort with ^G)
1> []
```

The first line is the command to run the shell. The last line is the prompt of the Erlang shell, the number 1 meaning that the shell is waiting for the first command. Note that the terminal prompt is denoted by a dollar sign ($). The character [] denotes the blinking prompt of the Erlang shell where typing will occur. If we want to close the shell and return to the operating system shell, just type 'q().' (standing for 'quit'). Each command must be terminated by a period (.) and followed by a pressure on the return key.

```
1> q().
ok
2> $ ⌴
```

The character ⌴ represents the place where text is to be typed in the operating system shell. But before quitting the **Erlang** shell, the first action usually consists in calling the **Erlang** compiler to process some module we want to use. This is done by the command 'c', whose argument is the module name. In our example, the filename is math1.erl:

```
1> c(math1).
{ok,math1}
2> ▯
```

The compilation was successful, as the atom ok says. Let us compute some factorials now:

```
2> math1:fact(4).
24
3> math1:fact(-3).
** exception error: no function clause matching
math1:fact(-3)
4> ▯
```

The error message is very legible. In this book, we will rarely copy and paste the input to and the output from the **Erlang** shell. We will not write complete modules as well because we want to focus on the programming itself and delegate the practical aspects to a user manual or a textbook oriented towards practice.

9.1 Memory

Let us review some programs under the angle of memory usage instead of cost. In the introduction, we stated that the essence of an expression is best captured by a bidimensional representation, namely a tree, as opposed to a line of punctuated text. In section 2.3 on page 44, we introduced the syntactic notions of context of a call and tail form of a definition. We also assumed that identical data structures occurring in the left-hand and right-hand sides of the same rule are actually shared.

In the present section, we elaborate on these concepts and representations, and show how they enable a better understanding of memory management by the run-time environment of a functional language, generated by a compiler. Nevertheless, these matters depend strongly on the compiler and the hardware architecture at hand, so it would be imprudent to pursue a description too detailed. Therefore, it is sufficient and appropriate here to provide a refined model based on the directed acyclic graphs only, to wit, abstract syntax trees with explicit sharing. Typically, we consider the number of nodes of these trees, or a particular kind, like cons-nodes, as a measure of how much memory needs to be allocated in total.

Summing integers Here is the definition of `sum/1`, which sums the integers in a given stack:

```
sum([N])   -> N;
sum([N|S]) -> N + sum(S).
```

For the sake of legibility, let us label the arrows:

$$sum([N]) \;\xrightarrow{\alpha}\; N;$$
$$sum([N|S]) \;\xrightarrow{\beta}\; N + sum(S).$$

We have, for instance,

$$
\begin{aligned}
sum([1|[2|[3|[]]]]) \;&\xrightarrow{\beta}\; 1 + sum([2|[3|[[]]]]) \\
&\xrightarrow{\beta}\; 1 + (2 + sum([3|[]])) \\
&\xrightarrow{\alpha}\; 1 + (2 + (3)) \\
&= 6.
\end{aligned}
$$

What can be said about the speed and the memory usage of the function `sum/1`? The number of rewrites clearly equals the number of integers in the stack because every integer is matched. Hence, if the initial function is called on a stack of n integers, the number of steps to reach the result is n: $n-1$ times using clause β, and once using clause α. Taking a slightly longer stack can provide a hint about memory usage:

$$
\begin{aligned}
sum([1|[2|[3|[4|[]]]]]) \;&\xrightarrow{\beta}\; 1 + sum([2|[3|[4|[]]]]) \\
&\xrightarrow{\beta}\; 1 + (2 + sum([3|[4|[]]])) \\
&\xrightarrow{\beta}\; 1 + (2 + (3 + sum([4|[]]))) \\
&\xrightarrow{\alpha}\; 1 + (2 + (3 + (4))) \\
&= 10.
\end{aligned}
$$

This prompts us to consider only the sizes of the right-hand sides:

It seems that the total memory usage increases slowly and then reduces sharply after the last rewrite step. But omitting blanks yields

```
sum([1|[2|[3|[4|[]]]]]) -> 1+sum([2|[3|[4|[]]]])
                        -> 1+(2+sum([3|[4|[]]]))
                        -> 1+(2+(3+sum([4|[]])))
                        -> 1+(2+(3+(4))).
```

It looks as if, now, the expressions are of constant size until clause α applies. Moreover, even if (+) were instead written plus, its occurrence should not be considered as taking more memory than (+) because names are only tags. Also, what about the parentheses and the blanks? Should they be considered meaningful, as far as memory allocation is concerned? All these considerations bring to the fore the need for a finer understanding of how Erlang functions and data are usually represented at run-time but, because these encodings depend strongly on the compiler and the hardware architecture, we should not rely on too detailed a description. The adequate model is the *abstract syntax trees* and the *directed acyclic graphs*, seen in the introduction. These allow us to draw conclusions about memory usage which hold up in proportion of a constant.

Concatenation of stacks   Definition in FIGURE 1.3 on page 7 is

$$\mathsf{cat}([\,],t) \overset{\alpha}{\rightarrow} t; \qquad \mathsf{cat}([x\,|\,s],t) \overset{\beta}{\rightarrow} [x\,|\,\mathsf{cat}(s,t)].$$

The relevant measure of memory usage here is the number of cons-nodes created by rule β. Clearly, the call $\mathsf{cat}(s,t)$ yields n such nodes, where n is the length of stack s.

Reversal of stacks   The definition of $\mathsf{rev}_0/1$ is found in section 2.2:

$$\mathsf{rev}_0([\,]) \overset{\gamma}{\rightarrow} [\,]; \qquad \mathsf{rev}_0([x\,|\,s]) \overset{\delta}{\rightarrow} \mathsf{cat}(\mathsf{rev}_0(s),[x]).$$

The empty stack on the right-hand side of rule γ is shared with the pattern. Of course, the same would hold for any constant. We already know how many such nodes are created by calls to $\mathsf{cat}/2$ and, since the length of s in the recursive call $\mathsf{rev}_0(s)$ decreases by 1 each time, the number of pushes is $\sum_{k=1}^{n-1} k = n(n-1)/2$, if the original stack contains n items. We need to add one push for each $[x]$, that is, n. In total: $n(n+1)/2$.

The alternative definition (2.2) of the reversal, on page 40, is

$$\mathsf{rev}(s) \overset{\epsilon}{\rightarrow} \mathsf{rcat}(s,[\,]). \qquad \mathsf{rcat}([\,],t) \overset{\zeta}{\rightarrow} t; \qquad \mathsf{rcat}([x\,|\,s],t) \overset{\eta}{\rightarrow} \mathsf{rcat}(s,[x\,|\,t]).$$

Clearly, the total number of pushes is n, the length of the input stack.

Merging Let us quantify the memory to sort by merging $n = 2^p$ keys, bottom-up. First, the number of stacks created is the number of nodes of the merge tree: $2^p + 2^{p-1} + \ldots + 2^0 = 2^{p+1} - 1 = 2n - 1$. There is one cons-node for each key, which leads us to determine the sum of the lengths of all the created stacks: $(p+1)2^p = n \lg n + n$. This is the total number of cons-nodes. In the case of top-down mergers, only the first half of the stacks, including the original one, are reversed, hence allocate cons-nodes. As a consequence, the total number of cons-nodes created is $(n \lg n)/2$.

Context of a call We want now to get a better understanding of how the context of a recursive call impact the evaluation. As a continued example, let us define a function sum/1 such that the call sum(s) is the sum of the integers in the stack s:

$$\mathsf{sum}([n]) \xrightarrow{\alpha} n; \qquad \mathsf{sum}([n\,|\,s]) \xrightarrow{\beta} n + \mathsf{sum}(s).$$

Consider in FIGURE 9.2a the abstract syntax tree of $1 + (2 + \mathsf{sum}([3,4]))$ and the function call it contains in FIGURE 9.2c. By taking as origin the node sum, the abstract syntax tree can be split into the part below it, that is, the argument in FIGURE 9.2d, and the part above, called *instances of the context*, in FIGURE 9.2b.

The main interest of abstract syntax trees is that no parentheses are required, because a sub-expression is denoted by a subtree, that is, a tree embedded into another. Moreover, blank characters are absent as well. Altogether, this brings the essential to the fore. To illustrate the gained legibility, consider again the previous computation in full, from left to right (the node to be rewritten is boxed), in FIGURE 9.3. It is now clear that the instances of the context accumulate so as to grow in inverse proportion to the argument's length: integers move one by one from the

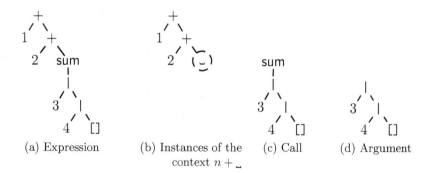

(a) Expression   (b) Instances of the   (c) Call   (d) Argument
                      context $n + \text{\textvisiblespace}$

Figure 9.2: $1 + (2 + \mathsf{sum}([3,4]))$

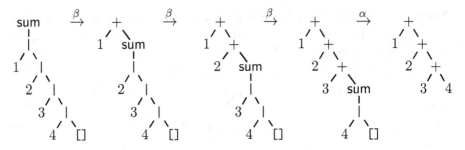

Figure 9.3: Evaluation of sum([1, 2, 3, 4])

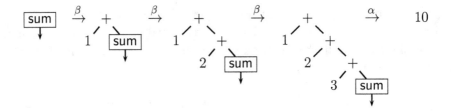

Figure 9.4: Contexts while computing sum([1, 2, 3, 4])

argument to the context and the associated operation changes from a cons-node to an addition. Therefore, if we use as memory unit a node, the total memory is indeed constant – except for the last step.

Consider again the running example and what happens to the context, step after step, in FIGURE 9.4. This example shows that the context instances grow, while the argument size decreases in such a way that the total memory remains constant.

Tail form   Let us consider the function sum/1, which sums the integers given in a stack:

```
sum([N])    -> N;
sum([N|S]) -> N + sum(S).
```

and look for an equivalent definition in tail form, called sum0/1. Very much like with the factorial in equation (1.1) on page 3, the idea is to use a supplementary argument which accumulates partial results. This kind of argument is called an *accumulator*. The new version should hence look like as follows:

```
sum0(T)          -> sum0(T,□).
sum0([M],N)    -> [            ];
sum0([M|S],N) -> [            ].
```

or, equivalently,

```
sum0(T)        -> sum0(□,T).
sum0(N,[M])    -> [            ];
sum0(N,[M|S])  -> [            ].
```

Notice that, just as with `sum/1`, the call `sum0([])` fails without a warning and we may find this behaviour questionable. Indeed, it can be considered inappropriate in the framework of software engineering, where programming large and robust applications is a requisite, but this book focuses primarily on programming in the small, therefore the programs introduced here are purposefully fragile; in other words, they may fail on some undesirable inputs instead of providing the user with some nice warnings, error messages or, even better, managing to get the compiler itself to reject such programs.

Since it was decided that an accumulator is needed, we must be clear on what kind of data it holds. As said previously, an accumulator usually contains a part of the final result. From a different perspective, an accumulator can be regarded as a partial trace of all the previous rewrite steps. Here, since the final result is an integer, we bear in mind that the accumulator ought to be a number as well.

There is no need to fill the above canvas (the boxes) from the first line to the last: this is a program, not an essay. Perhaps the best method is to first lie down the left-hand sides of the clauses and make sure none is missing and that none is useless (taking into account the implicit ordering from first to last). Second, we pick up the clause whose right-hand side seems the easiest to guess. For instance, the first clause of `sum/2` seems simple enough because it applies when only one number, M, remains in the input stack. Since the accumulator N holds the partial sum up to now, only M remains to be processed. Therefore, the answer is M+N or N+M:

```
sum0(T)        -> sum0(□,T).
sum0(N,[M])    -> M+N;
sum0(N,[M|S])  -> [            ].
```

The second clause of `sum0/2` is chosen next. It applies when the input stack is not empty and its first item is M and the remaining are in S. Until now, the partial sum is the accumulator N. It is clear that a recursive call is needed here, because if the body were M+N again, then the rest of the integers, S, would be useless. So the process must be resumed with another input:

```
sum0(T)        -> sum0(□,T).
sum0(N,[M])    -> M+N;
sum0(N,[M|S])  -> sum0([      ],□).
```

The question now is to find what the new stack and the new accumulator should be in this last clause. What is known about the stack? M and S. What can be done with M? Well, the same that was done before, in the first clause of `sum0/2`, that is, let us add it to the accumulator:

```
sum0(T)        -> sum0(□,T).
sum0(N,[M])    -> M+N;
sum0(N,[M|S]) -> sum0(M+N,□).
```

This way, the new accumulator is M+N, which is fine since the purpose of the accumulator is to hold the partial sum until the present number, which is M now. What new stack of numbers should be used? It is clear that M cannot be reused here, because it has already been added to the accumulator, and it must not be added twice. This means that it is not needed anymore. Remains S, which is what is sought, since it represents all the remaining numbers to be added to the accumulator:

```
sum0(T)        -> sum0(□,T).
sum0(N,[M])    -> M+N;
sum0(N,[M|S]) -> sum0(M+N,S).
```

The last unfinished business is the initial value of the accumulator. It is important not to rush and to deal with this value at the last moment. What kind of operation is being carried out on the accumulator? Additions. Without knowing anything about the integers in T, as it is the case in the clause of `sum0/1`, what integer could be taken as an initial value? It is well known that, for all n, $n + 0 = n$, thus 0 appears to be the only possible value here, since it does not change the total sum:

```
sum0(T)        -> sum0(0,T).
sum0(N,[M])    -> M+N;
sum0(N,[M|S]) -> sum0(M+N,S).
```

The last step consists in trying some examples after the labelling

```
sum0(T)        --α-> sum0(0,T).
sum0(N,[M])    --β-> M+N;
sum0(N,[M|S]) --γ-> sum0(M+N,S).
```

Consider our running example again:

```
sum0([1|[2|[3|[4|[]]]]])
  --α-> sum0(0,[1|[2|[3|[4|[]]]]])
  --γ-> sum0(1+0,[2|[3|[4|[]]]])     = sum0(1,[2|[3|[4|[]]]])
  --γ-> sum0(2+1,[3|[4|[]]])         = sum0(3,[3|[4|[]]])
  --γ-> sum0(3+3,[4|[]])             = sum0(6,[4|[]])
  --β-> 4 + 6                        = 10.
```

By contrast, let us recall here the run

```
sum([1|[2|[3|[4|[]]]]]) -> 1+sum([2|[3|[4|[]]]])
                        -> 1+(2+sum([3|[4|[]]]))
                        -> 1+(2+(3+sum([4|[]])))
                        -> 1+(2+(3+(4))).
```

The difference between sum0/1 and sum/1 lies not in the result (both functions are indeed equivalent) but in the way the additions are performed. They are equivalent because

$$4 + (3 + (2 + (1 + 0))) = 1 + (2 + (3 + 4)).$$

This equality holds because, for all numbers x, y and z,

1. the addition is associative: $x + (y + z) = (x + y) + z$,
2. the addition is symmetric: $x + y = y + x$,
3. zero is a right-neutral number: $x + 0 = x$.

To show exactly why, let us write $(\overset{1}{=})$, $(\overset{2}{=})$ and $(\overset{3}{=})$ to denote, respectively, the use of associativity, symmetry and neutrality, and lay out the following equalities:

$$
\begin{aligned}
4 + (3 + (2 + (1 + 0))) &\overset{3}{=} 4 + (3 + (2 + 1)) \\
&\overset{2}{=} (3 + (2 + 1)) + 4 \\
&\overset{2}{=} ((2 + 1) + 3) + 4 \\
&\overset{2}{=} ((1 + 2) + 3) + 4 \\
&\overset{1}{=} (1 + 2) + (3 + 4) \\
&\overset{1}{=} 1 + (2 + (3 + 4)).\square
\end{aligned}
$$

This seems a bit heavy for such a small program. Is there a way to rewrite further sum0/1 so that less hypotheses are needed to prove the equivalence with sum/1? Let us start with the most obvious difference: the use of zero. This zero is the initial value of the accumulator and its sole purpose is to be added to the first number in the stack. We could then simply first load the accumulator with this number, so the neutrality of zero is no more required:

```
sum0([N|T])    -> sum0(N,T).
sum0(N,[M])    -> M+N;
sum0(N,[M|S]) -> sum0(M+N,S).
```

But this definition of sum0/1 fails on stacks containing exactly one number, because T can be empty. Therefore, we must allow the stack to be empty in the definition of sum0/2:

```
sum0([N|T])    -> sum0(N,T).
sum0(N,    []) -> N;
sum0(N,[M|S]) -> sum0(M+N,S).
```

Now, we can easily get rid of the hypothesis that the addition is symmetric: by replacing M+N by N+M:

```
sum0([N|T])    -> sum0(N,T).
sum0(N,    []) -> N;
sum0(N,[M|S]) -> sum0(N+M,S).
```

Let us relabel the arrows

```
sum0([N|T])    --α-> sum0(N,T).
sum0(N,    []) --β-> N;
sum0(N,[M|S]) --γ-> sum0(N+M,S).
```

and consider again our running example:

```
sum0([1|[2|[3|[4|[]]]]])
       --α-> sum0(1,[2|[3|[4|[]]]])
       --γ-> sum0(1+2,[3|[4|[]]])   = sum0(3,[3|[4|[]]])
       --γ-> sum0(3+3,[4|[]])       = sum0(6,[4|[]])
       --γ-> sum0(4+6,[])           = sum0(10,[])
       --β-> 10.
```

This time, the series of additions corresponds to $((1 + 2) + 3) + 4$, which we can prove equal to $1 + (2 + (3 + 4))$ by means of associativity only:

$$((1 + 2) + 3) + 4 \overset{1}{=} (1 + 2) + (3 + 4) \overset{1}{=} 1 + (2 + (3 + 4)). \quad \square$$

What about the speed and the memory usage of sum0/1? It is easy to see that each step by means of clauses β and γ process exactly one integer from the input stack, so the total number of rewrite steps is the number of integers plus one due to the initial rewrite through clause α. In other words, if the initial input stack contains n integers, the number of rewrites is exactly $n + 1$.

Let us rename sum0/1 as $sum_0/1$ in FIGURE 9.5 on the next page. Consider in FIGURE 9.6 the abstract syntax trees of the rewritten expressions. The intermediary trees of $m + n$ have been skipped to emphasise that the size of the trees strictly decreases and the size of the context is constant.

$$\begin{array}{c}
\mathsf{sum}_0([n\,|\,t]) \xrightarrow{\gamma} \mathsf{sum}_0(n,t). \\
\mathsf{sum}_0(n,[\,]) \xrightarrow{\delta} n; \\
\mathsf{sum}_0(n,[m\,|\,s]) \xrightarrow{\epsilon} \mathsf{sum}_0(n+m,s).
\end{array}$$

Figure 9.5: Summing integers in a stack with $\mathsf{sum}_0/1$

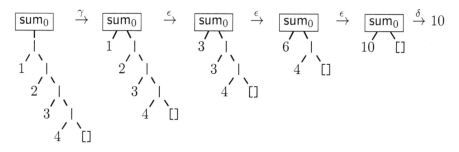

Figure 9.6: Abstract syntax trees of $\mathsf{sum}_0([1,2,3,4] \twoheadrightarrow 10$

Multiplication   Consider this time multiplying all the integers in a stack. The first thing that should come to the mind is that this problem is very similar to the previous one, only the arithmetic operator is different, so the following definition can be written immediately, by modification of `sum/1`:

```
mult([N])    -> N;
mult([N|S]) -> N * mult(S).
```

Similarly, a definition in tail form can be derived from `sum0/1`:

```
mult0([N|T])    -> mult0(N,T).
mult0(N,    []) -> N;
mult0(N,[M|S]) -> mult0(N*M,S).
```

The reason why `mult0/1` is equivalent to `mult/1` is the same reason why `sum0/1` is equivalent to `sum/1`: the arithmetic operator $(*)$ is associative, just as $(+)$ is.

What may be improved that could not be in `sum0/1`? In other words, what can speed up a long series of multiplications? The occurrence of at least one zero, for example. In that case, it is not necessary to keep multiplying the remaining numbers, because the result is going to be zero anyway. This optimisation can be done by setting apart the case when `N` is `0`:

```
mult0([N|T])    -> mult0(N,T).
```

```
mult0(N,    []) -> N;
mult0(N,[0|S]) -> 0;                                    % Improvement.
mult0(N,[M|S]) -> mult0(N*M,S).
```

How often a zero occurs in the input? In the worst case, there is no zero and thus the added clause is useless. But if it is known that zero is likely to be in the input with a probability higher than for other numbers, this added clause could be useful in the long term, that is, on the average time of different runs of the program. Actually, even if the numbers are uniformly random over an interval including zero, it makes sense to keep the clause.

Aliasing   In section 2.7, we assumed that the sharing between the pattern and the right-hand side of the same rule is maximal. In practice, compilers do not enforce that property and the programmers have to explicit the sharing beyond mere variables. For example, let us consider again FIGURE 2.8 on page 57 defining function $\mathsf{flat}_0/1$. In Erlang, maximum sharing in rule γ is achieved by naming $[x\,|\,s]$ in the pattern and reusing that name in the right-hand side. This name is called an *alias*. The syntax is self-explanatory:

```
flat0(             []) -> [];
flat0(         [[]|T]) -> flat0(T);
flat0([S=[_|_]|T]) -> cat(flat0(S),flat0(T));          % Aliasing
flat0(          [Y|T]) -> [Y|flat0(T)].
```

Another example is the function **red**/1 (*reduce*), seen in FIGURE 2.22 on page 73, copying its input stack, but discarding items which are successively repeated:

$$\mathsf{red}([\,]) \to [\,];$$
$$\mathsf{red}([x, x\,|\,s]) \to \mathsf{red}([x\,|\,s]);$$
$$\mathsf{red}([x\,|\,s]) \to [x\,|\,\mathsf{red}(s)].$$

For instance, $\mathsf{red}([4,2,2,1,1,1,2]) \twoheadrightarrow [4,2,1,2]$. The translation to Erlang with maximum sharing is

```
red(             []) -> [];
red([X|S=[X|_]]) -> red(S);
red(          [X|S]) -> [X|red(S)].
```

Another important example is merging in FIGURE 4.1 on page 120:

$$\mathsf{mrg}([\,],t) \to t;$$
$$\mathsf{mrg}(s,[\,]) \to s;$$
$$\mathsf{mrg}([x\,|\,s],[y\,|\,t]) \to [y\,|\,\mathsf{mrg}([x\,|\,s],t)], \text{ if } x \succ y;$$
$$\mathsf{mrg}([x\,|\,s],t) \to [x\,|\,\mathsf{mrg}(s,t)].$$

The best translation is

```
mrg(      [],     T)              -> T;
mrg(      S,     [])              -> S;
mrg(S=[X|_],[Y|T]) when X > Y -> [Y|mrg(S,T)];
mrg(    [X|S],    T)              -> [X|mrg(S,T)].
```

We must mind the abbreviations in the notations for stacks. For instance, tms/1 in FIGURE 4.7 on page 130 should be translated as

```
tms([X|T=[_|U]]) -> cutr([X],T,U);
tms(        T) -> T.
```

Yet another example is 2-way insertion in FIGURE 3.3 on page 106:

$$i2w(s) \xrightarrow{\xi} i2w(s, [], []).$$
$$i2w([], [], u) \xrightarrow{\pi} u;$$
$$i2w([], [y\,|\,t], u) \xrightarrow{\rho} i2w([], t, [y\,|\,u]);$$
$$i2w([x\,|\,s], t, [z\,|\,u]) \xrightarrow{\sigma} i2w([x\,|\,s], [z\,|\,t], u), \quad \text{if } x \succ z;$$
$$i2w([x\,|\,s], [y\,|\,t], u) \xrightarrow{\tau} i2w([x\,|\,s], t, [y\,|\,u]), \quad \text{if } y \succ x;$$
$$i2w([x\,|\,s], t, u) \xrightarrow{\upsilon} i2w(s, t, [x\,|\,u]).$$

In Erlang, maximum sharing requires an alias in clauses σ and τ:

```
i2w(S)                                   -> i2w(S,[],[]).
i2w(      [],     [],     U)             -> U;
i2w(      [],[Y|T],     U)             -> i2w([],T,[Y|U]);
i2w(V=[X|_],      T,[Z|U]) when X > Z -> i2w(V,[Z|T],U);
i2w(V=[X|_],[Y|T],     U) when Y > X -> i2w(V,T,[Y|U]);
i2w(    [X|S],     T,     U)             -> i2w(S,T,[X|U]).
```

Note that atoms (constant constructors), including the empty stack [], are automatically shared, so, for example, the alias S in f(S=[]) -> S. is useless.

Andersson's search with a tree candidate also benefits from using aliases. The definitions of FIGURE 8.7 on page 262 is best translated as

```
mem3(Y,T) -> mem4(Y,T,T).
```

```
mem4(Y,   {bst,X,T1,_},          T) when X > Y -> mem4(Y,T1,T);
mem4(Y,C={bst,_,_,T2},          _)             -> mem4(Y,T2,C);
mem4(Y,          ext,{bst,Y,_,_})             -> true;
mem4(_,          ext,          _)             -> false.
```

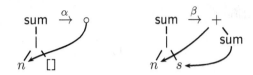

Figure 9.7: Definition of sum/1 with maximum sharing

Sometimes, aliasing is crucial. For instance, the whole discussion about persistence in section 2.7 hinges on having maximum sharing in each rewrite rule, but, here, **Erlang** needs aliasing to achieve this goal, so definitions (2.14) on page 74 *must* be implemented as follows:

```
push(X,H=[S|_]) -> [[X|S]|H].
pop(T=[[X|S]|_]) -> {X,[S|T]}.
```

Control stack and heap   The memory is under the exclusive supervision of the *garbage collector*. It is a process which has constantly full access to the directed acyclic graphs and whose task consists in finding the nodes which have become useless during evaluation. It consequently gets rid of them, so that subsequently created nodes can find enough room. This chapter hopefully demonstrates that the concept of *control stack* and *heap* arise naturally when a detailed analysis shows how some nodes can be automatically scheduled for deletion as soon as they become useless, thus relieving the garbage collector and improving the timing of memory management. Further investigation shows that calls to functions defined in tail form can be optimised so that the total amount of memory needed to evaluate a call is reduced.

For a better understanding of memory management, we need to make sharing explicit, as with the definition of **sum/1** in FIGURE 9.7. Let us compute **sum**([3, 7, 5]) and show the first rewrites in FIGURE 9.8, where the full state of the memory is given as snapshots between dashed arrows. (DAG is the abbreviation of *directed acyclic graph*.) The arrows

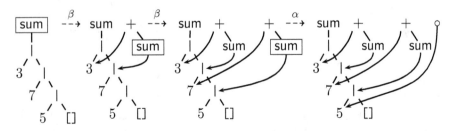

Figure 9.8: Evaluation of sum([3, 7, 5]) with a DAG (phase 1/2)

are dashed as to distinguish them from the ones in the definition, since rewrite rules apply in general only to parts of the trees, and we wanted to display all the data after each rewrite.

Naturally, a question arises on how the value of the original function call is finally computed (15). Examining FIGURE 9.8 and comparing memory snapshots from left to right, we realise that roots (+) have been accumulating at the right of the original call, until a reference to a value has been reached – here, the integer 5. This process is analogous to pushing items on a stack, although a stack containing not only values, but also expressions as $7 + \mathsf{sum}([5])$, and we name it 'pushing phase'. This invites us to perform the inverse operation, that is, popping the expressions in question, in order to finish the evaluation, or 'popping phase'. More precisely, we want to compute *values* from the trees composing the DAG from right to left, the roots of which are considered an item in a special stack, until the tree of the original call is reached and associated with its own value – which is, by definition, the final result. A value can either be an *immediate* value like integers, atoms and empty stacks, or a *constructed* value like non-empty stacks and tuples. We may also deal with *references* to values, which are graphically represented by edges; for instance, the rightmost tree in the DAG is a reference to the immediate value 5. *When the rightmost tree is an immediate value or a reference to a value, the second phase of the evaluation (leftward) can take place.* In the following, for the sake of conciseness, we shall write 'value' when a 'reference to a value' is also acceptable.

While our refined computational model forbids erasing nodes, because this is the exclusive task of the garbage collector, it does allow the edge ending in the latest rewritten call to be overwritten by its value. As explained before, these calls have been successively framed in FIGURE 9.8 on the preceding page. The popping phase consists here in replacing the edge to the previous node sum with an edge to the current value. Then the patched tree is evaluated, perhaps leading to more trees to be pushed and subsequent popping phases until one value remains in the stack.

The popping phase is shown at play in FIGURE 9.9 on the following page, which is to be read from right to left. The rightmost memory state is the result of the prior pushing phase, on the last state of FIGURE 9.8. Note how all the nodes sum and (+) become useless, step by step, that is, they cannot be reached from the stack (these nodes lie below the horizontal base line). For illustration purposes, we made all the nodes (+) disappear as soon as possible and three nodes sum are reclaimed by the garbage collector, including the original one, that is, the leftmost. The leftmost dashed arrow has the superscript 2 because it combines two steps $(3 + 12 \rightarrow 15$, and discarding the original node $\mathsf{sum})$ at once, for the sake of room. *A node is useful if it can be reached from one of the roots of the DAG.* Keep in mind that the argument of the original call, that is, $[3, 7, 5]$, may or may not be freed by the garbage collector, depending on it being shared or not (from outside the figure, that is, by some context). The intermediary node containing the value 12 has been freed as well along the way, to suggest that garbage collection is interleaved with the evaluation or, if adhering to a multiprocessing view, we would say that collection and evaluation run in parallel, sharing the same memory space but without interferences from the programmer's point of view – only nodes that are forever unreachable from a point onwards during the evaluation are swept away.

Our example is actually worth another, closer look. Indeed, we can predict exactly when the nodes sum can be reclaimed: after each step backwards (from right to left in FIGURE 9.9), the rightmost node sum becomes useless. Same for the intermediary value 12: it becomes unreachable from the roots of the DAG as soon as it has been used to compute 15. The same observation can be made about the nodes $(+)$. All these facts mean that, in our example, we do not need to rely on the garbage collector to identify these particular nodes as useless: let us really implement an isolated stack of expressions as a meta-object, instead of solely relying on an analogy and storing everything in the same space. The memory managed by the garbage collector is called the *heap*, in contrast with this special stack, called the *control stack*. The heap and the control stack are separate and complementary, making up the whole memory. Also, for implementation reasons, the control stack never contains constructed data but references to constructed data in the heap.

Consider how the evaluation in FIGURE 9.9 can be improved with automatic deallocation of nodes based on a stack-based policy ('Last In, First Out') in FIGURE 9.10 on the next page. Remember that the value $[3, 7, 5]$ is stored in the heap, not in the control stack, and that it may be shared. Also, due to space limitations on the page, the last step is actually twofold, as it was in FIGURE 9.9. We can seize the growth of the

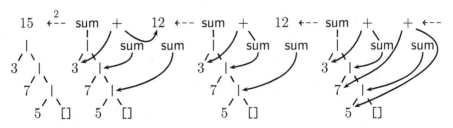

Figure 9.9: Evaluation of sum($[3, 7, 5]$) (phase 2/2)

control stack in FIGURE 9.11 on the next page. The poppings, from right to left, are presented in FIGURE 9.12.

The corresponding algorithm consists in the following steps. Let us first assume, as a result of the previous steps, that the control stack is not empty and that the top item is an immediate value or a reference to a value, although we shall refer to either as values.

1. While the control stack contains at least two objects, pop out the value, but without losing it, so another tree becomes the top;

    (a) if the root of the top tree is a node sum, then pop it and push instead the value;

    (b) else, the node sum in the tree has an incoming edge:

        i. change its destination so it reaches the value and discard the node sum;

        ii. evaluate the patched top tree and iterate.

2. The only item remaining in the control stack is the result.

Actually, we allowed integers to be stored in the control stack, so we could replace any tree which consists solely of a reference to such kind of value in the heap by a copy of the value. We can see in FIGURE 9.11 that the control stack grows at every step until a value is reached.

Tail call optimisation   Let us investigate what happens when using an equivalent definition in tail form like $sum_0/1$ in FIGURE 9.5 on page 299. FIGURE 9.13 only shows the first phase, which consists in pushing in the control stack the tree newly produced by a rule and sharing the subtrees denoted by variables (including aliases) occurring both in the pattern and the right-hand side. The second phase consists in popping the accumulated roots in order to resume suspended call contexts and, in the end, only the final result remains in the control stack.

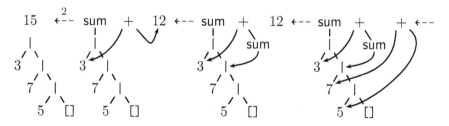

Figure 9.10: Evaluation of sum([3, 7, 5]) (phase 2/2, stack and heap)

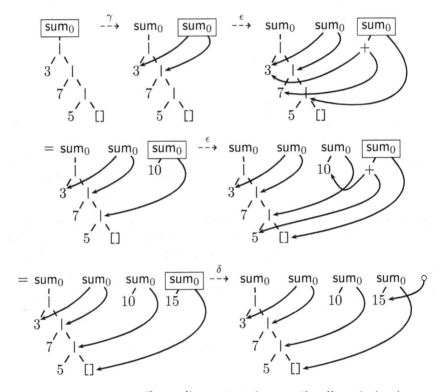

Figure 9.11: Control stack while computing sum([3, 7, 5]) (phase 1/2)

Figure 9.12: Control stack while computing sum([3, 7, 5]) (phase 2/2)

Figure 9.13: $sum_0([3, 7, 5]) \twoheadrightarrow 15$ without tail call optimisation

In the case of $sum_0/1$, we notice that we already found the result after the first phase: 15. Therefore, in this case, the second phase does not contribute to build the value, which raises the question: why keep the previous trees in the first place?

Indeed, they are useless after each push and a common optimisation,

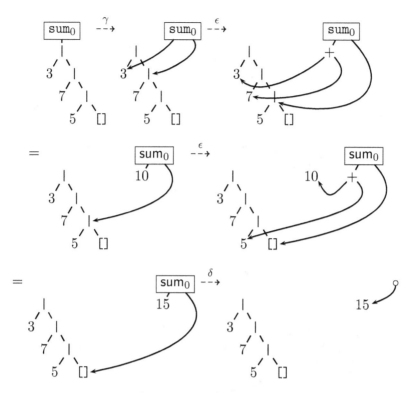

Figure 9.14: $sum_0([3, 7, 5]) \twoheadrightarrow 15$ with tail call optimisation

named *tail call optimisation* and implemented by compilers of functional languages, consists in popping the previous tree (matched by the pattern of the rule) and pushing the new one (created by the right-hand side of the rule). This way, the control stack contains only one item at all times. This optimisation is shown in FIGURE 9.14 and should be contrasted with the series in FIGURE 9.13 on the facing page.

Tail call optimisation can be applied to all functions in tail form.

Let us visualise another example: the evaluation of $cat([1, 2], [3, 4])$, using the definition in FIGURE 1.4 on page 7, which is not in tail form.

1. The first phase, consisting in pushing the newly created trees in the control stack is shown in FIGURE 9.15a on the following page.

2. The second phase of the evaluation of $cat([1, 2], [3, 4])$ is shown in FIGURE 9.15b on the next page. It consists in replacing from right to left the reference to the previous call by the current (reference to a) value, until the initial call itself is removed and only the final result remains. Notice how the second argument, $[3, 4]$, is actually shared with the output $[1, 2, 3, 4]$ and how no optimisation is possible.

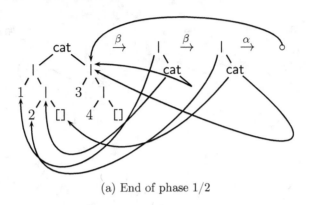

(a) End of phase 1/2

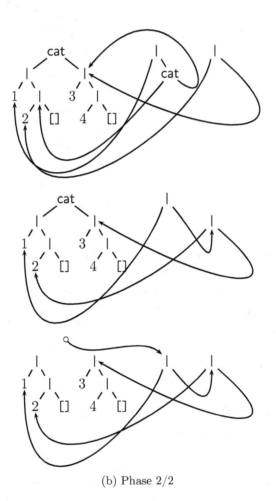

(b) Phase 2/2

Figure 9.15: cat([1, 2], [3, 4]) ↠ [1, 2, 3, 4]

Transformation to tail form Our definition of flat/1 with lifting in
FIGURE 2.12 on page 60, is easily translated to Erlang as follows:

```
flat(        []) -> [];
flat(    [[]|T]) -> flat(T);
flat([[X|S]|T]) -> flat([X,S|T]);
flat(     [X|T]) -> [X|flat(T)].
```

It is almost in tail form: only the last rule has a call with a non-empty
context. By adding an accumulator, this definition can be transformed
into an equivalent one in tail form. The purpose of this accumulator is
to store the variables which occur in the instances of the context, so
these can be rebuilt and computed after the current call is. So let us
add a stack accumulator A, unchanged in every clause, and add a new
flat_tf/1 definition calling the new flat/2 with the initial value of the
accumulator set to the empty stack:

$$
\begin{aligned}
\textbf{flat\_tf(T)} &\xrightarrow{\alpha} \textbf{flat(T,[])}.\\
\text{flat(} \quad [],A) &\xrightarrow{\beta} []; \qquad\qquad\qquad\qquad \text{\% A \textit{unused yet}}\\
\text{flat(} \quad [[]|T],A) &\xrightarrow{\gamma} \text{flat(T,A)};\\
\text{flat([[X|S]|T],A)} &\xrightarrow{\delta} \text{flat([X,S|T],A)};\\
\text{flat(} \quad [X|T],A) &\xrightarrow{\epsilon} [X|\text{flat(T,A)}].
\end{aligned}
$$

Now we must accumulate a value at each call which is not in tail form
(here, clause ϵ), and use the contents of the accumulator in all clauses
where there is no call (here, clause α). The technique consists in accu-
mulating in clause ϵ the values occurring in the call context, [X|_]; in
other words, we push X onto A:

$$
\begin{aligned}
\text{flat\_tf(T)} &\xrightarrow{\alpha} \text{flat(T,[])}.\\
\text{flat(} \quad [],A) &\xrightarrow{\beta} [];\\
\text{flat(} \quad [[]|T],A) &\xrightarrow{\gamma} \text{flat(T,A)};\\
\text{flat([[X|S]|T],A)} &\xrightarrow{\delta} \text{flat([X,S|T],A)};\\
\text{flat(} \quad [X|T],A) &\xrightarrow{\epsilon} \text{flat(T,[X|A])}. \qquad\qquad \text{\% \textit{Here}}
\end{aligned}
$$

When the input is fully consummated, in clause β, the accumulator contains all the non-stack items (all the Xs from clause ϵ) in the reverse order
of the original stack; therefore, they need to be reversed. That is to say:

$$
\begin{aligned}
\text{flat\_tf(T)} &\xrightarrow{\alpha} \text{flat(T,[])}.\\
\text{flat(} \quad [],A) &\xrightarrow{\beta} \textbf{rev(A)};\\
\text{flat(} \quad [[]|T],A) &\xrightarrow{\gamma} \text{flat(T,A)};\\
\text{flat([[X|S]|T],A)} &\xrightarrow{\delta} \text{flat([X,S|T],A)};\\
\text{flat(} \quad [X|T],A) &\xrightarrow{\epsilon} \text{flat(T,[X|A])}.
\end{aligned}
$$

The definition is now completed and in tail form. What about flat0/1 in FIGURE 2.8 on page 57?

```
flat0(            []) -> [];
flat0(        [[]|T]) -> flat0(T);
flat0([Y=[_|_]|T]) -> cat(flat0(Y),flat0(T));
flat0(         [Y|T]) -> [Y|flat0(T)].
```

That definition has the peculiarity that some of its clauses contain two or more calls – let us not forget that a call being recursive or not has nothing to do, in general, with being in tail form or not.

Let us start by adding the accumulative parameter to flat0/1 and initialise it with the empty stack:

```
flat0_tf(T)                  α→ flat0(T,[]).                        % Added
flat0(             [],A) γ→ [];                          % A unused yet
flat0(        [[]|T],A) δ→ flat0(T,A);
flat0([Y=[_|_]|T],A) ε→ cat(flat0(Y,A),flat0(T,A));
flat0(         [Y|T],A) ζ→ [Y|flat0(T,A)].
cat(    [],T)                η→ T;
cat([X|S],T)                θ→ [X|cat(S,T)].
```

Let us decide that, in clause ϵ, the first call to be rewritten is the leftmost recursive call flat0(Y,A), whose context is cat(_,flat0(T,A)). Therefore, in clause ϵ, let us save T in A so we can reconstruct the context in the right-hand side of γ, where the current stack to process is empty and thus the stacks saved in the accumulator enable resuming the flattening:

```
flat0_tf(T)                  α→ flat0(T,[]).
flat0(             [],[T|A]) γ→ cat([],flat0(T,A));       % Used
flat0(        [[]|T],    A) δ→ flat0(T,A);
flat0([Y=[_|_]|T],    A) ε→ flat0(Y,[T|A]);              % Saved
flat0(         [Y|T],    A) ζ→ [Y|flat0(T,A)].
cat(    [],T)                η→ T;
cat([X|S],T)                θ→ [X|cat(S,T)].
```

But a clause is now missing: what if the accumulator is empty? Therefore, a clause β must be added before clause γ to take care of this situation:

```
flat0_tf(T)                  α→ flat0(T,[]).
flat0(             [],    []) β→ [];
flat0(             [],[T|A]) γ→ cat([],flat0(T,A));
flat0(        [[]|T],    A) δ→ flat0(T,A);
flat0([Y=[_|_]|T],    A) ε→ flat0(Y,[T|A]);
```

```
flat0(         [Y|T],    A) ⁵↗ [Y|flat0(T,A)].
cat(    [],T)             ⁿ↗ T;
cat([X|S],T)             ⁿ↗ [X|cat(S,T)].
```

We can simplify the right-hand side of clause γ because the definition of
cat/2 has become useless:

```
flat0_tf(T)                       α↗ flat0(T,[]).
flat0(            [],    []) β↗ [];
flat0(            [],[T|A]) γ↗ flat0(T,A);        % Simplified
flat0(        [[]|T],    A) δ↗ flat0(T,A);
flat0([Y=[_|_]|T],    A) ε↗ flat0(Y,[T|A]);
flat0(         [Y|T],    A) ζ↗ [Y|flat0(T,A)].
```

Clause ζ is not in tail form. We cannot just push Y onto the accumulator

```
flat0(         [Y|T],    A) ζ↗ flat0(T,[Y|A]).          % Wrong
```

because the latter contains stacks to be flattened later (see clause ϵ) and
Y is not a stack – this modification would lead to a match failure just
after clause γ matches, because all patterns only match stacks. What can
we do? Perhaps the first idea which comes to the mind is to add another
accumulator to hold the non-stack items, like Y. Basically, this is exactly
the same method as before, except it applies to another accumulator,
say B. Let us first add B everywhere and initialise it with []:

```
flat0_tf(T)                       α↗ flat0(T,[],[]).
flat0(            [],    [],B) β↗ [];               % B unused yet
flat0(            [],[T|A],B) γ↗ flat0(T,A,B);
flat0(        [[]|T],    A,B) δ↗ flat0(T,A,B);
flat0([Y=[_|_]|T],    A,B) ε↗ flat0(Y,[T|A],B);
flat0(         [Y|T],    A,B) ζ↗ [Y|flat0(T,A,B)].
```

Now we can save the variables of the call context in clause ζ in B and
erase the context in question. In clause β, we know that B contains all the
non-stack items in reversed order, so we must reverse B. Since clause β
contained no further calls, this is the end:

```
flat0_tf(T)                       α↗ flat0(T,[],[]).
flat0(            [],    [],B) β↗ rev(B);
flat0(            [],[T|A],B) γ↗ flat0(T,A,B);
flat0(        [[]|T],    A,B) δ↗ flat0(T,A,B);
flat0([Y=[_|_]|T],    A,B) ε↗ flat0(Y,[T|A],B);
flat0(         [Y|T],    A,B) ζ↗ flat0(T,A,[Y|B]).
```

Further examination can lead to a simpler program, where the patterns
do not match embedded stacks:

```
flat0_tf(T)            -> flat0(T,[],[]).
flat0(   [],[],B) -> rev(B);
flat0(   [], A,B) -> flat0(A,   [],    B);
flat0(  [Y], A,B) -> flat0(Y,    A,    B);        % Optimisation
flat0([Y|T], A,B) -> flat0(Y,[T|A],    B);
flat0(   Y, A,B) -> flat0(A,   [],[Y|B]).
```

The shortcoming of this approach is that it requires many accumulators
in general and it is *ad hoc*. Instead of adding one more accumulator to
solve our problem, we can stick to only one but make sure that values in it
are distinguished according to their origin, so a value from a given context
is not confused with a value from another context. (This was previously
implemented by using different accumulators for different context values.)
The way of achieving this with only one accumulator consists in putting
in a tuple the values of a given context together with an atom, which
plays the role of a tag identifying the original expression containing the
call. Let us backtrack to

```
flat0_tf(T)                  α→ flat0(T,[]).
flat0(            [],A) γ→ [];                    % A unused yet
flat0(        [[]|T],A) δ→ flat0(T,A);
flat0([Y=[_|_]|T],A) ε→ cat(flat0(Y,A),flat0(T,A));
flat0(         [Y|T],A) ζ→ [Y|flat0(T,A)].
cat(    [],T)          η→ T;
cat([X|S],T)          θ→ [X|cat(S,T)].
```

Let us modify clause ϵ by choosing, as before, `flat0(Y,A)` as the first
call to be rewritten. We choose the atom `k1` to represent that call and
we pair it with the sole value of its context, that is, `T`. We remove the
context `cat(_,flat0(T,A))` and, in the remaining call, we push `{k1,T}`
onto the accumulator `A`:

```
flat0_tf(T)                  α→ flat0(T,[]).
flat0(            [],A) γ→ [];                    % A unused yet
flat0(        [[]|T],A) δ→ flat0(T,A);
flat0([Y=[_|_]|T],A) ε→ flat0(Y,[{k1,T}|A]);
flat0(         [Y|T],A) ζ→ [Y|flat0(T,A)].
cat(    [],T)          η→ T;
cat([X|S],T)          θ→ [X|cat(S,T)].
```

The key point is that `k1` must not be pushed in this accumulator anywhere else in the program, because it must denote unambiguously the

call in clause ϵ. Of course, this program is not correct anymore, as the erased context must be reconstructed somewhere else and applied to the value of the call `flat0(Y,[{k1,T}|A])`. The accumulator `A` represents, as before, the values of the contexts. Where should we extract its contents? Clause γ does not make any use of `A` and this is our cue. It means that, at that point, there are no more stacks to be flattened, so this is the right moment to wonder if there is some work left to be done, that is, examine the contents of `A`. In order to implement this task, a dedicated function should be created, say `appk/2`, so that `appk`(V, A) will compute whatever remains to be done with what is found in the accumulator A, the value V being a partial result, that is, the result up to this point. If there is nothing left to do, that is, if A is empty, then `appk`(V, A) rewrites into V and this is it. In other words:

```
appk(V,[{k1,T}|A]) -κ→ [                    ];
appk(V,          []) -ι→ V.                          % The end
```

The empty box must be filled with the reconstruction of the context which was erased at the point where `k1` was saved in the accumulator. The context in question was `cat(_,flat0(T,A))`, in clause ϵ, so we have

```
appk(V,[{k1,T}|A]) -κ→ cat([    ],flat0(T,A));
appk(V,          []) -ι→ V.
```

The remaining empty box is meant to be filled with the result of the function call `flat0(Y,[{k1,T}|A])`. To make this happen, two conditions must be fulfilled. Firstly, the accumulator in the pattern of `appk/2` must be the same as at the moment of the call, that is, it must be matched by `[{k1,T}|A]`. In theory, we should prove that the two occurrences of `A` indeed denote the same value, but this would lead us astray. Finally, we need to make sure that when a call to `flat0/2` is over, a call to `appk/2` is made with the result. When the whole transformation into tail form will be completed, no context will be found anymore (by definition), so all calls to `flat0/2` will end in clauses whose right-hand sides do not contain any further call to be processed. A quick examination of the clauses reveals that clause γ is the only clause of concern and that `A` was unused yet. So let us replace the right-hand side of this clause with a call to `appk/2`, whose first argument is the result of the current call to `flat0/2`, that is, the current right-hand side, and whose second argument is the accumulator which may contain more information about contexts to be rebuilt and applied. We have

```
flat0(          [],A) -γ→ appk([],A);
```

Now we understand that `V` in clause κ is the value of the function call `flat0(Y,[{k1,T}|A])`, so we can proceed by plugging `V` into the frame of clause κ:

```
appk(V,[{k1,T}|A]) -κ-> cat(V,flat0(T,A));
```

A glance is enough to realise that clause κ is not in tail form. Therefore, let us repeat the same method. The first call that must be rewritten is `flat0(T,A)`, whose context is `cat(V,␣)`. Let us associate the variable `V` in the latter with a new atom `k2` and push the two of them onto the accumulator:

```
appk(V,[{k1,T}|A]) -κ-> flat0(T,[{k2,V}|A]);
```

We need a new clause for `appk/2` which handles the corresponding case, that is, when the value of the call has been found and the context has to be reconstructed and resumed:

```
flat0_tf(T)                -α-> flat0(T,[]).
flat0(           [],A)     -γ-> appk([],A);
flat0(       [[]|T],A)     -δ-> flat0(T,A);
flat0([Y=[_|_]|T],A)       -ϵ-> flat0(Y,[{k1,T}|A]);
flat0(        [Y|T],A)     -ζ-> [Y|flat0(T,A)].
cat(    [],T)              -η-> T;
cat([X|S],T)               -θ-> [X|cat(S,T)].
appk(V,[{k2,W}|A])         -λ-> cat(W,V);                 % A unused yet
appk(V,[{k1,T}|A])         -κ-> flat0(T,[{k2,V}|A]);
appk(V,           [])      -ι-> V.
```

Notice how, in clause λ, we renamed `V` (in the accumulator) into `W`, so as to avoid a clash with the first argument of `appk/2`. Also, why is it `cat(W,V)` and not `cat(V,W)`? The reason is found by recollecting that `W` denotes the value of the call `flat0(Y)` (in the original definition), whereas `V` represents the value of `flat0(T)` (in the original definition). Nothing is done yet with the rest of the accumulator `A`, which entails that we must pass it to `cat/2`, just like the other functions:

```
flat0_tf(T)                -α-> flat0(T,[]).
flat0(           [],A)     -γ-> appk([],A);
flat0(       [[]|T],A)     -δ-> flat0(T,A);
flat0([Y=[_|_]|T],A)       -ϵ-> flat0(Y,[{k1,T}|A]);
flat0(        [Y|T],A)     -ζ-> [Y|flat0(T,A)].
cat(    [],T,A)            -η-> T;                        % A unused yet
cat([X|S],T,A)             -θ-> [X|cat(S,T,A)].
```

```
appk(V,[{k2,W}|A])   λ→  cat(W,V,A);                      % Passed A
appk(V,[{k1,T}|A])   κ→  flat0(T,[{k2,V}|A]);
appk(V,        [])   ι→  V.
```

After clause ϵ, the first clause not being in tail form is clause ζ. Let us pair the variable Y of the context [Y|_] with a new atom k3, and let us save the pair into the accumulator, while reconstructing the erased context in a new clause μ of appk/2:

```
flat0_tf(T)                   α→  flat0(T,[]).
flat0(            [],A)       γ→  appk([],A);
flat0(        [[]|T],A)       δ→  flat0(T,A);
flat0([Y=[_|_]|T],A)          ε→  flat0(Y,[{k1,T}|A]);
flat0(        [Y|T],A)        ζ→  flat0(T,[{k3,Y}|A]).          % Y saved
cat(     [],T,A)              η→  T;                    % A unused yet
cat([X|S],T,A)               θ→  [X|cat(S,T,A)].
appk(V,[{k3,Y}|A])           μ→  [Y|V];                 % A unused yet
appk(V,[{k2,W}|A])           λ→  cat(W,V,A);
appk(V,[{k1,T}|A])           κ→  flat0(T,[{k2,V}|A]);
appk(V,        [])           ι→  V.
```

Something interesting happens here: the brand-new right-hand side of clause μ makes no use of the remaining accumulator A. We encountered the exact same situation with γ: a right-hand side containing no further calls. In this case, we need to check whether there is more work to be done with the data saved earlier in A. This is the very aim of appk/2, therefore a call to it must be set within the right-hand side of clause μ:

```
flat0_tf(T)                   α→  flat0(T,[]).
flat0(            [],A)       γ→  appk([],A);
flat0(        [[]|T],A)       δ→  flat0(T,A);
flat0([Y=[_|_]|T],A)          ε→  flat0(Y,[{k1,T}|A]);
flat0(        [Y|T],A)        ζ→  flat0(T,[{k3,Y}|A]).
cat(     [],T,A)              η→  T;                    % A unused yet
cat([X|S],T,A)               θ→  [X|cat(S,T,A)].
appk(V,[{k3,Y}|A])           μ→  appk([Y|V],A);
appk(V,[{k2,W}|A])           λ→  cat(W,V,A);
appk(V,[{k1,T}|A])           κ→  flat0(T,[{k2,V}|A]);
appk(V,        [])           ι→  V.
```

The next clause to be considered is clause η, because its right-hand side contains no calls, so it requires now a call to appk/2 with the right-hand side T, which is the result of the current call to flat0/2, and the accumulator, that is, A:

```
flat0_tf(T)                    α→ flat0(T,[]).
flat0(             [],A)       γ→ appk([],A);
flat0(         [[]|T],A)       δ→ flat0(T,A);
flat0([Y=[_|_]|T],A)           ε→ flat0(Y,[{k1,T}|A]);
flat0(            [Y|T],A)     ζ→ flat0(T,[{k3,Y}|A]).
cat(     [],T,A)               η→ appk(T,A);
cat([X|S],T,A)                 θ→ [X|cat(S,T,A)].
appk(V,[{k3,Y}|A])             μ→ appk([Y|V],A);
appk(V,[{k2,W}|A])             λ→ cat(W,V,A);
appk(V,[{k1,T}|A])             κ→ flat0(T,[{k2,V}|A]);
appk(V,            [])         ι→ V.
```

Last but not least, clause θ must be fixed as we did for the other clauses not in tail form. Let us pick a new atom, say, k4, and tuple it with the sole variable Y of the context [Y|_] and push the resulting pair onto the accumulator A. Dually, we need to add a clause ν to appk/2 to catch this case, rebuild the erased context and apply it to the result of the current call to flat0/2, that is, its first argument:

```
flat0_tf(T)                    α→ flat0(T,[]).
flat0(             [],A)       γ→ appk([],A);
flat0(         [[]|T],A)       δ→ flat0(T,A);
flat0([Y=[_|_]|T],A)           ε→ flat0(Y,[{k1,T}|A]);
flat0(            [Y|T],A)     ζ→ flat0(T,[{k3,Y}|A]).
cat(     [],T,A)               η→ appk(T,A);
cat([X|S],T,A)                 θ→ cat(S,T,[X|A]).
appk(V,[{k4,X}|A])             ν→ [X|V];                % A unused yet
appk(V,[{k3,Y}|A])             μ→ appk([Y|V],A);
appk(V,[{k2,W}|A])             λ→ cat(W,V,A);
appk(V,[{k1,T}|A])             κ→ flat0(T,[{k2,V}|A]);
appk(V,            [])         ι→ V.
```

The right-hand side of the newly created clause contains no calls, so we must send it to appk/2 together with the rest of the accumulator, in order to process any pending contexts:

```
flat0_tf(T)                    α→ flat0(T,[]).
flat0(             [],A)       γ→ appk([],A);
flat0(         [[]|T],A)       δ→ flat0(T,A);
flat0([Y=[_|_]|T],A)           ε→ flat0(Y,[{k1,T}|A]);
flat0(            [Y|T],A)     ζ→ flat0(T,[{k3,Y}|A]).
cat(     [],T,A)               η→ appk(T,A);
cat([X|S],T,A)                 θ→ cat(S,T,[{k4,X}|A]).
```

```
appk(V,[{k4,X}|A])    ν→  appk([X|V],A);
appk(V,[{k3,Y}|A])    μ→  appk([Y|V],A);
appk(V,[{k2,W}|A])    λ→  cat(W,V,A);
appk(V,[{k1,T}|A])    κ→  flat0(T,[{k2,V}|A]);
appk(V,       [])     ι→  V.
```

The transformation is now finished. It is correct in the sense that the resulting program is equivalent to the original one, that is, flat0/1 and flat0_tf/1 compute the same values from the same inputs, and all the clauses of the latter are in tail form. It is also complete in the sense that any definition can be transformed. As announced, the main interest of this method lies in its uniformity and must not be expected to generate programs which are faster than the originals.

It is possible, upon close examination, to shorten a bit the definition of appk/2. Indeed, clauses ν and μ are identical, if not the presence of a different tag, k4 versus k3. Let us fuse them into a single clause and use a new atom k34 instead of every occurrence of k3 and k4.

```
flat0_tf(T)                 α→  flat0(T,[]).
flat0(          [],A)       γ→  appk([],A);
flat0(       [[]|T],A)      δ→  flat0(T,A);
flat0([Y=[_|_]|T],A)        ε→  flat0(Y,[{k1,T}|A]);
flat0(        [Y|T],A)      ζ→  flat0(T,[{k34,Y}|A]).
cat(    [],T,A)             η→  appk(T,A);
cat([X|S],T,A)              θ→  cat(S,T,[{k34,X}|A]).
appk(V,[{k34,Y}|A])         μ→  appk([Y|V],A);
appk(V, [{k2,W}|A])         λ→  cat(W,V,A);
appk(V, [{k1,T}|A])         κ→  flat0(T,[{k2,V}|A]);
appk(V,        [])          ι→  V.
```

Let us make a short digression and transform flat0_tf/1 further so that flat0_tf(T) is rewritten into a pair made of the value of flat0(T) and its cost. Because the definition is initially in tail form, we just have to add a counter and increment it where the clause corresponds to a clause in the original definition, else the counter is left unchanged. We also have to add a clause to set the first value of the counter. Let us recall first the original definition of flat0/1 (we rename the arrows here to ease the forthcoming steps):

```
flat0(          [])        γ→  [];
flat0(       [[]|T])       δ→  flat0(T);
flat0([Y=[_|_]|T])         ε→  cat(flat0(Y),flat0(T));
flat0(        [Y|T])       ζ→  [Y|flat0(T)].
```

```
cat(    [],T)          --η-->  T;
                         θ
cat([X|S],T)           -->  [X|cat(S,T)].
```

Let us identify and name identically in the tail form version `flat0_tf/1` the clauses that have their counterpart in the definition of `flat0/1`:

```
flat0_tf(T)                   --> flat0(T,[]).
flat0(           [],A)    --γ--> appk([],A);
flat0(      [[]|T],A)    --δ--> flat0(T,A);
flat0([Y=[_|_]|T],A)    --ε--> flat0(Y,[{k1,T}|A]);
flat0(       [Y|T],A)    --ζ--> flat0(T,[{k34,Y}|A]).
cat(    [],T,A)          --η--> appk(T,A);
                            θ
cat([X|S],T,A)          --> cat(S,T,[{k34,X}|A]).
appk(V,[{k34,Y}|A])    --> appk([Y|V],A);
appk(V, [{k2,W}|A])    --> cat(W,V,A);
appk(V, [{k1,T}|A])    --> flat0(T,[{k2,V}|A]);
appk(V,          [])    --> V.
```

Drawing from our practical understanding of the new, systematic transformation, we can try to summarise it as follows.

1. Consider all the definitions involved, that is, the one of immediate concern, but also all which it depends upon;
2. add a stack accumulator to all these definitions and add a definition setting the empty stack as the initial value of the accumulator;
3. for each body made of a call in tail form, just pass the accumulator unchanged;
4. replace each body containing no call by a call to a new function `appk/2`, with the body expression and the accumulator unchanged;
5. for each body not in tail form, including those of `appk/2`,

   (a) identify or choose the first call to be evaluated;
   (b) select all the values and variables in the call context which are parameters, except the accumulator, and group them in a tuple, together with a unique atom;
   (c) replace the body in question with the call to be done first and pass to it the accumulator on top of which the tuple of the previous step has been pushed;
   (d) create a clause for `appk/2` matching this case, whose body is the previously mentioned context;
   (e) replace the place-holder ␣ in the context by the first argument of `appk/2` and make sure that there is no clash of variables;

6. add the clause `appk(V,[]) -> V` to `appk/2`.

This algorithm is said to be *global*, insofar as *all* the steps must be achieved before a program equivalent to the original input is reached, because intermediary steps may not lead to correct definitions. It is possible to dynamically rearrange the order in which some steps are applied so the algorithm becomes *incremental*, but it is probably not worth the complication (based on the analysis of the call graph).

Let us apply the same methodological steps to another difficult definition like that of the Fibonacci function `fib/1`:

```
fib(0)                      β→  1;
fib(1)                      γ→  1;
fib(N) when N > 1  δ→  fib(N-1) + fib(N-2).
```

The steps are as follows.

1. This definition is self-contained.

2. Let us rename `fib/1` into `fib/2`, then add a stack accumulator to it so it becomes `fib/2`, next create a clause α defining `fib_tf/1` as a single call to `fib/2` where the initial value of the accumulator is the empty stack:

   ```
   fib_tf(N)                      α→  fib(N,[]).              % New
   fib(0,A)                       β→  1;
   fib(1,A)                       γ→  1;
   fib(N,A) when N > 1  δ→  fib(N-1,A) + fib(N-2,A).
   ```

3. There is no body in tail form which contains a call.

4. Clauses β and γ are in tail form and contain no call, so we must replace the bodies with a call to function `appk/2`, whose first argument is the original body (here, both are the value 1) and the second argument is the accumulator unchanged:

   ```
   fib_tf(N)                      α→  fib(N,[]).
   fib(0,A)                       β→  appk(1,A);
   fib(1,A)                       γ→  appk(1,A);
   fib(N,A) when N > 1  δ→  fib(N-1,A) + fib(N-2,A).
   ```

5. Clause δ is not in tail form and contains two calls, so we must choose which one we want to compute first. Let us arbitrarily choose the rightmost call, that is, `fib(N-2,A)`. Therefore, its context is `fib(N-1,A) + ⌴`. The values in the context, excluding the accumulator, are reduced to the sole value of `N`. Let us create a

unique atom identifying this call, `k1`, and form the pair `{k1,N}`. Let us replace the body of clause δ with `fib(N-2,[{k1,N}|A])`. Next, let us create a clause for `appk/2` matching this tuple. Its body is the context we just removed from the body of clause δ. In it, let us fill the hole ␣ with the first parameter.

```
fib_tf(N)                  α    fib(N,[]).
                           →
fib(0,A)                   β    appk(1,A);
                           →
fib(1,A)                   γ    appk(1,A);
                           →
fib(N,A) when N > 1        δ    fib(N-2,[{k1,N}|A]).
                           →
appk(V,[{k1,N}|A])         ε    fib(N-1,A) + V.
                           →
```

The body of ϵ is not in tail form, as it contains a function call not located at the root of the abstract syntax tree. The context of this call is ␣ + V and all the values it contains are limited to the one denoted by the variable V. Let us generate a new unique atom `k2` and pair it with V. We then replace the body of clause ϵ with the call to be computed first and we pass to it the accumulator A on top of which the pair has been pushed. We make a new clause of `appk/2` matching this case and in its body we put the context we just mentioned. We substitute the first parameter to the placeholder ␣. We have

```
appk(V,[{k2,W}|A])         ζ    V + W;
                           →
appk(V,[{k1,N}|A])         ε    fib(N-1,[{k2,V}|A]).
                           →
```

Note that we carefully renamed the variable V in the accumulator into W in order to avoid a clash with the first parameter V. This new body V+W is in tail form and contains no further function calls, so it must be embedded into a recursive call because the accumulator A may not be empty – so further calls may be waiting. We pass A to that call. Finally, all the clauses are in tail form:

```
fib_tf(N)                  α    fib(N,[]).
                           →
fib(0,A)                   β    appk(1,A);
                           →
fib(1,A)                   γ    appk(1,A);
                           →
fib(N,A) when N > 1        δ    fib(N-2,[{k1,N}|A]).
                           →
appk(V,[{k2,W}|A])         ζ    appk(V+W,A);
                           →
appk(V,[{k1,N}|A])         ε    fib(N-1,[{k2,V}|A]).
                           →
```

6. We must make sure to add a clause to match the case of the empty accumulator and rewrite to the first parameter:

```
fib_tf(N)                    α→  fib(N,[]).
fib(0,A)                     β→  appk(1,A);
fib(1,A)                     γ→  appk(1,A);
fib(N,A) when N > 1          δ→  fib(N-2,[{k1,N}|A]).
appk(V,          [])         η→  V;                    % Do not forget!
appk(V,[{k2,W}|A])           ζ→  appk(V+W,A);
appk(V,[{k1,N}|A])           ε→  fib(N-1,[{k2,V}|A]).
```

Let us apply now our general method to flat/1. Let us pick up here:

```
flat_tf(T)            -> flat(T,[]).
flat(          [],A) -> [];                    % A unused yet
flat(      [[]|T],A) -> flat(T,A);
flat([[X|S]|T],A) -> flat([X,S|T],A);
flat(      [Y|T],A) -> [Y|flat(T,A)].
```

The only body containing no calls is in the first clause of flat/2, so it must be passed to a call to appk/2, together with the accumulator. Only the last body is not in tail form. The only call to be performed has the context [Y|⌴], whose only values are reduced to the sole Y. So we generate a unique atom k1 and we pair it with Y. We replace the body not in tail form with the call to which we pass the accumulator on top of which the pair has been pushed. We consequently create a clause for appk/2 matching this case. Its body is the just erased context. The hole ⌴ is filled with the first parameter:

```
flat_tf(T)             -> flat(T,[]).
flat(          [],A)  -> appk([],A);
flat(      [[]|T],A)  -> flat(T,A);
flat([[X|S]|T],A)  -> flat([X,S|T],A);
flat(      [Y|T],A)  -> flat(T,[{k1,Y}|A]).
appk(V,[{k1,Y}|A]) -> [Y|V].
```

Since the body of the newly created clause of appk/2 is a value, it has to be wrapped into a recursive call because the accumulator A may not be empty, so perhaps some more calls have to be computed:

```
flat_tf(T)             -> flat(T,[]).
flat(          [],A)  -> appk([],A);
```

```
flat(    [[]|T],A)   -> flat(T,A);
flat([[X|S]|T],A)    -> flat([X,S|T],A);
flat(    [Y|T],A)    -> flat(T,[{k1,Y}|A]).
appk(V,[{k1,Y}|A])   -> appk([Y|V],A).
```

Finally, the definition of appk/2 must be completed by a clause corresponding to the case when the accumulator is empty and its body simply is the first argument, that is, by design, the result:

```
flat_tf(T)           -> flat(T,[]).
flat(         [],A)  -> appk([],A);
flat(    [[]|T],A)   -> flat(T,A);
flat([[X|S]|T],A)    -> flat([X,S|T],A);
flat(    [Y|T],A)    -> flat(T,[{k1,Y}|A]).
appk(V,          []) -> V;
appk(V,[{k1,Y}|A])   -> appk([Y|V],A).
```

If we compare this version with

```
flat_tf(T)           -> flat(T,[]).
flat(      [],A) -> rev(A);
flat(    [[]|T],A) -> flat(T,A);
flat([[X|S]|T],A) -> flat([X,S|T],A);
flat(    [Y|T],A) -> flat(T,[Y|A]).
```

we understand that the latter can be derived from the former if the pair {k1,Y} is replaced by Y. This is possible because it is the only atom which was generated. The definition of appk/2 then is equivalent to rcat/2 (section 2.2 on page 38):

```
rev(S)             -> rcat(S,[]).
rcat(    [],T) -> T;
rcat([X|S],T) -> rcat(S,[X|T]).
```

The philosophy underlying our general method to transform a given group of definitions into an equivalent in tail form consists in adding a parameter which is a stack accumulating the values of the different contexts and creating a function (appk/2) to reconstruct these when the call they contained is over. These rebuilt contexts are in turn transformed into tail form until all the clauses are in tail form. As a result, the number of clauses is larger than in the original source and the algorithm is obscured because of all the administrative work about the accumulator.

In order to save time and efforts, it is wise to consider tail forms useful *a posteriori*, when we run afoul of the maximum stack size because, except if very large inputs are, from the design phase, likely. Another reason may be to compile to low-level C (only using goto jumps).

Let us transform straight insertion (section 3.1 on page 95) and analyse the cost of the resulting definition. We start from

```
isrt(    [])                  β
                              ─→ [];
isrt([X|S])                   γ
                              ─→ ins(isrt(S),X).
ins([Y|S],X) when X > Y       δ
                              ─→ [Y|ins(S,X)];
ins(    S,X)                  ε
                              ─→ [X|S].
```

(the clauses have been renamed) and we add a stack accumulator to our functions and initialise it with the empty stack (new clause α):

```
isrt_tf(S)                    α
                              ─→ isrt(S,[]).
isrt(    [],A)                β
                              ─→ [];               % A unused yet
isrt([X|S],A)                 γ
                              ─→ ins(isrt(S,A),X,A).
ins([Y|S],X,A) when X > Y     δ
                              ─→ [Y|ins(S,X,A)];
ins(    S,X,A)                ε
                              ─→ [X|S].             % A unused yet
```

We can now inspect each clause and, depending on its body shape (that is: expression in tail form, either with or without a call, or not in tail form), some transformation is done. First, the body of clause β is in tail form and does not contain any function call. Thus, we transform it by calling the auxiliary function appk/2:

```
isrt(    [],A)                β
                              ─→ appk([],A);
```

Next is clause γ, which is not in tail form. The first call to be evaluated is isrt(S,A), whose control context is ins(_,X,A). Let us keep the call whilst saving into the accumulator A the variable X needed to rebuild the control context later, in a new clause of function appk/2. This variable needs *a priori* to be tagged by some unique atom, say k1:

```
isrt([X|S],A)                 γ
                              ─→ isrt(S,[{k1,X}|A]).
...
appk(V,[{k1,X}|A])            → ins(V,X,A).
```

The following clause is δ, which is not in tail form. The only call to be evaluated is ins(S,X,A), whose control context is [Y|_]. Let us associate Y with a unique atom k2, then save both of them in the accumulator A and, dually, add a clause to appk/2 to reconstruct the erased control context:

```
ins([Y|S],X,A) when X > Y     δ
                              ─→ ins(S,X,[{k2,Y}|A]);
...
appk(V,[{k2,Y}|A])            → appk([Y|V],A);
```

The last clause is ϵ, which is in tail form and contains no call, so we must pass its body to `appk/2` in order to check whether there are pending control contexts to rebuild and evaluate:

```
ins(    S,X,A)                    ϵ⟶ appk([X|S],A).
```

In order to complete the transformation, we must add a clause to `appk/2` to process the case when the accumulator is empty, so the final result is found. Finally, the resulting program is (last step in bold typeface)

```
isrt_tf(S)                        α⟶ isrt(S,[]).
isrt(    [],A)                    β⟶ appk([],A);
isrt([X|S],A)                     γ⟶ isrt(S,[{k1,X}|A]).
ins([Y|S],X,A) when X > Y         δ⟶ ins(S,X,[{k2,Y}|A]);
ins(    S,X,A)                    ϵ⟶ appk([X|S],A).
appk(V,         [])               ζ⟶ V;
appk(V,[{k2,Y}|A])                η⟶ appk([Y|V],A);
appk(V,[{k1,X}|A])                θ⟶ ins(V,X,A).
```

We can remark that the atom `k1` is not necessary in the definition of `isrt_tf/1`, since all other values in the accumulator are tagged `k2`:

```
isrt_tf(S)                        α⟶ isrt(S,[]).
isrt(    [],A)                    β⟶ appk([],A);
isrt([X|S],A)                     γ⟶ isrt(S,[X|A]).            % Here
ins([Y|S],X,A) when X > Y         δ⟶ ins(S,X,[{k2,Y}|A]);
ins(    S,X,A)                    ϵ⟶ appk([X|S],A).
appk(V,         [])               ζ⟶ V;
appk(V,[{k2,Y}|A])                η⟶ appk([Y|V],A);
appk(V,     [X|A])                θ⟶ ins(V,X,A).               % and here
```

It becomes obvious now that `isrt/2` reverses its first argument in the accumulator, which is initialised in clause α to the empty stack. Then, in clause β, `appk/2` is called with the same arguments. For instance, `isrt([3,8,2],[])` $\overset{3}{\rightarrow}$ `appk([],[2,8,3])`. Hence, we conclude that

$$\text{isrt}(S,[]) \equiv \text{appk}([],\text{rev}(S)),$$

which allows us to cut out the definition of `isrt/2` entirely as follows:

```
isrt_tf(S)                        α⟶ appk([],rev(S)).
ins([Y|S],X,A) when X > Y         δ⟶ ins(S,X,[{k2,Y}|A]);
ins(    S,X,A)                    ϵ⟶ appk([X|S],A).
appk(V,         [])               ζ⟶ V;
appk(V,[{k2,Y}|A])                η⟶ appk([Y|V],A);
appk(V,     [X|A])                θ⟶ ins(V,X,A).
```

We expect that sorting a stack or the same stack reversed is the same:

$$\mathtt{isrt\_tf}(S) \equiv \mathtt{isrt\_tf}(\mathtt{rev}(S)).$$

By clause α, and remarking that $\mathtt{rev}(\mathtt{rev}(S)) \equiv S$, we draw

$$\mathtt{isrt\_tf}(S) \equiv \mathtt{appk}([],\mathtt{rev}(\mathtt{rev}(S))) \equiv \mathtt{appk}([],S).$$

Therefore, we can simplify the body of clause α:

```
isrt_tf(S)                        α→  appk([],S).
ins([Y|S],X,A) when X > Y         δ→  ins(S,X,[{k2,Y}|A]);
ins(     S,X,A)                   ε→  appk([X|S],A).
appk(V,          [])              ζ→  V;
appk(V,[{k2,Y}|A])                η→  appk([Y|V],A);
appk(V,       [X|A])              θ→  ins(V,X,A).
```

We can get a shorter program at the expense of more comparisons. Remark that when clause η applies, Y is lower than the head of V, which exists because this clause is only used to compute the bodies of clauses ϵ and η, where the first argument is not the empty stack. Therefore, $\mathtt{appk}([Y|V],A) \equiv \mathtt{ins}(V,Y,A)$, because clause ϵ would apply. Accordingly, let us change clause η:

```
isrt_tf(S)                        α→  appk([],S).
ins([Y|S],X,A) when X > Y         δ→  ins(S,X,[{k2,Y}|A]);
ins(     S,X,A)                   ε→  appk([X|S],A).
appk(V,          [])              ζ→  V;
appk(V,[{k2,Y}|A])                η→  ins(V,Y,A);
appk(V,       [X|A])              θ→  ins(V,X,A).
```

We can see clearly now that `appk/2` calls `ins/3` in the same way in clauses η and θ, which means that it is useless to tag Y with k2 and we can get rid of clause θ (Z can either be a X or a Y):

```
isrt_tf(S)                        α→  appk([],S).
ins([Y|S],X,A) when X > Y         δ→  ins(S,[Y|A]);          % Here
ins(     S,X,A)                   ε→  appk([X|S],A).
appk(V,    [])                    ζ→  V;
appk(V,[Z|A])                     η→  ins(V,Z,A).            % and here
```

Perhaps it is clearer to get rid of `appk/2` by integrating its two operations in `isrt_tf/1` and `ins/3`. Let us split clauses α and ϵ to manifest the cases where, respectively, S and A are empty:

```
isrt_tf(    [])                          α0   appk([],[]);
isrt_tf([X|S])                           α1   appk([],[X|S]).
ins([Y|S],X,      A) when X > Y          δ    ins(S,X,[Y|A]);
ins(      S,X,[Y|A])                     ε0   appk([X|S],[Y|A]);
ins(      S,X,    [])                    ε1   appk([X|S],[]).
appk(V,    [])                           ζ    V;
appk(V,[Z|A])                            η    ins(V,Z,A).
```

We can now replace the bodies of clauses α_0 and ϵ_1 by their value, as
given by clause ζ, and we can remove ζ:

```
isrt_tf(    [])                          α0   [];
isrt_tf([X|S])                           α1   appk([],[X|S]).
ins([Y|S],X,      A) when X > Y          δ    ins(S,X,[Y|A]);
ins(      S,X,[Y|A])                     ε0   appk([X|S],[Y|A]);
ins(      S,X,    [])                    ε1   [X|S].
appk(V,[Z|A])                            η    ins(V,Z,A).
```

We saved one rewrite in case the input stack is empty. Lastly, the bodies
of clauses α_1 and ϵ_0 can be replaced by their value, as given by clause η,
which can be, finally, erased. We rename the accumulator A as T.

```
isrt_tf(    [])                          α0   [];
isrt_tf([X|S])                           α1   ins([],X,S).
ins([Y|S],X,      T) when X > Y          δ    ins(S,X,[Y|S]);
ins(      S,X,[Y|T])                     ε0   ins([X|S],Y,T);
ins(      S,X,    [])                    ε1   [X|S].
```

It is important to remember that these last steps, relative to the removal
of tag k2 and so forth, make sense only because, in assessing the cost,
we take into account only the number of function calls, not the number
of comparisons, which is now greater for not using the control context
[Y|_] in the original clause δ of ins/3. In other words, the keys saved in
the accumulator in the new clause δ have to be re-inserted in clause ϵ_0.

The same analysis used for assessing the cost of isrt/1 applies here as
well, except that the keys are inserted in their original order. So when the
keys are sorted increasingly, the cost is here *maximum* (that is, clause δ
is used maximally) and when it is sorted non-increasingly, the cost is
minimum (that is, clause δ is never used). *If keys are not repeated, the
best case of isrt/1 is the worst case of isrt_tf/1 and the worst case of
isrt/1 is the best case of isrt_tf/1.* This is true because 'nondecreasing'
means the same as 'increasing' when there is no repetition.

In order to find the minimum cost of the final version of isrt_tf/1, it
is helpful to get first a better understanding of the computational process

by unfolding a simple example like sorting $[4,3,2,1]$, which is a stack sorted in decreasing order:

```
isrt_tf([4,3,2,1])  ᵅ¹→ ins(     [],4,[3,2,1])
                    ᵉ⁰→ ins(     [4],3,  [2,1])
                    ᵉ⁰→ ins(  [3,4],2,    [1])
                    ᵉ⁰→ ins([2,3,4],1,     [])
                    ᵉ¹→ [1,2,3,4].
```

Let us note $\mathcal{B}_n^{\text{isrt\_tf}}$ the minimum cost of sorting n keys. Then $\mathcal{B}_0^{\text{isrt\_tf}} = 1$, by clause α_0. Let us assume next that $n > 0$. Then

- clause α_1 is used once;
- clause δ is not used, since we assume here that the keys are already sorted non-increasingly;
- clause ϵ_0 is used once for each key in its third argument, which, by clause α_1, means all keys except the first, that is $n - 1$ times;
- clause ϵ_1 is used once.

In sum, the evaluation trace is $\alpha_1 \epsilon_0^{n-1} \epsilon_1$, so the total cost is

$$\mathcal{B}_n^{\text{isrt\_tf}} = |\alpha_1 \epsilon_0^{n-1} \epsilon_1| = n + 1,$$

if $n > 0$. Since we found that $\mathcal{B}_0^{\text{isrt\_tf}} = 1 = 0 + 1$, we can extend the previous formula to $n = 0$. This result can be related directly to $\mathcal{W}_n^{\text{isrt}} = (n^2 + 3n + 2)/2$, because the best case of isrt_tf/1 corresponds to the worst case of isrt/1 when the keys are not repeated. We can further reckon that this minimum cost for isrt_tf/1 is also an absolute minimum for a sorting algorithm when the input is sorted non-increasingly, because it is simply the cost needed to reverse the input.

Let $\mathcal{W}_n^{\text{isrt\_tf}}$ be the maximum cost of isrt_tf(S), where the stack S contains n keys (in increasing order). For the empty stack, the evaluation trace is α_0. For singletons, for example, $[5]$, it is $\alpha_1 \epsilon_1$. To understand the general case $n > 1$, we can try

```
isrt_tf([1,2,3,4])  ᵅ¹→ ins(     [],1,[2,3,4])
                    ᵉ⁰→ ins(    [1],2,  [3,4])
                    ᵟ→ ins(     [],2,[1,3,4])
                    ᵉ⁰→ ins(    [2],1,  [3,4])
                    ᵉ⁰→ ins(  [1,2],3,    [4])
                    ᵟ→ ins(    [2],3,  [1,4])
                    ᵟ→ ins(     [],3,[2,1,4])
                    ᵉ⁰→ ins(    [3],2,  [1,4])
                    ᵉ⁰→ ins(  [2,3],1,    [4])
```

$$\begin{aligned}
&\xrightarrow{\epsilon_0}\ \texttt{ins([1,2,3],4,\qquad [])} \\
&\xrightarrow{\delta}\ \texttt{ins(\quad [2,3],4,\qquad [1])} \\
&\xrightarrow{\delta}\ \texttt{ins(\qquad [3],4,\quad [2,1])} \\
&\xrightarrow{\delta}\ \texttt{ins(\qquad\ [],4,[3,2,1])} \\
&\xrightarrow{\epsilon_0}\ \texttt{ins(\qquad [4],3,\quad [2,1])} \\
&\xrightarrow{\epsilon_0}\ \texttt{ins(\quad [3,4],2,\qquad [1])} \\
&\xrightarrow{\epsilon_0}\ \texttt{ins([2,3,4],1,\qquad [])} \\
&\xrightarrow{\epsilon_1}\ \texttt{[1,2,3,4].}
\end{aligned}$$

Notice the interplay of clauses δ and ϵ_0. A series of applications of clause δ ends with the first argument to be the empty stack. This is because the effect of clause δ is to save the contents of this argument by reversing it on top of the third argument. In other words, in the worst case, clause δ is equivalent to

```
ins([Y|S],X,T) when X > Y → ins([],X,rcat(S,[Y|T]));
```

A sequence of δ is followed by a series of ϵ_0 *of same length*, followed by another ϵ_0 or ϵ_1. The reason is that clause ϵ_0 restores on top of the first argument the keys saved previously by clause δ. Then, if there are some keys left in the last argument (to be sorted), one more application of clause ϵ_0 is required, otherwise the program ends with clause ϵ_1, that is, the evaluation trace when $n > 1$ is

$$\alpha_1 \prod_{p=0}^{n-2} \left(\delta^p \epsilon_0^{p+1} \right) \cdot \delta^{n-1} \epsilon_0^{n-1} \cdot \epsilon_1 = \alpha_1 \prod_{p=0}^{n-2} \left((\delta\epsilon_0)^p \epsilon_0 \right) \cdot (\delta\epsilon_0)^{n-1} \cdot \epsilon_1.$$

This observation is the key for finding the maximum cost as it hints at counting the rewrite steps of clause δ and of clause ϵ_0 *together*, as evinced in the right-hand side of the equality. We can now directly derive the maximum cost:

$$\mathcal{W}_n^{\text{isrt\_tf}} = \left| \alpha_1 \prod_{p=0}^{n-2} \left((\delta\epsilon_0)^p \epsilon_0 \right) \cdot (\delta\epsilon_0)^{n-1} \cdot \epsilon_1 \right|$$

$$= |\alpha_1| + \left| \prod_{p=0}^{n-2} \left((\delta\epsilon_0)^p \epsilon_0 \right) \right| + \left| (\delta\epsilon_0)^{n-1} \right| + |\epsilon_1|$$

$$= 1 + \sum_{p=0}^{n-2} |(\delta\epsilon_0)^p \epsilon_0| + (n-1)|\delta\epsilon_0| + 1$$

$$\mathcal{W}_n^{\text{isrt\_tf}} = 1 + \sum_{p=0}^{n-2} (2p+1) + 2(n-1) + 1 = n^2 + 1.$$

Since the worst case of `isrt_tf/1` and `isrt/1` are identical, we can compare their cost in this case, for $n \geqslant 0$:

$$\mathcal{W}_n^{\mathsf{isrt}} = \frac{1}{2}(n^2 + 3n + 2) \quad \text{and} \quad \mathcal{W}_n^{\mathsf{isrt\_tf}} = 2 \cdot \mathcal{W}_n^{\mathsf{isrt}} + 3n + 1.$$

Let us relate now the best and worst cases for `isrt/1` and `isrt_tf/1`. We have, for $n > 3$, $\mathcal{B}_n^{\mathsf{isrt\_tf}} < \mathcal{B}_n^{\mathsf{isrt}} < \mathcal{W}_n^{\mathsf{isrt}} < \mathcal{W}_n^{\mathsf{isrt\_tf}}$. If we note $\mathcal{C}_n^{\mathsf{isrt}}$ the cost of `isrt/1` on an input of length n, these inequalities are equivalent to say $\mathcal{B}_n^{\mathsf{isrt\_tf}} < \mathcal{C}_n^{\mathsf{isrt}} < \mathcal{W}_n^{\mathsf{isrt\_tf}}$. This is the best we can do because we only have the obvious inequalities $\mathcal{B}_n^{\mathsf{isrt\_tf}} \leqslant \mathcal{C}_n^{\mathsf{isrt\_tf}} \leqslant \mathcal{W}_n^{\mathsf{isrt\_tf}}$, which do not allow us to compare $\mathcal{C}_n^{\mathsf{isrt}}$ and $\mathcal{C}_n^{\mathsf{isrt\_tf}}$. In order to obtain a stronger result, we need an average cost analysis so we can tell apart `isrt_tf/1` from `isrt/1`. Indeed, it might be that, for a given input stack of length n, most configurations of the input lead to a cost for `isrt_tf/1` which is actually lower than for `isrt/1`. Let us note $\mathcal{A}_n^{\mathsf{isrt\_tf}}$ the average number of rewrites needed to compute $\mathsf{isrt\_tf}(S)$, where the length of stack S is n. Similarly, we note $\mathcal{A}_{p,q}^{\mathsf{ins}}$ for the average cost of the call $\mathsf{ins}(P,X,Q)$, where stack P has length p and stack Q has length q. The short story is this: because the keys are random, the average number of times clause δ is used is $p/2$. Since the aim of clause ϵ_0, as observed before, is to put back the keys previously moved by clause δ, we expect, in average, the same number $p/2$, plus 1, because clause ϵ_0 also prepares the possible following use of clause δ. In other words, the difference with the longest evaluation trace defining $\mathcal{W}_n^{\mathsf{isrt}}$ is that the subsequences $\delta\epsilon_0$ are expected to be 50% shorter in average, so the evaluation trace is, in average,

$$\alpha_1 \prod_{p=0}^{n-2} \left((\delta\epsilon_0)^{p/2} \epsilon_0 \right) \cdot (\delta\epsilon_0)^{(n-1)/2} \cdot \epsilon_1,$$

from which we deduce the average cost for $n > 1$:

$$\mathcal{A}_n^{\mathsf{isrt\_tf}} = 1 + \sum_{p=0}^{n-2} \left(2 \cdot \frac{p}{2} + 1 \right) + \left(2 \cdot \frac{n-1}{2} \right) + 1 = \frac{1}{2}n^2 + \frac{1}{2}n + 1.$$

Elegantly, this formula extends to cope with $n = 0, 1$ and we can compare now $\mathcal{A}_n^{\mathsf{isrt\_tf}}$ to $\mathcal{A}_n^{\mathsf{isrt}}$, for $n \geqslant 0$:

$$\mathcal{A}_n^{\mathsf{isrt\_tf}} = \frac{1}{2}n^2 + \frac{1}{2}n + 1 \sim \frac{1}{2}n^2 \sim 2 \cdot \mathcal{A}_n^{\mathsf{isrt}}.$$

In other words, `isrt_tf/1`, in spite of being optimised, is nevertheless 50% slower than the original function, *in average for large values of* n. This should not be too surprising, as a transformation to tail form should only be undertaken for the sake of the control stack, not efficiency.

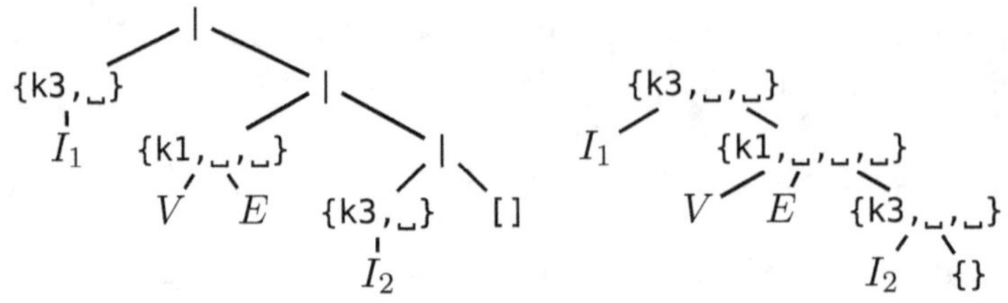

(a) With a stack of tuples   (b) With nested tuples

Figure 9.16: Two implementations of the same linear accumulator

Exercise   Consider the variation

```
isrt0(L)                                -> isrt0(    L,    [],    []).
isrt0(    [],    [],    Q)              -> Q;
isrt0(    [],[J|P],    Q)              -> isrt0(    [],    P,[J|Q]);
isrt0([I|L],      P,[K|Q]) when K > I  -> isrt0([I|L],[K|P],    Q);
isrt0([I|L],[J|P],    Q) when I > J   -> isrt0([I|L],    P,[J|Q]);
isrt0([I|L],      P,    Q)             -> isrt0(    L,    P,[I|Q]).
```

Here, one rewrite involves moving exactly one key, so the cost of isrt0/3 is the number of key movements to sort the original stack. Analyse the minimum, maximum and average number of key movements.

Light encoding of stack accumulators   The accumulators used to transform definitions into tail form are, in their most general instance, stacks of tuples. While using a stack brings to the fore the very nature of the accumulator, it incurs a penalty in the size of the memory required because, in the abstract syntax trees, a push corresponds to a node, just as a tuple. *By nesting tuples in tuples, we can get rid of the stack altogether.* For instance, instead of writing $[\{k3,X_1\},\{k1,V,E\},\{k3,X_2\}]$, we would write the nested tuples $\{k3,X_1,\{k1,V,E,\{k3,X_2,\{\}\}\}\}$. Both abstract syntax trees are easily compared in FIGURE 9.16. The encoding of a stack accumulator by means of tuples only supposes to add a component to each tuple, which holds what was the 'next' tuple in the stack. The memory saving consists in one edge for each initial tuple, plus all the push nodes, that is, if there were n tuples, we save n edges (often called *pointers* in imperative languages) and n nodes. This is a very significant amelioration. As an illustration, let us improve on the following code we derived earlier:

```
flat0_tf(T)                     α→  flat0(T,[]).
flat0(          [],A)  γ→  appk([],A);
flat0(     [[]|T],A)  δ→  flat0(T,A);
```

```
flat0([Y=[_|_]|T],A)  ϵ→  flat0(Y,[{k1,T}|A]);
flat0(      [Y|T],A)  ζ→  flat0(T,[{k34,Y}|A]).
cat(      [],T,A)     η→  appk(T,A);
cat([X|S],T,A)        θ→  cat(S,T,[{k34,X}|A]).
appk(V,[{k34,Y}|A])   μ→  appk([Y|V],A);
appk(V, [{k2,W}|A])   λ→  cat(W,V,A);
appk(V, [{k1,T}|A])   κ→  flat0(T,[{k2,V}|A]);
appk(V,          [])  ι→  V.
```

It results in the more economical

```
flat0_tf(T)           α→  flat0(T,{}).
flat0(           [],A) γ→  appk([],A);
flat0(       [[]|T],A) δ→  flat0(T,A);
flat0([Y=[_|_]|T],A)  ϵ→  flat0(Y,{k1,T,A});
flat0(       [Y|T],A)  ζ→  flat0(T,{k34,Y,A}).
cat(     [],T,A)      η→  appk(T,A);
cat([X|S],T,A)        θ→  cat(S,T,{k34,X,A}).
appk(V,{k34,Y,A})     μ→  appk([Y|V],A);
appk(V, {k2,W,A})     λ→  cat(W,V,A);
appk(V, {k1,T,A})     κ→  flat0(T,{k2,V,A});
appk(V,        {})    ι→  V.
```

Improvements   Just to illustrate the point that improvements on a definition which is not in tail form are much more beneficial than a mere transformation to tail form, let us consider again the Fibonacci function:

```
fib(0)                  -> 1;
fib(1)                  -> 1;
fib(N) when N > 1 -> fib(N-1) + fib(N-2).
```

The equations defining the cost of this function are simply:

$$C_0^{\text{fib}} := 1; \quad C_1^{\text{fib}} := 1; \quad C_n^{\text{fib}} := 1 + C_{n-1}^{\text{fib}} + C_{n-2}^{\text{fib}}, \text{ with } n > 1.$$

Adding 1 on both sides of the last equation and reordering the terms:

$$C_n^{\text{fib}} + 1 = (C_{n-1}^{\text{fib}} + 1) + (C_{n-2}^{\text{fib}} + 1).$$

This gives us the idea to set $D_n := C_n^{\text{fib}} + 1$, yielding, for $n > 1$,

$$D_0 = C_0^{\text{fib}} + 1 = 2, \quad D_1 = C_1^{\text{fib}} + 1 = 2, \quad D_n = D_{n-1} + D_{n-2}.$$

The recurrence is the same as the Fibonacci sequence (third clause of `fib/1`), except for D_0 and D_1 whose values are 2 instead of 1. In order to make it coincide with the values of `fib/1`, we need to set $F_n := D_n/2$:

$$C_n^{\text{fib}} = 2 \cdot F_n - 1.$$

Now we have $F_0 = F_1 = 1$ and $F_n = F_{n-1} + F_{n-2}$, for all $n > 1$; importantly, F_n computes the same values as `fib/1`, that is, $F_n \equiv \texttt{fib}(n)$. The *generating function* associated to the sequence $(F_n)_{n \geqslant 0}$ is

$$f(x) := \sum_{k \geqslant 0} F_k x^k. \tag{9.1}$$

Let us set aside for a moment the issue of the convergence and let us work out a closed form for $f(x)$. We have $xf(x) = \sum_{k>0} F_{k-1}x^k$ and $x^2 f(x) = \sum_{k>1} F_{k-2}x^k$, therefore

$$f(x) - xf(x) - x^2 f(x) = F_0 + F_1 x - F_0 x + \sum_{k>1} (F_k - F_{k-1} - F_{k-2})x^k = x.$$

Thus

$$f(x) = \frac{x}{1 - x - x^2}.$$

Now, let us expand $f(x)$ back into a power series by naming $\phi := \frac{1+\sqrt{5}}{2}$ and $\hat{\phi} := \frac{1-\sqrt{5}}{2}$ the roots of $1 - x - x^2$ and factoring the denominator:

$$f(x) = \frac{x}{(1 - \phi x)(1 - \hat{\phi} x)} = \frac{1}{\sqrt{5}} \left(\frac{1}{1 - \phi x} - \frac{1}{1 - \hat{\phi} x} \right).$$

We can now use the geometric power series $\frac{1}{1-\alpha x} = \sum_{k \geqslant 0} \alpha^k x^k$ to derive

$$f(x) = \sum_{k \geqslant 0} \frac{\phi^k - \hat{\phi}^k}{\sqrt{5}} x^k,$$

so, by identification with the coefficients in equation (9.1), we conclude

$$F_n = \frac{1}{\sqrt{5}}(\phi^n - \hat{\phi}^n).$$

(See Graham et al. (1994), § 6.6, for more details.) Of course, we may very well doubt the result, as the method neglects convergence issues, therefore let us prove now by means of complete induction on $n > 0$ that

$$F_0 = 1; \quad F_n = \frac{1}{\sqrt{5}}(\phi^n - \hat{\phi}^n).$$

First, let us verify that the formula works for the smallest value of n:

$$F_1 = \frac{1}{\sqrt{5}}(\phi - \hat{\phi}) = \frac{1}{\sqrt{5}}(\phi - (1 - \phi)) = 1,$$

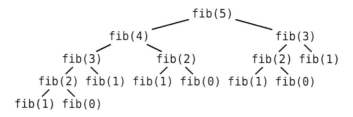

Figure 9.17: Call tree of `fib(5)`

where we used the fact $\hat{\phi} = 1 - \phi$. Let us suppose now that the equation to establish is valid for all values ranging from 1 to n (this is the complete induction hypothesis) and let us prove that it holds for $n + 1$. We have $F_{n+1} := F_n + F_{n-1}$. We can use the complete induction hypothesis for the cases $n - 1$ and n:

$$F_{n+1} = \frac{1}{\sqrt{5}}(\phi^n - \hat{\phi}^n) + \frac{1}{\sqrt{5}}(\phi^{n-1} - \hat{\phi}^{n-1})$$
$$= \frac{1}{\sqrt{5}}(\phi^{n-1}(\phi+1) - \hat{\phi}^{n-1}(\hat{\phi}+1)).$$

The key is that ϕ and $\hat{\phi}$ are the roots of $x^2 = x + 1$, therefore

$$F_{n+1} = \frac{1}{\sqrt{5}}(\phi^{n-1} \cdot \phi^2 - \hat{\phi}^{n-1} \cdot \hat{\phi}^2) = \frac{1}{\sqrt{5}}(\phi^{n+1} - \hat{\phi}^{n+1}),$$

which was the statement to be proved. The complete induction principle then implies that the equation holds for all $n > 0$. Now that we derived a closed form for F_n, let us study its asymptotic behaviour. This is straightforward if we start by noticing that $\hat{\phi} < 1$, therefore $\hat{\phi}^n \to 0$, as n gets large and, because $\phi > 1$,

$$F_n \sim \frac{1}{\sqrt{5}}\phi^n, \text{ implying } C_n^{\text{fib}} \sim \frac{2}{\sqrt{5}}\phi^n.$$

That is, this cost is *exponential* and, because $\phi > 1$, it will always be greater than any polynomial cost, except perhaps for a finite number of some small values of n. In other words, this is hopelessly slow.

How can we improve this definition?

We must resist the temptation to transform it into tail form because being in tail form only benefits the control stack, not the cost in general. By looking at the call tree of `fib(5)` in FIGURE 9.17, we realise that some small subtrees are duplicated, like the ones rooted at `fib(2)` and, even larger ones, like `fib(3)`. Let us examine the leftmost branch, from the leaf to the root. It is made of the successive nodes `fib(1)`, `fib(2)`, `fib(3)`, `fib(4)` and `fib(5)`, that is, all the values of `fib(N)` for N ranging from 1 to 5. Generalising this observation, we can say that the series $(\texttt{fib(N)})_N$ is entirely described, except `fib(0)`, by the leftmost branch in the call tree of `fib(N)`. Therefore, starting from the small tree

```
         fib(2)
        ╱      ╲
    fib(1)    fib(0)
```

we can obtain the complete call tree for `fib(5)` by growing the tree from the root, whilst sharing some subtrees, that is, reusing them instead of recomputing them, so the call tree looks now like in FIGURE 9.18 (technically, it is a directed acyclic graph), where the arrowed edges implement the reuse of subtrees. This graph representation leads us to think that if two successive Fibonacci numbers are kept at all times, we can achieve this maximal sharing. Let us denote by F_n the nth Fibonacci number in the series. Then each computational step is $(F_{n-1}, F_n) \to (F_n, F_{n+1}) := (F_n, F_n + F_{n-1})$. Let f be the function such that $f(x, y) := (y, x + y)$, then $(F_n, F_{n+1}) = f(F_{n-1}, F_n)$ and

$$(F_n, F_{n+1}) = f(F_{n-1}, F_n) = f(f(F_{n-2}, F_{n-1})) = f^2(F_{n-2}, F_{n-1})$$

etc. till we reach $(F_n, F_{n+1}) = f^n(F_0, F_1) := f^n(1, 1)$, for all $n \geqslant 0$. Let π_1 be the function such that $\pi_1(x, y) = x$, that is, it projects the first component of a pair, then $F_n = \pi_1 \circ f^n(1, 1)$, for all $n \geqslant 0$. The iteration of f is easy to define by the recurrences

$$f^0(x, y) = (x, y), \quad f^n(x, y) = f^{n-1}(f(x, y)) := f^{n-1}(y, x + y).$$

The **Erlang** code is now straightforward:

```
fib_opt(N) -> pi1(f(N,{1,1})).
pi1({X,_}) -> X.
f(0,{X,Y}) -> {X,Y};
f(N,{X,Y}) -> f(N-1,{Y,X+Y}).
```

A tail form definition is extremely easy to obtain, without even applying the general method:

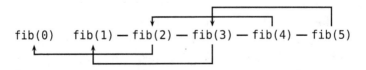

Figure 9.18: Call tree of `fib(5)` with maximal sharing

```
fib_opt_tf(N) -> f(N,{1,1}).
f(0,{X,_})    -> X;                      % Projection done here
f(N,{X,Y})    -> f(N-1,{Y,X+Y}).
```

We deduce that its cost is $n + 2$. This is a tremendous improvement over fib/1 and, as an unexpected bonus, the definition is in tail form and is made of the same number of clauses as the original.

The general algorithm we presented in this section transforms all the definitions of the functions used by a given definition. Assuming that the size of the control stack is a real issue, is it possible not to transform all the functions involved? Consider again slst0/2, defined in equation (2.7) on page 53:

```
slst0(S,X) -> rev(sfst(rev(S),X)).
```

If we use the alternative definition sfst0/2, which is in tail form, instead of sfst/2, and, since rev/1 is already in tail form, we reach

```
slst0(S,X) -> rev(sfst0(rev(S),X)).
```

where all the composed functions are in tail form. Of course, a function composition, like sfst0/2, is not, by definition, in tail form, but it is not a problem. The size of control stack needed to compute the calls to slst0/2 will be bounded by a small constant, because it is not recursive.

9.2 Higher-order functions

Polymorphic sorting There is an aspect of straight insertion sort with isrt/1 (section 3.1 on page 95) which deserves a second thought. Erlang functions are *polymorphic*, that is, they may process some of their arguments in a uniform manner, irrespective of its type. For example, reversing a stack does not depend on the nature of the keys it contains – it is a purely structural algorithm. By contrast, our definition of isrt/1 relies on the usage of the predefined comparison operator (>) in a guard. This implies that all keys in the stack must be pairwise comparable – for example, they can be integers. But what if we want to sort other kinds of values, like stacks? Consider the very practical need to sort a set of bills: each bill can be represented by a stack of prices rounded to the closest integer and the set in question by a stack itself; we would then want to sort by insertion the bills by, say, nondecreasing total amounts. If we set on writing a version of isrt/1 tailored to work only with keys which are stacks of integers, we are duplicating code and we would have to write a different instance every time a different kind of values to be sorted presents itself. As a consequence, what is needed here is polymorphism on *function parameters*, more precisely, the possibility of a function to be a value, thus suitable as an argument. **Erlang** provides this facility in a natural way and many functional languages do as well. In our case, we need the caller of `isrt/1` to provide an additional argument which is a comparison function between the keys. Then the new `isrt/2` would make use of this caller-defined comparison, instead of always applying the default operator (>) which works only (or mostly) on integers. Here is again the definition of `isrt/1`:

```
isrt(    [])                    β→ [];
isrt([X|S])                     γ→ ins(isrt(S),X).
ins([Y|S],X) when X > Y         δ→ [Y|ins(S,X)];
ins(    S,X)                    ε→ [X|S].
```

Then, our first attempt at modification leads us straightforwardly to

```
isrtf(    [],_)                 β→ [];
isrtf([X|S],F)                  γ→ ins(isrtf(S,F),X,F).
ins([Y|S],X,F) when F(X,Y)      δ→ [Y|ins(S,X,F)];
ins(    S,X,_)                  ε→ [X|S].
```

But the compiler would reject this program because **Erlang** does not allow a user-defined function to be called in a guard. The rationale is that the call `F(X,Y)` above may not terminate and **Erlang** guarantees that pattern matching always ends. Because it is impossible to automatically check whether any function call terminates on all inputs (this problem is equivalent to the famous *halting problem of a Turing machine*, which is *undecidable*), the compiler does not even try and prefers to reject all guards made of function calls. Thus we must move the call `F(X,Y)` inside the body of the same clause, which begets the question as how to merge clauses δ and ϵ into a new clause δ_0. A simple way out is to create another function, `triage/4`, whose task is to take the result of the comparison and proceed with the rest of the evaluation. Of course, this means that `triage/4` must also receive all necessary information to carry on:

```
isrtf(    [],_)                 β→ [];
isrtf([X|S],F)                  γ→ ins(isrtf(S,F),X,F).
ins([Y|S],X,F)                  δ₀→ triage(F(X,Y),[Y|S],X,F).
triage(⬚,[Y|S],X,F)             ζ→ [Y|ins(S,X,F)];
triage(⬚,[Y|S],X,F)             η→ [X|S].
```

The empty boxes must be filled with the result of a comparison. In our case, we want a comparison with two possible outputs, depending on the first argument being lower or greater than the second. By definition, the result of X > Y is the atom true if the value of X is greater than the value of Y and false otherwise. Let us follow the same convention for F and impose that the value of F(X,Y) is the atom true if X is greater than Y and false otherwise. It is even better to rename the parameter F into something more intuitive according to its behaviour, like Gt (*Greater than*):

```
triage( true,[Y|S],X,Gt) ↪ [Y|ins(Gt,X,S)];
triage(false,[Y|S],X,Gt) ↪ [X|S].
```

We notice that clause η makes no use of Y, which means we actually lose a key. What went wrong and when? The mistake came from not realising that clause ϵ covered two cases, S is empty or not, therefore we should have untangled these two cases before merging clause ϵ with clause δ, because in δ we have the pattern [Y|S], that is, the non-empty case. Let us rewind and split ϵ into ϵ_0 and ϵ_1:

```
isrtf(    [], _)                    ᵝ↪ [];
isrtf([X|S],Gt)                     ᵞ↪ ins(isrtf(S,Gt),X,Gt).
ins([Y|S],X,Gt) when Gt(X,Y) ᵟ↪ [Y|ins(S,X,Gt)];
ins([Y|S],X,Gt)                     ᵉ⁰↪ [X|[Y|S]];
ins(    [],X, _)                    ᵉ¹↪ [X].
```

Notice that we did not write

```
ins([],X,_) ᵉ¹↪ [X];
ins( S,X,_) ᵉ⁰↪ [X|S].
```

even though it would have been correct, because we had in mind the fusion with clause δ, so we needed to make the pattern [Y|S] conspicuous in ϵ_0. For even more clarity, we made apparent the parameter Gt: the patterns of clauses δ and ϵ_0 are now identical and ready to merge into a new clause δ_0:

```
isrtf(    [], _)                    ᵝ↪ [];
isrtf([X|S],Gt)                     ᵞ↪ ins(isrtf(S,Gt),X,Gt).
ins([Y|S],X,Gt)                     ᵟ⁰↪ triage(Gt(X,Y),[Y|S],X,Gt).
ins(    [],X, _)                    ᵉ¹↪ [X].
triage( true,[Y|S],X,Gt) ↪ [Y|ins(S,X,Gt)];
triage(false,[Y|S],X, _) ᵞ↪ [X|[Y|S]].
```

We can improve a little bit clause η by not distinguishing Y and S:

```
triage(false,    S,X, _) ᵞ↪ [X|S].
```

This transformation is correct because S is never empty. Instead of using an auxiliary function like triage/4, which takes many arguments and serves no purpose other than performing a test on the value of Gt(X,Y) and proceed accordingly, we can make good use of a case construct:

```
isrtf(   [], _) ─β→ [];
isrtf([X|S],Gt) ─γ→ ins(isrtf(S,Gt),X,Gt).
ins([Y|S],X,Gt) ─δ0→ case Gt(X,Y) of
                     true ─ς→ [Y|ins(S,X,Gt)];
                     false ─η→ [X|[Y|S]]
                   end;
ins(   [],X, _) ─ε1→ [X].
```

We can decrease the memory usage again in the clause η (case false), this time by means of an alias for the pattern [Y|S], so the best version of the code is

```
isrtf(   [], _)    ─β→ [];
isrtf([X|S],Gt)    ─γ→ ins(isrtf(S,Gt),X,Gt).
ins(T=[Y|S],X,Gt)  ─δ0→ case Gt(X,Y) of
                        true ─ς→ [Y|ins(S,X,Gt)];
                        false ─η→ [X|T]
                      end;
ins(   [],X, _) ─ε1→ [X].
```

How would we call isrtf/2 so the resulting value is the same as calling isrt/1? First, we need a comparison function which behaves exactly like the operator (>):

```
gt_int(X,Y) when X > Y -> true;
gt_int(_,_)            -> false.
```

If we try now to form the call

$$isrtf([5,3,1,4,2],gt\_int),$$

we find that an error occurs at run-time because gt_int is an atom, not a function. That is why Erlang provides a special syntax for denoting functions used as values:

$$isrtf([5,3,1,4,2],\textbf{fun } gt\_int/2).$$

Notice the new keyword fun and the usual indication of the number of arguments the function is expected to operate on (here, two).

What would happen if we passed as an argument the function lt_int/2 defined as follows?

```
lt_int(X,Y) when X < Y -> true;
lt_int(X,Y)               -> false.
```

The consequence is that the result is sorted non-increasingly and all we had to do was to change the comparison function, *not the sorting function itself.*

It may seem a burden to have to name even simple comparison functions like lt_int/2, which is none other than the predefined operator (<). Fortunately, Erlang provides a way to define functions without giving them a name. The syntax consists in using the keyword fun together with the keyword end and put the usual definition in-between, without a function name. Reconsider for example the previous calls but using such anonymous functions (sometimes called *lambdas*):

$$isrtf([5,3,1,4,2],\textbf{fun}(X,Y) \rightarrow X > Y\ \textbf{end})$$

results in [1,2,3,4,5] and

$$isrtf([5,3,1,4,2],\textbf{fun}(X,Y) \rightarrow X < Y\ \textbf{end})$$

results in [5,4,3,2,1].

Let us now use isrtf/2 to sort stacks of stacks of integers, according to the sum of the integers in each stack – this is the practical application of sorting bills we previously mentioned. As the example of sorting in non-increasing order hints at, we only need here to write how to compare two stacks of integers by means of the sum0/1 function in FIGURE 9.5 on page 299). We have $C_n^{\text{sum0}} = n + 2$. Now we can define the comparison function gt_bill/2, based upon the operator (>):

```
gt_bill(P,Q) -> sum0(P) > sum0(Q).
```

Notice in passing that the predefined Erlang comparison operator (>) results in either the atom true or false, so there is no need to use a case construct. Then we can sort our bills by calling

$$isrtf([[1,5,2,9],[7],[2,5,11],[4,3]],\textbf{fun}\ gt\_bill/2)$$

or, simply,

$$isrtf([[1,5,2,9],[7],[2,5,11],[4,3]],$$
$$\textbf{fun}(P,Q) \rightarrow sum0(P) < sum0(Q)\ \textbf{end}).$$

(By the way, do we expect [7] to appear before or after [4,3] in the answer? What would we have to modify so the relative order of these two stacks is reversed?) It is just as easy to sort the bills in non-increasing order. This great easiness in passing around functions as any other kind of values is what justifies the adjective *functional* for a language like Erlang and many others. A function taking another function as an argument is said to be a *higher-order function*.

Sorted association lists   There is something that we could improve
in the previous definition of isrtf/2. Sorting by comparison may imply that some keys are compared more than once, as the worst case of
insertion sort demonstrates eloquently. It may be that one comparison
has a small cost but, compounded over many uses, it leads to a significant cost. In the case of sorting bills, it is more efficient to compute all
the total amounts first and then only use these amounts during the sort
process, because comparing one integer to another is much faster than
recomputing the sum of many integers in a stack. So, what is sorted is a
stack of pairs whose first component, called the *key*, is a simple and small
representative of the second component, called the *value* (improperly, as
keys are Erlang values as well, but such is the traditional nomenclature).
This data structure is sometimes called an *association list*. Only the key
is used for sorting, not the value, therefore, if the key is an integer, the
comparison on the key is likely to be faster than on the values. The only
penalty is that all the keys must be precomputed in a first pass over the
initial data and they must be stripped from the final result in an additional postprocessing. This time we shall design these first and last passes
in the most general fashion by parameterisation upon the evaluation Mk
of the keys:

```
% Computing the keys
mk_keys( _,         []) -> [];
mk_keys(Mk,[V|Values]) -> [{Mk(V),V}|mk_keys(Mk,Values)].


% Eliminating the keys
rm_keys(                []) -> [];
rm_keys([{_,V}|KeyVal]) -> [V|rm_keys(KeyVal)].
```

The cost of mk_keys/2 depends on the cost of Mk. The cost of calling
rm_keys(S) is $n + 1$ if S contains n pairs key-value. Now we can sort by
calling isrtf/2 with a comparison on two keys and with the function to
build the keys, sum0/1. For instance:

```
rm_keys(isrtf(mk_keys(fun sum0/1,
                      [[1,5,2,9],[7],[2,5,11],[4,3]]),
             fun({K1,_},{K2,_}) -> K1 > K2 end))
```

It is very important to notice that we did not need to redefine isrtf/2.
Actually, isrtf/2, mk_keys/2 and rm_keys/1 would very well constitute a
library by grouping their definitions in the same module. The client, that
is, the user of the library, would then provide the comparison function
fitted to their data to be sorted and the function making the keys. This
modularisation is enabled by polymorphism and higher-order functions.

$$\boxed{\begin{aligned}
&\mathsf{len}_0(s) \rightarrow \mathsf{len}_0(s, 0).\\
&\mathsf{len}_0([\,], n) \rightarrow n;\\
&\mathsf{len}_0([x\,|\,s], n) \rightarrow \mathsf{len}_0(s, n+1).
\end{aligned}}$$

Figure 9.19: Computing the length of a stack (tail form)

As a last example proving the versatility of our program, let us sort stacks by their non-increasing lengths:

```
rm_keys(isrtf(mk_keys(fun len0/1,
                     [[1,5,2,9],[7],[2,5,11],[4,3]]),
             fun({K1,_},{K2,_}) -> K1 < K2 end))
```

where `len0/1` is specified in FIGURE 9.19. The result:

$$[[1,5,2,9],[2,5,11],[4,3],[7]].$$

Notice that [4,3] occurs before [7] because the former is longer.

Let us specialise further `isrtf/1`. Here is the definition again:

```
isrtf(   [], _)        ──β──▸ [];
isrtf([X|S],Gt)        ──γ──▸ ins(isrtf(S,Gt),X,Gt).
ins(T=[Y|S],X,Gt) ──δ₀──▸ case Gt(X,Y) of
                      true   ──ζ──▸ [Y|ins(S,X,Gt)];
                      false  ──η──▸ [X|T]
                  end;
ins(      [],X, _) ──ε₁──▸ [X].
```

It is clear that if keys are repeated in the input stack, the call `Gt(X,Y)` is expected to be rewritten to **false** at least once, therefore duplicates are kept by clause η and their relative order is preserved, that is, the sorting algorithm is stable. What if we do not want to preserve such duplicates in the output? We need to rewrite the definition to support this choice. The choice itself, that is, to keep them or not, would naturally be implemented as an additional functional parameter, say `Eq`. Also, we would need a 3-way comparison, so the equality case is explicit. Let us modify the variable `Gt` to reflect this increase in detail and call it more generally `Cmp` (*compare*). Its arguments should be values amongst the user-defined atoms `lt` (*lower than*), `gt` (*greater than*) and `eq` (*equal*). We have

```
isrtf(   [], _, _)       ──β──▸ [];
isrtf([X|S],Cmp,Eq)      ──γ──▸ ins(isrtf(S,Cmp,Eq),X,Cmp,Eq).
```

```
ins(T=[Y|S],X,Cmp,Eq) ──δ₀→ case Cmp(X,Y) of
                            gt ──ς→ [Y|ins(S,X,Cmp,Eq)];
                            lt ──η→ [X|T];
                            eq ──θ→ Eq(X,T)                    % New case
                          end;
ins(      [],X,  _, _) ──ε₁→ [X].
```

Now, let us say that we want to sort nondecreasingly a stack of integers and retain possible redundant numbers, just as the previous version allowed. We have (novelty in boldface type):

```
isrtf([5,3,1,4,3],fun(X,Y) -> X>Y end,fun(X,T) -> [X|T] end)
```

which results in `[1,3,3,4,5]`. If we do not want the numbers repeated, we form instead the call

```
isrtf([5,3,1,4,3],fun(X,Y) -> X>Y end,fun(_,T) -> T end)
```

resulting in `[1,3,4,5]`. In passing, this technique solves the problem of removing duplicates in a stack of keys for which there is a total order. However, if only successive duplicates have to be removed from a stack, the function `red/1`, defined in FIGURE 2.22 on page 73, is more efficient because its cost is linear in the input size.

We would be remiss if we do not mention that a higher-order function is not only a function whose at least one parameter is a function, but it also can be a function whose calls evaluate in a function. This kind of function is said to be *curried*, as an homage to the logician Haskell Curry. The possibility was already there when we introduced the keywords `fun` and `end`, because they allow us to define an anonymous function and use it just like another value, so nothing impeded us from using such a functional value as the result of a named function, like in the following function mathematically composing two functions:

```
compose(F,G) -> (fun(X) -> F(G(X)) end).
```

Actually, the parentheses around the functional value are useless if we remember that *the keywords* `fun` *and* `end` *play the role of parentheses when the anonymous function is not called*:

```
compose(F,G) -> fun(X) -> F(G(X)) end.
```

The higher-order function `compose/2` can be used to compute the composition of two other functions, the result being a function, of course.

Functional iterators We may desire a function which sums the images of a stack S of integers by a given function f. In mathematical notation, the final result would be expressed as

$$\sum_{k \in S} f(k).$$

In order to implement this in **Erlang**, we must proceed in two steps: firstly, we need a higher-order function which computes the images of the items of a stack by a function; secondly, we need a function summing the integers of a stack. We already have the latter, known from FIGURE 9.5 page 299 as `sum0/1`. The former is traditionally called `map/2`, such that the call `map(F,S)` applies function F to all the items of stack S and evaluates into the stack of the results. That is,

$$\mathtt{map}(F,[X_1,X_2,\ldots,X_n]) \equiv [F(X_1),F(X_2),\ldots,F(X_n)].$$

With this goal in mind, it is straightforward to define `map/2`:

```
map(_,    []) -> [];
map(F,[X|S]) -> [F(X)|map(F,S)].
```

The function we were looking for is now compactly defined as the composition of `map/2` and `sum0/1` as follows:

```
sumf(F) -> fun(S) -> sum0(map(F,S)) end.
```

For instance, the function call

```
sumf(fun(X) -> X*X end)
```

denotes the function which sums the squares of the numbers in a stack to be provided. It is equivalent to the value

```
fun(S) -> sum0(map(fun(X) -> X*X end,S)) end.
```

It is possible to call this function just after it has been computed by `sumf/1`, but *parentheses must be added around a function being called when it is anonymous.* For instance, see the boldface type and underlining in

```
(sumf(fun(X) -> X*X end))([1,2,3]).
```

The function `map/2` is often used because it captures a common operation on stacks. For example,

```
push(_,        []) -> [];
push(X,[P|Perms]) -> [[X|P]|push(X,Perms)].
```

is equivalent to

```
push(X,Perms) -> map(fun(P) -> [X|P] end,Perms).
```

This style leads to clearer programs as it shows the underlying recursive evaluation without having to read or write a definition for it. In other words, using a higher-order function like map/2 allows us to identify a common recursive pattern and let the programmer focus instead on the specific processing of the items. We shall encounter other examples in the next sections but, before we move on, imagine we typed instead

```
push(X,Perms) -> map(fun(Perms) -> [X|Perms] end,Perms).
```

The Erlang compiler would issue the following warning:

> Warning: variable 'Perms' shadowed in 'fun'.

What happens is that the parameter **Perms** (in boldface type) 'hides' the parameter Perms of push/2 in the sense that, in the body of the anonymous function, the occurrence of **Perms** refers to fun(**Perms**), but not push(X,Perms). In this case, it is not an error, but the compiler designers worried about programmers walking on the shadowy side of the street. For example,

```
push(X,Perms) -> map(fun(X) -> [X|X] end,Perms).        % Capture
```

is definitely wrong because the two variables X in [X|X], which is the body of the anonymous function, are the parameter of the anonymous function. A faulty shadowing is called a *capture*. Here, the parameter X bound by push(X,Perms) has been captured to mean instead the parameter of fun(X). As a guideline, it is best to avoid shadowing a parameter, as the Erlang compiler reminds us for our own sake. Note that

$$\text{sumf(fun(S) -> S*S end)}$$

is fine because it is equivalent to

$$\text{fun(S) -> sum0(map(fun(S) -> S*S end,S)) end}$$

which is a correct shadowing.

Folds　Some other useful and frequently recursive schemas can be conveniently reified into some other higher-order functions. Consider a function which traverses completely a stack while processing an accumulator depending or not on the current visited item. In the end, the result is the final value of the accumulator, or else another function is called to finalise it. A simple example is len0/1 in FIGURE 9.19 on page 341. In this case, the accumulator is an integer and the operation on it consists in incrementing it, whatever the current item is. Another function reverses a stack (equation (2.2) on page 40):

```
rev(S)          -> rcat(S,[]).
rcat(   [],T) -> T;
rcat([X|S],T) -> rcat(S,[X|T]).
```

Here, the accumulator is a stack and the operation on it consists in pushing the current item on top of it. Let us abstract separately these two concerns in a higher-order function

1. which takes as input the function creating a new accumulator from the current item and the previous accumulator and

2. which applies it successively to all the items of a parameter stack.

One famous function doing exactly this is called foldl/3 in Erlang, which stands for 'fold left', because once the new accumulator for some item has been computed, the prefix of the stack up to it can be folded back, as if the stack were written down on a sheet of paper, because it is no longer useful. So the name should be better read as 'fold from left to right' or *rightward fold*. We want

$$\text{foldl}(F, A, [X_1, X_2, \ldots, X_n]) \equiv F(X_n, \ldots, F(X_2, F(X_1, A)) \ldots),$$

where A is the initial value of the accumulator. FIGURE 9.20 shows the corresponding abstract syntax trees. The following definition implements the desired effect:

```
foldl(_,A,   []) -> A;
foldl(F,A,[X|S]) -> foldl(F,F(X,A),S).
```

Now we can rewrite new definitions of len0/1 and rev/1:

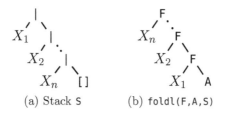

(a) Stack S   (b) foldl(F,A,S)

Figure 9.20: The result of foldl/3 on a non-empty stack

```
lenl(S) -> foldl(fun(_,A) ->    A+1 end, 0,S).
revl(S) -> foldl(fun(X,A) -> [X|A] end,[],S).
```

Function `foldl/3` is not in tail form because of the embedded call `F(X,A)`, but only a constant amount of control stack is used for the recursion of `foldl/3` itself (one node). In our two examples, `F` is in tail form, therefore these new definitions are *almost* in tail form and can stand against the originals. More definitions almost in tail form are

```
suml([N|S]) -> foldl(fun(X,A) ->      X+A end, N,S).
rcatl(S,T)  -> foldl(fun(X,A) ->    [X|A] end, T,S).
rmap(F,S)   -> foldl(fun(X,A) -> [F(X)|A] end,[],S).
```

Again, the reason why these definitions are not exactly in tail form is due to the call `F(X,A)` in the definition of `foldl/3`, *not* because of the functional arguments `fun(X,A) -> ... end` in the calls to `foldl/3`: these are not function calls but anonymous function definitions, that is, pieces of data. The main advantage of using `foldl/3` is that it allows the programmer to focus exclusively on the processing of the accumulator, whilst `foldl/3` itself provides the ride for free. Moreover, we can easily compare different functions defined by means of `foldl/3`.

When the accumulator is a stack on which values are pushed, the result is in reverse order with respect to the input. That is why `rmap/2`, above, is not equivalent to `map/2`. The former is to be preferred over the latter if the order of the items is not relevant, because `map/2` requires a control stack as long as the input stack. This leads us quite naturally to introduce another higher-order function: `foldr/3`, meaning 'fold from right to left', or *leftward fold*. We expect

$$\texttt{foldr}(F, A, [X_1, X_2, \ldots, X_n]) \equiv F(X_1, F(X_2, \ldots, F(X_n, A))\ldots).$$

FIGURE 9.21 shows the corresponding abstract syntax trees. We achieve this behaviour with the following definition:

```
foldr(_,A,   []) -> A;
foldr(F,A,[X|S]) -> F(X,foldr(F,A,S)).
```

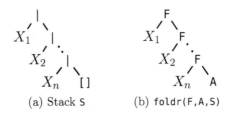

(a) Stack `S`　　　(b) `foldr(F,A,S)`

Figure 9.21: The result of `foldr/3` on a non-empty stack

This definition, like `foldl/3`, is not in tail form but, unlike `foldl/3`, it requires a control stack as long as the input stack.

With the help of `foldr/3`, we can redefine `map/2` and `cat/2` as

```
mapr(F,S) -> foldr(fun(X,A) -> [F(X)|A] end,[],S).
catr(S,T) -> foldr(fun(X,A) ->    [X|A] end, S,T).
```

Compare `rcatl/2`, defined above, with `catr/2`: the role of the accumulator and of the input stack have been exchanged, as well as `foldl/3` and `foldr/3`. It is also possible to define

```
lenr(S)     -> foldr(fun(_,A) -> 1+A end, 0,S).     % Bad
sumr([N|S]) -> foldr(fun(X,A) -> X+A end, N,S).     % Bad
isrtr(S)    -> foldr(fun(X,A) -> ins(A,X) end,[],S).  % Bad
```

but that would be unwise because `foldr/3` does not use a bounded amount of control stack, contrary to `foldl/3`. In the case of `isrt/1`, it is best to call `foldl/3` instead because the order of insertion does not matter in average (although it swaps the best and worst cases if the items are not repeated). Note also, in the case of `isrtr/1`, how the order of the arguments of the mapped function `ins/2` matters.

This leads us to formulate some guidelines about the transformation into tail form. We already know that a definition in tail form is worth having or even necessary if the maximum size of the control stack is smaller than that of some input recursively traversed in its greatest extension. No speed-up should be expected a priori from turning a definition into tail form – although this may happen sometimes. Usually,

- it is preferable, if possible, to use `foldl/3` instead of `foldr/3` because, provided the functional parameter is defined in tail form, the call will use a small limited amount of control stack (if the parameter is not in tail form, at least `foldl/3` won't burden further the control stack, contrary to `foldr/3`);

- when writing our own recursion, that is, without resorting to folds, it is best to have it in tail form if the accumulator is an integer, otherwise, the maximum size of the control stack may need to be proportional to the size of the input, despite the output being a single integer. (Contrast `sum/1` and `sum0/2`, as well as `len/1` and `len0/1`.)

Independently of stack allocation, there can be a significant difference in cost when using one fold instead of the other. Take for example the following two calls:

```
foldl(fun cat/2,[],S) ≡ foldr(fun cat/2,[],S).
```

The first one will be slower than the second, as shown by inequality (2.6) on page 43.

What cannot be programmed with folds? As the defining properties show, folds traverse the input stack in its entirety, hence there is no way to get off the bus while it is running. For instance, sfst/2 in section 2.3, on page 44, is, in Erlang,

$$
\begin{aligned}
\text{sfst(\quad [],X)} &\xrightarrow{\theta} \text{[];} \\
\text{sfst([X|S],X)} &\xrightarrow{\iota} \text{S;} \\
\text{sfst([Y|S],X)} &\xrightarrow{\kappa} \text{[Y|sfst(S,X)].}
\end{aligned}
$$

and cannot be implemented by means of a fold because there are two ends to the function calls: either the item has not been found and we ran afoul the end of the stack in clause θ, or it has been found somewhere inside the stack in clause ι. However, in theory, if we accept a full traversal of the stack for every call, then sfst/2 can be programmed by means of a rightward fold. The usual technique is to have an accumulator which is either an atom meaning 'not found' or a pair with an atom meaning 'found' and the rebuilt stack. If the result is 'not found', then we just give back the original stack. The following function makes a stronger case because it is really impossible to express by means of a fold, even inefficiently. It is the 'complete tail' function:

```
ctail(  []) -> [];
ctail([_|S]) -> S.
```

In general, a function F can be equivalently expressed by a call to a fold if, and only if, for all stacks S and T, for all item X, we have

$$F(S) \equiv F(T) \Rightarrow F([X|S]) \equiv F([X|T]).$$

(See Gibbons et al. (2001), Weber and Caldwell (2004).) For instance, we have ctail([]) ≡ ctail([2]) but ctail([1]) ≢ ctail([1,2]).

One positive side-effect of using maps and folds is that they sometimes allow the programmer to recognise some compositions that can be optimised by means of some equivalence. As an example, we have, for all functions F and G:

$$\text{map}(F,\text{map}(G,S)) \equiv \text{map}(\text{compose}(F,G),S).$$

Without counting in the costs of F and G, the left-hand side induces the cost $2n+2$, if S contains n items, whereas the right-hand side incurs the cost $n + 2$, so it is much preferable to the former. Another interesting equation is

$$\texttt{foldl}(F, A, S) \equiv \texttt{foldr}(F, A, S) \tag{9.2}$$

if F is associative and symmetric. Let us prove it. The first clauses of the definitions of `foldl/3` and `foldr/3` imply that, for all F and A,

$$\texttt{foldl}(F, A, [\,]) \equiv A \equiv \texttt{foldr}(F, A, [\,]).$$

For non-empty stacks, this equation means:

$$F(X_n, \ldots, F(X_2, F(X_1, A)) \ldots) \equiv F(X_1, F(X_2, \ldots, F(X_n, A)) \ldots).$$

Although the ellipses in the previous equation are intuitive, they are not a valid foundation for a rigorous mathematical argument. Instead, by definition, we have

$$\texttt{foldl}(F, A, [X \,|\, S]) \equiv \texttt{foldl}(F, F(X, A), S).$$

Dually, by definition, we also have

$$\texttt{foldr}(F, A, [X \,|\, S]) \equiv F(X, \texttt{foldr}(F, A, S)).$$

The original equation would thus be established for all stacks if we prove

$$\texttt{foldl}(F, F(X, A), S) \equiv F(X, \texttt{foldr}(F, A, S)).$$

Let us call this conjecture Fold and prove it by structural induction. In general terms, this principle states that, given a finite data structure S, a property $\mathsf{Fold}(S)$ to be proved about it, then

1. if $\mathsf{Fold}(S)$ is provable for all the atomic S, that is, configurations of S that cannot be decomposed;

2. if, assuming $\mathsf{Fold}(T)$ for all immediate substructures T of S, then $\mathsf{Fold}(S)$ is proved;

3. then $\mathsf{Fold}(S)$ is proved for *all* S.

Here, the data structure S being a stack, there is a unique atomic stack: the empty stack. So we must first prove $\mathsf{Fold}([\,])$. The first clauses of the definitions of `foldl/3` and `foldr/3` imply that, for all F and A,

$$\texttt{foldl}(F, F(X, A), [\,]) \equiv F(X, A) \equiv F(X, \texttt{foldr}(F, A, [\,])),$$

which is $\mathsf{Fold}([\,])$. Next, let us consider a non-empty stack $[Y \,|\, S]$. What are its immediate substructures? By construction of stacks, there is only one immediate substack of $[X|S]$, namely S. Therefore, let us assume Fold(S) for a given stack S and suppose that F is associative and symmetric (this is the structural induction hypothesis) and let us prove Fold($[Y|S]$), for all Y. For F to be associative means that, for all values I, J and K, we have

$$F(I, F(J, K)) \equiv F(F(I, J), K).$$

The symmetry of F means that, for all I and J, we have

$$F(I, J) \equiv F(J, I).$$

Let us start with the left-hand side of Fold($[Y|S]$):

$$
\begin{aligned}
&\texttt{foldl}(F, F(X, A), [Y|S]) \\
&\equiv \texttt{foldl}(F, F(Y, F(X, A)), S) \quad &&\text{Definition of } \texttt{foldl/3} \\
&\equiv \texttt{foldl}(F, F(F(Y, X), A), S) \quad &&\text{Associativity of } F \\
&\equiv \texttt{foldl}(F, F(F(X, Y), A), S) \quad &&\text{Symmetry of } F \\
&\equiv F(F(X, Y), \texttt{foldr}(F, A, S)) \quad &&\text{Induction hypothesis Fold}(S) \\
&\equiv F(X, F(Y, \texttt{foldr}(F, A, S))) \quad &&\text{Associativity of } F \\
&\equiv F(X, \texttt{foldr}(F, A, [Y|S])) \quad &&\text{Definition of } \texttt{foldr/3}. \qquad \square
\end{aligned}
$$

This proves Fold($[Y|S]$). The principle of structural induction then implies that Fold(S) is proved for all stacks S, hence the original equation (9.2) on the previous page. The previous derivation suggests a variation in the definition of `foldl/3`:

```
foldl_alt(_,A,   []) -> A;
foldl_alt(F,A,[X|S]) -> foldl_alt(F,F(A,X),S).
```

The difference lies in the order of the parameters of F. We would then have to prove a slightly different conjecture:

$$\texttt{foldl\_alt}(F, F(A, X), S) \equiv F(X, \texttt{foldr}(F, A, S)).$$

The previous derivation would read now as follows:

$$
\begin{aligned}
&\texttt{foldl\_alt}(F, F(A, X), [Y|S]) \\
&\equiv \texttt{foldl\_alt}(F, F(F(A, X), Y), S) \quad &&\text{Definition} \\
&\equiv \texttt{foldl\_alt}(F, F(A, F(X, Y)), S) \quad &&\text{Associativity of } F \\
&\equiv F(F(X, Y), \texttt{foldr}(F, A, S)), \quad &&\text{Induction hypothesis Fold}(S) \\
&\equiv F(X, F(Y, \texttt{foldr}(F, A, S))) \quad &&\text{Associativity of } F \\
&\equiv F(X, \texttt{foldr}(F, A, [Y|S])), \quad &&\text{Definition of } \texttt{foldr/3}. \qquad \square
\end{aligned}
$$

We see that the symmetry of F is not required anymore but in only one remaining place: when the stack is empty. Indeed, we have

$$\text{foldl\_alt}(F,F(A,X),[\,]) \equiv F(A,X), \quad \text{by definition;}$$
$$F(X,\text{foldr}(F,A,[\,])) \equiv F(X,A), \quad \text{by definition of } \text{foldr/3.}$$

Therefore, in order to prove the variant conjecture about foldl_alt/3 and foldr/3, we must have

$$F(A,X) \equiv F(X,A),$$

that is, A, which is the initial value of the accumulator, must commute with all items X under F. This is not a clear improvement over the first theorem about foldl/3, which required all pairs of successive items commute. Nevertheless, there is an interesting special case, which is when A is a neutral element for F, that is, for all X,

$$F(A,X) \equiv F(X,A) \equiv A.$$

Then symmetry altogether is no more required. Therefore, foldl_alt/3 is preferable over foldl/3, because it provides more opportunities when transforming applications of foldr/3. But, since the standard library of Erlang offers the definition foldl/3, we shall stick to it. The standard library of OCaml, however, proposes the function fold_left, which corresponds to foldl_alt/3.

Anyway, theorem (9.2) allows us to transform immediately some calls to foldr/3, which requires an amount of control stack at least proportional to the size of the input stack, into calls to foldl/3, whose parameter F is the only function possibly not using a constant amount of control stack (if it does, the gain is all the more obvious). This is why the following definitions are equivalent:

```
lenl(S) -> foldl(fun(_,A) -> A+1 end,0,S).
lenr(S) -> foldr(fun(_,A) -> A+1 end,0,S).
```

Proving that the following two definitions are equivalent happens to be a bit trickier:

```
suml([N|S]) -> foldl(fun(X,A) -> X+A end,N,S).
sumr([N|S]) -> foldr(fun(X,A) -> X+A end,N,S).
```

The reason is that the first item of the stack serves as the initial value of the accumulator in both cases, despite the order of traversal of the stack being reversed (rightward versus leftward). It is much more obvious to see that the following definitions are equivalent:

```
sum1(S=[_|_]) -> foldl(fun(X,A) -> X+A end,0,S).
sum2(S=[_|_]) -> foldr(fun(X,A) -> X+A end,0,S).
```

only because addition is associative and symmetric.

Functional encoding of maps In order to illustrate further the expressive power of higher-order functions, let us muse about a small, albeit unlikely, example. We mentioned on page 340 association lists being a collection of pairs key-value, straightforwardly implemented as stacks, for instance, [{a,0},{b,1},{a,5}]. A *mapping* is an association list which is searched based on the first component of the pairs. Typically, we have

```
find(_,        []) -> absent;
find(X,[{X,V}|_]) -> V;                % Associated value found
find(X,    [_|S]) -> find(X,S).        % Keep searching
```

Notice that if a key is repeated, only the first pair will be considered, for instance, find(a,[{a,0},{b,1},{a,5}]) evaluates to 0, not 5. These pairs are called *bindings*. Let us assume now that we want to present formally what a mapping is but without relying upon any particular programming language. In this case, we must count on mathematics to convey the concept, more precisely, on mathematical functions. We would say that a mapping M is a function from some finite set of values $\mathcal{K}$ to some finite set of values $\mathcal{V}$. Therefore, what was previously the conjunction of a data type (a stack) and a lookup function (find/2) is now a single function, representing the mapping *and* the lookup at the same time. A binding $x \mapsto y$ is just another notation for the pair (x, y), where $x \in \mathcal{K}$ and $y \in \mathcal{V}$. We need now to express how a mapping is updated, that is, how a mapping is extended with a new binding. With a stack, this is simply done by pushing a new pair but, without a stack, we would say that an update is a function itself, taking a mapping and a binding as arguments and returning a new mapping. *An update is thus a higher-order function.* Let the function ($\oplus$) be such that $M \oplus x_1 \mapsto y$ is the *update* of the mapping M by the binding $x_1 \mapsto y$, as defined by

$$(M \oplus x_1 \mapsto y)(x_2) := \begin{cases} y & \text{if } x_1 = x_2, \\ M(x_2) & \text{otherwise.} \end{cases}$$

We can check that we return the value associated to the first key matching the input, as expected. The empty mapping would be a special function returning a special symbol meaning 'not found', like $M_\varnothing(x) = \bot$, for all x. The mapping containing the binding $(1, 5)$ would be $M_\varnothing \oplus 1 \mapsto 5$. This is very abstract and independent of any programming language, whilst being totally precise. If now the need arises to show how this definition can be programmed, this is when functional languages can shine. An update would be directly written in Erlang as

```
update(M,{X1,Y}) -> fun(X2) -> case X2 of X1 -> Y;
                                          _ -> M(X2)
                              end
          end.
```

The correspondence with the formal definition is almost immediate, there is no need to introduce a data structure and its interpretation, nor prove its correctness. The empty mapping is simply

```
empty(_) -> absent.
```

For example, the mapping as stack [{a,0},{b,1},{a,5}] can be modelled with higher-order functions only as

```
update(update(update(fun empty/1,{a,5}),{b,1}),{a,0}).
```

Perhaps what needs to be learnt from all this is that stacks in functional languages, despite having a distinctive syntax and being used pervasively, are not a fundamental data type: functions are.

Functional encodings of tuples   Let us start by abstracting the tuple into its essence and, because in a functional language functions are the main feature, we should ask ourselves what is *done* with something we think of as a tuple. Actually, we rushed because we should have realised first that all tuples can be expressed in terms of the empty tuple and pairs. For instance, {5,foo,{fun(X) -> X*X end}} can be rewritten with embedded pairs as {5,{foo,{fun(X) -> X*X end,{}}}}. So let us rephrase the question in terms of pairs only. Basically, a pair is constructed (or *injected*) and matched, that is, deconstructed (or *projected*). This analysis leads to the conclusion that the functional encoding of pairs requires three functions: one for making, mk_pair/2, and two for unmaking, fst/1 and snd/1. Once a pair is built, it is represented as a function, therefore functions extracting the components take as an argument another function denoting the pair, thus they are of higher order. Consider

```
mk_pair(X,Y) --α--> fun(Pr) --β--> Pr(X,Y) end.      % Pr is a projection
fst(P) --γ--> P(fun(X,_) --δ--> X end).              % P denotes a pair
snd(P) --ε--> P(fun(_,Y) --ζ--> Y end).
```

We have the following expected behaviour:

$$\texttt{fst(mk\_pair(3,5))} \xrightarrow{\alpha} \texttt{fst(fun(Pr)} \xrightarrow{\beta} \texttt{Pr(3,5) end)}$$
$$\xrightarrow{\gamma} \texttt{(fun(Pr)} \xrightarrow{\beta} \texttt{Pr(3,5) end)(fun(X,\_)} \xrightarrow{\delta} \texttt{X end)}$$
$$\xrightarrow{\beta} \texttt{(fun(X,\_)} \xrightarrow{\delta} \texttt{X end)(3,5)}$$
$$\xrightarrow{\delta} \texttt{3.}$$

To proof the versatility of this encoding, let us define a function `add/1` which adds the components of the pair passed to it:

$$\texttt{add(P)} \xrightarrow{\eta} \texttt{fst(P) + snd(P).}$$

A call to `add/1` would unravel as follows, assuming that arguments are evaluated rightward:

$$\texttt{add(mk\_pair(3,5))}$$
$$\xrightarrow{\alpha} \texttt{add(fun(Pr)} \xrightarrow{\beta} \texttt{Pr(3,5) end)}$$
$$\xrightarrow{\eta} \quad \texttt{fst(fun(Pr)} \xrightarrow{\beta} \texttt{Pr(3,5) end)}$$
$$\texttt{+ snd(fun(Pr)} \xrightarrow{\beta} \texttt{Pr(3,5) end)}$$
$$\xrightarrow{\gamma} \quad \texttt{(fun(Pr)} \xrightarrow{\beta} \texttt{Pr(3,5) end)(fun(X,\_)} \xrightarrow{\delta} \texttt{X end)}$$
$$\texttt{+ snd(fun(Pr)} \xrightarrow{\beta} \texttt{Pr(3,5) end)}$$
$$\xrightarrow{\beta} \quad \texttt{(fun(X,\_)} \xrightarrow{\delta} \texttt{X end)(3,5)}$$
$$\texttt{+ snd(fun(Pr)} \xrightarrow{\beta} \texttt{Pr(3,5) end)}$$
$$\xrightarrow{\delta} \texttt{3 + snd(fun(Pr)} \xrightarrow{\beta} \texttt{Pr(3,5) end)}$$
$$\xrightarrow{\epsilon} \texttt{3 + (fun(Pr)} \xrightarrow{\beta} \texttt{Pr(3,5) end)(fun(\_,Y)} \xrightarrow{\varsigma} \texttt{Y end)}$$
$$\xrightarrow{\beta} \texttt{3 + (fun(\_,Y)} \xrightarrow{\varsigma} \texttt{Y end)(3,5)}$$
$$\xrightarrow{\varsigma} \texttt{3 + 5 = 8.}$$

The keen reader may feel cheated, though, because we could have simply defined `add/2` as

```
add(X,Y) -> X + Y.
```

Indeed, this critique is valid. The ability of functions to receive various arguments at once amounts to them receiving *one* tuple exactly, whose components are these various values. Therefore, we have to retry and make sure that our functions are *nullary* or *unary*, that is, take zero or one argument. This is achieved by taking one value as argument and rewrite the call into a function which will take in turn the next value as argument etc. This translation is called *currying*.

$$\texttt{mk\_pair(X)} \xrightarrow{\alpha} \texttt{fun(Y)} \xrightarrow{\beta} \texttt{fun(Pr)} \xrightarrow{\gamma} \texttt{(Pr(X))(Y) end end.}$$
$$\texttt{fst(P)} \xrightarrow{\delta} \texttt{P(fun(X)} \xrightarrow{\epsilon} \texttt{fun(\_)} \xrightarrow{\varsigma} \texttt{X end end).}$$
$$\texttt{snd(P)} \xrightarrow{\eta} \texttt{P(fun(\_)} \xrightarrow{\theta} \texttt{fun(Y)} \xrightarrow{\iota} \texttt{Y end end).}$$
$$\texttt{add(P)} \xrightarrow{\kappa} \texttt{fst(P) + snd(P).}$$

Let us recall that **fun**(X) -> **fun**(P) -> ... is equivalent to the expression **fun**(X) -> (**fun**(P) -> ...) The parentheses around Pr(X) are necessary in Erlang because this call is in the place of a function being called itself. Now

```
add((mk_pair(3))(5))
  α
  ⟶ add((fun(Y) ─β→ fun(Pr) ─γ→ (Pr(3))(Y) end end)(5))
  β
  ⟶ add(fun(Pr) ─γ→ (Pr(3))(5) end)
  κ
  ⟶   fst(fun(Pr) ─γ→ (Pr(3))(5) end)
    + snd(fun(Pr) ─γ→ (Pr(3))(5) end)
  δ
  ⟶   (fun(Pr)─γ→(Pr(3))(5) end)(fun(X) ─ε→ fun(_) ─ζ→X end end)
    + snd(fun(Pr) ─γ→ (Pr(3))(5) end)
  γ
  ⟶   ((fun(X) ─ε→ fun(_) ─ζ→ X end end)(3))(5)
    + snd(fun(Pr) ─γ→ (Pr(3))(5) end)
  ε
  ⟶ (fun(_) ─ζ→ 3 end)(5) + snd(fun(Pr) ─γ→ (Pr(3))(5) end)
  ζ
  ⟶ 3 + snd(fun(Pr) ─γ→ (Pr(3))(5) end)
  η
  ⟶ 3 +(fun(Pr)─γ→(Pr(3))(5) end)(fun(_) ─θ→ fun(Y) ─ι→ Y end end)
  γ
  ⟶ 3 + ((fun(_) ─θ→ fun(Y) ─ι→ Y end end)(3))(5)
  θ
  ⟶ 3 + (fun(Y) ─ι→ Y end)(5)
  ι
  ⟶ 3 + 5 = 8.
```

Of course, this encoding is usually not worth doing because the number of function calls is much greater than when using a data structure. Its main interest is to show the theoretical expressive power of higher-order functions.

Functional encoding of stacks   To gain more insight into the nature of stacks as data structures, we can encode stacks only with higher-order functions. In the former view, a stack is an infrastructure, a kind of inert container for data and functions are expected to operate on it. In the latter view, a stack is a composition of functions containing data as arguments and waiting to be called to *do* something with them. The difference between both points of view is not an imagined dichotomy between data and functions, which is blurred in object-oriented languages too, but the fact that higher-order functions *alone* can make up a stack.

Since we already know how to encode pairs with higher-order functions, a first approach to encoding stacks with functions simply consists in encoding them with pairs. Abstractly, a stack can either be empty or constructed by pushing an item into another stack, so all we need is to translate these two concepts. The empty stack can readily be represented by the empty tuple {} and pushing becomes pairing:

```
push(X,S) -> {X,S}.
```

This encoding was introduced in FIGURE 9.16 on page 330 to save memory on linear accumulators. Here, we want to go one step further and get rid of the pairs themselves by means of their functional interpretation seen above, so push/2 becomes a renaming of mk_pair/2:

```
push(X,S) -> fun(Pr) -> Pr(X,S) end.              % See mk_pair/2
```

To understand the status of the empty stack, we must consider projections on stacks. These are usually called *head* and *tail*. We implement them as the original versions of fst/2 and snd/2, where S, H and T denote, respectively, an encoding of a stack, a head and a tail:

```
head(S) -> S(fun(H,_) -> H end).                  % See fst/2
tail(S) -> S(fun(_,T) -> T end).                  % See snd/2
```

Let us now think *how* the empty stack is used. It is a stack such that any projection of its putative contents fails, that is, projecting the first component (the head) fails, as well as projecting the second component (the tail). A trick consists in defining

```
empty() -> fail.                    % The atom fail is arbitrary
```

The point is that empty/0 is nullary, so calling it with an argument fails, as in head(fun empty/0). For example, the stack [a,b,c] is encoded

```
          push(a,push(b,push(c,fun empty/0))).
```

This solution relies on the *arity*, that is, the number of parameters, of empty/0 to lead to failure. This failure is consistent with the way classic stacks, that is, stacks as data structures, are used: tail([_|S]) -> S and the call tail([]) fails to match a clause. The limit of this encoding is that, being based on functions, the encoded stacks cannot be matched by the heads of the clauses. For example, the function ctail/1 on page 348

```
ctail(   []) -> [];
ctail([_|S]) -> S.
```

cannot not be encoded because we would need a way to check whether an encoded stack is empty without crashing the program if it is not. If we prefer the caller to be gently informed of the problem instead, that is, we want the definition of the projections to be complete, we could allow empty/1 to take a projection which is then discarded:

```
empty(_) -> fail.
```

We would have the rewrite head(fun empty/1) $\rightarrow$ fail, which is not a failure insofar the run-time system is concerned, but is interpreted by the application as a *logical* failure. Of course, it becomes the burden of the caller to check whether the atom fail is returned and the burden of the stack maker to make sure not to push this atom in the encoded stack, otherwise a caller would confuse the empty stack with a regular item. (A better solution consists in using *exceptions*.)

Fixed-point combinators   Many functions need some other auxiliary functions to carry out subtasks. For example, consider FIGURE 9.19 on page 341 where len0/2 is the auxiliary function. To forbid its usage outside the scope of the module, it would be omitted in the -export clause at the beginning, but it still could be called from within the module it is defined. How could we avoid this as well? This is where anonymous functions comes handy:

```
len0(S) ->
  Len = fun(    [],N) -> N;
           ([_|S],N) -> Len(S,N+1)          % Does not compile
        end,
  Len(S,0).
```

This limits the visibility of the anonymous function bound to variable Len to the body of len0/1, which is exactly what we wanted. The problem here is that this definition is rejected by the **Erlang** compiler because the binding construct (=) does not make the variable on its left-hand side visible to the right-side, hence Len is unknown in the call Len(S,N+1). In some other functional languages, there is a specific construct to allow recursion on local definitions, for instance, let rec in OCaml, but the following hypotyposis is nevertheless theoretically relevant. The original problem becomes another one: how can we define anonymous *recursive* functions? A workaround is to pass an additional function parameter, which is used in stead of the recursive call:

```
len1(S) -> Len = fun(_,    [],N) -> N;
                    (F,[_|S],N) -> F(F,S,N+1)
               end,
            Len(Len,S,0).
```

Notice that we renamed len0/1 into len1/1 because we are going to envisage several variants. Moreover, the anonymous function is not equivalent to len/2 because it takes three arguments. Also, the compiler emits the following warning (we removed the line number):

Warning: variable 'S' shadowed in 'fun'.

We have seen this before, on page 344. Here, the shadowing is harmless, because inside the anonymous function denoted by Len, the original value of S, that is, the argument of len1/1, is not needed. Nevertheless, for the sake of tranquillity, a simple renaming will get rid of the warning:

```
len1(S) -> Len = fun(_,    [],N) -> N;
                     (F,[_|T],N) -> F(F,T,N+1)          % Renaming
              end,
           Len(Len,S,0).
```

We can alter this definition by currying the anonymous function and renaming it so Len now is equivalent to fun len/2:

```
len2(S) -> H = fun(F) -> fun(   [],N) -> N;
                            ([_|T],N) -> (F(F))(T,N+1)
                         end
              end,
           Len = H(H),                    % Equivalent to fun len/2
           Len(S,0).
```

Let us define a function u/1 which auto-applies its functional argument and let us make use of it in stead of F(F):

```
u(F) -> fun(X,Y) -> (F(F))(X,Y) end.           % Self-application
```

```
len3(S) -> H = fun(F) -> fun(   [],N) -> N;
                            ([_|T],N) -> (u(F))(T,N+1)
                         end
              end,
           (H(H))(S,0).                         % Expanded Len
```

Let us replace now u(F) by F. This transformation does not preserve the semantics of H, so let us rename the resulting function G and we redefine H to be equivalent to its prior instance:

```
len3(S) -> G = fun(F) -> fun(   [],N) -> N;
                            ([_|T],N) -> F(T,N+1)
                         end
              end,
           H = fun(F) -> G(u(F)) end,
           (H(H))(S,0).
```

The interesting point is that the anonymous function referred to by variable G is very similar to Len at the beginning. (It may sound paradoxical to speak of anonymous functions with names, but, in Erlang, variables and function names are two distinct syntactic categories, so there is no contradiction in terms.) Here it is again:

```erlang
len0(S) ->
  Len = fun(    [],N) -> N;
            ([_|S],N) -> Len(S,N+1)        % Unfortunately invalid
         end,
  Len(S,0).
```

The difference is that G abstracts over F instead of having a (problematic) recursive call. Let us expand back the call u(F) and get rid of u/1 altogether:

```erlang
len4(S) ->
  G = fun(F) -> fun(    [],N) -> N;
                   ([_|T],N) -> F(T,N+1)
               end
      end,
  H = fun(F) -> G(fun(X,Y) -> (F(F))(X,Y) end) end,
  (H(H))(S,0).
```

To gain some generality, we can extract the assignments to H and Len, put them into a new function x/1 and expand Len in place:

```erlang
x(G) -> H=fun(F) -> G(fun(X,Y)->(F(F))(X,Y) end) end, H(H).
```

```erlang
len5(S) -> G = fun(F) -> fun(    [],N) -> N;
                            ([_|T],N) -> F(T,N+1)
                        end
               end,
           (x(G))(S,0).
```

By putting the definition of function x/1 into a dedicated module, we can now easily define recursive anonymous functions. There is a limitation, though, which is that x/1 is tied to the arity of F. For instance, we cannot use it for the factorial:

```erlang
fact(N) -> G = fun(F) -> fun(0) -> 1;
                            (N) -> N * F(N-1)
                        end
               end,
           (x(G))(S,0).                     % Arity mismatch
```

Therefore, if we really want a general scheme, we should work with fully curried functions, so all functions are unary:

```
x(G) -> H = fun(F) -> G(fun(X) -> (F(F))(X) end) end, H(H).

len6(S) -> G=fun(F) -> fun(N) -> fun(    []) -> N;
                                    ([_|T]) -> (F(N+1))(T)
                          end
              end
          end,
          ((x2(G))(0))(S).
```

Notice that we swapped the order of the stack and the integer, since there is no pattern matching to be done on the latter. The grammar of Erlang obliges us to put parentheses around every function call resulting in a function being immediately called, so calling fully curried functions with all their arguments, like ((x2(G))(0))(S), ends up being a bit fastidious, although a good text editor can help us in paring properly the parentheses.

The theoretical point of this derivation is that we can always write a non-recursive function equivalent to a recursive one, since even x/1 is not recursive. In fact, nothing special is required as long as we have unrestricted function calls. Some strongly and statically typed languages like OCaml reject the definition of x/1 above, but other valid, albeit more complex, definitions are possible. (In the case of OCaml, the switch -rectypes allows us to compile the one above, though.) If we grant ourselves the use of recursion, which we never banned, we can actually write a simpler definition of x/1, named y/1:

```
y(F) -> fun(X) -> (F(y(F)))(X) end.                    % Recursive
```

This definition is actually very easy to come by, as it relies on the computational equivalence, for all X,

$$(y(F))(X) \equiv (F(y(F)))(X),$$

If we assume the mathematical property $\forall x.f(x) = g(x) \Rightarrow f = g$, the previous equivalence would yield

$$y(F) \equiv F(y(F)),$$

which, by definition, shows that y(F) is a fixed-point of F. Beware that

```
y(F) -> F(y(F)).                                       % Infinite loop
```

does not work because the call y(F) would *immediately* start evaluating the call y(F) in the body, therefore never ending. Some functional programming languages have a different evaluation strategy than Erlang and do not always start by evaluating the argument in a function call, which may make this definition directly workable. Another example:

```
fact(N) -> F = fun(F) -> fun(A) -> fun(0) -> A;
                                      (M) -> (F(A*M))(M-1)
                                   end
                         end
               end,
            ((y(F))(1))(N).
```

The technique we developed in the previous lines can be used to reduce the amount of control stack in some functions. For example, consider

```
cat(   [],T) -> T;
cat([X|S],T) -> [X|cat(S,T)].
```

Note how the parameter T is threaded until the first argument is empty. This means that a reference to the original stack T is duplicated at each rewrite until the last step, because the definition is not in tail form. In order to avoid this, we could use a recursive anonymous function which binds T not as a parameter but as part of the (embedding) scope:

```
cat(S,T) -> G = fun(F) -> fun(   []) -> T;           % T in scope
                             ([X|U]) -> [X|F(U)]
                          end
               end,
            (y(G))(S).
```

This transformation is called *lambda-dropping*, and its inverse *lambda-lifting*. The function y/1 is called the *Y fixed-point combinator*.

We sometimes may want to define two mutually recursive anonymous functions. Consider the following example, which is in practice utterly useless and inefficient, but simple enough to illustrate our point.

```
even(0) -> true;
even(N) -> odd(N-1).

odd(0) -> false;
odd(N) -> even(N-1).
```

Let us say that we do not want even/1 to be callable from any other function but odd/1. This means that we want the following pattern:

```
odd(I) -> Even = fun(☐) -> ⬜ end,
          Odd  = fun(☐) -> ⬜ end,
          Odd(I).
```

where `Even` and `Odd` depend on each other. As the canvas is laid out, `Even` cannot call `Odd`. The technique to allow mutual recursion consists in abstracting the first function over the second, that is, `Even` becomes a function whose parameter is a function destined to be used as `Odd`:

```
odd(I) -> Even = fun(Odd) -> fun(0) -> true;
                               (N) -> Odd(N-1)
                            end
          end,
          Odd  = fun(☐) -> ⬜ end,
          Odd(I).
```

The next step is more tricky. We can start naïvely, though, and let the problem come to the fore by itself:

```
odd(I) -> Even = fun(Odd) -> fun(0) -> true;
                               (N) -> Odd(N-1)
                            end
          end,
          Odd  = fun(0) -> false;
                     (N) -> (Even(Odd))(N-1)
                 end,
          Odd(I).
```

The problem is not unheard of and we already know how to define an anonymous recursive function by abstracting over the recursive call and passing the resulting function to the Y fixed-point combinator:

```
odd(I) -> Even = fun(Odd) -> fun(0) -> true;
                               (N) -> Odd(N-1)
                            end
          end,
          Odd  = y(fun(F) -> fun(0) -> false;
                               (N) -> (Even(F))(N-1)
                            end
                 end),
          Odd(I).
```

The technique presented here to achieve local recursion is interesting beyond compilation, as shown by Goldberg and Wiener (2009). Fixed-point combinators can also be shown to work in imperative languages, like C:

```
#include<stdio.h>
#include<stdlib.h>

typedef int (*fp)();

int fact(fp f, int n) {
  return n? n * ((int (*)(fp,int))f)(f,n-1) : 1; }

int read(int dec, char arg[]) {
  return ('0' <= *arg && *arg <= '9')?
         read(10*dec+(*arg - '0'),arg+1) : dec; }

int main(int argc, char** argv) {
  if (argc == 2)
    printf("%u\n",fact(&fact,read(0,argv[1])));
  else printf("Only one integer allowed.\n");
  return 0;
}
```

Continuations In section 9.1, the transformation into tail form applies to first-order programs, that is, those without higher-order functions, and its result are first-order programs as well. Here, we explain briefly a transformation to tail form which results in higher-order functions in *continuation-passing style* (often abbreviated CPS). The main advantage is that programs are shorter. The first example was flat/1:

```
flat(       []) -> [];
flat(   [[]|T]) -> flat(T);
flat([[X|S]|T]) -> flat([X,S|T]);
flat(   [X|T]) -> [X|flat(T)].
```

Applying the algorithm of section 9.1, the tail form we found was

```
flat_tf(T)           -> flat(T,[]).
flat(       [],A)    -> appk([],A);
flat(   [[]|T],A)    -> flat(T,A);
flat([[X|S]|T],A)    -> flat([X,S|T],A);
flat(   [Y|T],A)     -> flat(T,[{k1,Y}|A]).

appk(V,          []) -> V;
appk(V,[{k1,Y}|A]) -> appk([Y|V],A).
```

(This is the version using a stack accumulator instead of embedded tuples.) The driving idea consists in adding a stack A which accumulates the variables of all the call contexts, each occurrence being uniquely tagged, and an auxiliary function appk/2 then reconstructs the contexts.

The idea behind continuation-passing style is to not separate the variables of the contexts and their reconstruction. Instead, what is saved is a function, named *continuation*, corresponding to one clause of appk/1 reconstructing a context. This way, there is no need for appk/1. First, just like an empty accumulator was created, an initial continuation is needed. For the moment, we will ignore it. Just like an extra argument was added for the accumulator, an extra argument is added for the continuation:

```
flat_k(T)                -> flat_k(T,[          ]).
flat_k(        [],K) -> [];                         % K unused yet
flat_k(    [[]|T],K) -> flat_k(T,K);
flat_k([[X|S]|T],K) -> flat_k([X,S|T],K);
flat_k(    [X|T],K) -> [X|flat_k(T,K)].
```

Just like before, each right-hand side is examined in order. If it contains no function call, the expression (where appk/2 was called): is applied to the continuation K:

```
flat_k(        [],K) -> K([]);
```

If it is a function call in tail form, nothing is done, just like before:

```
flat_k(    [[]|T],K) -> flat_k(T,K);
flat_k([[X|S]|T],K) -> flat_k([X,S|T],K);
```

If the right-hand side is not in tail form, we identify the first call to be evaluated. Here, there is only one: flat_k(T,K). Now is the main difference with the original transformation. Instead of extracting the variables from the context and generating a clause of appk/2 reconstructing that context, we pass to the call a new continuation which applies the context to the result of the call and then calls K, just like appk/2 was called recursively:

```
flat_k(    [X|T],K) -> flat_k(T,fun(V) -> K([X|V]) end).
```

Finally, we need to determine what is the continuation counterpart of the empty accumulator. More precisely, we want to find an equivalent to appk(V,[]) -> V. That is, we want a continuation such that, provided with V, returns V: it is the identity function. We now have completed the transformation to continuation-passing style:

```
flat_k(T)                 -> flat_k(T,fun(V) -> V end).
flat_k(          [],K) -> K([]);
flat_k(      [[]|T],K) -> flat_k(T,K);
flat_k([[X|S]|T],K) -> flat_k([X,S|T],K);
flat_k(      [X|T],K) -> flat_k(T,fun(V) -> K([X|V]) end).
```

The number of rewrites is the same as with `flat_tf/1`; the main interest is that the resulting code is shorter, as each clause of `appk/2` is encoded as an anonymous function at each location not in tail form. (Note that it is tradition to name the continuations with the letter K.)

Let us consider another related example, `flat0/1`:

```
flat0(              []) -> [];
flat0(        [[]|T]) -> flat0(T);
flat0([Y=[_|_]|T]) -> cat(flat0(Y),flat0(T));
flat0(          [Y|T]) -> [Y|flat0(T)].
```

The first-order tail form we derived was

```
flat0_tf(T)                  -> flat0(T,[]).
flat0(                [],A) -> appk([],A);
flat0(          [[]|T],A) -> flat0(T,A);
flat0([Y=[_|_]|T],A) -> flat0(Y,[{k1,T}|A]);
flat0(        [Y|T],A)    -> flat0(T,[{k34,Y}|A]).
cat(    [],T,A)              -> appk(T,A);
cat([X|S],T,A)              -> cat(S,T,[{k34,X}|A]).
appk(V,[{k34,Y}|A])     -> appk([Y|V],A);
appk(V,  [{k2,W}|A])     -> cat(W,V,A);
appk(V,  [{k1,T}|A])     -> flat0(T,[{k2,V}|A]);
appk(V,              []) -> V.
```

Again, for the sake of the argument, we use the non-optimised version without embedded tuples for the stack accumulator. First, we generate the identity continuation:

```
flat0_k(T) -> flat0_k(T,fun(V) -> V end).
```

The right-hand side of the first clause of `flat0/1` contains no calls so we apply to it the current continuation:

```
flat0_k(              [],K) -> K([]);
```

The right-hand side of the second clause of `flat0/1` is a call in tail form, so its transform just passes around the current continuation:

```
flat0_k(        [[]|T],K) -> flat0_k(T,K);
```

The third clause is more complicated because it contains three calls. Let us decide that the first to be evaluated will be `flat0(Y)`. (Erlang does not specify the order of evaluation of arguments.) We start by setting the framework of the new continuation:

```
flat0_k([Y=[_|_]|T],K) -> flat0_k(Y,fun(V) -> ⬛ end);
```

The parameter `V` will hold, when the new continuation will be called, the value of `flat0(Y)`. Next, we must evaluate the call `flat0(T)`, so we set

```
flat0_k([Y=[_|_]|T],K) ->
  flat0_k(Y,fun(V) -> flat0_k(T,fun(W) -> ⬛ end) end);
```

We have to prepare the future call to `cat/2`, which must also be transformed in continuation-passing style. What must be concatenated are the values of `flat0(Y)` and `flat0(T)`. The former will be bound by the parameter `V` and the latter by `W`, therefore:

```
flat0_k([Y=[_|_]|T],K) ->
  flat0_k(Y,fun(V) ->
                flat0_k(T,fun(W) -> cat_k(V,W,⬛) end) end);
```

Finally, we must put to good use the continuation `K` by keeping in mind its meaning: 'Call `K` with the value of `cat(flat0(Y),flat0(T))`'. At this point, we do not know the value of this call, so we have to pass `K` to `cat_k/3`, which will know that value:

```
flat0_k([Y=[_|_]|T],K) ->
  flat0_k(Y,fun(V) ->
                flat0_k(T,fun(W) -> cat_k(V,W,K) end) end);
```

Now, we must transform `cat_k/3` in continuation-passing style. The original `cat/2` is

```
cat(   [],T) -> T;
cat([X|S],T) -> [X|cat(S,T)].
```

We have

```
cat_k(   [],T,K) -> K(T);
cat_k([X|S],T,K) -> cat_k(S,fun(V) -> K([X|V]) end).
```

Note that we did not care for introducing the identity continuation, as there is only one call to `cat_k/3`. Remains to transform the last clause of `flat0/2`, which contains one call whose context is `[Y|_]`:

```
flat0_k(      [Y|T],K) -> flat0_k(T,fun(V) -> [Y|V] end).
```

Summing up all previous steps, we arrive at

```
flat0_k(T)                   -> flat0_k(T,fun(V) -> V end).
flat0_k(          [],K) -> K([]);
flat0_k(       [[]|T],K) -> flat0_k(T,K);
flat0_k([Y=[_|_]|T],K) ->
  flat0_k(Y,fun(V) ->
                flat0_k(T,fun(W) -> cat_k(V,W,K) end) end);
flat0_k(         [Y|T],K) -> flat0_k(T,fun(V) -> [Y|V] end).

cat_k(   [],T,K) -> K(T);
cat_k([X|S],T,K) -> cat_k(S,fun(V) -> K([X|V]) end).
```

All functions are now in tail form, because a continuation is an anonymous function, that is, it is a value.

Our next example is `fib/1`, the straightforward but extremely inefficient implementation of the Fibonacci function:

```
fib(0) -> 1;
fib(1) -> 1;
fib(N) -> fib(N-1) + fib(N-2).
```

The corresponding continuation-passing style is

```
fib_k(N)    -> fib_k(N,fun(V) -> V end).
fib_k(0,K) -> K(0);
fib_k(1,K) -> K(1);
fib_k(N,K) ->
  fib_k(N-1,fun(V) -> fib_k(N-2,fun(W) -> K(V+W) end) end).
```

Continuation-passing style is also interesting because it makes some optimisations easier to spot (Danvy, 2004). The design of sfst$_0$/2 in FIGURE 2.4 on page 52 was motivated by the need to share the input in case the sought item was missing. This kind of improvement is common in algorithms combining a search and an optional local update. For example, let us consider again leaf insertion *without duplicates* in a binary search tree in FIGURE 8.9 on page 262:

```
insl0(Y,{bst,X,T1,T2}) when X > Y -> {bst,X,insl0(Y,T1),T2};
insl0(Y,{bst,X,T1,T2}) when Y > X -> {bst,X,T1,insl0(Y,T2)};
insl0(Y,          ext)          -> {bst,Y,ext,ext};
insl0(Y,            T)          -> T.
```

In case Y is present in the tree, the last clause will share the subtree below the found occurrence of Y in the input tree, but the two first clauses,

corresponding to the search phase, will duplicate all the nodes from the
input root to Y (excluded). This can be avoided by threading the original
tree through the recursive calls and transforming the function in tail
form, so if Y is found, the entire input is shared and the evaluation stops
immediately (no pending contexts). First, let us transform the definition
into continuation-passing style (new continuations set in boldface type):

```erlang
insl0(Y,T)                      -> insl0(Y,T,fun(V) -> V end).
insl0(Y,{bst,X,T1,T2},K) when X > Y ->
                        insl0(T1,Y,fun(V) -> K({bst,X,V,T2}) end);
insl0(Y,{bst,X,T1,T2},K) when Y > X ->
                        insl0(T2,Y,fun(V) -> K({bst,X,T1,V}) end);
insl0(Y,        ext,K) -> K({bst,Y,ext,ext});
insl0(Y,          T,K) -> K(T).
```

Second, we thread the original search tree T (renamed U):

```erlang
insl0(Y,T)                      -> insl0(TmT,fun(V) -> V end,T).
insl0(Y,{bst,X,T1,T2},K,U) when X > Y ->
                        insl0(T1,Y,fun(V) -> K({bst,X,V,T2}) end,U);
insl0(Y,{bst,X,T1,T2},K,U) when Y > X ->
                        insl0(T2,Y,fun(V) -> K({bst,X,T1,V}) end,U);
insl0(Y,        ext,K,U) -> K({bst,Y,ext,ext});
insl0(Y,          T,K,U) -> K(T).
```

Finally, we discard the continuation in the last clause of insl0/4 and the
right-hand side shares the input:

```erlang
insl0(Y,T)                      -> insl0(Y,T,fun(V) -> V end,T).
insl0(Y,{bst,X,T1,T2},K,U) when X > Y ->
                        insl0(T1,Y,fun(V) -> K({bst,X,V,T2}) end,U);
insl0(Y,{bst,X,T1,T2},K,U) when Y > X ->
                        insl0(T2,Y,fun(V) -> K({bst,X,T1,V}) end,U);
insl0(Y,        ext,K,U) -> K({bst,Y,ext,ext});
insl0(Y,          T,K,U) -> U.                  % Input shared
```

In functional languages featuring *exceptions*, as Erlang does, the same
effect can be achieved without continuations:

```erlang
insl0(Y,T)                  -> try insl_(Y,T) catch throw:dup -> T end.
insl_(Y,{bst,X,T1,T2}) when X > Y -> {bst,X,insl_(Y,T1),T2};
insl_(Y,{bst,X,T1,T2}) when Y > X -> {bst,X,T1,insl_(Y,T2)};
insl_(Y,        ext)           -> {bst,Y,ext,ext};
insl_(Y,          T)           -> throw(dup).
```

This style is to be preferred over CPS because it preserves most of the original program ('direct style'). Nevertheless, this shows that continuations are useful when writing a compiler, so features like exceptions can be removed, as long as higher-order functions are available (Appel, 1992). These, in turn, can be transformed into first-order functions by *defunctionalisation* (Reynolds, 1972, Danvy and Nielsen, 2001).

Continuations can also be a design pattern. Consider the problem of determining whether a given stack is a *palindrome*, that is, given s, whether $s \equiv \mathsf{rev}(s)$. The obvious

```
pal(S) -> S == rev(S).
```

works in $n + 2$ rewrites because the cost of the operator (==) is not accounted for. Internally, though, what happens is that S is traversed (completely if it is a palindrome). If we do not allow ourselves the use of the equality operator on stacks, we may try

```
pal(S)   -> eq(S,rev(S)).
eq(S,S) -> true;
eq(_,_) -> false.
```

which is cheating in the same way: the non-linear pattern eq(S,S) requires that its arguments are traversed, without impacting the cost. If we also give up such patterns on stacks, we may come up with a solution based on continuations (Danvy and Goldberg, 2001):

```
pal(S)                   -> pal(S,S,fun(_) -> true end).
pal(    S,      [],K) -> K(S);                    % Even length
pal([_|S],     [_],K) -> K(S);                    % Odd length
pal([X|S],[_,_|T],K) ->
                     pal(S,T,fun([Y|U]) -> X == Y andalso K(U) end).
```

We reuse here an idea we saw in FIGURE 4.7 on page 130: duplicating the reference to S and moving into the second copy twice as fast as in the first (last clause); when reaching the end of the second copy (first and second clause of pal/3), the first copy holds the second half of the original stack, which is applied to the current continuation. The continuation was constructed by keeping a reference X to the current item in the first copy and scheduling an equality test with the first item of its parameter (the operator andalso is *sequential*, to wit, if its first argument evaluates to false, its second argument is not evaluated, so the continuation is dropped). Indeed, the idea is to compare the second half of the original stack with the items of the first half *in reverse order*, and this is the very purpose of the continuation. Note that the continuation takes a stack as an argument, but evaluates into a boolean, contrary to previous uses of continuations, where the initial continuation was the identity function (compare with par/1). Notice also how we also find out the parity of the length of the original stack, without using integers. It is easy to write an equivalent first-order function:

```
pal0(S)                    -> pal0(S,S,[]).
pal0(    S,       [],A) -> eq(S,A);
pal0([_|S],      [_],A) -> eq(S,A);
pal0([X|S],[_,_|T],A) -> pal0(S,T,[X|A]).


eq(   [],   []) -> true;
eq([X|S],[X|T]) -> eq(S,T);
eq(    _,    _) -> false.
```

The difference is that pal0/3, instead of constructing a continuation holding the items of the first half and preparing a test, explicitly reverses the first half and compares it to second half by means of eq/2. The cost of pal/1 and pal0/1 is the same.

The minimum cost is $\mathcal{B}_n^{\text{pal}} = \mathcal{B}_n^{\text{pal0}} = \lfloor n/2 \rfloor + 2$, if S is not a palindrome and a difference lies in the middle.

The maximum cost is $\mathcal{W}_n^{\text{pal}} = \mathcal{W}_n^{\text{pal0}} = 2\lfloor n/2 \rfloor + 1$, if S is a palindrome.

Further comparison of their memory consumption would require a way to quantify the store needed for a functional value, but it is likely that, in this case, the memory usages of pal/1 and pal0/1 are similar, so choosing one or the other is purely a matter of style, for instance, conciseness may be preferred.

Another entertaining example is provided again by Danvy (1988, 1989). The purpose is to make all the prefixes of a word, for example,

$$\text{allp}([a,b,c,d]) \twoheadrightarrow [[a],[a,b],[a,b,c],[a,b,c,d]],$$

where allp/1 stands for *all prefixes*. Building the suffixes with a linear cost would be much easier, in particular, it is straightforward to maximise memory sharing with an alias:

```
alls(    []) -> [];
alls(S=[_|T]) -> [S|alls(T)].
```

(The name alls means *all suffixes*.) We have $\mathcal{C}_n^{\text{alls}} = n + 1$ and

$$\text{alls}([a,b,c,d]) \twoheadrightarrow [[a,b,c,d],[b,c,d],[c,d],[d]].$$

A solution for prefixes, based on continuations, is

```
allp(S)         -> allp(S,fun(X) -> X end).
allp(   [],_) -> [];
allp([X|S],K) -> [K([X])|allp(S,fun(T) -> K([X|T]) end)].
```

Another higher-order solution `allp0/1` relies on a map (see page 343):

```
allp0(   []) -> [];
allp0([X|S]) -> [[X]|map(fun(T) -> [X|T] end, allp0(S))].
```

We have

$$C_n^{\mathsf{allp0}} = (n+1) + \sum_{k=1}^{n-1} k = \frac{1}{2}n^2 + \frac{1}{2}n + 1. \tag{9.3}$$

Exercise   Write a first-order version of `allp0/1`.

Chapter 10

Translation to Java

In this chapter we show how to translate simple functional programs to Java, illustrating what may be called a functional style in an object-oriented language. We will make no use of side-effects, so all variables are assigned only once. Objects programmed in this manner are sometimes called *functional objects*. The difficulties we face have to do with the type system of Java, since our functional language is untyped. As a consequence, some programs cannot be translated and others require intermediary translations, called *refinements*, before the equivalent Java program is produced.

In the introduction, on page 16, we laid out the design pattern for modelling stacks: an abstract class Stack<Item> parameterised over the type of its contents Item and two extensions, EStack<Item> for empty stacks and NStack<Item> for non-empty stacks. It is important to understand the rationale behind this pattern, because it is perhaps more likely to find an imperative implementation in the following lines:

```
public class Stack<Item> {                          // Stack.java
  private Item head;
  private Stack<Item> tail;

  public Stack() { head = null; tail = null; }

  public boolean empty() { return head == null; }

  public Item pop() throws EmptyStack {
    if (empty()) throw new EmptyStack();
    final Item orig = head;
    if (tail.empty()) head = null; else head = tail.pop();
    return orig; }
```

```
  public void push(final Item item) {
    Stack<Item> next = new Stack<Item>();
    next.head = head;
    next.tail = tail;
    head = item;
    tail = next; }
}
```

```
// EmptyStack.java
public class EmptyStack extends Exception {}
```

This encoding has several defaults. Firstly, it is incorrect if the top of a stack (head) is a null reference. This can be remedied by adding a level of indirection, that is, by creating a private class holding head and tail or modelling the empty stack with null, which entails to check for null before calling any method. Secondly, pervasive use of null references increases the risk of an invalid access. Thirdly, the code for pop and push already suggests that further operations will lead to lengthy reference manipulations. Fourthly, persistence, for example, keeping successive versions of a stack, is not easy.

A thorough study of the issues of null references in programming language design is given by Chalin and James (2007), Cobbe (2008) and Hoare (2009). One practical inconvenience of such references is that they render the composition of methods cumbersome and, for example, instead of writing s.cat(t).push(x).rev(), we would have to check if each call returns null or not.

The design we presented in the introduction avoids all the problems and limitations previously mentioned. Of course, this comes with a cost, which we will discuss in a couple of occasions. For now, let us recall the Java program of the introduction, which will be completed further in this chapter:

```
// Stack.java
public abstract class Stack<Item> {
  public final NStack<Item> push(final Item item) {
    return new NStack<Item>(item,this); }
  public abstract Stack<Item> cat(final Stack<Item> t); }
```

```
// EStack.java
public final class EStack<Item> extends Stack<Item> {
  public Stack<Item> cat(final Stack<Item> t) { return t; }
}
```

```
// NStack.java
public final class NStack<Item> extends Stack<Item> {
  private final Item head;
  private final Stack<Item> tail;

  public NStack(final Item item, final Stack<Item> stack) {
    head = item; tail = stack;
  }

  public NStack<Item> cat(final Stack<Item> t) {
    return tail.cat(t).push(head);
  }
}
```

Notice that we eschewed defining any method **pop**. The reason is that
it is intrinsically a partial function, undefined when its argument is the
empty stack, and this is why we had to resort to the exception **EmptyStack**
above. In practice, anyway, this method is hardly useful as it would be
implicit in an algorithm, for example, in the definition of **cat** in class
NStack<Item>. More fundamentally, because **head** and **tail** are part of
the data structure itself, there is no need for a **pop** method.

10.1 Single dispatch

Stack reversal As we have seen in equation (2.2) on page 40, the
efficient manner to reverse a stack in our functional language consists in
using an accumulator as follows:

$$\mathsf{rev}(s) \xrightarrow{\epsilon} \mathsf{rcat}(s, [\,]). \quad \mathsf{rcat}([\,], t) \xrightarrow{\zeta} t; \quad \mathsf{rcat}([x\,|\,s], t) \xrightarrow{\eta} \mathsf{rcat}(s, [x\,|\,t]).$$

Function **rev/1** is defined with one rule which does not discriminate on
the nature of its parameter. Therefore, its translation will be one method
in the abstract class **Stack<Item>**:

```
// Stack.java
public abstract class Stack<Item> {
  ...
  public Stack<Item> rev() {
    return rcat(new EStack<Item>()); }
}
```

An examination of the patterns defining the rules of function **rcat/2** shows
that only the first parameter is constrained, more precisely, it is either

expected to be an empty stack or a non-empty stack. This simple kind of functional definition is easily translated by relying upon the *single dispatch* feature of Java, that is, the dynamic class of an object determines the method being called. When, in a rule, exactly one parameter is constrained, it is thus the natural candidate for single dispatch. For example,

```java
// Stack.java
public abstract class Stack<Item> {
  ...
    public abstract Stack<Item> rcat(final Stack<Item> t);
}
```

Class `EStack<Item>` contains the translation of rule ζ:

```java
// EStack.java
public final class EStack<Item> extends Stack<Item> {
  ...
    public Stack<Item> rcat(final Stack<Item> t) { return t; }
}
```

Class `NStack<Item>` holds the translation of rule η (`tail` is s, `head` is x):

```java
// NStack.java
public final class NStack<Item> extends Stack<Item> {
  ...
  public Stack<Item> rcat(final Stack<Item> t) {
    return tail.rcat(t.push(head));
  }
}
```

Skipping Let us recall the function sfst/2 in section 2.3 on page 44:

$$\mathsf{sfst}([], x) \xrightarrow{\theta} [];\quad \mathsf{sfst}([x\,|\,s], x) \xrightarrow{\iota} s;\quad \mathsf{sfst}([y\,|\,s], x) \xrightarrow{\kappa} [y\,|\,\mathsf{sfst}(s, x)].$$

This definition cannot be translated as it is because it contains an implicit equality test in its patterns ι and κ, hence it cannot solely rely on single dispatch. Perhaps the easiest way to proceed is to extend our functional language with a conditional expression if ... then ... else ... and refine the original definition to use it. Here, we obtain

$$\mathsf{sfst}([], x) \xrightarrow{\theta} [];\quad \mathsf{sfst}([y\,|\,s], x) \xrightarrow{\iota + \kappa} \text{if } x = y \text{ then } s \text{ else } [y\,|\,\mathsf{sfst}(s, x)].$$

Now that pattens do not overlap anymore, we can translate to Java. First, we must not forget to expand the abstract class `Stack<Item>`:

```
// Stack.java
public abstract class Stack<Item> {
  ...
  public abstract Stack<Item> sfst(final Item x);
}
```

The translation of rule θ goes into the class EStack<Item>:

```
// EStack.java
public final class EStack<Item> extends Stack<Item> {
  ...
  public EStack<Item> sfst(final Item x) { return this; }
}
```

The joint translation of ι and κ is

```
// NStack.java
public final class NStack<Item> extends Stack<Item> {
  ...
  public Stack<Item> sfst(final Item x) {
    return head.compareTo(x) == 0 ?
            tail : tail.sfst(x).push(head); }
}
```

This last step reveals a mistake and a limitation of our method: in order to compare two values of class Item like head and x, we need to specify that Item extends the predefined class Comparable. Therefore, we must rewrite our class definitions as follows:

```
public abstract
class Stack<Item extends Comparable<? super Item>> {
  ...
}
public class EStack<Item extends Comparable<? super Item>>
      extends Stack<Item> {
  ...
}
public class NStack<Item extends Comparable<? super Item>>
      extends Stack<Item> {
  ...
}
```

It is a limitation because we must constrain Item to be comparable even if some methods do not require this, like rev, which is purely structural. Also, the abstract class must be updated every time a new operation is added. (For a detailed understanding of generics in Java, see Naftalin and Wadler (2006).)

Insertion sort   Insertion sort was defined in section 3.1 on page 95 as

$$\mathsf{ins}([y\,|\,s], x) \xrightarrow{\kappa} [y\,|\,\mathsf{ins}(s, x)], \text{ if } x \succ y; \qquad \mathsf{isrt}([\,]) \xrightarrow{\mu} [\,];$$
$$\mathsf{ins}(s, x) \xrightarrow{\lambda} [x\,|\,s]. \qquad\qquad \mathsf{isrt}([x\,|\,s]) \xrightarrow{\nu} \mathsf{ins}(\mathsf{isrt}(s), x).$$

Function isrt/1 is easy to translate because it only needs single dispatch. Function ins/2 too, but first requires a refinement introducing a conditional. Easy things first:

```java
// Stack.java
public abstract
class Stack<Item extends Comparable<? super Item>> {
  ...
  public abstract Stack<Item> isrt();
}
// EStack.java
public class EStack<Item extends Comparable<? super Item>>
       extends Stack<Item> {
  ...
  public EStack<Item> isrt() { return this; }
}
// NStack.java
public class NStack<Item extends Comparable<? super Item>>
       extends Stack<Item> {
  ...
  public NStack<Item> isrt() {return tail.isrt().ins(head);}
}
```

Notice how ins(isrt(s), x) became `tail.isrt().ins(head)`. The general method consists, firstly, in translating x and s into x and `tail`; secondly, in finding a possible order of evaluation (there may be more than one) and laying out the translations of each function call from left to right, separated by full stops. In the case at hand, isrt(s) is evaluated first and becomes `tail.isrt()`, then ins($\_$, x), which yields `_.ins(head)`.

The refinement of ins/2 is

$$\mathsf{ins}([y\,|\,s], x) \rightarrow \text{if } x \succ y \text{ then } [y\,|\,\mathsf{ins}(s, x)] \text{ else } [x\,|\,s];$$
$$\mathsf{ins}([\,], x) \rightarrow [x].$$

Note how we split rule λ in two cases: $[\,]$ and $[y\,|\,s]$, so the latter can be merged with rule κ and partake to the conditional. We can now translate to Java:

```java
// Stack.java
public abstract
class Stack<Item extends Comparable<? super Item>> {
  ...
  protected abstract NStack<Item> ins(final Item x);
}
// EStack.java
public class EStack<Item extends Comparable<? super Item>>
      extends Stack<Item> {
  ...
  protected NStack<Item> ins(final Item x) {return push(x);}
}
// NStack.java
public class NStack<Item extends Comparable<? super Item>>
      extends Stack<Item> {
  ...
  protected NStack<Item> ins(final Item x) {
    return head.compareTo(x) < 0 ?
          tail.ins(x).push(head) : push(x); }
}
```

The method `ins` is declared `protected`, because it is erroneous to insert an item into a non-ordered stack.

Testing To test these definitions, we need a method `print`:

```java
public abstract void print();                        // Stack.java
public void print() { System.out.println(); }        // EStack.java
public void print() {                                // NStack.java
  System.out.print(head + " "); tail.print(); }
```

Finally, the `Main` class would look like

```java
public class Main {                                  // Main.java
  public static void main (String[] args) {
    Stack<Integer> nil = new EStack<Integer>();
    Stack<Integer> s = nil.push(5).push(2).push(7);
    s.print();                                       // 7 2 5
    s.rev().print();                                 // 5 2 7
    Stack<Integer> t = nil.push(4).push(1);          // 1 4
    s.cat(t).print();                                // 7 2 5 1 4
    t.cat(s).isrt().print(); }                       // 1 2 4 5 7
}
```

The properties we proved earlier on the functional source codes are trans-
ferred to the Java target codes. In particular, the costs are left invariant
and they count the number of method calls needed to compute the value
of a method call, *assuming that we do not account for the calls to* push:
this method, which was intended as a commodity, was declared final in
the hope that the compiler might inline its definition.

Cutting   In section 2.6 on page 69, we saw how to cut a stack in two
stacks by specifying the length of the prefix:

$$\mathsf{cut}(s,0) \to ([\,],s); \qquad\qquad \mathsf{push}(x,(t,u)) \to ([x\,|\,t],u).$$
$$\mathsf{cut}([x\,|\,s],k) \to \mathsf{push}(x,\mathsf{cut}(s,k-1)).$$

Here, we have another instance of a rule which covers two different cases:
in the first rule of cut/2, either s is empty or not. If the latter, the
translation of the rule must be merged with the translation of the second
rule. There is an additional difficulty in the fact that Java does not
provide native pairs to translate (t,u) immediately. Fortunately, it is not
difficult to devise a class for pairs if we realise that, abstractly, a pair is a
thing that has two properties: one informing about its 'first component'
and another about its 'second component'. We have

```
// Pair.java
public class Pair<Fst,Snd> {
  protected final Fst fst;
  protected final Snd snd;
  public Pair(final Fst f, final Snd s) {fst = f; snd = s;}

  public Fst fst() { return fst; }
  public Snd snd() { return snd; }
}
```

Now we can proceed as follows:

```
// Stack.java
public abstract
class Stack<Item extends Comparable<? super Item>> {
  ...
  public abstract
  Pair<Stack<Item>,Stack<Item>> cut(final int k);
}
```

Notice that, as usual, a function with n parameters is translated into a
method with $n-1$ parameters because one of them is used to perform

the single dispatch or, in terms of the type system, it supports *subtype polymorphism* (Pierce, 2002).

```java
// EStack.java
public class EStack<Item extends Comparable<? super Item>>
        extends Stack<Item> {
  ...
  public Pair<Stack<Item>,Stack<Item>> cut(final int k) {
    return new Pair<Stack<Item>,Stack<Item>>(this,this);
  }
}
// NStack.java
public class NStack<Item extends Comparable<? super Item>>
        extends Stack<Item> {
  ...
  public Pair<Stack<Item>,Stack<Item>> cut(final int k) {
    if (k == 0)
      return new Pair<Stack<Item>,Stack<Item>>
                      (new EStack<Item>(),this);
    Pair<Stack<Item>,Stack<Item>> p = tail.cut(k-1);
    return new Pair<Stack<Item>,Stack<Item>>
                    (p.fst().push(head),p.snd());
  }
}
```

Finally, the `Main` class could look like

```java
// Main.java
public class Main {
  public static void main (String[] args) {
    Stack<Integer> nil = new EStack<Integer>();
    Stack<Integer> s = nil.push(5).push(2).push(7);       // 7 2 5
    Stack<Integer> t = nil.push(4).push(1);               // 1 4
    Pair<Stack<Integer>,Stack<Integer>> u = s.cat(t).cut(2);
    u.fst().print();                                      // 7 2
    u.snd().print();                                      // 5 1 4
  }
}
```

A translation may or must enjoy different interesting properties. For example, it must be correct in the sense that the result of the evaluation of a call in the source language is, in a certain sense, equal to the result of the evaluation of the translated call. This is what we wanted for our translation from our functional language to Java. Additionally, it could be required that erroneous behaviours also translate into erroneous behaviours. For example, it may be desirable that infinite loops translate into infinite loops and that run-time errors in evaluations in the source langage correspond to similar errors in the target. (The translation of cut/2 does not preserve all errors. Why?)

10.2 Binary dispatch

Functions defined by matching two or more stacks in the same pattern call for *multiple dispatch* in a target object-oriented language. Unfortunately, Java only features single dispatch, in other words, only one parameter of the source function supports subtype polymorphism in the target. In case of *binary dispatch*, we can refine the source definition into an equivalent definition which can, in turn, be translated with single dispatch alone. This technique was proposed a long time ago by Ingalls (1986) and a practical overview was published by Muschevici et al. (2008).

Merge sort For example, let us consider again the definition of mrg/2 in FIGURE 4.7 on page 130:

$$mrg([], t) \rightarrow t;$$
$$mrg(s, []) \rightarrow s;$$
$$mrg([x \mid s], [y \mid t]) \rightarrow [y \mid mrg([x \mid s], t)], \text{ if } x \succ y;$$
$$mrg([x \mid s], t) \rightarrow [x \mid mrg(s, t)].$$

We need to rewrite this definition so only one stack is inspected in the patterns. In order to do so, we choose arbitrarily one stack parameter, let us say the first, and match it against the empty and non-empty patterns as follows:

$$mrg([], t) \rightarrow t;$$
$$mrg([x \mid s], t) \rightarrow mrg_0(x, s, t).$$

$$mrg_0(x, s, []) \rightarrow [x \mid s];$$
$$mrg_0(x, s, [y \mid t]) \rightarrow \text{if } x \succ y \text{ then } [y \mid mrg([x \mid s], t)] \text{ else } [x \mid mrg(s, [y \mid t])].$$

Note how we had to introduce an auxiliary function $mrg_0/3$ to handle the matching of the second argument, t, of mrg/2. We also made use of a conditional construct in the last rule of $mrg_0/3$, where we can also avoid the memory-consuming pushes $[x \mid s]$ and $[y \mid t]$ by, respectively, calling $mrg_0(x, s, t)$ and $mrg_0(y, t, s)$. The latter call is a consequence of the theorem that merging is a symmetric function: $\mathsf{mrg}(s,t) \equiv \mathsf{mrg}(t,s)$. We have now

$$\mathsf{mrg}([\,],t) \rightarrow t;$$
$$\mathsf{mrg}([x\,|\,s],t) \rightarrow \mathsf{mrg}_0(x,s,t).$$

$$\mathsf{mrg}_0(x,s,[\,]) \rightarrow [x\,|\,s];$$
$$\mathsf{mrg}_0(x,s,[y\,|\,t]) \rightarrow \text{if } x \succ y \text{ then } [y\,|\,\mathsf{mrg}_0(x,s,t)] \text{ else } [x\,|\,\mathsf{mrg}_0(y,t,s)].$$

Then we have two functions that can be translated to Java only using single dispatch:

```java
// Stack.java
public abstract
class Stack<Item extends Comparable<? super Item>> {
  ...
  public abstract Stack<Item> mrg(final Stack<Item> t);
  public abstract
  Stack<Item> mrg0(final Item x, final Stack<Item> s);
}
// EStack.java
public class EStack<Item extends Comparable<? super Item>>
      extends Stack<Item> {
  ...
  public Stack<Item> mrg(final Stack<Item> t) { return t; }
  public Stack<Item> mrg0(final Item x,final Stack<Item> s){
    return s.push(x); }
}
// NStack.java
public class NStack<Item extends Comparable<? super Item>>
      extends Stack<Item> {
  ...
  public Stack<Item> mrg(final Stack<Item> t) {
    return t.mrg0(head,tail); }

  public Stack<Item> mrg0(final Item x,
                          final Stack<Item> s) {
    return x.compareTo(head) > 0 ?
           tail.mrg0(x,s).push(head)
         : s.mrg0(head,tail).push(x); }
}
```

Keep in mind that the pattern $\mathsf{mrg}_0(x,s,[y\,|\,t])$ means that $[y\,|\,t]$ translates as this, so the target code should go in the class NStack<Item>, where head is the translation of y and tail is the image of t. Finally,

```java
public class Main {                                          // Main.java
  public static void main (String[] args) {
    Stack<Integer> nil = new EStack<Integer>();
    Stack<Integer> s = nil.push(5).push(2).push(7);          // 7 2 5
    Stack<Integer> t = nil.push(4).push(1);                  // 1 4
    s.isrt().mrg(t.isrt()).print();                          // 1 2 4 5 7
    t.isrt().mrg(s.isrt()).print();                          // 1 2 4 5 7
  }
}
```

At this point, it could be argued that our translation scheme leads to cryptic Java programs. But this critique is valid only because it forgets to take into account any specification. We propose that the functional program *is* the specification of the Java program and should accompany it. A translation to Erlang could be performed first, due to its simplicity, and it would in turn be translated into Java, while remaining as a comment in the target code and its documentation. For example, we would write

```java
// NStack.java
public class NStack<Item extends Comparable<? super Item>>
       extends Stack<Item> {
  ...
  // mrg0(X,S,[Y|T]) -> case X > Y of
  //                          true  -> [Y|mrg0(X,S,T)];
  //                          false -> [X|mrg0(Y,T,S)]
  //                     end.
  //
  public Stack<Item> mrg0(final Item x,
                          final Stack<Item> s) {
    return x.compareTo(head) > 0 ?
           tail.mrg0(x,s).push(head)
         : s.mrg0(head,tail).push(x); }
}
```

(We could even go a step further and rename the Erlang parameters Y and T, respectively, as Head and Tail.) This has the additional advantage that the specification is executable, so the result of running the Erlang program can be expected to be equal to the result of the translated run in Java, which is a significant help for the test phase.

Let us finish now the translation of top-down merge sort in FIG-URE 4.7 on page 130. We have

$$\text{tms}([x,y\,|\,t]) \xrightarrow{\alpha} \text{cutr}([x],[y\,|\,t],t); \qquad \text{tms}(t) \xrightarrow{\beta} t.$$

A refinement is necessary because rule β covers the case of the empty stack and the singleton stack. Let us make all these cases explicit and reorder them as follows:

$$\mathsf{tms}([\,]) \to [\,]; \quad \mathsf{tms}([x]) \to [x]; \quad \mathsf{tms}([x, y\,|\,t]) \to \mathsf{cutr}([x], [y\,|\,t], t).$$

Now, we must fuse the two last rules because they are covered by the case 'non-empty stack' and introduce an auxiliary function $\mathsf{tms}_0/2$ whose role is to distinguish between the singleton and longer stacks. Whence

$$\mathsf{tms}([\,]) \xrightarrow{\gamma} [\,]; \qquad\qquad \mathsf{tms}_0(x, [\,]) \xrightarrow{\epsilon} [x];$$
$$\mathsf{tms}([x\,|\,t]) \xrightarrow{\delta} \mathsf{tms}_0(x, t). \qquad \mathsf{tms}_0(x, [y\,|\,t]) \xrightarrow{\zeta} \mathsf{cutr}([x], [y\,|\,t], t).$$

At this point, both $\mathsf{tms}/1$ and $\mathsf{tms}_0/2$ can be translated into Java using single dispatch but, before doing so, we must check whether the final refinement is indeed equivalent to the original program. We can test some calls whose partial evaluations make use, as a whole, of all the rules in the refined program and then compare them with the partial evaluations in the original program. (This is an instance of *structural testing*, more precisely, *path testing*.) Here, we found out that three cases are distinguished: empty stack, singleton and longer stacks. In the refined program, we have the interpretations

$$\mathsf{tms}([\,]) \xrightarrow{\gamma} [\,].$$
$$\mathsf{tms}([x]) \xrightarrow{\delta} \mathsf{tms}_0(x, [\,]) \xrightarrow{\epsilon} [x].$$
$$\mathsf{tms}([x, y\,|\,t]) \xrightarrow{\delta} \mathsf{tms}_0(x, [y\,|\,t]) \xrightarrow{\zeta} \mathsf{cutr}([x], [y\,|\,t], t).$$

We can now compare with the same calls being partially computed with the original program:

$$\mathsf{tms}([\,]) \xrightarrow{\beta} [\,].$$
$$\mathsf{tms}([x]) \xrightarrow{\beta} [x].$$
$$\mathsf{tms}([x, y\,|\,t]) \xrightarrow{\alpha} \mathsf{cutr}([x], [y\,|\,t], t).$$

These calls agree and cover all the arrows in all the definitions. We can now translate the refined program:

```java
// Stack.java
public abstract
class Stack<Item extends Comparable<? super Item>> {
    ...
    public abstract Stack<Item> tms();
    protected abstract Stack<Item> tms0(final Item x);
}
```

```java
// EStack.java
public class EStack<Item extends Comparable<? super Item>>
      extends Stack<Item> {

  ...
  public Stack<Item> tms() { return this; }

  protected Stack<Item> tms0(final Item x) {
    return push(x); }
}
```

```java
// NStack.java
public class NStack<Item extends Comparable<? super Item>>
      extends Stack<Item> {

  ...
  public Stack<Item> tms() { return tail.tms0(head); }

  protected Stack<Item> tms0(final Item x) {
    return tail.cutr(new EStack<Item>().push(x),this); }
}
```

Notice again how auxiliary functions result in `protected` methods and how they add to the overall cost, compared to the functional program: this is a limitation on how properties on the source transfer to the target. However, the asymptotic cost is the same as in the original functional program. A closer look at `tms0` shows that we translated $[y \mid t]$ by `this` instead of `tail.push(head)`, as an optimisation. Moreover, we dispatch `cutr` on `tail` because we already know that this is the parameter we are going to distinguish when translating `cutr/3` defined in FIGURE 4.7 on page 130:

$$\mathsf{cutr}(s, [y \mid t], [a, b \mid u]) \rightarrow \mathsf{cutr}([y \mid s], t, u);$$
$$\mathsf{cutr}(s, t, u) \rightarrow \mathsf{mrg}(\mathsf{tms}(s), \mathsf{tms}(t)).$$

We remark that two stacks are matched by the first pattern so some refinement is called for and we must choose one parameter to start with. A little attention reveals that the third one is the best choice, because if it does not contain at least two items, it is simply discarded. We need to introduce two auxiliary functions, $\mathsf{cutr}_0/3$ and $\mathsf{cutr}_1/3$, that check, respectively, whether the third parameter contains at least two items and whether the second contains at least one. The result is shown in FIGURE 10.1.

Note how $\mathsf{cutr}_1(s, [\,], u) \rightarrow \mathsf{mrg}(\mathsf{tms}(s), \mathsf{tms}([\,]))$ was simplified using the theorems $\mathsf{tms}([\,]) \equiv [\,]$ and $\mathsf{mrg}(s, [\,]) \equiv s$. The translation is now direct:

$$\begin{aligned}
\mathrm{cutr}(s, t, [\,]) &\to \mathrm{mrg}(\mathrm{tms}(s), \mathrm{tms}(t)); \\
\mathrm{cutr}(s, t, [a \,|\, u]) &\to \mathrm{cutr}_0(s, t, u).
\end{aligned}$$

$$\begin{aligned}
\mathrm{cutr}_0(s, t, [\,]) &\to \mathrm{mrg}(\mathrm{tms}(s), \mathrm{tms}(t)); \\
\mathrm{cutr}_0(s, t, [b \,|\, u]) &\to \mathrm{cutr}_1(s, t, u).
\end{aligned}$$

$$\begin{aligned}
\mathrm{cutr}_1(s, [\,], u) &\to \mathrm{tms}(s); \\
\mathrm{cutr}_1(s, [y \,|\, t], u) &\to \mathrm{cutr}([y \,|\, s], t, u).
\end{aligned}$$

Figure 10.1: Cutting and merging top-down

```java
// Stack.java
public abstract
class Stack<Item extends Comparable<? super Item>> {
  ...
  public abstract
  Stack<Item> cutr(final Stack<Item> s, final Stack<Item> t);

  protected abstract
  Stack<Item> cutr0(final Stack<Item> s, final Stack<Item> t);

  protected abstract
  Stack<Item> cutr1(final Stack<Item> s, final Stack<Item> u);
}

// EStack.java
public class EStack<Item extends Comparable<? super Item>>
extends Stack<Item> {
  ...
  public
  Stack<Item> cutr(final Stack<Item> s, final Stack<Item> t) {
    return s.tms().mrg(t.tms()); }

  protected
  Stack<Item> cutr0(final Stack<Item> s, final Stack<Item> t) {
    return s.tms().mrg(t.tms()); }

  protected
  Stack<Item> cutr1(final Stack<Item> s, final Stack<Item> u) {
    return s.tms(); }
```

```
}

// NStack.java
public class NStack<Item extends Comparable<? super Item>>
        extends Stack<Item> {
  ...
  public
  Stack<Item> cutr(final Stack<Item> s, final Stack<Item> t) {
    return tail.cutr0(s,t); }

  protected
   Stack<Item> cutr0(final Stack<Item> s, final Stack<Item> t) {
    return t.cutr1(s,tail); }

  protected
  Stack<Item> cutr1(final Stack<Item> s, final Stack<Item> u) {
    return u.cutr(s.push(head),tail); }
}
```

Note that it is of the utmost importance to constantly mind the parameter in the source function whose translation will be the base for dispatch. Finally, the Main class might look like

```
// Main.java
public class Main {
  public static void main (String[] args) {
    Stack<Integer> nil = new EStack<Integer>();
    Stack<Integer> s = nil.push(5).push(2).push(7);      // 7 2 5
    Stack<Integer> t = nil.push(4).push(1);                 // 1 4
    s.tms().print();                                                  // 2 5 7
    s.cat(t).tms().print();                                    // 1 2 4 5 7
  }
}
```

Chapter 11

Translation to XSLT

Recursion is a programming technique often neglected in undergraduate curricula, rushed at the end of the semester, except when the programming language is functional, that is, if it prominently features immutable data and a control flow mostly defined by the composition of mathematical functions. Examples of such languages are Scheme, Haskell, OCaml, Erlang and XSLT (Kay, 2008). Amongst them, XSLT is rarely taught in college, so professionals without prior exposure to functional programming are likely to face the double challenge of learning a new programming paradigm and using XML: while the former put forth recursion, the latter obscures it because of its inherent verbosity. The syntactic difficulty is inevitable with XSLT because its grammar *is* XML, as well as it is the grammar of its input and, usually, of its output.

This is why this chapter introduces the basics of XSLT by relying on our understanding of our abstract functional programming language or, concretely, a small subset of Erlang, a language chosen for its plain and regular syntax, as well as its native pattern matching, yielding very compact programs. Hopefully, the mental model of an Erlang programmer will ease the transition to thinking recursively in XSLT, having then to overcome only the obstacle of XML. Accordingly, a tiny subset of XSLT is presented and previous examples in Erlang are systematically stripped of their use of pattern matching so they become easily translatable into XSLT, which lacks that feature. At the same time, new exercises on unranked trees, that is, trees where internal nodes can have a variable number of children, are worked out directly in XSLT, aiming at a transfer of skills from Erlang.

The purpose of this chapter is not to present as many features of XSLT as possible, but to think recursively in XSLT, which can be conceived as a functional language specialised for the processing of XML documents.

389

11.1   Documents

We start our journey with a very brief presentation of the basics of XML, HTML and DTD, based on our lecture notes. The reader already a bit familiar with these languages may skip it and use it as a reference for the following chapters.

XML   The acronym XML stands for *eXtensible Markup Language*. It is a language for defining unranked trees with plain text, with a minimum number of syntactic constructs. These trees are used to model *structured documents*. Database programmers would perhaps call them *semi-structured data* because they are then conceived in opposition to data that fit well into tables, the fundamental structure of relational databases. These tables implement a mathematical model of *relations* satisfying *schemas*, whilst XML represents *unranked trees* and *formal grammars*. (To add to the confusion, XML also can be adjoined schemas of their own.) Anyway, to understand what XML is and how this modelling works, it is probably easier to start with a small example, like an email. What are the different *elements* and what is the *structure*, that is, how are the elements related to each other? As far as the elements are concerned, an email contains at least

- the sender's address,
- a subject or title,
- the recipient's address,
- a body of plain text.

The elements correspond to the tree nodes and the structure is modelled by the shape of the tree itself (its topology). For example:

```
From: Me
Subject: Homework
To: You

    A deadline is a due date for a homework.
```

This email can be modelled by a tree in FIGURE 11.1 on the facing page.

Note that the (boxed) leaves, called *text nodes*, contain text whereas the inner nodes contain information *about* their subtrees, in particular the leaves. Since the information in the inner nodes describes the information actually laid out, it is called *metadata* or *mark-up*, which explains part of the acronym 'XML'. The corresponding XML document is:

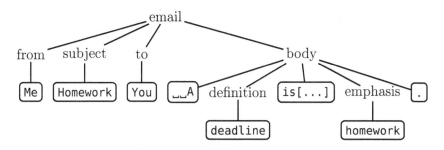

Figure 11.1: An email viewed as an XML tree

```
<email>
  <from>Me</from>
  <subject>Homeworks</subject>
  <to>You</to>
  <body>
  A <definition>deadline</definition> is a due date for a
<emphasis>homework</emphasis>.
  </body>
</email>
```

Elements   Each subtree is denoted by an opening and a closing *tag*. An opening tag is a name enclosed between < and >. A closing tag is a name enclosed between </ and >. A pair of opening and closing tags constitute an *element*; in other words, a subtree corresponds to an element. In particular, the element including all the others is called the *root element* (here, it is named email). The *element name* is not part of the text, it is metadata, so it suggests the meaning of the data contained in the subtree. For example, the whole XML document is an element whose name is email because the document describes a email. A preorder traversal of the XML tree (see page 209 for binary trees) yields nodes in the same order as their corresponding elements, when read in the XML document. (We shall comment on this.) The data (as opposed to the metadata) is always contained in the leaves, and is always text. Note, in particular, how the contents of the text nodes who are children of elements definition and emphasis have been respectively typeset with a bold typeface and in italics, but other interpretations would have been possible. It is important to understand that visual interpretations of mark-up are *not* defined in XML. This is why we wrote earlier that XML is purely a formal grammar, without semantics.

Actually, our example is not a correct XML document because it lacks a special element which says that the document is indeed XML, and, more precisely, what is the version of XML used here, for instance:

```
<?xml version="1.0"?>
```

This special element is actually not an element per se, as the special markers <? and ?> show. It is more a declaration, carrying some information about the current file to destination of the reader, whether it is a parsing software, usually called an *XML processor*, or a human. As such, it is a *processing instruction* (more to come on this).

For now, consider the following element:

```
<axiom>
The empty set <varnothing/> contains no elements.
</axiom>
```

which could be interpreted as

Axiom: The empty set ∅ contains no elements.

This <varnothing/> is an *empty element*, it features a special tag terminator, />, which is absent in normal opening and closing tags. It is useful for denoting things, as symbols, that cannot be written with the Roman alphabet and need to be distinguished from plain text. The associated tree is

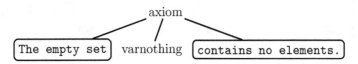

An empty element corresponds to a leaf in the XML tree, despite it is mark-up and not data.

Nodes do not need to be unique amongst siblings. For instance, if we want to send an email to several recipients, we would write:

```
<email>
  <from>Me</from>
  <subject>Homeworks</subject>
  <to>You</to>
  <to>Me</to>
  <body>
  A <definition>deadline</definition> is a due date for a
<emphasis>homework</emphasis>.
  </body>
</email>
```

The XML tree associated to this XML document is

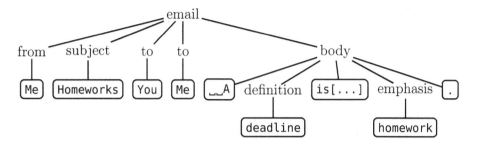

Note that there are two nodes to and that their order must be the same as in the XML document.

Attributes It is possible to annotate each mark-up node with some labelled strings, called *attributes*. For example, we may want to specify that our email is urgent, which is a property of the email as a whole, not a part of the contents per se:

```
<email priority="urgent">
  <from>Me</from>
  <subject>Homeworks</subject>
  <to>You</to>
  <body>
  A <definition>deadline</definition> is a due date for a
<emphasis>homework</emphasis>.
  </body>
</email>
```

That XML document may be represented by the following annotated tree:

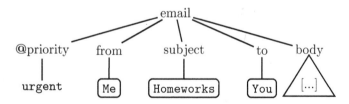

Note the symbol @ preceding the attribute name, which distinguishes it from element nodes. Amongst siblings, attribute nodes are found *before* element nodes. We may attach several attributes to a given element:

```
<email priority="urgent" ack="yes">
  <from>Me</from>
  <subject>Homeworks</subject>
```

```
<to>You</to>
<body>
 A <definition>deadline</definition> is a due date for a
<emphasis>homework</emphasis>.
 </body>
</email>
```

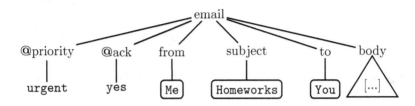

The order of the attributes matters. Any element can have attributes, including empty elements. Attributes are considered to be a special kind of node, although they are not often represented in the XML tree for lack of room.

The xml processing instruction too can hold other predefined attributes besides version:

```
<?xml version="1.0" encoding="UTF-8"?>
<?xml version='1.1' encoding="US-ASCII"?>
<?xml version='1.0' encoding='iso-8859-1'?>
```

The encoding is the *character encoding* of the XML document, which is particularly useful when using Unicode or some dedicated Asian font, for instance. Note that the attribute names must be in lowercase and the attribute *values* must be enclosed in single or double quotes. In the case of version and encoding, only some standardised values are valid.

Escaping   Most programming languages offer strings of characters to the programmer to use. For instance, in C, the strings are enclosed between double quotes, like "abc". Thus, if the string contains double quotes, we must take care of distinguishing, or *escaping*, them, so the compiler (or, more precisely, the parser) can recognise the double quotes in the contents from the enclosing double quotes. In C, escaping a character is achieved by adding a backslash just before it. This way, the following is a valid C string: "He said: \"Hello!\"."

In XML, there is a similar problem. The attribute values can either be enclosed by single or double quotes. If the latter, the double quotes in the contents need escaping; if the former, the quotes need escaping. Problems also stem from the characters used for the mark-up. For example, the following element

```
<problem>For all integers n, we have n < n + 1.</problem>
```

is not valid because the text between the tags contains the character '<', which is confused by the XML parsers with the (expected) start of a tag:

```
<problem>For all integers n, we have n ⟨<⟩ n + 1.</problem>
```

The way in which XML escapes this character is by using the special sequence of characters < so the previous element, once corrected, is

```
<valid>For all integers n, we have n &lt; n + 1.</valid>
```

Predefined named entities   The sequence < is called a *predefined named entity*. Such entities always

1. start with an ampersand (&),
2. continue with a predefined name (here, lt),
3. end with a semicolon (;).

Of course, the use of the ampersand to mark the start of an entity entails that this very character must itself be escaped if used to only denote itself. In that case, we should use & instead. There are some other characters which can *sometimes* cause a problem to XML parsers (as opposed to always create a problem, as < and & do). A summary of all the predefined named entities is given in the following table.

Character	Entity	Mandatory
&	&amp;	always
<	&lt;	always
>	&gt;	in attribute values
"	&quot;	between double quotes
'	&apos;	between single quotes

As an illustration, consider the following document:

```
<?xml version="1.0" encoding="UTF-8"?>
<escaping>
  <amp>&amp;</amp>
  <lt>&lt;</lt>
  <quot>&quot;</quot>
  <quot attr="&quot;">"</quot>
  <apos attr='&apos;'>&apos;</apos>
  <apos>'</apos>
  <gt>&gt;</gt>
```

```
<gt attr="&gt;">></gt>
<other>&#100;</other>
<other>&#x00E7;</other>
</escaping>
```

The two last entities are *predefined numbered entities* because they denote characters by using their Unicode point (http://www.unicode.org/). If the code is given in decimal, it is introduced by &#, for instance, &#100. If the code is given in hexadecimal, it is introduced by &#x, for example, &#x00E7.

Internal entities   It can be annoying to use numbers to refer to characters, especially if one considers that Unicode requires up to six digits. To make life easier, it is possible to bind a name to an entity representing a character, and get a *user-defined internal entity*. They are called internal because their definition must be in the same document where they are used. For example, it is easier to use &n; rather than &#241, especially if the text is in Spanish (this represents the letter ñ). This kind of entity must be declared in the *document type declaration*, which is located, if any, just after the declaration <?xml ... ?> and before the root element. A document type declaration is made of the following components:

1. the opening <!DOCTYPE,
2. the root element name,
3. the opening character [,
4. the *named character entity* declarations,
5. the closing]>.

A named character entity declaration is made of

1. the opening <!ENTITY,
2. the entity name,
3. the numbered character entity between double quotes,
4. the closing >

For example: <!ENTITY n "ñ"> Here is a complete example:

```
<?xml version="1.0"?>
<!DOCTYPE spain [
  <!ELEMENT spain (#PCDATA)>
  <!ENTITY n "&#241;">
]>
<spain>
Viva Espa&n;a!
</spain>
```

One can think such an entity as being a macro in cpp, the C preprocessor language. It is indeed possible to extend user-defined internal entities to denote any character string, not just a single character. Typically, if one wishes to repeat a long or difficult piece of text, like a foreign company name or the genealogy of the kings of Merina, it is best to name this text and put an entity with that name wherever one wants its contents. The syntax for the declaration is fundamentally the same. For example,

```
<!ENTITY univ "Konkuk University">
<!ENTITY motto "<spain>Viva Espa&n;a!</spain>">
<!ENTITY n "&#241;">
```

External entities Sometimes the XML document needs to include other XML documents, but copying and pasting of those is not a good strategy, since this precludes us from automatically following their editing. Fortunately, XML allows us to specify the inclusion of other XML documents by means of *external entities*. The declaration of these entities is as follows:

1. the opening <!ENTITY,
2. the entity name,
3. the keyword SYSTEM,
4. the full name of the XML file between double quotes,
5. the closing >

For example,

```
<?xml version="1.0"?>
<!DOCTYPE longdoc [
  <!ENTITY part1 SYSTEM "p1.xml">
  <!ENTITY part2 SYSTEM "p2.xml">
  <!ENTITY part3 SYSTEM "p3.xml">
]>
<longdoc>
  The included files are:
  &part1;
  &part2;
  &part3;
</longdoc>
```

At parsing time, the external entities are fetched by the underlying operating system and copied into the main XML document, replacing their associated entity. Therefore the included parts cannot contain any prolog, that is, no XML declaration <?xml ... ?> and no document type declaration `<!DOCTYPE ... ]>`. When reading an external entity, XML processors are required to copy verbatim the contents of the referenced external document and then to parse it as if it always belonged to the main document.

Unparsed entities   *Unparsed entities* allow us to refer to binary objects, like images, videos, sounds, or to some text which is not XML, like a program or a play by Shakespeare. They are declared by

1. the opening `<!ENTITY`,
2. the entity name,
3. the keyword `SYSTEM`,
4. the full name of the non-XML external file between double quotes,
5. the keyword `NDATA`,
6. a *notation* (the kind of the file),
7. the closing `>`

The following is an example.

```
<?xml version="1.0"?>
<!DOCTYPE doc [
  <!ELEMENT doc (para,graphic)>
  <!ELEMENT para (#PCDATA)>
  <!ELEMENT graphic EMPTY>
  <!ATTLIST graphic image   CDATA #REQUIRED
                    alt     CDATA #IMPLIED>
  <!NOTATION gif
     SYSTEM "CompuServe Graphics Interchange Format 87a">
  <!ENTITY picture SYSTEM "picture.gif" NDATA gif>
  <!ENTITY me "Christian Rinderknecht">
]>
<doc>
  <para>The following element refers to my picture:</para>
  <graphic image="picture" alt="A picture of &me;"/>
</doc>
```

Had we used external entities, the object would have been copied in place of the reference and parsed as XML – which it is not. Notice the notation `gif`, which is the kind of the unparsed entity. Notations must be defined in the document type declarations as follows:

1. the opening `<!NOTATION`,
2. the notation name,
3. the keyword `SYSTEM`,

   4. a description of the kind of unparsed entity the notation refers to
      (it can be a MIME type, an URL, plain English...)
   5. the closing >

Notice also that unparsed entities must be used either

   - as attribute values (in our example, the attribute name is `image`),
   - or as names (`picture`), instead of the entity syntax (`&picture;`).

For example, the next document is *not* well-formed:

```
<?xml version="1.0"?>
<!DOCTYPE doc [
  <!NOTATION jpeg SYSTEM "image/jpeg">
  <!ENTITY pic "pictures/me.jpeg" NDATA jpeg>
]>
<doc>
  &pic;
</doc>
```

Unparsed character data   It is sometimes tiresome to have to escape
characters, that is, to use character entities. To avoid the need of escaping, there is a special construct: *CDATA sections* (short for 'Character
DATA'), made of

   1. the opening `<![CDATA[`,
   2. some text without escaping and without the sequence `]]>`,
   3. the closing `]]>`.

For example

```
<paragraph>An example of conditional in C:
  <c><![CDATA[if (x < y) return &r;]]></c>
</paragraph>
```

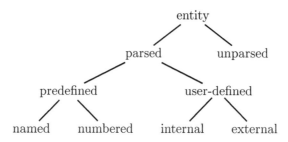

Figure 11.2: Summary of the different kinds of entities

Internal linking Consider a document representing a technical book,
like a textbook. It is common to find cross-references in such kind of
books, that is, references in some chapters to other chapters or sections,
or bibliographical entries. One easy way to achieve this is to use some
attributes as labels, that is, names unambiguously identifying a location
in the structure, and some attributes as references (to the labels). The
problem is that the writer is then in charge of checking whether

- a given label is unique throughout the whole document, including
  external entities,
- every reference corresponds to an existing label (linking).

XML provides a way to ensure that any validating parser will check this
kind of internal linking automatically: using the predefined attributes `ID`
and `IDREF`. The former is the kind of all the (attribute) labels and the
latter is the kind of all the (attribute) references. The attributes used
either as labels or references must be declared in the `DOCTYPE` section
using `ATTLIST` ('attribute list').

To declare labels, we must write

1. the opening `<!ATTLIST`,
2. the name of the element being labelled,
3. the names of the label attributes separated by spaces,
4. the keyword `ID`,
5. the keyword `#REQUIRED` if the element must always be labelled, otherwise `#IMPLIED`,
6. the closing `>`

For the references, we must write

1. the opening `<!ATTLIST`,
2. the name of the referring element,
3. the names of the reference attributes separated by spaces,
4. the keyword `IDREF`,
5. the keyword `#REQUIRED` if the element must always carry a reference,
   otherwise `#IMPLIED`,
6. the closing `>`

For example,

```
<?xml version='1.0'?>
<!DOCTYPE map [
   <!ATTLIST country code   ID    #REQUIRED
                     name   CDATA #REQUIRED
                     border IDREF #IMPLIED>
```

```
]>
<map>
  <country code="uk" name="United Kingdom" border="ie"/>
  <country code="ie" name="Ireland" border="uk"/>
</map>
```

Comments It is possible to include comments in an XML document. They are made of

1. the opening `<!--`,
2. some text without the sequence `--`,
3. the closing `-->`.

For example

```
<p>Our store is located at</p>
<!-- <address>Eunpyeong-gu, Seoul</address> -->
<address>Gangnam-gu, Seoul</address>
```

Contrary to programming languages, comments are *not* ignored by the parsers and are nodes of the XML tree.

Namespaces Each XML document defines its own element names, which we collectively call its *vocabulary*. In case we use external entities which refer to other XML documents using, by coincidence, the same names, we end with an ambiguity in the main document. A good way to avoid these name clashes is to use *namespaces*. A namespace is a user-defined annotation of each element names and attribute names. Therefore, if two XML documents use two different namespaces, that is to say, two different element name annotations, there is no way to mix their elements when importing one document into the other, because each element name carries an extra special annotation which is different (ideally unique in the set of documents of interest).

The definition of a namespace can be done at the level of any element by using a special attribute with the following syntax:

```
xmlns:prefix = "URL"
```

where *prefix* is the space name and *URL* (*Universal Resource Location*) points to a web page describing in natural language (for example, in English) the namespace. Consider the namespace `course` in the following:

```
<?xml version="1.0"?>
<course:short
```

```
 xmlns:course="http://konkuk.ac.kr/~rinderkn/Mirror/XML">
 <course:date>26 August 2006</course:date>
 <course:title>Some XML-centric languages</course:title>
 <course:topic course:level="advanced">
   We study XML, XPath and XSLT.</course:topic>
</course:short>
```

The scope of a namespace, that is, the part of the document where it is usable, is the subtree whose root is the element declaring the namespace. By default, if the prefix is missing, the element and all its sub-elements without prefix belong to the namespace. So, the previous example could be simply rewritten

```
<?xml version="1.0"?>
<short xmlns="http://konkuk.ac.kr/~rinderkn/Mirror/XML">
 <date>26 August 2006</date>
 <title>Some XML-centric languages</title>
 <topic level="advanced">We study XML, XPath and XSLT.</topic>
</short>
```

Note that the colon is missing in the namespace attribute: 'xmlns=...'. This example illustrates the important fact that what ultimately defines a namespace is a URL, not a prefix (like course).

As an example of a name clash and how to avoid it, let us consider a file fruits.xml containing the following HTML fragment:

```
<table>
  <tr>
    <td>Bananas</td>
    <td>Oranges</td>
  </tr>
</table>
```

HTML will be sketched in a coming subsection, but, for now, suffice it to say that the elements have an implicit meaning if the file is indeed interpreted as HTML. For example, table refers to a typographical layout.

Imagine now a file furniture.xml containing a description of pieces of furniture, like

```
<table>
  <name>Round table</name>
  <wood>Oak</wood>
</table>
```

Now, the main document main.xml includes both files:

```
<?xml version="1.0"?>
<!DOCTYPE eclectic [
  <!ENTITY part1 SYSTEM "fruits.xml">
  <!ENTITY part2 SYSTEM "furniture.xml">
]>
<eclectic>
  &part1;
  &part2;
</eclectic>
```

The problem is that `table` has a different meaning in the two included files, so they should not be confused: this is a clash name. The solution consists in using two different namespaces. First:

```
<html:table xmlns:html="http://www.w3.org/TR/html5/">
  <html:tr>
    <html:td>Bananas</html:td>
    <html:td>Oranges</html:td>
  </html:tr>
</html:table>
```

Second:

```
<f:table xmlns:f="http://www.e-shop.com/furnitures/">
  <f:name>Round table</f:name>
  <f:wood>Oak</f:wood>
</f:table>
```

But this is a heavy solution. Fortunately, namespaces can be defaulted:

```
<table xmlns="http://www.w3.org/TR/html5/">
  <tr>
    <td>Bananas</td>
    <td>Oranges</td>
  </tr>
</table>
```

Second:

```
<table xmlns="http://www.e-shop.com/furnitures/">
  <name>Round table</name>
  <wood>Oak</wood>
</table>
```

The two kinds of tables can be safely mixed now. For example

```
<mix xmlns:html="http://www.w3.org/TR/html5/"
     xmlns:f="http://www.e-shop.com/furnitures/">
<html:table>
  ...
  <f:table>
  ...
  </f:table>
...
<html:table>
</mix>
```

Note that element `mix` has no associated namespace (it is neither `html` nor `f`). It is possible to unbind or rebind a prefix namespace (the following examples are found at `http://www.w3.org/TR/REC-xml-names/`):

```
<?xml version="1.1"?>
<x xmlns:n1="http://www.w3.org">
  <n1:a/> <!-- valid; the prefix n1 is bound to
                http://www.w3.org -->
    <x xmlns:n1="">
      <n1:a/> <!-- invalid; the prefix n1 is not bound here -->
      <x xmlns:n1="http://www.w3.org">
        <n1:a/> <!-- valid; the prefix n1 is bound again -->
      </x>
    </x>
</x>

<?xml version='1.0'?>
<Beers>
  <table xmlns='http://www.w3.org/1999/xhtml'>
    <!-- default namespace is now XHTML -->
    <th><td>Name</td><td>Origin</td><td>Description</td></th>
    <tr>
      <!-- Unbinding XHTML namespace inside table cells -->
      <td><brandName xmlns="">Huntsman</brandName></td>
      <td><origin xmlns="">Bath, UK</origin></td>
      <td><details xmlns="">
            <class>Bitter</class>
            <hop>Fuggles</hop>
            <pro>Wonderful hop, good summer beer</pro>
            <con>Fragile; excessive variance pub to pub</con>
          </details></td>
    </tr>
```

```
    </table>
</Beers>

<?xml version="1.0" encoding="UTF-8"?>
<!-- initially, the default namespace is "books" -->
<book xmlns='http://loc.gov/books'
      xmlns:isbn='http://isbn.org/0-395-36341-6'
      xml:lang="en" lang="en">
  <title>Cheaper by the Dozen</title>
  <isbn:number>1568491379</isbn:number>
  <notes>
    <!-- make HTML the default namespace
         for a hypertext commentary -->
    <p xmlns='http://www.w3.org/1999/xhtml'>
       This is also available
       <a href="http://www.w3.org/">online</a>.
    </p>
  </notes>
</book>
```

An element may have children elements with the same name (like the element to in the email example above), but an element may not have attributes with identical names or identical namespaces (URL) and identical names. For example, each of the **bad** empty elements is invalid in the following:

```
<!-- http://www.w3.org is bound to n1 and n2 -->
<x xmlns:n1="http://www.w3.org" xmlns:n2="http://www.w3.org" >
  <bad a="1"    a="2"/>      <!-- invalid -->
  <bad n1:a="1" n2:a="2"/>  <!-- invalid -->
</x>
```

However, each of the following is valid, the second because *default namespaces never apply to attribute names*:

```
<!-- http://www.w3.org is bound to n1 and is the default -->
<x xmlns:n1="http://www.w3.org" xmlns="http://www.w3.org" >
  <good a="1" b="2"/>      <!-- valid -->
  <good a="1" n1:a="2"/> <!-- valid -->
</x>
```

Namespaces will be very important when learning XSLT. Although namespaces are declared as attributes, they are present in the XML tree corresponding to the document as a special node, different from the attribute nodes.

Processing instructions In some exceptional cases, it may be useful to include in an XML document some data that are targeted to a specific XML processor. These data are then embedded in a special element, and the data themselves are called a *processing instruction* because they tell a particular processor, for instance, Saxon, what to do at this point. The syntax is

```
<?target data?>
```

The *target* is a string supposed to be recognised by a specific XML processor and the *data* is then used by this processor. Note that the data takes the shape of attribute values, and may be absent. For example:

```
<?xml version="1.0"?>
```

Validation All XML processors must check whether the input document satisfy the *syntactical* requirements of a well-formed XML document. In particular,

- pairs of tags making up an element must be present, except for empty elements which are closed with /> (this has to be contrasted with HTML, which is very lax in this regard),
- the predefined entities must really be predefined (unicodes are automatically checked),
- internal entities must be declared in the prolog, etc.

Validating processors also check that the external entities are indeed found (their well-formedness is checked after they have been inserted in the main document). There are several XML parsers available free of charge over the internet, implemented in several languages. Most of them are actually libraries (API), so an application processing XML would only need to be interfaced with one of them. A good standalone, validating parser is xmllint.

HTML The *Hyper-Text Markup Language* (*HTML*) is used to describe web pages. See the W3C Draft Recommendation at http://www.w3.org/TR/html5/. Let us skim over this vast language and illustrate it with some small examples. For instance, all HTML file containing English should at least follow the pattern

```
<!DOCTYPE html>
<html lang="en-GB">
  <head>
    <title>the title of the window</title>
```

```
    </head>
    <body>
        ...contents and markup...
    </body>
</html>
```

Elements h1, h2, ..., h6 enable six kinds of headers, of decreasing font sizes. Consider opening in a web browser the following document:

```
<!DOCTYPE html>
<html lang="en-GB">
    <head>
        <title>Comparing heading sizes</title>
    </head>
    <body>
        <h1>The biggest</h1>
        <h2>Just second</h2>
        <h3>Even smaller</h3>
    </body>
</html>
```

Other useful elements are the following:

- The empty element <br/> is interpreted by user agents as a *line break*;
- element em marks text to be *emphasised* (for example, by using an italic font);
- element strong marks text to be emphasised stronger than with em (for instance, by using a bold font);
- element p delimits a *paragraph*.

Lists are a common way to typeset closely related sentences, like enumerations. There are three kinds of lists:

1. unordered lists;
2. ordered lists;
3. lists of definitions.

Unordered lists are the well-known 'bullet lists', where each line is displayed after an indentation followed by a bullet, like the following.

- element ul contains an unordered list;
- element li ('list item') contains an item in the list.

Try the following recipe:

```
<h3>Ingredients</h3>
<ul>
  <li>100 g. flour,</li>
  <li>10 g. sugar,</li>
  <li>1 cup of water,</li>
  <li>2 eggs,</li>
  <li>salt and pepper.</li>
</ul>
```

Ordered lists are lists whose items are introduced by an indentation followed by a number, in increasing order. They require

1. the element ol, which contains the ordered list,
2. elements li, as in unordered lists.

For example,

```
<h3>Procedure</h3>
<ol>
  <li>Mix dry ingredients thoroughly;</li>
  <li>Pour in wet ingredients;</li>
  <li>Mix for 10 minutes;</li>
  <li>Bake for one hour at 300 degrees.</li>
</ol>
```

A list of definitions is a list whose items are introduced by a few words in a bold font followed by the contents of the item itself. Consider

---

hacker
> A clever programmer.

nerd
geek
> A technically bright but socially misfit person.

The elements involved are

- dl ('definition list'), which contains the whole list of definitions;
- dt ('definition term'), which contains every term to be defined;
- dd ('definition description'), which contains every definition of a term.

The previous example corresponds to the following HTML excerpt:

```
<dl>
  <dt><strong>hacker</strong></dt>
    <dd>A clever programmer.</dd>
  <dt><strong>nerd</strong></dt>
  <dt><strong>geek</strong></dt>
    <dd>A technically bright but socially misfit person.</dd>
</dl>
```

A *table* is a rectangle divided into smaller rectangles, called *cells*, which contain some text. When read vertically, cells are said to belong to *columns*, whilst horizontally, they belong to *rows*. A row or a column can have a *header*, that is, a cell at their beginning containing a name in bold face. A table can have a *caption*, which is a short text describing the contents of the table and displayed just above it, like a title. Columns can be divided themselves into subcolumns, when needed. The following example is taken from `http://www.w3.org/TR/html4/struct/tables.html`.

A test table with merged cells

	Average		Red
	height	**weight**	**eyes**
Males	1.9	0.003	40%
Females	1.7	0.002	43%

Males and **Females** are row headers. The column headers are **Average**, **Red eyes**, **height** and **weight**. The column **Average** spans two columns; in other words, it contains two subcolumns, **height** and **weight**. The caption reads *A test table with merged cells*. The corresponding HTML code is

```
<table border="1">
  <caption><em>A test table with merged cells</em></caption>
  <tr>
    <th rowspan="2"/>
    <th colspan="2">Average</th>
    <th rowspan="2">Red<br/>eyes</th>
  </tr>
  <tr><th>height</th><th>weight</th></tr>
  <tr><th>Males</th><td>1.9</td><td>0.003</td><td>40%</td></tr>
  <tr>
    <th>Females</th>
    <td>1.7</td>
    <td>0.002</td>
    <td>43%</td>
```

```
  </tr>
</table>
```

The meaning of the elements is as follows:

- Element `table` contains the table; its attribute `border` specifies the width of the table borders, that is, of the lines separating the cells from the rest.
- Element `caption` contains the caption.
- Element `th` ('table header') contains a row or column header, that is, the title of the row of column in bold type.
- Element `td` ('table data') contains the data of a cell (if not a header).
- Element `tr` ('table row') contains a row, that is, a series of `td` elements, perhaps starting with a `th` element.

Notice the attributes `rowspan` and `colspan` of the `th` element. Attribute `rowspan` allows us to specify how many rows the current cell spans. For example, the first row, that is, the one on the top-left corner, is empty and covers two rows because `<th rowspan="2"/>`. Attribute `colspan` allows us to declare how many columns the current cell spans. For example, the second cell contains the text **Average** and covers two columns because `<th colspan="2">Average</th>`. Notice the line break `<br/>` in the third cell (first row, last column) and how **height** and **weight** are automatically at the right place

Hyperlinks in HTML are defined by the element 'a' with its mandatory attribute `href` ('hyper-reference'). For example, consider the following hyperlink:

```
<a href="http://konkuk.ac.kr/~rinderkn/">See my web page.</a>
```

XHTML　The current working draft of HTML is HTML 5. Until it becomes a standard supported by web browsers and XSLT processors, it is best for beginners to use a simpler version of HTML, called XHTML (*eXtensible Hyper-Text Markup Language*), whose W3C Recommandation is found at `http://www.w3.org/TR/xhtml1/`. Basically, XHTML is XML, but the elements which are found in HTML have the same meaning (instead of none). For example, the previous examples are valid XHTML, with the provision that a specific `DOCTYPE` is declared. The pattern is the following:

```
<?xml version="1.0" encoding="encoding"?>
<!DOCTYPE html
    PUBLIC "-//W3C//DTD XHTML 1.0 Strict//EN"
    "http://www.w3.org/TR/xhtml1/DTD/xhtml1-strict.dtd">
```

```
<html xmlns="http://www.w3.org/1999/xhtml"
      xml:lang="en" lang="en">
  <head>
    <title>the title of the window</title>
  </head>
  <body>
     ...contents and markup...
  </body>
</html>
```

Just like XML documents, XHTML documents can be and should be validated before being published on the web, for example using the site at http://validator.w3.org/.

DTD We saw on page 396 that the *Document Type Declaration* may contain markup which constrains the XML document it belongs to (elements, attributes etc.). The content of a Document Type Declaration is made of a *Document Type Definition*, abbreviated DTD. So the former is the container of the latter. It is possible to have all or part of the DTD in a separate file, usually with the extension '.dtd'. We already saw *attribute lists* on page 400 when setting up internal linking. In general, the special element ATTLIST can be used to specify any kind of attributes, not just labels and references. Consider the attribute declarations for element memo:

```
<!ATTLIST memo ident     CDATA          #REQUIRED
               security  (high | low)   "high"
               keyword   NMTOKEN        #IMPLIED>
```

CDATA stands for *character data* and represents any string. A *named token* (NMTOKEN) is a string starting with a letter and which may contain letters, numbers and certain punctuation. In order for a document to be validated, which requires more constraints than to be merely well-formed, all the elements used must be declared in the DTD. The name of each element must be associated a *content model*, that is, a description of what it is allowed to contain, in terms of textual data and sub-elements (mark-up). This is achieved by means of the DTD ELEMENT declarations. There are five content models:

1. the *empty element*:

   ```
   <!ELEMENT padding EMPTY>
   ```

2. elements with *no content restriction*:

```
<!ELEMENT open ALL>
```

3. elements containing *only text*:

```
<!ELEMENT emphasis (#PCDATA)>
```

which means *parsed-character data*.

4. elements containing *only elements*:

```
<!ELEMENT section (title,para+)>
<!ELEMENT chapter (title,section+)>
<!ELEMENT report (title,subtitle?,(section+ | chapter+))>
```

where `title`, `subtitle` and `para` are elements.

5. elements containing *both text and elements*:

```
<!ELEMENT para (#PCDATA | emphasis | ref)+>
```

where `emphasis` and `ref` are elements.

The definition of a content model is akin to *regular expressions*. Such an expression can be made up by combining the following expressions:

- $(e_1, e_2, \ldots, e_n)$ represents the elements represented by e_1, followed by the elements represented by e_2 etc. until e_n;
- $e_1 \mid e_2$ represents the elements represented by e_1 or e_2;
- (e) represents the elements represented by e;
- $e?$ represents the elements represented by e or none;
- $e+$ represents a non-empty repetition of the elements represented by e;
- $e*$ represents the repetition of the elements represented by e.

Warning: When mixing text and elements, the only possible regular expression is either `(#PCDATA)` or `(#PCDATA | ...)*`

The part of a DTD which is included in the same file as the XML document it applies to is called the *internal subset*. See again the example on page 400. The part of a DTD which is in an independent file (`.dtd`) is called the *external subset*. If there is no internal subset and everything is in the external subset we have a declaration like

```
<!DOCTYPE some_root_element SYSTEM "some.dtd">
```

In order to validate an XML document, its DTD must completely describe the elements and attributes used. This is not mandatory when well-formedness is required. Therefore, the example on page 400 is well-formed but not valid in the sense above, because the elements `map` and `country` are not declared. To validate the document, it is enough, for example, to add

```
<!ELEMENT map (country*)>
<!ELEMENT country EMPTY>
```

11.2 Introduction

Given one or several XML documents, it may be useful

- to search the documents and output what has been found in a format suitable for another application or reader, in particular, XML (filtering in);

- to copy the input, perhaps without certain parts (filtering out), and/or adding data (updating).

When such needs arise, it is a good idea to use the functional programming languages XQuery or XSLT (*eXtensible Stylesheet Language Transformations*). Even if both languages share a great deal of common use cases (to the point of having in common a sublanguage, XPath), the first application, which is more oriented towards database management, is more commonly tackled with XQuery, whilst the second usage is often undertaken with XSLT.

An XSLT processor reads an XML document and an XSLT program, then applies the *transformations* defined in XSLT to the document, and the result is printed, usually in plain text, XML or HTML. The twist is that an XSLT file is actually an XML document, which enables XSLT to transform XSLT programs. For example, if we use an element book in an XML document, XML itself does not necessarily imply that this element models a book, although some application using the document perhaps will precisely do that. One can think of XML as merely syntactic rules, in other words, a formal grammar, with no semantics attached to the constructs. An XSLT document is thus XML with a performative declaration.

To enable the interpretation of XML as XSLT, XSLT programs require the predefined namespace http://www.w3.org/1999/XSL/Transform, which is often (but not necessarily) named xsl, as shown in

```
<?xml version="1.0" encoding="UTF-8"?>
<xsl:transform version="2.0"
              xmlns:xsl="http://www.w3.org/1999/XSL/Transform">
  <xsl:output method="text"/>
</xsl:transform>
```

The first line states that this is an XML document. The second defines the interpretation as XSLT by declaring the namespace for XSLT and

using the *root element* xsl:transform (xsl:stylesheet is also accepted).
The version of XSLT is set to 2.0, which is the version current at the
time of writing. Moreover, the element xsl:output states that the output
is to be plain text. Other than that, the program says nothing else, so
we might expect the transformation to do nothing. Assume then the
following XML document, cookbook.xml, to be transformed:

```
<?xml version="1.0" encoding="UTF-8"?>
<cookbook author="Salvatore Mangano">
  <title>XSLT Cookbook</title>
  <chapter>XPath</chapter>
  <chapter>Selecting and Traversing</chapter>
  <chapter>XML to Text</chapter>
  <chapter>XML to XML</chapter>
  <chapter>XML to HTML</chapter>
</cookbook>
```

The application of the empty transformation to this document yields

```
XSLT Cookbook
XPath
Selecting and Traversing
XML to Text
XML to XML
XML to HTML
```

Perhaps surprisingly, something did happen: the contents of the *text
nodes* of the input XML document were extracted *in the same order*,
but not the attribute values. (Note that if <xsl:output method="text"/>
were missing, the output would be considered XML and <?xml ... ?>
would be outputted by default.) More precisely, the order corresponds to
a preorder traversal of the corresponding XML tree: this is the implicit
traversal of XSLT processors, also called *document order*. The rationale
is that, since the aim is often to rewrite a document into another, this
traversal corresponds to the order in which a book is read and written,
cover to cover. Furthermore, the reason why the text nodes are extracted
by default is due to XSLT favouring a filtering style: if part of the input
should be ignored or augmented, the programmer must say so. Finally,
let us remark that there is no need for explicit printing instructions in
XSLT: the programmer assumes that the result is XML or text and the
run-time system ensures automatic *serialisation* of the result.

Matching   Let us complete our empty transformation as follows:

```
<?xml version="1.0" encoding="UTF-8"?>
<xsl:transform version="2.0"
            xmlns:xsl="http://www.w3.org/1999/XSL/Transform">
  <xsl:output method="text"/>
  <xsl:template match="chapter">A chapter</xsl:template>
</xsl:transform>
```

Note the predefined element xsl:template defining a *template*. It bears
the attribute match, whose value is the name of the element we want to
transform. During the preorder traversal, if a chapter element is found
(that is, matched), the contents of the text node of the template (A
chapter) becomes the result. (Let us not confuse the text node and its
contents.) Applying the previous transformation to the document in the
file named cookbook.xml yields

```
XSLT Cookbook
A chapter
A chapter
A chapter
A chapter
A chapter
```

Let us match now the root element with the following:

```
<?xml version="1.0" encoding="UTF-8"?>
<xsl:transform version="2.0"
            xmlns:xsl="http://www.w3.org/1999/XSL/Transform">
  <xsl:output method="text"/>
  <xsl:template match="cookbook">Chapters:</xsl:template>
  <xsl:template match="chapter">A chapter</xsl:template>
</xsl:transform>
```

The result is now:

```
Chapters:
```

The reason is that when a template matches a node, called the *context
node* from within the template, that node is processed (here, the text
Chapters: or A chapter is produced) and the preorder traversal resumes
without visiting the children of the context node. Therefore, after the
element cookbook is matched and done with, the XSLT processor ignores
everything else since it is the root element.

In order to visit and try to match the children of the context node,
one must tell so the processor by using the special empty element

```
<xsl:apply-templates/>
```

Let us add this element as a child of the template matching the root
element:

```
<?xml version="1.0" encoding="UTF-8"?>
<xsl:transform version="2.0"
                xmlns:xsl="http://www.w3.org/1999/XSL/Transform">
  <xsl:output method="text"/>
  <xsl:template match="cookbook">
    Chapters:
    <xsl:apply-templates/>
  </xsl:template>
  <xsl:template match="chapter">A chapter</xsl:template>
</xsl:transform>
```

The result is now:

```
    Chapters:

    XSLT Cookbook
    A chapter
    A chapter
    A chapter
    A chapter
    A chapter
```

It is striking that the text 'Chapters:' is not aligned with the title. It
is a sad fact that the handling of whitespace and newlines can be very
confusing in XML and XSLT, in particular when we want or not some
space if the output, like here, is plain text. We will not discuss this thorny
issue here and refer the reader to the book by Kay (2008), page 141. As
for the rest, the title appears after 'Chapters:', which is confusing.

If we simply want to get rid of the title, we could simply define an
empty template matching title:

```
<?xml version="1.0" encoding="UTF-8"?>
<xsl:transform version="2.0"
                xmlns:xsl="http://www.w3.org/1999/XSL/Transform">
  <xsl:output method="text"/>
  <xsl:template match="cookbook">
    Chapters:
    <xsl:apply-templates/>
  </xsl:template>
```

```
  <xsl:template match="chapter">A chapter</xsl:template>
  <xsl:template match="title"/>
</xsl:transform>
```

The result is now:

```
    Chapters:


    A chapter
    A chapter
    A chapter
    A chapter
    A chapter
```

If we want to retain the title, we need to extract the text from the text node which is a child of the title element, and put it before 'Chapters:'. One way is to apply the templates on title alone using the special attribute select, whose value is the child's name, then produce 'Chapters:', and finally apply the templates to the chapters:

```
<?xml version="1.0" encoding="UTF-8"?>
<xsl:transform version="2.0"
                 xmlns:xsl="http://www.w3.org/1999/XSL/Transform">
  <xsl:output method="text"/>
  <xsl:template match="cookbook">
    <xsl:apply-templates select="title"/>
    Chapters:
    <xsl:apply-templates/>
  </xsl:template>
  <xsl:template match="chapter">A chapter</xsl:template>
</xsl:transform>
```

The result is now:

```
XSLT Cookbook
    Chapters:

  XSLT Cookbook
  A chapter
  A chapter
  A chapter
  A chapter
  A chapter
```

This is not quite it, because we must not apply the templates to all the children of **cookbook**, only to the chapters:

```
<?xml version="1.0" encoding="UTF-8"?>
<xsl:transform version="2.0"
                 xmlns:xsl="http://www.w3.org/1999/XSL/Transform">
  <xsl:output method="text"/>
  <xsl:template match="cookbook">
    <xsl:apply-templates select="title"/>
    Chapters:
    <xsl:apply-templates select="chapter"/>
  </xsl:template>
  <xsl:template match="chapter">A chapter</xsl:template>
</xsl:transform>
```

The result is now:

```
XSLT Cookbook
    Chapters:
    A chapterA chapterA chapterA chapterA chapter
```

We just hit another quirk with the newlines. What happened is that the *selection* (via the attribute **select**) gathered all the **chapter** nodes in a linear structure called a *sequence*, the templates have been applied to all of the nodes in it, then each of the results has been serialised, concatenated to the others and, finally, a newline character has been added. The reason why we had newlines after each 'A **chapter**' before is because each of these texts constituted a singleton sequence. In order to recover the newlines, we could use the special element **xsl:text**, whose purpose is to output the content of its unique text node *as it is*, without tweaking blanks and newlines. Here, we could force a newline after each 'A **chapter**'. In XML, the newline character is the numbered entity **
**

```
<?xml version="1.0" encoding="UTF-8"?>
<xsl:transform version="2.0"
                 xmlns:xsl="http://www.w3.org/1999/XSL/Transform">
  <xsl:output method="text"/>
  <xsl:template match="cookbook">
    <xsl:apply-templates select="title"/>
    Chapters:
    <xsl:apply-templates select="chapter"/>
  </xsl:template>
  <xsl:template match="chapter">
    <xsl:text>A chapter&#10;</xsl:text>
```

```
  </xsl:template>
</xsl:transform>
```

The result is now:

```
XSLT Cookbook
    Chapters:
    A chapter
A chapter
A chapter
A chapter
A chapter
```

Still not perfect, but let us abandon this example and spend some time understanding sequences.

11.3 Transforming sequences

As we already know from part I, the linear structure of choice in functional languages is the stack, also called list. In XSLT, it is the *sequence*. The empty sequence is written () and the non-empty sequence is written $(x_1, x_2, \ldots, x_n)$, where the x_i are items, or $x_1, x_2, \ldots, x_n$. The difference with stacks is twofold. First, sequences are always flat, so when an item of a sequence is itself a sequence, it is replaced by its contents, if any. For instance, (1,(),(2,(3)),4) is actually evaluated in (1,2,3,4). In particular, a singleton sequence is the same as the unique item it contains: ((5)) is 5. Second, no cost is incurred when concatenating two sequences (in contrast with the linear cost in the length of the first stack when concatenating two stacks), so the previous evaluation costs 0. The reason is that concatenation of sequences, being frequently needed, is a built-in operation. Therefore, in XSLT, concatenation is the primary operation, not pushing, as it is the case with stacks.

Just like in Erlang, sequences can contain any kind of items, not just integers. We will use sequences to hold XML elements and attributes, for instance. Another thing to know about sequences is that if seq is the name of a sequence, then $seq represents the sequence: *note the dollar sign*. If we write seq in the value of an attribute match or select, it means the *element* seq. Furthermore, the first item in $seq is written $seq[1], the second $seq[2] etc. where the natural number is the *position* of the item. If we select an item missing in a sequence, the result is the empty sequence, for example, if $seq[2] is (), it means that $seq contains at most one item. It is often very useful to extract a subsequence, similarly to projecting the substack (the tail) of a given stack. This is done with the predefined function `position`: `$seq[position()>1]` or `$seq[position() != 1]`.

Length   Let us recall here a functional program computing the length of a stack:

$$\mathsf{len}_0([]) \to 0; \quad \mathsf{len}_0([x\,|\,s]) \to 1 + \mathsf{len}_0(s).$$

In view of a translation to XSLT, let us add to our source language a conditional expression and rewrite the program without pattern matching:

$$\mathsf{len}_0(s) \to \mathbf{if}\ s = []\ \mathbf{then}\ 0\ \mathbf{else}\ 1 + \mathsf{len}_0(\mathsf{tl}(s)). \qquad (11.1)$$

where $\mathsf{tl}(s)$ (*tail*) returns the immediate substack of s. Note that we cannot define `tail/1` without pattern matching, so it has to be translated into a predefined function. In order to start writing the XSLT program, we need to be more specific about the input. Let us suppose that we obtain our sequence by selecting the children nodes `chapter` of the root element `book`. In other words, we want to count the number of chapters in a book. For instance,

```
<?xml version="1.0" encoding="UTF-8"?>
<!DOCTYPE book SYSTEM "book.dtd">
<book>
  <author>Priscilla Walmsley</author>
  <title>Definitive XML Schema</title>
  <chapter>Schema: An Introduction</chapter>
  <chapter>A quick tour of XML Schema</chapter>
  <chapter>Namespaces</chapter>
  <chapter>Schema composition</chapter>
  <chapter>Instances and schemas</chapter>
</book>
```

The DTD is as follows:

```
<!ELEMENT book (author?,title?,chapter+)>
<!ELEMENT author (#PCDATA)>
<!ELEMENT title (#PCDATA)>
<!ELEMENT chapter (#PCDATA)>
```

The style we recommend in XSLT consists in explicitly typing as much as we can the data and the templates. In order to do so, we need to use a tiny part of a standard called XML Schema (Walmsley, 2002), by means of a namespace, just like we enable XSLT through a namespace. This explains the canvas of our program:

```
<?xml version="1.0" encoding="UTF-8"?>
<xsl:transform version="2.0"
                xmlns:xsl="http://www.w3.org/1999/XSL/Transform"
                xmlns:xs="http://www.w3.org/2001/XMLSchema">
  <xsl:output method="text" encoding="UTF-8"/>
  ...
</xsl:transform>
```

In all our XSLT programs whose output is text, we would like to have a newline character at the end to improve readability. Because the root element is likely to vary, we match the *document root*, noted /, which is an implicit node whose only child is the root element. We then apply any available templates to the root element and put a newline:

```
<xsl:template match="/">
  <xsl:apply-templates/>
  <xsl:text>&#10;</xsl:text>
</xsl:template>
```

Now we need to match the root element and call the translation of $\mathsf{len}_0/1$. To translate functions, we will use a special kind of template, called a *named template*, which differs from the *matching templates* we saw earlier. There are two sides to their usage: their definition and their call.

The canvas for defining a named template is

```
<xsl:template name="f" as="t">
  <xsl:param name="x₁" as="t₁"/>
  ...
  <xsl:param name="xₙ" as="tₙ"/>
  ...
</xsl:template>
```

The name of the template is f, each x_i is a parameter of type t_i, the type of the value computed by f is t.

The canvas for calling a named template is as follows:

```
<xsl:call-template name="f">
  <xsl:with-param name="x₁" select="v₁" as="t₁"/>
  ...
  <xsl:with-param name="xₙ" select="vₙ" as="tₙ"/>
</xsl:call-template>
```

The template named f has n parameters x_1, x_2, ..., x_n, such that the type of x_i is t_i and its value is v_i. Binding values to parameters in this way is featured in programming languages like Ada (*named association*) and OCaml (*labels*), and it allows the programmer to forget about the parameters order, which is particularly useful when they are numerous.

At this point it is important to know that there exists functions in XSLT, defined by the element xsl:function, and, although we chose named templates for the translation, plain XSLT functions would do as well.

Resuming our translation, we need to call the named template which will be the translation of len0/1:

```
<xsl:template match="book" as="xs:integer">
  <xsl:call-template name="len0">
    <xsl:with-param name="chapters" select="chapter"
                    as="element(chapter)*"/>
  </xsl:call-template>
</xsl:template>
```

As mentioned previously, we had to name the parameter we pass a value to, that is, chapters. Perhaps more puzzling is the meaning of the attribute value 'element(chapter)*': it is the type of a sequence (possibly empty) of chapter elements. Although it may not be necessary in this instance to provide this type because it is implicit in the selection select="chapter", we recommend to always use the attribute as with xsl:with-param. Furthermore, note that the result of the template matching book is also typed as xs:integer because it is the same result as that of the called template len0. (In the template matching the document root (/), we did not specify the return type because we wanted that template to work with every transformation.)

Let us focus now on the definition of the called template, that is, the translation of $len_0/1$ (at last!). We expect the following pattern:

```
<xsl:template name="len0" as="xs:integer">
  <xsl:param name="chapters" as="element(chapter)*"/>
  ...
</xsl:template>
```

The parameter named chapters corresponds to s in the definition (11.1) of $len_0/1$; we changed the name to fit more closely the specialised meaning, limited to chapters here. We need now to translate the conditional expression **if** ... **then** ... **else** ... into XSLT. Unfortunately, tests in XSLT are quite verbose in general. Let us introduce three elements that allow us to write general tests in the style of the switch constructs of Java:

```
<xsl:choose>
```

```
<xsl:when test="b₁">e₁</xsl:when>
...
<xsl:when test="bₙ">eₙ</xsl:when>
<xsl:otherwise>eₙ₊₁</xsl:otherwise>
</xsl:choose>
```

The values b_i of the test attributes are evaluated (The apparent tautology is due to the XSLT vocabulary: an attribute value is actually not a value in general, but an expression.) in order until one, say b_j, results in the boolean true, causing the sequence e_j to be evaluated; otherwise the sequence e_{n+1} (children of xsl:otherwise) is processed. Resuming our exercise, we fill a bit more the blanks:

```
<xsl:template name="len0" as="xs:integer">
  <xsl:param name="chapters" as="element(chapter)*"/>
  <xsl:choose>
    <xsl:when test="empty($chapters)">
      ... <!-- Translation of 0 -->
    </xsl:when>
    <xsl:otherwise>
      ... <!-- Translation of 1 + len₀(s) -->
    </xsl:otherwise>
  </xsl:choose>
</xsl:template>
```

Note the built-in XSLT function empty, which returns true if its argument is an empty sequence, and false otherwise. The translation of 0 is not so simple, though! Indeed, the obvious 0 would mean that we actually produce a *text* containing the character 0, instead of the expected integer. There is a very useful XSLT element which may come handy here – although more versatile than it seems here, as we shall see later. Let us introduce the *sequence constructor*:

```
<xsl:sequence select="..."/>
```

The selected value must evaluate into a sequence which is then substituted in place of the element xsl:sequence. One may wonder why this is so convoluted, and the reason is that the value of the select attributes belongs to a sublanguage of XSLT, called XPath, and XPath can only be used for selections or tests (empty is an XPath function). In a select attribute, 0 means 0, not the text made of the single character 0, and xsl:sequence allows us to inject in XSLT the XPath values, so we can construct a sequence made with XPath. Of course, we have to keep in mind that any item is equivalent to a singleton sequence, in particular (0) is the same as 0 in XPath. Therefore, the translation of 0 is

```
<xsl:when test="empty($chapters)">
  <xsl:sequence select="0"/>
</xsl:when>
```

The expression $1+\mathsf{len}_0(s)$ is made of three parts: the stack s, the function call $\mathsf{len}_0(s)$ and the addition of 1 to the value of the call. We already know that stacks are translated as sequences, we also know that function calls become calls to named templates. It is simple to add 1 to a function call in XPath, for instance `1 + f($n)`, but this syntax is not valid outside a selection or a test and, anyway, we defined a named template, not a function in XSLT (which must be called in XPath). Therefore, we have to hold temporarily the value of the recursive call in a variable, say x, then use `xsl:sequence` to compute (in XPath) the value of `1 + $x`. The element which defines a variable in XSLT is `xsl:variable` and it has two possible forms: either with a `select` attribute or with children. In the former case, we have the pattern

```
<xsl:variable name="x" select="v" as="t">
```

and the latter is

```
<xsl:variable name="x" as="t">
  ... <!-- Children whose value is v and has type t -->
</xsl:variable>
```

where the value of the variable x is v, of type t. The reason for the dual syntax is due again to the territory delimited by XPath: if v can be computed in XPath alone, we should use the first form, otherwise we need the second. In our problem, we need the second form because v is the value of a recursive call *not* expressed in XPath, as we use `xsl:call-template`. We can now complete the program:

```
<?xml version="1.0" encoding="UTF-8"?>
<xsl:transform version="2.0"
              xmlns:xsl="http://www.w3.org/1999/XSL/Transform"
              xmlns:xs="http://www.w3.org/2001/XMLSchema">

  <xsl:output method="text" encoding="UTF-8"/>

  <xsl:template match="/">
    <xsl:apply-templates/>
    <xsl:text>&#10;</xsl:text>
  </xsl:template>
```

```
<xsl:template match="book" as="xs:integer">
  <xsl:call-template name="len0">
    <xsl:with-param name="chapters" select="chapter"
                    as="element(chapter)*"/>
  </xsl:call-template>
</xsl:template>


<xsl:template name="len0" as="xs:integer">
  <xsl:param name="chapters" as="element(chapter)*"/>
  <xsl:choose>
    <xsl:when test="empty($chapters)">
      <xsl:sequence select="0"/>
    </xsl:when>
    <xsl:otherwise>
      <xsl:variable name="x" as="xs:integer">
        <xsl:call-template name="len0">
          <xsl:with-param name="chapters"
                          as="element(chapter)*"
                          select="$chapters[position()>1]"/>
        </xsl:call-template>
      </xsl:variable>
      <xsl:sequence select="1 + $x"/>
    </xsl:otherwise>
  </xsl:choose>
</xsl:template>


</xsl:transform>
```

The result of running it on our table of contents is, as expected:

5

After we recover from the sustained effort and the disappointment from such an incredible verbosity in comparison to **Erlang**, we may find out that there exists a built-in function in **XPath**, named `count`, which is basically a translation of $\text{len}_0/1$. Nevertheless, our purpose is to address beginners, so the didactic usefulness primes other considerations.

Let us work on the translation of a better version of $\text{len}_0/1$:

$$\text{len}_1(s) \rightarrow \text{len}_1(s, 0). \qquad \text{len}_1([\,], n) \rightarrow n;$$
$$\text{len}_1([x\,|\,s], n) \rightarrow \text{len}_1(s, n+1).$$

Function $\text{len}_1/1$ is better than $\text{len}_0/1$ because its cost is the same as the latter *and* it uses a constant amount of memory, being in tail form. The

tail form implies that we do not need a variable, because the addition is
performed in XPath (parameter of the recursive call):

```xml
<?xml version="1.0" encoding="UTF-8"?>

<xsl:transform version="2.0"
               xmlns:xsl="http://www.w3.org/1999/XSL/Transform"
               xmlns:xs="http://www.w3.org/2001/XMLSchema">

  <xsl:output method="text" encoding="UTF-8"/>

  <xsl:template match="/">
    <xsl:apply-templates/>
    <xsl:text>&#10;</xsl:text>
  </xsl:template>

  <xsl:template match="book" as="xs:integer">
    <xsl:call-template name="len2">
      <xsl:with-param name="chapters" select="chapter"
                                      as="element(chapter)*"/>
      <xsl:with-param name="n"        select="0"
                                      as="xs:integer"/>
    </xsl:call-template>
  </xsl:template>

  <xsl:template name="len2" as="xs:integer">
    <xsl:param name="chapters" as="element(chapter)*"/>
    <xsl:param name="n"        as="xs:integer"/>
    <xsl:choose>
      <xsl:when test="empty($chapters)">
        <xsl:sequence select="$n"/>
      </xsl:when>
      <xsl:otherwise>
        <xsl:call-template name="len2">
          <xsl:with-param name="chapters"
                          select="$chapters[position()>1]"
                          as="element(chapter)*"/>
          <xsl:with-param name="n" select="1 + $n"
                          as="xs:integer"/>
        </xsl:call-template>
      </xsl:otherwise>
    </xsl:choose>
```

```
  </xsl:template>
```

```
</xsl:transform>
```

Note how we did not have to define a named template for $len_0/1$.

As a last variation, consider a variant input where the chapters are all children of a `contents` element and their names are held in a `title` attribute, instead of a text node:

```
<?xml version="1.0" encoding="UTF-8"?>

<!DOCTYPE book SYSTEM "book_att.dtd">

<book>
  <author>Priscilla Walmsley</author>
  <title>Definitive XML Schema</title>
  <contents>
    <chapter title="Schema: An Introduction"/>
    <chapter title="A quick tour of XML Schema"/>
    <chapter title="Namespaces"/>
    <chapter title="Schema composition"/>
    <chapter title="Instances and schemas"/>
  </contents>
</book>
```

Of course, the DTD `boot_att.dtd` has to be changed:

```
<!ELEMENT book (author,title,contents)>
<!ELEMENT author (#PCDATA)>
<!ELEMENT title (#PCDATA)>
<!ELEMENT contents (chapter+)>
<!ELEMENT chapter EMPTY>
<!ATTLIST chapter title CDATA #REQUIRED>
```

To solve this problem, we must modify a previous XSLT transformation, not think from the abstract functional language. First, we should modify the call to the template so as to select the chapters where they are now:

```
  <xsl:template match="book" as="xs:integer">
    <xsl:call-template name="len3">
      <xsl:with-param name="elm" select="contents/chapter"
                                  as="element(chapter)*"/>
      <xsl:with-param name="n" select="0" as="xs:integer"/>
    </xsl:call-template>
  </xsl:template>
```

The expression `contents/chapter` is a selection in XPath which means: 'Gather all the children `contents` of the context node (`book`), preserving their relative order (here, there is only one), then select all the children named `chapter` of all those nodes, also preserving their relative order'. Other than that, there is no need to change the template (apart from its name, now `len3`). Notice also that using `title` attributes made no difference.

But let us take this opportunity to make slight variations and learn something new. Let us say that we want the template to be able to work on any kind of elements, not just `chapter`, and we would like to use a *default parameter*. Indeed, the type of the template parameter `chapters` is `element(chapter)*`, so it is not enough general. The solution is the type `element()*`, which means 'A sequence, possibly empty, of elements.' Moreover, the original value of the parameter `n` must always be `0`, so we could make this value a default by adding a `select` attribute to the corresponding `xsl:param` element:

```
<xsl:template name="len3" as="xs:integer">
  <xsl:param name="elm" as="element()*"/>
  <xsl:param name="n" as="xs:integer" select="0"/>
  ...
</xsl:template>
```

In passing, we renamed the parameter to the neutral `elm`. Of course, the call to the template is now shorter:

```
<xsl:template match="book" as="xs:integer">
  <xsl:call-template name="len3">
    <xsl:with-param name="elm" select="contents/chapter"
                               as="element(chapter)*"/>
  </xsl:call-template>
</xsl:template>
```

Note that it is still possible to impose an initial value to `n` that would not be `0`. Also, it is possible now to reuse the template `len3` for computing the length of any sequence of elements.

In the end, the new transformation is

```
<?xml version="1.0" encoding="UTF-8"?>

<xsl:transform version="2.0"
            xmlns:xsl="http://www.w3.org/1999/XSL/Transform"
            xmlns:xs="http://www.w3.org/2001/XMLSchema">
```

```
<xsl:output method="text" encoding="UTF-8"/>

<xsl:template match="/">
  <xsl:apply-templates/>
  <xsl:text>&#10;</xsl:text>
</xsl:template>

<xsl:template match="book" as="xs:integer">
  <xsl:call-template name="len3">
    <xsl:with-param name="elm" select="contents/chapter"
                               as="element(chapter)*"/>
  </xsl:call-template>
</xsl:template>

<xsl:template name="len3" as="xs:integer">
  <xsl:param name="elm" as="element()*"/>
  <xsl:param name="n" as="xs:integer" select="0"/>
  <xsl:choose>
    <xsl:when test="empty($elm)">
      <xsl:sequence select="$n"/>
    </xsl:when>
    <xsl:otherwise>
      <xsl:call-template name="len3">
        <xsl:with-param name="elm" as="element()*"
                   select="$elm[position()>1]"/>
        <xsl:with-param name="n" as="xs:integer"
                   select="1 + $n"/>
      </xsl:call-template>
    </xsl:otherwise>
  </xsl:choose>
</xsl:template>

</xsl:transform>
```

Summing   Given a stack of integers, we can compute their sum as
follows

$$\mathsf{sum}([x\,|\,s]) \to \mathsf{sum}_0([x\,|\,s], 0). \qquad \mathsf{sum}_0([\,], n) \to n;$$
$$\mathsf{sum}_0([x\,|\,s], n) \to \mathsf{sum}_0(s, n + x).$$

Immediately, we see that there is just a small difference between $\mathsf{sum}_0/2$
and $\mathsf{len}_1/2$: instead of adding 1, we add x. Thus, we can expect a tiny

modification of the corresponding XSLT template. Let us assume the following input:

```
<?xml version='1.0' encoding='UTF-8'?>
<!DOCTYPE numbers SYSTEM "sum.dtd">
<numbers>
  <num>18</num>
  <num>1</num>
  <num>3</num>
  <num>5</num>
  <num>23</num>
  <num>3</num>
  <num>2</num>
  <num>7</num>
  <num>4</num>
</numbers>
```

with the DTD

```
<!ELEMENT numbers (num*)>
<!ELEMENT num (#PCDATA)>
```

The change we would like to make to len3 is

```
<xsl:call-template name="sum">
  <xsl:with-param name="elm" as="element()*"
                select="$elm[position()>1]"/>
  <xsl:with-param name="n" as="xs:integer"
                select="$elm[1] + $n"/>
</xsl:call-template>
```

Unfortunately, the compiler Saxon returns the following warning about the change:

```
The only value that can pass type-checking is an empty sequence.
Required item type of value of parameter $n is xs:integer;
supplied value has item type xs:double
```

and the wrong result 18135233274, which is just the concatenation of the contents of the text nodes of the num elements. What happened? From the message, one thing is clear: the problem has to do with the type system, that is why we did not anticipate it from the untyped $\text{sum}_0/2$. It is also clear that the compiler understands that $n is an integer, therefore the culprit can only be our modification, $elm[1]. We would like it to be of type xs:integer too, but is it? The type of $elm is element()*, as declared, which means that the items it contains are elements, not integers, hence the issue. We need to force the type of `$elem[1]` to become `xs:integer`, that is, we *cast* it. First, we need to select the text node of `$elem[1]` and then cast it by using `xs:integer` like an XPath *function*: `xs:integer($elm[1]/text())`. There is no warning now:

18135233274

The wrong result is still there. It is time to understand why! It is clearly made of the all text nodes, in document order and serialised without any separation. We know from the start that, by default, this is what XSLT is meant to do, therefore we failed to specify that *we* actually want. A look back at the first call to `sum` reveals

```
<xsl:template match="book" as="xs:integer">
  <xsl:call-template name="sum">
    <xsl:with-param name="elm" select="contents/chapter"
                    as="element(chapter)*"/>
  </xsl:call-template>
</xsl:template>
```

Because we do not have `chapter` elements in the input now, an empty sequence is selected by `contents/chapter`. It should be num. But this does not change the wrong result. The reason is that there is no context node because there is no `book` element in the document. Therefore, we should write:

```
<xsl:template match="numbers" as="xs:integer">
  <xsl:call-template name="sum">
    <xsl:with-param name="elm" select="num"
                    as="element(num)*"/>
  </xsl:call-template>
</xsl:template>
```

This time, the correct result comes out:

66

There is still a subtle error, which becomes apparent when inputting the empty sequence. (Among other values, we recommend to test programs with extreme values of the input.) Indeed, the result is then 0, which is not what is expected if we consider the abstract function `sum/1` as a specification.

$$\mathsf{sum}([x \,|\, s]) \rightarrow \mathsf{sum}_0([x \,|\, s], 0).$$

In XSLT, we forgot to forbid the empty sequence. This can be achieved by specifying a type 'non-empty sequence of elements': `element()+`.

```
<xsl:template match="numbers" as="xs:integer">
  <xsl:call-template name="sum">
    <xsl:with-param name="elm" select="num"
                              as="element(num)+"/>
  </xsl:call-template>
</xsl:template>
```

If we try the input

```
<?xml version='1.0' encoding='UTF-8'?>
<!DOCTYPE numbers SYSTEM "sum.dtd">
<numbers/>
```

we obtain now the expected error message

```
An empty sequence is not allowed as the value of parameter $elm
```

The transform is complete now:

```
<?xml version="1.0" encoding="UTF-8"?>
<xsl:transform version="2.0"
               xmlns:xsl="http://www.w3.org/1999/XSL/Transform"
               xmlns:xs="http://www.w3.org/2001/XMLSchema">
  <xsl:output method="text" encoding="UTF-8"/>

  <xsl:template match="/">
    <xsl:apply-templates/>
    <xsl:text>&#10;</xsl:text>
  </xsl:template>

  <xsl:template match="numbers" as="xs:integer">
    <xsl:call-template name="sum">
      <xsl:with-param name="elm" select="num"
                                as="element(num)+"/>
    </xsl:call-template>
  </xsl:template>

  <xsl:template name="sum" as="xs:integer">
    <xsl:param name="elm" as="element()*"/>
    <xsl:param name="n" as="xs:integer" select="0"/>
    <xsl:choose>
      <xsl:when test="empty($elm)">
        <xsl:sequence select="$n"/>
      </xsl:when>
```

```
        <xsl:otherwise>
          <xsl:call-template name="sum">
            <xsl:with-param name="elm" as="element()*"
                            select="$elm[position()>1]"/>
            <xsl:with-param name="n" as="xs:integer"
                 select="xs:integer($elm[1]/text()) + $n"/>
          </xsl:call-template>
        </xsl:otherwise>
      </xsl:choose>
    </xsl:template>

</xsl:transform>
```

If we would rather have no output instead of an error message at run-time, we could check for emptiness before the first call and do nothing. But there is a shorter way, easily understood on the abstract program:

$$\mathsf{sum}_1(s) \rightarrow \mathsf{sum}_2(s, 0). \qquad \mathsf{sum}_2([\,], n) \rightarrow \mathsf{nothing}();$$
$$\mathsf{sum}_2([x], n) \rightarrow x + n;$$
$$\mathsf{sum}_2([x \,|\, s], n) \rightarrow \mathsf{sum}_2(s, x + n).$$

The data constructor in case of empty stack, $\mathsf{nothing}()$, will be translated in XSLT as an empty element:

```
<xsl:when test="empty($elm)"/>
<xsl:when test="empty($elm[2])">
  <xsl:sequence select="xs:integer($elm[1]/text()) + $n"/>
</xsl:when>
```

The case for the singleton sequence is `empty($elm[2])`. Indeed, we know that `$elm` is not empty, because that is the previous case; therefore, all we have to do is to check for the existence of `$elm[2]`: if absent, this selection results in the empty sequence and, since we know that `$elm[1]` exists, the sequence `$elm` contains exactly one element. Still, there is a problem remaining with the types: the template matching `numbers` and the template named `sum` have to return a value of type `xs:integer`, which is not possible if `$elm` is empty, in which case, as we just saw, an empty sequence is returned (because of the empty element `xsl:when`). There is a way in XPath to express the type 'A sequence with no item or exactly one.' using the operator '?'. If we recall that a value can always be implicitly cast to a sequence containing that value, then `xs:integer?` means 'An integer or an empty sequence.' Therefore,

```
<?xml version="1.0" encoding="UTF-8"?>
```

```
<xsl:transform version="2.0"
               xmlns:xsl="http://www.w3.org/1999/XSL/Transform"
               xmlns:xs="http://www.w3.org/2001/XMLSchema">
  <xsl:output method="text" encoding="UTF-8"/>

  <xsl:template match="/">
    <xsl:apply-templates/>
    <xsl:text>&#10;</xsl:text>
  </xsl:template>

  <xsl:template match="numbers" as="xs:integer?">
    <xsl:call-template name="sum">
      <xsl:with-param name="elm" select="num"
                                 as="element(num)*"/>
    </xsl:call-template>
  </xsl:template>

  <xsl:template name="sum" as="xs:integer?">
    <xsl:param name="elm" as="element()*"/>
    <xsl:param name="n" as="xs:integer" select="0"/>
    <xsl:choose>
      <xsl:when test="empty($elm)"/>
      <xsl:when test="empty($elm[2])">
        <xsl:sequence select="xs:integer($elm[1]/text()) + $n"/>
      </xsl:when>
      <xsl:otherwise>
        <xsl:call-template name="sum">
          <xsl:with-param name="elm" as="element()*"
                          select="$elm[position()>1]"/>
          <xsl:with-param name="n" as="xs:integer"
                select="xs:integer($elm[1]/text()) + $n"/>
        </xsl:call-template>
      </xsl:otherwise>
    </xsl:choose>
  </xsl:template>

</xsl:transform>
```

Skipping We want to make a copy of a given stack, without its last item. A way to achieve this is to check first whether the stack contains zero, one or more items. In the first two cases, the result is the empty

stack; in the last, we know that the first item is not the last, so we keep
it and proceed recursively with the rest:

$$\mathsf{cutl}([x, y \,|\, s]) \rightarrow [x \,|\, \mathsf{cutl}([y \,|\, s])]; \quad \mathsf{cutl}(s) \rightarrow [\,].$$

In **Erlang**, this would be implemented as follows (header omitted):

```erlang
cutl([X|S=[_|_]]) -> [X|cutl(S)];
cutl(_)           -> [].
```

To see how to express it in **XSLT**, we need first to set some context of
use. For example, let us say that we have a table of contents complying
with the following DTD, book_bis.dtd:

```
<!ELEMENT book (author,title,contents)>
<!ELEMENT author (#PCDATA)>
<!ELEMENT title (#PCDATA)>
<!ELEMENT contents (chapter+)>
<!ELEMENT chapter EMPTY>
<!ATTLIST chapter title CDATA #REQUIRED>
```

For example, the input may be

```xml
<?xml version="1.0" encoding="UTF-8"?>
<!DOCTYPE book SYSTEM "book_bis.dtd">
<book>
  <author>Priscilla Walmsley</author>
  <title>Definitive XML Schema</title>
  <contents>
    <chapter title="Schema: An Introduction"/>
    <chapter title="A quick tour of XML Schema"/>
    <chapter title="Namespaces"/>
    <chapter title="Schema composition"/>
    <chapter title="Instances and schemas"/>
  </contents>
</book>
```

We want a copy of that XML document without the last chapter:

```xml
<?xml version="1.0" encoding="UTF-8"?>
<book>
  <author>Priscilla Walmsley</author>
  <title>Definitive XML Schema</title>
  <contents xmlns:xs="http://www.w3.org/2001/XMLSchema">
    <chapter title="Schema: An Introduction"/>
```

```
          <chapter title="A quick tour of XML Schema"/>
          <chapter title="Namespaces"/>
          <chapter title="Schema composition"/>
     </contents>
</book>
```

This is the first time we use XSLT to output XML, acting as a negative filter, that is, filtering out part of the input. We can start by reusing some code from previous transforms and then work on the translation of the function cutl/1 in XSLT, which will be a template named cutl. But first, the boilerplate and a twist:

```
<?xml version="1.0" encoding="UTF-8"?>
<xsl:transform version="2.0"
               xmlns:xsl="http://www.w3.org/1999/XSL/Transform"
               xmlns:xs="http://www.w3.org/2001/XMLSchema">
               exclude-result-prefixes="xs">

   <xsl:output method="xml" version="1.0"
               encoding="UTF-8" indent="yes"/>
```

Note that the output method is no longer text, but xml, as we wish to output XML. Of course, we then need to state which version of XML we want (here, 1.0), what the encoding of the file will be (here, UTF-8), and if we want the resulting XML to be indented (yes, because it greatly increases legibility, but if we would expect the output to be processed by another XSLT program, indentation could be dropped). There is another novelty, which is the attribute exclude-result-prefixes="xs" of xsl:transform. For the sake of clarity, we shall come back to it after we are finished.

On we go now with the rest of the canvas:

```
<xsl:template match="/">
  <xsl:apply-templates/>
  <xsl:text>&#10;</xsl:text>
</xsl:template>

<xsl:template match="book" as="element(book)">
  <xsl:copy>
    <xsl:sequence select="author"/>
    <xsl:sequence select="title"/>
    <contents>
      <xsl:call-template name="cutl">
```

```
        <xsl:with-param name="items" select="contents/chapter"
                        as="element(chapter)*"/>
      </xsl:call-template>
    </contents>
  </xsl:copy>
</xsl:template>

<xsl:template name="cutl" as="item()*">
  <xsl:param name="items" as="item()*"/>
  ...
</xsl:template>

</xsl:transform>
```

We used a bold typeface to bring forth a new XSLT element, namely
xsl:copy. Perhaps it was expected <book>...</book>, and this would
have worked indeed. Instead, we may prefer avoid copying the element
name too often, in case it changes in future versions. This is where
xsl:copy comes handy: it is *a shallow copy of the context node*. The context node is the node that was last matched by an element xsl:template,
so it is here book, and 'shallow' means that the children are not copied
(we want to copy but also modify the descendants).

Furthermore, notice how we used xsl:sequence with a selection of
an input element (author and title). This is where xsl:sequence shines:
what it does is to *refer to* the selected elements, without actually copying
them. In that sense, it acts like a pointer, as featured in some imperative
programming languages, like C, and thus saves memory.

Last, but not least, note how the output is constructed by recreating
an XML document; in particular, the juxtaposition of elements denotes
the concatenation of the singleton sequences they are (for instance, the
two aforementioned xsl:sequence are written one after the other).

Now we need to translate cutl/1. As we already know, XSLT does not
feature pattern matching, so we should rewrite our abstract functional
program without it:

$$\text{cutl}(t) \rightarrow \text{if } \text{tl}(t) \neq [] \text{ then } [\text{hd}(t) \,|\, \text{cutl}(\text{tl}(t))] \text{ else } [].$$

where $\text{hd}(t)$ (*head*) evaluates in the first item of the stack t and $\text{tl}(t)$ (*tail*)
in the immediate substack of t. (Of course, $\text{hd}([])$ and $\text{tl}([])$ could fail, so
we always must check that their argument is not the empty stack.) We
note the two occurrences of $\text{tl}(t)$, so, in XSLT, we should use a variable
to hold the value of this call to avoid recomputing it. We start like so:

```
<xsl:template name="cutl" as="item()*">
  <xsl:param name="items" as="item()*"/>
  <xsl:variable name="tail" select="$items[position()>1]"
                                 as="item()*"/>
  ...
</xsl:template>
```

Note that we did not specialise the template to process only chapter
elements, but any kind of item, including primitive types, like integers,
but also nodes and, in particular, elements.

Now we need to translate the conditional. We already have seen the
element xsl:choose and proceed to fill the previous ellipsis:

```
<xsl:choose>
  <xsl:when test="not(empty($tail))"> ... </xsl:when>
  <xsl:otherwise> ... </xsl:otherwise>
</xsl:choose>
```

The purpose of XPath functions empty and not is evident. The translation of the **else** alternative is the empty sequence in the xsl:otherwise
element. This is easily done without even the xsl:sequence element:

```
<xsl:choose>
  <xsl:when test="not(empty($tail))"> ... </xsl:when>
  <xsl:otherwise/>
</xsl:choose>
```

Indeed, an empty element can always be considered as having an empty
sequence of children. In XSLT, conditionals which have the form of one
xsl:when and an empty xsl:otherwise are better expressed using the
element xsl:if. For instance, our code becomes

```
<xsl:if test="not(empty($tail))"> ... </xsl:if>
```

Implicitly, if the test fails, the value of the conditional xsl:if is the empty
sequence. We need now to translate $[\mathsf{hd}(t)\,|\,\mathsf{cutl}(\mathsf{tl}(t))]$. We already have
at our disposal the translation of $\mathsf{tl}(t)$, which is the XSLT variable tail.
The translation of $\mathsf{hd}(t)$ is simply the singleton sequence <xsl:sequence
select="$items[1]"/>. Instead of pushing on a stack, we concatenate
two sequences and this concatenation is simply textual juxtaposition:

```
<xsl:if test="not(empty($tail))">
  <xsl:sequence select="$items[1]"/>
  <xsl:call-template name="cutl">
    <xsl:with-param name="items" select="$tail"
```

```
                             as="item()*"/>
        </xsl:call-template>
      </xsl:if>
```

In the end, the solution is

```
<?xml version="1.0" encoding="UTF-8"?>

<xsl:transform version="2.0"
               xmlns:xsl="http://www.w3.org/1999/XSL/Transform"
               xmlns:xs="http://www.w3.org/2001/XMLSchema">


  <xsl:output method="xml" version="1.0"
              encoding="UTF-8" indent="yes"/>

  <xsl:template match="/">
    <xsl:apply-templates/>
    <xsl:text>&#10;</xsl:text>
  </xsl:template>

  <xsl:template match="book" as="element(book)">
    <xsl:copy>
      <xsl:sequence select="author"/>
      <xsl:sequence select="title"/>
      <contents>
        <xsl:call-template name="cutl">
          <xsl:with-param name="items" select="contents/chapter"
                                       as="element(chapter)*"/>
        </xsl:call-template>
      </contents>
    </xsl:copy>
  </xsl:template>

  <xsl:template name="cutl" as="item()*">
    <xsl:param name="items" as="item()*"/>
    <xsl:variable name="tail" as="item()*"
                  select="$items[position()>1]"/>
    <xsl:if test="not(empty($tail))">
      <xsl:sequence select="$items[1]"/>
      <xsl:call-template name="cutl">
        <xsl:with-param name="items" select="$tail"
                        as="item()*"/>
```

```
      </xsl:call-template>
    </xsl:if>
  </xsl:template>
```

```
</xsl:transform>
```

At this point, we may wonder why we needed to set the attribute `exclude-result-prefixes="xs"` of element `xsl:transform`. If we remove it, we obtain the same result except for the element `contents`:

```
<contents xmlns:xs="http://www.w3.org/2001/XMLSchema">
   ...
</contents>
```

The reason is that when a namespace is declared, all the descendant elements inherit it, except the namespace associated to XSLT, here named `xsl`. Therefore, when we wrote

```
<contents>
   ...
</contents>
```

in the previous transform, the element `contents` *implicitly* had the namespace child node `xs`. The reason why `author` and `title` did not, is that we used `xsl:sequence` to reference the input, where that namespace is absent. The same happens with the elements `chapter`, which are selected in the input. The element `book` was actually copied with `xsl:copy`, and we saw that this element does not copy children, amongst whose the namespace nodes. The default behaviour of the XSLT processor is to set the inherited namespaces in case they are of some use in the output. In the present example, `xs` is useless, so it is best to exclude it from the (namespace) prefixes in the result: `exclude-result-prefixes="xs"`.

Skipping the penultimate item   The purpose of this exercise is to write an XSLT transform which takes as input a table of contents and outputs it in XML where the penultimate chapter is missing. If there is no chapter or only one, the output is identical to the input. The input should conform to the following DTD, named `book_bis.dtd`:

```
<!ELEMENT book (author,title,contents)>
<!ELEMENT author (#PCDATA)>
<!ELEMENT title (#PCDATA)>
<!ELEMENT contents (chapter+)>
<!ELEMENT chapter EMPTY>
<!ATTLIST chapter title CDATA #REQUIRED>
```

For example, the input may be

```
<?xml version="1.0" encoding="UTF-8"?>
<!DOCTYPE book SYSTEM "book_bis.dtd">
<book>
  <author>Priscilla Walmsley</author>
  <title>Definitive XML Schema</title>
  <contents>
    <chapter title="Schema: An Introduction"/>
    <chapter title="A quick tour of XML Schema"/>
    <chapter title="Namespaces"/>
    <chapter title="Schema composition"/>
    <chapter title="Instances and schemas"/>
  </contents>
</book>
```

The corresponding output is

```
<?xml version="1.0" encoding="UTF-8"?>
<book>
   <author>Priscilla Walmsley</author>
   <title>Definitive XML Schema</title>
   <contents>
      <chapter title="Schema: An Introduction"/>
      <chapter title="A quick tour of XML Schema"/>
      <chapter title="Namespaces"/>
      <chapter title="Instances and schemas"/>
   </contents>
</book>
```

The boilerplate XSLT code is the same, except the template, which we name here `cutp`. We do not start from an abstract functional program, but from the previous transform. We will need more cases, so `xsl:choose` is back. Perhaps the first difference is the case when `tail` is empty. This means that we need to keep the first item, instead of ignoring it:

```
<xsl:choose>
  <xsl:when test="empty($tail)">
    <xsl:sequence select="$items[1]"/>
  </xsl:when>
  ...
</xsl:choose>
```

As for the complementary case, when the tail is not empty, that is to say, when there are at least two items, we do not know whether the

first one is the penultimate or not, and the same can be said about the
second. Therefore, we need more information on the structure of the tail,
in particular, whether its tail is, in turn, empty (the tail of the tail of
the complete sequence), in other words, whether the sequence contains
at least three items or not. If it does, then we know that the first item is
not the penultimate, but we still can not say nothing about the others,
so a recursive call is in order; if it does not, then it means that the whole
sequence contains exactly two items, so we put in the result the second
one only, and ignore the first. In the end, we have

```
<xsl:template name="cutp" as="item()*">
  <xsl:param name="items" as="item()*"/>
  <xsl:variable name="tail" select="$items[position()>1]"
                          as="item()*"/>
  <xsl:choose>
    <xsl:when test="empty($tail)">
      <xsl:sequence select="$items[1]"/>
    </xsl:when>
    <xsl:when test="empty($tail[position()>1])">
      <xsl:sequence select="$items[2]"/>
    </xsl:when>
    <xsl:otherwise>
      <xsl:sequence select="$items[1]"/>
      <xsl:call-template name="cutp">
        <xsl:with-param name="items" select="$tail"
                                as="item()*"/>
      </xsl:call-template>
    </xsl:otherwise>
  </xsl:choose>
</xsl:template>
```

Notice that the case `<xsl:when test="empty($items)"/>` is actually missing because it is unnecessary: if `$items` is empty, then `$tail` is empty as
well, and the result is thus `$items[1]`, which is the empty sequence.

Reversal   The purpose of this exercise is to write an XSLT transform
which takes as input a table of contents with chapters and outputs the
same table of contents in XML where the chapters have been reversed
with respect to the document order (so, for example, the introduction is
listed last). In section 2.2 on page 38, we saw that the straightforward
definition of rev_0:

$$\mathsf{cat}([], t) \rightarrow t; \qquad\qquad \mathsf{rev}_0([]) \rightarrow [];$$
$$\mathsf{cat}([x\,|\,s], t) \rightarrow [x\,|\,\mathsf{cat}(s, t)]. \quad \mathsf{rev}_0([x\,|\,s]) \rightarrow \mathsf{cat}(\mathsf{rev}_0(s), [x]).$$

We saw that this definition yielded a quadratic cost and therefore should not be used for reversing stacks. In XSLT, the cost is linear because concatenation has cost zero. We would then write the following translation:

```
<xsl:template name="rev" as="item()*">
  <xsl:param name="items" as="item()*"/>
  <xsl:if test="not(empty($items))">
    <xsl:call-template name="rev">
      <xsl:with-param name="items" as="item()*"
                      select="$items[position()>1]"/>
    </xsl:call-template>
    <xsl:sequence select="$items[1]"/>
  </xsl:if>
</xsl:template>
```

Instead of producing an XML document, we could use this opportunity to see how to produce an XHTML document. Although the purpose may seem a bit foolish (reversing a table of contents), it is appropriate to start learning complicated languages such as XSLT and XHTML.

In order to instruct an XSLT processor to produce XHTML, we need to set some attributes of `xsl:transform` and `xsl:output` as follows:

```
<xsl:transform version="2.0"
               xmlns:xsl="http://www.w3.org/1999/XSL/Transform"
               xmlns:xs="http://www.w3.org/2001/XMLSchema"
               xmlns:xhtml="http://www.w3.org/1999/xhtml"
               exclude-result-prefixes="xs">

  <xsl:output method="xhtml"
              doctype-public="-//W3C//DTD XHTML 1.0 Strict//EN"
              doctype-system=
              "http://www.w3.org/TR/xhtml1/DTD/xhtml1-strict.dtd"
              indent="yes"
              omit-xml-declaration="yes"/>
```

Note that we defined a namespace `xhtml` for XHTML elements and that the XHTML version is `1.0` ('strict' means that it adheres strictly to XML). Perhaps the real novelty is setting `omit-xml-declaration="yes"`. Since XHTML (strict) is XML, the declaration `<?xml version="1.0"?>` is to be expected, but some web browsers are confused by this, so we prefer to be on the safe side and not have that declaration.

Given the previous table of contents, we now would like to obtain

```
<!DOCTYPE html
```

```
    PUBLIC "-//W3C//DTD XHTML 1.0 Strict//EN"
          "http://www.w3.org/TR/xhtml1/DTD/xhtml1-strict.dtd">
<html xmlns="http://www.w3.org/1999/xhtml"
      xml:lang="en" lang="en">
    <head>
        <meta http-equiv="Content-Type"
              content="text/html; charset=UTF-8" />
        <title>Definitive XML Schema</title>
    </head>
    <body>
        <h2>Definitive XML Schema</h2>
        <p>by Priscilla Walmsley</p>
        <h3>Reversed table of contents</h3>
        <ul>
            <li>Instances and schemas</li>
            <li>Schema composition</li>
            <li>Namespaces</li>
            <li>A quick tour of XML Schema</li>
            <li>Schema: An Introduction</li>
        </ul>
    </body>
</html>
```

which, interpreted by a web browser, would likely render as

Definitive XML Schema

by Priscilla Walmsley

Reversed table of contents

- Instances and schemas
- Schema composition
- Namespaces
- A quick tour of XML Schema
- Schema: An Introduction

First, here is the template matching book:

```
<xsl:template match="book" as="element(xhtml:html)">
  <html xmlns="http://www.w3.org/1999/xhtml"
        xml:lang="en" lang="en">
    <head>
```

```
      <title><xsl:sequence select="title/text()"/></title>
    </head>
    <body>
      <h2><xsl:value-of select="title"/></h2>
      <p>by <xsl:value-of select="author"/></p>
      <h3>Reversed table of contents</h3>
      <ul>
        <xsl:call-template name="rev">
          <xsl:with-param name="chap"
                          select="contents/chapter"/>
        </xsl:call-template>
      </ul>
    </body>
  </html>
</xsl:template>
```

Note first the selection `title/text()`, which means 'the text nodes of the element `title`, which is the child of the context node (`book`).' Second, we meet a new XSLT element, `xsl:value-of`, whose purpose is to create a text node from the selected items. If we select elements, like here the unique `title` element, its *descendant* text nodes (there is only one child here) are concatenated in document order and put in a new text node. Therefore, `<xsl:sequence select="title/text()"/>` has the same result as `<xsl:value-of select="title"/>`, although in the later case a new text node has been created (instead of being shared with the input). As a remark, we decided to specialise the types to make them fit as closely as possible the elements being processed, like `element(xhtml:html)`, which means: 'One element `html` in the namespace `xhtml`.'

Finally, the template doing the reversal is:

```
<xsl:template name="rev" as="element(xhtml:li)*">
  <xsl:param name="chap" as="element(chapter)*"/>
  <xsl:if test="not(empty($chap))">
    <xsl:call-template name="rev">
      <xsl:with-param name="chap" select="$chap[position()>1]"/>
    </xsl:call-template>
    <li xmlns="http://www.w3.org/1999/xhtml">
      <xsl:value-of select="$chap[1]/@title"/>
    </li>
  </xsl:if>
</xsl:template>
```

Again, we specialise the types, like `element(xhtml:li)*`, meaning: 'Sequence (possibly empty) of elements `li` in the namespace `xhtml`.' And element(chapter)* is a sequence of chapters, without namespace. But the two interesting excerpts are set in a bold typeface.

The first one is the declaration of the xhtml namespace in the element li: xmlns="http://www.w3.org/1999/xhtml". This is simply necessary to conform with the type of the value of the template. Indeed, this value should be, as we just saw, a sequence of elements li in the namespace xhtml. But <li> is actually outside all namespaces, because there is no default namespace declaration in any ascendant node, contrary to the template matching book, which we described previously. There, we had the declaration <html xmlns="http://www.w3.org/1999/xhtml" xml:lang="en" lang="en">, so any descendent element written without a namespace actually inherits the xhtml namespace. This is not the case in the template named rev, so an explicit declaration is necessary, otherwise a type error is raised by the XSLT compiler.

The second noteworthy excerpt is the selection of the xsl:value-of element, $chap[1]/@title, which means: 'The title attribute of the first element of the sequence $chap.' Here, we cannot substitute the element xsl:sequence, as with the text node before. Indeed, if we try <xsl:sequence select="$chap[1]/@title"/>, the result is

```
        . . .
      <li title="Instances and schemas"></li>
      <li title="Schema composition"></li>
      <li title="Namespaces"></li>
      <li title="A quick tour of XML Schema"></li>
      <li title="Schema: An Introduction"></li>
        . . .
```

Let us recall that xsl:sequence is an alias of, or a reference to, the input, in this case an attribute node, so we should expect a title *attribute* in the output. But we wanted the value of the attribute title, not the attribute itself, hence the need of xsl:value-of. If we wonder why we really need to create a text node, we must understand that *the value of an attribute is not a text node.* This can be seen by changing the selection to <xsl:sequence select="$chap[1]/title/text()"/>, in which case the result is

```
        . . .
      <li></li>
      <li></li>
      <li></li>
      <li></li>
      <li></li>
```

. . .

Attributes are special and often a source of confusion for beginners.

Comma-separated values   The purpose of this exercise is to write an XSLT transform which takes as input a sequence of elements containing each one text node and output their contents in the same order, separated by commas and ended by a period. If the input sequence is empty, the result is the empty sequence. More precisely, let us assume the following DTD:

```
<!ELEMENT numbers (hexa+)>
<!ELEMENT hexa (#PCDATA)>
```

and the conforming input

```
<?xml version='1.0' encoding='UTF-8'?>

<!DOCTYPE numbers SYSTEM "csv.dtd">

<numbers>
  <hexa>0</hexa>
  <hexa>1</hexa>
  <hexa>A</hexa>
  <hexa>B</hexa>
  <hexa>C</hexa>
</numbers>
```

Then we want

```
0,1,A,B,C.
```

The algorithm is simple enough: if the input sequence is empty, the result is the empty sequence; if the input is a singleton sequence, the result is the item it contains, followed by a period; otherwise, the first item of the result is the first in the input, followed by a comma and the value of a recursive call on the tail. Probably, the difficulty is to implement this scheme with XSLT. Here is how:

```
<?xml version="1.0" encoding="UTF-8"?>

<xsl:transform version="2.0"
            xmlns:xsl="http://www.w3.org/1999/XSL/Transform"
            xmlns:xs="http://www.w3.org/2001/XMLSchema">
```

```
<xsl:output method="text" encoding="UTF-8"/>

<xsl:template match="/" as="text()*">
  <xsl:call-template name="csv">
    <xsl:with-param name="items" select="numbers/hexa/text()"/>
  </xsl:call-template>
  <xsl:text>&#10;</xsl:text>
</xsl:template>

<xsl:template name="csv" as="text()*">
  <xsl:param name="items" as="item()*"/>
  <xsl:choose>
    <xsl:when test="empty($items)"/>
    <xsl:when test="empty($items[position()>1])">
      <xsl:value-of select="($items[1],'.')" separator=""/>
    </xsl:when>
    <xsl:otherwise>
      <xsl:value-of select="($items[1],',')" separator=""/>
      <xsl:call-template name="csv">
        <xsl:with-param name="items"
                        select="$items[position()>1]"/>
      </xsl:call-template>
    </xsl:otherwise>
  </xsl:choose>
</xsl:template>

</xsl:transform>
```

Note first that we merged the two templates that match the document root (/) and the root element (numbers) because we do not reconstruct an XML document. Furthermore, we may remark on the type text()*, which means 'A sequence (possibly empty) of text nodes.' The remaining titbits are the xsl:value-of elements, in particular a new attribute, separator. Its value must be a string which is used to separate the selected items. By default, that string is '␣', that is why we set it here to the empty string. Otherwise, we would obtain: '0␣,1␣,A␣,B␣,C␣.'. Note that the value of the attribute separator is the *contents* of a string, so if we use """, we are *not* specifying the empty string and produce instead: '0",1",A",B",C".'.

At this point it is perhaps pertinent to draw the relationships between the different types we have encountered, and learn a few more. Consider the tree in FIGURE 11.3 on the facing page. The ascendant reading of an edge from a node x to a node y is 'x is a [subtype of] y.' For instance,

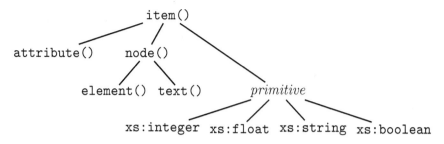

Figure 11.3: XPath subtypes

an element() is a node(). This models a subtyping relationship, which means that in any context where a node() is correct, a element() is also correct. This relationship is transitive, so anywhere an item() is expected, a text() is valid, which can be seen at work in the parameter of the template named csv. As an illustration, let us consider a slight variation of the input, where the content of interest is stored as attribute values, like so:

```
<?xml version='1.0' encoding='UTF-8'?>

<!DOCTYPE numbers SYSTEM "csv_att.dtd">

<numbers>
  <hexa val="0"/>
  <hexa val="1"/>
  <hexa val="A"/>
  <hexa val="B"/>
  <hexa val="C"/>
</numbers>
```

The DTD csv_att.dtd is

```
<!ELEMENT numbers (hexa+)>
<!ELEMENT hexa EMPTY>
<!ATTLIST hexa val CDATA #REQUIRED>
```

It is then enough to change the selection of the parameter item as follows:

```
<xsl:with-param name="items" select="numbers/hexa/@val"/>
```

The type of the selection is attribute()*, which is a subtype of item()*, therefore is a suitable value for the parameter of template csv and the result is the same as with the first XML input (no attributes).

While we are interested in the data types, let us pay attention to the selections of the elements `xsl:value-of`, for instance `($items[1],'.')`. Statically, the type of `$items[1]` is `item()`, although we know, from the initial template call, that it is actually `text()`. The type of `'.'` is `xs:string`. The sequence in question then has the type `item()*`, because `xs:string` is a subtype of `item()`, as seen in FIGURE 11.3 on the previous page. Since the result of the template is of type `text()*`, the strings it contains will be cast into text nodes, thus allocating memory. The serialiser is the back-end of the code generated by the XSLT compiler (the front-end is the XML parser) and its purpose is to produce text from all the values obtained. In this case, it will then destructure all these text nodes to generate strings (either displayed on a terminal or written in a file). If we want to avoid this boxing of strings in text nodes and their subsequent unboxing, we could plan ahead and opt for a return type `xs:string*`, so

```
<xsl:template match="/" as="xs:string*">
  ...
</xsl:template>

<xsl:template name="csv" as="xs:string*">
  ...
</xsl:template>
```

As a result of this change, we obtain '`0,␣1,␣A,␣B,␣C.`'. The extra spaces come from the fact that we forgot that the elements `xsl:value-of` create text nodes and the implicit serialisation of these (by casting to `xs:string*`) yields blank separators, here rendered as '`␣`'. The morale of this excursus is to keep working with non-primitive types, that is, attributes and nodes, if the input contains attributes and nodes, and let the serialiser manage the linearisation for the output. (It is possible to use XSLT for string processing, although this is not the main application domain of the language, in which case working with `xs:string*` makes sense.)

Let us give this exercise a last spin by remarking that the algorithm may be conceived as *working in parallel* on the sequence items, as long as we know how to distinguish the last item because it must be treated differently (it is followed by a period instead of a comma). But 'parallel' does not necessarily imply a temporal meaning, like multithreading, and can be also thought as processing in isolation, then fusion of the partial results, which is what a *map* does. We saw maps when introducing functional iterators in Erlang, on page 343:

$$\mathtt{map}(F,[X_1,X_2,\ldots,X_n]) \equiv [F(X_1),F(X_2),\ldots,F(X_n)].$$

A simple definition is

```
map(_,    []) -> [];
map(F,[X|S]) -> [F(X)|map(F,S)].
```

Note that `map` is a higher-order function and XSLT only features first-order templates and functions. Nevertheless, we can implement maps by using a kind a template we already have been using since the introduction to XSLT, starting on page 414: the *matching template*. The XSLT processor (by which we mean the run-time produced by the XSLT compiler) implicitly performs a preorder traversal of the input XML tree; when it finds an element *e*, it evaluates the corresponding matching template and carries on with the traversal. A matching template works as a rewrite rule for an implicit function in our abstract functional language, each rule being tried in turn when encountering a node in the XML tree.

Since we often select some children of the context node and apply to them the same treatment (as if in parallel), we need a mechanism to gather the results for each child into one sequence. In the running exercise, we wish to select a sequence of `hexa` elements, children of `numbers`, and expect a template matching `hexa`. We also want to group the results, just like a map would do. This is achieved twofold by the definition of a template

```
<xsl:template match="hexa" as="text()*">
  ...
</xsl:template>
```

which is analogous to the definition of the functional parameter *F* above and by

```
<xsl:apply-templates select="hexa"/>
```

which is analogous to calling `map` in Erlang.

The only problem remaining is to find out if the context node `hexa` is the last in the sequence upon which all templates were applied. This is where XPath comes handy in providing a function `last()`, which returns the position of the last item matched in the same sequence as the context node. Here is what the transform looks like now:

```
<?xml version="1.0" encoding="UTF-8"?>
<xsl:transform version="2.0"
            xmlns:xsl="http://www.w3.org/1999/XSL/Transform">

  <xsl:output method="text" encoding="UTF-8"/>
```

```
<xsl:template match="numbers" as="text()*">
  <xsl:apply-templates select="hexa"/>
  <xsl:text>&#10;</xsl:text>
</xsl:template>

<xsl:template match="hexa" as="text()*">
  <xsl:sequence select="text()"/>
  <xsl:choose>
    <xsl:when test="position() eq last()">
      <xsl:value-of select="'.'"/>
    </xsl:when>
    <xsl:otherwise>
      <xsl:value-of select="','"/>
    </xsl:otherwise>
  </xsl:choose>
</xsl:template>
```

```
</xsl:transform>
```

This reminds us that any item implicitly carries information about itself, including its position in a sequence, but also the position of the last item in that sequence. Notice that we do not need any parameter in the template matching hexa, because, inside, the context node is one of the original elements hexa, and we do not need to know which one is it or what are the others (think parallel processing, if you feel inclined to do so). For example,

```
<xsl:sequence select="text()"/>
```

means: 'Reference the text node of the context node,' (as opposed to copying it with xsl:value-of).

We will use matching templates in the forthcoming section about the transformation of trees, but we need first more practice to understand better named templates, because they are closer to the concept of first-order function in our abstract functional language.

Shuffling The purpose of this exercise is to write an XSLT transform which takes as input two sequences of elements and output one sequence containing the items of each sequence shuffled, or, more precisely, the first item of the resulting sequence is the first item of the first sequence, the second item is the first item of the second sequence, the third item is the second item of the first sequence, the fourth item is the second item of the second sequence etc. An enlightening analogy is interleaving two hands from a deck of cards.

If the first items of both sequences are taken out at the same time, then comes a moment when either both sequences are empty or only one of them is. The problem is actually underspecified: nothing is said about what to do if the two sequences are not of the same length. Actually, in the latter case, we will ignore the remaining items.

The DTD we have in mind is the following

```
<!ELEMENT persons (names,notes)>
<!ELEMENT names (name*)>
<!ELEMENT name (#PCDATA)>
<!ELEMENT notes (note*)>
<!ELEMENT note (#PCDATA)>
```

Then, this input:

```
<?xml version='1.0' encoding='UTF-8'?>
<!DOCTYPE persons SYSTEM "persons.dtd">

<persons>
  <names>
    <name>Alan Turing</name>
    <name>Kurt Gödel</name>
    <name>Donald Knuth</name>
    <name>Robin Milner</name>
  </names>
  <notes>
    <note>Defined a simple theoretical model of computers</note>
    <note>Proved the incompleteness of arithmetics</note>
    <note>Prolific author and creator of TeX</note>
    <note>Proposed a model of concurrency</note>
  </notes>
</persons>
```

yields this output:

```
<?xml version="1.0" encoding="UTF-8"?>
<persons>
    <name>Alan Turing</name>
    <note>Defined a simple theoretical model of computers</note>
    <name>Kurt Gödel</name>
    <note>Proved the incompleteness of arithmetics</note>
    <name>Donald Knuth</name>
```

```
    <note>Prolific author and creator of TeX</note>
    <name>Robin Milner</name>
    <note>Proposed a model of concurrency</note>
</persons>
```

The following input:

```
<?xml version='1.0' encoding='UTF-8'?>
<!DOCTYPE persons SYSTEM "persons.dtd">
<persons>
  <names>
    <name>Alan Turing</name>
    <name>Kurt Gödel</name>
  </names>
  <notes>
    <note>Defined a simple theoretical model of computers</note>
    <note>Proved the incompleteness of arithmetics</note>
    <note>Prolific author and creator of TeX</note>
    <note>Proposed a model of concurrency</note>
  </notes>
</persons>
```

yields this output:

```
<?xml version="1.0" encoding="UTF-8"?>
<persons>
    <name>Alan Turing</name>
    <note>Defined a simple theoretical model of computers</note>
    <name>Kurt Gödel</name>
    <note>Proved the incompleteness of arithmetics</note>
</persons>
```

This input:

```
<?xml version='1.0' encoding='UTF-8'?>
<!DOCTYPE persons SYSTEM "persons.dtd">
<persons>
  <names>
    <name>Alan Turing</name>
    <name>Kurt Gödel</name>
    <name>Donald Knuth</name>
    <name>Robin Milner</name>
  </names>
  <notes>
```

```
    <note>Defined a simple theoretical model of computers</note>
  </notes>
</persons>
```

yields this output:

```
<?xml version="1.0" encoding="UTF-8"?>
<persons>
    <name>Alan Turing</name>
    <note>Defined a simple theoretical model of computers</note>
</persons>
```

Following the strategy outlined above, we expect a template named shuffle to have two parameters, one for the names and one for the notes:

```
<xsl:template match="persons" as="element(persons)">
  <xsl:copy>
    <xsl:call-template name="shuffle">
      <xsl:with-param name="names" select="names/name"/>
      <xsl:with-param name="notes" select="notes/note"/>
    </xsl:call-template>
  </xsl:copy>
</xsl:template>

<xsl:template name="shuffle" as="element()*">
  <xsl:param name="names" as="element(name)*"/>
  <xsl:param name="notes" as="element(note)*"/>
  ...
</xsl:template>
```

Note that we use xsl:copy to copy the context node persons and that we had to use the return type element()* because we cannot express in XPath: 'A sequence of mixed elements name and note.' The body of that template follows our plan. If the parameters are both not empty, we do something, otherwise an implicit empty sequence will be produced. This test is performed in XPath using the Boolean connector and as follows:

```
<xsl:template name="shuffle" as="element(persons)*">
  <xsl:param name="names" as="element(name)*"/>
  <xsl:param name="notes" as="element(note)*"/>
  <xsl:if test="not(empty($names)) and not(empty($notes))">
    <xsl:sequence select="$names[1]"/>
    <xsl:sequence select="$notes[1]"/>
```

```
        <xsl:call-template name="shuffle">
          <xsl:with-param name="names"
                          select="$names[position()>1]"/>
          <xsl:with-param name="notes"
                          select="$notes[position()>1]"/>
        </xsl:call-template>
      </xsl:if>
    </xsl:template>
```

Another possibility, when confronted to dangling items, is to append them to the already outputted items. For instance, given the first input above yields now

```
<?xml version="1.0" encoding="UTF-8"?>
<persons>
   <name>Alan Turing</name>
   <note>Defined a simple theoretical model of computers</note>
   <name>Kurt Gödel</name>
   <note>Proved the incompleteness of arithmetics</note>
   <name>Donald Knuth</name>
   <note>Prolific author and creator of TeX</note>
   <name>Robin Milner</name>
   <note>Proposed a model of concurrency</note>
</persons>
```

The second input above leads to

```
<?xml version="1.0" encoding="UTF-8"?>
<persons>
   <name>Alan Turing</name>
   <note>Defined a simple theoretical model of computers</note>
   <name>Kurt Gödel</name>
   <note>Proved the incompleteness of arithmetics</note>
   <note>Prolific author and creator of TeX</note>
   <note>Proposed a model of concurrency</note>
</persons>
```

And the last input above results in

```
<?xml version="1.0" encoding="UTF-8"?>
<persons>
   <name>Alan Turing</name>
   <note>Defined a simple theoretical model of computers</note>
   <name>Kurt Gödel</name>
```

```
  <name>Donald Knuth</name>
  <name>Robin Milner</name>
</persons>
```

Here is a solution:

```
<xsl:template name="shuffle" as="element()*">
  <xsl:param name="names" as="element(name)*"/>
  <xsl:param name="notes" as="element(note)*"/>
  <xsl:choose>
    <xsl:when test="empty($notes)">
      <xsl:sequence select="$names"/>
    </xsl:when>
    <xsl:when test="empty($names)">
      <xsl:sequence select="$notes"/>
    </xsl:when>
    <xsl:otherwise>
      <xsl:sequence select="($names[1],$notes[1])"/>
      <xsl:call-template name="shuffle">
        <xsl:with-param name="names"
                        select="$names[position()>1]"/>
        <xsl:with-param name="notes"
                        select="$notes[position()>1]"/>
      </xsl:call-template>
    </xsl:otherwise>
  </xsl:choose>
</xsl:template>
```

Note how we placed $notes[1] after $names[1] in XPath with

```
<xsl:sequence select="($names[1],$notes[1])"/>
```

instead of working at the level of XSLT, as previously:

```
<xsl:sequence select="$names[1]"/>
<xsl:sequence select="$notes[1]"/>
```

As a variation, it is possible to achieve the same result by extracting one element at a time, instead of two. Of course, the program will be about twice as slow, but it is interesting nevertheless:

```
<xsl:template name="shuffle" as="element()*">
  <xsl:param name="names" as="element(name)*"/>
  <xsl:param name="notes" as="element(note)*"/>
  <xsl:choose>
```

```
      <xsl:when test="empty($names)">
        <xsl:sequence select="$notes"/>
      </xsl:when>
      <xsl:otherwise>
        <xsl:sequence select="$names[1]"/>
        <xsl:call-template name="shuffle">
          <xsl:with-param name="names" select="$notes"/>
          <xsl:with-param name="notes"
                          select="$names[position()>1]"/>
        </xsl:call-template>
      </xsl:otherwise>
    </xsl:choose>
  </xsl:template>
```

The point is to swap the arguments in the recursive call. Of course, the parameters' names are not pertinent anymore, and a neutral renaming would be fitting. In our abstract functional language, we would write

$$\mathsf{shuffle}([\,],t) \to t; \quad \mathsf{shuffle}([x\,|\,s],t) \to [x\,|\,\mathsf{shuffle}(t,s)].$$

This is actually almost the same definition as that of cat/1 (concatenation):

$$\mathsf{cat}([\,],t) \to t; \quad \mathsf{cat}([x\,|\,s],t) \to [x\,|\,\mathsf{cat}(\underline{s},\underline{t})].$$

Maximum   The aim of this exercise is to write an XSLT transform which takes as input a sequence of integers and outputs the maximum of these numbers as plain text. If an item is not castable to xs:integer, a dynamic type error is raised and the execution is stopped. If an item is an empty text node, for example, <num/>, it is skipped. If the sequence contains no integer, not text is outputted, because the maximum is undefined. The root element is numbers and the elements containing the numbers are named num. Any element other than num is ignored.

The DTD we have in mind is the following:

```
<!ELEMENT numbers (num,foo?)*>
<!ELEMENT num (#PCDATA)>
<!ELEMENT foo (#PCDATA)>
```

If the input document is

```
<?xml version='1.0' encoding='UTF-8'?>
<!DOCTYPE numbers SYSTEM "numbers.dtd">
<numbers>
  <num/>
```

```
        <num>18</num>
        <num>-1</num>
        <num>3</num>
        <num>5</num>
        <num/>
        <num>23</num>
        <foo>hello</foo>
        <num>-3</num>
        <num>2</num>
        <num/>
        <num>7</num>
        <num>4</num>
        <num></num>
</numbers>
```

the result is

23

First, let us set the types in the following schema:

```
<xsl:template match="numbers" as="xs:integer?">
  ...
</xsl:template>

<xsl:template name="max" as="xs:integer?">
  <xsl:param name="int" as="xs:integer*"/>
  <xsl:param name="cur" as="xs:integer?"/>
  ...
</xsl:template>
```

Let's recall the type operator '?' meaning 'One or none', so `xs:integer?` is either an empty sequence or a sequence containing one integer. This precaution is necessary because we are not certain that the input contains at least an integer (we even allowed for dummy elements `foo`, as a look back at the DTD confirms). The parameter `int` contains the remaining integers to examine, whilst `cur` is the current maximum, if any. That is why we should initialise the latter with the contents of the first number:

```
<xsl:template match="numbers" as="xs:integer?">
  <xsl:call-template name="max">
    <xsl:with-param name="int"
                    select="num[position()>1]/text()"/>
    <xsl:with-param name="cur" select="num[1]/text()"/>
```

```
  </xsl:call-template>
 </xsl:template>
```

Note that had we written `$num[1]/text()`, the selection would have been empty, as there is no *variable* num, but, instead, we meant the *child element* num. Next, we selected the text nodes, although the expected types are `xs:integer*` and `xs:integer?`. In fact, a cast at run-time will be performed. In the case of cur, if the cast fails, the empty sequence will result; otherwise, an integer (that is, a sequence containing a single integer). In the case of int, a cast is attempted for each element in the sequence and the resulting sequences are concatenated.

There are several ways to solve this problem. We could make the following cases:

- if there are no integers to examine, the result is the current integer, if any;

- if there is an actual, current integer, and if it is greater than the first integer to examine, we start over while discarding the latter;

- otherwise, the first integer to examine becomes the current maximum and we start over and discard the previous maximum.

This plan is implemented as follows:

```
<xsl:template name="max" as="xs:integer?">
  <xsl:param name="int" as="xs:integer*"/>
  <xsl:param name="cur" as="xs:integer?"/>
  <xsl:choose>
    <xsl:when test="empty($int)">
      <xsl:sequence select="$cur"/>
    </xsl:when>
    <xsl:when test="not(empty($cur)) and $cur ge $int[1]">
      <xsl:call-template name="max">
        <xsl:with-param name="int"
                        select="$int[position()>1]"/>
        <xsl:with-param name="cur" select="$cur"/>
      </xsl:call-template>
    </xsl:when>
    <xsl:otherwise>
      <xsl:call-template name="max">
        <xsl:with-param name="int"
                        select="$int[position()>1]"/>
        <xsl:with-param name="cur" select="$int[1]"/>
```

```
        </xsl:call-template>
      </xsl:otherwise>
    </xsl:choose>
  </xsl:template>
```

Notice how we checked for the presence of a current maximum with not(empty($cur)) and the XPath Boolean operator 'greater than or equal to' is ge. We may further remark that, in both recursive calls, the parameter int has the same value $int[position()>1], so we might want to share the code as follows:

```
<xsl:template name="max" as="xs:integer?">
  <xsl:param name="int" as="xs:integer*"/>
  <xsl:param name="cur" as="xs:integer?"/>
  <xsl:choose>
    <xsl:when test="empty($int)">
      <xsl:sequence select="$cur"/>
    </xsl:when>
    <xsl:otherwise>
      <xsl:call-template name="max">
        <xsl:with-param name="int" select="$int[position()>1]"/>
        <xsl:with-param name="cur">
          <xsl:choose>
            <xsl:when test="not(empty($cur)) and $cur ge $int[1]">
              <xsl:sequence select="$cur"/>
            </xsl:when>
            <xsl:otherwise>
              <xsl:sequence select="$int[1]"/>
            </xsl:otherwise>
          </xsl:choose>
        </xsl:with-param>
      </xsl:call-template>
    </xsl:otherwise>
  </xsl:choose>
</xsl:template>
```

This template contains less duplication and is more logically structured, but it is longer, which means that the usual reflexes gained from experience in other programming languages may be counterproductive in XSLT. Note in passing that this answer illustrates that xsl:with-param may have children instead of a select attribute.

Reducing   The purpose of this exercise is to write an **XSLT** transform
which takes as input a flat document tree, that is, the document root
has children but no grand-children. The children carry an attribute and
the output should be the same document without those children being
consecutively repeated. This is the same as the function **red/1** we saw in
FIGURE 2.22 on page 73:

$$\mathsf{red}([]) \to [];$$
$$\mathsf{red}([x, x\,|\,s]) \to \mathsf{red}([x\,|\,s]);$$
$$\mathsf{red}([x\,|\,s]) \to [x\,|\,\mathsf{red}(s)].$$

In XSLT, we need more constraints on the input and we must be take
into account data types. Let us opt for the following DTD:

```
<!ELEMENT numbers (num*)>
<!ELEMENT num EMPTY>
<!ATTLIST num val NMTOKEN #REQUIRED>
```

For example, this valid input

```
<?xml version='1.0' encoding='UTF-8'?>
<!DOCTYPE numbers SYSTEM "numbers_bis.dtd">
<numbers>
  <num val="8"/>
  <num val="1"/>
  <num val="two"/>
  <num val="two"/>
  <num val="two"/>
  <num val="2"/>
  <num val="one"/>
  <num val="2"/>
  <num val="4"/>
  <num val="4"/>
</numbers>
```

results in

```
<?xml version="1.0" encoding="UTF-8"?>
<numbers>
   <num val="8"/>
   <num val="1"/>
   <num val="two"/>
   <num val="2"/>
   <num val="one"/>
```

```
  <num val="2"/>
  <num val="4"/>
</numbers>
```

If we start from red/1, we need to remove the pattern matching and use instead conditionals. First, we separate the patterns depending on the number of items:

$$\begin{aligned}
\mathsf{red}([\,]) &\rightarrow [\,]; \\
\mathsf{red}([x]) &\rightarrow [x]; \\
\mathsf{red}([x, x \,|\, s]) &\rightarrow \mathsf{red}([x \,|\, s]); \\
\mathsf{red}([x, y \,|\, s]) &\rightarrow [x \,|\, \mathsf{red}([y \,|\, s])].
\end{aligned}$$

Now, we can remove pattern matching:

$$\mathsf{red}(t) \rightarrow \textbf{if } t = [\,] \textbf{ or } \mathsf{tl}(t) = [\,] \textbf{ then } t$$
$$\textbf{else if } \mathsf{hd}(t) = \mathsf{hd}(\mathsf{tl}(t)) \textbf{ then } \mathsf{red}(\mathsf{tl}(t)) \textbf{ else } [\mathsf{hd}(t) \,|\, \mathsf{red}(\mathsf{tl}(t))].$$

where $\mathsf{hd}(t)$ is the head of stack t and $\mathsf{tl}(t)$ is the tail of t, that is, its immediate substack. In XSLT, we may define a variable by means of the element xsl:variable, so we can improve the translation by computing only once the translation of $\mathsf{red}(\mathsf{tl}(t))$. We also know that $\mathsf{hd}(t)$ translates as $t[1]$, where t is the translation of t, and $\mathsf{tl}(t)$ translates as $t[position()>1]$ or $t[position()!=1]$. Here is the full transform:

```
<?xml version="1.0" encoding="UTF-8"?>

<xsl:transform version="2.0"
               xmlns:xsl="http://www.w3.org/1999/XSL/Transform"
               xmlns:xs="http://www.w3.org/2001/XMLSchema">

  <xsl:output method="xml" version="1.0" encoding="UTF-8"
              indent="yes"/>

  <xsl:template match="/">
    <xsl:apply-templates select="numbers"/>
    <xsl:text>&#10;</xsl:text>
  </xsl:template>

  <xsl:template match="numbers" as="element(numbers)">
    <xsl:copy>
      <xsl:call-template name="red">
        <xsl:with-param name="t" select="num"/>
      </xsl:call-template>
```

```
    </xsl:copy>
  </xsl:template>

  <xsl:template name="red" as="element(num)*">
    <xsl:param name="t" as="element(num)*"/>
    <xsl:choose>
      <xsl:when test="empty($t[position()>1])">
        <xsl:sequence select="$t"/>
      </xsl:when>
      <xsl:otherwise>
        <xsl:if test="$t[1]/@val ne $t[2]/@val">
          <xsl:sequence select="$t[1]"/>
        </xsl:if>
        <xsl:call-template name="red">
          <xsl:with-param name="t" select="$t[position()>1]"/>
        </xsl:call-template>
      </xsl:otherwise>
    </xsl:choose>
  </xsl:template>

</xsl:transform>
```

Note how we do not cast the attribute value to xs:integer, for example
with xs:integer($t[1]/@val) ne xs:integer($t[2]/@val), because we
want to allow any kind of value for comparison.

Merging   The purpose of this exercise is to write an XSLT transform
which takes as input two sequences of elements which are sorted by increasing values of the same integer attribute, and it outputs one sequence
containing all the items sorted increasingly. We can reuse for this the
function mrg/2 in FIGURE 4.1 on page 120, which merges two ordered
stacks:

$$\mathsf{mrg}([\,],t) \rightarrow t;$$
$$\mathsf{mrg}(s,[\,]) \rightarrow s;$$
$$\mathsf{mrg}([x\,|\,s],[y\,|\,t]) \rightarrow [y\,|\,\mathsf{mrg}([x\,|\,s],t)], \text{ if } x \succ y;$$
$$\mathsf{mrg}([x\,|\,s],t) \rightarrow [x\,|\,\mathsf{mrg}(s,t)].$$

We envisage the following simple DTD list.dtd:

```
<!ELEMENT lists (list,list)>
<!ELEMENT list (item*)>
<!ELEMENT item EMPTY>
<!ATTLIST item val CDATA #REQUIRED>
```

Given the following XML document

```xml
<?xml version="1.0" encoding="UTF-8"?>
<!DOCTYPE lists SYSTEM "list.dtd">
<lists>
  <list>
    <item val="1"/>
    <item val="7"/>
    <item val="13"/>
    <item val="15"/>
    <item val="28"/>
    <item val="33"/>
  </list>
  <list>
    <item val="8"/>
    <item val="9"/>
    <item val="16"/>
    <item val="19"/>
  </list>
</lists>
```

the output is

```xml
<?xml version="1.0" encoding="UTF-8"?>
<lists>
    <item val="1"/>
    <item val="7"/>
    <item val="8"/>
    <item val="9"/>
    <item val="13"/>
    <item val="15"/>
    <item val="16"/>
    <item val="19"/>
    <item val="28"/>
    <item val="33"/>
</lists>
```

Here, we can translate mrg/2 in XSLT without explicitly getting rid of pattern matching:

```xml
<?xml version="1.0" encoding="UTF-8"?>

<xsl:transform version="2.0"
               xmlns:xsl="http://www.w3.org/1999/XSL/Transform"
```

```
                 xmlns:xs="http://www.w3.org/2001/XMLSchema">
<xsl:output method="xml" version="1.0"
              encoding="UTF-8" indent="yes"/>

<xsl:template match="/">
  <xsl:apply-templates/>
  <xsl:text>&#10;</xsl:text>
</xsl:template>

<xsl:template match="lists" as="element(lists)">
  <xsl:copy>
    <xsl:call-template name="merge">
      <xsl:with-param name="seq1" select="list[1]/item"/>
      <xsl:with-param name="seq2" select="list[2]/item"/>
    </xsl:call-template>
  </xsl:copy>
</xsl:template>

<xsl:template name="merge" as="element(item)*">
  <xsl:param name="seq1" as="element(item)*"/>
  <xsl:param name="seq2" as="element(item)*"/>
  <xsl:choose>
    <xsl:when test="empty($seq1)">
      <xsl:sequence select="$seq2"/>
    </xsl:when>
    <xsl:when test="empty($seq2)">
      <xsl:sequence select="$seq1"/>
    </xsl:when>
    <xsl:when test="xs:integer($seq1[1]/@val)
                    lt xs:integer($seq2[1]/@val)">
      <xsl:sequence select="$seq1[1]"/>
      <xsl:call-template name="merge">
        <xsl:with-param name="seq1"
                        select="$seq1[position()>1]"/>
        <xsl:with-param name="seq2" select="$seq2"/>
      </xsl:call-template>
    </xsl:when>
    <xsl:otherwise>
      <xsl:sequence select="$seq2[1]"/>
      <xsl:call-template name="merge">
        <xsl:with-param name="seq1" select="$seq1"/>
        <xsl:with-param name="seq2"
```

```
                        select="$seq2[position()>1]"/>
      </xsl:call-template>
    </xsl:otherwise>
  </xsl:choose>
</xsl:template>
```

```
</xsl:transform>
```

If we would like instead produce text, we only have the changes

```
...
  <xsl:output method="text"/>
...
  <xsl:template match="lists" as="xs:integer*">
    <xsl:call-template name="merge">
      <xsl:with-param name="seq1" select="list[1]/item"
                                  as="xs:integer*"/>
      <xsl:with-param name="seq2" select="list[2]/item"
                                  as="xs:integer*"/>
    </xsl:call-template>
  </xsl:template>

  <xsl:template name="merge" as="xs:integer*">
    <xsl:param name="seq1" as="xs:integer*"/>
    <xsl:param name="seq2" as="xs:integer*"/>
    ...
  </xsl:template>
...
```

11.4 Transforming trees

After an extensive training with the transformation of sequences, it is time that we tackle the general case, that is, trees. As we have mentioned at the beginning of this chapter, XML trees are *unranked*, which means that an element node can have a variable number of children, if not invalidated by a DTD. This is in contrast with binary trees, for instance, whose nodes can only have two or no children.

Size The purpose of this exercise is to write an XSLT transform which takes as input a table of contents and computes the number of sections. But, contrary to a previous exercise, the table is not flat here, more precisely, the DTD we have in mind is as follows:

```
<!ELEMENT book (author, chapter+)>
<!ATTLIST book title CDATA #REQUIRED>
<!ELEMENT author EMPTY>
<!ATTLIST author first NMTOKEN #REQUIRED
                 last  NMTOKEN #REQUIRED>
<!ELEMENT chapter (section*)>
<!ATTLIST chapter title CDATA #REQUIRED>
<!ELEMENT section (section*)>
<!ATTLIST section title CDATA #REQUIRED>
```

An example of valid XML document is

```
<?xml version='1.0' encoding='UTF-8'?>

<!DOCTYPE book SYSTEM "book_deep.dtd">

<book title="Definitive XML Schema">
  <author first="Priscilla" last="Walmsley"/>
  <chapter title="A quick tour of XML Schema">
    <section title="An example schema"/>
    <section title="The components of XML Schema">
      <section title="Declarations vs. definitions"/>
      <section title="Global vs. local components"/>
    </section>
    <section title="Elements and attributes">
      <section title="The tag/type distinction"/>
    </section>
  </chapter>

  <chapter title="Instances and schemas">
    <section title="Using the instance attributes"/>
    <section title="Schema processing">
      <section title="Validation"/>
      <section title="Augmenting the instance"/>
    </section>
  </chapter>
</book>
```

Of course, we expect the result

```
10
```

Instead of going back to our abstract functional language, or **Erlang**, and then translating to XSLT, let us try to figure out the algorithm in plain English and move to write the transform.

The idea is to match the root element, then select the first level of sections, just below the chapters. This sequence of nodes `section` is passed to a template named `count`, whose job is to count all the sections in it. If this sequence of sections is empty, the answer is `0`. Otherwise,

1. we call recursively `count` on the subsections of the first section;

2. this number plus 1 is the number of sections in the first section (including itself) of the sequence;

3. finally we call recursively `count` on the rest of the sequence (that is, the remaining sections) and add this number to the previous one: the total is the result.

Note that the two recursive calls can be interchanged and the case described (call first on the children of the first node, then on the following siblings), is *depth-first* traversal of the tree, which we write first:

```
<?xml version="1.0" encoding="UTF-8"?>
<xsl:transform version="2.0"
               xmlns:xsl="http://www.w3.org/1999/XSL/Transform"
               xmlns:xs="http://www.w3.org/2001/XMLSchema"
               exclude-result-prefixes="xs">

  <xsl:output method="text" encoding="UTF-8"/>

  <xsl:template match="/">
    <xsl:apply-templates/>
    <xsl:text>&#10;</xsl:text>
  </xsl:template>

  <xsl:template match="book" as="xs:integer">
    <xsl:call-template name="count">
      <xsl:with-param name="sections" select="chapter/section"/>
    </xsl:call-template>
  </xsl:template>

  <xsl:template name="count" as="xs:integer">
    <xsl:param name="sections" as="element(section)*"/>
    <xsl:choose>
      <xsl:when test="empty($sections)">
        <xsl:sequence select="0"/>
      </xsl:when>
      <xsl:otherwise>
```

```
    <xsl:variable name="subsec" as="xs:integer">
      <xsl:call-template name="count">
        <xsl:with-param name="sections"
                        select="$sections[1]/section"/>
      </xsl:call-template>
    </xsl:variable>
    <xsl:variable name="subseq" as="xs:integer">
      <xsl:call-template name="count">
        <xsl:with-param name="sections"
                        select="$sections[position()>1]"/>
      </xsl:call-template>
    </xsl:variable>
    <xsl:sequence select="1 + $subsec + $subseq"/>
  </xsl:otherwise>
 </xsl:choose>
</xsl:template>

</xsl:transform>
```

Beware of selecting `$sections[1]/section`, but not `sections[1]/section`, which is empty, because `section` is a child element of the context node, whereas `$section` is the content of the variable `section`. Perhaps it is wise to avoid using variables which are also element names in the input. Note also that because we must call named templates at the XSLT level, not in XPath, we have to define variables `subsec` and `subseq` to hold the results of the two recursive calls. Had we use XSLT functions (`xsl:function`), we would have called them in XPath. For the sake of uniformity, let us stick to named templates, even though, in some contexts, they may add verbosity to an already verbose language.

   If we want to visit the siblings before the children, we just need to swap the declarations of the variables:

```
  ...
    <xsl:variable name="subseq" as="xs:integer">
     ...
    </xsl:variable>
    <xsl:variable name="subsec" as="xs:integer">
     ...
    </xsl:variable>
    ...
```

This makes no difference because the parts of the tree traversed by the two calls are complementary. It is nevertheless instructive to draw the

XML tree and follow the (descending) calls with one colour on the left side of the nodes, and the (ascending) results with another colour on the right side.

Instead of counting the sections in a bottom-up fashion, we can thread a counter during our traversal and increment it each time we encounter a section; the final result is then the current count when we are back at the root. (The counter is a kind of *accumulator*.) We have

```
<?xml version="1.0" encoding="UTF-8"?>

<xsl:transform version="2.0"
               xmlns:xsl="http://www.w3.org/1999/XSL/Transform"
               xmlns:xs="http://www.w3.org/2001/XMLSchema">

  <xsl:output method="text"/>

  <xsl:template match="/">
    <xsl:apply-templates/>
    <xsl:text>&#10;</xsl:text>
  </xsl:template>

  <xsl:template match="book" as="xs:integer">
    <xsl:call-template name="count">
      <xsl:with-param name="sections" select="chapter/section"/>
      <xsl:with-param name="current"  select="0"/>
    </xsl:call-template>
  </xsl:template>

  <xsl:template name="count" as="xs:integer">
    <xsl:param name="sections" as="element(section)*"/>
    <xsl:param name="current"  as="xs:integer"/>
    <xsl:choose>
      <xsl:when test="empty($sections)">
        <xsl:sequence select="$current"/>
      </xsl:when>
      <xsl:otherwise>
        <xsl:variable name="subsec" as="xs:integer">
          <xsl:call-template name="count">
            <xsl:with-param name="sections"
                            select="$sections[1]/section"/>
            <xsl:with-param name="current"
                            select="$current + 1"/>
```

```
        </xsl:call-template>
      </xsl:variable>
      <xsl:call-template name="count">
        <xsl:with-param name="sections"
                          select="$sections[position()>1]"/>
        <xsl:with-param name="current" select="$subsec"/>
      </xsl:call-template>
    </xsl:otherwise>
  </xsl:choose>
</xsl:template>
```

```
</xsl:transform>
```

Note how the case of the empty sequence $sections yields the current count instead of 0, as opposed to previous versions.

For the sake of practising with the XSLT syntax, we might remark that the variable subsec is only used to initialise the parameter current of second recursive call. We could avoid creating that variable if we expand its recursive call as a child of the parameter in question:

```
<xsl:template name="count" as="xs:integer">
  <xsl:param name="sections" as="element(section)*"/>
  <xsl:param name="current"  as="xs:integer" select="0"/>
  <xsl:choose>
    <xsl:when test="empty($sections)">
      <xsl:sequence select="$current"/>
    </xsl:when>
    <xsl:otherwise>
      <xsl:call-template name="count">
        <xsl:with-param name="sections"
                          select="$sections[position()>1]"/>
        <xsl:with-param name="current" as="xs:integer">
          <xsl:call-template name="count">
            <xsl:with-param name="sections"
                              select="$sections[1]/section"/>
            <xsl:with-param name="current"
                              select="$current + 1"/>
          </xsl:call-template>
        </xsl:with-param>
      </xsl:call-template>
    </xsl:otherwise>
  </xsl:choose>
</xsl:template>
```

Note the use of a default value for parameter `current`, thus avoiding its initialisation in the first call (in the template matching element `book`).

Summing The purpose of this exercise is to write an XSLT transform which takes as input a document made of one kind of element with one kind of attribute whose value is a positive integer, and computes the sum of all these numbers. More precisely, we think of the following DTD:

```
<!ELEMENT numbers (num+)>
<!ELEMENT num (num*)>
<!ATTLIST num val CDATA #REQUIRED>
```

and, for instance, of the following input:

```
<?xml version='1.0' encoding='UTF-8'?>
<!DOCTYPE numbers SYSTEM "numbers_tree.dtd">
<numbers>
  <num val="18"/>
  <num val="1">
    <num val="1"/>
    <num val="2"/>
  </num>
  <num val="3">
    <num val="4">
      <num val="1"/>
      <num val="1"/>
    </num>
  </num>
  <num val="5">
    <num val="23"/>
    <num val="3"/>
    <num val="2">
      <num val="7">
        <num val="4"/>
        <num val="4"/>
      </num>
    </num>
  </num>
</numbers>
```

The expected result is then

The key is to understand the difference between this exercise and the exercise where we had to count the number of sections in a table of contents. In the latter, we counted 1 for each section. In the former, we simply take the value of the attribute `val` instead of 1:

```
<?xml version="1.0" encoding="UTF-8"?>
<xsl:transform version="2.0"
               xmlns:xsl="http://www.w3.org/1999/XSL/Transform"
               xmlns:xs="http://www.w3.org/2001/XMLSchema">
  <xsl:output method="text"/>

  <xsl:template match="numbers">
    <xsl:call-template name="sum">
      <xsl:with-param name="numbers" select="num"/>
    </xsl:call-template>
    <xsl:text>&#10;</xsl:text>
  </xsl:template>

<xsl:template name="sum" as="xs:integer">
  <xsl:param name="numbers" as="element(num)*"/>
  <xsl:param name="current" as="xs:integer" select="0"/>
  <xsl:choose>
    <xsl:when test="empty($numbers)">
      <xsl:sequence select="$current"/>
    </xsl:when>
    <xsl:otherwise>
      <xsl:call-template name="sum">
        <xsl:with-param name="numbers"
                        select="$numbers[position()>1]"/>
        <xsl:with-param name="current" as="xs:integer">
          <xsl:call-template name="sum">
            <xsl:with-param name="numbers"
                            select="$numbers[1]/num"/>
            <xsl:with-param name="current"
            select="$current + xs:integer($numbers[1]/@val)"/>
          </xsl:call-template>
        </xsl:with-param>
      </xsl:call-template>
    </xsl:otherwise>
  </xsl:choose>
</xsl:template>
```

```
</xsl:transform>
```

Mirroring The purpose of this exercise is to write an XSLT transform
which takes as input a table of contents with sections only and output
the same table in XML where the sections have been reversed, level by
level, which means that the result tree is the image of the input tree in
a mirror. We already defined an abstract function mir/1 doing exactly
that appears in FIGURE 7.25 on page 225:

$$\mathrm{mir}(\mathrm{ext}()) \to \mathrm{ext}(); \quad \mathrm{mir}(\mathrm{int}(x, t_1, t_2)) \to \mathrm{int}(x, \mathrm{mir}(t_2), \mathrm{mir}(t_1)).$$

The DTD we have in mind have in mind here is the following:

```
<!ELEMENT book (author, section+)>
<!ATTLIST book title CDATA #REQUIRED>
<!ELEMENT author EMPTY>
<!ATTLIST author first NMTOKEN #REQUIRED
                 last  NMTOKEN #REQUIRED>
<!ELEMENT section (section*)>
<!ATTLIST section title CDATA #REQUIRED>
```

An example of valid input is the following table of contents:

```
<?xml version='1.0' encoding='UTF-8'?>
<!DOCTYPE book SYSTEM "book_simple.dtd">

<book title="Definitive XML Schema">
  <author first="Priscilla" last="Walmsley"/>

  <section title="[1] A quick tour of XML Schema">
    <section title="[1.1] An example schema"/>
    <section title="[1.2] The components of XML Schema">
      <section title="[1.2.1] Declarations vs. definitions"/>
      <section title="[1.2.2] Global vs. local components"/>
    </section>
    <section title="[1.3] Elements and attributes">
      <section title="[1.3.1] The tag/type distinction"/>
    </section>
  </section>

  <section title="[2] Instances and schemas">
    <section title="[2.1] Using the instance attributes"/>
    <section title="[2.2] Schema processing">
```

```
      <section title="[2.2.1] Validation"/>
      <section title="[2.2.2] Augmenting the instance"/>
    </section>
  </section>
</book>
```

Note that each section title has been numbered in order to better understand the corresponding output:

```
<?xml version="1.0" encoding="UTF-8"?>
<book title="Definitive XML Schema">
    <author first="Priscilla" last="Walmsley"/>
    <section title="[2] Instances and schemas">
        <section title="[2.2] Schema processing">
            <section title="[2.2.2] Augmenting the instance"/>
            <section title="[2.2.1] Validation"/>
        </section>
        <section title="[2.1] Using the instance attributes"/>
    </section>
    <section title="[1] A quick tour of XML Schema">
        <section title="[1.3] Elements and attributes">
            <section title="[1.3.1] The tag/type distinction"/>
        </section>
        <section title="[1.2] The components of XML Schema">
            <section title="[1.2.2] Global vs. local components"/>
            <section title="[1.2.1] Declarations vs. definitions"/>
        </section>
        <section title="[1.1] An example schema"/>
    </section>
</book>
```

The difference with the function mir/1 is that XML trees are unranked and there are no external nodes. The case mir(ext()) corresponds to empty sequence of subsections and its right-hand side ext() translates then as an empty sequence as well, which means that the structure of the named template is

```
<xsl:template name="mir" as="element(section)*">
  <xsl:param name="sections" as="element(section)*"/>
  <xsl:if test="not(empty($sections))">
     ...
  </xsl:if>
</xsl:template>
```

This is a typical use-case for `xsl:if`, instead of the general `xsl:choose`. Next, we focus on the second rewrite rule, whose right-hand side is $\text{int}(x, \text{mir}(t_2), \text{mir}(t_1))$. In XSLT, the parameter is a *sequence* of sections, that is, a forest, because we are dealing with unranked trees, so the children of the root make up a forest, not a pair (t_1, t_2) like in binary trees. Therefore, we need to generalise the mirroring to a stack. If we simply reverse it, this is not good because the children need reversing too, and so the grand-children etc. In other words, we need to traverse the whole tree, thus we should expect to perform two recursive calls: one horizontally (to process the current level `$sections`), and one vertically (to process the children of a node in the current level, usually the first).

The previous canvas then should be filled like so:

```
<xsl:template name="mir" as="element(section)*">
  <xsl:param name="sections" as="element(section)*"/>
  <xsl:if test="not(empty($sections))">
    <xsl:call-template name="mir">
      <xsl:with-param name="sections"
                      select="$sections[position()>1]"/>
    </xsl:call-template>
    <section>
      <xsl:sequence select="$sections[1]/@title"/>
      <xsl:call-template name="mir">
        <xsl:with-param name="sections"
                        select="$sections[1]/section"/>
      </xsl:call-template>
    </section>
  </xsl:if>
</xsl:template>
```

This template can be conceived as interleaving the reversal and the recursive mirroring of the children of the root. Note how `<xsl:sequence select="$sections[1]/@title"/>` is needed to rebuild the attribute of the mirrored image `<section>...</section>` of the first section. Recall that attribute nodes must be defined *before* the other kinds of nodes amongst the children (see page 393), that is, immediately after the opening tag `<section>`. The complete transform is

```
<?xml version="1.0" encoding="UTF-8"?>
<xsl:transform version="2.0"
               xmlns:xsl="http://www.w3.org/1999/XSL/Transform"
               xmlns:xs="http://www.w3.org/2001/XMLSchema"
               exclude-result-prefixes="xs">
```

```
<xsl:output method="xml" version="1.0"
            encoding="UTF-8" indent="yes"/>

<xsl:template match="/">
  <xsl:apply-templates select="book"/>
  <xsl:text>&#10;</xsl:text>
</xsl:template>

<xsl:template match="book" as="element(book)">
  <xsl:copy>
    <xsl:sequence select="@title"/>
    <xsl:sequence select="author"/>
    <xsl:call-template name="mir">
      <xsl:with-param name="sections" select="section"/>
    </xsl:call-template>
  </xsl:copy>
</xsl:template>

<xsl:template name="mir" as="element(section)*">
  <xsl:param name="sections" as="element(section)*"/>
  <xsl:if test="not(empty($sections))">
    <xsl:call-template name="mir">
      <xsl:with-param name="sections"
                      select="$sections[position()>1]"/>
    </xsl:call-template>
    <section>
      <xsl:sequence select="$sections[1]/@title"/>
      <xsl:call-template name="mir">
        <xsl:with-param name="sections"
                        select="$sections[1]/section"/>
      </xsl:call-template>
    </section>
  </xsl:if>
</xsl:template>

</xsl:transform>
```

Again, we have an illustration of the necessity of the attribute setting `exclude-result-prefixes="xs"`, or else the rebuilt section would needlessly inherit the namespace `xs`.

Now, let us answer the same question when the table of contents contains chapters, which in turn contain sections, and we do not want the chapters to be reversed, only the sections. More precisely, the DTD we want is `book_deep.dtd`:

```
<!ELEMENT book (author, chapter+)>
<!ATTLIST book title CDATA #REQUIRED>
<!ELEMENT author EMPTY>
<!ATTLIST author first NMTOKEN #REQUIRED
                 last  NMTOKEN #REQUIRED>
<!ELEMENT chapter (section*)>
<!ATTLIST chapter title CDATA #REQUIRED>
<!ELEMENT section (section*)>
<!ATTLIST section title CDATA #REQUIRED>
```

and a valid input would be

```
<?xml version='1.0' encoding='UTF-8'?>

<!DOCTYPE book SYSTEM "book_deep.dtd">

<book title="Definitive XML Schema">
  <author first="Priscilla" last="Walmsley"/>

  <chapter title="[I] A quick tour of XML Schema">
    <section title="[I.1] An example schema"/>
    <section title="[I.2] The components of XML Schema">
      <section title="[I.2.1] Declaration vs. definition"/>
      <section title="[I.2.2] Global vs. local components"/>
    </section>
    <section title="[I.3] Elements and attributes">
      <section title="[I.3.1] The tag/type distinction"/>
    </section>
  </chapter>

  <chapter title="[II] Instances and schemas">
    <section title="[II.1] Using the instance attributes"/>
    <section title="[II.2] Schema processing">
      <section title="[II.2.1] Validation"/>
      <section title="[II.2.2] Augmenting the instance"/>
    </section>
  </chapter>
</book>
```

We want the result

```
<?xml version="1.0" encoding="UTF-8"?>
<book title="Definitive XML Schema">
   <author first="Priscilla" last="Walmsley"/>
   <chapter title="[I] A quick tour of XML Schema">
      <section title="[I.3] Elements and attributes">
         <section title="[I.3.1] The tag/type distinction"/>
      </section>
      <section title="[I.2] The components of XML Schema">
         <section title="[I.2.2] Global vs. local components"/>
         <section title="[I.2.1] Declaration vs. definition"/>
      </section>
      <section title="[I.1] An example schema"/>
   </chapter>
   <chapter title="[II] Instances and schemas">
      <section title="[II.2] Schema processing">
         <section title="[II.2.2] Augmenting the instance"/>
         <section title="[II.2.1] Validation"/>
      </section>
      <section title="[II.1] Using the instance attributes"/>
   </chapter>
</book>
```

We mentioned that we had to write

```
<section>
  <xsl:sequence select="$sections[1]/@title"/>
  ...
</section>
```

to copy the attribute of the first section. Instead, we would like to write
`<section title="$sections[1]/@title">`, but the attribute value is then
considered as plain text, not as a selection. Therefore, the problem boils
down to performing a selection in an attribute which is neither test
nor select. The answer lies with an XPath operator {...}, which means
'Consider the text between braces as XPath, not plain text.' In other
words, we could write

```
<section title="{$sections[1]/@title}">
  ...
</section>
```

Clearly, we do not need to rewrite the template named mir because sections are to be processed in the same way as before, although it may be
interesting to use this new XPath operator for the sake of learning. Other

than that, all we need is a new named template to handle the chapters by reconstructing them *in the same order*, but with mirrored `section` children (if any). This means that we can reuse the same structure as `mir`, but without the reversal:

```
<xsl:template match="book" as="element(book)">
  <xsl:copy>
    <xsl:sequence select="@title"/>
    <xsl:sequence select="author"/>
    <xsl:call-template name="mk_chap">
      <xsl:with-param name="chapters" select="chapter"/>
    </xsl:call-template>
  </xsl:copy>
</xsl:template>

<xsl:template name="mk_chap" as="element(chapter)*">
  <xsl:param name="chapters" as="element(chapter)*"/>
  <xsl:if test="not(empty($chapters))">
    <chapter title="{$chapters[1]/@title}">
      <xsl:call-template name="mir">
        <xsl:with-param name="sections"
                        select="$chapters[1]/section"/>
      </xsl:call-template>
    </chapter>
    <xsl:call-template name="mk_chap">
      <xsl:with-param name="chapters"
                      select="$chapters[position()>1]"/>
    </xsl:call-template>
  </xsl:if>
</xsl:template>
```

Note that the `xsl:copy` element admit no `select` attribute: it only performs a shallow copy of the context node. Here it is clear that the context node is `book`, because `xsl:copy` is a child of the template matching `book`. But what if it is in a named template? How do we know the context node there, since we are not in a matching template? The answer is that the context node is the last matched node in the control flow up to the present instruction. For instance, in the template named `mir`, the context node is the root element `book`.

Because the order of the chapters must be left unchanged, it is interesting to use a template matching `chapter` to process them and call it with `<xsl:apply-templates select="chapter"/>`, instead of using the bulky template named `mk_chap`. It means:

1. select the elements `chapter` which are children of the context node;
2. for each element in the resulting sequence, in parallel, apply the first template in the stylesheet which matches `chapter`;
3. when finished, gather all the results in one sequence, in the same order as the original chapters.

As we saw on page 451, a matching template is like a map, the parallel application of a template to the items of a sequence. In other words, when *parallel* processing of elements is envisaged, we use `xsl:apply-templates`, otherwise *sequential* processing is chosen, that is `xsl:call-template`. (Please keep in mind that 'parallel' does not imply that an implementation of an XSLT processor must be multi-threaded, only that it could be. The function `map` in Erlang is clearly sequential, for instance, although it could be programmed using concurrent, even distributed, processes.) We have to rewrite the template matching `book` and the template named `mk_chap`, which becomes a template matching `chapter`:

```
<xsl:template match="book" as="element(book)">
  <xsl:copy>
    <xsl:attribute name="title" select="@title"/>
    <xsl:sequence select="author"/>
    <xsl:apply-templates select="chapter"/>
  </xsl:copy>
</xsl:template>

<xsl:template match="chapter" as="element(chapter)">
  <xsl:copy>
    <xsl:attribute name="title" select="@title"/>
    <xsl:call-template name="mir">
      <xsl:with-param name="sections" select="section"/>
    </xsl:call-template>
  </xsl:copy>
</xsl:template>
```

Note how the structure of the new template does not mimic anymore that of the template named `mir`, thus is shorter. Also, we introduced a new XSLT element:

```
<xsl:template match="book" as="element(book)">
  <xsl:copy>
    <xsl:attribute name="title" select="@title"/>
    ...
```

This is an alternative to using `xsl:sequence` as before. Also, we have now an element `xsl:copy` per matching template, the context node being **book** in one case, and **chapter**, in the other.

Comparing the contents of the template matching chapters with the following element in the template named `mir`,

```
...
<section title="{$sections[1]/@title}">
  <xsl:call-template name="flip">
  <xsl:with-param name="sections"
                  select="$sections[1]/section"/>
  </xsl:call-template>
</section>
...
```

it becomes apparent that both actions are the same: make a shallow copy of an element and mirror its children. Therefore it would be advantageous if the template matching chapters also matched sections. Because we used `xsl:copy` and `xsl:attribute`, it becomes possible to have a common template matching chapters and sections: `<xsl:template match="chapter|section">`, whose interpretation is as follows: 'Match either a **chapter** or a **section**.'

Here is the difference with the previous answer:

```
<xsl:template match="chapter|section" as="element()*">
  <xsl:copy>
    <xsl:attribute name="title" select="@title"/>
    <xsl:call-template name="mir">
      <xsl:with-param name="sections" select="section"/>
    </xsl:call-template>
  </xsl:copy>
</xsl:template>

<xsl:template name="mir" as="element(section)*">
  <xsl:param name="sections" as="element(section)*"/>
  <xsl:if test="not(empty($sections))">
    <xsl:call-template name="mir">
      <xsl:with-param name="sections"
                      select="$sections[position()>1]"/>
    </xsl:call-template>
    <xsl:apply-templates select="$sections[1]"/>
  </xsl:if>
</xsl:template>
```

Note how we have to apply templates to the first section in `mir` (see code in bold), instead of calling recursively `mir` (this call is now done in the template matching chapters and sections). Since the template applies to only one section, parallelism is lost, but code sharing is gained nonetheless.

The elements `xsl:call-template` and `xsl:apply-templates` differ also is that the former always results in a call while the latter may be a non-operation if the `select` attribute evaluates to an empty sequence. In other words, `<xsl:apply-templates select="..."/>` does nothing if the value of `"..."` is the empty sequence, whereas `<xsl:call-template name="t">` always calls the template named `t`, even if the parameters are empty sequences.

It is possible for a matching template to have parameters. Just put some `xsl:param` elements just after `<xsl:template match="...">` (this is the definition) and `xsl:with-param` just after `xsl:apply-templates` (this is the application). This is the same syntax as `xsl:call-template`.

Let us then change the call to template `mir` into a template application with a parameter and remove the definition of `mir` entirely. The shortest transform to achieve the same effects as the previous ones is

```
<?xml version="1.0" encoding="UTF-8"?>
<xsl:transform version="2.0"
               xmlns:xsl="http://www.w3.org/1999/XSL/Transform"
               xmlns:xs="http://www.w3.org/2001/XMLSchema"
               exclude-result-prefixes="xs">
  <xsl:output method="xml" version="1.0"
              encoding="UTF-8" indent="yes"/>

  <xsl:template match="/">
    <xsl:apply-templates select="book"/>
    <xsl:text>&#10;</xsl:text>
  </xsl:template>

  <xsl:template match="book" as="element(book)">
    <xsl:copy>
      <xsl:attribute name="title" select="@title"/>
      <xsl:sequence select="author"/>
      <xsl:apply-templates select="chapter"/>
    </xsl:copy>
  </xsl:template>

  <xsl:template match="chapter|section" as="element()*">
```

```
  <xsl:copy>
    <xsl:attribute name="title" select="@title"/>
    <xsl:call-template name="mir">
      <xsl:with-param name="sections" select="section"/>
    </xsl:call-template>
  </xsl:copy>
</xsl:template>

<xsl:template name="mir" as="element(section)*">
  <xsl:param name="sections" as="element(section)*"/>
  <xsl:if test="not(empty($sections))">
    <xsl:call-template name="mir">
      <xsl:with-param name="sections"
                      select="$sections[position()>1]"/>
    </xsl:call-template>
    <xsl:apply-templates select="$sections[1]"/>
  </xsl:if>
</xsl:template>

</xsl:transform>
```

Height   The purpose of this exercise is to write an XSLT transform
which takes as input a table of contents and outputs its height.

- The height of a table of contents is the largest height of its chapters.

- The height of a chapter (respectively, section) is 1 plus the largest
  height of its sections (respectively, subsections).

- The height of an empty sequence is 0.

For instance, a book with no chapters has height 0 (it is empty). A book
made only of chapters with no sections at all has height 1 (it is flat). We
will use the same DTD as in the previous exercise:

```
<!ELEMENT book (author, chapter+)>
<!ATTLIST book title CDATA #REQUIRED>
<!ELEMENT author EMPTY>
<!ATTLIST author first NMTOKEN #REQUIRED
                 last  NMTOKEN #REQUIRED>
<!ELEMENT chapter (section*)>
<!ATTLIST chapter title CDATA #REQUIRED>
<!ELEMENT section (section*)>
<!ATTLIST section title CDATA #REQUIRED>
```

The same input

```
<?xml version='1.0' encoding='UTF-8'?>

<!DOCTYPE book SYSTEM "book_deep.dtd">

<book title="Definitive XML Schema">
  <author first="Priscilla" last="Walmsley"/>

  <chapter title="[I] A quick tour of XML Schema">
    <section title="[I.1] An example schema"/>
    <section title="[I.2] The components of XML Schema">
      <section title="[I.2.1] Declaration vs. definition"/>
      <section title="[I.2.2] Global vs. local components"/>
    </section>
    <section title="[I.3] Elements and attributes">
      <section title="[I.3.1] The tag/type distinction"/>
    </section>
  </chapter>

  <chapter title="[II] Instances and schemas">
    <section title="[II.1] Using the instance attributes"/>
    <section title="[II.2] Schema processing">
      <section title="[II.2.1] Validation"/>
      <section title="[II.2.2] Augmenting the instance"/>
    </section>
  </chapter>
</book>
```

yields the result

3

The above definition is a parallel algorithm, because the heights of the chapters and sections can be computed separately. Therefore, let us write the transform using matching templates only and we reuse the template named max for finding the maximum of two integers.

```
<?xml version="1.0" encoding="UTF-8"?>

<xsl:transform version="2.0"
               xmlns:xsl="http://www.w3.org/1999/XSL/Transform"
               xmlns:xs="http://www.w3.org/2001/XMLSchema">
```

```
<xsl:output method="text" encoding="UTF-8"/>

<xsl:template match="/">
  <xsl:apply-templates select="book"/>
  <xsl:text>&#10;</xsl:text>
</xsl:template>

<xsl:template match="book" as="xs:integer">
  <xsl:call-template name="max">
    <xsl:with-param name="int" as="xs:integer*">
      <xsl:apply-templates select="chapter"/>
    </xsl:with-param>
    <xsl:with-param name="cur" select="0"/>
  </xsl:call-template>
</xsl:template>

<xsl:template match="chapter|section" as="xs:integer">
  <xsl:variable name="sub" as="xs:integer">
    <xsl:call-template name="max">
      <xsl:with-param name="int" as="xs:integer*">
        <xsl:apply-templates select="section"/>
      </xsl:with-param>
      <xsl:with-param name="cur" select="0"/>
    </xsl:call-template>
  </xsl:variable>
  <xsl:sequence select="1 + $sub"/>
</xsl:template>

<xsl:template name="max" as="xs:integer?">
  <xsl:param name="int" as="xs:integer*"/>
  <xsl:param name="cur" as="xs:integer?"/>
  <xsl:choose>
    <xsl:when test="empty($int)">
      <xsl:sequence select="$cur"/>
    </xsl:when>
    <xsl:when test="not(empty($cur)) and $cur ge $int[1]">
      <xsl:call-template name="max">
        <xsl:with-param name="int"
                        select="$int[position()>1]"/>
        <xsl:with-param name="cur" select="$cur"/>
      </xsl:call-template>
    </xsl:when>
```

```
    <xsl:otherwise>
      <xsl:call-template name="max">
        <xsl:with-param name="int"
                          select="$int[position()>1]"/>
        <xsl:with-param name="cur" select="$int[1]"/>
      </xsl:call-template>
    </xsl:otherwise>
  </xsl:choose>
</xsl:template>


</xsl:transform>
```

Same question but this time, instead of computing in parallel de heights of the children of a given node, let us compute them sequentially with a named template. The purpose is to avoid computing a sequence of heights and then taking their maximum. Instead, we would compute the current height along the traversal.

Two parameters are needed: a parameter `cur` representing the height of the sequence so far (the initial value is `0`) and a parameter `seq` holding the rest of the sequence whose height we want to know. Then

1. we compute the height of the sequence of the children of $seq[1];

2. we add `1` to obtain the height of $seq[1];

3. the maximum of this value and $cur is the value of `cur` in the recursive call with $seq[position()>1]. If $seq is empty, the maximum height of the nodes is $cur. (This scheme is similar to counting the number of sections.)

This is written in XSLT as follows:

```
<?xml version="1.0" encoding="UTF-8"?>


<xsl:transform version="2.0"
               xmlns:xsl="http://www.w3.org/1999/XSL/Transform"
               xmlns:xs="http://www.w3.org/2001/XMLSchema">

  <xsl:output method="text" encoding="UTF-8"/>

  <xsl:template match="/">
    <xsl:apply-templates select="book"/>
    <xsl:text>&#10;</xsl:text>
  </xsl:template>
```

```
<xsl:template match="book" as="xs:integer">
  <xsl:call-template name="height">
    <xsl:with-param name="seq" select="chapter"/>
    <xsl:with-param name="cur" select="0"/>
  </xsl:call-template>
</xsl:template>

<xsl:template name="height" as="xs:integer">
  <xsl:param name="seq" as="element()*"/>
  <xsl:param name="cur" as="xs:integer"/>
  <xsl:choose>
    <xsl:when test="empty($seq)">
      <xsl:sequence select="$cur"/>
    </xsl:when>
    <xsl:otherwise>
      <xsl:call-template name="height">
        <xsl:with-param name="seq"
                        select="$seq[position()>1]"/>
        <xsl:with-param name="cur" as="xs:integer">
          <xsl:variable name="sub" as="xs:integer">
            <xsl:call-template name="height">
              <xsl:with-param name="seq"
                              select="$seq[1]/section"/>
              <xsl:with-param name="cur" select="0"/>
            </xsl:call-template>
          </xsl:variable>
          <xsl:choose>
            <xsl:when test="$cur gt $sub">
              <xsl:sequence select="$cur"/>
            </xsl:when>
            <xsl:otherwise>
              <xsl:sequence select="1 + $sub"/>
            </xsl:otherwise>
          </xsl:choose>
        </xsl:with-param>
      </xsl:call-template>
    </xsl:otherwise>
  </xsl:choose>
</xsl:template>

</xsl:transform>
```

In the previous question, the height is computed *bottom-up*, that is, the increments on the height are performed just before the recursive calls end and new calls initialise the height parameter to 0. Instead, we can propose an alternate design where the height is incremented *top-down*, that is, the height parameter is added 1 just before the recursive calls start:

```
<?xml version="1.0" encoding="UTF-8"?>

<xsl:transform version="2.0"
               xmlns:xsl="http://www.w3.org/1999/XSL/Transform"
               xmlns:xs="http://www.w3.org/2001/XMLSchema">

  <xsl:output method="text" encoding="UTF-8"/>

  <xsl:template match="/">
    <xsl:apply-templates select="book"/>
    <xsl:text>&#10;</xsl:text>
  </xsl:template>

  <xsl:template match="book" as="xs:integer">
    <xsl:call-template name="height">
      <xsl:with-param name="seq" select="chapter"/>
      <xsl:with-param name="lvl" select="0"/>
    </xsl:call-template>
  </xsl:template>

  <xsl:template name="height" as="xs:integer">
    <xsl:param name="seq" as="element()*"/>
    <xsl:param name="lvl" as="xs:integer"/>
    <xsl:choose>
      <xsl:when test="empty($seq)">
        <xsl:sequence select="$lvl"/>
      </xsl:when>
      <xsl:otherwise>
        <xsl:variable name="sub" as="xs:integer">
          <xsl:call-template name="height">
            <xsl:with-param name="seq" select="$seq[1]/section"/>
            <xsl:with-param name="lvl" select="1 + $lvl"/>
          </xsl:call-template>
        </xsl:variable>
        <xsl:variable name="nxt" as="xs:integer">
```

```
          <xsl:call-template name="height">
            <xsl:with-param name="seq"
                            select="$seq[position()>1]"/>
            <xsl:with-param name="lvl" select="$lvl"/>
          </xsl:call-template>
        </xsl:variable>
        <xsl:choose>
          <xsl:when test="$nxt gt $sub">
            <xsl:sequence select="$nxt"/>
          </xsl:when>
          <xsl:otherwise>
            <xsl:sequence select="$sub"/>
          </xsl:otherwise>
        </xsl:choose>
      </xsl:otherwise>
    </xsl:choose>
  </xsl:template>

</xsl:transform>
```

Numbering The purpose of this exercise is to write an XSLT transform
which takes as input a table of contents and outputs it in XHTML, first
without numbering chapters and sections, then numbering them. The
DTD is still the same:

```
<!ELEMENT book (author, chapter+)>
<!ATTLIST book title CDATA #REQUIRED>
<!ELEMENT author EMPTY>
<!ATTLIST author first NMTOKEN #REQUIRED
                 last  NMTOKEN #REQUIRED>
<!ELEMENT chapter (section*)>
<!ATTLIST chapter title CDATA #REQUIRED>
<!ELEMENT section (section*)>
<!ATTLIST section title CDATA #REQUIRED>
```

The valid input is still

```
<?xml version='1.0' encoding='UTF-8'?>

<!DOCTYPE book SYSTEM "book_deep.dtd">

<book title="Definitive XML Schema">
  <author first="Priscilla" last="Walmsley"/>
```

```
<chapter title="[I] A quick tour of XML Schema">
  <section title="[I.1] An example schema"/>
  <section title="[I.2] The components of XML Schema">
    <section title="[I.2.1] Declaration vs. definition"/>
    <section title="[I.2.2] Global vs. local components"/>
  </section>
  <section title="[I.3] Elements and attributes">
    <section title="[I.3.1] The tag/type distinction"/>
  </section>
</chapter>

<chapter title="[II] Instances and schemas">
  <section title="[II.1] Using the instance attributes"/>
  <section title="[II.2] Schema processing">
    <section title="[II.2.1] Validation"/>
    <section title="[II.2.2] Augmenting the instance"/>
  </section>
</chapter>
</book>
```

The expected result (without numbering) is then

```
<!DOCTYPE html
  PUBLIC "-//W3C//DTD XHTML 1.0 Strict//EN"
  "http://www.w3.org/TR/xhtml1/DTD/xhtml1-strict.dtd">
<html xmlns:xhtml="http://www.w3.org/1999/xhtml"
      xmlns="http://www.w3.org/1999/xhtml"
      xml:lang="en" lang="en">
  <head>
    <meta http-equiv="Content-Type"
          content="text/html; charset=UTF-8"/>
    <title>Definitive XML Schema</title>
  </head>
  <body>
    <h2>Definitive XML Schema</h2>
    <p>by Priscilla Walmsley</p>
    <h3>Table of contents</h3>
    <ul>
      <li>[I] A quick tour of XML Schema
        <ul>
          <li>[I.1] An example schema</li>
          <li>[I.2] The components of XML Schema
```

```
            <ul>
              <li>[I.2.1] Declaration vs. definition</li>
              <li>[I.2.2] Global vs. local components</li>
            </ul>
          </li>
          <li>[I.3] Elements and attributes
            <ul>
              <li>[I.3.1] The tag/type distinction</li>
            </ul>
          </li>
        </ul>
      </li>
      <li>[II] Instances and schemas
        <ul>
          <li>[II.1] Using the instance attributes</li>
          <li>[II.2] Schema processing
            <ul>
              <li>[II.2.1] Validation</li>
              <li>[II.2.2] Augmenting the instance</li>
            </ul>
          </li>
        </ul>
      </li>
    </ul>
  </body>
</html>
```

which, interpreted by a web browser, would likely render as

Definitive XML Schema

by Priscilla Walmsley

Table of contents

I A quick tour of XML Schema

    I.1 An example schema

    I.2 The components of XML Schema

        I.2.1 Declaration vs. definition

        I.2.2 Global vs. local components

    I.3 Elements and attributes

        I.3.1 The tag/type distinction

The following solution should not be difficult by now:

```
<?xml version="1.0" encoding="UTF-8"?>
<xsl:transform version="2.0"
               xmlns:xsl="http://www.w3.org/1999/XSL/Transform"
               xmlns:xhtml="http://www.w3.org/1999/xhtml">

  <xsl:output method="xhtml"
              doctype-public="-//W3C//DTD XHTML 1.0 Strict//EN"
              doctype-system=
              "http://www.w3.org/TR/xhtml1/DTD/xhtml1-strict.dtd"
              indent="yes"
              omit-xml-declaration="yes"/>

  <xsl:template match="/">
    <xsl:apply-templates select="book"/>
    <xsl:text>&#10;</xsl:text>
  </xsl:template>

  <xsl:template match="book" as="element(xhtml:html)">
    <html xmlns="http://www.w3.org/1999/xhtml"
          xml:lang="en" lang="en">
      <head>
        <title><xsl:value-of select="@title"/></title>
      </head>
      <body>
        <h2><xsl:value-of select="@title"/></h2>
        <p>by <xsl:value-of select="author/@first,author/@last"/>
        </p>
        <h3>Table of contents</h3>
        <ul><xsl:apply-templates select="chapter"/></ul>
      </body>
    </html>
  </xsl:template>
```

```
<xsl:template match="section|chapter" as="element(xhtml:li)">
  <li xmlns="http://www.w3.org/1999/xhtml">
    <xsl:value-of select="@title"/>
    <xsl:if test="not(empty(section))">
      <ul><xsl:apply-templates select="section"/></ul>
    </xsl:if>
  </li>
</xsl:template>
```

```
</xsl:transform>
```

Perhaps it is worth noting `<xsl:value-of select="@title"/>`, since the titles are attribute values, so we need `xsl:value-of` to create a text node, just like for `"author/@first,author/@last"`, which is the same as `"(author/@first,author/@last)"`. Also possible here woud have been `"author/@*"`, which means 'All attribute values of the element `author`, child of the context node.'

Now, let us add a number between square brackets after the XHTML `<li>` tag, which is the position of the item in the list, like so:

```
<!DOCTYPE html
  PUBLIC "-//W3C//DTD XHTML 1.0 Strict//EN"
         "http://www.w3.org/TR/xhtml1/DTD/xhtml1-strict.dtd">
<html xmlns:xhtml="http://www.w3.org/1999/xhtml"
      xmlns="http://www.w3.org/1999/xhtml"
      xml:lang="en" lang="en">
  <head>
    <meta http-equiv="Content-Type"
          content="text/html; charset=UTF-8"/>
    <title>Definitive XML Schema</title>
  </head>
  <body>
    <h2>Definitive XML Schema</h2>
    <p>by Priscilla Walmsley</p>
    <h3>Table of contents</h3>
    <ul>
      <li>[1] [I] A quick tour of XML Schema
        <ul>
          <li>[1] [I.1] An example schema</li>
          <li>[2] [I.2] The components of XML Schema
            <ul>
              <li>[1] [I.2.1] Declaration vs. definition</li>
```

```
        <li>[2] [I.2.2] Global vs. local components</li>
        </ul>
      </li>
      <li>[3] [I.3] Elements and attributes
        <ul>
          <li>[1] [I.3.1] The tag/type distinction</li>
        </ul>
      </li>
    </ul>
  </li>
  <li>[2] [II] Instances and schemas
    <ul>
      <li>[1] [II.1] Using the instance attributes</li>
      <li>[2] [II.2] Schema processing
        <ul>
          <li>[1] [II.2.1] Validation</li>
          <li>[2] [II.2.2] Augmenting the instance</li>
        </ul>
      </li>
    </ul>
  </li>
  </ul>
 </body>
</html>
```

The added numbers have been set in a bold typeface. The only other change lies in the template matching chapters and sections:

```
<xsl:template match="section|chapter" as="element(xhtml:li)">
   <li xmlns="http://www.w3.org/1999/xhtml">
     <xsl:value-of select="('[',position(),'] ',@title)"
                   separator=""/>
     <xsl:if test="not(empty(section))">
       <ul><xsl:apply-templates select="section"/></ul>
     </xsl:if>
   </li>
</xsl:template>
```

The `separator` attribute must be set to the empty string, so the items in the selection (strings and integer) are converted to one text node without the default blank separator. For example, the result of evaluating `<xsl:value-of select="1,2,3">` is the string '1 2 3'.

Finally, we can complete the numbering so it becomes what is expected in a table of contents. Let us resume with an input *without* any numbers:

```
<?xml version='1.0' encoding='UTF-8'?>

<!DOCTYPE book SYSTEM "book_deep.dtd">

<book title="Definitive XML Schema">
  <author first="Priscilla" last="Walmsley"/>
  <chapter title="A quick tour of XML Schema">
    <section title="An example schema"/>
    <section title="The components of XML Schema">
      <section title="Declarations vs. definitions"/>
      <section title="Global vs. local components"/>
    </section>
    <section title="Elements and attributes">
      <section title="The tag/type distinction"/>
    </section>
  </chapter>

  <chapter title="Instances and schemas">
    <section title="Using the instance attributes"/>
    <section title="Schema processing">
      <section title="Validation"/>
      <section title="Augmenting the instance"/>
    </section>
  </chapter>
</book>
```

and, for making things a little bit easier, the output will number the chapters with Arabic numbers, like the sections:

```
<!DOCTYPE html
  PUBLIC "-//W3C//DTD XHTML 1.0 Strict//EN"
         "http://www.w3.org/TR/xhtml1/DTD/xhtml1-strict.dtd">
<html xmlns:xhtml="http://www.w3.org/1999/xhtml"
      xmlns="http://www.w3.org/1999/xhtml"
      xml:lang="en" lang="en">
  <head><meta http-equiv="Content-Type"
              content="text/html; charset=UTF-8"/>
        <title>Definitive XML Schema</title>
  </head>
```

```
<body>
  <h2>Definitive XML Schema</h2>
  <p>by Priscilla Walmsley</p>
  <h3>Table of contents</h3>
  <ul>
    <li>[1] A quick tour of XML Schema
      <ul>
        <li>[1.1] An example schema</li>
        <li>[1.2] The components of XML Schema
          <ul>
            <li>[1.2.1] Declarations vs. definitions</li>
            <li>[1.2.2] Global vs. local components</li>
          </ul>
        </li>
        <li>[1.3] Elements and attributes
          <ul>
            <li>[1.3.1] The tag/type distinction</li>
          </ul>
        </li>
      </ul>
    </li>
    <li>[2] Instances and schemas
      <ul>
        <li>[2.1] Using the instance attributes</li>
        <li>[2.2] Schema processing
          <ul>
            <li>[2.2.1] Validation</li>
            <li>[2.2.2] Augmenting the instance</li>
          </ul>
        </li>
      </ul>
    </li>
  </ul>
</body>
</html>
```

The idea is to add a parameter `prefix` to the template matching chapters
and sections, which receives the prefix numbering of the parent. For instance, when matching the section entitled 'Declarations vs. definitions',
the parameter value is the sequence (1,'.',2,'.'), so we simply concatenate the position of the section amongst its siblings, that is, 1. Then we
create a text node to format [1.2.1]. Here is the change:

```
<xsl:template match="chapter|section" as="element(xhtml:li)">
  <xsl:param name="prefix" as ="item()*"/>
  <xsl:variable name="current" select="($prefix,position())"/>
  <li xmlns="http://www.w3.org/1999/xhtml">
    <xsl:value-of select="('[',$current,'] ',@title)"
                  separator=""/>
    <xsl:if test="not(empty(section))">
      <ul>
        <xsl:apply-templates select="section">
          <xsl:with-param name="prefix"
                          select="($current,'.')"/>
        </xsl:apply-templates>
      </ul>
    </xsl:if>
  </li>
</xsl:template>
```

Note that the first application of this template is left unchanged:

```
...
<ul><xsl:apply-templates select="chapter"/></ul>
...
```

because, in XSLT, an empty sequence is implicitly passed, which is here convenient.

Sorting leaves   The purpose of this exercise is to write an XSLT transform which takes as input a document representing a binary tree whose leaves contain an integer and sort these in nondecreasing order. The integers in the sorted sequence must be separated by commas and terminated by a period in the resulting text. For instance, the following XML document

```
<?xml version="1.0" encoding="UTF-8"?>

<num>
  <num>
    <num val="9"/>
    <num>
      <num>
        <num val="33"/>
      </num>
      <num val="15"/>
```

```
      </num>
    </num>
    <num>
      <num>
        <num val="13"/>
        <num val="8"/>
      </num>
      <num>
        <num>
          <num>
            <num val="9"/>
            <num val="0"/>
          </num>
          <num val="16"/>
        </num>
        <num val="19"/>
      </num>
    </num>
  </num>
```

yields the following output:

`0,8,9,9,13,15,16,19,33.`

The format of the output should remind us of the comma-separated values (CSV), on page 447, and the ordering of the merging of ordered sequences, on page 464. Then, a first idea could be to traverse the tree and collect the numbers in ordered sequences which are merged together with the template named `merge` until one remains and, finally, we use the template named `csv`. More precisely, this traversal can be performed in parallel: the recursive template applications on the children yield two ordered sequences, which are merged; if the context node is the root element, then we call `csv`. In other words, the mergers are performed purely in a bottom-up fashion (that is, after the end of the recursive calls). Therefore, we start with

```
<xsl:template match="/" as="text()*">
  <xsl:call-template name="csv">
    <!-- The following cast is needed. -->
    <xsl:with-param name="items" as="xs:integer*">
      <xsl:apply-templates select="num"/>
    </xsl:with-param>
  </xsl:call-template>
```

```
    <xsl:text>&#10;</xsl:text>
  </xsl:template>
```

Note how the type annotation `xs:integer*` is necessary when invoking the template `csv`, whose type is

```
<xsl:template name="csv" as="text()*">
  <xsl:param name="items" as="item()*"/>
  ...
</xsl:template>
```

The rest is

```
<xsl:template match="num" as="xs:integer*">
  <xsl:choose>
    <xsl:when test="empty(@val)">
      <xsl:call-template name="merge">
        <xsl:with-param name="fst" as="xs:integer*">
          <xsl:apply-templates select="num[1]"/>
        </xsl:with-param>
        <xsl:with-param name="snd" as="xs:integer*">
          <xsl:apply-templates select="num[2]"/>
        </xsl:with-param>
      </xsl:call-template>
    </xsl:when>
    <xsl:otherwise>
      <xsl:value-of select="@val"/>
    </xsl:otherwise>
  </xsl:choose>
</xsl:template>
```

The template `merge` needs to be simplified and generalised because it was too specialised:

```
<xsl:template name="merge" as="element(item)*">
  <xsl:param name="seq1" as="element(item)*"/>
  <xsl:param name="seq2" as="element(item)*"/>
  ...
</xsl:template>
```

We need it to receive integers now:

```
<xsl:template name="merge" as="xs:integer*">
  <xsl:param name="fst" as="xs:integer*"/>
  <xsl:param name="snd" as="xs:integer*"/>
```

```
<xsl:choose>
  <xsl:when test="empty($fst)">
    <xsl:sequence select="$snd"/>
  </xsl:when>
  <xsl:when test="empty($snd)">
    <xsl:sequence select="$fst"/>
  </xsl:when>
  <xsl:when test="$fst[1] lt $snd[1]">
    <xsl:sequence select="$fst[1]"/>
    <xsl:call-template name="merge">
      <xsl:with-param name="fst"
                      select="$fst[position()>1]"/>
      <xsl:with-param name="snd" select="$snd"/>
    </xsl:call-template>
  </xsl:when>
  <xsl:otherwise>
    <xsl:sequence select="$snd[1]"/>
    <xsl:call-template name="merge">
      <xsl:with-param name="fst" select="$fst"/>
      <xsl:with-param name="snd"
                      select="$snd[position()>1]"/>
    </xsl:call-template>
  </xsl:otherwise>
</xsl:choose>
</xsl:template>
```

Exercise   Is example 2.2 in the book of Mangano (2006), page 39, really in tail form?

Part IV

Annex

Chapter 12

Overview of compilation

The function of a compiler is to translate texts written in a source language into texts written in a target language. Usually, the source language is a programming language, and the corresponding texts are programs. The target language is often an assembly language, *i.e.,* a language closer to the machine language (the language understood by the processor) than the source language. Some programming languages are compiled into a bytecode language instead of assembly. Bytecode is usually more abstract than an assembly language and is either interpreted by another program, called *virtual machine* (VM), or compiled to assembly.

Compilation chain

From an engineering point of view, the compiler is one link in a chain of tools, as shown in FIGURE 12.1. Let us consider the example of the *C language*. A widely used open-source compiler is GNU GCC. In reality,

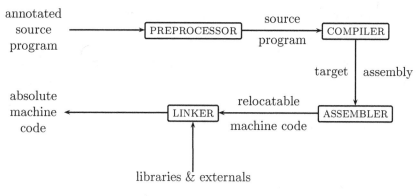

Figure 12.1: Compilation chain

GCC includes a complete compilation chain, not just a C compiler:

- to only preprocess the sources: `gcc -E prog.c` (standard output) (the C preprocessor `ccpp` can also be called directly);
- to preprocess and compile: `gcc -S prog.c` (output `prog.s`);
- to preprocess, compile and assemble: `gcc -c prog.c` (out: `prog.o`);
- to preprocess, compile, assemble and link: `gcc -o prog prog.c` (output `prog`). Linking can be directly called using `ld`.

There are two parts to compilation: *analysis* and *synthesis*.

1. The analysis part breaks up the source program into constituent pieces of an intermediary representation of the program.
2. The synthesis part constructs the target program from this intermediary representation.

Here, we shall concern ourselves only with analysis, which can itself be divided into three successive stages:

1. *linear analysis,* in which the stream of characters making up the source program is read and grouped into *lexemes,* that is, sequences of characters having a collective meaning; sets of lexemes with a common interpretation are called *tokens* (note that 'token' is often used when 'lexeme' would be correct, but the confusion is minimal);
2. *hierarchical analysis,* in which tokens are grouped hierarchically into nested collections (trees) with a collective meaning;
3. *semantic analysis,* in which certain checks are performed on the previous hierarchy to ensure that the components of a program fit together meaningfully.

In the following, we shall focus on linear and hierarchical analysis.

Lexical analysis   In a compiler, linear analysis is called *lexical analysis* or *scanning.* During lexical analysis, the characters in the assignment statement

```
position := initial + rate*60
```

would be grouped into the following lexemes and tokens (see facing table). The blanks separating the characters of these tokens are normally eliminated.

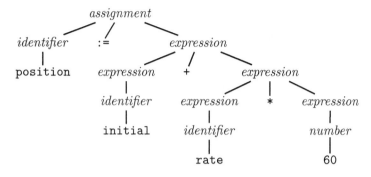

Figure 12.2: Parse tree of `position := initial + rate * 60`

TOKEN	LEXEME
identifier	`position`
assignment symbol	`:=`
identifier	`initial`
plus sign	`+`
identifier	`rate`
multiplication sign	`*`
number	`60`

Syntax analysis Hierarchical analysis is called *parsing* or *syntax analysis*. It involves grouping the tokens of the source program into grammatical phrases that are used by the compiler to synthesise the output. Usually, the grammatical phrases of the source are represented by a *parse tree* such as in FIGURE 12.2. In the expression `initial + rate * 60`, the phrase `rate * 60` is a logical unit because the usual conventions of arithmetic expressions tell us that multiplication is performed prior to addition. Thus, because the expression `initial + rate` is followed by a `*`, it is *not* grouped into the same subtree. The hierarchical structure of a program is usually expressed by *recursive rules*. For instance, an expression can be defined by a set of cases as follows:

1. any *identifier* is an expression;
2. any *number* is an expression;
3. if *expression₁* and *expression₂* are expressions, then so are

    (a) *expression₁* + *expression₂*,
    (b) *expression₁* * *expression₂*,
    (c) (*expression*).

Rules 1 and 2 are non-recursive base rules, while the others define expressions in terms of operators applied to other expressions:

- `initial` and `rate` are identifiers, therefore, by rule 1, `initial` and `rate` are expressions;
- `60` is a number, thus, by rule 2, we infer that `60` is an expression.

Next, by rule 3b, we infer that `rate * 60` is an expression. Finally, by rule 3a, we conclude that `initial + rate * 60` is an expression. Similarly, many programming languages define statements recursively by rules such as:

- if *identifier* is an identifier and *expression* is an expression, then we can form the statement

$$identifier := expression$$

- if *expression* is an expression and *statement* is a statement, then we can create the statements

```
while (expression) do statement
   if (expression) then statement
```

Let us keep in mind that the distinction between lexical and syntactic analysis is somewhat arbitrary. For instance, we could define the integer numbers by means of the following recursive rules:

- a *digit* is a *number* (base rule),
- a *number* followed by a *digit* is a *number* (recursive rule).

Imagine now that the lexer does *not* recognise numbers, only digits. The parser therefore would use the previous recursive rules to group in a parse tree the digits which form a number. For instance, the parse tree for the number `1234`, following these rules, is shown in FIGURE 12.3a on the facing page. Notice how that tree actually is almost a list: the structure, *i.e.*, the embedding of trees, is indeed not meaningful here. For example, there is no obvious meaning to the separation of `12` (same subtree at the leftmost part) in the number `1234`. Therefore, pragmatically, the best division between the lexer and the parser is the one that simplifies the overall task of analysis. One factor in determining the distinction is whether a source language construct is inherently recursive or not: lexical constructs do not require recursion, while syntactic constructs often do. For instance, recursion is not necessary to recognise identifiers, which are typically strings of letters and digits beginning with a letter: we can read the input stream until a character that is neither a digit nor a letter is found, then these read characters are grouped into an identifier token.

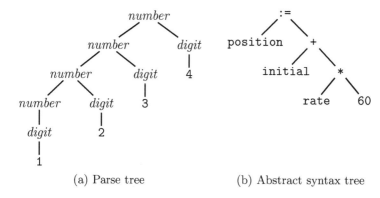

(a) Parse tree   (b) Abstract syntax tree

Figure 12.3: Parse tree vs. abstract syntax tree

On the other hand, this kind of linear scan is not powerful enough to analyse expressions or statements, like matching parentheses in expressions, or matching braces in block statements: a nesting structure is compulsory, as seen earlier in FIGURE 12.2 on page 507. The representation internal to the compiler of this syntactic structure is called an *abstract syntax tree* (or simply *syntax tree*), an example of which can be seen in FIGURE 12.3b. It is a compressed version of the parse tree, where only the most important elements are retained for the semantic analysis.

Semantic analysis The semantic analysis checks the syntax tree for meaningless constructs and completes it for the synthesis. An important part of semantic analysis is devoted to *type checking, i.e.,* checking properties on how the data in the program is combined. For instance, many programming languages require an error to be issued if an array is indexed with a floating-point number (called *float*). Some languages allow such floats and integers to be mixed in arithmetic expressions, some do not, because internal representation of integers and floats is very different, as is the cost of their corresponding arithmetic operations. In FIGURE 12.3b, let us assume that all identifiers were declared as being floats, that is, they are of type float. Typechecking then compares the type of `rate`, which is a float, with that of `60`, which is an integer.

Let us assume that our language permits these two types of operands for the multiplication ('*'). Then the analyser must insert a special node in the syntax tree which represents a *type cast* from integer to float for the constant `60`. At the level of the programming language, a type cast is the identity function (also called a non-operation in this context), so the value is not changed, but the type of the result is different from the type of the argument. This way the synthesis will know that the assembly

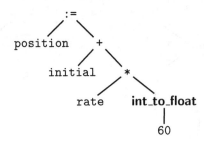

Figure 12.4: An annotated abstract syntax tree

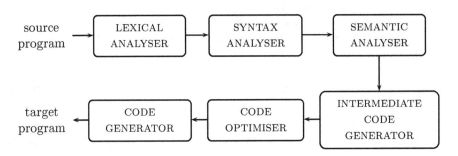

Figure 12.5: Decomposition of a compiler into phases

code for such a conversion has to be generated. The semantic analysis issues no error and produces an *annotated syntax tree* for the synthesis, displayed in FIGURE 12.4.

Phases   Conceptually, a compiler operates in *phases*, each transforming the program from one representation to another. This decomposition is shown in FIGURE 12.5. The first row makes up the analysis and the second is the synthesis.

Symbol table

FIGURE 12.5 does not depict another component which is connected to all the phases: the *symbol table manager*. A symbol table is a two-column table whose first column contains identifiers collected in the program and the second column contains any interesting information, called *attributes*, about their corresponding identifier. Example of identifier attributes are

- the allocated storage,
- the type,
- the *scope* (*i.e.*, where in the program it is valid),

- in case of procedures names, the number and type of the parameters, the method of passing each argument (*e.g.,* by reference) and the result type, if any.

When an identifier in the source program is detected by the lexer, this identifier is entered into the symbol table. However, some attributes of an identifier cannot normally be determined during lexical analysis. For example, in a Pascal declaration like

```
var position, initial, rate: real;
```

the type `real` is not known when `position`, `initial` and `rate` are recognised by the lexical analyser. The remaining phases enter information about the identifiers into the symbol table and use this information. For example, the semantic analyser needs to know the type of the identifiers to generate intermediate code.

Error detection and reporting

Another compiler component that was omitted from FIGURE 12.5 on the preceding page because it is also connected to all the phases is the *error handler*. Indeed, each phase can encounter errors, so each phase must somehow deal with these errors. Here are some examples:

- the lexical analysis finds an error if a series of characters do not form a token;
- the syntax analysis finds an error if the relative position of a group of tokens is not described by the grammar (abstract syntax);
- the semantic analysis finds an error if the program contains the addition of an integer and an array.

Lexing

Let us revisit the analysis phase and its sub-phases, following up on a previous example. Consider the following character string:

First, as we stated in section 12 on page 506, lexical analysis recognises the tokens of this character string, which can be stored in a file. Lexing results in a stream of tokens like

id⟨position⟩	**sym**⟨:=⟩	**id**⟨initial⟩	**op**⟨+⟩	**id**⟨rate⟩	**op**⟨*⟩
					num⟨60⟩

where **id** (*identifier*), **sym** (*symbol*), **op** (*operator*) and **num** (*number*) are the token names and between brackets are the *lexemes*. The lexer also outputs or updates a symbol table (Even if the table is named 'symbol table' it actually contains information about identifiers only.) like

Identifier	Attributes
position	...
initial	...
rate	...

The attributes often include the position of the corresponding identifier in the original string, like the position of the first character either counting from the start of the string or through the line and column numbers.

Parsing

The parser takes this token stream and outputs the corresponding syntax tree and/or report errors. In FIGURE 12.3b on page 509, we gave a simplified version of this syntax tree. A refined version is given in the facing column. Also, if the language requires variable definitions, the syntax analyser can complete the symbol table with the type of the identifiers.

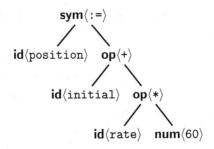

The parse tree can be considered as a *trace* of the syntax analysis process: it summarises all the recognition work done by the parser. It depends on the syntax rules (*i.e.*, the grammar) and the input stream of tokens.

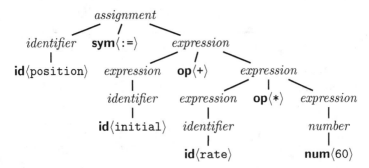

Semantic analysis

The semantic analysis considers the syntax tree and checks certain properties depending on the language, typically it makes sure that the valid syntactic constructs also have a certain meaning (with respect to the rules of the language). We saw in FIGURE 12.4 on page 510 that this phase can annotate or even add nodes to the syntax tree. It can as well update the symbol table with the information newly gathered in order to facilitate the code generation and/or optimisation. Assuming that our toy language accepts that an integer is mixed with floats in arithmetic operations, the semantic analysis can insert a type cast node. A new version of the annotated syntax tree is proposed in FIGURE 12.6. Note that the new node is not a token, just a (semantic) tag for the code generator.

The synthesis phase

The purpose of the synthesis phase is to use all the information gathered by the analysis phase in order to produce the code in the target language. Given the annotated syntax tree and the symbol table, the first sub-phase consists in producing a program in some artificial, intermediary, language. Such a language should be independent of the target language, while containing features common to the *family* the target language belongs to. For instance, if the target language is the PowerPC G4 microprocessor, the intermediary language should be like an assembly of the IBM RISC family. If we want *to port a compiler* from one platform to another, *i.e.,* make it generate code for a different OS or processor, such intermediary language comes handy: if the new platform share some features with the first one, we only have to rewrite the code generator component of the compiler – not the whole compiler. It may be interesting to have the same intermediary language for different source languages, allowing the sharing of the synthesis. We can think of an intermediary language as

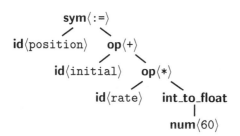

Figure 12.6: Refined annotated abstract syntax tree

an assembly for an *abstract machine* (or processor). For instance, our example could lead to the code

```
temp1 := inttoreal(60)
temp2 := id_rate * temp1
temp3 := id_initial + temp2
id_position := temp3
```

Another point of view is to consider the intermediary code as a tiny subset of the source language, as it retains some high-level features from it, like, in our example, variables (instead of explicit storage information, like memory addresses or register numbers), operator names etc. This point of view enables optimisations that otherwise would be harder to achieve (because too many aspects would depend closely on many details of the target architecture). This kind of assembly is called *three-address code*. It has several properties:

- each instruction has at most one operator (in addition to the assignment);
- each instruction can have at most three operands;
- some instructions can have less than three operands, for instance, the first and last instruction;
- the result of an operation must be linked to a variable;.

As a consequence, the compiler must order well the code for the subexpressions, *e.g.,* the second instruction must come before the third one because the multiplication has priority on addition.

Code optimisation The code optimisation phase attempts to improve the intermediate code, so that faster-running target code will result. The code optimisation produces intermediate code: the output language is the same as the input language. For instance, this phase would find out that our little program would be more efficient this way:

```
temp1 := id_rate * 60.0
id_position := id_initial + temp1
```

This simple optimisation is based on the fact that type casting can be performed at compile-time instead of run-time, but it would be an unnecessary concern to integrate it in the code generation phase.

Code generation The code generation is the last phase of a compiler. It consists in the generation of target code, usually relocatable assembly code, from the optimised intermediate code. A crucial aspect is the assignment of variables to registers. For example, the translation of code above could be

```
MOVF id_rate, R2
MULF #60.0, R2
MOVF id_initial, R1
ADDF R2, R1
MOVF R1, id_position
```

The first and second operands specify respectively a source and a destination. The F in each instruction tells us that the instruction is dealing with floating-point numbers. This code moves the contents of the address id_rate into register 2, then multiplies it with the float 60.0. The # signifies that 60.0 is a constant. The third instruction moves id_initial into register 1 and adds to it the value previously computed in register 2. Finally, the value in register 1 is moved to the address of id_position.

From phases to passes   An implementation of the analysis is called a *front-end* and an implementation of the synthesis *back-end*. A *pass* consists in reading an input file and writing an output file. It is possible to group several phases into one pass in order to interleave their activity.

- On the one hand, this can lead to a greater efficiency since interactions with the file system are much slower than with internal memory.

- On the other hand, this architecture leads to a greater complexity of the compiler – something the software engineer always fears.

Sometimes it is difficult to group different phases into one pass. For example, the interface between the lexer and the parser is often a single token. There is not a lot of activity to interleave: the parser requests a token to the lexer which computes it and gives it back to the parser. In the meantime, the parser had to wait. Similarly, it is difficult to generate the target code if the intermediate code is not fully generated first. Indeed, some languages allow the programmer the use of variables without a prior declaration, so we cannot generate immediately the target code because this requires the knowledge of the variable type.

Chapter 13

Automata theory for lexing

In this chapter, we present the basic notions of lexical analysis, also known as *lexing* or *scanning*.

13.1 Specification of tokens

FIGURE 13.1 shows that the lexical analyser is the first phase of a compiler. Its main task is to read the input characters and produce a sequence of tokens that the syntax analyser uses. Upon receiving a request for a token (*get token*) from the parser, the lexical analyser reads input characters until a lexeme is identified and returned to the parser together with the corresponding token. Usually, a lexical analyser is in charge of

- stripping out from the source program comments and white spaces, in the form of blank, tabulation and newline characters;
- keeping trace of the position of the lexemes in the source program, so the error handler can refer to exact positions in error messages.

A *token* is a set of strings which are interpreted in the same way, for a given source language. For instance, **id** is a token denoting the set of all possible identifiers. A *lexeme* is a string belonging to a token. For

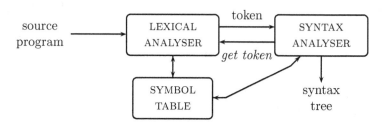

Figure 13.1: Lexer and parser

517

Token	Sample lexemes	Informal pattern
id	pi count D2 ...	letter followed by letters and digits
relop	< <= = >= >	< or <= or < or = or >= or >
const	const	const
if	if	if
num	3.14 4 .2E2 ...	numeric constant
literal	"message" "" ...	characters between " and " except "

Figure 13.2: Examples of tokens and lexemes

example, 5.4 is a lexeme of the token **num**. Tokens are defined by means of *patterns*. A pattern is a kind of compact rule describing all the lexemes of a token. A pattern is said to *match* each lexeme in the token. For example, in the Pascal statement

```
const pi = 3.14159;
```

the substring pi is a lexeme for the token **id** (*identifier*).

Most recent programming languages distinguish a finite set of strings that match the identifiers but are not part of the identifier token: the *keywords*. For example, in Ada, function is a keyword and, as such, is not a valid identifier. In C, int is a keyword and, as such, cannot be used as an identifier, for instance to declare a variable. Nevertheless, it is common not to create explicitly a **keyword** token and let each keyword lexeme be the only one of its own token, as displayed in FIGURE 13.2.

Regular expressions are an important notation for specifying patterns. Each pattern matches a set of strings, so regular expressions will serve as names for sets of strings. The term *alphabet* denotes any finite set of symbols. Typical examples of symbols are letters and digits, for example, the set $\{0, 1\}$ is the *binary alphabet*; ASCII is another example of computer alphabet.

A *string* over some alphabet is a finite sequence of symbols drawn from that alphabet. The terms *sentence* and *word* are often used as synonyms. The length of string s, usually noted $|s|$, is the number of occurrences of symbols in s. For example, banana is a string of length 6. The *empty string*, denoted ε, is a special string of length zero. More informal definitions are given in the table in FIGURE 13.3 on the facing page.

The term *language* denotes any set of strings over some fixed alphabet. The *empty set*, noted $\varnothing$, or $\{\varepsilon\}$, the set containing only the empty word are languages. The set of valid C programs is an infinite language. If x and y are strings, then the *concatenation* of x and y, written xy or $x \cdot y$,

TERM	INFORMAL DEFINITION
prefix of s	A string obtained by removing zero or more trailing symbols of string s; *e.g.,* ban is a prefix of banana.
suffix of s	A string formed by deleting zero or more of the leading symbols of s; *e.g.,* nana is a suffix of banana.
substring of s	A string obtained by deleting a prefix and a suffix from s; *e.g.,* nan is a substring a banana. Every prefix and every suffix of s is a substring s, but not every substring of s is a prefix or a suffix of s. For every string s, both s and ε are prefixes, suffixes and substrings of s.
proper prefix, suffix or substring of s	Any non-empty string x, that is, respectively, a prefix, suffix, substring of s such that $s \neq x$; *e.g.,* ε and banana are *not* proper prefixes of banana.
subsequence of s	Any string formed by deleting zero or more not necessarily contiguous symbols from s; *e.g.,* baaa is a subsequence of banana.

Figure 13.3: Formal language glossary

is the string formed by appending y to x. For example, if $x =$ dog and $y =$ house, then $xy =$ doghouse. The empty string is the identity element under concatenation: $s\varepsilon = \varepsilon s = s$. If we think of concatenation as a product, we can define string exponentiation as follows:

- $s^0 = \varepsilon$,
- $s^n = s^{n-1}s$, if $n > 0$.

Since $\varepsilon s = s$ and $s^1 = s$, we have $s^2 = ss$ and $s^3 = sss$, etc.

We can now revisit in FIGURE 13.4 on the next page the definitions we gave in FIGURE 13.3 using a formal notation, where L is the language under consideration.

Operations on languages It is possible to define operations on languages. For lexical analysis, we are interested mainly in *union, concatenation* and *closure*. Consider FIGURE 13.5 on the next page, where let L and M be two languages. L^* means 'zero or more concatenations of L', and L^+ means 'at least one concatenation of L'. Clearly, $L^* = \{\varepsilon\} \cup L^+$. For instance, let $L = \{A, B, \ldots, Z, a, b, \ldots, z\}$ and $D = \{0, 1, \ldots, 9\}$. Then

1. L is the alphabet consisting of the set of upper and lower case letters and D is the alphabet of the decimal digits;

TERM	FORMAL DEFINITION
x is a *prefix* of s	$\exists y \in L.s = xy$
x is a *suffix* of s	$\exists y \in L.s = yx$
x is a *substring* of s	$\exists u, v \in L.s = uxv$
x is a *proper prefix* of s	$\exists y \in L.y \neq \varepsilon$ and $s = xy$
x is a *proper suffix* of s	$\exists y \in L.y \neq \varepsilon$ and $s = yx$
x is a *proper substring* of s	$\exists u, v \in L.uv \neq \varepsilon$ and $s = uxv$

Figure 13.4: Formal definitions of FIGURE 13.3 on the preceding page

2. since a symbol is a string of length one, the sets L and D are finite languages too.

These two ways of considering L and D and the operations on languages allow us to create new languages from other languages defined by their alphabet. Here are some examples of new languages created from L and D:

- $L \cup D$ is the language of letters and digits;
- LD is the language whose words consist of a letter followed by a digit;
- L^4 is the language whose words are four-letter strings;
- L^* is the language made up on the alphabet L, *i.e.*, the set of all strings of letters, including the empty string ε;
- $L(L \cup D)^*$ is the language whose words consist of letters and digits and beginning with a letter;
- D^+ is the language whose words are made of one or more digits, *i.e.*, the set of all decimal integers.

13.2   Regular expressions

In Pascal, an identifier is a letter followed by zero or more letters or digits, that is, and identifier is a member of the set defined by $L(L \cup D)^*$. The

OPERATION	FORMAL DEFINITION
union of L and M	$L \cup M = \{s \mid s \in L \text{ or } s \in M\}$
concatenation of L and M	$LM = \{st \mid s \in L \text{ and } t \in M\}$
Kleene closure of L	$L^* = \bigcup_{i=0}^{\infty} L^i$ where $L^0 = \{\varepsilon\}$
positive closure of L	$L^+ = \bigcup_{i=1}^{\infty} L^i$

Figure 13.5: Operations on formal languages

notation we introduced so far is comfortable for mathematics but not for computers. Let us introduce another notation, called *regular expressions*, for describing the same languages and define its meaning in terms of the mathematical notation. With this notation, we might define Pascal identifiers as

letter (letter | digit)*

where the vertical bar means 'or', the parentheses group subexpressions, the star means 'zero or more instances of' the previous expression and juxtaposition means concatenation. A regular expression r is built up out of simpler regular expressions using a set of rules, as follows. Let Σ be an alphabet and $L(r)$ the language denoted by r. Then

1. ϵ is a regular expression that denotes $\{\varepsilon\}$;
2. if $a \in \Sigma$, then a is a regular expression that denotes $\{a\}$. This is ambiguous: a can denote a language, a word or a letter – it depends on the context;
3. assume r and s denote the languages $L(r)$ and $L(s)$; a denotes a letter. Then

   (a) $r \mid s$ is a regular expression denoting $L(r) \cup L(s)$;
   (b) rs is a regular expression denoting $L(r)L(s)$;
   (c) r^* is a regular expression denoting $(L(r))^*$;
   (d) (r) is a regular expression denoting $L(r)$;
   (e) $\bar{a}$ is a regular expression denoting $\Sigma \backslash \{a\}$.

A language described by a regular expression is a *regular language*. Rules 1 and 2 form the base of the definition. Rule 3 provides the inductive step. Unnecessary parentheses can be avoided in regular expressions if

- the unary operator * has the highest precedence and is left associative,
- concatenation has the second highest precedence and is left associative,
- $\mid$ has the lowest precedence and is left associative.

Under those conventions, $(a) \mid ((b)^*(c))$ is equivalent to $a \mid b^*c$. Both expressions denote the language containing either the string a or zero or more b's followed by one c: $\{a, c, bc, bbc, bbbc, \dots\}$. For example,

- the regular expression $a \mid b$ denotes the set $\{a, b\}$;
- the regular expression $(a \mid b)(a \mid b)$ denotes $\{aa, ab, ba, bb\}$, the set of all strings of a's and b's of length two. Another regular expression for the set is $aa \mid ab \mid ba \mid bb$;

LAW	DESCRIPTION
$r \mid s = s \mid r$	$\mid$ is commutative
$r \mid (s \mid t) = (r \mid s) \mid t$	$\mid$ is associative
$(rs)t = r(st)$	concatenation is associative
$r(s \mid t) = rs \mid rt$ $(s \mid t)r = sr \mid tr$	concatenation distributes over $\mid$
$\epsilon r = r$ $r\epsilon = r$	ϵ is the identity element for the concatenation
$r^{\star\star} = r^{\star}$	Kleene closure is idempotent
$r^{\star} = r^{+} \mid \epsilon$ $r^{+} = rr^{\star}$	Kleene closure and positive closure are closely linked

Figure 13.6: Algebraic laws on regular languages

- the regular expression $a^{\star}$ denotes the set of all strings of zero or more a's, i.e. $\{\varepsilon, a, aa, aaa, \dots\}$;
- the regular expression $(a \mid b)^{\star}$ denotes the set of all strings containing zero of more instances of an a or b, that is the language of all words made of a's and b's. Another expression is $(a^{\star}b^{\star})^{\star}$.

If two regular expressions r and s denote the same language, we say that r and s are *equivalent* and write $r = s$. In FIGURE 13.6, we show useful algebraic laws on regular languages.

Regular definitions

It is convenient to give names to regular expressions and define new regular expressions using these names as if they were symbols. If Σ is an alphabet, then a *regular definition* is a series of definitions of the form

$$d_1 \rightarrow r_1$$
$$d_2 \rightarrow r_2$$
$$\dots$$
$$d_n \rightarrow r_n$$

where each d_i is a distinct name and each r_i is a regular expression over the alphabet $\Sigma \cup \{d_1, d_2, \dots, d_{i-1}\}$, *i.e.*, the basic symbols and the previously defined names. The restriction to d_j such $j < i$ allows to construct a regular expression over Σ only by repeatedly replacing all the names in it. For instance, as we have stated, the set of Pascal identifiers can be defined by the regular definitions

$$\text{letter} \rightarrow A \mid B \mid \dots \mid Z \mid a \mid b \mid \dots \mid z$$

$$\textbf{digit} \rightarrow 0 \mid 1 \mid 2 \mid 3 \mid 4 \mid 5 \mid 6 \mid 7 \mid 8 \mid 9$$
$$\textbf{id} \rightarrow \textbf{letter (letter} \mid \textbf{digit)}^{\star}$$

Unsigned numbers in Pascal are strings like 5280, 39.37, 6.336E4 or 1.894E-4.

$$\textbf{digit} \rightarrow 0 \mid 1 \mid 2 \mid 3 \mid 4 \mid 5 \mid 6 \mid 7 \mid 8 \mid 9$$
$$\textbf{digits} \rightarrow \textbf{digit digit}^{\star}$$
$$\textbf{opt\_fraction} \rightarrow . \textbf{ digits} \mid \epsilon$$
$$\textbf{opt\_exponent} \rightarrow (\textbf{E} (+ \mid - \mid \epsilon) \textbf{ digits}) \mid \epsilon$$
$$\textbf{num} \rightarrow \textbf{digits opt\_fraction opt\_exponent}$$

Certain constructs occur so frequently in regular expressions that it is convenient to introduce notational shorthands for them:

- *Zero or one instance.* The unary operator '?' means 'zero or one instance of'. Formally, by definition, if r is a regular expression then $r? = r \mid \epsilon$. In other words, $(r)?$ denotes the language $L(r) \cup \{\varepsilon\}$.

$$\textbf{digit} \rightarrow 0 \mid 1 \mid 2 \mid 3 \mid 4 \mid 5 \mid 6 \mid 7 \mid 8 \mid 9$$
$$\textbf{digits} \rightarrow \textbf{digit}^{+}$$
$$\textbf{opt\_fraction} \rightarrow (. \textbf{ digits})?$$
$$\textbf{opt\_exponent} \rightarrow (\textbf{E} (+ \mid -)? \textbf{ digits})?$$
$$\textbf{num} \rightarrow \textbf{digits opt\_fraction opt\_exponent}$$

- It is also possible to write:

$$\textbf{digit} \rightarrow 0 \mid 1 \mid 2 \mid 3 \mid 4 \mid 5 \mid 6 \mid 7 \mid 8 \mid 9$$
$$\textbf{digits} \rightarrow \textbf{digit}^{+}$$
$$\textbf{fraction} \rightarrow . \textbf{ digits}$$
$$\textbf{exponent} \rightarrow \textbf{E} (+ \mid -)? \textbf{ digits}$$
$$\textbf{num} \rightarrow \textbf{digits fraction? exponent?}$$

If we want to specify the characters '?', '*', '+', '|', we write them with a preceding backslash, *e.g.,* '\?', or between double-quotes, *e.g.,* "?". Then, of course, the character double-quote must have a backslash: \". It is also sometimes useful to match against end of lines and end of files: \n stands for the control character 'end of line' and **$** is for 'end of file'.

Non-regular languages

Some languages cannot be described by any regular expression. For example, the language of balanced parentheses cannot be recognised by any regular expression: (), (()), ()(), ((())()) etc. Another example is the C programming language: it is not a regular language because it contains embedded blocs between '{' and '}'. Therefore, a lexer cannot recognise valid C programs: we need a parser.

Exercises

Question 1.   Let the alphabet $\Sigma = \{a, b\}$ and the following regular expressions:

$$r = a(a \,|\, b)^* ba,$$
$$s = (ab)^* \,|\, (ba)^* \,|\, (a^* \,|\, b^*).$$

The language denoted by r is noted $L(r)$ and the language denoted by s is noted $L(s)$. Find a word x such that

1. $x \in L(r)$ and $x \notin L(s)$,
2. $x \notin L(r)$ and $x \in L(s)$,
3. $x \in L(r)$ and $x \in L(s)$,
4. $x \notin L(r)$ and $x \notin L(s)$.

Answer 1.   The method to answer these questions is simply to try small words by constructing them in order to satisfy the constraints.

1. The shortest word x belonging to L(r) is found by taking ϵ in place of $(a|b)^*$. So $x = aba$. Let us check if $x \in L(s)$ or not. $L(s)$ is made of the union of four sub-languages (subsets). To make this clear, let us remove the useless parentheses on the right side:

   $$s = (ab)^* \,|\, (ba)^* \,|\, a^* \,|\, b^*.$$

   Therefore, membership tests on $L(s)$ have to be split into four: one membership test on $(ab)^*$, one on $(ba)^*$, one on a^* and another one on b^*. In other words, $x \in L(s)$ is equivalent to

   $$x \in L((ab)^*) \text{ or } x \in L((ba)^*) \text{ or } x \in L(a^*) \text{ or } x \in L(b^*).$$

   Let us test the membership with $x = aba$:

   (a) The words in $L((ab)^*)$ are ϵ, ab, $abab$... Thus $aba \notin L((ab)^*)$.

(b) The words in $L((ba)^*)$ are ϵ, ba, $baba\ldots$ Hence $aba \notin L((ba)^*)$.

(c) The words in $L(a^*)$ are ϵ, a, $aa\ldots$ Therefore $aba \notin L(a^*)$.

(d) The words in $L(b^*)$ are ϵ, b, $bb\ldots$ So $aba \notin L(b^*)$.

The conclusion is $aba \notin L(s)$.

2. What is the shortest word belonging to $L(s)$? Since the four sub-languages composing $L(s)$ are starred, it means that $\epsilon \in L(s)$. Since we showed at the item (1) that aba is the shortest word of $L(r)$, it means that $\epsilon \notin L(r)$ because ϵ is of length 0.

3. This question is a bit more difficult. After a few tries, we cannot find any x such that $x \in L(r)$ and $x \in L(s)$. Then we may try to prove that $L(r) \cap L(s) = \varnothing$, i.e., there is no such x. How should we proceed? The idea is to use the decomposition of $L(s)$ into for sub-languages and try to prove

$$L(r) \cap L((ab)^*) = \varnothing,$$
$$L(r) \cap L((ba)^*) = \varnothing,$$
$$L(r) \cap L(a^*) = \varnothing,$$
$$L(r) \cap L(b^*) = \varnothing.$$

If all these four equations are true, they imply $L(r) \cap L(s) = \varnothing$.

(a) Any word in $L(r)$ ends with a whereas any word in $L((ab)^*)$ finishes with b or is ϵ. Thus $L(r) \cap L((ab)^*) = \varnothing$.

(b) For the same reason, $L(r) \cap L(b^*) = \varnothing$.

(c) Any word in $L(r)$ contains both a and b whereas any word in $L(a^*)$ contains only b or is ϵ. Therefore $L(r) \cap L(a^*) = \varnothing$.

(d) Any word in $L(r)$ starts with a whereas any word in $L((ba)^*)$ starts with b or is ϵ. Thus $L(r) \cap L((ba)^*) = \varnothing$.

Finally, since all the four equations are false, they imply that

$$L(r) \cap L(s) = \varnothing.$$

4. Let us construct letter by letter a word x which does not belong neither to $L(r)$ not $L(s)$. First, we note that all words in $L(r)$ start with a, so we can try to start x with b: this way $x \notin L(r)$. So we have $x = b\ldots$ and we have to fill the dots with some letters in such a way that $x \notin L(s)$.

We use again the decomposition of $L(s)$ into four sub-languages and make sure that x does not belong to any of those sub-languages. First, because x starts with b, we have $x \notin L(a^\star)$ and $x \notin L((ab)^\star)$. Now, we have to add some more letters such that $x \notin L(b^\star)$ and $x \notin L((ba)^\star)$. Since any word in $L(b^\star)$ has a letter b as second letter or is ϵ, we can choose the second letter of x to be a. This way $x = ba \ldots \notin L(b^\star)$. Finally, we have to add more letters to make sure that

$$x = ba \ldots \notin L((ba)^\star).$$

Any word in $L((ba)^\star)$ is either ϵ or ba or $baba \ldots$, hence the third letter is b. Therefore, let us choose the letter a as the third letter of x and we thus have $x = baa \notin L((ba)^\star)$. In summary, $baa \notin L(r), baa \notin L(b^\star), baa \notin L((ba)^\star), baa \notin L(a^\star), baa \notin L((ab)^\star)$, which is equivalent to $baa \notin L(r)$ and $baa \notin L((ab)^\star) \cup L((ba)^\star) \cup L(a^\star) \cup L(b^\star) = L(s)$. Therefore, $x = baa$ is one possible answer.

Question 2.   Given the binary alphabet $\Sigma = \{a, b\}$ and the order on letters $a < b$, write regular definitions for the following languages.

1. All words starting and ending with a.
2. All non-empty words.
3. All words in which the third last letter is a.
4. All words containing exactly three a.
5. All words containing at least one a before a b.
6. All words in which the letters are in increasing order.
7. All words with no letter following the same one.

Answer 2.   When answering these questions, it is important to keep in mind that the language of words made up on the alphabet Σ is Σ^* and that there are, in general, several regular expressions describing one language.

1. The constraint on the words is that they must be of the shape $a \ldots a$ where the dots stand for 'any combination of a and b'. In other words, one answer is $a(a \mid b)^* a \mid a$.

2. This question is very simple since the language of all words is $(a \mid b)^*$, we have to remove ϵ, *i.e.,* one simple answer is $(a \mid b)^+$.

3. The question implies that the words we are looking for are of the form $\ldots a \_\_$ where the dots stand for 'any sequence of a and b' and each '$\_$' stands for a regular expression denoting any letter.

Any letter is described by $(a\,|\,b)$; therefore one possible answer is $(a\,|\,b)^\star a\,(a\,|\,b)\,(a\,|\,b)$.

4. The words we search contain, at any place, exactly three a, so are of the form $\ldots a \ldots a \ldots a \ldots$, where the dots stand for 'any letter except a', *i.e.*, 'any number of b'. In other words: $b^\star ab^\star ab^\star ab^\star$.

5. Because the alphabet contains only two letters, the question is equivalent to: 'All words containing the substring ab', *i.e.*, the words are of the form $\ldots ab \ldots$ where the dots stand for 'any sequence of a and b'. It is then easy to understand that a short answer is $(a\,|\,b)^\star ab(a\,|\,b)^\star$.

6. Because the alphabet is made only of two letters, the answer is easy: we put first all the a and then all the b: $a^\star b^\star$.

7. Since the alphabet contains only two letters, the only way to not repeat a letter is to only have substrings ab or ba in the words we look for. In other words: $abab \ldots ab$ or $abab \ldots aba$ or $baba \ldots ba$ or $baba \ldots bab$. In short: $(ab)^\star a?\,|\,(ba)^\star b?$ or, even shorter: $a?(ba)^\star b?$.

Question 3. Try to simplify the regular expressions $(\epsilon\,|\,a^\star\,|\,b^\star\,|\,a\,|\,b)^\star$ and $a(a\,|\,b)^\star b\,|\,(ab)^\star\,|\,(ba)^\star$.

Answer 3.

1. The first regular expression can be simplified in the following way:

$$\begin{aligned}
(\epsilon\,|\,a^\star\,|\,b^\star\,|\,a\,|\,b)^\star &= (\epsilon\,|\,a^\star\,|\,b^\star\,|\,b)^\star, &&\text{since } L(a) \subset L(a^\star);\\
&= (\epsilon\,|\,a^\star\,|\,b^\star)^\star, &&\text{since } L(b) \subset L(b^\star);\\
&= (\epsilon\,|\,a^+\,|\,b^+)^\star, &&\text{since } \{\epsilon\} \subset L(x^\star);\\
&= (a^+\,|\,b^+)^\star, &&\text{since } (\epsilon\,|\,x)^\star = x^\star.
\end{aligned}$$

Words in $L((a^+\,|\,b^+)^\star)$ are of the form ϵ or $(a \ldots a)\,(b \ldots b)\,(a \ldots a)\,(b \ldots b) \ldots$, where the ellipsis stands for 'none or many times'. So we recognise $(a\,|\,b)^\star$. Therefore $(\epsilon\,|\,a^\star\,|\,b^\star\,|\,a\,|\,b)^\star = (a\,|\,b)^\star$.

2. The second regular expression can be simplified in the following way. We note first that the expression is made of the disjunction of three regular sub-expressions (*i.e.*, it is a union of three sub-languages). The simplest idea is then to check whether one of these sub-languages is redundant, *i.e.*, if one is included in another. If so, we can simply remove it from the expression.

$$a(a\,|\,b)^\star b\,|\,(ab)^\star\,|\,(ba)^\star = a(a\,|\,b)^\star b\,|\,\epsilon\,|\,(ab)^+\,|\,(ba)^\star,$$

$$\text{since } (ab)^\star = \epsilon \,|\, (ab)^+;$$
$$= a(a\,|\,b)^\star b \,|\, (ab)^+ \,|\, (ba)^\star,$$
$$\text{since } \{\epsilon\} \subset L((ba)^\star).$$

We have:

$$(ab)^+ = (ab)(ab)\ldots(ab)$$
$$= a(ba)(ba)\ldots(ba)b \,|\, ab$$
$$= a(ba)^\star b.$$

Also $L((ba)) \subset L((a\,|\,b)^\star)$ and then $L((ba)^\star) \subset L((a\,|\,b)^\star)$, because $(a\,|\,b)^\star$ denotes all the words. Therefore

$$L(a(ba)^\star b) \subset L(a(a\,|\,b)^\star b)$$
$$L((ab)^+) \subset L(a(a\,|\,b)^\star b)$$

As a consequence, one possible answer is

$$a(a\,|\,b)^\star b \,|\, (ab)^\star \,|\, (ba)^\star = a(a\,|\,b)^\star b \,|\, (ba)^\star.$$

The intersection between $L(a(a\,|\,b)^\star b)$ and $L((ba)^\star)$ is empty because all the words of the former start with a, while all the words of the other start with b (or is ϵ). Therefore we cannot simply further this way.

13.3   Specifying lexers with Lex

Several tools have been built for constructing lexical analysers from special-purpose notations based on regular expressions. We shall now describe one of these tools, named Lex, which is widely used in software projects developed in C. Using this tool shows how the specification of patterns using regular expressions can be combined with actions, *e.g.*, making entries into a symbol table, that a lexer may be required to perform. We refer to the tool as the *Lex compiler* and to its input specification as the *Lex language*. Lex is generally used in the following manner:

Lex source lex.l	$\longrightarrow$ Lex compiler $\longrightarrow$	lex.yy.c
lex.yy.c	$\longrightarrow$ C compiler $\longrightarrow$	a.out
character stream	$\longrightarrow$ a.out $\longrightarrow$	token stream

Lex specifications

A Lex specification (or source or program) consists of three parts:

```
declarations
%%
translation rules
%%
user code
```

The *declarations section* includes declarations of C variables, constants and regular definitions. The latter are used in the translation rules. The *translation rules* of a Lex program are statements of the form

$$p_1 \quad \{action_1\}$$
$$p_2 \quad \{action_2\}$$
$$\cdots \qquad \cdots$$
$$p_n \quad \{action_n\}$$

where each p_i is a regular expression and each $action_i$ is a C program fragment describing what action the lexer should take when pattern p_i matches a lexeme. The third section holds whatever *user code* (auxiliary procedures) are needed by the actions. A lexer created by Lex interacts with a parser in the following way:

1. the parser calls the lexer;
2. the lexer starts reading its current input characters;
3. when the longest prefix of the input matches a regular expression p_i, the corresponding $action_i$ is executed;
4. finally, two cases occur whether $action_i$ returns control to the parser or not:

   (a) if so, the lexer returns the recognised token and lexeme;
   (b) if not, the lexer forgets about the recognised word and go to step 2.

Declarations

Let us consider the following excerpt of an example:

```
%{ /* definitions of constants
       LT, LE, EQ, GT, GE, IF, THEN, ELSE, ID, NUM, RELOP */
%}

/* regular definitions */
```

```
ws          [ \t\n]+
letter      [A-Za-z]
digit       [0-9]
id          {letter}({letter}|{digit})*
num         {digit}+(\.{digit}+)?(E[+\-]?{digit}+)?
```

First, we see a section where tokens are declared. If Lex is used in conjunction with a parser (as is the case in a compiler), those tokens may
be instead declared by the parser. In Lex, the token declarations are surrounded by %{ and %}, and anything between these brackets is copied
verbatim in lex.yy.c.

Second, we see a series of regular definitions, each consisting of a
name and a regular expression denoted by that name. For instance, delim
stands for the *character class* [\t\n], that is, any of the three characters:
blank, tabulation (\t) or newline (\n).

If we want to denote a set of letters or digits, it is often unwieldy to
enumerate all the elements, like the **digit** regular expression. So, instead
of 4 | 1 | 2 we would shortly write [142]. If the characters are consecutively
ordered, we can use *intervals*, called in Lex *character classes*. For instance,
we write [a-c] instead of a | b | c. Or [0-9] instead of 0 | 1 | 2 | 3 | 4 | 5 |
6 | 7 | 8 | 9. We can now describe identifiers in a very compact way:

$$[A\text{-}Za\text{-}z][A\text{-}Za\text{-}z0\text{-}9]^*$$

It is possible to have ']' and '-' in a character range: the character ']'
must be first and '-' must be first or last.

The second definition is of white space, denote by the name ws. Note
that we must write {delim} for **delim**, with braces inside regular expressions in order to distinguish it from the pattern made of the five letters
delim. The definitions of letter and digit illustrate the use of character classes (interval of (ordered) characters). The definition of id shows
the use of some Lex special symbols (or *metasymbols*): parentheses and
vertical bar.

The definition of num introduces a few more features. There is another metasymbol '?' with the obvious meaning. We notice the use of a
backslash to make a character mean itself instead of being interpreted
as a metasymbol: '\.' means 'the dot character', while '.' (metasymbol)
means 'any character'. This works with any metasymbol.

Note finally that we wrote [+\-] because, in this context, the character '-' has the meaning of 'range', as in [0-9], so we must add a backslash.
This action is called *to escape* (a character). Another way of escaping a
character is to use double-quotes around it, like ".".

Translation rules

The next section contains the translation rules.

```
%%
{ws}      { /* no action and no return */ }
if        { return IF; }
then      { return THEN; }
else      { return ELSE; }
{id}      { yylval = lexeme(); return ID; }
{number} { yylval = lexeme(); return NUM; }
"<"       { return LT; }
"<="      { return LE; }
"="       { return EQ; }
"<>"      { return NE; }
">"       { return GT; }
">="      { return GE; }
```

The translation rules follow the first %%. The first rule says that if the
regular expression denoted by the name ws maximally matches the input,
we take no action. In particular, we do not return to the parser. Therefore,
by default, this implies that the lexer will start again to recognise a token
after skipping white spaces. The second rule says that if the letters if are
seen, return the token IF. In the rule for {id}, we see two statements in
the action. First, the Lex predefined variable yylval is set to the lexeme
and the token ID is returned to the parser. The variable yylval is shared
with the parser (it is defined in lex.yy.c) and is used to pass attributes
about the token.

User code

Contrary to our previous presentation, the procedure lexeme takes here
no argument. This is because the input buffer is directly and globally
accessed in Lex through the pointer yytext, which corresponds to the
first character in the buffer when the analysis started for the last time.
The length of the lexeme is given via the variable yyleng. We do not show
the details of the auxiliary procedures but the trailing section should look
like as follows:

```
%%
char* lexeme () {
  /* returns a copy of the matched string
     between yytext[0] and yytext[yyleng-1] */
}
```

Longest-prefix match

If several regular expressions match the input, Lex chooses the rule which matches the most text. This is why the input if123 is matched, that is, recognised, as an identifier and not as the keyword if and the number 123. If Lex finds two or more matches of the same length, the rule listed *first* in the Lex input file is chosen. That is why we listed the patterns if, then and else before {id}. For example, the input if is matched by if and {id}, so the first rule is chosen, and since we want the token keyword if, its regular expression is written *before* {id}.

It is possible to use Lex without a parser. For instance, let count.l be the following Lex specification:

```
%{
int char_count=1, line_count=1;
%}
%%
.  {char_count++;}
\n {line_count++; char_count++;}
%%
int main () {
  yylex();  /* Calls the lexer */
  printf("There were %d characters in %d lines.\n",
         char_count,line_count);
  return 0;
}
```

We have to compile the Lex specification into C code, then compile this C code and link the object code against a special library named l:

```
lex -t count.l > count.c
gcc -c -o count.o count.c
gcc -o counter count.o -ll
```

We can also use the C compiler cc with the same options instead of gcc. The result is a binary counter that we can apply on count.l itself:

```
cat count.l | counter
There were 210 characters in 12 lines.
```

We can extend the previous specification to count words as well. For this, we need to define a regular expression for letters and bind it to a name, at the end of the declarations.

```
%{
int char_count=1, line_count=1, word_count=0;
%}
letter [A-Za-z]
%%
{letter}+ { word_count++; char_count += yyleng;
            printf ("[%s]\n",yytext); }
.           { char_count++; }
\n          { line_count++; char_count++; }
%%
...
```

We can also use more regular expressions with names.

```
letter [A-Za-z]
digit  [0-9]
alpha  ({letter}|{digit})      /* No space inside! */
id     {letter}([_]*{alpha})*  /* No space inside! */
%%
{id} { word_count++; char_count += yyleng;
       printf ("word=[%s]\n",yytext); }
.    { char_count++; }
\n   { line_count++; char_count++; }
```

By default, if there is no parser and no explicit `main` procedure, Lex will add one in the produced C code as if it were given in the user code section (at the end of the specification) as

```
int main () {
 yylex();
 return 0;
}
```

13.4 Token recognition

Until now we showed how to specify tokens. Now we show how to recognise them, *i.e.*, realise lexical analysis. Let us consider the following token definition:

$$\textbf{if} \rightarrow \texttt{if}$$
$$\textbf{then} \rightarrow \texttt{then}$$
$$\textbf{else} \rightarrow \texttt{else}$$
$$\textbf{relop} \rightarrow \texttt{<} \mid \texttt{<=} \mid \texttt{=} \mid \texttt{<>} \mid \texttt{>} \mid \texttt{>=}$$

$$\textbf{digit} \rightarrow [\text{0-9}]$$
$$\textbf{letter} \rightarrow [\text{A-Za-z}]$$
$$\textbf{id} \rightarrow \textbf{letter} \ (\textbf{letter} \mid \textbf{digit})^*$$
$$\textbf{num} \rightarrow \textbf{digit}^+ \ (. \ \textbf{digit}^+)? \ (\textsf{E} \ (+ \mid \ -)? \ \textbf{digit}^+)?$$

Reserved identifiers and white space   Keywords are commonly considered as *reserved identifiers, i.e.,* in this case, a valid identifier cannot be any token **if**, **then** or **else**. This is usually not specified, but, instead, programmed. In addition, let us assume that the lexemes are separated by white spaces, consisting of non-null sequences of blanks, tabulations and newline characters. The lexer usually strips out those white spaces by comparing them to the regular definition **white_space**:

$$\textbf{delim} \rightarrow \textbf{blank} \mid \textbf{tab} \mid \textbf{newline}$$
$$\textbf{white\_space} \rightarrow \textbf{delim}^+$$

If a match for **white_space** is found, the lexer does *not* return a token to the parser. Rather, it proceeds to find a token following the white space and return it to the parser.

Input buffer   The stream of characters that provides the input to the lexer comes usually from a file. For efficiency reasons, when this file is opened, a *buffer* is associated, so the lexer actually reads its characters from this buffer in memory. A buffer is like a *queue*, or *FIFO* (*First in, First out*), that is, a list whose one end is used to put elements in and whose other end is used to get elements out, one at a time. The only difference is that a buffer has a *fixed size* (hence a buffer can be full). An empty buffer of size three is depicted as follows:

$$\text{output side} \longleftarrow \boxed{\ \ | \ \ | \ \ } \longleftarrow \text{input side}$$

If we input characters A then B in this buffer, we draw

$$\text{lexer} \quad \longleftarrow \quad \boxed{\ \ |\text{A}|\text{B}} \quad \longleftarrow \quad \text{file}$$
$$\uparrow$$

The symbol $\upharpoonright$ is a pointer to the next character available for output. Let keep in mind that the blank character will now be noted '␣', in order to avoid confusion with an empty cell in a buffer. So, if we input now a blank in our buffer from the file, we get the full buffer

$$\text{lexer} \quad \longleftarrow \quad \boxed{\text{A}|\text{B}|␣} \quad \longleftarrow \quad \text{file}$$
$$\uparrow$$

and no more inputs are possible until at least one output is done. Let us be careful: a buffer is full if and only if ⌈ points to the leftmost character. For example,

$$\text{lexer} \longleftarrow \boxed{A\,B\,\lrcorner} \longleftarrow \text{file}$$
$$\uparrow$$

is *not* a full buffer: there is still room for one character. If we input C, it becomes

$$\text{lexer} \longleftarrow \boxed{B\,\lrcorner\,C} \longleftarrow \text{file}$$
$$\uparrow$$

which is now a full buffer. The overflowing character A has been discarded. Now, if we output a character (or, equivalently, the lexer inputs a character) we get

$$\text{lexer} \longleftarrow \boxed{B\,\lrcorner\,C} \longleftarrow \text{file}$$
$$\uparrow$$

Let us output another character:

$$\text{lexer} \longleftarrow \boxed{B\,\lrcorner\,C} \longleftarrow \text{file}$$
$$\uparrow$$

Now, if the lexer needs a character, C is output and some routine automatically reads some more characters from the disk and fill them in order into the buffer. This happens when we output the rightmost character. Assuming the next character in the file is D, after outputting C we get

$$\text{lexer} \longleftarrow \boxed{\lrcorner\,C\,D} \longleftarrow \text{file}$$
$$\uparrow$$

If the buffer only contains the *end-of-file* character (noted here **eof**), it means that no more characters are available from the file. So, if we have the situation

$$\text{lexer} \longleftarrow \boxed{\cdots\,\mathbf{eof}} \longleftarrow \text{empty file}$$
$$\uparrow$$

in which the lexer requests a character, it would get **eof** and subsequent requests would fail, because both the buffer and the file would be empty.

Transition diagrams   As an intermediary step in the construction of a
lexical analyser, we introduce another concept, called *transition diagram*.
Transition diagrams depict the actions that take place when a lexer is
called by a parser to get the next token. *States* in a transition diagram
are drawn as circles. Some states have double circles, with or without an
asterisk *. States are connected by arrows, called *edges*, each one carrying
an input character as *label*, or the special label *other*. An example of such
transition diagram is given in FIGURE 13.7. Double-circled states are
called *final states*. The special arrow which does not connect two states
points to the *initial state*. A state in the transition diagram corresponds
to the state of the input buffer, *i.e.*, its contents and the output pointer
at a given moment. At the initial state, the buffer contains at least one
character. If the only one remaining character is **eof**, the lexer returns a
special token **$** to the parser and stops. Let us assume that the character c
is pointed by $\uparrow$ in the input buffer and that c is not **eof**, depicted as
follows:

$$\text{lexer} \quad \longleftarrow \quad \boxed{\cdots\,|c|\,\cdots} \quad \longleftarrow \quad \text{file}$$
$$\uparrow$$

When the parser requests a token, if an edge to the state s has a label with
character c, then the current state in the transition diagram becomes s,
and c is removed from the buffer. This is repeated until a final state is
reached or we get stuck. If a final state is reached, it means the lexer
recognised a token – which is in turn returned to the parser. Otherwise
a lexical error occurred.

Let us consider again the diagram in FIGURE 13.7 and let us assume
that the initial input buffer is

$$\text{lexer} \quad \longleftarrow \quad \boxed{\;\;|>|=|\_|1|} \quad \longleftarrow \quad \text{file}$$
$$\uparrow$$

From the initial state 1 to the state 2 there is an arrow with the label
'>'. Because this label is present at the output position of the buffer, we
can change the diagram state to 2 and remove '<' from the buffer, which
becomes

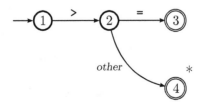

Figure 13.7: A transition diagram

$$\text{lexer} \longleftarrow \boxed{\;|>|=|\textvisiblespace|1|} \longleftarrow \text{file}$$

From state 2 to state 3 there is an arrow with label '=', so we remove it:

$$\text{lexer} \longleftarrow \boxed{\;|>|=|\textvisiblespace|1|} \longleftarrow \text{file}$$

and we move to state 3. Since state 3 is a final state, we are done: we recognised the token **relop**⟨>=⟩. Let us imagine now the input buffer is

$$\text{lexer} \longleftarrow \boxed{\;|>|1|+|2|} \longleftarrow \text{file}$$

In this case, we will move from the initial state to state 2:

$$\text{lexer} \longleftarrow \boxed{\;|>|1|+|2|} \longleftarrow \text{file}$$

We cannot use the edge with label '=', but we can use the one with '*other*'. Indeed, the '*other*' label refers to any character that is not indicated by any of the edges leaving the state. Hence, we move to state 4 and the input buffer becomes

$$\text{lexer} \longleftarrow \boxed{\;|>|1|+|2|} \longleftarrow \text{file}$$

and the lexer emits the token **relop**⟨>⟩. But there is a problem here: if the parser requests another token, we have to start again with this buffer but we already skipped the character $\boxed{1}$ and we forgot where the recognised lexeme starts. The idea is to use another arrow to mark the starting position when we try to recognise a token. Let ↿ be this new pointer. Then the initial buffer of our previous example would be depicted as

$$\text{lexer} \longleftarrow \boxed{\;|>|1|+|\cdots} \longleftarrow \text{file}$$

When the lexer reads the next available character, the pointer ↾ is shifted to the right of one position.

$$\text{lexer} \longleftarrow \boxed{\;|>|1|+|\cdots} \longleftarrow \text{file}$$

We are now at state 2 and the current character, that is, pointed by ↾, is 1. The only way to continue is to go to state 4, using the special label *other*. The pointer of the secondary buffer shifts to the right and, since it points to the last position, we input one character from the primary buffer:

$$\text{lexer} \longleftarrow \boxed{\quad |>|1|+|\cdots|} \longleftarrow \text{file}$$
$$\quad\quad\quad\quad\quad\quad\uparrow\quad\uparrow$$

State 4 is a final state a bit special: it is marked with '*'. This means that before emitting the recognised lexeme we have to shift the current pointer by one position *to the left*:

$$\text{lexer} \longleftarrow \boxed{\quad |>|1|+|\cdots|} \longleftarrow \text{file}$$
$$\quad\quad\quad\quad\quad\uparrow\;\uparrow$$

This allows to recover the character $\boxed{1}$ *as current character.* Moreover, the recognised lexeme now always starts at the pointer ↑ and ends one position before the pointer ⌐. So, here, the lexer outputs the lexeme '>'. Actually, we can complete our token specification by adding some extra information that are useful for the recognition process, as just described. First, it is convenient for some tokens, like **relop**, not to carry the lexeme verbatim, but a symbolic name instead, which is independent of the actual size of the lexeme. For instance, we shall write **relop**⟨GT⟩ instead of **relop**⟨>⟩. Second, it is useful to write the recognised token and the lexeme close to the final state in the transition diagram itself. See FIGURE 13.8. Similarly, FIGURE 13.9 on the facing page shows all the relational operators.

Identifiers and longest prefix match   A transition diagram for specifying identifiers is given in FIGURE 13.10 on the next page. lexeme is a function call which returns the recognised lexeme, as found in the buffer. The *other* label on the last step to final state force the identifier to be of *maximal length*. For instance, given counter+1, the lexer will recognise counter as identifier and not just count. This is called *the longest prefix* property.

Keywords   Since keywords are sequences of letters, they are exceptions to the rule that a sequence of letters and digits starting with a letter is an identifier. One solution for specifying keywords is to use dedicated

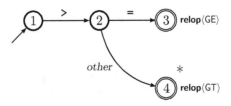

Figure 13.8: Completion of FIGURE 13.7 on page 536

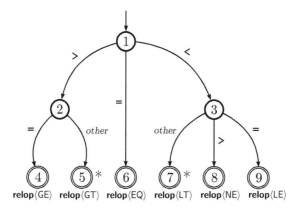

Figure 13.9: Relational operators

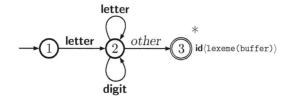

Figure 13.10: Transition diagram for identifiers

transition diagrams, one for each keyword. For example, the **if** keyword is simply specified in FIGURE 13.11. If one keyword diagram succeeds, *i.e.*, the lexer reaches a final state, then the corresponding keyword is transmitted to the parser; otherwise, another keyword diagram is tried after shifting the current pointer ⌐ in the input buffer back to the starting position, *i.e.*, pointed by ⌐.

There is a problem, though. Consider the OCaml language, where there are two keywords **fun** and **function**. If the diagram of **fun** is tried successfully on the input `function` and then the diagram for identifiers, the lexer outputs the lexemes **fun** and **id**⟨ction⟩ instead of one keyword **function**. As for identifiers, we want the longest prefix property to hold for keywords too and this is simply achieved by *ordering the transition diagrams*. For example, the diagram of **function** must be tried before the one for **fun** because **fun** is a prefix of **function**. This strategy implies that the diagram for the identifiers (given in FIGURE 13.10 on page 539)

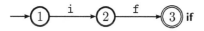

Figure 13.11: Transition diagram for **if**

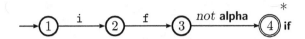

Figure 13.12: Completion of FIGURE 13.11 on the previous page

must appear *after* the diagrams for the keywords.

There are still several drawbacks with this technique, though. The first problem is that if we indeed have the longest prefix property among keywords, it does not hold with respect to the identifiers. For instance, iff would lead to the keyword **if** and the identifier f, instead of the (longest and sole) identifier iff. This can be remedied by forcing the keyword diagram to recognise a keyword and not an identifier. This is done by failing if the keyword is followed by a letter or a digit (remember we try the longest keywords first, otherwise we would miss some keywords — the ones which have prefix keywords). The way to specify this is to use a special label *not* such that *not c* denotes the set of characters which are *not c*. Actually, the special label *other* can always be represented using this *not* label because *other* means 'not the others labels'. Therefore, the completed **if** transition diagram would be as found in FIGURE 13.12. where **alpha** (which stands for alpha-numerical') is defined by the following regular definition:

$$\textbf{alpha} \rightarrow \textbf{letter} \mid \textbf{digit}$$

The second problem with this approach is that we have to create a transition diagram for each keyword and a state for each of their letters. In real programming languages, this means that we get hundreds of states only for the keywords. This problem can be avoided if we change our technique and give up the specification of keywords with transition diagrams.

Since keywords are a strict subset of identifiers, let us use only the identifier diagram but *we change the action at the final state, i.e.,* instead of always returning a **id** token, we make some computations first to decide whether it is either a keyword or an identifier. Let us call switch the function which makes this decision based on the buffer (equivalently, the current diagram state) and a *table of keywords*. The

Keywords	
Lexeme	Token
if	**if**
then	**then**
else	**else**

specification is shown in FIGURE 13.13 on the facing page. The table of keywords is a two-column table whose first column (the entry) contains the keyword lexemes and the second column the corresponding token. Let us write the code for switch in pseudo-language, in FIGURE 13.14

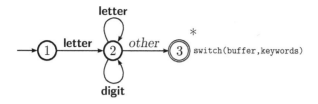

Figure 13.13: Transition diagram for keywords

SWITCH(*buffer*, *keywords*)

    str ← LEXEME(*buffer*)

    if *str* ∈ 𝒟(*keywords*)

        then SWITCH ← *keywords*[*str*]

        else SWITCH ← **id**⟨*str*⟩

Figure 13.14: Pseudo-code for function `switch`

on page 541. Function names are in uppercase, like LEXEME. Writing $x \leftarrow a$ means that we *assign* the value of the expression a to the variable x. Then the value of x is the value of a. The value $\mathcal{D}(t)$ is the first column of table t. The value $t[e]$ is the value corresponding to e in table t. SWITCH is also used as a special variable whose value becomes the result of the function SWITCH when it finishes.

Numbers   Let us consider now the numbers as specified by the regular definition

$$\textbf{num} \rightarrow \textbf{digit}^+ \ (\textbf{. digit}^+)? \ (\textsf{E} \ (\textbf{+} \ | \ \textbf{-})? \ \textbf{digit}^+)?$$

and propose a transition diagram in FIGURE 13.15 on the next page as an intermediary step to their recognition.

White spaces   The only remaining issue concerns white spaces as specified by the regular definition

$$\textbf{white\_space} \rightarrow \textbf{delim}^+$$

which is equivalent to the transition diagram in FIGURE 13.16 on the following page. The specificity of this diagram is that there is no action associated to the final state: no token is emitted.

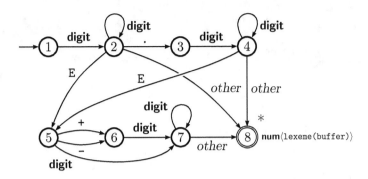

Figure 13.15: Transition diagram for numbers

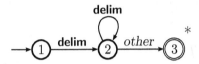

Figure 13.16: Transition diagram for white spaces

A simplification There is a simple away to reduce the size of the diagrams used to specify the tokens while retaining the longest prefix property: allow to pass through several final states. This way, we can actually also get rid of the '*' marker on final states. Coming back to the first example in FIGURE 13.8 on page 538, we would alternatively make up FIGURE 13.17. But we have to change the recognition process a little bit here in order to keep the longest prefix match: we do not want to stop at state 2 if we could recognise '>='.

The simplified complete version with respect to the one given in FIGURE 13.9 on page 539 is found in FIGURE 13.18 on the facing page. The transition diagram for specifying identifiers *and* keywords looks now like FIGURE 13.19 on the next page. The transition diagram for specifying numbers is simpler now, as seen in FIGURE 13.20 on the facing page.

How do we interpret these new transition diagrams, where the final states may have out-going edges (and the initial state have incoming edges)? For example, let us consider the recognition of a number:

$$\text{lexer} \longleftarrow \boxed{\text{a}\,|\,=\,|\,1\,|\,5\,|\,3\,|\,+\,|\,6\,|\,\cdots} \longleftarrow \text{file}$$

Figure 13.17: Alternative to FIGURE 13.8 on page 538

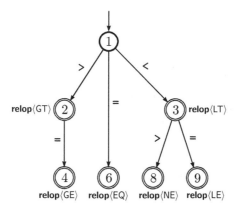

Figure 13.18: Simplification of FIGURE 13.9 on page 539

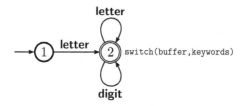

Figure 13.19: Simplification of FIGURE 13.13 on page 541

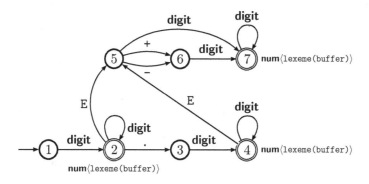

Figure 13.20: Simplification of FIGURE 13.15 on the facing page

As usual, if there is a label of an edge going out of the current state which matches the current character in the buffer, the pointer ⌈ is shifted to the right of one position. The new feature here is about final states. When the current state is final

1. the current position in the buffer is pointed to with a new pointer ⇑;
2. if there is an out-going edge which carries a matching character, we try to recognise a longer lexeme;

   (a) if we fail, *i.e.,* if we cannot go further in the diagram and the current state is not final, then we shift back the current pointer ⌈ to the position pointed by ⇑;
   (b) and return the then-recognised token and lexeme;

3. if not, we return the recognised token and lexeme associated to the current final state.

Following our example of number recognition:

- The label **digit** matches the current character in the buffer, *i.e.,* the one pointed by ⌈, so we move to state 2 and we shift right by one the pointer ⌈.

$$\text{lexer} \quad \longleftarrow \quad \boxed{a \mid = \mid 1 \mid 5 \mid 3 \mid + \mid 6} \cdots \quad \longleftarrow \quad \text{file}$$
$$\uparrow \ \uparrow$$

- The state 2 is final, so we set the pointer ⇑ to the current position in the buffer

$$\text{lexer} \quad \longleftarrow \quad \boxed{a \mid = \mid 1 \mid 5 \mid 3 \mid + \mid 6} \cdots \quad \longleftarrow \quad \text{file}$$
$$\uparrow \ \Uparrow\uparrow$$

- We shift right by one the current pointer and stay in state 2 because the matching edge is a loop (notice that we did not stop here).

$$\text{lexer} \quad \longleftarrow \quad \boxed{a \mid = \mid 1 \mid 5 \mid 3 \mid + \mid 6} \cdots \quad \longleftarrow \quad \text{file}$$
$$\uparrow \ \Uparrow \ \uparrow$$

- The state 2 is final so we set pointer ⇑ to point to the current position:

$$\text{lexer} \quad \longleftarrow \quad \boxed{a \mid = \mid 1 \mid 5 \mid 3 \mid + \mid 6} \cdots \quad \longleftarrow \quad \text{file}$$
$$\uparrow \qquad \Uparrow\uparrow$$

- The **digit** label of the loop matches again the current character (here **3**), so we shift right by one the current pointer.

$$\text{lexer} \longleftarrow \boxed{a\,|=|1|5|3|+|6|\cdots} \longleftarrow \text{file}$$

- Because state 2 is final we set the pointer $\Uparrow$ to the current pointer $\lceil$:

$$\text{lexer} \longleftarrow \boxed{a\,|=|1|5|3|+|6|\cdots} \longleftarrow \text{file}$$

- State 2 is final, so it means that we succeeded in recognising the token associated with state 2: **num**$\langle$lexeme(buffer)$\rangle$, whose lexeme is between $\lceil$ included and $\lceil$ excluded, *i.e.*, 153.

Let us consider the following initial buffer:

$$\text{lexer} \longleftarrow \boxed{a|=|1|5|.|+|6|\cdots} \longleftarrow \text{file}$$

Character 1 is read and we arrive at state 2 with the following situation:

$$\text{lexer} \longleftarrow \boxed{a|=|1|5|.|+|6|\cdots} \longleftarrow \text{file}$$

Then 5 is read and we arrive again at state 2 but we encounter a different situation:

$$\text{lexer} \longleftarrow \boxed{a|=|1|5|.|+|6|\cdots} \longleftarrow \text{file}$$

The label on the edge from state 2 to 3 matches '.' so we move to state 3, shift by one the current pointer in the buffer:

$$\text{lexer} \longleftarrow \boxed{a|=|1|5|.|+|6|\cdots} \longleftarrow \text{file}$$

Now we are stuck at state 3. Because this is not a final state, we should fail, *i.e.*, report a lexical error, but because the pointer $\Uparrow$ has been set (*i.e.*, we met a final state), we shift the current pointer back to the position of the pointer $\Uparrow$ and return the corresponding lexeme 15:

$$\text{lexer} \longleftarrow \boxed{a|=|1|5|.|+|6|\cdots} \longleftarrow \text{file}$$

13.5   Deterministic finite automata

Transition diagrams are useful graphical representations of instances of the mathematical concept of *deterministic finite automaton (DFA)*. Formally, a DFA $\mathcal{D}$ is a 5-tuple $\mathcal{D} = (Q, \Sigma, \delta, q_0, F)$ where

1. a finite set of *states*, often noted Q;
2. an *initial state* $q_0 \in Q$;
3. a set of *final (or accepting) states* $F \subseteq Q$;
4. a finite set of *input symbols*, often noted Σ;
5. a *transition function* δ that takes a state and an input symbol and returns a state: if q is a state with an edge labelled a, the edge leads to the state $\delta(q, a)$.

Recognised words

Independently of the interpretation of the states, we can define how a given word is accepted (or recognised) or rejected by a given DFA. For example, the word $a_1 a_2 \cdots a_n$, with $a_i \in \Sigma$, is recognised by the DFA $\mathcal{D} = (Q, \Sigma, \delta, q_0, F)$ if, for all $0 \leqslant i \leqslant n - 1$, there is a sequence of states $q_i \in Q$ such that $\delta(q_i, a_{i+1}) = q_{i+1}$ and $q_n \in F$. The language recognised by $\mathcal{D}$, noted $L(\mathcal{D})$ is the set of words recognised by $\mathcal{D}$. For example, consider the DFA in FIGURE 13.21. The word then is recognised because there is a sequence of states $(q_0, q_1, q_2, q_4, q_5)$ connected by edges which satisfies $\delta(q_0, \mathsf{t}) = q_1, \delta(q_1, \mathsf{h}) = q_2, \delta(q_2, \mathsf{e}) = q_4$ and $\delta(q_4, \mathsf{n}) = q_5$, with $q_5 \in F$, that is, q_5 is a final state.

Recognised language

It is easy to define formally $L(\mathcal{D})$. Let $\mathcal{D} = (Q, \Sigma, \delta, q_0, F)$. First, let us extend δ to words and let us call this extension $\hat{\delta}$:

- for all state $q \in Q$, let $\hat{\delta}(q, \varepsilon) = q$, where ε is the empty string;

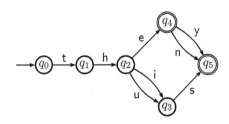

Figure 13.21: A trie recognising they, then, this and thus

- for all state $q \in Q$, all word $w \in \Sigma^*$, all input $a \in \Sigma$, let us define
$\hat{\delta}(q, wa) = \delta(\hat{\delta}(q, w), a)$.

Then the word w is recognised by $\mathcal{D}$ if $\hat{\delta}(q_0, w) \in F$. The language $L(\mathcal{D})$ recognised by $\mathcal{D}$ is defined as $L(\mathcal{D}) = \{w \in \Sigma^* \mid \hat{\delta}(q_0, w) \in F\}$. For example, in our last example:

$$\hat{\delta}(q_0, \epsilon) = q_0,$$
$$\hat{\delta}(q_0, \mathsf{t}) = \delta(\hat{\delta}(q_0, \epsilon), \mathsf{t}) = \delta(q_0, \mathsf{t}) = q_1,$$
$$\hat{\delta}(q_0, \mathsf{th}) = \delta(\hat{\delta}(q_0, \mathsf{t}), \mathsf{h}) = \delta(q_1, \mathsf{h}) = q_2,$$
$$\hat{\delta}(q_0, \mathsf{the}) = \delta(\hat{\delta}(q_0, \mathsf{th}), \mathsf{e}) = \delta(q_2, \mathsf{e}) = q_4,$$
$$\hat{\delta}(q_0, \mathsf{then}) = \delta(\hat{\delta}(q_0, \mathsf{the}), \mathsf{n}) = \delta(q_4, \mathsf{n}) = q_5 \in F.$$

Transition diagrams

We can also redefine transition diagrams in terms of the concept of DFA. A transition diagram for a DFA $\mathcal{D} = (Q, \Sigma, \delta, q_0, F)$ is a graph defined as follows:

1. for each state q in Q there is a *node, i.e.*, a single circle with q inside;
2. for each state $q \in Q$ and each input symbol $a \in \Sigma$, if $\delta(q, a)$ exists, then there is an *edge, i.e.*, an arrow, from the node denoting q to the node denoting $\delta(q, a)$ labelled by a; multiple edges can be merged into one and the labels are then separated by commas;
3. there is an edge coming to the node denoting q_0 without origin;
4. nodes corresponding to final states are doubly circled.

Here is a transition diagram for the language over alphabet $\{0, 1\}$, called *binary alphabet*, which contains the string 01:

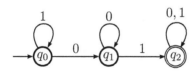

Transition table

There is a compact textual way to represent the transition function of a DFA: a *transition table*. The rows of the table correspond to the states and the columns correspond to the inputs (symbols). In other words, the entry for the row corresponding to state q and the column corresponding to input a is the state $\delta(q, a)$, as seen in FIGURE 13.22a. For instance,

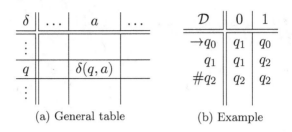

δ	$\ldots$	a	$\ldots$
$\vdots$			
q		$\delta(q, a)$	
$\vdots$			

(a) General table

$\mathcal{D}$	0	1
$\rightarrow q_0$	q_1	q_0
q_1	q_1	q_2
$\# q_2$	q_2	q_2

(b) Example

Figure 13.22: Transition tables

the transition table corresponding to the function δ of our last example is found in FIGURE 13.22b. Actually, we added some extra information in the table: the initial state is marked with $\rightarrow$ and the final states are marked with $\#$. Therefore, it is not only δ which is defined by means of the transition table here, but the whole DFA $\mathcal{D}$.

Let us consider another example. We want to define formally a DFA which recognises the language L whose words contain an even number of 0's and an even number of 1's (the alphabet is binary). We should understand that the role of the states here is to *not* count the exact number of 0's and 1's that have been recognised before, but, instead, this number *modulo 2*. Therefore, there are four states because there are four cases:

1. there has been an even number of 0's and 1's (state q_0);
2. there has been an even number of 0's and an odd number of 1's (state q_1);
3. there has been an odd number of 0's and an even number of 1's (state q_2);
4. there has been an odd number of 0's and 1's (state q_3).

What about the initial and final states?

- State q_0 is the initial state because before considering any input, the number of 0's and 1's is zero and zero is even;
- state q_0 is the lone final state because its definition matches exactly the characteristic of L and no other state matches.

We almost know now how to specify the DFA for the language L. It is

$$\mathcal{D} = (\{q_0, q_1, q_2, q_3\}, \{0, 1\}, \delta, q_0, \{q_0\}),$$

where the transition function δ is described by the transition diagram in FIGURE 13.23a on the next page. Notice how each input 0 causes the state to cross the horizontal line. Thus, after seeing an even number of

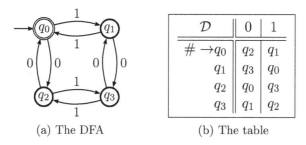

(a) The DFA (b) The table

$\mathcal{D}$	0	1
$\# \to q_0$	q_2	q_1
q_1	q_3	q_0
q_2	q_0	q_3
q_3	q_1	q_2

Figure 13.23: A deterministic finite automaton and its table

0's we are always above the horizontal line, in state q_0 or q_1, and after seeing an odd number of 0's we are always below this line, in state q_2 or q_3. There is a vertically symmetric situation for transitions on 1. We can also represent this DFA by the transition table in FIGURE 13.23b. We can use that table to illustrate the construction of $\hat{\delta}$ from δ. Suppose the input is 110101. Since this string has even numbers of 0's and 1's, it belongs to L, that is, we expect $\hat{\delta}(q_0, 110101) = q_0$, since q_0 is the sole final state. We can check this by computing step by step $\hat{\delta}(q_0, \texttt{110101})$, from the shortest prefix to the longest, which is the word $\texttt{110101}$ itself:

$$\hat{\delta}(q_0, \varepsilon) = q_0,$$
$$\hat{\delta}(q_0, \texttt{1}) = \delta(\hat{\delta}(q_0, \varepsilon), \texttt{1}) = \delta(q_0, \texttt{1}) = q_1,$$
$$\hat{\delta}(q_0, \texttt{11}) = \delta(\hat{\delta}(q_0, \texttt{1}), \texttt{1}) = \delta(q_1, \texttt{1}) = q_0,$$
$$\hat{\delta}(q_0, \texttt{110}) = \delta(\hat{\delta}(q_0, \texttt{11}), \texttt{0}) = \delta(q_0, \texttt{0}) = q_2,$$
$$\hat{\delta}(q_0, \texttt{1101}) = \delta(\hat{\delta}(q_0, \texttt{110}), \texttt{1}) = \delta(q_2, \texttt{1}) = q_3,$$
$$\hat{\delta}(q_0, \texttt{11010}) = \delta(\hat{\delta}(q_0, \texttt{1101}), \texttt{0}) = \delta(q_3, \texttt{0}) = q_1,$$
$$\hat{\delta}(q_0, \texttt{110101}) = \delta(\hat{\delta}(q_0, \texttt{11010}), \texttt{1}) = \delta(q_1, \texttt{1}) = q_0 \in F.$$

13.6 Non-deterministic finite automata

A *non-deterministic finite automaton* (*NFA*) has the same definition as a DFA except that δ returns a set of states instead of one state. Let us consider

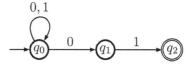

There are two out-going edges from state q_0 which are labelled 0, hence two states can be reached when 0 is input: q_0 (loop) and q_1. This NFA

recognises the language of words on the binary alphabet whose suffix
is 01.

Before describing formally what is a recognisable language by a NFA,
let us consider as an example the previous NFA and the input 00101.
Let us represent each transition for this input by an edge in a tree where
nodes are states of the NFA:

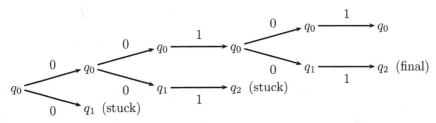

A NFA is represented essentially like a DFA: $\mathcal{N} = (Q_N, \Sigma, \delta_N, q_0, F_N)$,
where the names have the same interpretation as for DFA, except δ_N,
which returns a subset of Q – not an element of Q. For example, the
NFA above can be specified formally as

$$\mathcal{N} = (\{q_0, q_1, q_2\}, \{0, 1\}, \delta_N, q_0, \{q_2\})$$

where the transition function δ_N is given by the transition table

$\mathcal{N}$	0	1
$\rightarrow q_0$	$\{q_0, q_1\}$	$\{q_0\}$
q_1	$\varnothing$	$\{q_2\}$
$\#q_2$	$\varnothing$	$\varnothing$

Note that, in the transition table of a NFA, all the cells are filled: there
is no transition between two states if and only if the corresponding cell
contains $\varnothing$. In case of a DFA, the cell would remain empty. It is common
also to set that in case of the empty word input, ε, both for the DFA
and NFA, the state remains the same:

- for DFA: $\forall q \in Q.\delta_D(q, \varepsilon) = q$;
- for NFA: $\forall q \in Q.\delta_N(q, \varepsilon) = \{q\}$.

As we did for the DFAs, we can *extend the transition function* δ_N to
accept words and not just letters (labels). The extended function is noted
$\hat{\delta}_N$ and defined as

- for all state $q \in Q$, let $\hat{\delta}_N(q, \varepsilon) = \{q\}$;
- for all state $q \in Q$, all words $w \in \Sigma^*$, all input $a \in \Sigma$, let

$$\hat{\delta}_N(q, wa) = \bigcup_{q' \in \hat{\delta}_N(q,w)} \delta_N(q', a).$$

The language $L(\mathcal{N})$ recognised by a NFA $\mathcal{N}$ is defined as

$$L(\mathcal{N}) = \{w \in \Sigma^* \mid \hat{\delta}_N(q_0, w) \cap F \neq \varnothing\},$$

which means that the processing of the input stops successfully as soon as at least one current state belongs to F.

For example, let us use $\hat{\delta}_N$ to describe the processing of the input 00101 by the NFA on page 549:

1. $\hat{\delta}_N(q_0, \varepsilon) = q_0$,
2. $\hat{\delta}_N(q_0, \mathtt{0}) = \delta_N(q_0, \mathtt{0}) = \{q_0, q_1\}$,
3. $\hat{\delta}_N(q_0, \mathtt{00}) = \delta_N(q_0, \mathtt{0}) \cup \delta_N(q_1, \mathtt{0}) = \{q_0, q_1\} \cup \varnothing = \{q_0, q_1\}$,
4. $\hat{\delta}_N(q_0, \mathtt{001}) = \delta_N(q_0, \mathtt{1}) \cup \delta_N(q_1, \mathtt{1}) = \{q_0\} \cup \{q_2\} = \{q_0, q_2\}$,
5. $\hat{\delta}_N(q_0, \mathtt{0010}) = \delta_N(q_0, \mathtt{0}) \cup \delta_N(q_2, \mathtt{0}) = \{q_0, q_1\} \cup \varnothing = \{q_0, q_1\}$,
6. $\hat{\delta}_N(q_0, \mathtt{00101}) = \delta_N(q_0, \mathtt{1}) \cup \delta_N(q_1, \mathtt{1}) = \{q_0\} \cup \{q_2\} = \{q_0, q_2\} \ni q_2$.

Since q_2 is a final state, in fact $F = \{q_2\}$, we get $\hat{\delta}_N(q_0, \mathtt{00101}) \cap F \neq \varnothing$ thus the string 00101 is recognised by the NFA.

13.7 Equivalence of DFAs and NFAs

NFAs are easier to build than DFAs because one does not have to worry, for any state, of having out-going edges carrying a unique label. The surprising fact is that NFAs and DFAs actually have the same expressiveness, that is, all that can be defined by means of a NFA can also be defined with a DFA (the converse is trivial since a DFA is already a NFA). More precisely, there is a procedure, called *the subset construction*, which converts any NFA to a DFA.

Consider that, in a NFA, from a state q with several out-going edges with the same label a, the transition function δ_N leads, in general, to several states. The idea of the *subset construction* is to create a new automaton where these edges are merged. So we create a state p which corresponds to the set of states $\delta_N(q, a)$ in the NFA. Accordingly, we create a state r which corresponds to the set $\{q\}$ in the NFA. We create an edge labelled a between r and p. The important point is that *this edge is unique*. This is the first step to create a DFA from a NFA.

Graphically, instead of the non-determinism of FIGURE 13.24a on the following page, where we have $\delta_N(q, a) = \{p_0, p_1, \ldots, p_n\}$, we get the determinism of FIGURE 13.24b on the next page.

Let us present the complete algorithm for the subset construction.

Let us start from a NFA $\mathcal{N} = (Q_N, \Sigma, \delta_N, q_0, F_N)$. The goal is to construct a DFA $\mathcal{D} = (Q_D, \Sigma, \delta_D, \{q_0\}, F_D)$ such that $L(\mathcal{D}) = L(\mathcal{N})$.

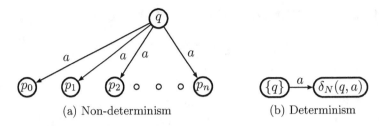

(a) Non-determinism   (b) Determinism

Figure 13.24: From non-determinism to determinism

Notice that the input alphabet of the two automata are the same and the initial state of $\mathcal{D}$ if the set containing only the initial state of $\mathcal{N}$.

The other components of $\mathcal{D}$ are constructed as follows. First, Q_D is the set of subsets of Q_N; that is, Q_D is the *power set* of Q_N. Thus, if Q_D has n states, Q_D has 2^n states. Fortunately, often not all these states are accessible from the initial state of Q_D, so these inaccessible states can be discarded.

Why is 2^n the number of subsets of a finite set of cardinal n?

Let us order the n elements and represent each subset by an n-bit string where bit i corresponds to the ith element: it is 1 if the ith element is present in the subset and 0 if not. This way, we counted all the subsets and not more (a bit cannot always be 0 since all elements are used to form subsets and cannot always be 1 if there is more than one element). There are 2 possibilities, 0 or 1, for the first bit; 2 possibilities for the second bit etc. Since the choices are independent, we multiply all of them: $\underbrace{2 \times 2 \times \cdots \times 2}_{n \text{ times}} = 2^n$, yielding the number of subsets of an n-element set.

Resuming the definition of DFA $\mathcal{D}$, the remaining components are defined as follows.

- F_D is the set of subsets S of Q_N such that $S \cap F_N \neq \varnothing$. That is, F_D is all sets of $\mathcal{N}$'s states that include at least one final state of $\mathcal{N}$.

- for each set $S \subseteq Q_N$ and for each input $a \in \Sigma$,

$$\delta_D(S, a) = \bigcup_{q \in S} \delta_N(q, a).$$

In other words, to compute $\delta_D(S, a)$, we look at all the states q in S, see what states of $\mathcal{N}$ are reached from q on input a and take the union of all those states to make the next state of $\mathcal{D}$.

Let us reconsider the NFA given by its transition table in FIGURE 13.25 on the facing page and let us create an equivalent DFA. Firstly, we form

NFA $\mathcal{N}$	0	1
$\rightarrow q_0$	$\{q_0, q_1\}$	$\{q_0\}$
q_1	$\varnothing$	$\{q_2\}$
$\# q_2$	$\varnothing$	$\varnothing$

Figure 13.25: Initial NFA table

DFA $\mathcal{D}$	0	1
$\varnothing$		
$\{q_0\}$		
$\{q_1\}$		
$\{q_2\}$		
$\{q_0, q_1\}$		
$\{q_0, q_2\}$		
$\{q_1, q_2\}$		
$\{q_0, q_1, q_2\}$		

(a) First stage

DFA $\mathcal{D}$	0	1
$\varnothing$		
$\rightarrow\{q_0\}$		
$\{q_1\}$		
$\#\{q_2\}$		
$\{q_0, q_1\}$		
$\#\{q_0, q_2\}$		
$\#\{q_1, q_2\}$		
$\#\{q_0, q_1, q_2\}$		

(b) Second stage

Figure 13.26: First two stages of the subset construction

all the subsets of the sets of the NFA and put them in the first column in FIGURE 13.26a.

Secondly, we annotate in this first column the states with $\rightarrow$ if and only if they contain the initial state of the NFA, here q_0, and we add a $\#$ if and only if the states contain at least a final state of the NFA, here q_2. See FIGURE 13.26b.

Thirdly, we form the subsets as follows:

DFA $\mathcal{D}$	0	1
$\varnothing$	$\varnothing$	$\varnothing$
$\rightarrow\{q_0\}$	$\delta_N(q_0, 0)$	$\delta_N(q_0, 1)$
$\{q_1\}$	$\delta_N(q_1, 0)$	$\delta_N(q_1, 1)$
$\#\{q_2\}$	$\delta_N(q_2, 0)$	$\delta_N(q_2, 1)$
$\{q_0, q_1\}$	$\delta_N(q_0, 0) \cup \delta_N(q_1, 0)$	$\delta_N(q_0, 1) \cup \delta_N(q_1, 1)$
$\#\{q_0, q_2\}$	$\delta_N(q_0, 0) \cup \delta_N(q_2, 0)$	$\delta_N(q_0, 1) \cup \delta_N(q_2, 1)$
$\#\{q_1, q_2\}$	$\delta_N(q_1, 0) \cup \delta_N(q_2, 0)$	$\delta_N(q_1, 1) \cup \delta_N(q_2, 1)$
$\#\{q_0, q_1, q_2\}$	$\delta_N(q_0, 0) \cup \delta_N(q_1, 0) \cup \delta_N(q_2, 0)$	$\delta_N(q_0, 1) \cup \delta_N(q_1, 1) \cup \delta_N(q_2, 1)$

Finally, we compute those subsets and obtain the table in FIGURE 13.27. The transition diagram of the DFA $\mathcal{D}$ is showed in FIGURE 13.28 on the next page where states with out-going edges which have no end are final states. If we look carefully at the transition diagram, we see that the DFA is actually made of two disconnected sub-automata. In particular, since

DFA $\mathcal{D}$	0	1
$\varnothing$	$\varnothing$	$\varnothing$
$\rightarrow \{q_0\}$	$\{q_0, q_1\}$	$\{q_0\}$
$\{q_1\}$	$\varnothing$	$\{q_2\}$
$\#\{q_2\}$	$\varnothing$	$\varnothing$
$\{q_0, q_1\}$	$\{q_0, q_1\}$	$\{q_0, q_2\}$
$\#\{q_0, q_2\}$	$\{q_0, q_1\}$	$\{q_0\}$
$\#\{q_1, q_2\}$	$\varnothing$	$\{q_2\}$
$\#\{q_0, q_1, q_2\}$	$\{q_0, q_1\}$	$\{q_0, q_2\}$

Figure 13.27: First DFA obtained

we have only one initial state, this means that one part is not accessible, therefore its states are never used to recognise or reject an input word, and we can remove this part, as shown in FIGURE 13.29a. It is important to understand that the states of the DFA are subsets of the NFA states. This is due to the construction and, when finished, it is possible to hide this by renaming the states. For example, we can rename the states of the previous DFA in the following manner: $\{q_0\}$ into A, $\{q_0, q_1\}$ in B and $\{q_0, q_2\}$ in C. So the transition table changes:

DFA $\mathcal{D}$	0	1
$\rightarrow \{q_0\}$	$\{q_0, q_1\}$	$\{q_0\}$
$\{q_0, q_1\}$	$\{q_0, q_1\}$	$\{q_0, q_2\}$
$\#\{q_0, q_2\}$	$\{q_0, q_1\}$	$\{q_0\}$

DFA $\mathcal{D}$	0	1
$\rightarrow A$	B	A
B	B	C
$\#C$	B	A

So, finally, the DFA is simply as in FIGURE 13.29b on the facing page.

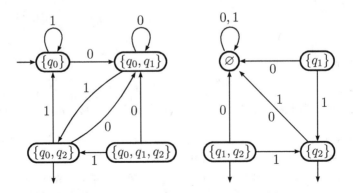

Figure 13.28: Transition diagram of FIGURE 13.27

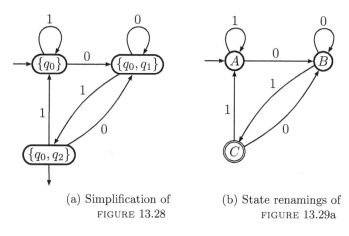

(a) Simplification of   (b) State renamings of
    FIGURE 13.28   FIGURE 13.29a

Figure 13.29: Simplifications

Optimisation

Even if in the worst case the resulting DFA has an exponential number
of states of the corresponding NFA, it is in practice often possible to
avoid the construction of inaccessible states.

- The singleton containing the initial state (in our example, $\{q_0\}$) is
  accessible;
- let us assume we have a set S of accessible states; then for each
  input symbol a, we compute $\delta_D(S, a)$: this new set is also accessible;
- let us repeat the last step, starting with $\{q_0\}$, until no new (accessible) sets are found.

Let us reconsider the NFA given by the transition table

NFA $\mathcal{N}$	0	1
$\rightarrow q_0$	$\{q_0, q_1\}$	$\{q_0\}$
q_1	$\varnothing$	$\{q_2\}$
$\# q_2$	$\varnothing$	$\varnothing$

Initially, the sole subset of accessible states is $\{q_0\}$:

DFA $\mathcal{D}$	0	1
$\rightarrow \{q_0\}$	$\delta_N(q_0, 0)$	$\delta_N(q_0, 1)$

that is

DFA $\mathcal{D}$	0	1
$\rightarrow \{q_0\}$	$\{q_0, q_1\}$	$\{q_0\}$

Therefore $\{q_0, q_1\}$ and $\{q_0\}$ are accessible sets, but $\{q_0\}$ is not a new set,
so we only add to the table entries $\{q_0, q_1\}$ and compute the transitions
from it:

DFA $\mathcal{D}$	0	1
$\rightarrow \{q_0\}$	$\{q_0, q_1\}$	$\{q_0\}$
$\{q_0, q_1\}$	$\{q_0, q_1\}$	$\{q_0, q_2\}$

This step uncovered a new set of accessible states, $\{q_0, q_2\}$, which we add to the table and repeat the procedure, and mark it as final state since $q_2 \in \{q_0, q_2\}$:

DFA $\mathcal{D}$	0	1
$\rightarrow \{q_0\}$	$\{q_0, q_1\}$	$\{q_0\}$
$\{q_0, q_1\}$	$\{q_0, q_1\}$	$\{q_0, q_2\}$
$\#\{q_0, q_2\}$	$\{q_0, q_1\}$	$\{q_0\}$

We are done since there are no more new accessible sets.

Tries

Lexical analysis tries to recognise a prefix of the input character stream (in other words, the first lexeme of the given program). Consider the C keywords **const** and **continue**:

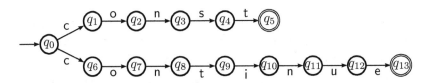

This example shows that a NFA is much more comfortable than a DFA for specifying tokens for lexical analysis: we design separately the automata for each token and then merge their initial states into one, leading to one, possibly large NFA. It is possible to apply the subset construction to this NFA.

After forming the corresponding NFA as in the previous example, it is actually easy to construct an equivalent DFA by sharing their prefixes, hence obtaining a tree-like automaton called *trie* (pronounced as the word 'try'):

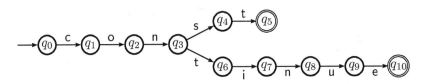

Note that this construction only works for a list of constant words, like keywords.

This technique can easily be generalised for searching constant strings (like keywords) in a text, that is, not only as a prefix of a text, but *at any position*. It suffices to add a loop on the initial state for each possible input symbol. If we note Σ the language alphabet, we get

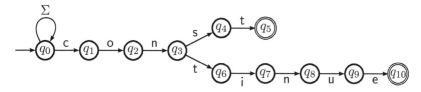

It is possible to apply the subset construction to this NFA or to use it directly for searching the two keywords at any position in a text. In case of direct use, the difference between this NFA and the trie one page 556 is that there is no need here to 'restart' by hand the recognition process once a keyword has been recognised: we just continue. This works because of the loop on the initial state, which always allows a new start. (The reader may try for instance the input `constantcontinue`.)

The subset construction can lead, in the worst case, to a number of states which is the total number of state subsets of the NFA. In other words, if the NFA has n states, the equivalent DFA by subset construction can have 2^n states (see page 552 for the count of all the subsets of a finite set). For instance, consider the following NFA, which recognises all binary strings which have 1 at the nth position from the end:

The language recognised by this NFA is $\Sigma^* 1 \Sigma^{n-1}$, where $\Sigma = \{0,1\}$, that is: all words of length greater or equal to n are accepted as long as the nth bit from the *end* is 1. Therefore, in any equivalent DFA, all the prefixes of length n should not lead to a stuck state, because the automaton must wait until the *end* of the word to accept or reject it. If the states reached by these prefixes are all different, then there are at least 2^n states in the DFA. Equivalently (by contraposition), if there are less than 2^n states, then some states can be reached by several strings of length n:

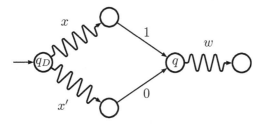

where words $x1w$ and $x'0w$ have length n. Let us define the DFA as follows: $\mathcal{D} = (Q_D, \Sigma, \delta_D, q_D, F_D)$, where $q_D = \{q_0\}$. The extended transition function is noted $\hat{\delta}_D$ as usual. The situation of the previous picture can be formally expressed as

$$\hat{\delta}_D(q_D, x1) = \hat{\delta}_D(q_D, x'0) = q, \qquad (13.1)$$
$$|x1w| = |x'0w| = n,$$

where $|u|$ is the length of u. Let y be a any string of 0 and 1 such that $|wy| = n - 1$. Then $\hat{\delta}_D(q_D, x1wy) \in F_D$ since there is a 1 at the nth position from the end:

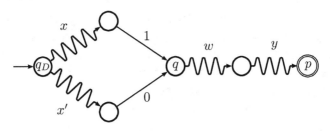

Also, $\hat{\delta}_D(q_D, x'0wy) \notin F_D$ because there is a 0 at the nth position from the end. On the other hand, equation (13.1) implies

$$\hat{\delta}_D(q_D, x1wy) = \hat{\delta}_D(q_D, x'0wy) = p.$$

So we stumble upon a contradiction because a state (p) must be either final or not final, it cannot be both. As a consequence, we must reject our initial assumption: there are at least 2^n states in the equivalent DFA. This is a very bad case, even if it is not the worst case (2^{n+1} states).

13.8   NFA with ϵ-transitions

We shall now introduce another extension to NFA, called ϵ-NFA, which is a NFA whose labels can be the empty string, noted ϵ. The interpretation of this new kind of transition, called ϵ-transition, is that the current state changes by following this transition *without reading any input*. This is sometimes referred as a *spontaneous transition*. The rationale is that $\epsilon a = a\epsilon = a$, so recognising ϵa or $a\epsilon$ is the same as recognising a. In other words, we do not need to read something more than a as input.

For example, the FIGURE 13.30 on the next page specifies signed natural and decimal numbers by means of the ϵ-NFA. This is not the simplest ϵ-NFA we can imagine for these numbers, but note the utility of the ϵ-transition between q_0 and q_1. In case of lexical analysers, ϵ-NFAs enable the separate design of a NFA for each token, then create an initial (respectively, final) state connected to all their initial (respectively, final) states with an ϵ-transition.

For instance, for keywords **fun** and **function** and identifiers, we have

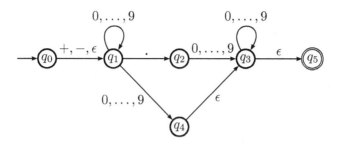

Figure 13.30: Signed natural and decimal numbers

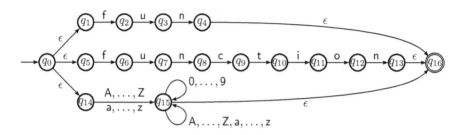

In lexical analysis, once we have a single ε-NFA, we can

- either remove all the ε-transitions and either create a NFA and then maybe a DFA, or create directly a DFA;

- or use a formal definition of ε-NFA that directly leads to a recognition algorithm, just as we did for DFAs and NFAs.

Both methods assume that it is always possible to create an equivalent NFA, hence a DFA, from a given ε-NFA. In other words, *DFA, NFA and ε-NFA have the same expressive power.*

The first method constructs explicitly the NFA and maybe the DFA, while the second does not, at the possible cost of more computations at run-time.

Before entering into the details, we need to define formally an ε-NFA, as suggested by the second method. The only difference between an NFA and an ε-NFA is that the transition function δ_E takes as second argument an element in $\Sigma \cup \{\epsilon\}$, with $\epsilon \notin \Sigma$, instead of Σ – but the alphabet still remains Σ.

ε-closure

We need now a function called *ε-close*, which takes an ε-NFA $\mathcal{E}$, a state q of $\mathcal{E}$ and returns all the states which are accessible in $\mathcal{E}$ from q with label ϵ. The idea is to achieve a *depth-first traversal* of $\mathcal{E}$, starting from q and following only ϵ-transitions. Let us call ϵ-DFS ('ϵ-Depth-First-Search') the function such that ϵ-DFS(q, Q) is the set of states reachable from q following ϵ-transitions and which is not included in Q, Q *being interpreted as the set of states already visited in the traversal.* The set Q ensures the termination of the algorithm even in presence of cycles in the automaton. Therefore, let

$$\epsilon\text{-close}(q) = \epsilon\text{-DFS}(q, \varnothing), \quad \text{if } q \in Q_E,$$

where the ϵ-NFA is $\mathcal{E} = (Q_E, \Sigma, \delta_E, q_0, F_E)$. Now we define ϵ-DFS as follows:

$$\epsilon\text{-DFS}(q, Q) = \varnothing, \qquad\qquad\qquad\qquad\qquad \text{if } q \in Q; \quad (13.2)$$

$$\epsilon\text{-DFS}(q, Q) = \{q\} \;\cup\; \bigcup_{p \in \delta_E(q,\epsilon)} \epsilon\text{-DFS}(p, Q \cup \{q\}), \quad \text{if } q \notin Q. \quad (13.3)$$

The ϵ-NFA in FIGURE 13.30 on the preceding page leads to the following ϵ-closures:

$$\epsilon\text{-close}(q_0) = \{q_0, q_1\}$$
$$\epsilon\text{-close}(q_1) = \{q_1\}$$
$$\epsilon\text{-close}(q_2) = \{q_2\}$$
$$\epsilon\text{-close}(q_3) = \{q_3, q_5\}$$
$$\epsilon\text{-close}(q_4) = \{q_4, q_3, q_5\} \quad \epsilon\text{-close}(q_5) \qquad\qquad = \{q_5\}.$$

Consider, as a more difficult example, the following ϵ-NFA $\mathcal{E}$:

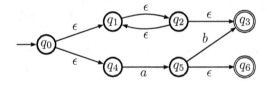

$$\epsilon\text{-close}(q_0) = \epsilon\text{-DFS}(q_0, \varnothing), \quad \text{since } q_0 \in Q_E$$

$$= \{q_0\} \cup \epsilon\text{-DFS}(q_1, \{q_0\}) \cup \epsilon\text{-DFS}(q_4, \{q_0\}) \quad \text{by eq. 13.3}$$

$$= \{q_0\} \cup \left(\{q_1\} \cup \bigcup_{p \in \delta_E(q_1,\epsilon)} \epsilon\text{-DFS}(p, \{q_0, q_1\}) \right) \quad \text{by eq. 13.3}$$

$$\cup \left(\{q_4\} \cup \bigcup_{p \in \delta_E(q_4,\epsilon)} \epsilon\text{-DFS}(p, \{q_0, q_4\}) \right) \quad \text{by eq. 13.3}$$

$$= \{q_0\} \cup \left(\{q_1\} \cup \bigcup_{p \in \{q_2\}} \epsilon\text{-DFS}(p, \{q_0, q_1\}) \right)$$

$$\cup \left(\{q_4\} \cup \bigcup_{p \in \varnothing} \epsilon\text{-DFS}(p, \{q_0, q_4\}) \right)$$

$$= \{q_0\} \cup (\{q_1\} \cup \epsilon\text{-DFS}(q_2, \{q_0, q_1\})) \cup (\{q_4\} \cup \varnothing)$$

$$= \{q_0, q_1, q_4\} \cup \epsilon\text{-DFS}(q_2, \{q_0, q_1\})$$

$$= \{q_0, q_1, q_4\} \cup \left(\{q_2\} \cup \bigcup_{p \in \delta_E(q_2, \epsilon)} \epsilon\text{-DFS}(p, \{q_0, q_1, q_2\}) \right)$$

$$= \{q_0, q_1, q_4\} \cup \left(\{q_2\} \cup \bigcup_{p \in \{q_1, q_3\}} \epsilon\text{-DFS}(p, \{q_0, q_1, q_2\}) \right)$$

$$= \{q_0, q_1, q_2, q_4\} \cup \epsilon\text{-DFS}(q_1, \{q_0, q_1, q_2\})$$
$$\cup \epsilon\text{-DFS}(q_3, \{q_0, q_1, q_2\})$$

$$= \{q_0, q_1, q_2, q_4\} \cup \varnothing \qquad \text{by eq. 13.2, since } q_1 \in \{q_0, q_1, q_2\}$$

$$\cup \left(\{q_3\} \cup \bigcup_{p \in \delta_E(q_3, \epsilon)} \epsilon\text{-DFS}(p, \{q_0, q_1, q_2, q_3\}) \right) \quad \text{by eq. 13.3}$$

$$= \{q_0, q_1, q_2, q_3, q_4\} \cup \bigcup_{p \in \varnothing} \epsilon\text{-DFS}(p, \{q_0, q_1, q_2, q_3\})$$

$$= \{q_0, q_1, q_2, q_3, q_4\}.$$

It is useful to extend ϵ-close to sets of states, not just states. Let us note $\overline{\epsilon\text{-close}}$ this extension, which we can easily define as

$$\overline{\epsilon\text{-close}}(Q) = \bigcup_{q \in Q} \epsilon\text{-close}(q),$$

for any subset $Q \subseteq Q_E$ where the ϵ-NFA is $\mathcal{E} = (Q_E, \Sigma, \delta_E, q_E, F_E)$.

Optimisation

Let us compute the ϵ-closure of q_0 in the following ϵ-NFA $\mathcal{E}$:

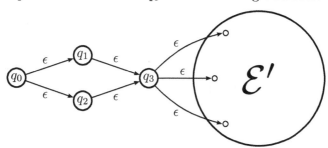

where the sub-ϵ-NFA $\mathcal{E}'$ contains only ϵ-transitions and all its Q' states are accessible from q_3.

$$\epsilon\text{-close}(q_0) = \epsilon\text{-DFS}(q_0, \varnothing)$$

$$= \{q_0\} \cup \epsilon\text{-DFS}(q_1, \{q_0\}) \cup \epsilon\text{-DFS}(q_2, \{q_0\})$$
$$= \{q_0\} \cup (\{q_1\} \cup \epsilon\text{-DFS}(q3, \{q_0, q_1\}))$$
$$\quad\quad \cup (\{q_2\} \cup \epsilon\text{-DFS}(q3, \{q_0, q_2\}))$$
$$= \{q_0, q_1, q_2\} \cup \epsilon\text{-DFS}(q3, \{q_0, q_1\}) \cup \epsilon\text{-DFS}(q3, \{q_0, q_2\})$$
$$= \{q_0, q_1, q_2, q_3, \} \cup (\{q_3\} \cup Q') \cup (\{q_3\} \cup Q')$$
$$= \{q_0, q_1, q_2, q_3, \} \cup Q'.$$

We compute $\{q_3\} \cup Q'$ twice, that is, we traverse twice q_3 and all the states of $\mathcal{E}'$, which can be inefficient if Q' is large. The way to avoid repeating traversals is to change the definitions of ϵ-close and $\overline{\epsilon}$-close. Dually, we need a new definition of ϵ-DFS and create a function $\overline{\epsilon}$-DFS which is similar to ϵ-DFS, except that it applies to set of states instead of one state:

$$\epsilon\text{-close}(q) = \epsilon\text{-DFS}(q, \varnothing), \quad\quad\quad \text{if } q \in Q_E;$$
$$\overline{\epsilon\text{-close}}(Q) = \overline{\epsilon\text{-DFS}}(Q, \varnothing), \quad\quad\quad \text{if } Q \subseteq Q_E.$$

We interpret Q' in ϵ-DFS(q, Q') and $\overline{\epsilon\text{-DFS}}(Q, Q')$ as the set of states that have already been visited in the depth-first search. Variables q and Q denote, respectively, a state and a set of states that have to be explored. In the first definition we computed the *new reachable states*, whilst, in the new one, we compute the *currently reached states*. Then let us redefine ϵ-DFS this way:

$$\epsilon\text{-DFS}(q, Q') = Q', \quad\quad\quad\quad\quad\quad \text{if } q \in Q'; \quad (1')$$
$$\epsilon\text{-DFS}(q, Q') = \overline{\epsilon\text{-DFS}}(\delta_E(q, \epsilon), Q' \cup \{q\}), \quad\quad \text{if } q \notin Q'. \quad (2')$$

Contrast with the first definition

$$\epsilon\text{-DFS}(q, Q') = \varnothing, \quad\quad\quad\quad\quad\quad\quad \text{if } q \in Q'; \quad (1)$$
$$\epsilon\text{-DFS}(q, Q') = \{q\} \quad \cup \bigcup_{p \in \delta_E(q, \epsilon)} \epsilon\text{-DFS}(p, Q' \cup \{q\}), \quad \text{if } q \notin Q'. \quad (2)$$

Hence, in (1) we return $\varnothing$ because there is no new state, that is, none not already in Q', whereas in (1') we return Q' itself. The new definition of $\overline{\epsilon}$-DFS is not more difficult than the first one:

$$\overline{\epsilon\text{-DFS}}(\varnothing, Q') = Q', \quad\quad\quad\quad\quad\quad\quad\quad (13.4)$$
$$\overline{\epsilon\text{-DFS}}(\{q\} \cup Q, Q') = \overline{\epsilon\text{-DFS}}(Q, \epsilon\text{-DFS}(q, Q')), \quad \text{if } q \notin Q. \quad (13.5)$$

Notice that the definitions of ϵ-DFS and $\overline{\epsilon}$-DFS are mutually recursive. In (2) we traverse states in parallel (consider the union operator), starting from each element in $\delta_E(q, \epsilon)$, whereas in (2') and (13.5), we traverse them sequentially so we can use the information collected (currently reached states) in the previous searches.

Coming back to our example on page 561, we find

$$
\begin{aligned}
\epsilon\text{-close}(q_0) &= \epsilon\text{-DFS}(q_0, \varnothing) & q_0 \in Q_E \\
&= \overline{\epsilon\text{-DFS}}(\{q_1, q_2\}, \{q_0\}) & \text{by eq. (2')} \\
&= \overline{\epsilon\text{-DFS}}(\{q_2\}, \epsilon\text{-DFS}(q_1, \{q_0\})) & \text{by eq. (4)} \\
&= \overline{\epsilon\text{-DFS}}(\{q_2\}, \overline{\epsilon\text{-DFS}}(\{q_3\}, \{q_0, q_1\})) & \text{by eq. (2')} \\
&= \overline{\epsilon\text{-DFS}}(\{q_2\}, \overline{\epsilon\text{-DFS}}(\varnothing, \epsilon\text{-DFS}(q_3, \{q_0, q_1\}))) & \text{by eq. (4)} \\
&= \overline{\epsilon\text{-DFS}}(\{q_2\}, \epsilon\text{-DFS}(q_3, \{q_0, q_1\})) & \text{by eq. (3)} \\
&= \overline{\epsilon\text{-DFS}}(\{q_2\}, \{q_0, q_1, q_3\} \cup Q') & \\
&= \overline{\epsilon\text{-DFS}}(\varnothing, \epsilon\text{-DFS}(q_2, \{q_0, q_1, q_3\} \cup Q')) & \text{by eq. (4)} \\
&= \epsilon\text{-DFS}(q_2, \{q_0, q_1, q_3\} \cup Q') & \text{by eq. (3)} \\
&= \overline{\epsilon\text{-DFS}}(\{q_3\}, \{q_0, q_1, q_2, q_3\} \cup Q') & \text{by eq. (2')} \\
&= \overline{\epsilon\text{-DFS}}(\varnothing, \epsilon\text{-DFS}(q_3, \{q_0, q_1, q_2, q_3\} \cup Q')) & \text{by eq. (4)} \\
&= \epsilon\text{-DFS}(q_3, \{q_0, q_1, q_2, q_3\} \cup Q') & \text{by eq. (3)} \\
&= \{q_0, q_1, q_2, q_3\} \cup Q' & \text{by eq. (1')}
\end{aligned}
$$

The important thing here is that we did not compute (traverse) several times Q'. Note that some equations can be used in a different order and q can be chosen arbitrarily in equation (4), but the result is always the same.

Extended transition functions

The ϵ-closure allows to explain how a ϵ-NFA recognises or rejects a given input. Let $\mathcal{E} = (Q_E, \Sigma, \delta_E, q_0, F_E)$. We want $\hat{\delta}_E(q, w)$ be the set of states reachable from q along a path whose labels, when concatenated, for the string w. The difference here with NFAs is that several ϵ can be present along this path, despite not contributing to w. For all state $q \in Q_E$, let

$$
\hat{\delta}_E(q, \epsilon) = \epsilon\text{-close}(q),
$$

$$
\hat{\delta}_E(q, wa) = \overline{\epsilon\text{-close}}\left(\bigcup_{p \in \hat{\delta}_E(q, w)} \delta_N(p, a) \right), \quad \text{for all } a \in \Sigma, w \in \Sigma^*.
$$

This definition is based on the regular identity $wa = ((w\epsilon^*)a)\epsilon^*$.

As an illustration, let us consider again the ϵ-NFA in FIGURE 13.30 on page 559 and compute the states reached on the input 5.6:

$$\hat{\delta}_E(q_0, \epsilon) = \epsilon\text{-close}(q_0) = \{q_0, q_1\};$$

$$\hat{\delta}_E(q_0, 5) = \overline{\epsilon\text{-close}}\left(\bigcup_{p \in \hat{\delta}_E(q_0, \epsilon)} \delta_N(p, 5)\right)$$

$$= \overline{\epsilon\text{-close}}(\delta_N(q_0, 5) \cup \delta_N(q_1, 5)) = \overline{\epsilon\text{-close}}(\varnothing \cup \{q_1, q_4\})$$

$$= \{q_1, q_3, q_4, q_5\};$$

$$\hat{\delta}_E(q_0, 5.) = \overline{\epsilon\text{-close}}\left(\bigcup_{p \in \hat{\delta}_N(q_0, 5)} \delta_N(p, .)\right)$$

$$= \overline{\epsilon\text{-close}}(\delta_N(q_1, .) \cup \delta_N(q_3, .) \cup \delta_N(q_4, .) \cup \delta_N(q_5, .))$$

$$\hat{\delta}_E(q_0, 5.) = \overline{\epsilon\text{-close}}(\{q_2\} \cup \varnothing \cup \varnothing \cup \varnothing) = \{q_2\};$$

$$\hat{\delta}_N(q_0, 5.6) = \overline{\epsilon\text{-close}}\left(\bigcup_{p \in \hat{\delta}_E(q_0, 5.)} \delta_N(p, 6)\right)$$

$$= \overline{\epsilon\text{-close}}(\delta_N(q_2, 6)) = \overline{\epsilon\text{-close}}(\{q_3\}) = \{q_3, q_5\} \ni q_5.$$

Since q_5 is a final state, the string 5.6 is recognised as a number.

Subset construction for ϵ-NFAs

Let us present now how to construct a DFA from a ϵ-NFA such that both recognise the same language. The method is a variation of the subset construction we presented for NFA: we must take into account the states reachable through ϵ-transitions, with help of ϵ-closures. Let us assume that $\mathcal{E} = (Q, \Sigma, \delta, q_0, F)$ is an ϵ-NFA. Let us define as follows the equivalent DFA $\mathcal{D} = (Q_D, \Sigma, \delta_D, q_D, F_D)$.

1. Q_D is the set of subsets of Q_E. More precisely, all accessible states of $\mathcal{D}$ are ϵ-closed subsets of Q_E, that is to say, sets $Q \subseteq Q_E$ such that $Q = \epsilon\text{-close}(Q)$;

2. $q_D = \epsilon\text{-close}(q_0)$, in other words, we get the start state of $\mathcal{D}$ by ϵ-closing the set made of only the start state of $\mathcal{E}$;

3. F_D is those sets of states that contain at least one final state of $\mathcal{E}$, that is to say, $F_D = \{Q \mid Q \in Q_D \text{ and } Q \cap F_E \neq \varnothing\}$;

4. For all $a \in \Sigma$ and $Q \in Q_D$, let $\delta_D(Q, a) = \overline{\epsilon\text{-close}}\left(\bigcup_{q \in Q} \delta_E(q, a)\right)$.

Let us consider again the ε-NFA in FIGURE 13.30 on page 559. Its transition table is

$\mathcal{E}$	$+$	$-$	$0,\dots,9$	$.$	ϵ
$\to q_0$	$\{q_1\}$	$\{q_1\}$	$\varnothing$	$\varnothing$	$\{q_1\}$
q_1	$\varnothing$	$\varnothing$	$\{q_1,q_4\}$	$\{q_2\}$	$\varnothing$
q_2	$\varnothing$	$\varnothing$	$\{q_3\}$	$\varnothing$	$\varnothing$
q_3	$\varnothing$	$\varnothing$	$\{q_3\}$	$\varnothing$	$\{q_5\}$
q_4	$\varnothing$	$\varnothing$	$\varnothing$	$\varnothing$	$\{q_3\}$
$\#q_5$	$\varnothing$	$\varnothing$	$\varnothing$	$\varnothing$	$\varnothing$

By applying the subset construction to this ε-NFA, we get the table

$\mathcal{D}$	$+$	$-$	$0,\dots,9$	$.$
$\to\{q_0,q_1\}$	$\{q_1\}$	$\{q_1\}$	$\{q_1,q_3,q_4,q_5\}$	$\{q_2\}$
$\{q_1\}$	$\varnothing$	$\varnothing$	$\{q_1,q_3,q_4,q_5\}$	$\{q_2\}$
$\#\{q_1,q_3,q_4,q_5\}$	$\varnothing$	$\varnothing$	$\{q_1,q_3,q_4,q_5\}$	$\{q_2\}$
$\{q_2\}$	$\varnothing$	$\varnothing$	$\{q_3,q_5\}$	$\varnothing$
$\#\{q_3,q_5\}$	$\varnothing$	$\varnothing$	$\{q_3,q_5\}$	$\varnothing$

Let us rename the states of $\mathcal{D}$ and get rid of the empty sets:

$\mathcal{D}$	$+$	$-$	$0,\dots,9$	$.$
$\to A$	B	B	C	D
B			C	D
$\#C$			C	D
D			E	
$\#E$			E	

The transition diagram of $\mathcal{D}$ is shown in FIGURE 13.31.

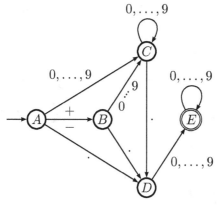

Figure 13.31: Determinisation of the ε-NFA in FIGURE 13.30 on page 559

13.9   From regular expressions to ε-NFAs

We left behind the regular expressions when we informally introduced the transition diagrams for token recognition. Now let us show that regular expressions when used in lexers to specify tokens can be converted to ε-NFAs, and therefore to DFAs. This proves that regular languages are recognisable languages. Actually, it is possible to prove that any ε-NFA can be converted to a regular expression denoting the same language, but we will not do so. Therefore, keep in mind that the regular languages are the same as the recognisable languages. In other words, the choice of using a regular expression or a finite automaton is only a matter of convenience.

The construction we present here to build an ε-NFA from a regular expression is called *Thompson's construction*. Let us first associate an ε-NFA to the basic regular expressions.

- For the expression ϵ, construct the following NFA, where i and f are new states:

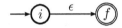

- For $a \in \Sigma$, construct the following NFA, where i and f are new states:

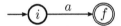

Now let us associate NFAs to complex regular expressions. In the following, let us assume that $N(s)$ and $N(t)$ are the NFAs for regular expressions s and t.

- For the regular expression st, construct the following NFA $N(st)$, where no new state is created:

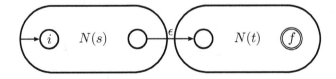

The final state of $N(s)$ becomes a normal state, as well as the initial state of $N(t)$. This way only remains a unique initial state i and a unique final state f.

- For the regular expression $s \mid t$, construct the following NFA $N(s \mid t)$

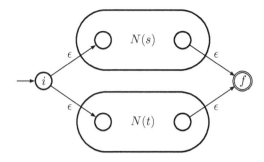

where i and f are new states. Initial and final states of $N(s)$ and $N(t)$ become normal.

- For the regular expression $s^{\star}$, construct the following NFA $N(s^{\star})$, where i and f are new states:

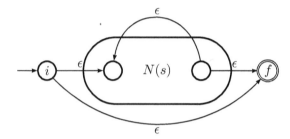

Note that we added two ϵ transitions and that the initial and final states of $N(s)$ become normal states.

How do we apply these simple rules when we have a complex regular expression, having many level of nested parentheses and other constructs? Actually, the abstract syntax tree of the regular expression directs the application of the rules. If the syntax tree has the shape shown in FIG-URE 13.32a, then we construct first $N(s)$, $N(t)$ and finally $N(s \cdot t)$. If the syntax tree has the shape found in FIGURE 13.32b, then we construct first $N(s)$, $N(t)$ and finally $N(s \,|\, t)$. If the syntax tree has the shape shown in FIGURE 13.32c, then we construct first $N(s)$ and finally $N(s^{\star})$. These

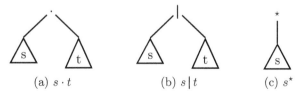

$\qquad$ (a) $s \cdot t$ $\qquad\qquad$ (b) $s \,|\, t$ $\qquad\qquad$ (c) $s^{\star}$

Figure 13.32: Three tree patterns for three regular expressions

pattern matchings are applied first at the root of the abstract syntax tree of the regular expression.

Bibliography

Arne Andersson. A note on searching in a binary search tree. *Software–Practice and experience*, 21(20):1125–1128, October 1991. (Short communication).

Arne Andersson. Balanced search trees made simple. In *Proceedings of the workshop on Algorithms and Data Structures*, volume 709/1993 of *Lecture Notes in Computer Science*, pages 60–71, 1993.

Arne Andersson, Christian Icking, Rolf Klein, and Thomas Ottmann. Binary search trees of almost optimal height. *Acta Informatica*, 28 (2):165–178, 1990.

Andrew Appel. *Compiling with Continuations*. Cambridge University Press, 1992.

Margaret Archibald and Julien Clément. Average depth in a binary search tree with repeated keys. In *Proceedings of the fourth colloquium on Mathematics and Computer Science Algorithms, Trees, Combinatorics and Probabilities*, pages 209–320, September 2006.

Joe Armstrong. *Programming Erlang*. The Pragmatic Bookshelf, July 2007.

Joe Armstrong. Erlang. *Communications of the ACM*, 53(9):68–75, September 2010.

Thomas Arts and Jürgen Giesl. Termination of constructor systems. Technical report, Technische Hochschule Darmstadt, July 1996. ISSN 0924-3275.

Thomas Arts and Jürgen Giesl. Automatically proving termination where simplification orderings fail. In *Proceedings of the seventh International Joint Conference on the Theory and Practice of Software Development*, Lecture Notes in Computer Science 1214, pages 261–272, Lille, France, 1997. Springer-Verlag.

Thomas Arts and Jürgen Giesl. Termination of term rewriting using dependency pairs. *Theoretical Computer Science*, 1-2(236):133–178, April 2000.

Thomas Arts and Jürgen Giesl. A collection of examples for termination of term rewriting using dependency pairs. Technical report, Aachen University of Technology, Department of Computer Science, September 2001. ISSN 0935-3232.

Javed A. Aslam. A simple bound on the expected height of a randomly built binary search tree. Technical Report TR 2001-387, Deparment of Computer Science, Dartmouth College, 2001.

Franz Baader and Tobias Nipkow. *Term Rewriting and all that*. Cambridge University Press, 1998.

Hendrik Pieter Barendregt. *Handbook of Theoretical Computer Science*, volume B (Formal Models and Semantics), chapter Functional Programming and Lambda Calculus, pages 321–363. Elsevier Science, 1990.

Paul E. Black George Becker and Neil V. Murray. Formal verification of a merge-sort program with static semantics. In Kamal Karlapalem Amin Y. Noaman and Ken Barker, editors, *Proceedings of the ninth International Conference on Computing and Information*, pages 271–277, Winnipeg, Manitoba, Canada, June 1998.

Yves Bertot and Pierre Castéran. *Interactive Theorem Proving and Program Development*. Texts in Theoretical Computer Science. Springer, 2004.

Richard Bird. *Pearls of Functional Algorithm Design*, chapter The Knuth-Morris-Pratt algorithm, pages 127–135. Cambridge University Press, October 2010.

Patrick Blackburn, Johan Bos, and Kristina Striegnitz. *Learn Prolog now!*, volume 7 of *Texts in Computing*. College Publications, June 2006.

Stephen Bloch. Teaching linked lists and recursion without conditionals or null. *Journal of Computing Sciences in Colleges*, 18(5):96–108, May 2003. ISSN 1937-4771.

Peter B. Borwein. On the irrationality of certain series. In *Mathematical Proceedings of the Cambridge Philosophical Society*, volume 112, pages 141–146, 1992.

Ivan Bratko. *Prolog Programming for Artificial Intelligence.* Addison-Wesley, third edition, September 2000.

Gerald G. Brown and Bruno O. Shubert. On random binary trees. *Mathematics of Operations Research*, 9(1):43–65, February 1984.

Robert Creighton Buck. Mathematical induction and recursive definitions. *American Mathematical Monthly*, 70(2):128–135, February 1963.

William H. Burge. An analysis of binary search trees formed from sequences of nondistinct keys. *Journal of the ACM*, 23(2):451–454, July 1976.

F. Warren Burton. An efficient functional implementation of FIFO queues. *Information Processing Letters*, 14(5):205–206, July 1982.

L. E. Bush. An asymptotic formula for the average sum of the digits of integers. *The American Mathematical Monthly*, 47(3):154–156, March 1940.

David Callan. Pair them up! A visual approach to the Chung-Feller theorem. *The College Mathematics Journal*, 26(3):196–198, May 1995.

Patrice Chalin and Perry James. Non-null references by default in Java: Alleviating the nullity annotation burden. In *Proceedings of the twenty-first European Conference on Object-Oriented Programming (ECOOP)*, pages 227–247, Berlin, Germany, 2007.

Christian Charras and Thierry Lecroq. *Handbook of Exact String Matching Algorithms.* College Publications, February 2004.

Brigitte Chauvin, Michael Drmota, and Jean Jabbour-Hattab. The profile of binary search trees. *The Annals of Applied Probability*, 11 (4):1042–1062, November 2001.

Wei-Mei Chen, Hsien-Kuei Hwang, and Gen-Huey Chen. The cost distribution of queue-mergesort, optimal mergesorts, and power-of-2 rules. *Journal of Algorithms*, 30(2):423–448, February 1999.

Richard C. Cobbe. *Much ado about nothing: Putting Java's null in its place.* PhD thesis, College of Computer and Information Science, Northeastern University, Boston, Massachusetts, USA, December 2008.

Charles Consel and Olivier Danvy. Partial evaluation of pattern matching in strings. *Information Processing Letters*, 20(2):79–86, January 1989.

Curtis R. Cook and Do Jin Kim. Best sorting algorithm for nearly sorted lists. *Communications of the ACM*, 23(11), November 1980.

Thomas Cormen, Charles Leiserson, Ronald Rivest, and Clifford Stein. *Introduction to Algorithms*. The MIT Press, third edition, 2009.

Guy Cousineau and Michel Mauny. *The Functional Approach to Programming*. Cambridge University Press, October 1998.

Maxime Crochemore, Christophe Hancart, and Thierry Lecroq. *Algorithms on strings*. Cambridge University Press, 2007.

Joseph Culberson and Patricia A. Evans. Asymmetry in binary search tree update algorithms. Technical Report TR 94-09, Department of Computing Science, University of Alberta, Edmonton, Alberta, Canada, May 1994.

Joseph Culberson and J. Ian Munro. Explaining the behaviour of binary search trees under prolonged updates: A model and simulations. *The Computer Journal*, 32(1):68–75, 1989.

Olivier Danvy. On some functional aspects of control. In *Proceedings of the Workshop on Implementation of Lazy Functional Languages*, pages 445–449. Program Methodology Group, University of Göteborg and Chalmers University of Technology, Sweden, September 1988. Report 53.

Olivier Danvy. On listing list prefixes. *List Pointers*, 2(3/4):42–46, January 1989.

Olivier Danvy. Sur un exemple de Patrick Greussay. BRICS Report Series RS-04-41, Basic Research in Computer Science, University of Aarhus, Denmark, December 2004.

Olivier Danvy and Mayer Goldberg. There and back again. BRICS Report Series RS-01-39, Basic Research in Computer Science, University of Aarhus, Denmark, October 2001.

Olivier Danvy and Lasse R. Nielsen. Defunctionalization at work. BRICS Report Series RS-01-23, Basic Research in Computer Science, University of Aarhus, Denmark, June 2001.

B. Dasarathy and Cheng Yang. A transformation on ordered trees. *The Computer Journal*, 23(2):161–164, 1980.

Hubert Delange. Sur la fonction sommatoire de la fonction « somme des chiffres ». *L'Enseignement Mathématique*, XXI(1):31–47, 1975.

Nachum Dershowitz. Termination of rewriting. *Journal of Symbolic Computation*, 3(1-2):69–115, February 1987. Corrigendum: Journal of Symbolic Computation (1987) **4**, 409–410.

Nachum Dershowitz. *Functional Programming, Concurrency, Simulation and Automated Reasoning*, volume 693 of *Lecture Notes in Computer Science*, chapter A taste of rewrite systems, pages 199–228. Springer, 1993.

Nachum Dershowitz. 33 examples of termination. In *Proceedings of the French Spring School of Theoretical Computer Science*, volume 909 of *Lecture Notes in Computer Science*, pages 16–26. Springer, 1995.

Nachum Dershowitz and Jean-Pierre Jouannaud. *Handbook of Theoretical Computer Science*, volume B (Formal Models and Semantics), chapter Rewrite Systems, pages 243–320. Elsevier Science, 1990.

Nachum Dershowitz and Christian Rinderknecht. The Average Height of Catalan Trees by Counting Lattice Paths. *Mathematics Magazine*, 88(3):187–195, June 2015. 18 pages (preprint, including supplement).

Nachum Dershowitz and Shmuel Zaks. Enumerations of ordered trees. *Discrete Mathematics*, 31(1):9–28, 1980.

Nachum Dershowitz and Shmuel Zaks. Applied tree enumerations. In *Proceedings of the Sixth Colloquium on Trees in Algebra and Programming*, volume 112 of *Lecture Notes in Computer Science*, pages 180–193, Berlin, Germany, 1981. Springer.

Nachum Dershowitz and Shmuel Zaks. The Cycle Lemma and some applications. *European Journal of Combinatorics*, 11(1):35–40, 1990.

Luc Devroye. A note on the height of binary search trees. *Journal of the Association for Computing Machinery*, 33(3):489–498, July 1986.

Luc Devroye. Branching processes in the analysis of the heights of trees. *Acta Informatica*, 24(3):277–298, 1987.

Edsger Wybe Dijkstra. Recursive Programming. *Numerische Mathematik*, 2(1):312–318, December 1960. Springer, ISSN 0029-599X.

Edsger Wybe Dijkstra. *A discipline of programming*. Series on Automatic Computation. Prentice Hall, October 1976.

Edsger Wybe Dijkstra. Why numbering should start at zero. University of Texas, Transcription EWD831, August 1982.

Kees Doets and Jan van Eijck. *The Haskell Road to Logic, Maths and Programming*, volume 4 of *Texts in Computing*. College Publications, May 2004.

Olivier Dubuisson. *ASN.1 Communication between heterogeneous systems*. Morgan Kaufmann, 2001.

Jefrey L. Eppinger. An empirical study of insertion and deletion in binary search trees. *Communications of the ACM*, 26(9):663–669, September 1983.

Vladmir Estivill-Castro and Derick Wood. A survey of adaptive sorting algorithms. *ACM Computing Surveys*, 24(4):441–476, December 1992.

Yuguang Fang. A theorem on the k-adic representation of positive integers. *Proceedings of the American Mathematical Society*, 130(6): 1619–1622, June 2002.

Matthias Felleisen and Daniel P. Friedman. *A little Java, a few patterns*. The MIT Press, December 1997.

James Allen Fill. On the distribution of binary search trees under the random permutation model. *Random Structures and Algorithms*, 8 (1):1–25, January 1996.

Philippe Flajolet and Mordecai Golin. Mellin transforms and asymptotics: The Mergesort Recurrence. *Acta Informatica*, 31(7): 673–696, 1994.

Philippe Flajolet and Andrew M. Odlyzko. The average height of binary trees and other simple trees. Technical Report 56, Institut National de Recherche en Informatique et en Automatique (INRIA), February 1981.

Philippe Flajolet and Andrew M. Odlyzko. Limit distributions of coefficients of iterates of polynomials with applications to combinatorial enumerations. *Mathematical Proceedings of the Cambridge Philosophical Society*, 96:237–253, 1984.

Philippe Flajolet and Robert Sedgewick. Analytic combinatorics: Functional equations, rational and algebraic functions. Technical Report 4103, Institut National de Recherche en Informatique et en Automatique (INRIA), January 2001.

Philippe Flajolet and Robert Sedgewick. *Analytic Combinatorics*. Cambridge University Press, January 2009.

Philippe Flajolet, Xavier Gourdon, and Philippe Dumas. Mellin Transforms and Asymptotics: Harmonic Sums. *Theoretical Computer Science*, 144:3–58, 1995.

Philippe Flajolet, Markus Nebel, and Helmut Prodinger. The scientific works of Rainer Kemp (1949–2004). *Theoretical Computer Science*, 355(3):371–381, April 2006.

Robert W. Floyd. Assigning meanings to programs. In J. T. Schwartz, editor, *Proceedings of the Symposium on Applied Mathematics*, volume 19 of *Mathematical Aspects of Computer Science*, pages 19–31. American Mathematical Society, 1967.

Daniel P. Friedman and Mitchell Wand. *Essentials of Programing Languages*. Computer Science/Programming Languages Series. The MIT Press, third edition, 2008.

Jaco Geldenhuys and Brink Van der Merwe. Comparing leaf and root insertion. *South African Computer Journal*, 44:30–38, December 2009.

Thomas E. Gerasch. An insertion algorithm for a minimal internal path length binary search tree. *Communications of the ACM*, 31(5): 579–585, May 1988.

Jeremy Gibbons and Geraint Jones. The under-appreciated unfold. In *Proceedings of the third ACM SIGPLAN International Conference on Functional Programming*, pages 273–279, Baltimore, Maryland, USA, September 1998.

Jeremy Gibbons, Graham Hutton, and Thorsten Altenkirch. When is a function a fold or an unfold? *Electronic Notes in Theoretical Computer Science*, 44(1):146–160, May 2001.

Jürgen Giesl. Automated termination proofs with measure functions. In *Proceedings of the Nineteenth Annual German Conference on Artificial Intelligence: Advances in Artificial Intelligence*, pages 149–160. Springer-Verlag, 1995a.

Jürgen Giesl. Termination analysis for functional programs using term orderings. In *Proceedings of the second international Symposium on Static Analysis*, pages 154–171. Springer-Verlag, 1995b.

Jürgen Giesl. Termination of nested and mutually recursive algorithms. *Journal of Automated Reasoning*, 19(1), August 1997.

Jürgen Giesl, Christoph Walther, and Jürgen Brauburger. *Automated deduction: A basis for applications*, volume III (Applications) of *Applied Logic Series*, chapter Termination analysis for functional programs, pages 135–164. Kluwer Academic, Dordrecht, 1998.

Mayer Goldberg and Guy Wiener. Anonymity in Erlang. In *Erlang User Conference*, Stockholm, November 2009.

Mordecai J. Golin and Robert Sedgewick. Queue-mergesort. *Information Processing Letters*, 48(5):253–259, December 1993.

Ronald L. Graham, Donald E. Knuth, and Oren Patashnik. *Concrete Mathematics*. Addison-Wesley, third edition, 1994.

Daniel H. Greene and Donald E. Knuth. *Mathematics for the Analysis of Algorithms*. Modern Birkhäuser Classics. Birkhäuser, Boston, USA, third edition, 2008.

Godfrey Harold Hardy. *Divergent series*. The Clarendon Press, Oxford, England, United Kingdom, 1949.

Michaela Heyer. Randomness preserving deletions on special binary search trees. *Electronic Notes in Theoretical Computer Science*, 225 (2):99–113, January 2009.

J. Roger Hindley and Jonathan P. Seldin. *Lambda-calculus and Combinators*. Cambridge University Press, 2008.

Konrad Hinsen. The Promises of Functional Programming. *Computing in Science and Engineering*, 11(4):86–90, July/August 2009.

Ralf Hinze. A fresh look at binary search trees. *Journal of Functional Programming*, 12(6):601–607, November 2002. (Functional Pearl).

Yoichi Hirai and Kazuhiko Yamamoto. Balancing weight-balanced trees. *Journal of Functional Programming*, 21(3):287–307, 2011.

Charles A. R. Hoare. Proof of a program: FIND. *Communications of the ACM*, 14(1):39–45, January 1971.

Tony Hoare. Null references: The billion dollar mistake. In *The Annual International Software Development Conference*, London, England, United Kingdom, August 2009.

John E. Hopcroft, Rajeev Motwani, and Jeffrey D. Ullman. *Introduction to Automata Theory, Languages, and Computation*. Pearson Education, 2nd edition, 2003.

Gérard Huet. The zipper. *Journal of Functional Programming*, 7(5): 549–554, September 1997.

Gérard Huet. Linear Contexts, Sharing Functors: Techniques for Symbolic Computation. In *Thirty Five Years of Automating Mathematics*, volume 28 of *Applied Logic Series*, pages 49–69. Springer Netherlands, 2003.

John Hughes. Why functional programming matters. *The Computer Journal*, 32(2):98–107, April 1989.

Katherine Humphreys. A history and a survey of lattice path enumeration. *Journal of Statistical Planning and Inference*, 140(8): 2237–2254, August 2010. Special issue on Lattice Path Combinatorics and Applications.

Hsien-Kuei Hwang. Asymptotic expansions of the mergesort recurrences. *Acta Informatica*, 35(11):911–919, November 1998.

Daniel H. H. Ingalls. A simple technique for handling multiple polymorphism. In *Proceedings of the conference on Object-Oriented Programming Systems, Languages and Applications*, pages 347–349, Portland, Oregon, USA, September 1986.

Geraint Jones and Jeremy Gibbons. Linear-time breadth-first tree algorithms: An exercise in the arithmetic of folds and zips. Technical Report 71, Department of Computer Science,University of Auckland, New Zealand, May 1993.

Michael Kay. *XSLT 2.0 and XPath 2.0 Programmer's Reference*. Wiley Publishings (Wrox), fourth edition, 2008.

Reiner Kemp. *Fundamentals of the average case analysis of particular algorithms*. Wiley-Teubner Series in Computer Science. John Wiley & Sons, B. G. Teubner, 1984.

Charles Knessl and Wojciech Szpankowski. The height of a binary search tree: The limiting distribution perspective. *Theoretical Computer Science*, 289(1):649–703, October 2002.

Donald E. Knuth. *Selected papers on Computer Science*, chapter Von Neumann's First Computer Program, pages 205–226. Number 59 in CSLI Lecture Notes. CSLI Publications, Stanford University, California, USA, 1996.

Donald E. Knuth. *Fundamental Algorithms*, volume 1 of *The Art of Computer Programming*. Addison-Wesley, third edition, 1997.

Donald E. Knuth. *Sorting and Searching*, volume 3 of *The Art of Computer Programming*. Addison-Wesley, second edition, 1998a.

Donald E. Knuth. *Sorting and Searching*, chapter Binary Tree Searching, 6.2.2, pages 431–435. Addison-Wesley, 1998b.

Donald E. Knuth. *Selected Papers on the Analysis of Algorithms*, chapter Textbook Examples of Recursion, pages 391–414. Number 102 in CSLI Lecture Notes. CSLI Publications, Stanford University, California, USA, 2000.

Donald E. Knuth. *Selected Papers on Design of Algorithms*, chapter Fast pattern matching in strings, pages 99–135. Number 191 in CSLI Lecture Notes. CSLI Publications, Stanford University, California, USA, 2010.

Donald E. Knuth. *Combinatorial algorithms*, volume 4A of *The Art of Computer Programming*. Addison-Wesley, 2011.

Donald E. Knuth, Nicolaas Govert de Bruijn, and S. O. Rice. *Graph Theory and Computing*, chapter The Average Height of Planted Plane Trees, pages 15–22. Academic Press, December 1972. Republished in Knuth et al. (2000).

Donald E. Knuth, James H. Morris Jr., and Vaughan R. Pratt. Fast pattern matching in strings. *SIAM Journal on Computing*, 6(2): 323–350, June 1977. Society for Industrial and Applied Mathematics.

Donald E. Knuth, Nicolaas Govert de Bruijn, and S. O. Rice. *Selected Papers on the Analysis of Algorithms*, chapter The Average Height of

Planted Plane Trees, pages 215–223. Number 102 in CSLI Lecture Notes. CSLI Publications, Stanford University, California, USA, 2000.

Đuro Kurepa. On the left factorial function !*n*. *Mathematica Balkanica*, 1:147–153, 1971.

John Larmouth. *ASN.1 Complete*. Morgan Kaufmann, November 1999.

Chung-Chih Li. An immediate approach to balancing nodes in binary search trees. *Journal of Computing Sciences in Colleges*, 21(4): 238–245, April 2006.

Naomi Lindenstrauss, Yehoshua Sagiv, and Alexander Serebrenik. Unfolding the mystery of mergesort. In *Logic Program Synthesis and Transformation*, volume 1463 of *Lecture Notes in Computer Science*, pages 206–225. Springer, 1998.

M. Lothaire. *Applied Combinatorics on Words*, chapter Counting, Coding and Sampling with Words, pages 478–519. Number 105 in Encyclopedia of Mathematics and its Applications. Cambridge University Press, United Kingdom, July 2005.

Hosam M. Mahmoud. *Evolution of random search trees*. Discrete Mathematics and Optimization. Wiley-Interscience, New York, USA, 1992.

Erkki Mäkinen. A survey on binary tree codings. *The Computer Journal*, 34(5), 1991.

Sal Mangano. *XSLT Cookbook*. O'Reilly, 2nd edition, 2006.

George Edward Martin. *Counting: The art of enumerative combinatorics*. Springer, 2001.

John McCarthy. Recursive functions of symbolic expressions and their computation by machine (Part I). *Communications of the ACM*, 3 (4):184–195, April 1960.

John McCarthy. Towards a mathematical science of computation. In *IFIP Congress*, pages 21–28. North-Holland, 1962.

M. D. McIlroy. The number of 1's in the binary integers: Bounds and extremal properties. *SIAM Journal on Computing*, 3(4):255–261, December 1974. Society for Industrial and Applied Mathematics.

Kurt Mehlhorn and Athanasios Tsakalidis. *Algorithms and Complexity*, volume A of *Handbook of Theoretical Computer Science*, chapter Data Structures, pages 301–341. Elsevier Science, 1990.

Alistair Moffat and Ola Petersson. An overview of adaptive sorting. *Australian Computer Journal*, 24(2):70–77, 1992.

Sri Gopal Mohanty. *Lattice path counting and applications*, volume 37 of *Probability and mathematical statistics*. Academic Press, New York, USA, January 1979.

Shin-Chen Mu and Richard Bird. Rebuilding a tree from its traversals: A case study of program inversion. In *Proceedings of the Asian Symposium on Programming Languages and Systems*, LNCS 2895, pages 265–282, 2003.

Radu Muschevici, Alex Potanin, Ewan Tempero, and James Noble. Multiple dispatch in practice. In *Proceedings of the 23rd ACM SIGPLAN conference on Object-Oriented Programming Systems, Languages and Applications*, pages 563–582, Nashville, Tennesse, USA, October 2008.

Maurice Naftalin and Philip Wadler. *Java Generics and Collections*. O'Reilly, October 2006.

Jürg Nievergelt and Edward M. Reingold. Binary search trees of bounded balance. In *Proceedings of the fourth annual ACM symposium on Theory of Computing*, pages 137–142, Denver, Colorado, USA, May 1972.

Andrew M. Odlyzko. Some new methods and results in tree enumeration. *Congressus Numerantium*, 42:27–52, 1984.

Chris Okasaki. Simple and efficient purely functional queues and dequeues. *Journal of Functional Programming*, 5(4):583–592, October 1995.

Chris Okasaki. *Purely Functional Data Structures*, chapter Fundamentals of Amortization, pages 39–56. Cambridge University Press, 1998a. Section 5.2.

Chris Okasaki. *Purely Functional Data Structures*. Cambridge University Press, 1998b.

Chris Okasaki. Breadth-first numbering: Lessons from a small exercise in algorithm design. In *Proceedings of the fifth ACM SIGPLAN*

International Conference on Functional Programming, pages 131–136, Montréal, Canada, September 2000.

A. Panayotopoulos and A. Sapounakis. On binary trees and Dyck paths. *Mathématiques et Sciences Humaines, No. 131*, pages 39–51, 1995.

Wolfgang Panny. Deletions in random binary search trees: A story of errors. *Journal of Statistical Planning and Inference*, 140(8): 2335–2345, August 2010.

Wolfgang Panny and Helmut Prodinger. Bottom-up mergesort: A detailed analysis. *Algorithmica*, 14(4):340–354, October 1995.

Tomi A. Pasanen. Note: Random binary search tree with equal elements. *Theoretical Computer Science*, 411(43):3867–3872, October 2010.

Dominique Perrin. *Handbook of Theoretical Computer Science*, volume B (Formal Models and Semantics), chapter Finite Automata, pages 3–57. Elsevier Science, 1990.

Benjamin C. Pierce. *Types and Programming Languages*. The MIT Press, 2002.

Bruce Reed. The height of a random binary search tree. *Journal of the ACM*, 50(3):306–332, May 2003.

Mireille Régnier. Knuth-Morris-Pratt algorithm: An analysis. In *Proceedings of the conference on Mathematical Foundations for Computer Science*, volume 379 of *Lecture Notes in Computer Science*, pages 431–444, Porubka, Poland, 1989.

Mireille Régnier. Average performance of Morris-Pratt-like algorithms. Technical Report 2164, Institut National de Recherche en Informatique et en Automatique (INRIA), January 1994. ISSN 0249-6399.

Marc Renault. Lost (and Found) in Translation: André's Actual Method and Its Application to the Generalized Ballot Problem. *American Mathematical Monthly*, 155(4):358–363, April 2008.

John C. Reynolds. Definitional interpreters for higher-order programming languages. In *Proceedings of the 25th ACM annual conference*, volume 2, pages 717–740, 1972.

John C. Reynolds. *Theories of Programming Languages*. Cambridge University Press, 1998.

Christian Rinderknecht. Une analyse syntaxique d'ASN.1:1990 en Caml Light. Technical Report 171, INRIA, April 1995. English at `http://crinderknecht.free.fr/pub/TR171-eng.pdf`.

Christian Rinderknecht. A Didactic Analysis of Functional Queues. *Informatics in Education*, 10(1):65–72, April 2011.

Raphael M. Robinson. Primitive recursive functions. *Bulletin of the American Mathematical Society*, 53(10):925–942, 1947.

Raphael M. Robinson. Recursion and double recursion. *Bulletin of the American Mathematical Society*, 54(10):987–993, 1948.

Frank Ruskey. A simple proof of a formula of Dershowitz and Zaks. *Discrete Mathematics*, 43(1):117–118, 1983.

Jacques Sakarovitch. *Éléments de théorie des automates*. Les classiques de l'informatique. Vuibert Informatique, 2003.

Robert Sedgewick and Philippe Flajolet. *An introduction to the analysis of algorithms*. Addison-Wesley, 1996.

David B. Sher. Recursive objects: An object oriented presentation of recursion. *Mathematics and Computer Education*, Winter 2004.

Iekata Shiokawa. On a problem in additive number theory. *Mathematical Journal of Okayama University*, 16(2):167–176, June 1974.

David Spuler. The best algorithm for searching a binary search tree. Technical Report 92/3, Department of Computer Science, James Cook University of North Queensland, Australia, 1992.

Richard P. Stanley. *Enumerative Combinatorics*, volume 1 of *Cambridge Studies in Advanced Mathematics (No. 49)*. Cambridge University Press, July 1999a.

Richard P. Stanley. *Enumerative Combinatorics*, volume 2 of *Cambridge Studies in Advanced Mathematics (No. 62)*. Cambridge University Press, April 1999b.

C. J. Stephenson. A method for constructing binary search trees by making insertions at the root. *International Journal of Computer and Information Sciences (now International Journal of Parallel Programming)*, 9(1):15–29, 1980.

Leon Sterling and Ehud Shapiro. *The Art of Prolog.* Advanced Programming Techniques. The MIT Press, second edition, 1994.

Kenneth B. Stolarsky. Power and exponential sums of digital sums related to binomial coefficient parity. *SIAM Journal of Applied Mathematics*, 32(4):717–730, June 1977.

J. R. Trollope. An explicit expression for binary digital sums. *Mathematics Magazine*, 41(1):21–25, January 1968.

Franklin Turbak and David Gifford. *Design Concepts in Programming Languages.* Computer Science/Programming Languages Series. The MIT Press, 2008.

Franklyn Turbak, Constance Royden, Jennifer Stephan, and Jean Herbst. Teaching recursion before loops in CS1. *Journal of Computing in Small Colleges*, 14(4):86–101, May 1999.

Jeffrey Scott Vitter and Philippe Flajolet. *Algorithms and Complexity*, volume A of *Handbook of Theoretical Computer Science*, chapter Average-Case Analysis of Algorithms and Data Structures, pages 431–524. Elsevier Science, 1990.

Patricia Walmsley. *Definitive XML Schema.* The Charles F. GoldFarb Definitive XML Series. Prentice-Hall PTR, 2002.

Tjark Weber and James Caldwell. Constructively characterizing fold and unfold. *Logic-based program synthesis and transformation*, 3018/2004:110–127, 2004. Lecture Notes in Computer Science.

Herbert S. Wilf. *Generatingfunctionology.* Academic Press, 1990.

Glynn Winskel. *The Formal Semantics of Programming Languages.* Foundations of Computing Series. The MIT Press, 1993.

Index